# REGRESSION THERAPY:

# A HANDBOOK FOR PROFESSIONALS

## Volume I

# Regression Therapy: A Handbook for Professionals

## Volume I: Past-Life Therapy

**WINAFRED BLAKE LUCAS, Ph.D.**

Regression work is beginning to be recognized as a powerful therapeutic addition to conventional therapy. Its inclusion is like placing doors and windows in a house formerly without vistas.

Interest in past lives has grown among both clients and therapists, fueled by a paradigm shift that recognizes imagery as significant and transpersonal perception as a valid, credible, and dynamic resource for healing.

In order for psychotherapists to move into the field competently, sound regression approaches need to be documented and described. Volume I, written for the professions of psychiatry and psychology, deals with the process of tuning into and modifying past-life influences on current life patterns. It presents accounts by thirteen credentialed therapists. Each contributor discusses philosophical hypotheses and therapeutic assumptions, the preparation and induction of the patient, and deepening and transformational techniques. The approaches of the therapists are compared in a series of integrating chapters.

Cases have been chosen to cover a range of therapeutic situations. The cases are of compelling interest and the scope and variety of remissions and transformations suggest that this new area of therapy may significantly extend our understanding of healing, both physical and psychological.

Contributors were chosen from the fields of clinical psychology and psychiatry to act as models in regression techniques. Their personal regression experiences provide further evidence that the process is a viable modality for all.

**Winafred Blake Lucas,** Ph.D., a diplomate of the American Board of Professional Psychology, began her academic training at the University of Washington in the early 30's, with majors in Greek, philosophy, and writing, since clinical psychology did not exist at that time. In Munich, where she went to complete a doctorate in Sanskrit, she became involved in a Jungian analysis. When her major professor fell victim to the Nazis, she shifted to the new discipline of clinical psychology and later completed her doctorate in psychology at UCLA under the Rorschach specialist, Dr. Bruno Klopfer.

Dr. Lucas served on the faculties of Los Angeles State University and the California School of Professional Psychology. Concurrently she provided workshops in holistic health and transpersonal issues at various University of California campuses. Her clinical work has spanned 45 years and recently has included the transpersonal areas of imagery and regression therapy. She served as editor of *The Journal of Regression Therapy* during its early years. She has now retired to her mountain home to write.

*Cover art*: Amanda Goodenough
*Cover design*: Kacey Fansett
*Photo credit*: Mara Magliarditi

Volume I & Volume II Published by Infinity Institute International, Inc.

# REGRESSION THERAPY
## A HANDBOOK FOR PROFESSIONALS
### VOLUME I: PAST~LIFE THERAPY

Winafred Blake Lucas Ph.D.

BookSolid Press
div. Transpersonal Publishing, AHU, LLC
PO Box 7220, Kill Devil Hills, NC 27948

Copyright ©1992, by Winafred Blake-Lucas
First printing: January, 1993
Second printing: 2001
Third printing: February, 2005
Fourth printing: March, 2007

Cover Art: Amanda goodenough
Jacket Design: Kacey Fansett
Photo Credit: Mara Magliarditi

ISBN Two Volumes (softcover edition)
Volume I: 978-1-929661-17-6
Volume II: 978-1-929661-18-3

All Rights Reserved. No part of this book may be reproduced in any form or by any means, without prior written consent from the publisher, with the exception of brief quotes used in reviews.

Unattributed quotations are by Winafred Blake-Lucas.

All of the publisher's titles, imprints, and distributed lines are available at special quantity discounts for bulk purchases for sales promotions, premiums, fund-raising, and educational or institutional use. Special book excerpts or customized printings can also be created to fit specific needs. For details, contact the publisher.

Orders:
Wholesale—www.BookSolidPress.com
www.TranspersonalPublishing.com
Retail—www.Holistictree.com (Zen Cart)
(800) 296-MIND

Printed in the United States of America

# *Acknowledgments to Volume I*

*Grateful acknowledgement is made to the following for permission to quote previously published material:*

Doubleday, a division of Bantam, Doubleday, Dell Publishing Group, Inc. for permission to quote from *Other Lives, Other Selves* by Roger Woolger. Copyright © 1987 by Roger Woolger.

Hickman Systems for permission to quote from *Mind Probe—Hypnosis* by Irene Hickman. Copyright © 1983 by Irene Hickman.

M. Evans and Company, Inc., New York. for permission to quote from *Voices from Other Lives* by Thorwald Dethlefsen. Copyright © 1977 by Thorwald Dethlefsen.

Putnam Publishing Group for permission to quote from *You have Been Here Before* by Edith Fiore. Copyright © 1978 by Edith Fiore.

Warner Brothers Music. Special Rider Music for permission to reprint the poem "A Hard Rain's A'Gonna Fall" by Bob Dylan. Copyright © 1963 by Warner Bros. Music. Copyright renewed 1991 by Special Rider Music. All rights reserved. International copyright secured.

The Association for Past-Life Research and Therapies for permission to reprint the following articles from *The Journal of Regression Therapy*:

    Denning, Hazel. "Philosophical Assumptions Underlying Successful Past-Life Therapy," Vol. 1, No. 2, 1986.
    ———. "Dialogue with Cancer," Vol. II, No. 2, 1987.
    ———. "Guilt: Facilitator and Inhibitor in the Growth of the Soul," Vol. III, No. 2, 1988.
    Findeisen, Barbara. "The Psyche and the Body: Partners in Healing," Vol. II, No. 1, 1987.
    Jue, Ronald Wong. "Past-Life Therapy: Assumptions, Stages and Progress," Vol. I, No. 1, 1986.
    Lucas, Winafred. "Mind Mirror Research on the Retrieval of Past Lives," Volume IV, No. 1, 1989.
    Pecci, Ernest. "Opening the Way for Healing," Vol. II, No. 2, 1987.
    Pecci, Ernest and Joanne Walsh, "Separating from the Source as an Indicator of Guilt," Vol. II, No. 2, 1988.
    Reynolds, Edward. "Humanistic Considerations in Regression Therapy," Vol. 1, No. 2, 1986.
    Woolger, Roger. "Theoretical Aspects of Past-Life Bodywork: Understanding Subtle Energy Fields. Part I: Theory," Vol. II, No. 1, 1987.
    ———. "Theoretical Aspects of Past-Life Bodywork: Understanding Subtle Energy Fields. Part II: Practical Aspects," Vol. II, No. 2, 1987.

# In Memory Of
# Winafred Blake-Lucas

## (1911-2006)

### A Message from the Publisher

Winafred left us for her rightful place in the light December, 2006. Shortly before, we promised to keep her books in print in the years to come and acquired the publishing rights. As a result, this book is being reprinted using short print runs by a progressive publishing company owned by Winafred's friends.

On a personal note, we will miss our private discussions about her very colorful life, which included: her encounters with Sigmund Freud and thereby dating various therapeutic theories relative to the evolution of psychotherapy; her comprehension of the destiny of the soul; and her personal hardships—including her WWII experiences when her professors were led to concentration camps, never to be seen again. We will also miss her annual Christmas letters, which were sent to friends she made along the journey. We truly feel blessed to have known her and be able to pass on her work in this way.

Like us, if you feel that the information contained herein is timeless and invaluable to the profession, and you would like to help keep these books in print, please copy the coupon on the last page of this book and pass it on to bookstores, practitioners, and educational institutions, so that together we may furhter her work and hold her vision to improve life on earth.

The author's personal web site can be found at:

www.DrWinafredLucas.com

*This book is dedicated to*

***Hazel M. Denning, Ph.D.***

*the first lady of regression therapy,*

*mentor and friend to all who know her.*

# Contents

## *Volume I - Past-Life Recall*

| | |
|---|---:|
| *Table of Contents* | *ix* |
| *Foreword by C. Norman Shealy, M.D., Ph.D.* | *xiii* |
| *Preface* | *xv* |

### *Introduction*

| | | |
|---|---|---:|
| **Chapter I.** | **The History of Regression Therapy** | 3 |

        Psychological Foundations
        Early Steps in Past-Life Therapy
        The Paradigm Shift
        The Formation of the Association for Past-Life Research and Therapies
        New Areas of Altered-State Therapy
        Past-Life Therapy Comes of Age

### *Theory*

| | | |
|---|---|---:|
| **Chapter II.** | **Philosophical Hypotheses** | 25 |

        The Journey of the Soul
        Karmic Patterns
        The Wisdom of the Core Self
        The Energic Nature of Experience and Transformation

| | | |
|---|---|---|
| Chapter III. | Psychotherapeutic Assumptions | 35 |

        General Principles
        The First Stage: Identification with a Previous Lifetime
        The Second Stage: Disidentification
        The Third Stage: Transformation
        Theories of Intervention

| | | |
|---|---|---|
| Chapter IV. | Indications and Contraindications for Use | 46 |

        Transpersonal Goals
        Focusing on Symptoms
        Working with Patterns
        Contraindications for Regression Work

## *Induction*

| | | |
|---|---|---|
| Chapter V. | Preparation | 57 |

        Exploring the Patient's History and Patterns
        Examining the Patient's Philosophy of Life
        Establishing Rapport
        Introducing Induction Techniques

| | | |
|---|---|---|
| Chapter VI. | Induction Techniques | 65 |

        The Nature of Altered States
        Hypnosis
        Brainwave Research
        Hypnosis or Its Accessories?
        Induction through Relaxation, Breathing and Visualization
        Entering a Past Life
        Age Regression as an Entry Technique
        The Emotional-Somatic Bridge as Induction and Entry

| | | |
|---|---|---|
| Chapter VII. | Supportive and Deepening Techniques | 86 |

                          The Role of the Therapist
                          Techiques for Eliciting Material
                          Blocking
                          Moving within Time
                          Dealing with Stress

## *Processing*

| | | |
|---|---|---|
| Chapter VIII. | Psychotherapeutic and Transformational Techniques | 107 |

                          The Stage of Identification: Abreaction
                          The Stage of Disidentification: Exploring
                              Patterns
                          The Stage of Disidentification: Cognitive
                              Techniques
                          Emotional and Transformational Techniques
                          The Importance of the Death Experience

| | | |
|---|---|---|
| Chapter IX. | Integration into the Therapeutic Process | 134 |

                          The Long Path of Transformation
                          Techniques of Integration
                          Transformation of the Personality

| | | |
|---|---|---|
| Chapter X. | Failures | 146 |

                          Realistic Limitations
                          Limitations Brought by the Patient
                          Sources of Failure Contributed by the Therapist

## *Contributors*

| | | |
|---|---|---|
| Chapter XI. | Ronald Wong Jue, Ph.D. | 155 |
| Chapter XII. | Hazel M. Denning, Ph.D. | 184 |
| Chapter XIII. | Roger J. Woolger, Ph.D. | 216 |
| Chapter XIV. | Edith Fiore, Ph.D. | 249 |

| | | |
|---|---|---|
| Chapter XV. | Chet B. Snow, Ph.D. | 280 |
| Chapter XVI. | Rob Bontenbal, M.A. and<br>Tineke Noordegraaf, M.M. (The Netherlands) | 320 |
| Chapter XVII. | Irene Hickman, D.O. | 377 |
| Chapter XVIII. | Edward N. Reynolds, Ph.D. | 403 |
| Chapter XIX. | Barbara Findeisen, M.F.C.C. | 422 |
| Chapter XX. | Thorwald Dethlefsen, Ph.D. (Germany) | 445 |
| Chapter XXI. | Winafred B. Lucas, Ph.D. | 480 |
| Chapter XXII. | Ernest F. Pecci, M.D. | 517 |

## *Appendices*

| | |
|---|---|
| *Appendix A. Profile of the Contributors* | 553 |
| *Appendix B. Group Induction—Helen Wambach, Ph.D.* | 559 |
| *Appendix C. Mind Mirror Research on the Retrieval of Past Lives* | 565 |
| *Notes* | 579 |
| *Bibliography* | 590 |
| *Index* | 595 |

# Foreword to Volume I

In 1972 I had one of the peak experiences of my life, my first past-life therapy session with Dr. Lindsey Jacob, a psychiatrist from Pittsburgh, Pennsylvania. Not only did I gain tremendous insight into my personal life at that time, but for some two hours following the session I experienced a cosmic peak awareness. During the years since then I have personally conducted hundreds of past-life therapy sessions and consider them to be the single most effective psychotherapeutic tool that I have experienced. Sometimes one past-life therapy session is enough to help a patient gain insight and make a big turnaround in his or her life.

I have also experienced many additional past-life experiences done with talented therapists around the world. Every one of them has given me increasing personal insight. The question is not whether the images and apparent memories evoked during such a session are "real" and actually happen in chronological time, but more importantly, I believe that each episode provides an allegory from the subconscious, much more intense and vivid than any dream could possibly convey.

Winafred Lucas is one of the world experts in past-life therapy. Her contributions to the field have been quite remarkable, and although the Journal of Regression Therapy will miss her expertise since she has recently resigned as its Chief Editor, more importantly her work will have even wider distribution with the publication of this book. May it serve you as a catalyst for your own inner awareness.

C. Norman Shealy, M.D., Ph.D.
1992, Springfield, Missouri

> Founder and Director, Shealy Institute for Comprehensive Health Care
> Founding President, American Holistic Medical Association
> Research and Clinical Professor of Psychology, Forest Institute of Professional Psychology

# Preface to Volume I

In this book I seek to meld the assumptions and methods of past-life therapy into a theoretical matrix. The book presents the field, not as I saw it in the beginning but as it appears to me after four years of examining the theories and ideas of my contributors. From their shared perceptions a pattern has emerged.

The first chapter has gone through numerous drafts over the years and has transformed itself several times. After reading widely in the field and mulling over the plethora of impressions and theories, I came to realize that there was a history and a continuity to altered-state work. This history appeared to progress hand in hand with a contemporary search for meaning; with the same tempo that past-life work evolved, so also did this thrust toward a new paradigm in understanding.

It became clear, also, that though past-life work began as an effort to remit symptoms more speedily and effectively than other therapeutic modalities were able to do, currently it is moving in the direction of clarifying the spiritual nature of our existence. My cognitive side has been embarrassed to discover this, but the trend cannot be denied.

The contributors to this book have two minds about past-life work. One derives from our university training, necessary if we are to deal cognitively with a field permeated with ambiguities—we flinch at what seems to be an unscientific thrust and we are not entirely comfortable with our own data. But we cannot deny the second impact, our inner experiences. After wrestling with the conflict, I have conceded that we will have to live with this split. We are trained scientists, but we know that we are on a journey of the soul.

In the beginning a single volume dealing with past lives appeared sufficient, but peripheral regression fields kept emerging and birthed a second volume. Meanwhile Chet Snow and the Dutch therapists became contributors and Thorwald Dethlefsen consented to allow the profound and stimulating views expressed in his first two books, *Voices from Many Lives* and *The Challenge of Fate*, to be presented. He has preferred to take no part in the preparation of his section, so the material may not represent his current thinking. Biographical data about him have not been available.

To the many therapists formerly unknown to me who have become known since this book found its final form, may I say that I am sorry not to have known of you sooner. I urge you to join the Association for Past-Life

Research and Therapies and to contribute to *The Journal of Regression Therapy* so that your work can be appreciated and shared by others.

Two matters of style. For the most part I have retained the conventional use of he and him to imply both genders—a continued attempt to use non-sexist pronouns proved too burdensome. I was reared in a home where there was no sex discrimination so I am less sensitive about this than perhaps I should be.

In the dialogue reported from patients' transcripts I have tried to follow the therapist's preference for use of "C" for client or "P" for patient. The designation does not change the relationship!

I wish to acknowledge a debt to Raymond Corsini for the structure of this first volume. Using such a format made clear to me how unified the area of past-life work is in spite of surface differences.

My especial appreciation goes to Chet Snow, who has provided invaluable suggestions concerning style, editing, and content. I thank Joanne Garland for always believing that the struggle to integrate so much material was worthwhile, for her painstaking formulation of the index, and for her final editing, which assured that the pages would flow smoothly. Without the patience of my secretary, Teri Stanton, during the interminable revisions, this book would undoubtedly have been delayed several more years!

I am grateful for the support and encouragement of my contributors, who remained patient during the long effort to bring these volumes to publication.

Winafred Blake Lucas, Ph.D.<br>
Crest Park, California

# *Introduction*

*We are really lighted beings.*

*Edith Fiore*

*Reincarnation therapy is a hard route to purification. In repeated incarnations we see no source of comfort but rather a challenge to develop toward completeness and thus become free. We must say "yes" to this earthly existence as long as it is necessary for our path of development.*

*Thorwald Dethlefsen*

*All is both one* **and** *many and everything is in its place in the ever-transforming play of creation.*

*Roger Woolger*

**Chapter I**

# The History of Regression Therapy

Regression therapy, the matrix of past-life work, did not emerge intact and complete. It is an intricate tapestry, still in the process of being woven, with many threads of theory and practice. Some of these are ancient, dating back to the Greek dream incubation centers and to the Greek and Egyptian mystery schools. In modern times, trips into the forbidden unconscious have replaced the dream schools.

## Psychological Foundations

The grandfather of present-day regression work was Freud, with his innovative idea that making the unconscious conscious would restore choice and bring healing. This concept emerged during a period of trial and error when Freud was tapping repressed memories of early childhood, first through hypnosis and then through free association. We can appreciate the innovation and the courage of that search when we conceptualize a world in which only novelists were sure that there *was* an unconscious.

Freud abandoned his original attempt to recover traumatic memories through hypnosis, a nebulous technique at that time, because the connection between original trauma and later symptoms was not yet evident. He himself discovered this link while working with free association. He called it *psychic determinism*. It was his conceptual masterpiece, and it has influenced nearly all subsequent psychotherapy and is the foundation of regression work. Current suggestions in regression therapy, such as "Go back to the time when this problem first occurred," are based on this certainty that what we experienced earlier determines our current behavior.

Freud's theory that memories of early childhood could be recovered and

Note: References are included in the bibliography except where subscripts refer to notes.

used therapeutically drew scornful reactions, but he persisted, though near the beginning he had to jettison his original conception of child abuse. As Galileo, who, in order to avoid being burned at the stake, agreed that the sun moved around the earth, Freud, to avoid being driven from Vienna, was forced to say that the tortured memories of his patients were fantasies. The importance of such memories currently permeates psychological thinking—witness to the often long hiatus between innovative proposals and their eventual acceptance.

Jung, in postulating a spiritual aspect to man's nature and the existence of universal patterns (archetypes), was even more removed from comfortable professionalism than Freud, and it took still longer for him to become accepted. In the 20's very few in the academic world had heard Jung's name. In the 50's his theories were still not welcome on American campuses. By the late 70's some Jungian concepts were beginning to be respectable, though they were still more likely to be considered exotic. Then, just as Plato's absolutes had provided soil in which the Jungian archetypes could emerge, so in the 80's Jung's theories flowed into the more scientific formulation of Sheldrake's morphogenetic fields,[1] finally gaining respectability. In a sense Jung ran interference for the spiritual thrusts of regression therapy because his concepts importuned the professional world throughout this century to become aware of this added aspect of existence. His use of "active imagination" influenced a spectrum of transformational techniques, and it rooted the emergence of the exciting flowering of imagery techniques in the 70's, which established an acceptable modality for reporting past-life impressions.

Freud lived long enough to see the conception that early childhood experience determines later behavior become acceptable, and gradually the focus of controversy moved backward to birth memories. Rank, who pioneered this new focus, appeared prematurely, and it was not until the 50's that Stanislav Grof reintroduced the concept, following his research with LSD.[2] The acceptance of birth memories lagged even at that time because it was assumed that memory depended on the existence of myelinated sheaths, which are undeveloped in the newborn. Moreover, the fact that in the beginning birth memories were recovered during drug experiences made them especially suspect. But Grof, after the banning of LSD in the early 60's, found that patients recovered similar birth memories through using an induction of music and breathing, demonstrating that these memories were not dependent on a drug for their retrieval.

Work with prenatal memories was not initiated until the 70's, and the concept of past life recall was not seriously explored until this time. Acceptance that past lives could be retrieved was especially grudging. This was not only because the concept of reincarnation did not fit into the scientific thinking of the time or because there appeared to be no viable vehicle to carry such memories, but even more because from early times past lives had been unhelpfully linked with the psychic community.

Psychics became involved because of the difficulty of accessing past lives. Prior to the late 60's there was little report of individuals remembering their own past lives except under hypnosis, where the depth of trance considered necessary to push memory back was not available to everyone and where it often left no conscious awareness of the experience. Even in India, where past lives are taken for granted, adults as a rule have not remembered them, though Ian Stevenson and others have documented young children clearly remembering their immediate previous past lives.[3]

In 1927 Paul Brunton wrote about a technique that the yogis developed to tune into past lives.[4] A Buddhist monk described to him a daily practice of turning memory backwards that he claimed had been taught by the Buddha. The meditator's recall of events flowed back first over days, then weeks, until the events of an entire year were remembered. This backward flow could then reach as far as birth. With many years of work, the monk said, one could go into former embodiments. Brunton felt that so many years of meditation did not justify the end.

During the 20's and 30's Edgar Cayce, well-known for his channeling of innovative healing approaches, began, to his own discomfort, to channel the past lives of some of his subjects. His extensive and enthusiastic following escalated interest in reincarnational theories in the United States. Though Cayce's channelings were for therapeutic purposes, they did not use the subjects' personal recovery of past-life material.[5]

In the late 50's a more direct approach to accessing past lives was proposed by a movement called Dianetics, but it was not taken seriously, partly because the professional image of its proponents became tarnished and partly because the intellectual climate was not ready to receive such a concept. However, the highly innovative approach has covertly impacted much of the past-life work we know today.

Dianetics emerged on the therapeutic scene apparently without warning, promising enlightenment and healing after five weeks of "auditing." It is still unclear how this divergent approach originated, although it has many concepts in common with the thinking of Wilhelm Reich. Those of us then in practice saw patients leave to embrace this attractive panacea, only to return after five weeks, distressed and anxious and sometimes psychotic. We realized that our patients had been pressured to recover distressing aspects of their lives by an uninvolved machine-like "auditor" who gave no therapeutic support. The absence in the Dianetic movement of awareness of the need for a therapeutic relationship combined with its cult-like grip on its followers caused the foundering of a technique that contained some innovative components.

As the therapeutic approach of Dianetics (later merged with Scientology) rapidly became discredited by the professional community, other aspects of Dianetics also became invalidated. These included the proposal, startling at the time, that past lives existed and could be contacted by traveling backwards on an emotional-physical bridge searching for an engram (an original traumatic situation still influencing behavior). The past lives recovered by this technique that L. Ron Hubbard reported in *Have You Lived Before This Life?* (1958) were in part similar to those found in contemporary regressions and in part were fanciful—a number of them took place on other planets or millions of years ago—but the technique of inducing them by flowing backward on a feeling or physical sensing was to surface in Morris Netherton's work. Netherton grounded and established the affect bridge as a form of induction, and under his tutelage many of our current therapists, including Woolger and the Dutch group led by Hans ten Dam, have demonstrated its clinical worth.

Meanwhile, hypnotic techniques had become more standardized and had developed an increasing range of applications. In the 60's this greater facility in hypnosis led to attempts to retrieve past lives. The case exploited by the media that provoked the greatest impact was a Colorado housewife's detailed account of a previous life in Ireland as a woman named Bridey Murphey.[6] The controversy regarding its validity opened up awareness of past lives to an extended audience. Following the Bridey case, increasing numbers of hypnotists undertook such past-life explorations, not with therapy in mind but through interest and curiosity.

## Early Steps in Past-life Therapy

By the late 60's and early 70's the use of age regression, the process of moving backward chronologically under hypnosis to tap early childhood memories, became generally acceptable. Increasingly sophisticated hypnotherapy techniques resulted in the patient being able to perceive and process experiences concurrently.

Denys Kelsey and Joan Grant were among the first to report such data in a professional way. Kelsey, a British psychiatrist, had for many years used hypnosis in his practice to regress patients to early childhood. Like other therapists of that time, he found that he could also uncover memories of birth and even return to pre-natal experience. Then he found patients remembering the time of their conception when there was no developed nervous system to retain the memories. At this point Kelsey concluded that there must exist in human beings an element that is capable of functioning and recording events, even in the absence of a physical body. It was this hypothesis, brought forward by a respected and conscientious professional, that initiated the acceptance of past-life therapy.

At the time when Kelsey concluded that there must be an aspect of personality that exists beyond the body, he heard about Joan Grant's experiences in remembering past lives, which she had recorded in *Far Memory* and *Winged Pharaoh*. He immediately went to visit Joan, who lived only 40 miles away. She had been an assistant to a psychiatrist and was familiar with psychiatric concepts and treatment, and she and Denys Kelsey found many common areas of interest. They set up a working relationship, which escalated into marriage six months later. From then on, Kelsey included past lives in much of his therapeutic work, often helped by Joan, who could psychically monitor patients and give helpful suggestions.

The Kelseys' joint book, *Many Lifetimes*, published in 1967, describes their work together. Because Joan was already a well-known author, this book was widely read, and the fact that Kelsey was a reputable psychiatrist encouraged readers to take the material seriously. The book opened an area of exploration that had been on the threshold for some time, and it constituted one of the first records of responsible regression therapy.

When we scan the period from the late 60's on, the barrier that excluded memories of the earlier periods of childhood (including sexual abuse), birth and prenatal experiences, and past lives, appears to thin. The immediacy with which such periods could be accessed was in striking contrast to their lack of availability in earlier times. Moreover, it became possible while in an altered state for one part of consciousness to retrieve memories while another part processed them. Could such memories have been recovered with more skillful techniques before the 60's? Or does the fact that past-life memories are increasingly more available constitute evidence that the nature of consciousness is undergoing a shift? Sheldrake proposed in his theory of morphic resonance that the growing number of people able to access such a level of consciousness increases the potential of everyone to do so.

Several other thrusts of the time have documented this thinning of the barrier to memory. In addition to Grof, other therapists found that deep breathing and imaging and other techniques could trigger birth memories, and this led to the formation of schools of rebirthing.[7] Barriers to prenatal memories that had seemed impermeable for many people, became bypassed by the new induction techniques.

There were experiments in the early 70's in the retrieval of past-life memories. In Australia a well-known novelist and playwright, G.M. Glaskin, worked with the Christos Technique, a powerful form of imaging and massage that enabled participants to go out-of-body and return to other lifetimes. In 1974 this account appeared as *Windows of the Mind*. More conservative but still innovative was Marcia Moore's *Hypersentience*, published in 1976. Hypersentience was Moore's term for the state of consciousness in which paranormal material is contacted: past lives, knowledge of the future, and psychic phenomena in general. Moore had already published and was well-known on radio shows, and *Hypersentience* became popular because, as was true of *Windows of the Mind*, it spelled out inductions that anybody could try.

In 1978 the energy that had been building up around past-life therapy exploded in four innovative books published the same year. The best known author at that time was a psychologist, Helen Wambach, who was concerned primarily with research. For some time she had been conducting large workshops, gathering data about artifacts, customs, and clothing of various time periods, and also material on future lifetimes. The first part of her research was summarized in a popular book *Reliving Past Lives*. Her statistical approach was an appropriate beginning for research in the new field and attracted attention because it dealt with homespun data and not with metaphysical claims. The material she gathered on the prenatal period was released subsequently in *Life Before Life*. Her investigation into future lifetimes was continued by her student, and later colleague, Chet Snow.

A book that exploded like a shooting star over an amazed and delighted public was *You Have Been Here Before* by Edith Fiore, a clinical psychologist and highly trained hypnotist. Like Kelsey, she had come upon past-life memories in the process of age regression. Putting a hold on her disbelief, she explored the past lives of a number of patients, some of whose experiences she included in her book. So effective did she find this method for achieving remission of symptoms that her psychological practice shifted to a focus on past lives. She provided an impetus for past-life work, not only through the impact of her book, which is a classic, but through the many training workshops she offered where she generously shared with other therapists her carefully conceived techniques. Later, *The Unquiet Dead* increased the scope of her work to include releasement of entities. In both books she suggested ways in which individuals could carry out the processes themselves, which was important, not so much as a practical approach, but as reassurance that such areas were available and respectable for the average person. A recent book, *Encounters*, concerns patients who have experienced UFO abductions.

It was also in 1978 that Morris Netherton released his book *Past Lives Therapy*. Netherton had worked outside the professional community while he was solidifying his concept of bridging. His first teaching was at the Healing Light Center in Glendale, California, and from there he gradually built his own school and eventually gave training workshops around the world. Many of our contributors started their work with him, or with both him and Fiore, and from these strikingly divergent techniques each therapist gradually incorporated what seemed useful into his/her own therapeutic approach. Netherton gave workshops in Europe and Brazil and is the dominant influence behind Hans ten Dam and the Dutch School. He has retained essentially the same core concepts over the years.

The fourth book, by a Munich psychologist, Thorwald Dethlefsen, had a strong impact on European psychologists but was less known here, although it was translated and appeared as *Voices from Other Lives*. It was a thoughtful book by a careful thinker. Dethlefsen was flexible in his conceptions and later changed direction and modified his ideas where data did not support his original concepts or when he saw a better way. In the beginning he used hypnosis as a form of induction but eventually realized that it was contraindicated because it gave control to the therapist instead of to the patient. He had employed varied forms of altered-state imagery while inducing hypnosis and simply removed the hypnotic suggestions, retaining a variety of images similar to those used by many American therapists. His revised understanding of altered state induction was described in *The Challenge of Fate*, his second book, where he included a brilliant and succinct discussion of the relationship between hypnosis and altered states in general. His most recent book, *The Healing Power of Illness* (translated in 1986), moved into a related area, healing and health, and stressed the theme of his second book, that we create our fate, including that of our bodies. It is a powerful and provocative treatise on psycho-somatic medicine.

These four books on past lives have one thing in common: they concern themselves with symptoms, a natural carry-over from conventional therapy, and do not stress spiritual implications. In the next decade the emphasis was gradually to shift, and with the exception of Netherton, these authors, and other past-life therapists along with them, began to include in their conceptualizations a concern for the meaning of life.

## The Paradigm Shift

The growing impulse to explore the nature of existence and to enter extended areas of consciousness reflected a massive paradigm shift, of which the transformation of the psychological perspective was only one aspect.[8] Small stirrings of this emerging shift had been evident from early in the century but had met with the resistance that any new paradigm inevitably encounters from a society, including most of its scientists, that finds the giving up of long accepted conceptualizations to be too painful. Because of the compelling need that has been felt in society to uncover meaning, the resistance to extended states of consciousness, dense and almost immovable at the beginning of the century, has gradually thinned. There have been three contributing thrusts that facilitated this paradigm shift: three strange bedfellows, each of which postulates and explores extended states of consciousness, which Kenneth Ring in his *Heading Toward Omega* calls "planetary consciousness" or Omega because it seeks to define our planetary as well as our individual lives.

The first thrust was an escalating interest in ancient philosophical theories from India and other Eastern countries, encouraged as early as the 20's and 30's by two credible observers, one an ace reporter turned philosopher, Paul Brunton, who reported his *Search in Secret India* (1934) and related explorations.[9] The second was the novelist L. Adams Beck, who reinforced the fragile initial interest in yoga in the 30's and opened up the obscure area of Zen.[10] She was one of the first thinkers to tie in Eastern concepts with the emerging theories of relativity and a broader understanding of the nature of consciousness proposed by innovative thinkers in physics.

Concurrently, after Germany had been devastated by World War I and needed a breakthrough in the search to find meaning in its suffering, Hermann Hesse, a Nobel Prize winner, reflected back the wisdom of the East in two profound novels, *Siddhartha* and *Journey to the East,* books that permeated the seeking of several generations of young people, in the United States as well as in Europe.[11] Another novel of this period that strongly impacted the thrust toward inner experience but stemmed from the neo-Platonic tradition rather than from Eastern wisdom was Charles Morgan's *The Fountain,* which went through numerous editions and was considered by Havelock Ellis to be the greatest novel in the English language. It opened up the feasibility and respectability of non-religious introversion.

Covering the same time span has been the apparently diametrically opposite exploration of modern physics and biology. No one would have expected that in the end the cutting edge of science would come to the same conclusions as the yogic philosophers, but from the early part of the century onward Einstein began talking about consciousness as a fundamental aspect of existence, and he was joined by other physicists, such as Jeans and Eddington, the latter of whom remarked succinctly that "the stuff of the world is mind stuff." Throughout the century other fellow travelers emerged to join these early paradigm breakers—Max Planck, David Bohm, and Rupert Sheldrake among them, all unashamedly talking about energy as constituting the nature of existence. In 1983 Peter Russell in the *The Global Brain* described our planet as Gaia, an alive consciousness with which human consciousness interacts.

Many popular books emerged from this scientific thrust. A book written by a physicist that had special impact because it successfully melded theoretical physics with the ancient Vedantic conceptualizations, was *The Tao of Physics* (1975) by Fritjof Capra. *The Dancing Wu Li Masters* (1979) by Gary Zukov, a Harvard scholar, covered a similar area and appealed to a different group of readers. Interestingly, the most successful work of fiction to emerge from the scientific approach was a trilogy written by Madeleine L'Engle for children. The first volume, *A Wrinkle in Time* (1962), a Newberry Award winner, became a classic beloved by all ages.

The third contribution to the emerging paradigm was the psychedelic thrust of the 60's, which gave direct experience of extended areas of perception to so many people that it became impossible that we could ever as a society return to the sterile limits of ordinary consciousness. Even the misuse of such explorations and the resultant legal restrictions could not dim the exciting landscape that had been unveiled. The brief glimpse of altered states had shaken perception into new patterns, and past-life memories seemed less alien as a result. Serious researchers in the area of psychedelic exploration documented their work, Jean Houston in *Varieties of Psychedelic Experiences* in 1966 and Stanislav Grof in a series of books beginning with *Realms of the Human Unconscious: Observations from LSD Research* ten years later in 1976. In his book Grof devoted several pages to the recovery of past-life patterns. What LSD therapy demonstrated was that other levels of consciousness were more available than had formerly been thought, and this helped to open the way to past-life recovery and other altered-state experiences.

Two books with strong impact on the more thoughtful public appeared in 1972. One was a novel by Aldous Huxley, called simply *Island*, in which he created a society built on psychedelic experiences. The other, *The Natural Mind* by Andrew Weil, gave a historical perspective of the impact of drugs on society and described the void it fills. Weil was certain that there is an innate human drive to experience periodic episodes of nonordinary consciousness and that these altered states of consciousness have a clear potential for psychic development. He felt that dealing with the drug problem involved, not control of drugs or punishment for their use, but offering safer and more productive ways of experiencing altered states. No one listened to his suggestions, and society is still chasing the expensive red herring of drug control.

During the 60's and early 70's when marijuana was the available drug for young people, I conducted adolescent groups where I took the participants on "trips" using guided meditation in a deep altered state. No member ever missed such a session, and extensive follow-up showed that the use of marijuana was discontinued or never started, suggesting that it was not the drug but the altered-state experience that was valued. The members with whom I was able to keep in touch became integrated and strikingly creative adults, even though at the time of the group they had been dysfunctional.[12]

We must determine whether experiences of altered states are a basic human need. If so, we must provide means more creative and positive than drugs for the experience of such states. Drugs seem as yet to be the most available resource, and the power of drugs to expand human consciousness continues to birth books by credible scientists and thinkers. A recent example is *Trialogues at the Edge of the West* (1992) by Ralph Abraham, Terence McKenna, and Rupert Sheldrake.

Threads of the constantly escalating new paradigm can be traced in many areas, but no transformation has been more dramatic than the shift in attitude toward physical health and medicine. It seems impossible now that there was ever an era without recognition that each person is responsible for his own health, but until the 70's the task of keeping well was considered a physician's responsibility. There had been thrusts toward conceiving medicine in terms of the changing paradigm, beginning with Ramacharaka in the beginning of this century. Ramacharaka wrote of the impact of good nutrition and of health practices in general—he was too wise to present to an unperceptive public what he obviously knew about the energy fields of the body.[13] He was one of the initiators of the paradigm shift in attitudes toward health largely through his influence on the physical culturist Bernard McFadden, who adopted Ramacharaka's proposals and couched them in good American language.

An early creative work that moved the medical thrust of the paradigm transformation forward was *The Medium, the Mystic and the Physicist* by Lawrence LeShan (1956). He had originally been convinced that paranormal phenomena could not stand up under scientific investigation, and he designed careful research to prove this. To his consternation, his data indicated that there was no way the phenomena could be considered invalid, and good scientist that he was, he courageously presented his findings. He then designed a successful new experiment in energy healing, using himself as a guinea pig, and after several years of working to understand what happened in such healing, he found that he could both demonstrate it and teach others to do the same. His research produced incontrovertible evidence of healing forces beyond those generally accepted. Conventional medicine should have had difficulty in dismissing his evidence because of the fine-tuned quality of his research, but, like those who refused to look through Galileo's new telescope at the craters of the moon because they were sure such craters did not exist, the medical profession dismissed LeShan's findings by shrugging their shoulders, not knowing what else to do with evidence that did not fit.

More than a decade later Elmer and Alyce Green brought out the Menninger-based book, *Beyond Biofeedback* (1978), which, in spite of its dry title, sparkled with innovation and courageous exploration. Their proposed control of autonomic processes by biofeedback merged into an exploration of body consciousness and extended the foundation of body-mind medicine. Their hypothesis that the body is the laboratory in which we learn to handle the energies of life is a profound concept that grounds regression therapy as well as the majority of spiritual and energic healing systems. Both this book and that of LeShan meshed modern medical concepts with Eastern philosophical points of view. To gather data for this, the Greens spent considerable time in India talking with its greatest current sages, especially with the followers of Auribindo.

The Greens' work with biofeedback was one of various experiments in alternative medicine, such as acupuncture and homeopathy. In the 70's in *Getting Well Again* the Simontons demonstrated the possibility of using imagery for healing cancer—such a radical suggestion that Carl Simonton was temporarily removed from the American Medical Association, though much later, when his ideas began to have credence, he was invited back to the staff of a large hospital. Pioneers such as Norman Shealy proposed other new models of healing, such as the innovative biogenic concepts in *Ninety Days to Self Health* (1976). Many of the ideas presented in Shealy's book that seemed extreme at that time are now taken for granted—witness to the long way we have come in little over a decade. His more recent book, *The Creation of Health* (1988), written with Carolyn Myss, reflects over a decade of growth in understanding of psychic diagnosis, the nature of illness, and the mechanics of healing.

Three other innovative and creative physicians who contributed to the revamping of the medical model released books in the late 80's. Larry Dossey anticipated his more definitive book *Recovery of the Soul* (1989) by a popular forerunner, *Space, Time and Medicine* (1982). Dossey's courageous presentation of the concept of the soul, so long *persona non grata* in scientific halls, was one more support for the unfolding concepts of regression work. He presented the concept of the nonlocal mind (a contemporary equivalent of the soul) as a place of interaction and connection that could lay a new foundation for ethical and moral behavior. An important hypothesis the book presents is that love is endemic to the genuine nonlocal sense of wholeness, a concept that is becoming increasingly evident in regression work. Dossey's concept of love meshed with those of the beloved physician, Bernie Siegel, in *Love, Medicine, and Miracles* (1988), who helped to make the concept of love energy credible and acceptable. The scientifically innovative work of Deepak Chopra, which reached its theoretical culmination in *Quantum Healing* (1989), finally provided a framework for mind-body medicine through the concept of an "intelligence" programming the DNA. This opened the way for understanding how programming in the energy body (which Woolger proposes is at least in part done in other lifetimes) can impact the physical body of today, an invaluable contribution to basic regression theory.

Gradually alternative medicine became linked with modern physics to declare finally what the yogis had known from the beginning, that the physical body is an energy field. Hiroshi Motoyama, a Japanese scientist, began to demonstrate instrumentally the nature of the body's energy fields and shifts in its energy centers. His findings were reported in English in 1978 in *Science and the Evolution of Consciousness: Chakras, Ki, and Psi*. Richard Gerber summarized the findings of Motoyama and other researchers in *Vibrational Medicine* (1988). His insistence that everything is composed of various energy frequencies opened medicine to even more radical concepts of healing.

The contribution of modern medicine to understanding healing as a transformation of energy has helped to provide a theoretical grounding for therapy involving past lives. Roger Woolger worked from ancient yogic conceptions of energy to explain the nature, storage, and transmission of experiences of other lifetimes. Chet Snow made maximum use of the concepts of energy in modern physics. The final positions of Woolger and Snow have much in common, and together they provide a theoretical matrix for understanding the formation and persistence of patterns and the nature of therapeutic change, not only in regression work but in psychotherapy in general.

The escalating paradigm shift was first defined and documented in 1980 by Marilyn Ferguson in her book *The Aquarian Conspiracy*. In it she postulated that numbers of people had begun "breathing together" (the literal meaning of con-spire) as they moved into a new state of consciousness. She founded the *Brain-Mind Bulletin*[14] as a clearinghouse for various professional thrusts—medical, psychological, educational, political, and personal—that were involved in the making of this new paradigm.

Meanwhile, various associations emerged to bring cohesion to these specialized thrusts: the Institute of Noetic Sciences, the Association of Transpersonal Psychology, the Association of Humanistic Psychology, the Association for Holistic Medicine, and many others. Journals for reporting research and discussing theory appeared, some sponsored by the associations, others more inclusive, such as *Revision* and *The Common Boundary*.

## The Formation of the Association for Past-Life Research and Therapies

One of the associations that was birthed by this paradigm shift was the Association for Past-Life Research and Therapies. By the 80's there was enough interest in the recovery of past lives as a method of therapy to encourage the formation of such a group to support organized communication in the field. The process began when Ronald Jue arranged a conference the weekend of May 14, 1980, at University of California, Irvine, to present ideas of reincarnation and past-life therapy. The only stipulation of the university was that all speakers be professionally credentialed, and those who spoke included Ernest Pecci, Edith Fiore, Helen Wambach, Gina Cerminara, and Morris Netherton. At the close of the first day, a group remained and appointed a committee, including Hazel Denning, Ronald Jue, and Barbara Findeisen, to work on the formation of a past-life therapy association. The purposes that were structured by this founding group included that the organization should be a clearing house for information, should establish professional status, set standards and determine ethics, help to articulate the concept of past lives to the professional community, publish a journal, and be involved in a training program. It was also to serve as a support group for its members and as a referral source for the public.

The following October the association was officially brought into existence at a conference in Anaheim. At this time the committee presented a constitution and organizational plans. Hazel Denning was elected the first president, with Barbara Findeisen the vice-president and Ronald Jue the secretary. A board of 15 was named, including Edith Fiore, Helen Wambach, Ernest Pecci, Jason Levine, and Morris Netherton.

Many of the original professionals have supported the association during its decade of growth. Pecci became the second president. Hazel Denning functioned as Executive Director for many years and it was under her guidance that the *Association for Past-life Research and Therapy* (APRT), as the new organization was known in its early years, grew from a struggling group who scarcely knew each other to a viable international society. Fiore left the board to complete her second book but since then has appeared many times as a lecturer on APRT conference programs. Netherton served on the original board and supported the new group by giving several workshops but eventually left, preferring to stress involvement with his center. Jason Levine edited the association's first newsletter. Helen Wambach gave totally to the new group with her warm and brilliant self, and her 1985 death, which she had long anticipated, dimmed the APRT world.

At the request of University of California at San Diego, the third conference was held there. The Executive Committee and Board had whittled away at the tasks set for them and had much to report to the new membership, beginning with thoughts about training.

Up to that time only a handful of licensed therapists had entered a field considered to lie beyond the perimeters of conventional psychology, and except for Fiore's and Netherton's workshops, there was no training. APRT gradually developed training seminars and worked to establish criteria of who should practice regression therapy. A preponderance of those doing regressions at that time were uncredentialed—many were psychics who did readings rather than practiced therapy. In addition to the handful of credentialed therapists, there was a small but important segment of professionals, many of them hypnotherapists, who were not credentialed in academic psychology but were gifted in past-life work, and these needed to be included.

Lack of credentialing meant that the young society would not be professionally recognized, so the trend has been toward more rigorous requirements, but the situation is still in flux. It has been complicated by different perceptions as to whether regression work is sufficient in itself or whether it is part of the larger discipline of psychotherapy. There has not been a clear answer, and those with diverse opinions have learned to accommodate each other. In July of 1963 Ronald Jue, Hazel Denning, and I formed the Professional Institute for Regression Therapy, an ongoing and credentialing institute for professional therapists. Roger Woolger, Irene Hickman, Edith Fiore, hypnotherapy institutes, and others, offer workshops open to non-licensed participants, and the semi-annual APRT conferences that include brief training workshops, have been a partial solution.

Research was named in the beginning as a major area of focus for the association. I asked to be the first research chairman and spent the year finding out that there was no research in progress and ending up empty-handed. Adequate techniques for research in therapy using past lives did not exist; no one knew how to pin down such a nebulous field. Ian Stevenson's books had concentrated on the credibility of reincarnation and Helen Wambach's innovative investigation of the parameters of past lives had been statistical and not involved with psychotherapy. The young association needed to develop tools for investigating therapeutic procedure and efficacy rather than concern itself with past-life validation. Since the type of temperament and interest that makes a good therapist does not often lend itself to research proclivity, progress has been slow and without much fruit. Most of the development in the field has been through experience and has been documented by anecdotes.

Woolger, Jue, Snow, and ten Dam in the Netherlands have been major contributors to a theoretical foundation for regression work. Woolger, especially, who was trained in philosophy at Oxford, has contributed far-reaching theoretical concepts that have grounded the understanding of past lives and provided structure for effective therapeutic techniques. Jue's contribution has been in differentiating the stages of past-life work and the interventions appropriate for each stage. His conceptions have become so much a part of the thinking of today that most people assume that the different levels have always been obvious, a tribute to a careful, clear, and helpful theorist.

Ten Dam explored holographic theory in his book *Exploring Reincarnation*, translated in 1990 from the Dutch *Een Ring van Licht*. He based his therapeutic approach on an understanding that all levels of experience are equally available and a change of focus permits a shift from one level to another. Woolger, also, considers holographic theory an underpinning for concepts of regression therapy, and Snow has extended the holographic conception to future progressions. Snow has contributed most to tying concepts of regression into such current scientific thinking as quantum physics. He has been an invaluable facilitator in working toward the recognition of past-life therapy as a legitimate and scientifically based form of therapy.

Hazel Denning's extensive research correlating physical healing with altered state work, including past-life recovery, has recently been statistically analyzed and presented in an APRT monograph entitled *Altered States of Consciousness: A Technique for Healing the Body*. In a five year follow-up 64% of her sample of volunteers experienced from mild to complete relief, including total remission in cases where severe pathology was present. [15]

A promising research proposal, never funded, was proposed by the Psychology Department of Colorado State University in 1987.[16] It hypothesized that the Post-Traumatic Stress Disorder found in Vietnam veterans, which has confounded every therapeutic approach, is the result of attachment by soldiers killed in battle to comrades still alive, a situation that cannot be dealt with in conventional therapy.

Research with the Mind Mirror into the brain states accompanying regression work has been my ongoing contribution, with the support of Chet Snow. Our research has dealt with the question of where past lives are stored and the mechanism for retrieving them, and it has thrown added light on the relationship between patient and therapist.[17]

In an effort to give cohesion to the association and to provide an opportunity to share therapeutic procedures, experiences, and research, APRT developed *The Journal of Regression Therapy* in 1986. The instructions of the Board were to include reactions from members, new research, innovative treatment techniques, and personal experiences, as well as articles and book reviews. The first editor was Irene Hickman. Her volume, unfortunately now out of print, contained some of the best articles on regression work ever printed. After the first volume, submissions were few, and the next six issues, which I edited, dealt with particular areas, such as physical healing, the roots of relationship patterning, guilt, and childhood patterns. Following my editorship, Garrett Oppenheim birthed one issue, then resigned due to ill health. The Journal now is in the competent hands of Russell Davis, a psychologist who is also an experienced editor. The Journal serves not only as a unifying agent for the association but has helped to define the nature and parameters of the regression field. The challenge has been to develop a professional journal in an area where scholarly boundaries are only in the process of being staked out.

## New Areas of Altered-State Therapy

Meanwhile, as psychotherapeutic techniques using past-life recall gathered momentum, other areas involving altered states found definition. Among these was exploration of the prenatal period. In the late 70's Thomas Verney proposed that *the fetus is aware* and that it stores memories. Prenatal memories were even more difficult to ground than birth memories for those who thought that the mind was equivalent to the brain and that both mind and brain were non-functional without myelinated sheaths. Verney was low-keyed in his proposals, however, and the professional community, impacted by the explorations of Grof, restrained its skepticism. Even in this more tolerant milieu Verney did not venture to propose the existence of memories before the development of the nervous system in the fourth month. His book, *The Secret Life of the Unborn Child*, appeared in 1981.[18]

Throughout the 80's many regression therapists investigated this prenatal area, adding new evidence to confirm Verney's hypotheses and extending perception back to the time of conception. Two who have made especial impact are David Chamberlain, who wrote *Babies Remember Birth*,[19] and David Cheek.[20] Therapists began to work more skillfully at this level but few were writers, and it was not until 1992 that Michael Gabriel, a seasoned therapist, summarized the area in an organized and insightful book, *Return to the Womb*. This book is a needed chart for exploring the important months of prenatal patterning.

A new thrust in the prenatal area with important implications for the controversy over abortion is the possibility of dialoguing with the unborn child. The first published discussion appeared in 1980 in Gladys McGarey's holistic approach to childbirth, *Born to Live*. It is difficult to understand why this simple, direct, and available resource of dialoguing, effective not only for dealing with decisions about abortion but also for deepening bonding with children who *are* wanted, is still largely neglected.

The theoretical groundwork for retrieval of more deeply hidden early childhood memories, especially those of abuse, was presented by Alice Miller in a series of books written between 1981 and 1984, the best known of which is *Thou Shalt Not Be Aware* (1984). Thomas Armstrong's *The Radiant Child* (1985) postulated the existence of a spiritual aspect of childhood seldom considered in the literature on children. The first book reporting psychotherapeutic techniques using altered states for early childhood distress appeared in 1992, *The Process of Healing* by Alice Givens.[21] The actual use of altered state exploration of childhood has not emerged as an area of regression therapy in its own right but is still employed as peripheral to past-life or prenatal retrieval.

The area of death and dying, on the other hand, experienced an explosion of interest as early as the 70's as the result of two remarkable pioneers.[22] The first of these, Elisabeth Kübler-Ross, opened up the discussion and exploration of death, which before this time had been subject to heavy taboo. In *On Death and Dying* (1969), she delineated the stages of dying. Following the publication of her book she retaught the art of dying in an uninterrupted succession of conferences and workshops, making the dying themselves more comfortable and acceptant, teaching family and friends and physicians to be helpful, and aiding those who were grieving over loss. Single-handedly she turned around the *attitude toward dying*.

Our understanding of the *nature of death* has been transformed by another pioneer, Raymond Moody, whose book *Life After Life* has been a classic best-seller since its publication in 1975. His data, gleaned from reports of near-death experiences, provided evidence that we do not cease to exist because our bodies die. This finding in one breathtaking leap confirmed the assumptions of regression therapists about the ongoing nature of existence and reinforced the description of the transition after death as it had consistently been reported in regression work. The significance of this research for increasing the credibility of past-life therapy cannot be overstated.

The first modern definitive report of interlife exploration was published in 1986 in *Life Between Life*, researched and written by Joel Whitton, a Toronto psychiatrist, in collaboration with Joe Fisher.[23] This book, which was also an excellent treatise on past lives, opened up a sensitive discussion of the nebulous area of the experience between lives and explored its therapeutic potential. Brian Weiss, whose book *Many Lives, Many Masters* appeared in 1989, further explored the interlife that Joel Whitton had investigated. Weiss's high professional visibility and persuasive personality have moved the field in the direction of more acceptance by the scholarly community. His recent book, *Through Time into Healing*, (1992) reports his forays into other transpersonal areas and is being received with even greater interest. He is becoming a high-profile television guest who presents regression work in an unflamboyant but convincing manner.

Progression into the future was long considered by most therapists to be either off-limits or not pertinent. Chet Snow's summary of his and Helen Wambach's research appeared in *Mass Dreams of the Future* in 1989 and opened up this largely unexplored dimension. Snow's book has both the charm and pace of an exciting novel and the scientific rigor of new-age physics. It provokes a careful analysis of where our current life-style and our lack of concern for our planet are leading us.

An area that persists in demanding attention is the releasement of those who after death have not completed their transition to the next state.[24] A social worker, Anabel Chaplin, discovered this situation while working with patients and documented it in 1975 in her book *The Bright Light of Death*. Through the following years, evidence accumulated of startling healings and remissions of symptoms following releasement, and there were scattered reports in journals about these, but it was not until Edith Fiore's *The Unquiet Dead* appeared in 1987 that the field became constellated and defused of its historically negative mystique. As she had done with past lives, Fiore made this difficult area simple and easily accessible as a therapeutic technique.

The thrust to bring the consideration of releasement into a sound therapeutic framework was continued by Adam Crabtree, a Toronto psychologist, in his recently released *Multiple Man: Explorations in Possession and Multiple Personality*.[25] His book is slowly coming into the acceptance and regard that it so much deserves. It is particularly valuable for the regression therapist, who frequently encounters spirit attachments and needs help to deal with them. Crabtree's approach is sensitive to the plight of the spirit and gives clear guidelines for dealing with it therapeutically. His approach is corrective for those who feel that releasement can be a brief process.

## Past-Life Therapy Comes of Age

Around the early 80's the area of past-life work progressed on many fronts. Following the work of the four pioneers, a number of other books appeared that reflected the experiences of their authors and little by little added to the foundation of regression work. Frederick Lenz, a competent psychologist and author who later turned guru, wrote *Lifetimes: True Accounts of Reincarnation* (1979), which had a built-in publicity boost because of Lenz's former successful book on guided imagery and meditation.[26] His book was followed in 1984 by Irene Hickman's *Mind Probe—Hypnosis*. Dr. Hickman, an osteopathic physician, was herself a longtime pioneer in past-life work who slowly and carefully developed reliable techniques, which she shared in her book.

More recent contributions to the field have included Roger Woolger's stimulating book *Other Lives, Other Selves*, published in 1987. Woolger had written articles for *The Journal of Regression Therapy* and in his book gathered together his psychotherapeutic assumptions and hypotheses and illustrated them by carefully chosen cases. His chapters on theory are the most innovative in the field, and his book is currently the one most used in training. During that same year Karl Schlotterbeck published *Living Your Past Lives*, which reexamines old territory while opening up interesting new areas.

In 1990 two well-established professionals brought out books that deepened and grounded the field of regression by their perceptive observations and reporting. Raymond Moody's *Coming Back: A Psychiatrist Explores Past-Life Journeys* is rich in clinical documentation and contains innovative induction techniques, such as skrying,[27] and fresh perspectives on processing, such as searching in past lives for one's personal myth. Garrett Oppenheim's *Who Were You Before You Were You?* reflects the literary polish of a senior writer. The moving personal experience of the author provides a model by which other therapists can analyze and synthesize their own dynamics.

Meanwhile the focus of regression work has been shifting. Through the 70's the objective, at least as stated by books released during that time, was the remission of symptoms, either by cathartic abreaction of a related traumatic situation or by scanning patterns. Through the 80's this emphasis on remission of symptoms continued—people entered regression therapy because they were suffering in some way—but increasing emphasis has become focused on the concept of the soul's journey. Not all therapists acknowledge this because not all are concerned with the spiritual aspect of life. However, it is becoming clear that where regression therapy supersedes other therapies is in its more profound perspective on the meaning of life.

Regression therapy has been carried along on a collective current that can neither be hurried nor stemmed. While gathering up each thrust in understanding during the decades of its flow this current has gradually become a river that carries in it the making of a new age. The next thrust may well be an expansion of interlife experience. Those who have been able to contact this state have perceived profound and appropriate sources of wisdom and an aura of love that is recognized by them to be the ground of being. Such perceptions are identical to those sensed in spontaneous near-death experiences or in cosmic consciousness.

The interlife is our controlled connection with the essence of life—a low-key transformational source that will become increasingly available, just as the recovery of past lives, once so difficult, can now be experienced by nearly everyone. Our planet is falling apart with negativity—from crime and self-involvement as well as from natural disasters resulting from our neglect of the environment—and work in the interlife may become the easily contacted transformational modality needed to bring in a new era. The focus must shift from self-involvement to the more life-enhancing goal of love and service. In the process our planet will be able to progress on its journey of the soul as a collective unit.

The Association for Past-Life Research and Therapies remains a fragile society. It is handicapped not only by the distances separating its core of members but by lack of a training mandate that would determine who is a candidate for the practice of past-life therapy and under what circumstances such therapy is appropriate. The young association provides an exchange of information at its semi-annual conferences and in its Journal and Newsletter, and without these, regression work would suffer loss of form and direction. However, acceptance of past lives is an integral part of the total paradigm shift, having been both spawned and nourished by it, and the concept of individual lives existing as segments of a soul journey will increasingly impact the thinking of our planet.

The intense concern over whether or not past lives exist has finally wound down. As Dethlefsen says, "Reincarnation is not a belief; it is a philosophy of life." A recent book that sums up this attitude, or perhaps even states an attitude that we will share more fully five years from now, is *Life Cycles: Reincarnation and the Web of Life* by Christopher Bache, a philosopher with degrees from Cambridge and Brown Universities who teaches philosophy at Youngstown State University. Bache bypasses the concern as to whether past lives exist by stating simply that reincarnation is the only description of life that makes sense and fits facts.

Bache, in addition to helpfully and unceremoniously closing the door on validation concerns, offers a perceptive review of the doctrine of karma and its current implications and at the same time explores the ramifications of adopting a reincarnationist perspective. Bache thinks of our lifetimes as an energy web underlying the causalities of our lives. Reincarnation, he says, makes us aware that we are essentially spiritual beings and can understand ourselves only when we look beyond our physical bodies and perceive ourselves in the frame of our own histories and beyond time itself. With this statement he becomes the eloquent spokesman of regression therapy as it is today—or as it will be tomorrow.

# *Theory*

*Life is like a string of pearls, the self being the thread and the pearls side by side are life experiences, births and deaths beings a continuum, all opportunities for growth in consciousness.*

*Barbara Findeisen*

*There is a primordial Essence characterized by unconditional love, joy, serenity, and wisdom, from which we have become separated and to which we can return by moving out into the vaster realities of awareness.*

*Ernest Pecci*

*In human beings the most powerful emotion is love. Love vibrates in a special way and serves as a kind of universal lubricant. Perhaps it defines harmony among the relationship of irregular wave patterns, what Pythagoras called "the music of the spheres."*

*Chet Snow*

# Chapter II

# Philosophical Hypotheses

We are multi-personalities, and there are two sides of us that evaluate the world. The scientific and rational approach is ingrained in us, the contributors to this book, who have been educated at Oxford, Harvard, Stanford, Columbia, Tufts, Oberlin, Mt. Holyoke, the University of Amsterdam, and various University of California campuses. We are committed to scientific observation, but at the same time our perception of life is permeated by the intuitive approach with its unfathomable and mysterious depths. The physical sciences in the centers of learning in which we were educated have tentatively reached in this direction by postulating the existence of a universe of energy that is never lost and can undergo transformation. However, this concept has not yet been integrated into conventional psychological thinking: the data of intuition is still suspect, and it is with reluctance that we produce hypotheses about such a clouded area as past lives. I appreciate the willingness of all of our contributors to express concepts that at times appear ungrounded, not only to our colleagues, but even to our own rational and professional selves.

## The Journey of the Soul

It is our intuition that leads us to realize that we are on a journey of the soul back to our Source and that what occurs in each lifetime is appropriate for the stage of that individual's journey.

Pecci states the underlying assumption:

> There is a primordial Essence characterized by unconditional love, joy, serenity, and wisdom, from which we have become separated and to which we can return by moving out into the vaster realities of awareness.

Journeying toward this universal flow of energy is the meaning of spirituality and the purpose of our stream of lifetimes. It embraces a consciousness essentially unlimited, that is continuous, has no boundaries, knows everything, and forms our essential core.

Snow reaffirms this transpersonal quality of past-life experience:

> The process is at heart a profoundly spiritual one. It implies the existence and accessibility of deep spiritual wisdom within each of us. This wisdom may carry a myriad of names and faces: it may even at times seem contradictory on the surface, yet underneath all the apparent contradictions is a fundamental unity behind our definition of being human.

Woolger describes this unity in non-linear terms:

> When we gain the perspective of the great wheel of existence, we can see that all spokes emanate from the Center—only at the rim are spokes seen as separate and in a sequential relationship with each other. The Self is at the heart of all beings and all Being.

He discusses the relationship between individual roles and the Self:

> At the unitive level all past lives are present to the Self and all roles are known aspects of the Self, like an actor playing many parts. Good and evil roles exist, but merely as parts of the greater drama, not as absolutes in themselves. Good and evil create that dynamic tension of opposites necessary for created reality to become conscious of itself.

To this Findeisen adds that the Self does not begin at birth or conception, nor does it end with death:

> Life is like a string of pearls, the Self being the thread and the pearls side by side are life experiences, births and deaths being a continuum, all of them opportunities for growth in consciousness.

Reynolds stresses that the journey to the Self is a drive toward wholeness and completion. Pecci says that coming to a place of peace and harmony with the Self allows us to live a more complete life; in the process we must reactivate our capacity to love and to accept the universal love that continually nourishes us and awaits our recognition of it. Jue postulates that we have an innate drive or instinct toward wholeness, integration, and equilibrium, and Denning adds that man is a spiritual being endowed with unlimited creative potentials and the capacity to know who he is and where he is going. Pain and disharmony focus our attention on the non-aligned aspects of our psyches so that we are eventually forced to create a homeostatic balance. All contributors agree that on a spiritual level the journey through our various lifetimes is movement toward karmic homeostasis.

Snow concedes that it is this spiritual aspect of past-life therapy that makes it suspect to the professional world:

The development of transpersonal psychology and past-life therapy as recognized and distinct psychological modalities marks a watershed in the search for new patterns and hypotheses beyond the traditional Western paradigms of belief in evolutionary or linear progress and in the primacy of material over spiritual reality. It is this spiritual aspect of regression therapy that is a stumbling block for the ordinary professional because for many, "spiritual" is equated with "illusory."

## Karmic Patterns

Our contributors accept the term "karmic" to describe the patterns that we establish in our drive toward wholeness and that either hinder or facilitate our journey.[1] It is the existence of these patterns that is the basic hypothesis underlying regression therapy; just to tap into past lives without postulating that they reveal patterns would be a hollow effort. Karma is a subtle form both of cause and effect and of relationship. Probably it is better thought of as constituting *patterns that need to be changed* because, although there is such a thing as positive karma, we seldom focus on it.

Karma, by mechanisms that are far from clear, establishes the perfect setting for each person's journey of the soul and underlies the therapeutic potential that is to be found in the recovery of other lifetimes. Dethlefsen describes the patterning involved:

> The sum of all incarnations forms our learning history, which makes us whatever we happen to be and stamps our conduct and emotions.... The fate of this life is therefore a result of the previous chain of lives, a consequence of what was previously learned or not learned. Everyone at times goes through these problems that he did not conquer in the past through conscious learning, and in the future he will again be confronted with one and the same problem until he has solved it for himself. This regularity is known in India as karma, which requires that a problem be experienced continuously until it is understood.

All of our contributors agree that the basic ground of regression therapy is the existence of these karmic patterns in our living. Most current thinkers extend the concept of karma from its early simplistic assumption of cause and effect to a broader understanding of its effect on the life setting of each individual, not only what he has earned but *what is most appropriate for his growth.*

Pecci feels that our acceptance of karmic patterns makes us more comfortable with life's seeming vicissitudes.

> The objective of viewing past lives is identifying such patterns. We can gain a great deal by studying the vivid pictures that come out as past-life memories.... An appreciation of our patterns takes the sting from our pain and makes of life an interesting adventure and one in which a new sense of harmony with the flow of universal life energy becomes possible.

Jue says that past-life therapy helps us to understand more profoundly the mind-body-spirit connection and how we as evolving souls are responsible for creating our universe for our own spiritual growth, another definition of karma.

Woolger calls these residues from previous lifetimes by the Hindu term *samskaras* and says that past-life aspects of a complex (samskaras) arise when there are events in another lifetime producing pain, hurt, loss, grief, bitterness, etc. that are brought forward to the present life. Samskaras (psychic residues) are the psychological equivalent of karma. Psychic residues may also arise from fresh events in the current lifetime (the biographical aspect of the complex), which creates new karma.

Specific repetition of patterns for the purpose of learning is often found in relationships. Denning feels that each person has chosen his lesson or lessons for a particular lifetime and in connection with this has determined the personalities and setting that will most effectively help him learn that lesson. Relationships become a part of one's karma and weave back and forth through lifetimes until the emotional entanglements are resolved. Most therapists agree that individuals tend to incarnate with others with whom they are karmically connected, though not always the same individuals in each lifetime. We continue to make contact with the same people as long as we have mutual problems to solve.

The process of repeating patterns and working through them until we achieve wholeness (on a more subtle level than we experienced wholeness in the original state of unity before the process of individuation began) assumes a series of lives. It postulates that the life we live today gives us a chance to rectify the mistakes we made in previous lives or to complete some of the unfinished business we left behind—the lessons that we failed to learn in previous incarnations, as Hickman suggests. That we are born again and again in physical bodies in order to perfect ourselves is the more inclusive goal formulated by Fiore.

Probably our multiplicity of lifetimes is not as simple as the linear model often used. Snow suggests that we may not be developed enough to understand what the progression really is, or if there is a progression rather than an integration of various roles. However, in our limited understanding of the nature of reality, most of us think in terms of a sequence of past lives, and this seems currently to offer the most understandable way to conceptualize the inner journey.

Many conceive of soul growth as including a variety of what seem to be contradictory roles. In various lives we experience the opposites—aggression and victimization, wealth and poverty, arrogance and humility. This concept, called *polarity*, is espoused especially by Woolger, the Dutch school, and Dethlefsen. According to them, the soul needs a spectrum of experiences to become complete. Therefore, we should not judge actions and attitudes negatively that lead to karmic repercussion but should consider them to be valuable facets of soul experience. All of them exist as potentials in each person, and it is only when we own these potentials that we become free.

Woolger points out that this is a concept similar to Jung's shadow:

> The integration of the opposites, or wholeness, is preferred to a goal of perfection or of "overcoming" negativity. Following Jung, the dark or shadow sides of the personality are to be integrated into consciousness, not banished or exorcised as if they were "possessing" entities.... Until a person can acquire a witness point outside patterns on all levels of the complex, he or she may experience a continuing spiral of lives of action, reaction, and counter-reaction that elude any resolution. The aim, therefore, is non-attachment to the complex.

Dethlefsen stresses the healing aspect of this process:

> Facing our individual and collective polarity and accepting it in its true sense ends judging ourselves and others and helps with transformation, both individually and collectively. Awareness of this heals body, mind, and soul.

One basic hypothesis on which our contributors agree is that *soul patterns repeat themselves on many levels*. To present a theoretical grounding for this assumption Findeisen, Woolger, and the Dutch therapists mention Pribram and his holographic theory. Pribram postulates that within each of us is a fragment of the whole and each fragment reflects the whole. One field contains both the past and the present, and an individual can work with and transform patterns on any level. The therapist can deal with a current pattern or work with a sub-personality, as in Gestalt or Psychosynthesis, or explore pre-birth experiences or go back to a past life.

Woolger, Bontenbal, and Noordegraaf stress the holographic nature of their approaches and have developed holographic models. They feel that work on any particular level is indicated when such work can amplify awareness of patterns and demonstrate continuity and repetition. Woolger extends the concept of the hologram to include not only current childhood, birth, perinatal, and past-life experiences, but also somatic complaints and archetypal aspects. He feels that none of these is temporarily prior or more fundamental. Snow conceptualizes the future as a further aspect of the hologram.

## The Wisdom of the Core Self

One hypothesis that is made by most contributors is that in an altered state we have access to a source that is all-knowing and possessed of deep wisdom. This wisdom is connected to the memory banks or the mind field and can produce information we need. Denning calls this the Inner Mind or Higher Self, depending on the background of her client. Hickman postulates a deep level of understanding and insight. Findeisen says there is a Basic Self that knows the answers. Pecci names this part the Superconscious Orchestrator. Jue says there is a transcendent function within the psychological makeup of the individual that knows the origin of problems and their resolution. Insight and wisdom, Woolger feels, come when one can reach a "witness point" and evaluate lives from a point outside the personal self.

The Kahunas hypothesize that we have a Body Self that can go into the memory banks and retrieve any memory (if the request is made courteously!).[2] It can even go into a more transcendent state and find answers to abstract questions. Guides, and possibly power animals, may be imaginal representatives of the Inner Mind. (Or guides may be wise teachers from other lifetimes who remain nearby and are ready to help.)

Why, if there is a deep place of knowing within us, a reliable and wise Inner Mind, do we use it so little? Why do people go to the trouble to employ derivatives—astrology, the Tarot cards, the I Ching, the pendulum, psychic readings, automatic writing? These are accurate only to the extent that the operator is tuned into the Inner Mind.

The answer may be that not everyone is close enough to whatever this state of wisdom is to address it directly. Perhaps the quiescent, listening stance required is incompatible with our hurrying lives—some patients cannot become quiet enough to imagine or perceive a deep source within themselves. Perhaps there needs to be an inner readiness, and training through meditation in contacting one's inner experience may help. Those who can contact this inner source of wisdom find that it contains highly accurate information, and there is some evidence, as Pecci suggests, that past-life journeys are difficult for people who cannot find an Inner Mind to help them perceive and evaluate.

## The Energic Nature of Experience and Transformation

Most of our contributors have been influenced by the current thrusts of modern physics and psycho-biology. Physics postulates that energy fields, which include behavior patterns, cannot simply cease to be: they can only be transmuted. This suggests that energy fields generated in previous lifetimes are brought forward into the current one, perhaps in the form of subpersonalities (repeated vibrational patterns), and it is these patterns that must be transmuted. Rupert Sheldrake hypothesizes a mind field that is the repository for such experience.[3] Information on any level is stored in this mind field, not in the brain. Such a field forms a continuity between one lifetime and another, and material from it can be recovered while in an altered state.

Snow considers that the theory of electromagnetic resonance best explains the storing of energy fields and their psychic transmission from lifetime to lifetime:

> According to this theory the basis of all reality is the interplay of cosmic waves of force of an electromagnetic nature. As these forces play together they vibrate energy. As we transit from one level of reality to another at death, all the emotional patterns previously created coalesce into a resonant energy field and survive. At the birth of our next incarnation in space/time, they are transmitted to the new individual's psyche according to a process still little understood. Apparently some choice is involved, as well as some determinism.
>
> The emotional programming received seems to be independent of linear space/time. It apparently includes not only past-life data but also archetypical models, the particular irregularities of a variety of vibrational energy patterns (other life forms), and human genetic predispositions. Stored at various levels of the subconscious, this programming profoundly influences future emotional and even physical reactions. New experiences are created during each incarnation and are added to the program at death.

Woolger feels that past lives are imprinted on three levels. The etheric body (which is the pattern for the physical body), the emotional body, and the mental body manifest different levels of energy and are separately imprinted in each lifetime. Physical traumas from past lives can become embedded at an organic (etheric) level and affect the physical body in the current life. Unresolved emotional complexes from past lives become imprinted on an emotional level but can affect the body as well. Beliefs or attitudes from past lives become imprinted in the mind. In a sense the etheric body and its emotional overtones create the physical body.

The concept of the creation of the body by the etheric self was formulated by Dethlefsen in 1976 in *The Challenge of Fate,* and his most recent book *The Healing Power of Illness* expands his initial understanding.[4] The concept has also been developed by Deepak Chopra in his book *Quantum Healing.* Chopra postulates an intelligence (quantum self) which directs the DNA so that it affects our body and at the same time impacts our thoughts and feelings. Any comprehensive change must touch this deep core of us, our quantum substrate.

The requirement that initial change take place in the quantum substrate explains why various forms of energy healing sometimes work and at other times have no effect, and why affirmations about health, such as Carl and Stephanie Simonton[5] and Jeanne Achterberg[6] suggest for healing cancer, have uneven impact. *Healing must take place in the etheric body.* If belief systems and images that interfere with healing or health, especially those set during the death process in other lifetimes, can be transformed, and if new images and affirmations are put into the etheric body through extensive meditation, changes become reflected in the physical body.

At times dramatic interventions impact the etheric body in a single occurrence, but in most cases persistent long-term work is needed. It is possible to bring about remarkable and permanent modifications in our physical body when we work diligently and lovingly with the etheric body, which is its model. Through an ongoing meditational process and through working in past lives we can encourage emotional blocks to emerge so that they can be skimmed off and no longer obstruct change in the etheric body. We have to be willing, also, to implement such modifications as our Body Self makes clear are necessary. Reluctance to change interfering physical factors, such as lack of exercise, smoking, overwork, or inappropriate diet, makes it difficult for us to perceive our etheric body healed and whole. *The physical body impacts the etheric body, as well as vice versa.* Changing our physical bodies through working with the etheric body is not easy and takes persistence, perhaps over years, but it *can* take place.

Elmer and Alyce Green, in their discussion of healing in *Beyond Biofeedback* (1978), state that "the physical body is the laboratory in which we learn to handle the energies of life." A part of being able to deal effectively with our energies is becoming sensitive to the interaction of the etheric body with our physical body. Not only will this bring about health and healing, but it will help us to master the lesson about dealing with energy that eventually, in some lifetime, we are going to have to learn. While scanning past lives we become aware of the patterns of these energies and begin to realize that we can direct and transform them in the same way that we can turn a light switch on and off or use a dimmer. Energy slowly loses its amorphous unpredictability, allowing us to assume more conscious governance of our lives.

It has often been puzzling that a past life in which one has lived as a healer or priest or a person of some other deep spiritual competence can be "followed" by or embedded in, a matrix of more chaotic lifetimes. Snow comments in his autobiography:

> I cannot say that this learning process is in any way one of linear chronological progress. As others have noted, some of the earlier lifetimes seem to have been both spiritually and philosophically richer. Still, there

seem to be both gains and losses in each experience. Furthermore, each reflects a facet of who I am in this current lifetime at some level.

An observation of past lives suggests that a soul may gain maximal growth on one level but must come back to learn to handle the energies of whatever level he has not yet addressed. It is not enough to have gained spiritual perspective if we lack development on other levels—if we are emotionally isolated or our thinking is naive or, as happens frequently, if our bodies fail to support our spiritual perspective and are open to becoming overwhelmed by cancer or other physical disorders.

In an effort to help seekers develop the various energy bodies more evenly, ancient yogic philosophy proposed disciplines on many fronts and considered Hatha Yoga, with its work on body energy, to be the basis for development of other levels. It is no accident that in our current paradigm shift toward forward movement on the journey of the soul, we increasingly stress awareness of the body, and that current emphasis in regression work is on recovering and transforming old tapes that have been stamped into the etheric body (the ongoing pattern of the physical body).

In trying to understand psychological transformation we have usually relied on words, not taking into account the *quality of energy* behind them. Carl Rogers suggested that unconditional positive regard is a therapeutic enhancer, a concept later espoused by Norman Cousins in his book *Anatomy of an Illness*,[7] and even more forcefully in *The Healing Heart*,[8] where the simpler but less scholarly term "love" finally became respectable. Jampolsky and others who work in *The Course of Miracles*,[9] as well as those involved in Psychosynthesis and other transpersonal approaches, reinforce this idea that love is not a feeling but an expression of positive energy.

Snow summarizes the conclusions of many therapists:

> Perhaps the most refined form of creating is that of emotional states. It is only through the medium of our emotions that we actually relate to consciousness. Therefore, it seems that we incarnate primarily to experience emotions. Why this is so, still remains a mystery. Perhaps it is to learn or to grow.... Emotions, or particular vibrational patterns, connect different levels of creation. Obviously, in human experience at least, the most powerful emotion is love. Love vibrates in a special way and serves as a kind of universal lubricant. Perhaps it defines harmony among the relationships of irregular wave patterns, what Pythagoras called "the music of the spheres.

As the field of regression therapy comes of age, its theoretical foundations emerge more clearly and are made more meaningful by new concepts of energy proposed in current physics and biology. Evidence has been gathered from research by Valerie Hunt (formerly at UCLA)[10] and by

Hiroshi Motoyama in Japan[11] that energy has different vibrational levels, which may eventually confirm age-old theories about the energy centers of the body (called chakras). Each of the chakras is considered a connector and transformer of the central source of energy and is geared to different types of experience.

Richard Gerber considers the physical body to be a complex network of interwoven energy fields, organized and nourished by subtle energetic pathways that coordinate the life-force with the body. Health and illness originate on these subtle levels, which include programs originating in past lives. Gerber, like Motoyama, conceives the chakras to function as transformers of this subtle energy, stepping down the vibrational frequency to appropriate mental, emotional, and physical levels. Because the spirit animates the physical framework, the spiritual dimension thus becomes the energetic basis of all life. Gerber suggests that vibrational healing works by rebalancing disturbances of structure and flow within these multilevel interactive energy fields.[12]

Snow talks about vibrational patterns that make up our being, both our physical body and the more subtle body:

> These living irregularities can be compared to the harmonics of sound waves detectable when a taut guitar string is plucked. These energies manifest themselves into our space/time universe and also into other dimensions that we can only deduce mathematically. Within these created dimensions, and particularly that of our space/time, these living energy waves, our own energy "selves," continue vibrating, interacting together, and creating ever denser physical manifestations of themselves. This is the "cosmic dance" so poetically evoked in many ancient traditions. Through this we are constantly creating new life experiences.

The existence of vibrational levels is important for therapy because emotions and attitudes on lower levels may be able to be transformed into others on higher levels.[13]

In summary, there is a consensus of understanding among our contributors regarding past-life work. They see it as contributing to the journey of the soul through dealing with the patterns that flow and repeat through lifetimes. As we re-experience these patterns, working through feelings and reframing understanding, we can transform our lives and free our energy for progress on our journey. Overseeing our struggles on the soul journey with its flux of patterns is an all-knowing Essence, which we can contact and which in actuality, on a deeper level, we are.

**Chapter III**

# Psychotherapeutic Assumptions

Psychotherapy is the process of assisting the patient to bring his energy field into a state of harmony and balance. In past-life work the short-term results are similar to those found in other forms of psychotherapy: alleviation of crises and conflicts, improvement in relationships, and augmentation of the patient's sense of competence and self-worth. A long term objective is acceptance of who one is on every level, leading to a pervasive sense of well-being and comfort with one's place in the skein of life. The principle of past-life therapy by which these changes are implemented is the same as that of psychoanalysis—to make the unconscious conscious in order to restore choice. Viewing a sequence of lifetimes brings about an understanding of problems, facilitating their alleviation, and it augments self-acceptance through an expansion of awareness.

## General Principles

Regression work differs from conventional therapies in that it is conducted in an altered state of consciousness—past-life memories cannot be retrieved in the beta state, though beta is necessary for their processing. In this altered state the patient retrieves the experience of another personality that is both himself and yet not himself. It is an autonomous personality that has its own history and tragedies and makes its own decisions. All the patient can do is watch the drama of this personality unfold—he cannot determine what the script will be. And yet, because this autonomous personality is also in some way himself, he is drawn into its strivings and sufferings. In this process the patient becomes aware that he is not to be identified totally with the personality of the other lifetime and probably he is not who he seems to be in this lifetime, either. Woolger describes some of the characteristics and vicissitudes of such personalities:

By using a straightforward induction process it is possible to arouse ancestral images from the collective unconscious and vividly recall detailed memories of other eras through an ego consciousness different from our present identity. This ego consciousness has all the characteristics of a full autonomous secondary personality or part-soul. This other self can be of either sex and complements the living ego psychologically in the same way as the familiar shadow, anima, and animus figures from dreams. The difference is that these secondary figures reveal, when asked, detailed and consistent historical biographies, the content of which is often mundane, rarely glamorous, but always full of situations where the subject's complexes are vividly enacted within the constraints of that historical period.

There is a clear three-step process in the retrieval and processing of such memories. Jue, who was the first to document these stages, describes these as follows:

**Stage I: Identification**

Here the patient relegates the control of his own unconscious process so that he can begin to experience an internal scenario, a mythic journey, an identifiable figure perceived as a personal projection or subpersonality.

**Stage II: Disidentification**

Nothing is what it appears to be. Re-living a past-life experience is like going into the backstage room of a theater where the player removes or puts on the accoutrements of the role. In this special room one realizes his/her true nature as distinguished from the role being played. It is this realization that is at the heart of the disidentification process.

**Stage III: Transformation**

Life takes on a different perspective as the patient becomes both a participant and witness to life processes. Seeing life as holotropic, a patient begins to shift attitudes and perceptions regarding past traumas and events, psychological scripts, particular parents as necessary factors for growth, and attraction or repulsion for certain individuals. Past-life scripts can be rewritten or released, depending on the choice of the client.

Woolger's description of the three levels varies somewhat but the underlying assumptions are the same.

**Stage I: Re-living**

First is the re-living of past lives as though they were real. In this level there is real pain. Real executions are experienced.

### Stage II: Symbolic and metaphorical exploration

In the second level the symbolic or metaphorical content is explored. The pains in the neck, experienced in the first level as beheading, indicate a feeling of being cut off from life, feeling crippled and being starved for love. Past lives are seen to be metaphors for our current life patterns.

### Stage III: Insight leading to creative productivity and service

There is also a third level that is symbolized by the well-known series of Zen ox-herding pictures where the person who has received enlightenment returns to the market place. Insight is here understood to be in the service of creative productivity. It does not exist as an end in itself.

Snow perceives the third stage as a reframing or rebalancing of material that has been brought to the surface, which is his equivalent of moving into a transperonal perspective. His approach probably represents the more usual experience of patients.

### Stage I: Identification

First comes identification with and replaying of significant past-life issues and/or traumas. Emphasis is placed on the key moments of death and rebirth.

### Stage II: Search for patterns

There follows a search for recurrent negative emotional response patterns between past and current lifetimes and their release through mutual forgiveness, when appropriate.

### Stage III: Integration of new models

Finally, positive and affirmative emotional patterns are discovered and can be integrated as alternative models for past and/or future responses.

In the research of Kenneth Ring on the near-death experience the same three stages emerge as are evidenced in regression work. First there is the experience of the death process and of leaving the body behind. This is followed by a time of disidentification and scanning of the lifetime just left. And then, for many, there is a realization of the nature of the One, which leaves the experiencer changed forever.[1]

Past-life therapy, even more than therapy dealing with current lifetimes, is focused on pertinent patterns or core issues. Pecci states:

Out of past-life work, patterns begin to emerge that give special meaning to existence and timing to all trauma, suffering, and life challenges. All of these come to be seen as unique opportunities for making a shift in attitude toward current life patterns.

The Dutch therapists show how these patterns are basic issues that are compelled to repeat themselves on various levels of experience:

All problems are merely symptoms of core issues. Each core issue or theme has its own character postulate or basic belief structure. In its essence such a character postulate is a self-judgment, usually formed in a prior existence, which actualizes connecting traumas in all four main areas of recall: transpersonal, past lives, prenatal, and biographical (contemporary). The task of therapy is to recover the originating and reinforcing components of the core issue.

Jue reiterates that past-life patterns are utilized to understand more deeply and broadly the dynamics of existing problems and situations. They are parts of the "implicate order" behind the "explicate order" that David Bohm addresses.[2] They also allow the client to become aware of unconscious motivational factors behind the choices he makes in his everyday life.

Snow adds:

Consciously held symptoms and patterns are often related to deeper primary issues in symbolic or metaphorical ways. These patterns frequently have origins in a series of past-life traumas and are an expression of the individual's unconscious attempt to uncover and resolve the underlying issues.

Findeisen confirms this:

Our reactions and the way in which we respond to problems are rooted in the past. In therapy we work to bring old memories to consciousness so that the old repressed material may be seen in the light of the present and we may choose our responses rather than be driven to react from old patterns.

All of the therapists emphasize the repetition of patterns on the various levels of experience, one of the strongest assumptions in regression therapy.

## The First Stage: Identification with a Previous Lifetime

The first stage consists of being in the past-life experience, feeling its feelings, being the person one was then. Woolger describes this as "being the reality." Whether this is tapping into past lives or constructing metaphors, one slips into the body, emotions, and mind of the person one is imaging, feeling the hurts, the alienation, the love, the terror of that life. Deepening techniques are used in an effort to help the patient identify maximally with the role he is playing.

Woolger describes this process:

> The past-life approach entails using a therapist to focus the story and ask the questions "as if" it were a literal lifetime and not a fantasy, thus subjecting the story to the constraints of time, space, personal identity, and history. It acknowledges, also, the limitations of the death experience and treats this as a literal, bodily event when it occurs. The psyche responds with great facility to the *as if* of such suggestions and frequently gives quite spontaneous and surprising historical data. Past-life remembering entails a deep projected identification with an inner or secondary personality. This involves imagination, as all remembering does, but in the fullest sense, so that the current personality must put himself in the place of the earlier ones....
>
> It is as if there were a linear cause-and-effect sequence that operates within and across lives. Here the story behind the complex is seen as absolutely real, a product of hidden trauma that is in need of healing through being brought to consciousness. By bringing the traumatic incident to consciousness in all its horror and pain there is often a strong cathartic release and remission of symptoms.[3]

Most of our therapists agree with Woolger that it is important during this stage that the patient experience the body feelings, especially if these have been traumatic. Fiore explains that in the process of remembering we discharge the energy tied up with the memory so that it does not continue to create a state of disease. Because she is interested primarily in the remission of symptoms and this takes place with the abreaction during the period of identification, transformational techniques are considered by her to be superfluous. Although many of her cases include cognitive reframing and other therapeutic techniques, she does not consider these to be the actual therapeutic agents. This approach is tied to the statement of her therapeutic goal, namely, the working through of a symptom.

Hickman's explanation, which is also concerned with symptoms, is that it is not the memory but the emotional charge on the memory that causes the problem, and the charge may stem from childhood, the prenatal state, or past lives. These emotions can be vented, discharged, or expended so that they no longer cause a problem. She considers that emotions are the special characteristic of physical experience and the reason that we have to come back in our bodies instead of making the journey of consciousness in some easier way. Remission of symptoms seems to her to be interwoven with contacting and abreacting the emotions.

Woolger postulates that in most illness traumatic experiences from earlier times, including past lives, have set a karmic residue in a complex that becomes so repressed as to be embodied psychosomatically. This has to be re-lived in its full range of somatic and emotional aspects:

> If bodily sensations and their concomitant emotions are not fully experienced, the complex seeking to express itself will remain lodged in the body because of the imaginal imprinting. No amount of methodical understanding of the meaning or symbolic content of the "karmic" ramifications of the experience will help unless this bodily imagery is allowed to surface as well. On the other hand, if the physical and emotional levels of the trauma are released without a full understanding of their meaning in whatever framework the subject is open to (psychological, karmic, spiritual), then the subject will tend to remain stuck in a meaningless repetition of the emotions of the past-life scenario and the recurrence of whatever psychosomatic symptoms exist.

Woolger's theory that the etheric body carries the pattern of what happens in the physical body and in a sense programs it, has extensive implications for therapy. He feels that the opportunity to experience imaginal scenarios that include violent injuries (whether actual past lives or metaphoric representations) has a potent effect on releasing or rebalancing the etheric body, and this makes possible a release of symptoms in the current physical body.

In general, our contributors agree that body functioning, its health and illness, has roots in the experience of other lifetimes. Allopathic healing is difficult when the perception of the body is limited to its condition and experience in the current lifetime.

## The Second Stage: Disidentification

The second stage, called "disidentification," "the search for patterns," or "symbolic and metaphorical exploration," has to do with taking a *witness position* in order to observe the patterns of a past life. Dethlefsen summarizes this:

Knowledge of former lifetimes effects an enormous increase in a person's conscious knowledge. The individual suddenly learns how to interpret and understand details of his present life in a new manner. He recognizes associations and receives insights that greatly expedite his learning process. When the experiences are recovered, he becomes able to see reality as it is now, without confusing it with feelings from the distant past. This makes it possible for him to live always, completely, and consciously in the present.

The same understanding of the goal of the second stage is discussed by Pecci:

Regression therapy is helpful because it loosens the rigidity of the intellect and opens the door to a new experience of reality. In it one experiences a body that has been conditioned by a somewhat different personality configuration, and one becomes able to see the arbitrary nature of the current personality. This heightened awareness makes possible a review of current life from a more objective perspective. It also reduces survival fear, enabling us to be more comfortable with the current life, since we are reminded that there will be others.... As each problem or symptom is experienced, it is not so important that we learn to alleviate the symptom as to understand what it is we need to know to bring us to that place of peace and harmony with the inner self that will enable us to live more fully.

Many therapists do not consider remembering and abreaction to be sufficient for healing and change but instead they stress this cognitive restructuring. They feel that a patient who draws on the wisdom of the Inner Mind becomes able to see past-life situations in a different perspective and to modify, often significantly, programs made at the time of the earlier life. Pecci and Jue call such cognitive re-evaluation *reframing*.

Fiore and Denning feel that beneath each symptom is energy-sustained guilt, and they seek to identify sources of guilt. Denning puts emphasis on the death process as a way of revealing this, and on the last conscious thought as programming future patterns. To facilitate this re-evaluation, many therapists have the patient go back to the time when patterns were set for that lifetime. Here they can see what lessons were chosen and decide whether they were learned. In the process of such a re-evaluation the individual learns how to interpret and understand details of his present life in a new manner. Dethlefsen, Findeisen, and Woolger stress that body-emotional experiences and restructuring go hand in hand.

Woolger feels that all types of experience are necessary in the evolution of our consciousness. The thrust of past lives is to reveal the elements of our polarities, the opposites that are rejected and concealed in shadow but which we need if we are to approach wholeness. This understanding of polarity as a major aspect of our psychic structure is becoming increasingly emphasized by other past-life therapists.

After years of working only with patterns, Dethlefsen became convinced that it is the integration of the polarities that is the major work of therapy:

> The alleviation of symptoms is not the final goal. True healing depends on confronting the polarity back of the symptoms. By exploring the chain of symptoms, the sick person is continually confronted with similar situations until finally he discovers the originating source of guilt. Through his act of recognition, he can dissolve the guilt, turning it into a transformative agent and solving his basic problem.

The Dutch school feels that facing our individual and collective polarity and accepting it in its true sense ends judging ourselves and others and helps with transformation, both individually and collectively. Such awareness heals body, mind, and soul.

Three of the contributors put special stress on decisions made by the ego. Pecci, Denning and Findeisen state that ego decisions made in time of stress are imprinted as programs in a computer, and as with programs that are no longer useful, we must replace them with more positive ones. Pribram provided theoretical grounding for such a process when he described the billions of neurons in the limbic system as having different frequencies, each pattern of response being made up of connections that make an image, (for instance, "I am a victim"). Our task as therapists is to transform the valences between the neurons making up the undesirable program (i.e., the victim) into a new valence (i.e., "I can take my own power") in order to construct a more felicitous program.

The computer programs inserted during the dying process are especially important. Evaluations and decisions made at that time may influence later lifetimes and maintain patterns of behavior, which are often reinforced by guilt. Through cognitive intervention, re-evaluation, and forgiveness such programs can be replaced by appropriate and productive ones. As a rule, work on ego decisions takes place during the disidentification stage of the regression.

Often these patterns and affirmations that are lifetimes old are reconstellated and reinforced during the pre- and perinatal experience, birth and childhood. At such times they set up the lifetime for a repetition of former hurts and disasters. Expressions that have taken place in early childhood can be identified by reviewing the childhood years, as Pecci found, particularly responses and reactions to parents. Then the patient can become aware that this repetition was determined by previous experiences and that these experiences are no longer needed and can be replaced by more appropriate and productive ones.

## The Third Stage: Transformation

Many of our therapists, but not all, propose a third state, difficult to define: the level of transformation, a term used by both Pecci and Jue. This seems to be a spiritual level that is not available to all patients. Woolger describes it as a "realization of the One." Pecci describes this transformation as a "process of coming to a place of peace and harmony with the Self that is attained by experiencing the primordial Essence from which we have become separated." He has many techniques for helping his patients reach such a position. Dethlefsen feels that "past-life therapy embraces the entire human being and touches the deepest levels of his essence. Its goal is to help him find and understand himself and make himself a significant part of the universe."

Snow stresses the increase in perspective mediated by the spiritual self:

> The final phases of the regression process involve adopting a wider perspective than that of any one past-life personality. As the spiritual self displays the various parallels between events, emotions, and attitudes of the past-life character(s) and those of the current personae, support is given for releasing pent-up judgment, guilt, hate, and denial.

Woolger comments that:

> When the client has identified with the opposite personalities in past lives, either in the after-life review stage or at the end of a session while their symbolic meaning is explored, a major piece of the work is done. A shadow figure becomes integrated, a split is healed, a lost part of the soul is redeemed through love and acceptance.

This increased insight is mediated by what Jue calls the transcendent function that understands the origin of the problem and effects its resolution. Snow agrees that during both the second and third phases the client's Higher Self or counselor part can be called upon for its innate wisdom in seeking creative, lasting solutions to the problems uncovered. Jue and Snow both observe that such solutions are often accompanied by synchronistic events and also by a deeper sense of self-esteem and worthiness.

For Denning and others, the first step on the ladder is forgiveness, which is conceived of as a leavening of various levels of negativity, whether these concern oneself or others. Denning stresses forgiveness of the self as a way of working through guilt, which she sees as the basis of continued patterns of distress and failure.

## Theories of Intervention

In the early development of techniques for exploring past lives and processing them, the fact that various types of intervention all brought about change was difficult to explain. The first professional regression therapists who emerged with hypotheses, Fiore, Hickman, and Netherton, felt that simply living out a regression with its physical and emotional aspects led to remission of the presenting symptom. When the types of symptoms they treated are examined, many of them are strongly connected with the body and emotions, such as physical symptoms, phobias, etc.

Woolger ties his understanding of the subtle body, the part of us that goes from lifetime to lifetime, into the most advanced (and also the most ancient) understanding of the part energy plays in the creation and perpetuation of our bodies. His hypothesis that the various aspects of the subtle body (somatic, emotional, and mental) require specific types of interventions is of paramount importance for regression work and may eventually contribute to an understanding of change in all therapeutic work:

> Programs in other lifetimes are set in one or more of these three bodies, and the type of intervention required may depend on which body is affected. Simple recall may be sufficient to release trauma done to the etheric body in another lifetime. Deep emotional living out may be sufficient for programs in the emotional body, and cognitive restructuring may be necessary for the mental body where affirmations and beliefs are involved.

Woolger feels that many times the imprinting of past-life traumas onto the body is transmitted at a subtle emotional level, also, and this emotional aspect becomes linked to the etheric level of a complex in the current life. Cases where past-life residues in the emotional body penetrate and deform the etheric system (and with it the physical body) are often complex and difficult to work with because such patients tend to somaticize their emotional problems.

Woolger's explanation of the various types of healing can be subjected to research, even to as simple a design as noting the type of techniques that are used, if they work, and if they can be correlated to the perceived level of the problem. Time and research will determine connections between the levels of the felt dysfunction or problem and the type of intervention that is most beneficial. Experiencing emotions and bodily feelings may at one time be enough for healing, and at other times transformational work with insight may be indicated. The stage of development in the patient and his perceived goals may also be a factor.

All the contributors stress the role of the therapist. Denning verbalizes the basic stance that the therapist's attitude should be such that the patient can feel safe and confident in verbalizing all that is seen in the unconscious while he is in an altered state. She feels that unless the therapist is able to make the patient know that these conditions of trust exist between them, much valuable and important material will not surface. Findeisen emphasizes that the major responsibility for creating a trusting space is the therapist's and that he/she is also responsible for the energy level between therapist and client. The emotional and spiritual well-being of the therapist is crucial (a comment that takes some thinking about, since this is a stance not usually taken in psychotherapy).

Bontenbal and Noordegraaf suggest that techniques used in therapy should obviate any control by the therapist over the client. It should always be the client doing the work, assisted by the therapist. Awareness helps to avoid transference and counter-transference. Jue states that unconscious projections and processes on the part of the therapist play an important role in the therapeutic context and affect the response of the patient.

According to Snow, altered state work connects therapist and patient on a deep level:

> The therapist-client relationship is especially crucial in regression therapy. Such altered-state work necessarily connects *both* parties at several energy levels. Regression therapists play a more active role in eliciting hidden past-life issues and patterns from clients than do surface-level analysts. Therefore they must remain especially open and accepting of whatever material emerges from the client's subconscious and must not allow transference and counter-transference problems to interfere with the healing process. The regression therapist must remain an active yet flexible participant. His or her loving empathy allows the client to establish enough self-trust to permit transformation.

Reynolds feels that the quality of energy between patient and therapist may be the actual healing agent and that what is said and done may turn out to be secondary to this energy field. Several of us suggest that in a regression the therapist needs to be in an altered state along with the patient in order to deepen and facilitate the process through shared energy.

The therapists in the sample appear even more aware of the patient-therapist relationship and the quality of energy that exists between them than is the general psychotherapist. Getting in touch with the deep levels of the unconscious that make up past lives and pre-and perinatal experiences is a sensitive interaction that needs all the facilitating energy available in order to be successful.

Chapter IV

# Indications and Contraindications for Use

When past-life regressions were done through psychics and were equivalent to a parlor trip, anyone could try the experience, whether or not he believed in past lives. There was never any question about when past lives were appropriate, and nobody needed to take the results seriously. Current past-life exploration has to contend with this—the assumption, carried over from the past, that regression work can be tried by anyone. We have only gradually become aware, now that regression has become a therapeutic modality and past lives are recovered by the subject and not by a psychic, that regression is not appropriate or helpful for everyone.

We have now reached a point where we can take a careful look at just who is helped by regression work and who is not. Every therapeutic approach has gone through this process. Freud gradually realized that psychoanalysis is not for everyone (and possibly not for very many). Analytic Jungian therapy also has a restricted clientele—Jung came to consider this modality to be most useful for those in a midlife crisis where an introversive thrust is needed to bring balance after years of extraversive activity. Regression therapy, also, has its limits and these need to be respected.

But, on the other hand, if regression therapy is like opening up windows in a closed room, a metaphor commonly used to describe it, then does not everyone deserve this extended perspective? It is a little like having the right to life, liberty, and the pursuit of happiness. Can everyone make use of this prerogative?

## Transpersonal Goals

In psychotherapy the modality of regression work runs the gamut from being used in special circumstances with patients who are looking for broad patterns or a spiritual basis for life, to being considered appropriate for the treatment of almost all dysfunctions. Ernest Pecci represents the most conservative and careful approach when he writes:

> I attempt to regress into past lives only a small percentage of the patients with whom I work. I use this modality only when I am convinced it would be of some use and when my patient has explored to the fullest all of the experiences in this lifetime.... Past-life therapy is not a therapy for the narrow-minded or skeptical but for the already partially awakened spiritual traveller who is ready to embrace the reality of spirit guides and the existence of other dimensions and other worlds, and who is unafraid to explore consciousness in all of its unlimited varieties and forms.

What personality structure enables one person and not another to make use of this transpersonal mode? One explanation is suggested by Caroline Myss, the intuitive who works with Norman Shealy.[1] She diagnoses physical imbalances and describes the levels of development in terms of the chakras, postulating that patients concerned with the three lower chakras are not able to work on transpersonal levels. It takes an open heart and an awakened intuition, characteristic of the upper four chakras, to move into spiritual levels. Pecci has a technique for ascertaining on what level a patient is working by asking for a formulation of ten questions. The nature of the questions (not their answers) reveals on what level a patient is functioning.[2]

A patient's level will have impact on the effectiveness of regression work. *Symptoms* may remit for those functioning on a limited space-time level (the lower chakras), but *the potential for transforming life and reframing perception* will not necessarily be actualized. Anyone wanting to move into a transpersonal and spiritual view of life can do so if he wants to expend the necessary effort, but it is up to the patient to decide this, not the therapist, who must often remain patiently stuck with his patient.

The ability to work at a transpersonal level seems to be correlated with an introversive thrust in the personality, and this potential for exploring within is the foundation for regression work. Most patients do possess introversive capacity, but women have come to my workshops bringing their husbands—professionals or business men—who cannot achieve imaging, even though they want to. Some therapists, such as Woolger, will not work in past lives with clients who have not had considerable therapy and experience in going within. However, introversion, with the resulting ability to go into altered states, is at least in part a learned ability.

The question of persistence is an important one. In our enthusiasm to demonstrate the effectiveness of regression, we often oversell by demonstrating seemingly miraculous results, which do happen, but not all the time and perhaps not a great percentage of the time. Such enthusiasm has led people to expect a miracle cure, a total remission after one, or at most two, sessions. Fiore, as a result of her first book, found that many people coming to her assumed a session or two would be sufficient. After four sessions, half her clientele dropped out because this expectation was not fulfilled. The striking remissions reported by therapists, especially after other modalities have proven ineffective, make good reading but do not accurately present the long and patient working through of patterns that underlie change.

## Focusing on Symptoms

In the beginning of therapy many patients focus on specific symptoms. All sorts of problems are good entering wedges, and surprisingly, for some reason we are only beginning to understand, many of these symptoms remit after the recovery of a focal memory, with or without subsequent transformational work. (However, without therapeutic work on the matrix in which the symptom is embedded, it may recur or another symptom with similar dynamics may emerge.)

Fiore considers that symptoms are a legitimate area of regression work and do not need to lead to expanded insight. She has had success in treating a wide range of problems by intense recall and re-living of past-life experiences. Included are phobias, compulsions, physical problems of all kinds, and various emotional, mental, and spiritual problems. Because of her willingness to treat all kinds of symptoms, she feels that regression work is indicated for a broad spectrum of patients. In her experience, special ability to work in a transpersonal mode is not necessary. However, as one scans her sessions with patients, it is evident that she does notice and point out patterns, even though she considers them unimportant.[3]

Our contributors mention a wide range of treatable conditions. Physical symptoms are dramatic entering wedges for regression work, though a physical problem may turn out to be penetrated with emotional threads of anger, guilt, or anxiety. Allergies are often tied into some specific past-life incident or a sequence of incidents of a repetitive nature and form an opening wedge into regression work. Phobias of various sorts, along with headaches and allergies, constitute presenting symptoms that yield to past-life therapy. Fear (with or without conversion into an allergy or phobia) is often grounded in another lifetime. Findeisen mentions treating not only the usual phobias and compulsions and problems in relationships but also the problems of women in pregnancy, birth, chronic miscarriages, infertility, etc. She feels these conditions have both psychological and physical components that may be relieved in regressing to earlier experiences.

Are solutions to symptoms explored in past lives more effective than those found in conventional therapy? If we take anger as an example, we find that regression often pinpoints the root of the anger, allowing it to become transformed. Ferreting up old angers in other lifetimes will not in itself accomplish this, but understanding and reframing past-life situations can do so. Guilt, closely related to anger, is difficult to deal with in the context of this lifetime if the origin lies in an earlier one; the reprogramming of such guilt is more effectively done at the level where it began. Regression work can also be helpful for depression, for the anger that underlies depression can often be found in a previous lifetime.

## Working with Patterns

Many therapists are willing to start with symptoms but feel that the major gain from regression work is insight into patterns. Denning is willing to take as a starting point the whole range of psychological and emotional dysfunctions, including stress, fears, irrational behavior, and rage that is the result of past injustice, but she feels that the special potential of regression work is the promoting of insight into the patterns. Her experience is that it is especially effective with clients who have lost all sense of self-worth or who are experiencing strong personality clashes in their relationships. However, it is interesting that some of her most striking remissions have been in the field of physical healing, including cancer.

Findeisen and Reynolds both start with symptoms but explore the underlying patterns. They consider that regression work helps to ferret out and resolve patterns in the current life that are rooted in the past and that often cannot be dealt with in conventional therapy. Reynolds feels that regression is also helpful for those working in the current lifetime who have had only superficial results and need to discover underlying patterns in order to alleviate their symptoms.

To Snow, a willingness to assume responsibility for looking at patterns is a necessary precondition, though he, too, willingly begins with a symptom:

> The decision to use regression therapy must be reached jointly by client and therapist after discussion, so that each understands its possibilities and limits. Past-life insights have greatest impact on those clients who are ready to assume greater responsibility for their lives and who sincerely wish to understand how current problems relate to deeply embedded emotional response patterns that they have long been avoiding or denying.

He goes on to define a number psychological complaints and blocks, long-term patterns that eventuate in psychospiritual breakdowns where there are feelings of lack of self-worth, hopelessness, and sometimes excessive grieving for a deceased loved one, all of which are appropriate entry points for treatment.

According to Hickman, even though she works particularly effectively with symptoms, especially with phobias, the benefits from regression therapy are more pervasive and far-reaching than the relief of specific problems:

> Patients see how past mistakes are still interfering with their optimum functioning and how they can make new choices to improve the old error-filled record. It is particularly helpful to those who strain against life with an attitude that life is unfair, that, in a sense, God plays favorites and they are not the favorites.... They are directed by their deeper wisdom to make the choices that will lead to greater awareness, harmony and creativity.

Dethlefsen deals with such incidents as accidents, illnesses, torture and death as important targets of recall. Since such anxiety is a part of everyone's life, almost any presenting symptom is grist for his mill, but symptoms are for him only an entering wedge. His thrust is to free his patients from bondage to outworn patterns that are grounded in the past and are no longer appropriate:

> Man never lives completely in the present but always somewhat in the past, and when the past obtrudes upon the present and distorts it, return to the original distorting incident can release and free the present. If the experiences from earlier years are made known, the filter disappears and the person is able to see reality as it is now, without confusing it with feelings from the distant past.

Bontenbal and Noordegraaf start with any presenting symptom that seems to them to be a core issue, but they then move into integration work through an exploration of the patterns of that issue and the polarities involved:

> We have found reincarnation therapy most effective when used for diagnosing, facing, processing, and integrating core-issues and their character-postulates. The therapy can very well be used for dealing with symptoms, but so can a lot of other therapies. Reincarnation therapy proves itself when it not only deals with causality but with polarity as well. Then the healing starts.

Their emphasis on polarity, the integration of the opposite and negative aspects, is an evolving thrust in regression work that is also strongly emphasized by Woolger. Working with polarities is not an easy experience and it may reduce the number of patients who are willing and able to go through the regression process in order to reach integration.

Patterns in relationships are a rewarding area of exploration. Woolger feels that parental complexes reveal themselves in a different light within the power dynamics of an entirely different family constellation in another age. He has found that current family struggles occur when there have been abuse of power, inheritance injustices, rivalry, etc., in earlier lifetimes. Such exploration of relationship difficulties is an especially fruitful entrance into past-life work.

Jue considers that an exploration of patterns totally overshadows symptom consideration:

> I do not consider the primary concern of any therapy to be only the alleviation of symptoms. Far more important is an examination of the dynamics and attitudes that support the symptoms, and this must be explored on physical, emotional, and mental levels in order to support any occurrence of symptom relief. Simply temporarily pinpointing the origin of a symptom in a past life and relieving it does not bring about much real change. Therefore I do not undertake regression therapy with patients whose primary motivation is the alleviation of a symptom without working on the underlying matrix.

In areas where conventional therapy proves inadequate, regression work can be helpful, such as in genuine blocks where nothing comes forward or where a problem cannot be formulated in terms of anything known about the patient's life. Patients who have experienced such a blocking and cannot find the origin of a problem often embrace what they find during regression and use it well; they tend to search for a pattern or to expand their understanding of basic patterns that lie in the deep unconscious. There are also times when resolution of the more obvious discords through conventional therapy may lead to a wish to find more inclusive patterns, and this can most fruitfully be done in the broader context of other lifetimes.

A further step beyond an identification of patterns is the thrust toward spiritual growth discussed earlier, emphasized by Pecci most strongly among our contributors. Eventually we get tired of living in that room without windows and without vistas of living gardens and move outward. One cannot always separate the resolution of a problem from the spiritual journey in which it is embedded.

## Contraindications for Regression Work

The most obvious barrier to regression work is a belief system that is strongly skeptical of the concept of past lives, even if they are seen as a metaphor. Such skepticism has been promoted by the scientific community and by the medical profession. Although the attitude of our cultural milieu is gradually changing so that there is now more openness to new approaches, patients whose security lies in adopting the intellectual framework of their time may be uncomfortable with an approach not yet in vogue.

Another contraindication, the result of psychic readings of past lives, is focus on supposed past incarnations of power and glory. Very few lifetimes are ego-enhancing. Helen Wambach found that in those regressed to any century or place there is the same proportion of kings to artisans to serfs as there were in actuality at that period and time.[4] Most of us have had humble lives and most of us have experienced violence, war, and hunger, since these have been around from the beginning of time. The wish for past-life situations that will be ego-enhancing is bound to bring disappointment. (In contrast, some patients who have actually had great power resist remembering it, since power is difficult to handle well, and most of us have failed.)

Regression work is contraindicated for patients who are in stuck positions of guilt and a need to be victimized. Sometimes no amount of work will shake such a position. Those who fall into this group are not willing to take responsibility for their lives but see themselves as undeserving victims. It is the world and the "others" who are at fault. Nothing can be accomplished in regression work unless the patient is willing to take responsibility for what happens to him.

Denning describes some specific attitudes that block therapy:

> If the individual is unwilling to be honest and blocks attempts at self-revelation, there will be no significant result. In such cases, the skill of the therapist may overcome the resistance, but until the individual is ready to face the truth about the self, there is probably no therapy that will be effective. Fear of exposure, religious conflicts, an inability to assume responsibility for oneself and one's actions and feelings and situation, and a feeling that one has a pre-determined destiny to suffer, all contraindicate regression therapy.

Various therapists have found other contraindications. Almost all agree that sufficient ego-strength is a prerequisite, and this rules out psychotics or borderline personalities, though Pecci feels that some of these patients, after a long period of conventional therapy to build up ego strength, can safely be regressed.[5]

Various personality deficits, such as lack of a capacity for introversion, which has been mentioned earlier, handicap regression. Noordegraaf and Bontenbal mention difficulty in working with people who have lost touch with their emotions. Fiore has found that fear of hypnosis causes difficulty in some patients and she has had to develop ways of bypassing this. Reynolds considers that conventional psychotherapy is more appropriate and helpful in times of crisis. Many therapists mention that when a general life situation is going well, there seems to be little motivation to look deeper except where there is a compelling drive toward a deeper experience.

Most therapists consider that regression work is contraindicated for children, but Noordegraaf has had unusual success with children from four to 15. She feels that work with older people depends entirely on whether they are inwardly flexible and still thrusting for growth.

# *Induction*

*Be in touch with your feelings, begin to be in touch with the part of you that you need to look at. Because there is a part of you that really yearns for understanding, for reconciliation, for a broadening of awareness.... Begin to see a shift now, a shift in seeing. It's almost as if you begin to walk through another dimension of time and space.*

Ronald Wong Jue

*Feel your mind expanding, down into your subconscious, out into your superconscious, expanding like the circles in a pool when you drop in a pebble. Your mind expands and expands, bringing into the conscious self that wonderful knowledge and information that is available to you about the rest of your lives.*

Hazel Denning

**Chapter V**

# Preparation

Past-life therapy can be set in two contexts, and the context chosen determines the nature of the preparation. One context is ongoing conventional psychotherapy where past-life exploration is used to highlight and explore problems that have already been identified. The second context is one in which past-life therapy is used as a modality in itself. In the absence of reliable outcome research it is not possible to say that one context is preferable. There are many factors to be weighed, not the least of which is the economic one—ongoing psychotherapy involves considerable investment and is not an option for everyone.

Our contributors fall into three groups. Pecci, Jue, Reynolds and I *use past-life work in the matrix of ongoing therapy*—it may or may not be included as a therapeutic approach for a specific patient. We tend to use regression work sparsely but feel that when used, it moves the therapy into deep and healing perceptions. Four others—Snow, Findeisen, Woolger and Denning —*stress past-life work*, and most of their patients come expecting to work in this modality, but these therapists embed the regression experience in general therapeutic procedures. Fiore, Noordegraaf and Bontenbal, Hickman, and Dethlefsen *employ past-life work as the specific modality that can best achieve their therapeutic goals*, and contacts with patients are structured with this in mind, though integrating therapeutic work supports the insight achieved in regressions.

Regardless of the context, according to all our contributors past-life therapy requires preparation. When the regression sessions are embedded in a broader therapeutic context, much of this preparation is covered in ongoing therapeutic sessions, with perhaps a few points specific to regression work discussed before actual past-life experience. For therapists where past-life work is the primary modality, biographical material is covered in a conventional manner but usually leads into a regression experience. When the patient is coming solely for past-life work and has had little or no experience in therapy, therapists feel that the preparation has to be particularly complete and informative. Bontenbal and Noordegraaf, who head a school of reincarnation therapy, spend the first several months of their training dealing with this preparation.

## Exploring the Patient's History and Patterns

The first step in the preparation of the patient is often, but not always, an exploration of the life history. This can include not only objective data about family background, developmental experiences, health history, education and social development, but also an exploration of inner dynamics: early memories, fantasies, fears, goals, and vicissitudes of the self-image. Attitudes and conceptions of sex, intimacy, love, power, money, and dependence versus independence, need examination. Whatever is known about pre- and peri-natal material is grist for the interview. This is a deeper intake than is usual in therapeutic work and gathers extensive information regarding the dynamics that have led up to the complaint.

Several therapists, because they feel that the current body state and physical symptoms are often embedded in earlier experiences, especially in past lives, seek detailed information about this state. This is especially true of Woolger:

> In the first session I take a detailed personal history from birth through childhood up to the present, noting illnesses, accidents, or impairments, such as deafness, the need for glasses, high blood pressure, etc. I ask if any emotional upheaval occurred shortly before or around the same period of life that these physical problems began. This is my procedure for all patients, whether or not past-life work is be undertaken.

Snow inquires about such areas as birth memories or feelings, recent or strongly felt deaths of family or friends, and any paranormal experiences or unexplained reactions to ordinary stressful events. Snow and others feel that the detailed history of physical symptoms, including any supporting script and key words, may be useful later in helping the patient go into a linked past life. Noordegraaf and Bontenbal, for example, make use of such material, especially from childhood periods, for the mental-emotional-somatic bridge. They say that the interview should include specification of symptoms, core-issues (themes), and underlying character-postulates (beliefs) in order to bring focus to the therapeutic process.

Some therapists use special techniques for eliciting information that may be helpful in understanding the level on which a regression will take place—whether it will focus on symptoms or move into an exploration of patterns and transpersonal areas. Pecci's ten questions, described in the preceding chapter, is such a technique. Jue stresses the importance of having profiles of the parents, and especially of the injunctions and non-verbal messages they have projected onto the patient. He encourages patients to image each parent standing in front and giving an injunction. This is helpful in determining themes and core issues.

The most abbreviated period of preparation is that of Dethlefsen. He postulates that since all current problems have their roots in the past and information about them comes up naturally, there is no need to cover them ahead of time. In contrast, the most thorough preparation may be that of Pecci, who from years of experience feels that past-life work is only for the well-prepared:

> I may work for many weeks or even months with a patient before I feel that he is ready to integrate a past-life experience into his present life situation. To determine readiness I assess the patient's current level of intellectual insight into his inner psychological conflicts, his openness to acknowledging and expressing feelings, and his willingness to look at his present circumstances with some objectivity. This includes a basic understanding of how his personality structure has set up his present problems and stressful life situation. Finally, there must be courage and a strong desire to change.

## Examining the Patient's Philosophy of Life

These explorations lead naturally into the next aspect of preparation, which is an examination of the patient's philosophy of life. In earlier times most therapists did not consider this important and seldom asked about it, but regression therapy becomes a wraith without some conceptual background. It is true that a belief in past lives is not a prerequisite, but some sort of metaphysical set that considers that individuals consciously or unconsciously program their lives is a necessary underpinning if the regression is to have meaning. It is part of the more general concept that we make our own destiny and create our own meaning. There needs to be recognition, also, that all experiences are subconsciously retained or recorded and that everyone has the capacity to contact this recording.

The need for such a set is a new problem for the wide-spectrum therapist. Formerly his general belief system and that of his patients matched fairly well. People came because they already believed the basic tenets of therapy as they were known. Now this cannot be taken for granted, and it is not efficient to plunge patients into a philosophic milieu for which they have no preparation and toward which they may even have high resistance. This difficulty in explicating the philosophical basis is probably one of the reasons that regression work is being accepted so slowly.

When patients have a rational and scientific perspective or religious predilection that rule out reincarnation as a concept, it is acceptable to structure the process as a metaphor, or, as Jue does, as a parable. Unnecessary resistance can be bypassed by not insisting on the term "past lives." What matters is that the process taps dynamics and brings about healing.

There is a reassuring openness in the scientific atmosphere at this time that is mitigating resistance to the concept of past lives. Various new concepts are being considered as a result of the theories put forth in theoretical physics and biology.[1] Such scientific formulations have been translated into more humanistic areas by others, who come from scientific backgrounds.[2] These pioneers are opening up new ways of looking at the world that strain and shatter our too-limited approach to the universe. Popularizers like Shirley MacLaine encourage people to look at new paradigms.[3]

In addition to searching for philosophical presuppositions, part of the preparation consists in examining the patient's set in regard to the therapeutic experience. He should be encouraged to have no expectations and should allow what wants to emerge from the unconscious to come up as a part of the therapeutic data. He must not expect a magic cure but instead be ready for extended work with whatever emerges. He needs to be instructed that in all likelihood there will be no clear TV image but little shreds of data that will increase like the image on a lottery ticket as one rubs it, until a wealth of appropriate details emerges. The images must be *invited to manifest*, and for some patients used to *making* things happen, this is a hard concept to accept. The patient must always look for his own responsibility in everything that happens; he has to be willing to see in what way he has been the director of his own script.

Some, but not all, of our contributors feel that it is helpful to discuss the concept of past-life patterns and karma before the regression begins. Snow feels that patients need to know about karmic law before they open to past-life experiences. He and Woolger and Dethlefsen and others alert clients to watch for lifetimes where they played roles opposite to what they are playing today. It is a surprise to many patients to find that behind every present-day victim is a past-life aggressor or an indifferent witness to aggression. Such a discussion of polarity can make the emerging of distressing past lives more palatable and forestall endless stories of victimization. Snow, when he discusses change and integration, describes the karmic continuity of life scripts or patterns as resembling grooves in a record. Often a person became stuck in a particular groove before he came into his present life. Then, unaware of alternate choices, he kept replaying the established unsatisfactory pattern. He needs to know that he does not have to stay stuck.

Denning opens up the concept of karma with her patients (though not necessarily using the term) and feels that a discussion of the patient's philosophy of life is of great importance. She stresses what all regression work indicates, that we make our destiny and create our own environment, and adds:

> This therapy is transpersonal in the truest sense of the work, and much of it will make little sense to the client who has no knowledge of mind dynamics. There are a number of areas that should be explored, and this exploration can take anywhere from half an hour to a number of sessions to satisfy the therapist that the client is ready for actual regression. Until this readiness is recognized by the therapist, it is not only a waste of time but unwise to lead a client into traumatic material when he is unprepared to deal with it.

Reynolds confirms the necessity and value of preparation and feels that an open discussion of the beliefs and assumptions that the patient holds regarding past lives, as well as disclosure regarding the therapist's own views, is a desirable preliminary step. Snow, also, is willing to discuss with his patients his views regarding past lives, and he and Denning and Reynolds all feel that being open and revealing may stimulate the patient's thinking about these areas and deepen and help the therapy.

Denning, who has had many years of practice as a regression therapist, has come to the conclusion that not everyone is ready for regression work. That is a point of view that more and more past-life therapists are reluctantly accepting. We need to know how much an appropriate philosophy of life throws the die in the direction of success.

## Establishing Rapport

The establishment of rapport with the patient is another function of the preparation. The Dutch therapists call this making "a safe and trustful relationship." Snow feels that it is important that this trust and rapport be established in the initial interview. Fiore makes it an article of faith to be totally open with patients throughout treatment.

Rapport is a key concept in altered state work. It involves reflecting back to clients their concerns and ways of dealing with the world so that they feel understood and so that they sense that the therapist is sympathetically in touch with their distress and with their outlook on life. Jue quotes Helen Wambach as saying that when patients come into one's office, the first thing they want to know is, "Do you love me?" Jue emphasizes that acceptance and empathic listening are important factors in allowing the patient to disclose himself and suggests that the depth of exploration possible with patients seems to correlate with the degree of unconditional regard the therapist gives.

While working in altered states patients sense the feelings of the therapist to a highly intuitive degree. If a therapist does not examine his own fears and internal blind sports, these factors will create an emotional impasse between him and the patient. Any sense on the part of the patient that the therapist will have more respect or approval if something different is produced will stop the flow of the actual material. The same defenses that keep patients from clear revelation of current events that are seen as unacceptable, function regarding events of other lifetimes, and similar work with defenses is in order.

## Introducing Induction Techniques

An important part of the preparation for many therapists is the presentation of the method of induction that will be used. The more this induction approaches formal hypnosis, the more discussion there must be in order to explore and allay any fears. Fiore, who uses a classical form of hypnosis, presents this clearly:

> During the second session (the first has been taken up with the interview) I explain the nature of hypnosis, especially emphasizing that the patient may not feel at all hypnotized, will not be "unconscious," and generally will have total recall of all that is experienced. I make it clear that there is no loss of consciousness; therefore the patient is not under the control of anyone else. Next, I outline my procedures for the regression, describing briefly the induction techniques, and present a viewpoint that is helpful in dealing with what will be experienced. I give the analogy of the court reporter who takes down everything that the witness says without judging the material that comes to mind. With just such objectivity the patient is to report verbally everything that is experienced.

At the end of this session Fiore makes a self-hypnosis tape including the induction that will be used, which has imbedded in it suggestions that the inner mind should bring up therapeutic dreams that will be remembered. A final experience establishes a "yes" finger and a "no" finger to use in future sessions.

Hickman, also, includes post-hypnotic suggestions in the initial session. One of these is a statement that when she takes the patient's left hand in her left hand and counts slowly from one to 21, that will be the signal to relax and go into deep trance. She finds that subsequent sessions can be devoted to therapy without having to take time for a lengthy induction.

Findeisen, in her discussion of the regression process with her clients, gives assurance of her support and makes it clear that the client will be able to communicate with her. Because she works in intra-uterine and birth memories, she is especially careful to help the client anticipate periods when verbalizations may be minimal. She assures the client that she does not have to know everything that is being experienced; she will make herself available for processing later:

> I invite the client to allow any image that wants to come up, any feeling response or any physical sensation. I explain that past-life material often surfaces in any one of many ways and we will work with it as it appears. I request that any experiences be reported, and I let the client know that this can be done usually without interfering with whatever is being experienced. I explain there are circumstances, especially uterine or birth, that are non-verbal and very physical and I will not stop the client's experience to ask for an explanation of what is occurring. In the process, tensions, energy blocks, and repressed material may emerge and be released with virtually no words and no discussion.

Snow, in his preparatory work during the initial session, offers a short "energy reading" whenever enough rapport has been established and if he feels this is appropriate. This reading involves his briefly entering a light trance and using that state to access information about the client's current energy patterns. After this he explains his induction technique, which usually, but not always, consists of controlled breathing accompanied by visualization of energy being channeled through the chakras. After a few moments of practicing this breathing he takes the client on a short guided imagery trip to test the response to different sensory stimuli and to note any personal symbols or metaphors that arise. Like Fiore, he requests that his clients note any dreams, insights, or daydreams that occur the following night or day. Sometime during the session he asks for higher guidance for each client so that the client can access his own wisdom.

Therapists who use relaxation and guided imagery or affect bridges as their induction often omit discussion of these processes, which on the whole are perceived as non-threatening, and go directly into the induction, which shortens the time of preparation.

In general, preparation time can vary, according to our therapists, from a half hour to a number of sessions. It should conclude, as the Dutch therapists point out, with therapist and client being aware of the goals the client wants to reach in regression work and some concept of how to obtain them.

Pecci sums it up:

> The preparation period should conclude with both patient and therapist having gained a fairly clear idea of the basic pattern of the patient's life, his ego stance, and his basic state of mind that has led to his projection and transference of his inner programs and patterns onto all the aspects of his life.

**Chapter VI**

# Induction Techniques

## The Nature of Altered States

Entering an altered state is a process of restricting and intensifying the focus of attention. Increase in inner focus, which by definition implies a progressive limiting of concern with outer events, is correlated with the appearance of lower brain wave frequencies on the electroencephalogram. Altered states are not unusual. Most of us are in a light altered state much of the time, as, for instance, when we miss our off-ramp while we are thinking of something else as we drive along the freeway.

Altered states result in two major modifications of consciousness that seem to be at variance with each other. The first is suggestibility. Altered states have been found to affect areas of brain functioning, such as the hippocampus, which is often conceived to be a computer that stores up programs. In altered states the hippocampus is especially open to reprogramming, a characteristic that has led to extensive research and to theories about mind control.

The second potential of altered states is their ability to tune into other levels of consciousness. Some of the areas that are contacted include dreaming, various types of meditation, visualization and imagery, energy healing, cosmic consciousness, and paranormal perceptions and abilities of various sorts. The scope of this contact with other areas of consciousness is as yet not well mapped and the implications of such contact are little understood.

## Hypnosis

Hypnosis is a technique known throughout history but brought to the attention of the professional western world in the mid-19th century by Braid, an English eye specialist. He found that if he asked a person to stare fixedly for a few minutes at a glittering object that was held slightly above eye-level at a distance of about 20 centimeters, the eyelids closed automatically and a strange, sleep-like condition was induced, which he called hypnosis, from the Greek word for sleep. (This is important to remember when we are considering the appropriateness of hypnosis as an induction for past-life work.) Later hypnotists were successful in inducing hypnotic sleep by verbal suggestion, and suggestion became the essential ingredient at the center of hypnotic techniques, especially the suggestion that the patient is tired or sleepy.

Hypnosis and its derivative, hypnotherapy, exploited this suggestible potential of the brain. We constantly modify programs unconsciously, but hypnotherapy offers an opportunity, with more or less success, to modify programs consciously. Its limitation as a method lies in the fact that often the program slated for change is only one in a related matrix of programs, all of which have to be modified if significant change is to take place in any of them. This is the reason that overweight, which is usually embedded in a complex web of programs, is less amenable to hypnosis than behavior with simpler etiology.

When the effects of hypnosis were first highlighted, the potential for suggestibility received predominant attention. At that time hypnosis was considered the royal road into altered states. While in hypnosis subjects often moved into other types of consciousness as the result of suggestions by the therapist, and for a time attainment of these states appeared to be dependent on hypnosis, although altered states induced through other means, such as drugs, chanting, trance-dancing, etc., had long been characteristic of other cultures. In Sri Lanka I watched a young priestess enter an immediate self-induced trance by beating her third eye with her fist.

It was while working in hypnotherapy that the ability of patients to retrieve past lives in therapeutic situations was first discovered. Therapists, trying to modify early childhood patterns by recovery and processing, suggested that their patients move further and further back, and often, to their surprise, the patient ended up in the prenatal state or in an earlier lifetime. The original element of suggestibility had caused the patient to move, not into a true hypnotic condition, but into an altered state of perception.

Because of this original tie between hypnosis and past-life recall, for a long time many therapists felt that past lives could be contacted only through hypnosis. However, experimentation with LSD, various types of visualization and imagery, certain modes of breathing, the use of light, or using a strong emotional charge as a bridge, made it obvious that there were other effective ways to go into altered states. Hypnotherapists had used many of these techniques to accompany and deepen the hypnotic trance. Gradually they focused on these peripheral methods and omitted a pure hypnotic induction, though they were often unaware that what they were using were supporting techniques only, not the essential components of hypnosis. Today, most, but not all types of induction into past lives share the common characteristics of relaxation, visualization, and the use of light. Some therapists deny using hypnosis and others assume they are still hypnotherapists, but they use similar techniques.

There are a number of reasons why regression therapists prefer not to use true hypnosis. Hypnosis operates by suggesting feelings of tiredness and sleepiness, as distinct from relaxation, and limits itself to suggestibility rather than moving into deeper areas of perception. It also assumes that the power is carried by the hypnotist, who takes the lead and tells the patient what to think. If hypnotic trance induction is stripped of the basic characteristics of suggestibility and control by the therapist, the result is no longer hypnosis. In all but the initial contact, which does take place through suggestion, the retrieval of past lives requires just the opposite ability: to move recall in the direction the Inner Mind of the patient finds most helpful, with the therapist assisting in a non-pressuring way. In regression it is possible, and perhaps preferable, to move beyond or to bypass hypnotic techniques altogether.

## Brainwave Research

We can learn much about altered states from observing brainwave patterns. Four levels of brainwave frequency have been identified: beta, alpha, theta, and delta, each with an individual range that reduces in frequency as beta is left behind. Dethlefsen describes what happens as the vibration frequencies become slower.

> There is a narrowing of consciousness to one point, as if, when a wide angle lens is replaced with converging lenses, the light becomes more and more concentrated, and a strongly focused light beam picks out a tiny point, plunging the surrounding areas into increasing darkness. The intensity of light at this point is far greater than when the light was diffused.

All the techniques we have mentioned produce, or aid in producing, more and more focused attention, and *this is the altered state.*

A common misconception, which may have been responsible for some of the emphasis on hypnosis, is that we are in only one range of brain waves at a time. Instead, it is possible to be in one or several or all levels of brainwaves simultaneously. There is no reason to lose beta just because we have gone into deeper levels, and the potential for processing past-life recovery relies on the ability of the patient to retain strong beta while he is in the other states. It is possible to be in an ancient lifetime and go into the next room to answer the telephone and come back and go on where one left off. It is possible to shift from experiencing a past life to observing it, then to processing it, then to observing it again, and weave back and forth.

The same phenomenon is being developed in lucid dreaming by Patricia Garfield and Steven LaBerge,[1] where by retaining beta one can enter one's own dream and control and guide it. Lucid dreaming and the capacity to be in beta and process deeper states at the time one is contacting them are relatively recent accomplishments. They are akin to controlling blood pressure and temperature, which we formerly considered to be impossible except by some yogis in the Himalayas. As the result of research by such centers as the Menninger Clinic, many people are now capable of influencing autonomic functions. The ability to remain in different brainwave frequencies can also be learned by an individual, but at the present time a therapist's assistance is usually needed. Therapists are also needed to help with processing the material unless we can emulate Freud, who dealt with dreams by becoming the observer outside himself, a possible but difficult achievement.

Considerable information about brain waves characteristic of meditation, energy healing, and past-life recovery has been contributed by a biofeedback device called the Mind Mirror, developed in England about 20 years ago by C. Maxwell Cade.[2] The Mind Mirror consists of a modified television screen, onto which are flashed EEG amplitudes of brainwaves. Electrodes are attached to both sides of a subject's head, and a continuous record of brain activity shows the functioning of each side of the brain in beta, alpha, theta, and delta frequencies. The Mind Mirror has been used extensively to research various types of meditation, most of which show a similar brainwave pattern characterized by low alpha, high theta, and little or no beta. Observing the pattern made by brain waves acts as a bio-feedback device to help the subject develop capacity for deep and sustained meditation. Cade called the optimal pattern of meditation, which consists of broader amplitudes of alpha and theta with some beta (which is usually lacking in meditation), the Awakened Mind.

Snow and I have conducted research with the Mind Mirror in regression work and have found several interesting phenomena.[3] Both the therapist and patient show flares of *delta* frequencies while in a regression, *but all the other levels are also present.* As a rule, one is dominant at a time but the dominance constantly shifts. Subjects in deep meditation or relaxation make alpha and theta waves, and this turns out to be true of regression subjects, also, especially as they proceed through the induction process; but once the regression starts, delta flares out, and beta, which diminished as the initial visualization began, returns more strongly.

What happens when a subject goes so deep into an hypnotic state that he cannot remember what has taken place, as often happened in earlier times? One hypothesis is that he has lost beta, perhaps as a result of his willingness to let the therapist take over control.

In the Mind Mirror research the most effective past-life work took place in brainwave entrainment. Snow defines this state:

> All forms of induction tend to become more effective when brainwave entrainment is present. This is a term that describes the development of a unified electromagnetic energy field between therapist and client during a session. This is something which occurs in all inductions to some extent, almost as if there were two strings vibrating and one picks up the vibrations of the other. I consider it a measurable manifestation of the interplay of the universal electromagnetic forces which I describe in my section on "Philosophical Hypotheses."

In our research it was found that therapists and patients moved more or less together into delta to contact past lives. When both therapists and patients entered in the same manner, either both going directly into delta from beta or, in contrast, both experiencing alpha and theta imagery as they moved from beta to delta, the entrainment took place easily and the regression appeared to be more successful. However, when the therapist moved directly into delta, patients who needed the imagery transition felt unsupported and even pressured. On the other hand, therapists who employed imaging, intending to help the patient (and perhaps themselves) move into delta, provoked impatience in subjects who preferred to go into delta more directly.

Abraham Kaplan, a philosopher noted for his cognitive approach, once asked me to take him into a past life. I agreed in spite of his skepticism because years before he had been on my doctoral committee, and not only did I have a warm place in my heart for his support but I was used to doing what he said! With a wicked gleam in his eye he informed me that he had been Don Quixote. I presumed (falsely) that he would have trouble attaining a level deep enough for a regression and began to take him carefully through all the images of my garden induction. After a few sentences he interrupted me rudely with, "Cut out the garbage! I'm already there." Nonplussed, I quickly entered a lifetime with him where for several years he was a poor and wandering idealistic soldier trying to get to his home farm after the war fizzled out. Finally he found his dilapidated house and began to farm again. A writer from a nearby village, Cervantes, often invited him to visit and got him to talk, eventually making him the prototype for Don Quixote. (This clever switch by his unconscious startled my skeptical subject, who urged me to share his experience.) That incident, where my subject went directly into delta and *I* spent time with imaging, made me aware of the differences that exist in the process of therapeutic induction and how discrepancies between patient and therapist may affect a regression, though the sensitive therapist can quickly adapt to the patient wherever he is.

Why regressions produce delta flares along with strong alpha and theta (needed to bring through the images and make possible the remembering of the experiences) must remain speculative. Mind Mirror research opens the possibility that delta is not a sleep state, as has been theorized, but a radar state tapping into what Rupert Sheldrake calls the mind field.[4] If there are past lives, they must be stored somewhere as a form of energy, to be contacted through one or more states of human consciousness. Delta, since it is strongly present, not only in regression work but in all paranormal activity, such as precognition and out-of-body states, may well be that contact.

Sleep research at the Menninger Clinic explored the hypothesis that dreamless sleep, which occurs in delta, is actually not unconsciousness but contact with a universal consciousness that is necessary for survival.[5] This contact is not as a rule remembered—that is, beta and delta do not manifest simultaneously. However, Swami Rama, a highly evolved yogi who founded and heads the Himalayan Institute and who for an extended period functioned as a research subject at Menningers, was able experimentally to produce delta waves at will. During what was apparently a sound sleep, complete with snoring, he retained various items of information that had been spoken during the period of "sleep" and reproduced them almost faultlessly when awakened. His explanation was that his consciousness continued to be active while his body, nervous system, and brain remained completely relaxed.[6] Unfortunately the encephalographic equipment in this experiment recorded only the dominant delta brainwaves, but beta must also have been present in order for him to process the conversation. Obviously we do not yet understand the nature of sleep.

The research suggests that in regression therapy we are moving into a new frontier where we can produce simultaneous beta and delta. Rama's experience offers support for the hypothesis of the Mind Mirror research that delta is our conscious contact with the mind field that is postulated by Sheldrake. Such contact provides an initial step in conceptualizing where past lives are stored and how they can be retrieved.

Dreams seem not to occur in the delta state. Perhaps a person goes into delta in sleep, but dreaming registers only after he has pulled back into theta or alpha to produce images. Or dreams may not contact the same level as past lives. Perhaps the meaning that they carry is primarily an alpha-theta phenomenon that does not call for a radar connection. If one could tap brainwaves during a profound archetypal dream, the situation might appear different.

## Hypnosis or Its Accessories?

About half of our contributors feel that they use hypnotic techniques to achieve induction into past-life memory. However, even including Reynolds, who still uses a classical hypnotic induction, they all disregard or even deny the basic assumptions back of hypnosis: control by the therapist and the use of specific suggestions. They stress that control is fully in the hands of the patient and are careful to give few direct orders, preferring to make open-ended suggestions or give choices. Relaxation, breathing and visualization are the matrix in which regression inductions are embedded and have now become *primary agents*. Reynolds, who feels he is authoritarian in the induction process, still remains careful to say, "We might start... If you are willing...etc." What cannot be documented by his words is his attitude of unconditional acceptance and a pure energy that draws his patients immediately into an altered state, regardless of what he is saying.

Hickman feels a strong investment in hypnotherapy, which was her initial road into the unconscious, but even she concludes that it does not matter whether one or another method is used if results are attained and that more important than choice of method is an understanding of the process and a comprehension that there are unexplored areas in every human consciousness. Her technique is characterized by extreme permissiveness and an honoring of where the person is. Fiore, who has also remained loyal to classical hypnosis in theory, in practice has shortened her actual induction and now depends strongly on the same imagery that many of our contributors use, such as visualizing light and walking down a staircase.

Pecci, a master of visualization, retains some hypnotic techniques, such as looking into a prism to focus trance, but depends primarily on specific images to attain the depth he feels necessary for a regression. An interesting and effective image that he uses to determine and deepen trance is that of a mirror in which a number appears suggesting the depth that has been reached. The patient replaces each number by a higher one until one appears that seems sufficient for the particular regression desired. Pecci sometimes takes patients back to very ancient lives and feels that maximum depth (symbolized by the number ten) is necessary to achieve this. In his so-called use of hypnosis he emphatically rejects the idea that the patient is in a state of helpless passivity or sleep. He feels that his technique, which often elicits vivid scenes of past-life recall, involves a particularly active participation by the subject, an approach that is contraindicative of hypnosis.

A final contributor endorsing hypnotic induction is Snow, who combines the best of hypnotic suggestions with rich and varied imagery approaches. He notes hypnotic considerations such as eye closure, body stillness, and mental shift to the interior world, and he is aware of the effectiveness of stimulating various sensory modes of perception, but he follows these with dramatic imagery. An image involving an element of choice that he uses frequently consists of advancing along a corridor and picking out "just the right door for today's session," behind which is to be found the appropriate past life. His induction through breathing and harmonizing the chakras, a technique also used by Denning, is appropriate for patients with a transpersonal philosophy. In this, bringing light into the chakra centers is used to draw the patient into an altered state. Another of his induction techniques, almost the opposite of classical hypnosis, is induction through arousal, which will be discussed presently.

Snow conducts many group regression and progression sessions throughout Europe and the United States, and effective group induction is important to him. He has modified the induction of Helen Wambach,[7] with whom he worked for a number of years, to include his new images, and sometimes with a sophisticated group he even uses the chakra induction. He, like the others still considering their inductions to be hypnotic techniques, is thoroughly trained in hypnotherapy and has retained some of its imaging and tone while actually renouncing its most basic principles.

From the beginning Denning was particularly troubled by the issue of control on the part of the therapist, since she places a high premium on personal freedom. She came to see, accurately I believe, that what is involved in regression work is an altered state of consciousness, of which hypnosis is only one example, and this allowed her to give control back to the patient. She uses breathing and relaxation and energy to bring patients into an altered state, and her inductions have a strong transpersonal flavor. She feels that it is unnecessary for the therapist to share alpha and theta with her patients and goes into delta with them when they are ready.

Findeisen postulates correctly that hypnotic states, trance states, and altered states are similar, perhaps a continuum, and can be induced effectively by deep breathing, counting, and other relaxation techniques, followed by visualization. She feels that often little induction is necessary because the patient comes in already in an altered state.

In the beginning of his work, Dethlefsen used hypnosis exclusively, following his standard hypnotic induction with the Leuner symbol drama.[8] This is a series of visualizations that teaches the patient to project inner pictures without conscious assistance and to accept the material rising to the surface as it appears, reporting it without criticism or comment. When Dethlefsen ceased using hypnotic techniques, he retained the symbol drama alone as his form of entrance.

Jue's inductions into an altered state are preceded by relaxation. The extent of his emphasis on relaxation depends on the patient; he finds that some need considerably more guidance and others are almost immediately ready to connect to a past life. In general, he focuses on body awareness, which at times leads to the Ericksonian approach, his closest association with actual hypnotic techniques. He often establishes areas of visualization in his initial interview and so weaves images effective for a particular patient into his induction. Control is given to the patient and is lovingly supported. On the Mind Mirror this shows up in his strong involvement, along with his patient, in alpha and theta.

Jue says:

> I do not use formal hypnosis in my practice, as I find it quite unnecessary for getting people into past-life memories. From years of dream work I can easily get clients to focus on their inner images, feelings, breath, or body sensations. No doubt this is trance-inducing in the Ericksonian sense, but I do not offer it as such or claim it to be hypnosis. I would prefer to call it a kind of guided meditation....

## Induction through Relaxation, Breathing, and Visualization

Most therapists, but excluding those who use emotional or other bridging techniques, begin regression work with relaxation. Relaxation approaches are myriad. An initial generally accepted approach, sometimes still used, was introduced by Jacobsen in the 50's.[9] It brought about relaxation as a reaction to tension that had been deliberately induced in various parts of the body. At the time, this approach was innovative and startling to a culture focused on achievement and unused to relaxation following striving, but now it is seen by many therapists as unnecessarily repetitive and lengthy (and a little boring). It is being replaced by a number of imaging techniques, usually including breathing and visualizing. Such inductions focus on a spectrum of bodily impressions, sounds, fragrances, feelings of the sun's warmth, as well as visual imaging. Various images of light are common and also perceptions of energy, often connected with light and color.

There is no doubt that light is a potent image and actually transforms the energy fields of the body. It is far more than a casual image—it is increasingly apparent that the influence of light is direct and "real." Most of our contributors use some special imaging of light to deepen contact. The patient may be asked to breathe in light and see light flooding every part of the body. Light may be visualized as coming into the feet and gradually relaxing the body as it flows upward, or it may be seen as a ball of light above the head that breaks and streams down, filling and surrounding the body.

Fiore has the subject image a miniature sun over the solar plexus, permeating the whole body with its rays:

> As you breath, gently imagine a bright light in the center of your solar plexus, just above your navel. It is like a miniature sun shining in the middle of your body. You are now completely protected by the white light of this sun, which is expanding softly to fill your whole body with bright light. It is expanding out to your fingertips and up to above the top of your head and down through the soles of your feet. Your whole body is softly glowing with protective while light. You are quite safe. You are deeply still.

The image of light may prove to be the most effective way of bringing a patient into an altered state. I find that having patients walk through a tunnel of light into an inner garden effects an immediate entry into an altered state. Snow's visualization of light being breathed into the various chakra centers is gradually replacing the more conventional induction techniques of Helen Wambach with which he began his regression work.

Snow and Denning are two forerunners who are putting increasing stress on energy techniques, including light, with which energy is often, probably correctly, identified. Denning has an especially effective energy meditation:

> Close your eyes and take a deep breath and just let go. I'd like you to take a second deep breath and this time bring energy into your body. With your mind send energy to every cell in your body.... And now with a third breath, bring energy to all the chakra centers. Image that you are sending energy to all the chakra centers and feel them come into synchronicity, each center vibrating at its normal rate so that all of them are vibrating like the cogs of a watch, each of them is vibrating at its own special rate. When you do this there is a synchronization of all the energy of all the energy centers, which is a wonderful feeling. So feel yourself balanced, centered, and when you do this, you feel yourself in tune with universal energy. You are vibrating in harmony with the energy of the universe. When you do this, it is an easy thing for you to slip into a deep altered state and get in tune and in touch with your own deeper all-knowing self.

Sensory imagery is characteristic of most inductions. This is well illustrated in Jue's inductions, where his safe and healing place is full of sensory overtones. These are woven into suggestions for relaxation:

> Allow yourself to be in your healing place and allow all your senses to be open to all the things there, looking around, being aware of the textures and colors of the flora around you, even being aware of the smells, the fragrances that seem to permeate this special place. So with every breath you take, with every sensing of this place, you seem to feel yourself going deeper and deeper, feeling the ground under your feet, and with every step you take you release more and more of your bodily tension.
>
> You even begin now to look around. You're noticing whether it's warm or cool. Is the sun shining on your head? Get in touch with that. Put yourself in

*the day where the sun is shining. You can feel the sun coming down over your body, penetrating your skin to the very bone, releasing all tension, feeling the warmth, the nurturance, the comfort of being in this place, so that as you walk through this place you become more and more aware of being relaxed. What sounds are in this place? Even the sounds seem to add to the deep sense of calmness that is coming over you. Become aware of the sounds, the insects, the birds, the wind. (Etc...) You will be noticing your breath now and your breathing is becoming more and more calm. You're breathing more slowly now as you begin to release all the tension.*

This induction points up the constant repetition of elements and the weaving of them into a web of relaxation in order to intensify the focus needed for an altered state. Therapists who have been trained in hypnosis and hypnotherapy emphasize this tendency to repeat. They also maintain an even and uninterrupted flow of words, and these techniques contribute to depth and continuity of trance. Observation shows that gaps of silence on the part of the therapist in the beginning stages of induction result in the patient moving up into beta rather than continuing immersion into deeper states.

It is important when a patient has followed a feeling backward and is already in a past life, that the therapist not intrude some cherished image into the process but follow the lead of the patient. The tendency to force a technique on a patient is characteristic of less-skilled therapists. It is one of the things Reynolds warns against as a violation of the therapeutic relationship.

Many therapists feel that it is important to establish a safe place to which the patient can return at the end of the regression or if his experiences seem overwhelming. The safe place can be both an entrance and an exit, thus circumscribing the experience so that there are safe boundaries. This place assures that the journeyer will return safely back into his body and recover his grounding. Pecci used his image of a mirror in such a way. My Tibetan garden meditation provides a safe entry into a past life and a definite and comfortable exit. The patient must be brought back to a normal state of consciousness. Moving back through the mirror or leaving the garden and returning along the tunnel into one's body brings about such a return.

In the process of returning, many therapists use hypnotic techniques to take advantage of the deeply altered state by injecting suggestions. These may be affirmations of energy and joy or a washing away of tensions with light, or they may concern an interim deepening of the lifetime being worked on. Some therapists add suggestions for easy entrance into a succeeding session and recovery of additional pertinent details. Many suggest that the pain and trauma that have been uncovered not follow the patient back into the current lifetime. Whether these suggestions are appropriate or not depends on how much of the matrix supporting them has been worked through and clarified.

In reviewing the process of induction the possibility arises that it is not so much the actual words that bring a patient into an altered state as the tone of the therapist's voice and the quality of energy that he emits. The Mind Mirror research suggests that the quickest way to take a patient into an altered state is for the therapist to go into that state himself and communicate it through his voice and his general quality of energy. Sometimes a hand clasp, such as Pecci and Hickman use, can communicate this, or a hand on the shoulder can transmit energy, though often this altered-state energy may best be communicated vocally. Induction techniques may turn out to be of benefit primarily to the therapist, making it possible for him as he goes into an altered state to draw his patient in after him. In the Mind Mirror research all effective therapists went into altered states similar to those of their patients, including delta, which ordinarily they would not make, and often their entry into these states preceded that of their patients.

A therapist's effectiveness may be linked to the quality of his energy and to his competence in accessing altered states himself. It is unclear whether a therapist who cannot enter an altered state can do effective regression therapy. If this turns out to be the case it may explain why not everyone in the field of psychotherapy is comfortable in working with past lives.

## Entering a Past Life

Many of the visualization processes used for induction into an altered state successfully lead the patient into a past life or prenatal or birth state. These visualizations usually suggest going from one level or state of consciousness into another where the earlier experience can be contacted. The practice of counting the subject down a stairway is a simple and effective entry that can be embellished by the imagination. In lieu of stairways there are elevators going down floors to the level where the lifetime lies. There are also tunnels, dark or filled with light, and doorways—in the tunnel, in a room, in a passageway. With such techniques one goes directly into another lifetime.

Fiore uses the image of the stairway especially skillfully:

> *Each breath is taking you deeper. As you breathe out, you feel yourself sinking deeper. Each out breath is taking you down, deeper down into an inner state.*

> *Now you are at the top of a flight of stairs that is covered with a thick plush carpet of your favorite color. Feel its softness with your toes. As you stand at the top, take hold of the bannister railing to steady yourself gently.*
>
> *You are now going to walk slowly down the steps, one at a time, and with each step and each out-breath, you will sink even deeper inside yourself, even deeper into your mind. As you walk down I will count slowly backwards from 20 to one, and you will go down one step with each count. (Counts down, interspersing numbers with suggestions for deepening.)*
>
> *Now I am going to count to ten and you will go to an event before you were born where you experienced...(state symptom or troublesome situation).*

Findeisen has her clients fly in a golden spaceship and land in another lifetime:

> *You are completely surrounded with warm golden energy. It forms around you a golden space ship! You feel the space ship beginning to lift. It lifts you up...it lifts you up...it lifts you up.... It is taking you high above the planet and back in time, higher and higher. Perhaps you can see the planet turning in space. You are going back in time, back to an important time for you to experience. You feel a pull to a particular place, a particular time. You feel yourself going down to this particular place. You are beginning to see the terrain. Closer and closer you see the place. You see a familiar figure. You are very close now. The space ship has landed. At the count of three you will step out of the space ship and tell me the first thing of which you are aware. Step into that body. Look down at your feet. What is there?...*

A similar image is that of floating on a cloud, which Wambach and Snow suggest in their group inductions:

> *As you look at the horizon you may find that there is a familiar object there, a fluffy, puffy, white cloud just your size, warm and secure. It's coming for you. Because you're weightless, it's a wonderfully supportive, welcoming sight. You relax completely. Fly on over to your cloud now...allow yourself to stretch out on it. Stretch out in whatever position is most comfortable as you lie on the cloud. And relax completely as I count. (Counts) Now you are floating on your cloud. Just allow yourself to float for a moment feeling relaxed and dreamy.*

Pecci often uses the magic mirror to take the patient to a depth of trance where the slightest suggestion will immediately bring the required lifetime. But at other times, following the period of relaxation, he uses a somatic state to help with the induction, as in this regression:

> T: *Get in touch with the anxiety and discomfort. Put them into one strong feeling and let this feeling build a scene that will give us a clue about your present condition. I will count from one to ten, and while I do this, let your feelings take you into that scene.*
>
> P: *There's a room, a great empty cold kind of room. A low light. There seems to be nothing in it but a table.*

Sometimes he concentrates on a feeling:

> T: *Let yourself focus on that feeling that you've been telling me about. Describe what you're feeling.*
>
> P: *Remorse...I'm astonished. The word is just there, a word I rarely use, and it fits precisely!*
>
> T: *Okay. We're going to trace the roots of this remorse...deep down feelings of remorse. Now I'm going to count down from ten to one and I want you to see a scene in which you had this feeling of remorse.*
>
> P: *Children. Children hurting. (Tears are streaming down her face so that it is difficult to speak.)*

Denning follows her energy induction with an image of a pool, which leads into recovery of a past lifetime:

> *Feel yourself getting in touch with your own deeper all-knowing Self, going deeper and deeper into the altered state. Feel your mind expanding, down into your subconscious, out into your superconscious, expanding like the circles in a pool when you drop in a pebble. Your mind expands and expands, bringing into the conscious self all that wonderful knowledge and information that is available to you about the rest of your lives.*
>
> *Let us focus now on (describing the present problem) and with that thought, putting all the energy into it that you can, let that thought take you back in time, through space, to some incident, some event, some trauma, that occurred a long time ago that you are still expressing in life today. Go back and back and back....*

Like Denning, I find the pool image effective for going into another life and combine it with images of energy and light. My pool is set in a garden, which allows practice in visualization:

> *Go up through the golden core and find yourself in a white tunnel. Walk along the tunnel, feeling it vibrating around and through you with light. As you walk along you will see a door on the side of the tunnel. Look at it carefully, noticing its size, the material it is made of, its shape, and how it is opened. (Allow time for the patient's response.) Open the door and go through and you will find yourself in a garden. Close the door behind you and look around.*

> *What is the shape of your garden and what are its boundaries? (Following this give ample time for exploration of the garden, its flowers, and any water that can be imaged.)*
>
> *In the center of your garden put a clear pool. Surround it with golden flowers if you like or let it be set in some grass. Then rest. Rest deeply in your garden. After a while go and look into your pool. You will see a star shimmering in its depth and as you look at this star it will blur and gradually you will see yourself at the bottom of the pool, but it is a long time ago, before you were born. Go to the lifetime that has to do with...(Here name the pattern or issue that has previously been decided on for exploration.)*

Following the image of the safe or healing place previously selected by the patient, Jue begins the actual regression:

> *See yourself walking through that special place, and as you walk you begin to see a shift now, a shift of seeing. It's almost as if as you walk through this place you begin to walk through another dimension of space and time. Your unconscious mind is now allowing you to go beyond this place, to know that beyond this place is another place, a time that you were once familiar with. In it is the answer to the question we asked about (name problem). Go back now.*

The focus for the regression, the problem to be addressed or the pattern to be explored, is usually determined by patient and therapist in the period of preparation, but it is restated in the actual entry into the past life. The therapist weaves the statement of the problem into the actual mode of entry. "At the bottom of the steps you will move into a lifetime that will help us understand your anger at your mother." Or, "When you look into the pool you will see yourself in a lifetime that contributed to this anxiety."

Jue describes this:

> In a relaxed state of light trance a number of simple guided imagery exercises or thematic phrases will lead easily and effortlessly into a past-life story where the client is the protagonist. Sometimes I encourage the client to focus on a recent memory or a person and start to say whatever comes to mind, as if that situation were being confronted. I may feed Gestalt-wise a phrase to sum up or intensify the affect, such as "I've had enough of this. Leave me alone!" Sometimes we may focus on a pain in the body, such as backache or stomach cramp, and allow images to emerge from that area.
>
> As soon as images, words, and feelings start to intensify, I suggest they be followed into any story that emerges in this or another life. I tell my client that it doesn't matter whether you believe in reincarnation, or not. Simply follow the story as if it were real for the duration of the session. The unconscious mind automatically produces a story that reflects current life issues.

## Age Regression as an Entry Technique

In the early days of past-life work there were two approaches that constituted entries into past lives. They are well described by Dethlefsen. Both are forms of age regression and involve moving backward in increments, starting with the current time. In the first of these approaches no specific theme or focus is followed but whatever incident in each time frame wants to emerge is allowed to do so. This approach puts minimal pressure on the patient as he travels backward through young adulthood, childhood, infancy, birth, the prenatal months, into the most recent lifetime, and even further backward. Eventually themes and patterns begin to take shape. This procedure has the advantage of allowing whatever is most important in the unconscious to emerge. Pertinent themes and issues arise on their own.

Dethlefsen illustrates this with a patient whose return to the prenatal state through age regression set off a regression to a traumatic lifetime where the bouncing that was felt in the uterus during the current lifetime's prenatal experience was the same bouncing that had been experienced during a carriage ride in a past life:

T: *We shall go backward through your life because time means nothing to us. Time is only a means of communication, a measure, but you will re-live the past as if it were happening now. The past will become the present. We shall go backward in your life. You are getting younger; you will be 25 years old.... We shall go back further; you will be 20 years old.... Let us go back further—you are 15, 10 years old. Today is your 10th birthday. How do you feel?*

P: *Not particularly well.*

T: *Why not?*

P: *I have the flu.*

T: *Did you get any presents?*

P: *Not many. My mother sent me a package—a red blouse and a pleated grey skirt with straps—it has red and blue dots in it—they took it away from me.*

T: *Who took it?*

P: *My sister. (Describes the situation and cries.)*

T: *Let us dissolve this birthday and go further back in time—we shall go further back in time. You are getting younger. You are now six years old. Are you going to school now? (Explores this.)*

T: *Good. Let us go back farther. You are getting younger—five, four, three, two, one. Let us return to the moment of your birth. Today is April 13, 1946. You are just being born. What time is it?*

P: *4:52. It's a Saturday.*

T: *Good. You are just being born. What do you feel? What is happening?*

P: *(Describes the details of a difficult Caesarian birth.)*

T: Let us go back further in time. Let us return to the cave from which you came—to the time of conception. Why are you laughing? Tell me.
P: Hmm (laughs), nothing—but it keeps bouncing. (The bouncing she felt while in the uterus triggered the memory of being in a wagon rolling over stones where she was an illegitimate child dying of consumption.)

The regression backward led immediately to a core issue, even though one had not been stated and probably had not even been discussed in the brief preparation work that Dethlefsen felt was sufficient. The specificity of detail in this account is not unusual but is always surprising.

Irene Hickman, also, often moves into a past life through this type of age regression. She finds that, among other things, it can throw light on family relationships. In the case of Justin, his relationship with his father emerged as the result of a series of close and loving, though often traumatic, lifetimes full of loss. His sixth Christmas when he was with a little girl friend provided entry into the age regression:

T: What's your girl friend's name?
P: Jean. (Gives details.)
T: I am going to count back one more year and you will be five. One...two...three...four...five. Now you are five years old. Find a happy time and tell me about it.
P: I'm with my grandma. (Answers questions about activities in this year.)
T: One...two...three...four. You are now four. Tell me what you are doing now.
P: (Begins to cry.) Nobody wanted me.
T: Why didn't they want you? If you talk about it you will feel much better.
P: (Sobs deeply, then tells about being left alone and constantly changing homes.)
T: Let's go back to a time when you were three. Go back until you are three years old and tell me about it. Is it happier when you are three?
P: No. (Tells about living in New Mexico and going to church.)
T: Now let's go back to the time you were two years old. Now you are two. Look around you and tell me what is happening.
P: It's better. Grandpa is here. He loves me. He sings. (Describes this.)
T: That is pretty good, isn't it. So now we will go back to one year—in the time you are one year old. Now you are one year old. Tell me exactly how you feel, and what's happening all around you. You will be able to speak about it as an adult, but you are actually living the experience as a baby one year old.
P: (Begins to cry and sob.) I'm all alone...in a room. I'm locked in. (Tells about being neglected and locked in a room by his mother.)
T: Now let's go forward a little bit—until someone comes and unlocks the door. You will know who it is, and what they do and say. (Pause.) Who is it that comes in?

> P: My daddy. He picks me up. He loves me. He's holding me. He's saying, "Everything's going to be all right."
> T: Now you feel better. Now we're going back a little further to the time just before you were born. (Takes him through his birth.)
> T: Well, we can go back a little further—back to the time before the birth, back to the time when you know why you are coming back to live this life. You will know why you are coming back to this particular mother and father. So go back through time until the time of this decision. Now you know why you came to these parents. Why did you come?
> P: For my daddy.
> T: Had you known him before?
> P: Yes.
> T: Let us now go back to the time when you knew your daddy before. Your subconscious knows and it can search through your memory until it finds the time when you and this daddy were together before. When I reach the count of seven you will have found this time. (Counts.) Look around you and tell me what's happening.
> P: He's my brother. (Goes on to describe two lifetimes where as a brother and girl-sweetheart he knew his current father and was separated from him.)

This type of age regression is often used effectively to recover lost childhood memories, especially of sexual abuse. It is also a way into prenatal and birth memories.

A modification of this unstructured backward regression consists of following a specific theme, symptom, feeling, or bodily state backward through the various age frames, disregarding extraneous material and focusing on the area of concern. This is a more cognitive version of the bridging technique.

## The Emotional-Somatic Bridge as Induction and Entry

The technique of following a feeling, body sensation, or core issue backward into a past life was originally proposed by Morris Netherton, building on techniques originated by Dianetics. Netherton has given many training workshops in the Netherlands, and his influence has been especially strong in the Dutch school. Hans ten Dam formulated the principles of this induction for his students, and currently Noordegraaf and Bontenbal have deepened and expanded them. Focus is achieved by concentration on what is called the Mental-Emotional-Somatic bridge. Any of the components—mental, emotional, or somatic—can be used separately and usually one is chosen as an entering wedge, but the bridge has its strongest impact when all the components are used together. The intense focus serves to precipitate the patient into another lifetime without any initial relaxation or imaging.

Woolger uses the technique of having the patient follow a feeling or memory back and then say Gestalt-wise whatever comes to mind. As soon as the feelings, images, or words start to intensify, he suggests that they be followed into any story that emerges in this or another life, whether or not the story is considered to be real. The unconscious mind automatically produces a story that reflects current life concerns. As a Jungian analyst, Woolger easily gets clients to focus on their inner images, feelings, breath, or body sensations in a guided meditation. He considers formal hypnosis unnecessary for getting people into past-life memories.

Woolger makes frequent use of entry through a somatic bridge, using breathing, massage, and abreaction. He feels that somatic disturbances contain deeply repressed feelings that either express themselves symbolically or else mirror a past-life trauma. To access them requires taking sensate consciousness into the area of disturbance:

> T: *I want you to close your eyes and take your awareness right down into your hips, right into the painful area. Good. What does it feel like down there?*
> P: *It's as though I'm wedged, as though I can't move from side to side.*
> T: *Does it feel like anything is restricting you from the outside, or is it held on the inside?*
> P: *It feels like I'm stuck between something like rocks. I can't move.*
> T: *Good. Repeat: "I can't move," and stay with the image of the rocks.*
> P: *Oh, it hurts! I've been thrown down here. It's a crevasse! They wanted to kill me!... My neck feels very tight. I'm tensing my shoulders.*
> T: *What are your shoulders trying to say, if they could speak?*
> P: *No, don't do this, don't do this!*
> T: *Exaggerate your shoulders—bring them up higher. Now say that again.*
> P: *Don't do this! No, no, no! They're going to cut my head off!...*

It always seems miraculous when someone, as this patient, becomes precipitated into a past life by intensification of emotions and bodily postures along with mental components such as the statement, "I can't move!" Apparently touching on an appropriate trigger releases such memories. Breathing is often used to intensify the triggers, as in the following examples by the Dutch therapists.

The first is a session by Bontenbal. In it he worked with a young woman whose life had been strongly impacted by a fear of rape that had been set off several years before when a man had jumped out of the bushes at her as she was riding her bicycle home after dark. She first went into that memory to deepen it and retrieve details.

T: You are cycling home, feeling good. What are you thinking cycling there?
C: Thinking? Nothing special. It's rather dark and cold. I had fun, but I long for my warm room.
T: Okay, move to the very first moment you see that man.
C: (Panicking.) He is right there! He suddenly jumps out of the bushes, pulling me off my bike! I fall. Oh, God! I feel so frightened!... (Starts sobbing.)
T: Feel how frightened you are, really feel it, as deep as you can....
C: (Still sobbing a little) And then those two people are there and he runs away...but I am still so frightened...
T: Breathe into the feeling. Feel it once more as deeply as you can, then breathe it out, all of it....

After a couple of minutes the client released some of her fear.

T: Move once more to the moment you are cycling...just before the man jumps...but move through it this time in slow motion...and just realize what you thought the moment he jumped.
C: He jumps...God it really startles me....
T: What are you thinking right there. Right there.
C: Oh God, he's going to rape me!
T: Say that again, and feel what is happening within you, within your body....
C: Oh, God, he's going to rape me...I freeze...
T: Realize that and then breathe yourself through that freeze, keep on breathing, until you come out of that freeze.

She realized that some time had elapsed between when the man appeared and when he touched her, but she had been frozen into shock by her exclamation that he was going to rape her.

C: No, no, please...no, no, don't rape me! No...please...no...noooo!!

She moaned louder and louder and then suddenly jumped from the couch, shrieked, and became motionless.

T: What are you experiencing right now?
C: (Deep sigh, still motionless) I believe I am dead. They killed me.
T: They?
C: Those men. They came upstairs, jumped on me, raped me, then killed me.
T: Repeat those words, listen to them!

A pertinent past life opened up for this patient through this brief induction.

Noordegraaf's 12-year-old patient, Ludovic, relived a terrifying lifetime in a similar manner. He had experienced fright during his entire lifetime and went into physical tremors whenever he was exposed to an emotional scene or to physical happenings such as thunder and lightning.

> C: *Something is terribly wrong, you know. I am even terribly scared of a thunderstorm, of the thunder and lightning. I scream and I shout as if it were a nightmare, as if a disaster were going to happen. I tell myself over and over that I am not a little baby anymore and I don't have to be afraid, but it doesn't work. Something is wrong with me. I just don't know what it is.*
> 
> T: *Well, let's find out then what is wrong. And before we start working on being wrong, just tell me what you mean by "wrong"? How would it be to be "right" then...?*
> 
> C: *(Shocked.) Are you crazy? Don't you know? Feeling at ease of course, feeling all right, not having to be alert all the time. Not to wait for the next time these tremors will show up...for the next terrible fight with my mother. (Sobbing.) I just want it to stop.... Please help me.... (Desperation is coming through strongly.)*

After repeating that sentence "I want it to stop" a number of times, the typical tremors started. Ludovic accessed the moment that was most traumatic for him. He was a young Japanese boy playing in the streets in early morning when his world fell apart. Everything he cared for went to pieces in a fraction of a minute. He landed back in World War II in August, 1945, at the moment that Hiroshima was bombed.

The wall between current awareness and past-life memory is fragile. I asked my grandson once, when he paused thoughtfully while telling me about a lifetime in Egypt, if he would like me to relax him. His answer was, "Why? It's right there (pointing into the air)!" Apparently, when we have the right key, the induction can be minimal. Have we failed to be aware of this in the past? Or is it that the consciousness of the planet is transforming and we have only to open ourselves to our new potential?

## Chapter VII

# Supportive and Deepening Techniques

Once an altered state has been reached and an initial image encountered, whether by counting, walking through a tunnel, going down a stairs, looking into a pool, or following an emotional-somatic charge backward, the patient enters the first stage of the regression, which is identification with the person imaged. It is now the objective of the therapist to help him relive the body, mind, and emotions of the person to such an extent that he *is* the person, and the vicissitudes of that lifetimes are *his* vicissitudes. Whether one assumes that what is being imaged is past life or metaphor, it is important, in order to achieve the maximum therapeutic benefit, that the patient totally identify with the person he is imaging.

There are two further considerations beyond assisting the actual process of identification. It is necessary to establish techniques for moving within the time frame of the recovered material in order to reveal patterns and motivations. And the therapist must be skilled in handling stress, which inevitably accompanies the emergence of past material, since we tend to recover traumatic memories rather than comfortable ones.

## The Role of the Therapist

The same supportive techniques that characterize any good therapy are necessary here. Foremost is a respect for the patient's process and acceptance of what he is revealing. It is just as important for a therapist in a regression process to give up expectations about what should happen as it is in a more conventional therapy. Atypical situations must be handled non-judgmentally. Sometimes the patient is not in a past life but in a metaphor, and this must be taken as his reality at the moment. At other times, two or more past lives are juxtaposed, and as more and more details emerge to contradict each other, the therapist needs to determine with great sensitivity which life the patient wishes to stress at the time.

If a patient describes details in a lifetime that obviously do not fit the period, the tendency to try and make sense of the material must be released in order to avoid making the patient self-conscious and hesitant about revealing other details. Patients are often themselves skeptical of what they are producing and do not need to be made self-conscious by critical overtones in the therapist's intervention. Whether through voice quality or comment, these overtones can make patients skeptical of what they are saying or of the direction their imaging is taking. Reflection of feelings is a therapeutic tool that can both give support and enable a patient to go more deeply into a situation.

As in most forms of therapy, there is nothing that has a more supportive effect on the patient than a modulated, unhurried, caring quality to the therapist's voice. Most of our contributors mention the important effect of voice, and some supplement supportive voice quality with a hand touch, especially in distressing episodes. Most regression therapists notice the way patients speak, and they formulate their questions and comments in language that is appropriate for a particular patient, avoiding any words that are too colloquial or too formal and might prove jarring. The quality of a therapist's voice becomes modulated when he is in an altered state, which is another reason for him to share such a state with his patient. In fact, through his voice he can often draw his patient into an altered state without supporting techniques, and by his voice he can also deepen trance.

Awareness of the heightened suggestibility of the altered state increases the responsibility of the therapist to be a sensitive companion and requires him to become fine-tuned to the patient's process. Snow describes this growing sensitivity:

> Once the client is perceiving information from a past-life scenario, my questions are guided by a co-mingling of the original information gleaned from the interview and my own intuitive perceptions. At this point we are sharing an intensified energy field.... As the session progresses, I pay close attention to the client's own responses and use them to mold further questions. I feel that following the client in his internal scenario is essential for a successful regression....

Jue talks about this connectedness:

> In working with clients I tend to hold back in the beginning and wait to see how things develop, but mid-way I feel connected and then it is as though my internal television set goes on. I tend to get more directive later when I make the connection. This comes as a result of feeling clarity about what needs to be done. However, any directiveness is modified because it is communicated with a heart connection. If the therapist doesn't feel connected when he is doing that kind of clarifying, even though he is

positive he is right, what he says becomes technique oriented, a sort of going through a protocol sheet, which prevents what he says from being effective. There must be an energy connection with the client for transformation to take place.

Reynolds feels that unconditional positive regard in itself brings healing and is transformational in the regression process, just as it is when therapy is set in the current lifetime. Healing is embedded in the experience of being guaranteed an unconditional attitude, which makes reframing possible. Unconditional positive regard and congruence on the part of the therapist encourage deep exploration of material. Reynolds comments:

> When thinking about what effects change, it appears that support helps people face frightening aspects of their lives. This support may play a part in helping people examine and resolve material in a past lifetime much as it does in the present.... I try to create an atmosphere that is essentially unrushed in its exploration of past-life memories that the client sees as important. I have found that emotional release seems to play a part, and a good bit of support, encouragement and reassurance are offered in these times.

There are numerous personal variables that affect therapist-patient energy interaction, as I learned when, as a part of my preparation for this book, I was regressed by nearly all of the major contributors, by some several times. No one experience remotely resembled any other, especially in the nature of the energy exchange between each therapist and myself and in the resulting transference. The extent and depth of the insight that I gained through the regressions also varied.

## Techniques for Eliciting Material

Every therapist develops personal techniques for eliciting material and moving a regression ahead, but there are some general approaches that are especially effective. The process of describing everything *in the present* not only yields details of feeling and invention but also helps to keep recall moving fluently. Woolger describes this process as being similar to voicing stage instructions:

*A light is shining above the doorway. The farmer and his son enter arguing fiercely.*

If the patient slips into the past tense, the therapist can bring back the sense of immediacy by repeating what has been said in the present tense. This technique is similar to the way many therapists work with dreams.

It is possible to recover details and rich material just by asking or suggesting, and this is the most common method of eliciting information. Counting and suggesting that at a final number, as "five," the information will be there usually works well. Suggestions may be non-directive or they may have the flavor of a command, as when Fiore moved a young man deeper into the lost feelings he had experienced while on a hunting trip in order to find out who he was. The confidence that there *is* an answer encourages patients to come up with one:

> P: Well...there's darkness all around me. I can't seem to see anything.
> T: In a few moments it will become very clear to you what is happening.
> P: (Sadly) It's cold...it's dark and cold. I'm outside. It's snowing, and I think...I think there's rocks and trees...it's snowing and cold.
> T: Just get in touch with who you are. You'll know you name and all about yourself.
> P: I was hunting...and I'm lost and I think I'm gonna' freeze! I don't know my name (voice very raspy and shaky).
> T: On the count of three you will know. One...two...three.
> P: Fred.

Specific questions elicit material more easily than open-ended ones, and the therapist needs to encourage small impressions by asking about simple things. Many therapists, for example, start by asking what the person has on his feet, if anything. Feet are relatively easy to see, and from them one can go on to articles of clothing, sex, age, and whatever the material suggests. Such a beginning serves to get the patient well-oriented into his personality in the other lifetime. Jue's patient, whose husband was killed riding horses, gave many details, beginning with her feet:

> T: I want you to look down and look at yourself and see who you are.
> P: I have brown sandals on my feet. I can see my toes. I think I see some sort of a long garment. Kind of a rough, gauzy sort of a pattern on it. I think it is a dress. The sandals are kind of rough. Peasanty, sort of, I think. There is a sort of a buckle. The garment comes down to my feet.
> T: Bring your awareness now to your whole stature and what you are addressing. Can you tell me who you are? I presume you are a woman.
> P: Yes. I think I am...I suddenly now get the sense that I am fairly old and not straight. I am sort of bent or slouched a bit. I feel frail. I feel bent and frail, and the skirt is sort of uneven, as if my body is not a straight, tall body. It is sort of uneven because of my body.
> T: I want you to feel your energy in this woman's body. Get a feeling of who you are. As this woman, who are you? And what are you doing here?

> P: I have a sense that I am old and not very useful. I have just sort of been left behind. Like everybody is gone, and I am here because they didn't think that I could keep up with them.

"How?" questions yield excellent material, and "When?" and "What?" are usually helpful, but questions introduced by "Why?" seldom produce anything useful and tend to stop material because they throw the patient into a cognitive state.

Since most therapists feel that deep trauma is lodged in the body and needs to be re-lived in order to be released, effective therapeutic support and patience are necessary to help the patient recover these bodily feelings. Woolger demonstrated this in his case with the little girl walking toward the gas chamber where sensitive coaching about bodily feelings and sensations helped her become released from her frozen state.[1]

Snow skillfully taps and releases emotions. His patient Margo came to understand her situation primarily through becoming aware of the spread of emotions that had gripped her in that lifetime:

> T: Now stay in that same body and approximately that time frame and move to a moment when you are having some strong feeling, either feeling very good or very bad, something emotional, something that you're watching, that you begin to become a part of. Move there. Where are you?
> P: I'm there in the same place.
> T: Let yourself move into the moment you begin to feel. What's happening?
> P: Well, there's a man coming out of the woods. I'm holding some flowers.
> T: What's the first thought that comes through your mind as you see him?
> P: I'm excited.
> T: Get in touch with that excitement for a moment. Get in touch with the excitement in your body. Where does it come?
> P: Up around my heart and my chest. And my throat. And my thighs. My thighs feel real warm. Real quivery.
> T: Okay. Stay with that feeling. Feel it even more strongly.

Such anchoring of feeling in the body intensified and deepened the experience. Later on, feelings of guilt proved an additional anchor for Margo:

> T: Move through—touch exactly your feelings. Get into the guilt feelings that you're having there along with the wonderful sensations. I want you to let yourself flow into those now.
> P: I can't believe that I'm really his. It's like he wants me to be his but he can't really be mine. It's not fair, but it's so exquisite. It means so much to be with him but I feel conflict at the back of my neck.
> T: Okay. Feel that feeling at the back of your neck. Now I want you to move forward one year from that date. Get in touch. Now where are you?

Key words help to move patients along on the theme of the lifetime. "Abandonment" and "rejection" were key words in the presentation of a young woman Jue treated who irrationally felt deserted by her husband when he was away on a business trip. Bringing these words frequently into the process of regression helped to move her into the lifetime where she had felt deserted and into the event in that lifetime that precipitated the abandonment. Jue uses this technique frequently:

> P: *It's like somebody else is taking away what was so wonderful and I have nothing to say about it. It is completely out of my hands. It feels like a betrayal. It's just not fair. It hurts—just hurts. I feel a real emptiness and darkness and despair. I feel my voice changing, struggling for some kind of control over these feelings. There is a profound sense of loss and unfairness.*
> T: *Could you stay with that profound sense of loss. What are the words that are coming into your mind over and over again? What is being repeated?*
> P: *It's going away. It's gone. It's going. It's empty.*
> T: *The connectiveness.*
> P: *Yes, the connectiveness. The wonderful connectiveness is going. It's stretching. It feels like it is stretched so much that it suddenly just popped. It feels like it's gone and the goneness is just a big sinking. A big thud.*
> T: *Stay with that sense of disconnectiveness in thinking to yourself, "It isn't fair." Now it is time for you to go back, because there have been other times that you felt this, and I want your psyche now, and using your own inner resources, to go back to another time when you felt this same kind of feeling, as if the whole floor has been sort of dropped from underneath you. Go back to another time when you experienced this.*
> P: *It is just grayish and darkish—not distinct. I look like I'm in...maybe some sort of hallway...*

Hickman is a master of detail. It is worth reading the account of her patient with the cat allergy to see how, over four regressions, she managed, giving excellent support, to get more and more details until finally the highly charged material was desensitized:

**First account:**

> P: *I'm running back to tell my chief that there are intruders down by the river. Then right in front of me is a tiger. I stop in my tracks.*
> T: *What happens next?*
> P: *He's lying down looking at me. He's crouched down ready to spring.*

**Second account:**

P: *I'm going to tell my chief that there are strangers going to the river. I'm running. I come to a spot and hear this growling sound and it's a tiger—a huge thing. He's staring at me. I stand and watch him. He's watching me. I stand there for a long time. He's calmed down now. Somehow I gotta' get around him.*

**Third account:**

P: *I'm running and 10 yards in front of me crouching down is a tiger. His hair is raised and his ears are up and his eyes are looking right at me. I stop right in my footsteps. I stand there for a long time looking at him—a long time.*

In the fourth account most of the details were dropped as the affect lessened and disappeared.

Specific situations can be set up to extend the framework. For instance, the therapist can move the patient ahead to dinner time and ask about his house, family members and other relationships, food, customs, etc. These details often set the period in which the lifetime takes place, introduce other characters, and in general move forward the action of that lifetime.

In my regression with Carrie dinner time produced a wealth of detail:

P: *I see myself in wooden shoes, a long blue skirt, short white blouse. Looks like Holland. I'm outside. Someone is near, my mother...*
T: *Go to your house at dinner time and tell me who is there.*
P: *It has a large eating area for such a small house. The table is wooden. The chairs are high-backed. The bowls are metal. There's a man there, my father—he's sitting across from me. My brother and I are near each other. My brother is 10. My father is a farmer. He's withdrawn, so dinner is a quiet affair because nobody dares to talk.*

## Blocking

Blocking can occur at any point in a regression and for many reasons. There may be initial blocking at getting into a lifetime. In that case a simple technique is to ask the patient to make up a story or to suggest that the material is a metaphor or a parable, which in a very true sense it is. Jue, whose clientele consists largely of cognitively oriented business executives who frequently feel that past lives are unorthodox, falls back on metaphors and parables routinely and gets the same type of material as others do when the framework is structured to be a past life.

## Supportive and Deepening Techniques

It is helpful to tell the patient, whenever he is at a loss, that he should say the first thing that occurs to him without intellectual scrutiny. When a patient begins to question what is coming through, to ask whether it is really that or something else, it is easy for him to end up with nothing. It is necessary for the patient to trust that the unconscious will throw up a valid memory and not feel it has to be scrutinized first.

When material seems difficult to verbalize or is obscure, Fiore uses finger signals to give information, perhaps even to say that the patient does not want to go on. In her work with William on his problem of obesity she used finger signals to establish that his craving for chocolate originated in another lifetime and to rule out that it began in this one.[2] Finger signals told her regarding another patient, Roger, that there were six lifetimes involved in forming the pattern of his indecision.[3] These techniques may bring information from the unconscious by bypassing the cognitive mind, though therapists agree that the message is not always reliable.

Woolger discusses two methods of dealing with resistance using highly sophisticated techniques. In the first, he suggests that a subject who is reliving a painful event and having difficulty be moved forward in time, overshooting large sections of the story. The painful event can then be described as in the past and finished. After that the patient can move backward until he is finally able to experience the painful event as currently happening. Woolger moved back and forth in the death incident of the anarchist in order to recover the details and feelings he felt were necessary:

T: *Go back and re-live the events leading up to the explosion.*
P: *I'm with a group of young men. I'm about 19, a man. It's Russia. We're going to kill them. We hate them. They killed my father!* They killed my father! *Several of our group has been killed but we go on fighting. No more of this tyranny. It's time to fight back.*
T: *What are you doing now?*
P: *We're carrying bombs. They're for those bastards (soldiers) who killed my father.*
T: *Go forward and tell me what happens.*
P: *It's all black. I'm not in my body.*
T: *Go back and tell me how you died.*
P: *I'm looking down from outside my body. Oh, my God! It has no arms and legs. There's been an explosion. It's still moving.*
T: *Go back inside your body and tell me exactly how it feels.*
P: *I'm dying, lying here on the street. The pain is terrible. No arms, no legs...(Cries.)... Now I'm dead. No more movement. I'm leaving my body.*
T: *Be aware of your last words as you are dying and go to the point where your heart finally stops beating.*
P: *My arms and legs will never work again. Oh, no!*

The opposite can occur: the unconscious of the patient may hesitate to go ahead because of the trauma it anticipates and therefore drags out earlier scenes. Then Woolger makes use of such connectors as, "What do you find when you go up the stairs?" or, even more sensitively, "What would you find if you went up the stairs?" He feels that the image encapsulates the event and once the event is in consciousness it is possible to work with the scene.

## Moving within Time

With relatively simple types of suggestions and questions the therapist can help the patient move within the time frame of the life being examined, or even to previous lives. It is comparatively simple to move him backward to a preceding incident or a time when an event was planned or to a happier time when he can gather himself together to face a traumatic incident. It is also possible to go ahead to the consequences of some event in the life or to the death in that lifetime, or to explore related lifetimes by moving on some emotional, cognitive, or somatic bridge.

Sometimes it is helpful to intersperse suggestions for moving forward in specific time intervals by combining counting with the suggestion that the patient go to the "next significant incident." This technique of moving from one incident to another often locates a crucial memory without an extended analysis of details that do not yield pertinent material. Here the suggestibility of the altered state is useful. Instructions should be open-ended.

My patient Rosemary responded well to simple suggestions and counting:

> T: *I will count to five and at five you will go to the next significant incident in that lifetime. (Counts.)*
> P: *I'm starting to feel fear. It's in London on the street at night. The fire! It seems to be a panic and a lot of people are running. Everything's on fire* (very excited and disturbed), *and the sky's red.*

One can move a definite number of years ahead, making a guess or having an informed opinion that a certain period will yield material. I took Rosemary ahead a half hour and she was in a crowd by the river and everyone was talking about whom they had lost. An hour later she was being taken care of by the equivalent of the Red Cross. Then I moved her into the future:

## Supportive and Deepening Techniques

T: Move ahead five years and tell me what's happening.
P: It's as though I couldn't have children and John got impatient. Feels like—ah, it is, it's a cemetery. I'm looking at the tombstones. I don't seem to be alive. I think that girl committed suicide.

Five years had evidently been too long a span. She was already dead.

T: Go backward to an hour before your death in that lifetime.
P: It's a knife. I hate to say this—it's a room. It's almost like John...killed me. It's in a study, in a library. I see his hatred. I'm pleading with him to stay, not to leave. I'm not old, not ugly. I just can't have kids. He needs kids for social prestige—he needs an heir. He stabs me in the stomach and walks out of the room.
T: Go through your death and tell me where you are.
P: I'm a little above her body and to the side.

Precursors to a situation can be found either in earlier incidents in the lifetime being examined or in an earlier lifetime. Pecci tends to start with very early lifetimes and move forward in order to locate the thread of cause and effect. But if the lifetime is recovered by means of a symptom, the therapist can move backward from the first lifetime recovered into other lifetimes to try to find roots and explanations of that symptom. Pecci did this with a young man suffering from a chest ailment and who first went back to a relatively recent lifetime where as a doctor he failed to save his friend:

T: His friend doesn't want to leave when this doctor is so guilty. Make a love bond, not a bond of pain and suffering. Can you feel this?
P: Yes, a little.
T: Now I'd like you to take a deep breath and relax and go back even further to where you began with this chest difficulty. Is there any other thing related to this?
P: It's a kind of open court within a building, a courtyard—Grecian or Roman. And there's a taper burning on the wall. There are two figures...

General or inevitable incidents, such as the end of a battle or the death of a person, can be recovered, either by counting or simply by suggesting that the patient go ahead to that time. A death experience can often be moved into more easily by going to an hour before the actual event and picking up the setting and people present. Then the death itself can be moved through and a scan made from the after-death state.

Dethlefsen's patient Claudia was able to report significant material when she was asked to go to the time just before her death:

T: How old will you get to be?
P: I will not get to be very old; I may have about another half year to live, not much more.
T: Very well, let us go forward in time until just before your death.
P: Yes.
T: Tell me what happens.
P: Well, I am lying on the bed and I'm terribly thin and frail, I...hmm...and the doctor is there and says he can't help me anymore—I'll have to die.
T: Very well, let's do that.

Bontenbal, in order to find the actual cause of his patient Henny's death in an earlier life, which was suicide, had to move her ahead, then back, then slightly ahead again.

P: I feel so depressed! I don't want to live anymore. I don't want to hear the children crying, to see the dirt, to look at myself in the mirror, to wait for him to come home in a bad mood. (Too far back.)
T: What do you do next?
P: I don't know. I am just sitting there. It feels like I am sitting in that kitchen forever. (She is already dying from an overdose.)
T: Just move backward a little bit in time. Until you feel you are moving again. Doing anything.
P: (After a minute) I actually move very slowly, like a zombie. I feel very strange. (Not far enough back. She has already taken the pills.)
T: Move back a little more. Before the slow moving as a zombie starts.
P: I am standing now. In the kitchen. (This is the moment of decision.)
T: What are you doing?
P: I don't know. I give up.
T: Repeat that!
P: What?
T: I give up. Say it again.
P: I give up (six times).... Oh, God (starts to cry)! I have pills in my hand. Oh God, no!

Very slowly she recalled taking the pills. She was sitting at the kitchen table. She heard her children crying but she was not able to respond. The zombie feeling was already there.

P: I can't move anymore. They are crying. I feel terrible. I have let them down. I want to stop it. But I can't, I can't anymore!

Bontenbal processed the slow dying by moving through it a number of times. At the end, the patient cried freely, letting out the distress, the fear, the anger, the guilt.

Moving backward in this current lifetime often includes the uterine and birth experiences. It is surprising how vividly the details of these can be recovered. A birthing experience may serve as a step backward into another lifetime with the same pattern or as an intermediate but reinforcing step between a pattern set in another lifetime and its repetition in this. Findeisen feels that this intermediate step amplifies insight and healing. In her account of the twins, an earlier lifetime where Joni as a younger sister had fallen to her death while climbing a cliff with Joy established the dependency relationship. In the current birth process Joni hung onto Joy's ankle, and Joy became agitated and repeated, "Baby, go 'way!" The birth replayed and clarified their strong bonds of ancient guilt and resentment and Joni's fear of being abandoned. As the twins realized this pattern, they were able to separate emotionally from each other.[4]

## Dealing with Stress

An important component in supporting and deepening the regression process is dealing with stress, and there is no aspect of regression work where the approaches of various therapists differ more widely. The spectrum runs from removing the patient from the distressing situation to intensification of the stressful experience. All of these are effective at times, and at other times all of them fail.

### 1. Changing the Time Frame

Some therapists wish to avoid stress in their patients and so remove them from a disturbing situation. One technique is to take the patient back to a more positive experience in that same lifetime and then bring him forward to look again at the distressing situation. Reynolds' patient, who was trying to break a smoking addiction, became deeply disturbed when she remembered dying of typhoid fever:

T: *Let's explore where the anxiety really began.*
P: *(In great anguish) I'm on fire. Someone please help me!*
T: *Are you in a fire?*
P: *No, I'm sick. I have the fever.*
T: *What kind of fever?*
P: *Typhoid fever.*
T: *Leave that and go back to a happier time in that lifetime.*

The patient then moved back to a time during her relatively benign earlier years. Later she was able to return to that death and see how her father, who had sat smoking at her bedside, had comforted her while she was dying, so that smoking and comfort became identified.

Findeisen used the same technique in a regression where a young chieftain was murdered while trying to save his people:

> T: *Go back to an earlier time when you had these feelings.*
> P: *I'm in a deep pit and there's no way I can get out. I'm trapped.*
> T: *Tell me who you are.*
> P: *I'm a dark-skinned man. I am the leader of my island. My people depend on me (sounds upset and desperate).*
> T: *Let's go back further to a time when you and your people are peaceful and happy, when you are safe.*

This regression backward in time not only gave a chance for emotional recouping but also supplied important information about the situation. The patient described a peaceful, almost idyllic life, which was interrupted when men from another island came in canoes to their island paradise and proceeded to kill and destroy.

It is also possible to go ahead following deep stress to relatively quieter waters, which allows one to return and explore a turbulent situation, knowing that it is not the end. This is true whether the future is in that life or in the state beyond death, or even in a succeeding lifetime. But even in the lifetime being scanned it is rare that there are not some bright days, and in addition to providing an opportunity for courage and energy to be recovered, it is good to find this sort of balance in a lifetime.

## 2. Detachment

Establishing a safe place before the regression provides a detached haven when things become threatening. This is an established procedure with Reynolds, who regularly uses it when the patient seems overwhelmed by stress. An example is where a woman saw herself as a young warrior being chased.

> P: *They're going to get me. I just can't get away (very agitated)!*
> T: *Who is going to get you?*
> P: *The men with clubs. They followed me to the big water. (Starts shaking violently and crying.)*
> T: *What's happening now?*
> P: *(No response, but more crying.)*
> T: *Imagine you're looking at it on a movie screen and just describe it without emotion.*
> P: *(Unable to do this.)*
> T: *Would you like to come out of this for right now?*

P: Yes.
T: Let your thoughts go that beautiful spot in the desert where you used to camp. (Pause.) Now on the count of five, feeling fully refreshed and alert, awaken in the present moment.

In the next session, the patient was able to go back to the events that had led up to the death and that made the death seem understandable.

A technique used by almost all of our therapists is one of becoming an observer. Patients seem immediately able to detach and observe unemotionally when the therapist gives permission for this. Often a few moments of such objectivity make it possible for the patient to step back into the experience.

Snow mentions support and not pressuring patients to actually re-experience overwhelming trauma but instead helping them to gain detachment from what they are experiencing until they are more able to deal with it. His supportive stance and his use of options is reassuring:

> When a situation is too painful, I remind the client that this is a past life and I suggest that he imagine he is looking at a movie of his past, so to speak, and he need not experience pain. I may suggest that the mind is like a great library and that the client can move through it and find a book about this particular incident.

He gives an example of how he encourages detachment:

T: *Just move forward into the next scene. What happens when George arrives?*
P: *(Sobbing now.) He's dead; he's dead. How could it come to that? (Sobs violently.)*
T: *Just take a couple of deep breaths. Now let yourself detach slightly from the intensity of that scene. You can just be an observer for a moment. George is dead? What happened?*

Noordegraaf suggested to Ludovic that he look at the Hiroshima destruction from a distance:

P: *Please help me. I am so scared. It hurts so much.... My skin is burning. My body is burning...I can't hold still.... The earth is trembling, or is it my body? Oh, please help me!... I don't know what happens to me. I don't know how to stop this. But I can't. It just occurs to me. I have no control over it.*
T: *Imagine that you can see from a distance, from some place where fear is not so frightening. See what happens to you and your body that makes you cry and scream. What would you see?*

Reynolds uses an old metaphor of watching a movie when his patient appeared to be in the grip of such terror and anguish that he even thought of taking her out of the hypnotic state. His suggestion provided the surcease needed, and they were able to go on and recover the distress:

> P: *Why doesn't my daddy move? I want him to move (very distressed).*
> T: *Tell me what it going on as if you are watching it in a movie.*

Another method of gaining detachment is to suggest to the patient that he summon an outside figure, such as a guide or even his own current self, which has hopefully become wiser over the intervening lifetimes! Such intervention not only provides relief from stress but tends to move the patient into a transformational process. Pecci frequently uses intervention by a Higher Source or the more mature self for insight or to provide emotional mothering:

> T: *I'd like you to go into that scene now and hold that little girl so she won't be so afraid. Let's help the little girl get over the shock. Tell her she doesn't have to stay in shock. You've got to convince her not to close off. She doesn't have to.*

### 3. Therapeutic Support without Withdrawal

The importance of deep therapist-patient rapport and bonding and respect for the patient's process is emphasized by Reynolds. In his experience with an agoraphobic patient the material was processed over eight sessions.[5] Time and care were given to the distressing emotional aspects. He assumed that the therapeutic agent enabling this patient to let go of her agoraphobic reaction was the supportive stance that made it possible for her to explore in depth such charged material. In general, it would seem that not rushing a patient, giving plenty of time to look at material and thoroughly enter into it, provides an optimum setting for examining it. Not all lifetimes need to be examined over many sessions, but it is important that a patient not feel rushed and that he be allowed to enter into painful re-experiencing when he is ready. Many times just this offer of support from the therapist is enough to enable the patient to stay with a distressing situation and work through it.

Support can to be communicated with minimal words when the patient feels secure with the therapeutic situation. When Denning's patient, who saw himself dying in an automobile accident, became distressed, Denning's voice and brief suggestions to release the pain were enough for him to go on.

Hickman's permission to a patient to scream, plus her warm support, made it possible for the patient finally to look through a window and see her own suicide:

> T: *It's all right. You can scream about this, but you do not need to be afraid of it. Whatever it is, it is now in the past. Just relax and tell me what you see.*
>
> P: *(With tension gradually lessening) I see my body hanging by a rope from the rafters. I see my baby crawling across the floor and reaching up toward the body. I see my real self over in the corner observing the scene and helpless to do anything about it.*

Noodegraaf, in the session with Ludovic, which has been mentioned several times because it provides an excellent model of therapist support, not only assured her young patient that she was staying with him but also touched him as well:

> P: *As if everything is shaking. As if the world is falling to pieces. As if...I don't know what is happening anymore...I am falling...it hurts.... Oh, God, please help me! Help me! What is going on.... This is too much. I don't know where I am anymore (panicking, sobbing, trembling).*
>
> T: *(Touching him to let him know I'll be with him, no matter what happens.) Feel what is happening there. Watch your body, watch your feet, just stay in touch with what is happening...let it happen. Let your body remember what happened so that your brain will start to understand as well. Stay with the feelings. Let your body do what it has to on order to understand why these movements make sense. Move through it. I will stay with you. Keep on moving through it.*

Touching patients is a controversial area in psychotherapy. Many of us, trained in the days when psychoanalysis was the most respected therapeutic technique, were taught never to touch a patient, largely because it destroyed the objectivity of the relationship and encouraged a dependent or erotic transference. However, modern psychotherapy is not so sure about this. In times of stress certain patients, and especially children, find concerned touch reassuring. It depends on the therapist, the patient, and the dynamics involved.

Other techniques that help a patient through emotional distress but do not take him out of the situation include repetition, counting, and breathing. Fiore combined these techniques in helping her acrophobic patient go through his death by falling from a roof he was mending:

T: *Where is your body?*
P: *I'm off the side, hanging...just...I'd say, arm on the gutter or...one hand in the gutter and the other arm on the top of the...but I stay right there. I don't seem to...fall (face bathed in sweat).*
T: *You're still dangling, you're hanging onto the gutter and your body is dangling and your arm is grasping for tiles.*
P: *(Nods head.)*
T: *I'm going to ask you to concentrate on your breathing. I'm going to count from one to three and you'll become much more relaxed and calm and your inner mind will let you proceed step by step so that you can see what happens to yourself. One...just becoming very relaxed as you experience what's happening...two...three. What are you aware of?*
P: *There are some people trying to help...standing on the other side letting down something...a rope or something.*

Through such assistance he was able to go through his actual death, which, because of the stress, he had been bypassing.

Some therapists relieve stress by reframing the situation. This is particularly true of Snow, Jue, and Dethlefsen. By helping the patient perceive the situation in a different context, often the terror can go out of it, or at least be diminished. An amusing example of this is Dethlefsen's work with a young women who was terrified of rats. In an earlier lifetime they had attacked her as she was starving to death and she had perceived them as killing her:

P: *Yes, and every time I see a rat...*
T: *You re-live what you experienced a long time ago.*
P: *No, I don't know whether I re-live it, but, in any case, it disgusts me terribly. (Screws up her face in distate.)*
T: *And this aversion started at that time?*
P: *Yes.*
T: *Now every time you see a rat, you must coordinate the time correctly. You know that this aversion goes back two hundred years; it has no business in your current life. You will learn to like rats. You will find them pleasant, beautiful.*
P: *Ah...*
T: *This feeling belongs back two centuries.*
P: *Do you really believe that? Learn to like rats?*
T: *Rats disgust you?*
P: *Yes.*
T: *Very well, where does this aversion belong? Dissolve back!*
P: *Yes, 1725.*
T: *Return to that situation!*
P: *No.*

> T: *You must learn to look at it—not so much disgust, not so much emotion. Don't show your feelings. Look at it and describe it. Look at it objectively. What is happening? The rats are nibbling on you, correct?*
> P: *Yes, at my feet.*
> T: *Yes, and why? Because they are hungry.*
> P: *Yes, because they are hungry.*

Claudia was led into an overview of her relationship with rats, realizing that she herself had killed a rabbit because she was hungry and that rats did not actually kill her; she died from starvation. Reframing is a major therapeutic technique in its own right, but here its use not only provided therapeutic insight but was helpful in relieving the stress experienced in the regression.

## 4. Encouraging the Release of Stress by Abreaction

Some of our therapists, especially Woolger and the Dutch therapists, and to a lesser extent Hickman and Fiore, feel that emotional stress should not be attenuated but increased and lived through, and in this way it will be released. For them emotions must be sharpened and bodily distress intensified, and often they suggest breathing to help this take place.

Bontenbal stresses the repetition of beliefs until it has been possible to deal with *any* anger attached to them. He tells of a rather privileged young woman who walked innocently into a trap and after being raped three times was murdered. He processed the rape and murder with her on all levels (mental, emotional, and physical), but she still seemed stressed:

> T: *What is the most difficult to accept of what just happened?*
> P: *I don't know. The innkeeper was one of them. I trusted him. The bastard!*
> T: *Say it again! And let all the feeling connected to that word come out.*

She screamed out this phrase 10 times and in the process released anger, sadness, and fear.

Woolger is experienced in breath work and through having his patients breathe, he helps them deepen and intensify experiences and connect with feelings that have been buried. A young woman who saw herself as an artist in an earlier life could not connect with her suicide until deep breathing released her feeling:

> T: *Where are you now?*
> P: *I'm wandering along the canals. I can't find my wife. She's left me for good.*
> T: *Where do you go now?*

> P: *I think, back to the house. Oh, no! I don't want to go back there. (Her shoulders begin to tense up noticeably.)*
> T: *Breathe deeply and go back to the house and see what happens.*

At this point the young woman, who had been lying on the couch, shot up to a sitting position and grabbed her neck and began to scream.

> T: *What has happened?*
> P: *Oh, God! I hanged myself. (Sobs deeply.)*

It is difficult for some patients to get in touch with feelings, and in such cases the use of breathing techniques is a proven stimulus to release.

How the therapist deals with the stress seems to depend both on his personality and on his therapeutic assumptions. Opposite techniques work with different patients. Relief from stress combines the emotional support of the therapist with trust on the patient's part in the therapist's wisdom and compassion in handling the situation. If the therapist communicates to the patient that he feels the stress can be endured, that is motivation to go ahead and plough through it. If the therapist feels that temporary surcease is a good idea, the patient gratefully uses that.

Retreating to a safe place or a happier time or just to the position of observer does not mean the stressful situation will not be entered later and re-lived. The immersion in it has merely been postponed while the patient gathers his resources. There may be advantages to this. The added strength of being more ready to approach a difficult situation may enable the patient to work with it more easily, and postponement of the abreaction may encourage a readiness to open up to deeper feelings.

# *Processing*

*Past lives are like threads in a skein. All my threads have worked toward increasing my ability to become an integral and competent part of the fabric of humanity with its stresses and strains.*

*Edward Reynolds*

*Facing our individual and collective polarity and accepting it in its true sense ends judging ourselves and others and helps with transformation, both indivual and collective. Awareness of this heals body, mind, and soul.*

*Thorwald Dethlefsen*

*We sat there for a while, the two of us, understanding well what had happened. He didn't need any renovation techniques. He had figured it out for himself. A little boy wonder instead of a little boy lost. And he knew that I knew, a wordless understanding.... Thank you for working with me, Ludovic. Thank you for your ability to change your world. Thank you for your courage. You taught me a lot.*

*Tineke Noordegraaf*

**Chapter VIII**

# Psychotherapeutic and Transformational Interventions

Past lives were originally recovered out of curiosity and interest, and it was accidental that there were beneficial results. In earlier times just the recovery of the material was in itself an achievement, and if remission of symptoms took place or relationships became improved, these concerns were subordinate to the recovery of the memory. Then, as therapists using hypnotherapy increasingly uncovered the potential of regression work for bringing about healing and transformation, a search began for techniques to supplement simple recall.

To begin with, it became increasingly clear that change in the patient depended not only on his ability to recover the actual feelings and experiences of a past life but on his willingness to acknowledge his responsibility for them. This approach was directly opposed to that of hypnotherapy, where responsibility and power belonged to the therapist. In his new role the therapist became relegated to the position of a co-explorer.

Reynolds points out that this less authoritarian and more cooperative role reflected the general therapeutic thrust of the time toward client-centered therapy and highlighted the importance of the patient-therapist relationship. He observes:

> The humanistic approach to therapy, as developed by Carl Rogers and Abraham Maslow, shifted the focus in the therapeutic process from the patient as an object to be "fixed" to the relationship between therapist and the patient as a powerful agent in producing therapeutic results. Nearly half the research in psychotherapy and five years of observing and documenting the process has grounded this shift in focus. In a new modality such as regression therapy, where the dominant legacy comes from the authoritarian approach of hypnotic induction, it is important that these gains in psychotherapy as a total field not be overlooked or lost.

Next, it gradually became apparent that there are three distinct stages in regression work and that each of these stages requires specific therapeutic approaches. The nature of these stages and their therapeutic challenges have been described and clarified by Jue.[1]

The first level involves the identification of the patient with the past-life role, so initial techniques, discussed in the preceding chapter, have been focused on implementing this identification and dealing with the suffering and stress that frequently result from immersion in another personality.

## The Stage of Identification: Abreaction

Abreaction is considered by most therapists to be the initial therapeutic agent, although therapists differ as to the importance of abreaction and the circumstances in which it will be effective. The expression of stress in a therapeutic matrix merges imperceptibly into an experience of healing and transformation as the patient cathects the physical reactions and emotional anguish of a past life.

The discrepant approaches to abreaction are the result of theoretical differences regarding the mechanisms involved in healing and change. On one end of the therapeutic spectrum, abreaction is conceded to be useful, but not if it takes place at the expense of rapport between therapist and patient. Reynolds, for instance, draws a troubled client out of an altered state and postpones the abreaction until a later time rather than sacrifice rapport. When one woman patient found herself as a man being chased by angry warriors and started shaking violently, crying, and unable to speak, Reynolds considered that abreaction at that time was inappropriate and offered the patient the opportunity to emerge from the regression:

T: *What was going on?*
P: *I don't really know but I felt as if I had been pursued for many days by people who wanted to do me harm. They might have been slave traders but I'm not sure.*
T: *Do you want to do more work on it today or resume it in our next session?*
P: *Let's wait until our next session.*

He initiated the next session by taking her to the beginning of the lifetime that had been so frightening, and she was able to approach the terrifying scene gradually and re-live it. Apparently nothing was lost by allowing the patient to withdraw and try again later—she was able to abreact intensively, and at her own pace she recovered insights that were cathartic and resulted in significant change. Abreaction remained a therapeutic agent but the timing of it was flexible.

At the other end of the therapeutic spectrum is Woolger, who presses his patients to live out both the emotions of a traumatic situation and the actual physical experiences. He offers forms of support, such as breathing or body work. One patient recalled going into a gas chamber in a concentration camp, distressed and frozen, holding the hand of a stranger. Woolger, by coaching her breathing, supported her in letting out all the feelings she had been trying to hold back:

> T: Where are you now?
> P: We're in a line outside this building. I'm no longer with my mother.
> T: What exactly are you doing?
> P: I'm holding the hand of this older woman.
> T: How do you feel?
> P: Terrible!
> T: Do you cry?
> P: No, I can't.
> T: All right. Then breathe very deeply and let any feelings you may be holding back come to the surface. (Coaches breathing.)
> P: (Breathes deeply.) I don't want to go in there. (Trembles, heaves.)
> T: Say that louder.
> P: I don't want to go in there! (Sobs loudly.)

From then on a flood of emotion emerged and she described in detail the gassing, how it tasted, smelled, and which parts of the body it affected. For several minutes she went through the convulsions of choking, vomiting, and doubling up as she re-lived her death. By the end of the session, she had released so much fear, grief, and despair, as well as physical pain, that her chest had opened up to a much fuller pattern of breathing, a release similar to that experienced in Reichian therapy and rebirthing.

Woolger gives his rationale:

> I always insist that the past-life story be experienced fully in the body, not from the viewpoint of a detached observer. There will often be quite intense bodily convulsions and contortions that are part of the somatic process of spontaneous release—sweating, hot and cold flushes, cramping, temporary paralysis, sharp pains, and other sensations, such as numbness, trembling, shaking or tingling. I tell patients that this is the release of blocked energy associated with an old trauma. The trauma at a physical level may be from birth, a past life, or a surgical operation in this life, and often all three. Whatever it is, the body is encouraged to express and let go of the shock and the trauma. Although to an observer seeing a session for the first time, this may seem frightening or even a little crazy, it has been the repeated and consistent finding that such release at a somatic as well as emotional level is absolutely crucial to the full healing process.

Is the healing contained in the abreaction, or in the cognitive re-evaluation following the experience that helps the patient to perceive the situation in a different way? Dethlefsen attempts to clarify this when he differentiates between the healing of symptoms, which he feels can take place in the abreaction, and a spiritual type of healing which requires additional cognitive and emotional intervention:

> The transformative power of regression work in the matter of symptoms does not depend on any specific type of intervention but is inherent in the process itself. This procedure of recovering and living out repressed and forgotten incidents is frequently applied in behavior therapy under the designation of "systematic desensitization," especially in the case of phobias. The core problem has gradually accrued energy in the form of subsequent experiences, and these subsequent layers must be released one by one in order for the final kernel of hurt and distortion to be approached and relived. The re-living of the nuclear trauma effects a complete release.
>
> Treatment of symptoms must be differentiated from true healing. Symptoms can be dealt with by first connecting an emotion with an incident in the present time that encourages its projection. When the projection can find its true place in the past, the projection is released, and the symptom disappears. Such release of symptoms and freedom from projection lead to a feeling of well-being and serenity.
>
> However, for true healing, for coming to the place where we perceive that we are cradled in a cosmos guided by meaning and purpose and that our sole task is to serve it, we need to go deeper.

Bontenbal and Noordegraaf have found that though processing trauma (abreacting) is often an integrating experience in itself, there are times when, in addition, a cognitive re-evaluation or emotional healing is necessary:

> The literature about reincarnation therapy shows that even dissociated recall sometimes integrates incidents that have previously been unresolved and thus effects a remission of symptoms. In a few cases, even core issues are impacted.... Many clients are able to understand how traumas from the past relate to their present problems, but other clients have to be helped with that. Cognitive integration is then necessary, executed with the help of rational-emotive methods.

Noordegraaf guided her 12-year-old patient Ludovic, to an intense abreaction after recalling the bombing of Hiroshima. In addition, when he got in touch after his death with anger over the dead corpses lying around, he was able to obtain additional emotional release through expressing his anger against those who had done the bombing:

C: It drives me mad, it drives me really mad. *We are all destroyed. All the people are destroyed, and the houses, and the trees, and...everything.*
T: What would you like to do most now, if you were able to....
C: *I wish I was stronger...I wish I could help them...I wish I could teach them a lesson by taking them apart...I wish I had that much energy.*
T: Then you have to come out of that blackness of yours to be able to do that, won't you? You have to come out of your safe hiding place into the open a little bit in order to do that.
C: *Well, that would be worth it....*
T: Give it a try then and tell them as loud as you're able to what you're so angry about. Start telling them, let nothing stop you this time.... Feel that you're right in doing that. Tell them they're *crazy and wrong* instead of you. Make clear to them that you know what happened there with you, with your body, and with the world, with everything.... Use your lungs, use your energy, use your body, and use your muscles in the right way. Do everything you feel you need to do in order to get rid of all the things that are still bothering you. Come on! Do your utmost!

Ludovic gave a good try, screaming and crying and trembling until he felt exhausted. Afterward he had a strong sense of relief. For him, re-living the incident had not been enough. The anger he had taken with him from death also had to be released.

Fiore stresses that for her the therapeutic factor in regression is the living out of the physical and emotional trauma, but nearly all her cases have in addition specific instances of cognitive work or additional emotional release. Joe, whose insomnia was handicapping his life, recovered a lifetime where he escaped from the Indians by traveling through the night and later as marshall in a western town was killed in the night in a moment of carelessness. Fiore had him contact guides following his death, and with their assistance he not only saw why he couldn't sleep but was able to release an underlying anger that had permeated his current life as well as that former one:

T: *How do you feel within yourself right now?*
P: *I feel good. I...feel the lack of anger.*
T: *You were aware of being angry before—is that what you're saying?*
P: *Yeah. I've always been angry with people.*
T: *From this spiritual state, tell me why you have always been angry with people? I'm going to ask you to tell me at the count of three. One... two... three... What comes to mind?*
P: *They go through life so unprepared. They're vulnerable. (Short laugh.) And then I get killed!*
T: *What were the events that have resulted in the sleep problems in your life as Joe? What are the significant events that contributed to that, or caused that? Whatever comes to mind?*

P: *(Long pause.)* Most of my awareness had to be at night, alert...someone was always trying to make a name for themselves.
T: In what way?
P: They...if they could say they killed me.

Fiore felt that though Joe did gain insight, this was *not* what cured his insomnia. Relief from insomnia came from the recall of the experiences themselves. She explains this in a metaphor:

> I consider that by simply remembering, the patient is getting rid of the problem and that is a transformation. The analogy I use is of a light bulb in human shape with a bulb inside shining perpetually, like the image of the sun in the solar plexus which I use in the induction. We are really lighted beings. This light is shining perfectly, but here and there on our bodies we have smudges. In therapy, through remembering, we are taking a sponge and wiping off the smudges so that the light can shine through perfectly. That is both the transformational and psychotherapeutic technique.

Hickman stresses not only re-living of emotions but often makes use of repetition as a form of systematic de-sensitization without any cognitive work. She has a thoughtful rationale for this:

> When strong feelings are long suppressed, communication with our inner selves is prevented. The primary thrust is to re-establish this lost contact with inner thoughts and wisdom. The subconscious mind, when probed, explored, drained of buried painful records, and restored to balance, becomes a source of strength and insight. Digging into areas of repressed feelings and thoughts enables us to purge the emotional charge from these areas. Once a contributing event has been found and re-lived, I ask if the emotions expressed are still there. If any painful feeling remains, the subject is requested to go back over the entire happening again, adding any details that may have been left out in the first telling. Each time the incident is re-lived and retold, its emotional intensity is diminished until finally the story can be related with complete composure. All that remains is a memory; the painful emotion is neutralized and the cause is removed.

Sometimes this systematic desensitization is effective without cognitive follow-up, as in the case of the woman with a cat phobia,[2] but most of Hickman's cases include not only somatic and emotional abreaction but also transpersonal work. An example of this is Rose Morgan, who was a recent widow at the time she came for consultation.[3] She considered obesity to be her problem, but actually she needed help for severe depression. When regressed to a former life in which she had a husband who was a fisherman, she was happy until her husband was drowned at sea, at which time she became increasingly distraught, ignored her infant son, and eventually drowned herself. Hickman reviewed periods of Rose's former life with her again and again, always urging her to express fully any emotions she had felt. With each review the emotions diminished in intensity until she could talk about the incident calmly.

Following this, Rose realized that she was repeating the same pattern at the present time, with the difference that in that life she had been beautiful but in this one she had allowed herself to become overweight, her way of avoiding love so that she would not be exposed to loss. In her current life she had met the same entity who had been her husband then, and she gave birth to the same son. Once more she had been left a widow—she was repeating the pattern and failing once again. With this insight Rose became able to accept her situation and live more creatively, and an added gain was her ability to control her weight. Two years later she met and married a man who suited her well. The intense abreaction had been only a prelude to a search for patterns, for cognitive re-evaluation, and for profound transformational work. For Hickman, the remission of symptoms remains the reason for referral and the goal of treatment, but she is able to go far beyond this into a transpersonal domain where not only do patterns become clear but the spiritual journey of the patient is exposed and facilitated.

It is important to note that in most of the cases where the living out of strong bodily feelings and emotions is encouraged, there is also a search for patterns of similar traumatic experiences. As we shall see in the next section, patterns encourage processing, and it is difficult to know whether remission and healing occur because of abreaction or as the result of reframing or some other cognitive process.

The fact that there is a significant amount of abreaction on the part of patients who are given only gentle support opens the question as to the appropriateness of a more pressured approach. In an altered state the patient is so suggestible that just the request to tap the appropriate feelings may be enough. The question may concern the timing of such an experience. Reynolds helps his patients catch their breath and make a new try. Snow gives permission for distancing. Woolger and the Dutch therapists and many others use supportive techniques to help patients challenge the crisis here and now.

## The Stage of Disidentification: Exploring Patterns

The second stage begins when the patient emerges from his absorption in the role he has been playing and can observe and evaluate what he has been through. The therapist can help him facilitate this shift to the witness position. Jue addresses this:

> It is helpful, and sometimes necessary to go to an earlier period of that lifetime or to antecedent lifetimes in order to understand the decision-making process. For instance, one may suggest, "Go back and see why you made this decision, to choose a mother who is unloving. What did you do to her in the past? Like a bridge, go back to another time when you knew your mother." It is necessary to go back and forth between lifetime experiences in order to understand the pattern of cause and effect. The therapist needs to help the patient see the aspects of past lives that are mirrored in this present one. Why did he need to bring that feeling into this lifetime? How does this lifetime serve the experiences of the past? What is the patient hanging onto in crossing over into this life? It is extremely important for the patient to see that he has set the stage and at some time made a decision that he needed to experience what he, in this lifetime, is now experiencing.

In the stage of disidentification, the salient factor to be explored and dealt with therapeutically is the existence of patterns. Without patterns, there would be no regression therapy. It is the existence of patterns that makes it possible for us to be aware that nothing is chance—we have been there before.

Pecci describes the benefits of working with patterning:

> Seeing the event or attitude in the context of another lifetime tends to give it a different meaning, and the therapist can point this out and extend its impact by comments and questions. This can lead to a reversal of the ego decisions that have been running one's life. However, such a reversal should not be taken for granted but should be carefully explicated within the therapeutic process. As the pattern of the person from his various lifetimes becomes more and more clear, there can also take place a disidentification with negative states, giving the person more room to make positive and helpful decisions.

Patterning can occur on any of the levels of experience, somatic, emotional, or cognitive, and the clearing of them needs to take place on all levels. Woolger gives this theoretical grounding:

> In all my past-life therapy I aim to clear negative samskaras (past-life patterning) at three levels: mental, emotional, and physical. There is no particular order to this process, but the key principle is that the patient must fully experience the bodily sensations as well as the emotions until they are completely released. In addition to this, full mental understanding of the karmic or symbolic meaning of the patterns must occur or else the

symptoms will simply recur in physical and/or emotional form. Directing the patient to re-live a seeming past-life story *in the body of the past-life personality* amounts to enabling the patient to become aware of the subtle body of the subpersonality as if it were his or her present body.

The purpose of understanding patterns is to become aware that much of our life is strongly, but not inevitably, predetermined by what we have done in other lifetimes. Denning compares a single lifetime experience to one scene in a play:

> The therapeutic goal is to restructure understanding of our current life in the light of our extended experience from other lifetimes. When we have only the present lifetime on which to base our interpretations, it is like trying to understand the theme and plot of a play when we have only one scene by which to go. Therefore, all therapeutic and transformational techniques are focused on extending perception of the lessons and limitations which the individual has chosen to help him along the journey toward higher consciousness. Incidents are not recovered for their intrinsic interest but only to implement this understanding.

The *karmic core* of patterns gives a focus for their recovery. Patterns are seen not just as repetitions of similar events but as a working out of our learning process, a *meaningful* connection. Dethlefsen says:

> If we trace thoughts we have developed in this life to an earlier incarnation, we find that the traumatic experience was certainly no chance occurrence but an expression of a pattern that was brought into that life. The soul of a person who drowns in one life is likely to have fear of water in the next, but we should not conclude from this that the drowning was the *cause* of the later fear of water. The drowning was itself part of a meaningful pattern, a demonstration of an inherent problem.

Karmic patterns strongly influence relationships. Denning comments on this:

> Many of our attitudes toward significant people in our lives—spouses, parents, children, even close friends—apparently stem from incidents and relationships in other lifetimes. Traditional therapy often results in minimal ameliorating effect. The affect seems to resist the usual interpretations and conventional understanding of its etiology. Sometimes these attitudes have influenced many lifetimes, especially if there are patterns of anger or deep attraction, and searching them out takes time.

Reynolds, also, focuses on the impact of former relationships:

Routinely I ask about relationships in past lives in terms of their relevance to relationships in this time and what possible karmic issues are present to be resolved. I have found it helpful in instances of extreme distress or anger to trace the origins of those emotions within the context of a past life, and I have found that frequently release comes with understanding. Many times this cannot be done in one session but is worked on over a period of time.

Often there are role reversals in various lifetimes, and many times an attitude toward someone in the current life is a reaction or a correction of an attitude toward that person in another life, a pattern not so much of repetition as of balancing. Denning tells of a patient whose presenting complaint was of anger, especially toward her husband and sister-in-law. Though she was financially able to separate from her abusive husband, she could not bring herself to do so. In her one regression she found herself as Edna, an eight-year-old girl locked in a closet for three days without food or water because her mother thought she had eaten a piece of cake that had actually been eaten by her brother, Edward. By the time the father returned, the child was unconscious and never recovered her health. After the father's death Edward forfeited his own marriage plans in order to take care of her. As the woman was dying of a high fever she explored her feelings:

T: *Can you tell me, please, your very last thought before your spirit leaves your body? What is your last conscious thought?*
P: *I feel very sad. I think I can never make up to Edward for all the years he took care of me.*
T: *Now look at this very carefully. What does that life have to do with your present one? Is there any relationship between the two, that one and this one?*
P: *Oh my goodness! My husband was Edward before—no wonder I can't leave him. I have to take care of him now. He is having a terrible time in this life and he doesn't mean to be the way he is...(long pause).... Oh, no! My sister-in-law was my mother! No wonder I hate her so. I feel as though I can never forgive her.*

It had seemed as though Edna could not make her marriage work, but once she realized what Edward/her husband had done for her she decided to do everything she could to help him. Moved by her new intention, her husband even consented to go to a psychologist. She came to understand her rage at her former mother/sister-in-law, also, and she realized that this woman had learned something in her intervening lifetimes. With work she was able to reach a more dispassionate and forgiving position. Major shifts in relationships often come about through scanning previous roles and determining the karmic pattern between two people. In this process irrational hates as well as irrational loves find explanation and grounding.

Reversal of roles in relationships is a half-way step toward the concept of polarity, which postulates that all of us need to play many opposite roles, not just in our relationships but in all our stances in living. The integration of roles that we consider negative (our shadow, as Jung put it) is the basis of true integration. Woolger says:

> To work with the shadow when it has surfaced is a process of constant inner dialogue with this secondary consciousness. I am convinced that our past-life identifications with personalities whose lives have been far from illustrious or creative are a profoundly helpful extension of this process. Past-life remembering is possibly the most vivid and extensive way of facing the shadow—seeing and knowing the murderer, the prideful priest, the cruel soldier, the abandoning mother, the greedy merchant, the sadistic slave-owner—which we may carry in us. These are personifications of the darker but necessary parts of the psyche that all stand in need of acceptance, forgiveness, and redemption. Jung said that we do not become enlightened by imaging figures of light but by making the darkness conscious.
>
> Not all shadows of the ego personality are dark, however. A person with a poor self-image—an abused wife, or a violent rapist—may find in their shadow personalities creative and fulfilled images of self. They may remember successful past lives as artists, leaders, innovators. The psyche compensates the ego personality as part of its tendency to seek balance and stability. Persons who feel powerless or inadequate may be shown lives with extremely powerful political or religious status, power that may have been abused and for which the ego in this or another life feels a need for atonement.

Woolger gives a brief account of dealing with polarity in the case of a young teacher who had been experiencing stage fright whenever he lectured to audiences larger than a small class. He manifested a seemingly unrelated body problem in the form of poor circulation in his hands and feet and constant stiff necks. This patient re-lived a life where as an influential and arrogant wandering teacher he had threatened the stability of a small caliphate and was arrested and martyred by having his hands and feet cut off, being crucified overnight on a gibbet, and then beheaded. When he went through the death in that lifetime, a loving group of guides showed him the polarities he had not looked at:

> *You lost your hands because you were out of touch with the people.*
> *You lost your feet because you were off the earth.*
> *You lost your head because it was too puffed up with knowledge.*

After much meditation on these words and an integration of their meaning, he was able to change. As a result, he found his outer life expanding and becoming more confident. The circulation returned to his hands and feet. He came to understand how the polarization of that teacher's complex was evidenced even in the past life itself: spiritual pride had constellated its opposite in an utterly humiliating death.

The objective of dealing with our polarities is to reach an integration where no aspect of ourselves is rejected or found to be without value. In the process we come to see that our earthly sojourns are merely lessons that need not be judged in themselves. This understanding enables us to move gradually into an experience of harmony and self-acceptance.

An early theory of intervention was that it was necessary to expose and understand the originating cause of a pattern in order to transform it. But what was the originating cause? Was it the first time the pattern manifested itself (usually in a traumatic situation)? Or was it the lifetime or lifetimes where the subject set up a karmic reaction that resulted in a polarity pattern having to be played out? Most therapists take the position that the source of patterns is the karmic event that requires balancing.

Dethlefsen states this clearly:

> The more one goes back, the more situations one finds that would seem to qualify as the "primal" trauma. Thus, a patient with an arrow in his left eye will find many more events in which he lost that eye. All these events are links in a chain whose totality forms the problem common to all the situations. When we have followed a chain of symptoms back as far as it seems to go, we need then to take the decisive therapeutic step and regress the patient back to the moment when he originally set up the cause of the chain of suffering and introduced the basic theme that was to emerge in many different forms.
>
> This is the step with which the individual confronts his own karmic guilt by which he himself has made necessary all the painful situations he has been through. Up to now he has always regarded himself as an unfortunate victim. When he is confronted with his own karmic guilt something quite different happens. The sufferer has to integrate his shadow. He experiences himself as an agent, doing to others the very thing that he complained was being done to him over several thousand years. To confront his own guilt is no easy matter for the patient, but it is a major step in the direction of healing if he is able to take it. If one wants to insist on looking for a "cause," then it is to be found in karmic guilt.

There are different theories about how to treat the karmic source once it has been uncovered. Fiore feels that though it is helpful for the person to deal with the causative event, it is not necessary for him to forgive himself, to accept the incident, or to believe that it really happened. For her, therapy is achieved at the moment a person remembers. But most therapists employ a spectrum of therapeutic techniques to deal with repeated patterns and with polarity.

## The Stage of Disidentification: Cognitive Techniques

When the groundwork of recognizing patterns and polarities has been thoroughly laid and the patient can disidentify and observe, a number of therapeutic and transformational techniques, many of them borrowed from more conventional therapy, are available. One of the most frequently used is *reframing*, a process whereby the patient can observe the pattern in a different perspective. Jue discusses and defines reframing:

> The focus of reframing is either to separate the intention behind a specific set of symptoms and to reframe that intention in a more beneficial pattern, or to reframe an inappropriate behavior pattern so that it occurs in a useful context. Besides intention and inappropriate behavior patterns, many basic life patterns, such as relationships, talents, handicaps, and physical illnesses can be reframed within a past-life scenario in order to provide a different and meaningful perspective. Such a perspective can offer not only insight into a situation but cathartic release and freedom from self-defeating patterns. Thus, reframing is the act of changing a frame by which a person perceives and experiences events in order to change the meaning. When the meaning of an event changes, behaviors and responses also change.

When perception of the situation becomes reframed, its emotional impact is transformed or dissolved. Jue provides an example in the case of Dawn, a woman who had never married but had a child through a sperm-bank. Her experience with her child was fulfilling but she wondered why she had never been able to make a bonding with a man. She went back to a lifetime in Egypt where she was betrothed to a cousin. Just before they were to have been married, she was given by her father to be a priestess in a temple. She felt betrayed, and anger covered all her feelings of love:

> *T: I want you to go back and look at that situation and see the circumstances of that love and also the change of plans. I want you to go to that scene where you decided that somehow he had betrayed you and I want you to see if that was really the case. There was his energy in loving and feeling very much in touch with you and having a great deal of joy in expressing and experiencing his and yours both, both your energies. I want you just to see another scene now....*

Dawn came to realize that her father owed something to the temple and had his choice between giving his daughter as a priestess or having his entire family killed:

> P: To accompany whoever it was who had just died. Either our whole family went with him (died) or I went as a priestess.
> T: You became the sacrificial one.
> P: Yes. And I never saw or heard from this boy or his family again. I knew nothing about them. But now I'm seeing that he killed himself. (Deep crying.)
> T: Because he really loved you, too, didn't he? He felt the loss.
> P: (Crying.) He took poison.
> T: Uh huh. It seems almost as though both of you became victims of filial duty here.
> P: (Deep crying.) I don't know why I felt his family had done it, because I see now it wasn't so.
> T: Seeing it now as it is, where is that energy, that anger? Do you feel that you're releasing it, now that you've seen this as it really is, that there was no one who really wanted to reject you.?

In that lifetime Dawn grieved for a few years and then competently took up her duties as a priestess. When she died she felt fulfilled in her priestess role but still unfinished about the relationship:

> T: I have a feeling that there's more here. I want you to take this life and see yourself moving out of it and into a space where you can look and view that entire life and compare it to where you are now and see how the energies and the unresolved relationship had an effect upon the decisions you have made in this lifetime. What do you see? Take a moment and see yourself now reviewing that entire scenario and look at what you're unfolding right now. What is it that you see?
> P: Somehow it seems—I don't know—that I had some reparative work to do in having my son, that I cannot have my son and have a relationship, too. That's the feeling that I have, that I've chosen in this lifetime to do something with my son.
> T: With your son. Do you feel any of your son's energy from that lifetime?
> P: (Voice breaking.) Well, I'm almost thinking he was the man. (Crying.)
> T: You feel that?
> P: I think...at least from my sadness...this time it was safer to have him as a son.
> T: Because in this way you could protect him, love him, love him in a way that would not have any intrusive factors coming in.
> P: It seems that he won't hurt me this way.
> T: He can't hurt you as your son.
> P: I have to look at my relationship with my son. I'm making it so there wouldn't be room for a man.

T: *That's right. There wouldn't be room for a man. It's almost as though you have created a very sacred space and that's part of your decision, and that space between you and him is not to be violated.*
P: *Yes. Well, I get that feedback from people, too, and I don't know what's right and what's wrong. I don't know.*
T: *I think it will be more clear to you as he grows up.*

In this case we can see how, with support and intervention from the therapist, Dawn reframed the incident and came to an understanding of her intense bonding with her son and the lack of space for another relationship. But the major piece of work in this lifetime, as Jue commented, lay in the reframing of her interpretation that the young man she loved had betrayed her and that no one cared for her. This reframing made it possible for her to re-experience the deep love she had felt for him and eventually to connect him with her son. She realized that the reason a significant, loving man doesn't come into her life is that her son is her significant, loving man, the one with whom she has a deep but unfinished relationship.

In the case of Dawn, no particular wisdom figure was requested—she simply went into herself and found the answers, but often Guides are employed to help in this reassessment. Sometimes it is the Inner Mind or Higher Self that provides the insight. Almost all of our therapists use a transpersonal aspect of the patient as a source of wisdom. In addition, Pecci often asks the current self to go back into the lifetime and help that floundering self understand what is going on. His assumption is that we have gained a little wisdom along the way! He relied on this type of intervention in his work with Lydia when she needed support in processing the reframing of her addiction to over-responsibility:

P: *I know what is wrong. I feel selfish because of that other lifetime. So I doubt myself even though I was right. I kind of mixed it up.*
T: *Philomen needs a little therapy from someone. Let's have the Lydia of today come into the scene. Let's have her go to Philomen as his teacher. You can tell him, "Look, you've got it mixed up. You're really right."*
P: *(To Philomen) Don't mix up being right with the fact that you were uninvolved or self-involved. You're right, so feel good about it.*
T: *You're right, so you can even take it to Egypt or some other place. You can feel good about that, too. You couldn't hold onto it there because there was too much pressure, but you can't be blamed for taking it to Egypt and being helpful in the Temple Beautiful with your ideas. Right?*
P: *Yes, that's right.*

It is possible to have the patient get into the mind of a person whose motivations have been misunderstood and tap into what he really thought, as Dawn did with her father when she perceived he had acted out of necessity to save the lives of his family. When asked—in an altered state a patient seldom volunteers such information—a patient can even come up with the life history of a person, as happened when I asked my patient Carrie to see if she could understand why her father in another lifetime had treated his family the way he did. I had her identify with her Inner Mind (but any other phrasing of the part of her that knows would have been as good) and expected some generalization, but instead, Carrie came up with a brief biography—from birth to death:

> P: He didn't have a family that stayed in one place. No roots. So he came to feel that if you are ever going to get ahead you have to work through your family, and that's why he didn't want me leaving. He was angry at his mother for being so weak. I can see that his own father took everything and ran away—he even forced the mother to sign the deed so that he got the land. He learned to get what he wanted through physical violence, and that was a way of life in his household. My father then learned from him to get what he wanted by being angry.

I repeated her explanation of the dynamics of the father and his anger, and I asked if she could release her expectations about him, since she now understood why he had acted as he had. Carrie was not ready to do this, so I asked her to look down on that father at the time of his death in the snow and understand why he had died then and what he had been thinking:

> P: He knew he was making his family unhappy and didn't know how to do anything different. He felt he couldn't control himself. He knew he had caused a terrible breach with my brother and that this hurt my mother, and he didn't know how to stop from hurting us so he decided to die.
> T: How do you feel about him now?
> P: I see for the first time that he really was trapped. I respect him for his early death. That feels nice. I see it differently.

As is often the case, reframing through going into the mind of a character in one's past life to determine his true motivations was transformational for Carrie, just as it had been for Dawn.

Another cognitive technique is called *rescripting* by Snow and Findeisen and *renovation* by the Dutch school. These therapists find that this approach produces healing and restores self-confidence. Snow defines rescripting as a device where, under the therapist's guidance, a regressed client intervenes at a critical point in his or her recalled experience to change that experience in such a way as to eliminate the conflict and achieve durable growth. This technique is seldom used in regression therapy, but it can sometimes speed conflict resolution as victory replaces defeat in the client's consciousness.

Snow warns that it should be used with caution and only when in agreement with the client's Higher Self or Counselor Part. He illustrates rescripting with a client, Anne-Marie, a French woman whose presenting symptoms were uncontrollable procrastination and intense panic in her relationship with a new medical director. Her first past lifetime was as a young page who was determined to win the favor of his lady. Though woefully unprepared, he tried to fight an experienced knight in a tournament and was killed:

> T: *Now, let yourself experience the spirit leaving the body.... Rise up out of that body.*
> P: I can't seem to do that. His eyes are terrible, so dark. He's towering over me. I was a fool to think I could beat him! I needed more time!
> T: *Move ahead until your spirit has left that body....*
> P: (Sighing.) It's okay now. I'm out of there.
> T: *Continue moving forward and upward. Remember now that your consciousness expands again as you leave that body; your spirit's always in touch with your inner wisdom. Let your Higher Self come forward now and help you see how that experience related to what's happening now to Anne-Marie, in this lifetime.*
> P: Yes, I see it now. Those dark eyes, they're the same as Dr. X's! Good grief, that's who it was! I didn't want to fight him—I wasn't ready but he made it a question of honor. I still feel that way! If only I'd not turned around; I was foolish.
> T: *I'm talking to the Higher Self now, am I not? (Assent.) Good. Now I want to know if it would serve Anne-Marie to go back to that tournament, but this time with more training and experience, ready for combat. Could she learn the same life lesson from preparing for success as from failing?*

The Higher Self agreed that Anne-Marie would go further ahead if she replayed the incident with more training and confidence. Snow had her visualize long training hours until she had a feeling of being ready for the decisive test. This time the page was stronger and with true aim knocked his opponent off his horse by a clean hit on the shield, thereby winning the tournament and the promise of knighthood. The week following this regression Anne-Marie proudly announced that she had finished a report a day early and that she could now face her new supervisor without fear and trembling. Rescripting was a part of her integrative process and widened her perspective, making change possible.

Bontenbal and Noordegraaf describe renovation in a similar way:

> After working through death in a past life, feelings and thoughts about certain incidents during the life or about the death experience itself can prevent moving on to a sphere where integration, healing, and transformation can take place. Renovation techniques should then be used. It can

help finally to do what could not be done in the life itself—for example, defending one's family bravely against a bunch of robbers, something that was not possible in the real situation because of severe shock or because strength was not available at that moment. Helping the client to experience that he is able to defend himself when not in shock or when strength is available can be deeply healing. Renovation is also used when death has been painful or when the body has been injured in a terrible and/or humiliating way.

This process of reconceptualizing a disastrous or ill-advised event and making it turn out more positively is not generally accepted, perhaps because it smacks too much of current thrusts into mind control. However, if the original incident has been well processed, rescripting often brings healing. Since there are only energy fields, we should be able to restructure them directly in the form of rescripting as well as indirectly in reframing and other techniques, provided that the elements that make up the rescripting are well understood. Findeisen gives a thoughtful rationale for the process:

> Sometimes I intervene to change the negative beliefs and attitudes that form the life scripts. During the regression to a trauma, I ask if there could have been other choices made, or how the client would have liked it to be. This suggests the option of completing or modifying relationships and communications. One could argue that this is not the truth. I would counter that the truth is that the past is *no longer present except in our minds.*

Returning to a positive lifetime, joyous or productive or creative, is another method of centering and tuning in to a more integrated position. Findeisen remarks about this:

> Another transformational technique that I often use is to return to a lifetime of fulfillment, of service, of peace, where love is experienced. This sort of lifetime is just as real as are painful lifetimes, and memories of happy lives can act as a ground when we are struggling with lifetimes where we seem to have missed the mark badly. It is a severe limitation, when working with past lifetimes, to fail to notice the good decisions we have made, the love we have shown, and the transpersonal qualities we have slowly developed.

Therapists seldom return to such lifetimes, but my own experience is that to do so has an integrating effect and enables one to deal with the more troubled shadow aspects of oneself. Recently a friend and I who knew that we had had a fulfilling mutual ancient lifetime as gopis (herdsgirls) had Pecci regress us together. We recovered many aspects of that life, including our devotion to a great teacher and our tenderness toward each other, and the remembrance of that life still lights up my heart. When we are dealing with guilt and anger and misdirection, it is helpful to know that there were other times when we did better!

Snow, in reflection on his own extensive series of past lives, comes to the same conclusion after re-living life as a wise woman shaman in a primitive social group:

> It can be profoundly healing to get in touch with this spiritual foundation of the collective unconscious as it has been lived through past personal experiences. Consequently, while I agree that many therapy sessions must be devoted to extirpating negative imprinting and symptoms originating in previous lifetimes, I also insist on the value of finding and raising the psyche's cache of positive spiritual resources so that the client can build for the future from as solid a base as possible.

## Emotional and Transformational Techniques of Intervention

Transformational techniques are concerned for the most part with anger and guilt. In our lifetime we experience a broad spectrum of emotions. Many of them, such as bitterness, despair, and grieving, are perceived as negative, but there is no emotion that causes more difficulty on our soul journey than anger. In its basic aspect as a facilitator of our survival, anger has its place, though even in that role it can cause trouble when the threat to survival is misperceived. Usually, however, anger is a reaction to *a failure of our expectations.* We carry an expectation of what life and people ought to be, and when they let us down, we become angry.

Deepset anger that has come down through lifetimes is not easy to release. Only rarely can it be dealt with in a single session; usually work on it must be integrated into extensive ongoing therapy. Anger against parents who have played various roles in former lifetimes (usually all bad!) is especially difficult to transform. It is not possible in this brief discussion to illustrate the process, but a number of cases are scattered throughout these two volumes that can demonstrate step-by-step effective intervention techniques.[4]

Pecci gives a broad general outline of the process of forgiveness as it relates to parents and stresses both cognitive re-evaluation and an emotional transformation:

> Regression to childhood and tracing interactions with parents in the roles they played in other lifetimes can and must eventually lead to a re-evaluation of the parents. As we come to see that we have chosen our parents in order to play out complementary roles and that we failed in love for them just as they failed in love for us, we gain an expanded perspective

that makes possible both compassion and subsequent re-evaluation. Old patterns of anger can be loosened and eventually released as we understand both the roles we played and how we brought anger about. In the end we learn to be grateful both for the lessons we have chosen in order to help us grow in consciousness and to the people who have clustered in our various lifetimes to help us learn them. It is the work of the therapist to take an active part in this process of re-evaluation, facilitating a letting go of old attachments to negative states and yielding to the process of inner growth.

The emotional release of anger must begin with thorough abreaction; the energy of anger cannot be transformed until it is first felt. Anger is connected to the first chakra, and the transformation lies in bringing the energy up from the base chakra to the heart chakra. The initial statement that emerges from a strong feeling of anger needs to be followed by a statement of what would have been preferable, which raises the energy to the second chakra and on to the third. Here through an act of will the patient makes a statement releasing his expectation and accepting the person the way he is. Eventually some patients move to the heart chakra where they can send love to the object of their anger, though this is difficult and often hits the snag of a destructive sub-personality constellated early in life. Sometimes when there is deep anger, it is helpful to identify with that person—get inside his head, so to speak, in order to reach an attitude of forgiveness.[5]

Even more destructive than anger at others is anger at ourselves for our perceived (and often actual) deficiencies. Anger at ourselves results in guilt. In its deepest aspect, guilt arises when actions are seen as contrary to the path of the soul. Awareness of this deviation is the force that keeps us on our soul path. But when guilt is too strong, reinforced usually by the social and moral fabric in which we are enmeshed, it becomes crippling and puts a prison around us. Therapists must help to remove this.

Most of our therapists are concerned with guilt, and Denning feels that dealing with guilt is the focus of regression work:

> If it were possible to step back and take a long penetrating look at life as it is lived out by most people, one would be appalled at the wasted time and energy unwittingly spent in trying to absolve guilt. That same energy spent in purposeful, creative pursuits could make a great deal of difference in individual destinies, as well as contribute to a more productive civilization. When one considers the evidence that the guilt not only stems from the errors in the present life but is an accumulation from an untold number of past lives, the burden is staggering to contemplate. It is no wonder that creativity is stifled in many people and that the world is full of those who do not feel worthy of loving or being loved....

It must be pointed out that even if the guilt is appropriate to the past-life behavior, which it often is, it still has to be released. The individual's need to bring about punishment and suffering in lifetime after lifetime has to be concluded so that the soul can get on with its journey toward higher consciousness. The process of canceling expectations that one should have behaved differently is often difficult, but facilitating such a process is one of the responsibilities of the regression therapist.

Pecci feels that guilt arises not only from sins of commission but from those of omission:

Out of all the themes that have arisen during my 20-plus years of doing past-life therapy, the most pervasive is that of guilt and of the resultant need for self-forgiveness. We feel responsible or guilty, not only for our motives and intentions and our negligence, but also for our legitimate helplessness. It is as if we cannot accept the limitations imposed upon us by a three-dimensional reality and so feel responsible for everything that goes wrong or that leads to the pain and suffering of others within our environment. The sins of omission often press more heavily upon our soul than do the sins of commission.... The soul in its learning punishes itself for hurting others, for cowardice, for being inadequate, and for negligence. Once we have deemed ourselves guilty, the cycles of self-imposed punishment never seem to end until we consciously arrive at an understanding that permits self-forgiveness. We are disciplined by guilt, we are taught by comparisons that engender guilt, and we have religious institutions that heavily reinforce guilt. The average person, in the natural condition of daily activities, feels subconsciously like a condemned criminal, awaiting fearfully the inevitable moment of exposure, as in Camus' *The Trial*.

Denning identifies two kinds of guilt. The first, which she calls "state guilt," refers to guilt over violations of various injunctions in this lifetime. Conventional therapy can often dispel this type of guilt. The second type of guilt is not so easily dealt with. She describes this:

A pervasive type of guilt, called "trait guilt," is often so deep-seated that it does not respond to any current therapies, including psychoanalysis.[6] This sort of guilt is entrenched in a past-life episode, carried in the unconscious mind through one or more physical experiences, and manifests in the current life from very early childhood, polluting the individual's entire life experience. The assumption by the traditional therapist regarding this sort of guilt is that an early childhood trauma (in the current life) is responsible. However, past-life work indicates that feelings of guilt have been brought in from other lives and are merely triggered by some early childhood experience.

The differentiation between these types of guilt is important because it helps to explain why conventional therapeutic interventions cannot release a patient from the burden of self-recrimination if the cause lies in a former lifetime.

How do we release such guilt and free ourselves to go on our soul path without carrying such a burden? Reframing often helps, as in Denning's case of Lois, who was burned at the stake believing she had committed an unpardonable sin. Denning initiated the reframing by having Lois get into the minds of her persecutors, a technique that she feels promotes forgiveness:

> T: *So they burn you?*
> P: *Yes, and I tell them I am sorry, but they say I can never be forgiven; that I am the Devil's handmaiden now and I will always burn in hell. I did a really bad thing and I can never be forgiven.*
> T: *Go to the last moment before your spirit leaves your body. What is your last conscious thought?*
> P: *I have committed an unpardonable sin. I can never be forgiven. My soul will burn in hell forever.*
> T: *Looking at it now, do you believe they were right?*
> P: *Of course not. I was right.*
> T: *Let's look at why they did that cruel thing to you. Use your intuition and get into their minds and feelings at that time and see what prompted their actions.*
> P: *I feel their fear (surprised). They are afraid of me. They really believe that I am working with the Devil. That is why they are screaming at me the way they are. They are terrified of me. I thought they hated me, but they don't. They are just afraid of me.*

Lois was able to reframe the situation and release unnecessary guilt.

But what about situations where the subject is really guilty? Essentially the same approach is needed as was used to deal with anger at others. *We need to forgive ourselves.* We need to let go of the expectations that we have for ourselves, especially those about being perfect (often stamped in during childhood). We need to accept ourselves as we are with all our limitations and from this place of acceptance love ourselves. Pecci feels strongly about this:

> The greatest crime, and perhaps the only crime, is not loving and valuing ourselves. Cowardly passivity, the fear of being true to oneself, leads to anguish, disillusionment, and despair. We must learn to live with courage, to live what we believe. Otherwise, we insult the indwelling Self, which leads to guilt and the need to set up similar situations in the hope that finally we will prove ourselves. Thus arise our karmic patterns and we

feel guilty and set up another trial with one more hope on an inner level that we will do better.

Eventually in the transformative process the patient begins to differentiate between his personal self and his soul self, known as "the Traveler," who continues from lifetime to lifetime on the journey of the soul. It is not appropriate to conclude that one has failed when the personal self makes mistakes or takes wrong paths. *The personal self is not supposed to be perfect*—it is a vehicle in which the soul self can learn and grow. Regression work helps one to take the stance of the soul self and observe the personal self in all its difficulties without judgment. It is the witness position that Jue talks about raised to a transpersonal level.

## The Importance of the Death Experience

Both birth and death are times when karmic programs are constellated. The time of death and the experience following it become important transformational opportunities. Most therapists feel that no matter what else must be omitted, the death process needs to be included because it offers more insights and scope for change than any other event in a lifetime. Denning explains this:

> Much of the work of insight and integration of the learning from any lifetime can best be uncovered and expressed at the time that a person leaves his body in that lifetime. Also, the last conscious thought before a person has actually left his body often sets an intention that he carries into the next lifetime and possibly through subsequent lifetimes, often being amplified by each new lifetime until that intention programs behavior and attitudes in the current lifetime. Therefore, I always ask that the situation of the death in the earlier lifetime be described, including the last conscious thought.

Snow explains this in a similar way. He feels that at the time of death the patterns that have been formed in the energy body during the lifetime are in a sense set and in this form are carried on into the next lifetime:

> As we transit from one level of reality to another at death, all the emotional patterns previously created coalesce into a resonant energy field and survive. At the birth of our next incarnation in space/time, they are transmitted to the new individual's psyche according to a process still little understood. Apparently some choice is involved, as well as some determinism.

Woolger feels that not only are the patterns that have been set during a lifetime imprinted at this time but the experience of the death, since it usually occurs in a heightened energy state, also becomes imprinted, often dragging pain, suffering, and anger into the next life:

> In most sessions I will attempt to complete the memory of a life story by taking the rememberer through the death of that particular personality. When a death agony is unfinished and is recorded in the imaginal body memory, it becomes re-imprinted in the current life body as if it were any other physical trauma. Also, going through the death brings a sense of completion and, more importantly, of detachment. The death transition is an opportunity to let go consciously of the obsessive and repetitive thoughts, feelings, or fears of that other self. In the after-death period of recall there is usually valuable comparison of the themes of the other life with unresolved issues in this one. Every patient is encouraged to see the story as now finished, as a pattern that need not be repeated.

The cases reported by our therapists are replete with examples of the influence of the death experience on lives to follow. Such imprinting is often back of phobias, obsessions, physical symptoms, overweight, and patterns of anger. Nearly all of Fiore's patients found the origin of particular symptoms in this lifetime in their deaths in previous ones, whether it was acrophobia, insomnia, or an inability to make decisions. In addition to the emotional and physical states induced by the death experience, cognitive decisions made at death have a strong influence on following lifetimes. One of my most tortured patients, abused and dying from starvation in a concentration camp in his last lifetime, declared that in the life to come he wanted only vengeance and food. He chose a father who built up a million-dollar food distribution business but whom he hates, and he has only slowly become able to make relationships.[7] Occasionally a death will be mellow and joyous, and this, also, leaves its mark on the future. Whatever the death is like, it impacts the life to come.

Besides setting patterns for another lifetime, death offers the opportunity for a review of the life just lived and makes reframing possible through an expanding of perspective. Polarities can be observed, and the therapist can aid in helping these become accepted and the shadow side of the personality reframed and integrated. Jue describes his technique of reframing a death:

> After the death, I suggest advancing to a post-life review where any other key incidents or relationships can be examined. At this point I remind clients, now in "spirit," of their timeless connection to higher guidance and I ask that they be joined by their "Higher Self" or "Counselor Part" or "Guide," using whatever terminology seems appropriate for each client. With this assistance, the client and I proceed to widen the context of

whatever trauma or "unfinished business" developed during the past-life scenario and to look for parallels in the current symptomology. In most cases obvious connections are rapidly perceived.

This helpful technique of placing a former lifetime side by side with this current one and noting similarities and differences amplifies an understanding of the patterns that have been uncovered.

Denning takes her patients out of the body of the past life and asks them to consider what lessons were planned for that lifetime and whether the goals that had been set were accomplished. The objective is to help the patient take responsibility for programming and implementing that life as well as to explore the effect of that lifetime on the current one. She also uses an imaginal technique to help this expansion of insight:

> A technique that I often use to help tie things together and integrate and consolidate a client's insight is to ask the client to imagine an altar with a presence behind it surrounded in light—the client's guide or Higher Self, whichever seems appropriate. I have the client approach this guide and receive a message. The guide will often summarize or heighten the understanding gained from the regression.

She feels that in this perspective forgiveness is especially appropriate. This includes self-forgiveness:

> If the client feels that in the lifetime under consideration something has been done that can never be forgiven, this attitude must be explored until it is clear that this event is a part of the soul's growth, that it, too, is an aspect of being on the path to self-discovery. Both the incident and the judgment about it must be reframed.

Pecci, who also works intensively with forgiveness during the death process, adds:

> What we cannot forgive in ourselves we cannot forgive in others. Thus our own guilt becomes projected upon others, resulting in judgments that perpetuate the emotions of anger and rage. This, in turn, results in progressive self-isolation, feelings of alienation, and fear. Guilt, anger, and fear create a locked triangle which cannot be broken without self-forgiveness and forgiveness of others. Unfortunately, in our most intimate relationships, such as the family, our communications tend to reinforce each member's sense of guilt.
>
> This is the foundation upon which I have based my model of therapy. I strive for a depth of understanding that will lead to compassion for self and others within a given situation. We need to accept others as trying desperately to work out their own salvation in the only way they know.

From this understanding we can arrive at both self-forgiveness and forgiveness of others, a position that will open the gate to self-love and brotherly love.

The next step after taking the patient out of his body and from that perspective re-evaluating the lifetime he has just passed through, is to go with him into the interlife. This is not a period of time but a state of consciousness, and what each person perceives in it depends upon what he is ready to perceive. Only for those who are ready to experience light and insight are these available. My patient Brad rushed through his memory of the interlife after his death in the concentration camp and saw nothing the first time.[8] It was only after returning a number of times that he became able to attribute wisdom to judges that he only gradually came to be aware of and to touch into deep insights in himself. Not everyone can report the events in the interlife because apparently these cannot be described in conventional language but must be translated into images and metaphors. Those who are on a soul path and are able to bring these images up to consciousness find the experience profound, and extensive learning can take place.

Bontenbal and Noordegraaf feel that experiencing the more enlightened state beyond death is a necessary condition for integration:

> Part of the integration process is to get the former personality out of surroundings, spheres, and places where it still feels painful, unhappy, restless, revengeful, humiliated, etc. Only when the projections change into ones in which safety, rest, warmth, love, and healing are experienced, does the therapist know that integration has started.

All transformational techniques that take place from the broader perspective of the death review in the interlife eventuate in a reduction of striving for ego-gratification and tend to move the patient into a life of service, which seems to be the ultimate good in human existence. This release of attachment for mundane concerns that are usually held important resembles the transformation that takes place in those who have gone through the near-death experience. Interlife perception may become our next area of focus—a perception of deep levels of being that, unlike the near-death experience or states of cosmic consciousness which they resemble, are open to everyone.

A final therapeutic concern is that of bringing the patient back into ordinary consciousness. Each therapist has his unique way to help a patient emerge from a regression, and many give positive affirmations and suggestions while aiding the patient's return into his body. The therapist needs to be aware of the vulnerability that characterizes the altered state and give protection in the transition back. He needs to facilitate the re-entry with caring and sensitivity. He may tie in the re-entry with the images of the induction.

Snow points out that the patient has been opened up through the induction process and must be restored to his original energy state. Since Snow induces an altered state by opening the chakras, he helps chakra energy become restored to a normal level:

> It is vital that the therapist take each client back into his current body and energy field after each session. The same applies to group inductions. Whenever the chakras are opened and harmonized or worked on during a therapy session, they must be restored to their normal functioning by direct suggestion as the client is being brought back from the altered state. Thus, if a client or group has been brought up through his chakras into an altered state during induction, the therapist needs to work back down the chakras in reverse order with suggestions of harmony and balance so that they end the session at a normal level again, fully reintegrated and in equilibrium.

Denning has an especially supportive re-entry:

> After that, I ask the client if there is anything further that needs to be seen or dealt with. Sometimes there is, and time must be allowed for this. If there is nothing further, I bring the client back by suggesting that an enclosing bubble of white light be imaged, that all the colors be visualized. I ask if there is any part of the body that needs extra energy, and I suggest that all the wonderful energy of the bubble melt into the body for healing. Then I slowly count back from five to one, observing the body response in order to determine the pacing of the return.

Chapter IX

# Integration into the Therapeutic Process

## The Long Path of Transformation

We are a synthesis of energy fields, many of them originating in past lifetimes and brought forward through various lives, finally to become constellated in the prenatal, birth, and current experiences of this life. Reconstellating the distortions in the original energy fields modifies difficulties experienced in the current lifetime and may effect a remission of symptoms.

But this is only a taste of the potential of regression therapy. There is a broader transformation that deals with integrating the individually transformed fields so that the patient can change as a whole, a long and demanding process. The goal of balancing and harmonizing the energy fields is teleological: it is concerned with our progress on the path of the soul. Apparently our purpose in life is to meld into an infinite field of goodness and love.

Snow stresses the time that is needed to balance and harmonize these fields:

> The client needs to be helped to understand that integration seldom develops immediately. It may take several sessions involving the examination of a number of related life themes from various past lives. It takes time for significant patterns to develop and impress themselves on the client's consciousness.... The therapist assists in bringing insights gained during regressions into the present through pre- and post-session discussions. These provide the client with a forum for testing new ideas and attitudes, and they help him or her to put such new viewpoints into practice in everyday life. Moreover, as inner healing develops, synchronous positive changes in surrounding conditions often take place. It is as if an energy-level shift has occurred in the client's nexus of relationships.

Noordegraaf and Bontenbal emphasize the importance, not only of fully integrating new insights cognitively, but also of modifying outer behavior to bring it into line with the insights:

> It is important to understand that integration and transformation often take time, especially when physical symptoms are involved.... It will help clients, impatiently waiting for their life to change, to realize that their core issue created participation in structures and networks (family, work, living environment, friendships, etc.) that are felt and seen as part of the problem. Some of these structures and networks will change with the client, others will even disappear. Others seem more resistant to change. Often one can't just step out of the family one chose when incarnating. A new house, new work, new friends, or even a new partner, needed when it is obvious that the old ones are a product of character postulate and slow down transformation, can't be achieved all at once. Quite often clients start feeling the final transformation taking place months after closing the therapeutic process.

Findeisen feels that this long process of integration, which changes energy patterns and therefore the behavior of the current lifetime, can best be implemented in a therapeutic situation:

> In general, though there are some regression sessions that seem almost to produce a magical cure, on the whole this modality is a psychological tool to be integrated along with other techniques in a therapeutic process. During the discussion that follows a regression, the meanings and lessons learned are evaluated and ways perceived in which the good of such lessons can be integrated into the current life process.... Uncovering the past is usually only the first step. Old habit patterns need to be confronted and changed. New ways of responding need to be discovered and tested. Resistance and fears of change need to be handled. Clients are encouraged to avail themselves of further psychological counseling for support and continuing growth.

Insights recovered in the regression process demand an adequate working through if their messages and the lessons they contain are to contribute to inner growth. They need to be probed at length for the range of their meaning and implications. Often the therapist can be misled that this has already occurred because impressions and insights he has gained while guiding his patient in an altered state tend to be so compelling that it is difficult to believe that the patient lacks an equally clear perception. After a session in which patterns appear to have emerged with startling clarity, the therapist must guard against his assumption that the patient has understood the dynamics and will easily and inevitably integrate them; therapeutic work may appear to be finished when in reality it has only been started. For this reason follow-ups are imperative so that the therapist can know what has been accomplished.

Day-by-day experience, especially in regard to relationships, provides the opportunity to choose different modes of response. Relationships offer opportunities to test out growth so that once a lesson has been learned it can be seen that it is unnecessary to repeat unfortunate or painful or unproductive patterns. This is true both of relationship patterns in general and of patterns of reaction to specific persons who appear in various lifetimes in different roles.

Resolving and releasing an unhelpful pattern of relationship requires a continuous integrative effort, as Denning notes:

> There are other instances wherein past lifetimes have exposed a long-standing personality pattern that has been reinforced in this lifetime in many ways. Such a pattern will not disappear immediately but must be identified continuously as it reappears, when further work on integrating the insight can go on. Often during the actual regression a different perspective has been reached, resulting in a new statement of purpose or a revised understanding, but old patterns often resurface and they carry sufficient energy to obscure or push back into the unconscious the insights and new perspectives that have been reached regarding the judgments of the self made in other lifetimes. These recriminations must be exposed again, and the insights and new perspectives must be reinforced. This reinforcement process may require numerous additional sessions.

There are many examples of the resolution or dissolution of patterns of relationship throughout this book. Findeisen's case of twins sisters, where in an earlier lifetime the tragic death of the younger sister imprinted guilt in the older one and led to the current neurotic interaction, is one such a relationship.[1] Denning gives an account of a young wife who could not control inappropriate feelings for her husband and brother who had played out reversed roles in an earlier lifetime.[2] My own patient Carrie brought anger from an earlier lifetime against her father of today.[3] Rosemary's anger toward the husband of an earlier lifetime who had killed her, continued against her mother of today who had been that husband.[4]

A release of patterns follows understanding that they are not inevitable and that there are other choices. Patients become freed from an emotional and cognitive stalemate and gain an awareness of new options. Understanding the reason for reactions to specific people in one's life encourages dealing with them in a different way. The more patterns that are understood and integrated, the more options open up for new ways of dealing with both the world and oneself.

A word of caution. Often a patient will recognize someone in another life as playing a role in this one. This recognition may be accurate, but there are times when the past-life character triggers a karmic pattern that becomes projected onto a similar personality in the current life. The patient needs to use recognition of the similarity for awareness of his own patterns unless the other person has recognized the repetition of the relationship. It is important to remind patients that *it is the personal lesson learned from the relationship and not the relationship itself* that is important. Each individual needs to avoid intruding on another's soul space.

There has been surprisingly sparse research in this area. When one person feels he has known another in a past life, it should be easy to regress the second person and check on the data, but such instances are seldom reported aside from regressions of groups who have known each other, such as the Cathar group Arthur Guirdham treated (1970 and 1974), the Civil War villagers in *Mission to Millboro* (1991), and Janet Cunningham's Indian tribe documented in *A Tribe Returned* (1993).

In addition to sensing that repetition of a relationship is primarily a karmic situation, we need to be aware that patterns do not originate accidentally, even in dramatic incidents, but evolve out of deeper dynamics in which we have set a direction for ourselves. Guilt tends to constellate patterns, and a lack of forgiveness, for oneself or others, may force their repetition until the discordance is resolved. Forgiveness is concerned, not so much with another person as with transformation of ourselves, the raising of our emotional selves to a higher frequency where we can experience what it is to love.

Findeisen warns about the complicated process of forgiveness, which often takes time and needs to be worked at from many angles:

> The place of forgiveness as a transformational agent is complex. It is certainly an essential ingredient in releasing guilt, but it cannot be hurried or forced. Release and understanding of the nature of our behavior and feelings from other lifetimes provide fertile soil for forgiveness to take place. Pressure for forgiveness, either of oneself or of others, before the soil is ready, is at best ineffective and may even be destructive, especially as it tends to generate more guilt. Sometimes the struggle to forgive is a necessary component of the client's process, which we must respect. Sometimes looking for lifetimes in which one experienced a problem both as a victim and as victimizer enables one to forgive more easily and let go of present negative patterns. Karmic reaction is not to punish but to generate sensitivity and awareness of our actions, and when such awareness has been learned, we can let go of judgments of ourselves and the guilt that accompanies them.

Dethlefsen points out that constant involvement with the shadow is one of the most difficult but indispensable aspects of this process of integration and he feels this is often related to a need for power:

## 138 *Processing*

Through integrating step by step into his consciousness all his hitherto totally suppressed shadow, a person becomes complete and whole.... Not until the patient has re-experienced, with full clarity, the power urges of his earlier incarnations will he begin to unmask them in the here and now. Only when he has seen how over thousands of years he has heaped suffering upon himself in order to buy power, will he slowly begin to be ready to understand the doctrine of humility.

Such understanding does not come about through an intellectual process but through an experience of reality that produces a trans-polarization in the individual. The changes in consciousness take place in the present, and thereby the person becomes healed. Reincarnation therapy is a hard route to purification. In repeated incarnations we see no source of comfort but rather a challenge to develop toward completeness and thus become free. We must say "yes" to this earthly existence as long as it is necessary for our path of development.[5]

## Techniques of Integration

Constant cognitive reframing and the working through of encrusted emotional patterns by such a technique as forgiveness, loosen up old energy fields and prepare them for transformation into a different pattern, much as a kaleidoscope shifts into a new pattern when it is turned. In addition, there are other techniques, for the most part transpersonal but some conventional, that assist in bringing outer behavior into congruence with new inner perceptions and patterns. These techniques facilitate the step-by-step modification of the external experience of the patient so that his perception comes to reflect the new inner awareness. Each therapist assembles his personal selection of techniques to facilitate the integrative process.

*Behavior modification* is frequently used in conventional therapy but is not generally considered appropriate in past-life work. However, as we come to see that insight needs to be grounded and reinforced by conventional relearning approaches, behavior modification may gain acceptance as an auxiliary tool. An example of its use is Fiore's work with her obese patient William.[6] Past-life recall had loosened up the patterns that were responsible for his being overweight, but various behavior modification techniques, including plotting his weight on a chart, assisted his weight loss. It was from watching the vicissitudes of this chart that patient and therapist gained clues that led them to recover a lifetime where an addiction to chocolate had begun in cold weather. The understanding of this link broke the stalemate that had kept Roger's weight stationary. Fiore feels that though hunger in another lifetime may underlie a problem of compulsive overeating in this life, there may be more than one life of starvation and there are inevitably complex behavioral factors superimposed on and reinforcing the overeating.

A therapist must work with the behavioral factors if insight gained from regression work is to help. Fiore considered that her good rapport with William, the reinforcing influence of the chart, and the hope given by the use of a new and untried approach, each played a part in his success.

Fiore employs other conventional interventions. She often offers therapeutic counseling, especially in terms of bodily well-being, and she suggests helpful books on diet and exercise. She asks patients to observe events carefully in between sessions, keep a journal of anything untoward that happens, and write down dreams and bring them in. Although she minimizes dream interpretation in itself, she uses dreams as focal points in work on the patient's material. She feels that such related investigations and discussions help to open up areas of memory where both the precipitating cause and therefore the source of healing are to be found.

Other therapists influenced by Jungian theory, as Woolger, find dreams to be important tools in the integrative process. Woolger feels that for patients whose goal is a broad integration of personality, dream work helps the transition to the symbolic level. Or dreams may be fragments of past lives and can lead into them, as occurred with Jue's patient, who had a dream of dying in Vietnam and as a consequence of the dream was able to return to what had been a Vietnamese lifetime and release destructive patterns that originated there.[7] Snow encourages his patients to note significant dreams, daydreams, or flashes of insight that occur either just after a therapy session or within 40 hours prior to the next session. He feels that frequently the client's subconscious provides material which, when correctly interpreted, penetrates long-standing psychological defenses. Tracing the impact of regression work from the dream work of patients provides important material for working on the integrative process.

Hickman has worked out individual approaches to dream work. She puts the burden of interpretation on the patient:

> Past-life work can be interspersed with other techniques, such as dream analysis. Through using a non-directive hypnotherapy approach the inner wisdom can be asked to analyze the dream, to recall a dream partially or totally forgotten, or even to present a new dream during the hypnotherapy session, and then give the dream's meaning.

Many regression therapists suggest that their patients keep a journal. The type of patient who wishes to work deeply in his life has probably already been writing in a journal prior to coming for regression work. Previous journal writing may even have touched on indications of what has later emerged as a past life. Journal writing not only opens up new details and insights but reinforces what has already been worked through; often perceptions that bubble up from the unconscious tend to sink back and be lost when focus on them ceases. New details may emerge in the process of writing. Pecci, Fiore, and others use journal writing to integrate a series of experiences, which not only clarifies the patterns that have been unearthed but moves the patient into a transformational perception of them.

One of the most effective approaches to writing in a journal is the Intensive Journal Process of Ira Progoff.[8] The dialogue process, which is stressed in this method, lends itself well to interactions with the selves of other lifetimes. The counsel of Guides or of one's Higher Self is easily integrated into the Progoff dialogue process, which includes a section for dialoguing with transpersonal figures. It is important that the patient be helped to feel that he is not being graded on his writing skill and that whatever comes up can be recorded without judgment.

Pecci's patient Joanne, whose recall of past lifetimes extended over several years, reached an even more comprehensive understanding of her life through her journal work than she had done in her sessions.[9] Outwardly she became more comfortable with her role as mother and wife, but in addition, on an inner level, through her journal she came to a place of synthesis. She summarized this new state in her journal near the conclusion of her therapy work:

> *After that session I knew that all the life experiences I've had here in this body and on this earth came after the first experience. I knew beyond all doubt that we, each of us, are more than beings in bodies. We are beings of awesome potentiality. We are beings whose heritage it is to live in harmony and beauty that exist beyond our present ability to perceive. I knew that each of us is more than we have believed ourselves to be. And my view of myself can never be quite the same.*

Though one cannot stay for long on such a high plane, one knows it is there and never again feels that life is without meaning.

Meditation is another form of deepening and grounding insight. A form of meditation popular in the West is the use of affirmations. Although affirming what we want is often futile because of the plethora of unconscious patterns that sabotage such an effort, when patterns have been loosened up in therapeutic sessions so that they no longer interfere, it is helpful to put out appropriate affirmations. Therapist and patient can work together to frame these affirmations so that the patient is able to incorporate them into his thinking.[10] Norman Shealy was one of the first to point out the power of positive affirmations in changing behavior and health and to show that affirming new insights while in an altered state helps to integrate them into one's life pattern.[11]

A transpersonal technique that is involved with the Higher Self and is appropriate for those starting on the path of self-discovery is Psychosynthesis. This approach places a helpful emphasis on the development of the will.[12] Because of the tendency to equate the will with only one of its aspects, its strength, it has generally been neglected by psychotherapists. In Psychosynthesis the will is developed through the use of affirmations, and although, as has been pointed out, affirmations have limited effectiveness if conflicting underlying patterns have not been resolved, they become a powerful instrument when correctly used.

Pecci, especially, works with the will:

> In therapeutic contacts following a regression, further exploration is helpful to see the way the current life reflects past lives. Current difficulties can be reviewed in the setting of the broader perspective now available and new choices can be considered. Patients can alert themselves as to how they are drawing things to happen. Meanwhile, with the material and compulsions of the unconscious so much loosened, it is possible to work on the development of the will. Gradually the patient becomes more aware that one attitude doesn't work and another does and his will can implement a new choice and a new direction.

Pecci discusses how he helped Jack to program his intellect and will in order to change.[13] He routinely has patients do homework in order to deepen understanding of their problems and strengthen the will so that affirmations will stand a better chance of success. Jack wrote out affirmations that resulted from insights gained in his regression work:

> *I have felt the presence of my Spirit Guide all around me, assuring me that I am not alone and asking me if I now see my task clearly, which I do. I am encouraged to have the courage of my convictions, day by day, to break the chain here and now. My Guide assures me I can do this and that I now have the strength of purpose for this realization. I can see that my present lifetime does not provide the opportunity for a dramatic demonstration of loyalty and courage through giving up my life, as I was given the opportunity to do twice before, but perhaps that would be too easy. That would be like the fantasy I always have that I can win the game by throwing a touchdown pass in the last play.*

Jack could not maintain this high level of insight at the time and needed additional work, but though for a while he became discouraged over losing what he thought he was grasping, with more work he regained that level of integration and from then on was able to retain it. A second journal entry recorded the recovery of his insight and a reinforcement of his affirmation to face his problems with courage:

142  *Processing*

> *Even a play that doesn't gain much ground, if devised and executed with conviction and courage, opens the way for the next play to achieve its objective. The game is won or lost every day in everything I do, at work or play or home with my family. I am determined to be true to myself, loyal to others, and have the courage of my convictions to face any situation in this life.*

Once the will is freed from the blocks that programs of earlier lifetimes have made, there are various ways to develop it. In *The Act of Will* Assagioli describes techniques for developing the will and lists qualities of the will, which include patience and skill.[14] Taking responsibility for change is a major method of developing the will. Every patient has to bring about his own changes; dependency must not be fostered, no matter how much the patient might like it or the therapist be flattered by it. It is the developed will that helps guide the patient into a more self-actualizing way of life.

Sub-personalities are energy fields from other lifetimes that continue in this one as sub-selfs.[15] Identifying those personalities in other lifetimes makes it easier to transform them. Fiore's patient Roger had lived a number of lives where his personal self was unassertive, so this lack of assertion became a strong sub-personality in the current life, but it yielded to transformational processes after the pertinent past lives were scanned.[16]

Denning's patient Lois, though in many ways her current life was harmonious and fulfilling and characterized by successful relationships, had a strong guilty sub-personality stemming from accepting the judgments of her accusers in the life when she was viewed as a witch. In regression the sub-personality became exposed in the lifetime where it originated, and it was then worked through.[17] The aspect of my patient Rosemary that propelled her into situations where she became abused, although only a sub-self in this current lifetime, was the dominant personal self in that earlier lifetime in England.[18]

Bontenbal and Noordegraaf talk about working with sub-personalities as "Inner Children," a concept popular in recovery programs:

> Old traumas often have resulted in the creation of traumatic Inner Children or other sub-personalities.... Gestalting a "sane" parent or adult is almost never possible without resolving childhood traumas. Integrating Inner Children in short- or long-term therapy is therefore essential for the integration and healing process.

Working with sub-personalities conceived of as past-life figures offers a new potential in the integrative process. Our shadow selves do not originate out of thin air. They are not just negative aspects that have appeared without reason but selves with histories and justifications for their behavior, contemporary equivalents of personae we have lived out in other times. Dialoguing with them and sensing how they came to be makes it easier to understand and accept them. Little by little the energy field of a former lifetime can be released, diffused, transformed, and finally accepted as a shadow aspect that can be integrated.

Woolger makes use of various auxiliary techniques, giving his patients a rich smorgasbord of peripheral experiences, including work with sub-personalities:

> In affecting these integrating and transformation processes I have drawn from many modalities. Most important have been the contributions of Jung, especially his view that all complexes manifest as sub-personalities that can be envisioned and dialogued with. Moreno's psychodrama has been extremely helpful because it aims for the catharsis of conflicting complexes. I have taken a great deal from the Gestalt theories of Fritz Perl because of their insistence on the contiguity of all complexes to awareness, which was a reinforcement of similar ideas I had practiced in the Buddhist Vipassana meditation. Finally, Reich's insight into bodily armoring and how the body holds attitudes at an organic level confirmed my impression of how trauma is imprinted into the imaginal body and helped me work out techniques for releasing this.

## Transformation of the Personality

Regression work has the potential for a comprehensive transformation of the personality. People seek transformation from many sources—workshops, meditation, conventional therapy, and following gurus—and find in each of these perhaps a taste, a touch of what they are seeking. It takes time and humility to realize that transformation is a lifelong process and can be watered and nourished by many streams. The broader perspective offered in regression experience and the insight into karmic law that it provides over an extended period can accelerate the transformational process. Jue describes this ongoing development:

> This is not a one-time burst of insight but a continuing recontextualizing of the patient's life. His life is now perceived from a different perspective and a different realm of consciousness. He begins to re-vision his personal life, his psychological scripts, how he perceives his parents, how he has been attracted to or repulsed by certain individuals. During this stage the therapist takes the opportunity to guide the patient through his past-life experiences in retrospect in order to bring him to an awareness of the necessity of each life's experiences in relation to his personal spiritual growth. Past-life scripts are rewritten and worked through, and in that change of patterning the present life becomes transformed. Released from the past unworkable patterns, the patient becomes more attuned to living

in the present and seeing the importance and meaning of what is in his world.

Woolger describes the deepening perception of patients who seek in regression work, not the remission of symptoms, but an experience of transformation:

> When a patient begins to understand his own past-life scenarios, his own inner stories and his own inner life, he begins to understand his existing scenarios. When that happens, the world becomes his teacher. Relationships carry a deeper meaning when it is realized that all relations are opportunities for growth. Seeing life as moving toward wholeness reinforces the shift in attitudes and perceptions regarding past-life traumas and events and facilitates a change in psychological scripts....
>
> This is what I call the *integrative level*, and it closely resembles what Jung called the individuation process—the process of becoming who one uniquely is. A subtle and almost indescribable movement of the recentering of the personality is experienced, which often brings spiritual openings and manifestations of the Greater Self in dreams and meditation.

In both past-life experience and meditation we come to perceive both the personal and transpersonal aspects of ourselves. In the beginning we tend to identify with the personal self and consider the Higher Self to be abstract, a little apart, perhaps even judgmental of our failings. Most of us begin by struggling to bring the personal self into a state closer to perfection. Our thrust, reinforced by injunctions from our childhood, is to "clean up the act" of the personal self.

As we expand our understanding and become able to discriminate between our soul self and our personal self, it becomes possible in meditation to enter a perspective in which we have less judgment about our lives. It is like shifting gears from a limited time-space perspective to another level. Work in past lives assists this shift, and meditation implements it.

After some years of meditation we no longer identify completely with the personal self. The variety of these other selves experienced over many lifetimes has loosened the identification with our current self. We find ourselves perceiving the Higher Self, not as someone apart from us but as in some sense ourselves. This Higher Self is seen as acceptant of the personal self, which diminishes our futile struggle toward perfection.

Finally we come to a time when we identify spontaneously with our Higher Self, our Soul, and from this new perspective we look upon the struggling personal self with compassion. We finally realize that the personal self is a vehicle for learning and is not supposed to be perfect. From this vantage point we are transformed. We can release judgment about ourselves and simply bear witness to the vicissitudes of our journey. It is a place of centeredness and serenity.[19]

Woolger describes the process this way:

> Nothing is what it appears to be. Life mirrors paradoxes and other levels of meaning. A patient comes to the paradoxical realization that "I'm all that I experience and yet I'm not that, either." Seeing the function of various roles in the spiritual development of one's being or soul, a person begins to release the investment of energy into rigid roles. He begins to free himself to a point where he can play with that energy, not taking himself so seriously. He can begin to feel the freedom to choose and to integrate the energy with other parts of himself.

This more acceptant attitude toward ourselves generalizes, according to Woolger, and becomes a global perspective:

> When we can achieve such a consciousness, all is seen as both one *and* many, and everything is in its place in the ever-transforming play of creation. The human comedy of all lives past and present is then seen from a perspective of understanding, compassionate acceptance, and non-attachment. We are called simply to know and embrace our part of this whole, to know that this part is perfect in and of itself.

In this place of extended consciousness we become able to connect with the world's pain with the same attitude of simultaneous involvement and detachment that we feel for our personal selves and their vicissitudes. Grief over the thousands of children dying of hunger in Somalia would be too great to bear except that from a transpersonal perspective what is happening is all right. Tears fall. We send planeloads of food to relieve the hunger. And at the same time we rest in the awareness of this "ever-transforming play of creation."

# Chapter X

# Failures

In any new technique the emphasis is on success. There is an attempt made to lure stray comers into the fold by underlining its potentials and virtues. Only as a modality comes of age does a willingness evolve to critique it more impartially and to look at its limitations honestly, not just at its assets. Regression work is an approach relatively new to the field of psychotherapy—in fact, there are probably many who have never heard of it or who associate past lives with crystal balls or, at best, with Shirley MacLaine's experiences.

Still, as a form of therapy, regression work *has* evolved, and just *because* it is on the edge of credibility with so many, and especially in the psychotherapeutic community, it is necessary that its liabilities and its areas of failures be looked at candidly. Those of us who have worked with it as a modality know that it has many limitations and is not always a successful therapeutic agent, but the many times when it makes possible striking change and brings about almost miraculous healing, urge us to properly evaluate its limits and potentials and to set up criteria for its use.

The limitations of regression work fall into three areas: built-in realistic limitations, limitations brought by the patient, and those that must be laid on the doorstep of the therapist.

## Realistic Limitations

The problem the patient brings may not lie in a past life, and if it does not, regression work will be only an intellectual trip or an escape from looking at the here and now. For this reason, most regression therapists work first in the current life and only when that does not yield enough material look further back.

The lack in certain patients of sufficient strength to integrate insights is a limitation. Jue's experience is that borderline clients and other types with ego-deficit and object relations problems, though often in touch with their primary process and having easy access to past-life material, are handicapped by poor ego strength and find it difficult to make necessary changes. My own experience is somewhat similar: borderline patients tend to tap into a fluid conglomeration of past lives and cannot focus on any one long enough to make therapeutic work possible.

The third consideration, brought forward by Fiore, is that there are times when entities, people who have died and not quite made it to the next stage, interfere. I wish I could say that I have never found that to be true, but I have. It complicates the situation.

## Limitations Brought by the Patient

There are a number of limitations that patients bring with them. The first of these is the difficulty of getting into an altered state in such a way that past-life material can be contacted. Sometimes patients cannot fix on a past life. Images from various lives come and go, changing periods, changing characters, seemingly totally confused. At other times the patient is not able to get into any life at all and sees at best a series of unrelated images. More intensive preparation and gentler induction techniques sometimes help. Other patients are so ingrained in a static religious system that there is no openness to the unconscious. Jue found this to be true in his practice and has had success with this sort of patient by asking that a parable, or perhaps an allegory, be produced—moving within the theoretical framework of a conventional religious system often bypasses this sort of resistance.

Some patients need to control the regression. If the therapist goes along with the flow, usually it proceeds properly. One would expect that high-powered people would have especial difficulty in giving up conscious control, but this is not necessarily so. Many of these people walk with confident strides through their unconscious, though sometimes responding impatiently or a little rudely to a therapist's attempt at guidance. The people who are most afraid of losing control are those who perceive their unconscious as a time bomb and do not dare to take a chance on its being set off. They are the ones who are particularly afraid of hypnosis (and for whom other forms of induction into altered states may be preferable). Fiore thinks this often has to do with deaths under surgery in a previous lifetime. Dethlefsen finds a similar source of failure in the patient's not trusting the therapeutic process in a way that will allow unconscious material to emerge.

Woolger mentions the need for the body to be involved if the regression is to be meaningful. He feels that failure results when patients have had many lifetimes, such as those of monks or nuns, without contact with their bodies or their feelings and the therapist allows this dissociation to continue.

Energy patterns anchored in the etheric and emotional bodies need to be re-experienced in order to be released; without this abreaction therapeutic work will fail. Most therapists agree that lack of identification with the body experience can limit therapeutic effectiveness.

Traumatic situations of deep suffering and anger may block the regression process. When a patient moves into scenes of great anger that he dares not confront, he may wander off in thin threads of recall that say nothing pertinent, or he may blank out completely. For such a person modern techniques of getting in touch with anger, such as the Radix process, can be effective as a preliminary step.

Violent traumas in past-life deaths can also block recovery of memories. Snow reports Helen Wambach's research dealing with people who after three workshops had not contacted either past-life or pre-natal experiences.[1] When she worked with them privately, every one of those who could eventually progress back beyond childhood memories was immediately caught up in the violent emotional storm of a past-life death. Once this was faced and processed, none had further trouble with regression work.

The next group of limitations patients bring has to do with their expectations. First comes the expectation of speedy change, in short, a miracle—one or two sessions at most! This expectation has been built up by psychics and the currently popular channels, who tell people what their past lives have been, usually not very accurately. People who are in a hurry for change do not go deep enough to find the core of their problems and patterns. Dethlefsen feels that a significant source of failure lies in being content with the outer layers of experience, allowing the core of the complex, such as the experience of primal guilt and the power urges connected with it, to remain unresolved.

Next in the area of expectations is the anticipation, built up by movies and literature, of glamorous lifetimes. Ninety percent of any social group consists of peons, but few people hear that. Moreover, some of the saddest and most lamented lifetimes have come when in positions of power we failed in our responsibilities and sometimes led lives lonelier and less fulfilled than the peons. Often a patient, because he feels that he ought to produce a glamorous lifetime, resists a drab past life, fearing to be seen as unimportant.

Patients who are in "stuck positions" are not uncommon, as both Denning and Fiore point out. One stuck position that is frequently seen is that of the victim. So ingrained in some patients is this expectancy of being victimized that sometimes it is not possible to budge it. One of the most striking things that we learn from regression work is that we are not victims: we ourselves bring into this life our need to be a victim. Knowing this, the regression therapist struggles to help this victim pattern become changed, but sometimes he does not succeed.

The need to hold onto symptoms, not just of being victims but of problems in general, such as illnesses, may have too many secondary gains for the patient to be willing to give them up. Just as one cannot demand that anyone, such as a cancer patient, hang on to life because one wants him to, so one cannot demand that a patient give up a symptom or a stuck position until he is ready. Findeisen tells the sad story of a man whose regression successfully exposed the source of his exhibitionism, but he could not release it because he was not ready to give up the pleasure involved, and he finally ended up in prison.

Occasionally a patient who has not dealt adequately with the source of his dysfunction will move temporarily into a state where a symptom is remitted or there is apparently improved functioning. The patient's unconscious motivation is to please the therapist. In analytic circles this is known as a transference cure, and once contact with the therapist ceases, the symptom returns or the dysfunction becomes reestablished. The therapist needs to be cautious when a patient shows minimal involvement with his material, especially if he over-praises the effectiveness of past-life work or of his therapist.

The major contribution that a patient makes toward failure in regression work is his lack of willingness to take responsibility for his life, which may overlap with one or more of the other situations discussed. The patient may resist taking responsibility because he has a conviction that unless he is special, in this life and past ones, he won't be loved or doesn't deserve to live. He may resist responsibility because that would mean giving up symptoms or stances that bring secondary gain. He may feel that he is hopelessly inadequate and the only way he can survive is to make others responsible. Whatever the source of his unwillingness, it negates ability to make use of regression work to bring about change and growth.

## Sources of Failure Contributed by the Therapist

It goes without saying that training in regression work is necessary. Though this is limited in availability as yet, if there is the interest, training programs will be set up in the United States as they have been in the Netherlands. Regression therapy is more difficult than any other type of therapy and cannot be successful unless its techniques are built on the framework of sound psychotherapy. Regression work *is* a form of therapy: it is not a gimmick to be picked up in a weekend workshop and tried out on someone.

Therapist training includes an ability to evaluate the patient's potential for regression, as Pecci points out. Establishing clear goals is especially important to him and also to Noordegraaf, who find that failures occur when objectives are not clearly perceived.

Pecci assumes that a patient needs to be able to contact a deeper level of himself and even to have guides to protect and help, and he is not willing to risk a past-life exploration if these conditions are not met because failure is all too possible. He warns also about the risks of regressing fellow therapists when there is no clear therapeutic matrix in which goals can be established and where personality patterns can be explored. He explains the reason:

> Colleagues who have had a great deal of analytic work and self-exploration and whose therapists are not trained in regression work and often do not even consider it a modality, come to me asking for regression because they wish to deepen their understanding of themselves. I find it difficult to refuse them, since they often have no other recourse, but the results are not always satisfactory. Without knowing clearly the basic patterns they are working on, it is difficult to tune in intuitively to where they need to go and the way they can best be helped. After several regression sessions—and sometimes only one—there are times when neither of us has the feeling that we have worked on significant material. When the majority of our healing profession is trained to use regression techniques, it will not be so necessary for the few of us now doing regression work to risk such a situation.

One of the few times Pecci broke his own rule and worked with a fellow therapist (because the man had come from a distance), he found himself precipitated into a massive negative transference because the subject, who had actually come for the undeclared objective of finding out more details about a life of prominence, instead found himself confronted by a mass of shadow material. We all want to help our fellow therapists, but we have to decide what is appropriate.

Besides lack of adequate training, both in general psychotherapy and in regression work, there are other therapist deficits. Denning feels that a faulty philosophy of life, or, as I think, no philosophy at all, militates against success in regression therapy. Regression work leads inevitably to an expanded perception of oneself and the universe, and there needs to be some kind of matrix into which the experiences can be fitted. A superficial or negativistic attitude toward living on the part of the therapist is not a good bedfellow for regression work.

Failure can also result because the therapist is deficient in time management. He needs to structure time well, and if he is functioning within a 50-minute hour, he must allow enough time to work through an experience of the death, even though other areas must be dealt with in a later session. He needs to allow sufficient time, also, to help the patient emerge from the altered state and become adequately grounded. Failure to structure time appropriately can leave a patient feeling roughly handled and unsatisfied.

The same sensitivity that deals well with time also provides the humanistic considerations that Reynolds feels are so important for the success of regression work. The therapist is primarily a guide and needs to be supportive and non-judgmental about any material that is recovered. A more authoritarian or judgmental stance seriously inhibits the flow of remembering. Snow feels that at times even a supportive stance is not enough: the core vibrational energy patterns of therapist and patient may be too far apart to allow sufficient rapport for an effective regression. This is a surprising concept that needs to be considered.

Jue points out that the same countertransference aspects that affect more conventional therapy also affect regression work. Picking up the need of a patient to be dependent and responding to this out of one's own need to be nurturing is an example. This pattern may interfere with the patient's taking responsibility for himself and may continue his expectation that someone will make it come out all right. Another type of countertransference occurs when the therapist feels unspoken dissatisfaction with the material the patient is producing. In the sensitive altered state a patient often senses this dissatisfaction and easily transfers to the therapist the image of the critical parent he has known in the past. When transferences occur, the trained therapist must be aware of them and work through them with the patient, congruently conceding his own part in their occurrence if there is one. Otherwise, the patient will leave dissatisfied or angry, often not knowing why.

In conducting the actual regression the therapist may limit success of the process in several ways. Fiore and others observe that many patients cannot produce visual imagery. Requests as to what they are "seeing" bring no response. This error is easy to correct by changing one's questions to deal with *what is happening* and avoiding an emphasis on visual recovery.

Pacing material is another area where difficulties can arise. If the response of the patient seems stuck or slow, there are many questions and suggestions that can help the process along. Some patients need to take time to let impressions emerge, and being pushed may make them close up. Experience and sensitivity, as Hickman points out, are needed to handle the pacing of a session in a maximally helpful way. The therapist must keep his own enthusiasm for regression from pushing the patient faster than is comfortable for him.

In dealing with the material, there are several ways in which therapists are inadequate in the interventions that are needed for a successful conclusion. One frequent failure consists of missing the connections between a past life and the current life. Usually a pattern is highly visible, but sometimes it is not. This is not always the fault of the therapist. The patient may bring into the situation some of his own agenda, as has been discussed, and may not want a pattern to emerge, but there are many techniques for extracting such a pattern, and the therapist needs to know these and sense which is appropriate to use. Even if the pattern is perceived clearly, the therapist may fail to help the patient integrate his new understanding into his current life processes. In general, the more adequately trained a therapist is and the more experience he has had, the better he can help this integration to occur.

One area of resolution that is emerging as increasingly important is polarity. Therapists need to have the experience of unearthing and integrating the shadow (polarity) material in their own lives in order to help the patient perceive and deal with his own. If the patient cannot effect such an integration, the regression work will peter out. Denning and Findeisen are particularly concerned with anger as an aspect of the shadow. A patient who is left with a heavy residue of anger has a difficult time making use of insights from a regression.

Pecci stresses as an overall goal, working to obtain an increasingly comprehensive viewpoint that can change the meaning and importance of life experience. Most regression therapists agree with this transformational objective and try to find ways of implementing it. If this is not done, and especially if no pattern is uncovered, the patient is left with a handful of dust, memories that are discrete from his experience, all that remains of an hour or more that may have been pleasant but is more likely to have contained sadness and distress.

Jue reviews some of these sources of failure:

> Failures...bring a sense of humility to the therapeutic context and a realization that, at best, therapy is a collaboration, with tacit agreements and mutually held assumptions as to what direction one takes in the therapy process. To prevent failures, there is a need for greater appreciation of the importance of accepting clients as they are without setting unrealistic therapeutic goals, and to maintain a lead and pace approach in the therapeutic relationship. In that way, one focuses and gives more importance to process rather than to goals, even though it is recognized that the basic goal for therapy is toward personal integration.

# *Contributors*

*When I talk with you,*
*Whom am I addressing?*

    *The Inner Child,*
    *Seeking so hopefully for some sign that it is loved?*

    *Or the Teenager,*
    *Buttressed against an unfriendly world,*
    *Searching desperately for the Truth?*

    *Or is it the Adult Intellect,*
    *Struggling so hard to hold everything together?*

*Let me speak to your Soul*
*Wandering through space like a castaway,*
*Caught up in a psychophysiological trap*
*Created by eons of suffering,*

*The imprisoned Splendor*
*Of this remote planet.*

                                        *Ernest Pecci*

Chapter XI

# Ronald Wong Jue, Ph.D.

## *Biographical Data*

### Personal Background

The antecedents to my involvement with past-life therapy stem from early experiences of childhood where I maintained a strong sense of synchronicity about life. Many people appeared who provided key elements in addressing specific issues with which I was dealing. When I was 14, I read Yoganada's *Autobiography of a Yogi,* a book that made a strong impact on my life in affirming a world view proclaiming life as a pure expression of the Godhead governed by life cycles, universal laws, and principles. In college, when a roommate left a copy of the Katha Upanishads for me to read, the truths in these sixth- to eighth-century Hindu treatises resonated within me a deeper sense of self. Though these views were not in alignment with the expectations and values of my parents and peers, my bicultural upbringing provided a state and motivation for blending the teachings of the East and West.

I am a third generation Chinese-American, born in San Francisco and raised in the San Francisco Bay area. My parents had a Baptist orientation and strong feelings as to what I needed to do to succeed in the world. I went to California State University in San Jose and majored in the biological sciences, but I found momentary relief from Western Newtonian-Cartesian thinking in selecting elective courses in Eastern philosophy.

After I had graduated from college, I left the United States and went on an 18-month trip around the world, spending a great part of my time in India, Burma, Thailand, and Japan, where I met many teachers who validated my inner life and knowingness. Participating in Vipassana meditation in Burma and Thailand, and Zen meditation in Japan, helped me to develop an inner basis for understanding my projections and the workings of my inner world. When I came back to the United States, I still had difficultly integrating my experiences with the practicality of developing a profession, but eventually I decided to go into teaching.

After four years of teaching, I still felt restless. I applied for and received a Fulbright Teaching Fellowship to Indonesia, where I was assigned the development of a science program for an embassy school in Djakarta. While completing my fellowship assignment, I became involved with the spiritual tradition of the Indonesian culture, did a film study of the trance dancers of Bali, and studied the religious art of the culture. The experience became important to me in that it provided a deeper understanding of the transpersonal dimensions in reality. In all of these cultures I found that altered states function to affirm faith in a higher power and to re-establish ties to mankind's spiritual heritage in order to establish harmony within a society.

After one year abroad I returned to California and set a different direction for my life by majoring in clinical psychology. I felt that psychology could be the forum and context for bringing together my various interests in cultural anthropology, religious studies, and science. At the United States International University in San Diego I found a program that had a strong humanistic orientation where I was able to combine many of my interests.

After earning my doctorate degree in 1976 I accepted a position as director of a day treatment program for latency-aged children in Fullerton, California. This position became a crucible for understanding the process of transformation. In working with mentally disturbed children I found that I could apply my knowledge of altered states in training children to take control of their lives through inner discipline and the use of imagery. Within the context of the program I found ways of utilizing intuitive methods and altered states of consciousness to create change and move children toward establishing emotional integrity. Biofeedback, imagery techniques, and the basic principles of the martial arts became vehicles of change. In working with the families of these children I became aware of the prenatal conditions and early developmental factors that fostered various forms of childhood pathology. Awareness of the impact of early childhood experiences later led me to regression work with adults and hypnotherapy as a vehicle for tapping deeper layers of unconscious material and examining the internalized prenatal imagery that was operational within the patient. All of these became important preliminary components to my interest in past-life therapy.

These explorations of my psyche were a part of a journey on which I felt like Jason and the Argonauts looking for the Golden Fleece. As a result of the progression of images in my own therapy and of pushing forward the realms of exploration with patients, past-life images began to emerge.

Because I worked within a culture that does not embrace the notion of reincarnation or the legitimacy of past-life images, I knew that I had a choice, either of working with this type of material in isolation or of bringing it out for open inquiry. I chose the latter, and in the period between 1979 and 1980 I developed several conferences on past-life therapy at the University of California in Irvine and San Diego. The purpose in holding them at universities was to create an open forum for examining and studying these experiences. From these conferences a group of interested individuals came together and created the Association for Past-Life Research and Therapy (APRT).

Because of my experience with meditation and altered states, I have been interested not only in integrating Eastern conceptual frameworks into traditional psychotherapy, but also in applying various trance and altered states. Due to my interest in the efficacy of trance states to create change and transformation in therapy, I began looking at various shamanic traditions in a generic manner. In my approach to reincarnation I have avoided the Western tradition that overstresses ego-enhancing aspects of past-life recall. I see the doctrine of reincarnation within the context of self-discovery and the illumination of the present as the "Eternal Now."

About seven years ago I started actively doing past-life therapy because it seemed to me the logical next step in the evolution of therapy. The process just evolved for me, as I think it has for many therapists. In directing a patient to go back to the event that was responsible for a symptom or attitude or pattern of life, often he would automatically go back to another lifetime, even when that had not been my intention. Since I do not believe that past-life exploration is the primary focus of therapy, I use it only in special cases where a patient needs to see the broader pattern or matrix of what is happening currently. Because life scripts and problems can be tapped on many different levels, an initial exploration of the present is my choice of focus; and at any rate, a thorough consideration of what is going on in this lifetime always precedes any past-life work.

## *Theory*

### Philosophical Hypotheses

Even though I have been instrumental in establishing APRT, I have yet to identify myself as a past-life therapist. My early training in the sciences has resulted in my remaining extremely pragmatic, even while working with altered states. I maintain a healthy skepticism, especially in the area of interpretation. Working with past-life images provides an epistomological challenge in that what comes up from the psyche can be interpreted by many conceptual models. For example, I found Rupert Sheldrake's concept of morphic resonance,[1] David Bohm's "implicate order,"[2] and Karl Pribram's holographic hypothesis[3] helpful in conceptualizing the dynamics of the psyche within the past-life therapy context.

My philosophical assumptions have emerged both from my own life experiences and from my work with patients. When I started to work with past-life scenarios, I had no particular philosophic assumptions to guide me, but as certain scenarios repeated themselves with patients during their self-exploration, I began to see patterns that had common features. However, as one examines past-life material, I believe it is extremely important that a person involved with such material be grounded in solid therapeutic work; otherwise one can easily participate in a *folie a deux* whereby a patient and a therapist participate and support mutual avoidance and delusions.

The hypotheses that have emerged from my therapeutic experience include the following:

1. We are multi-level conscious beings with many levels of awareness, ego-states, and past-life scenarios actively at play at any given moment in time.[4] Even though the process of exploring past-life patterns is linear, the patterns from another perspective can be seen as exerting concurrent influence upon present behavior.

2. The physical, mental, emotional, and spiritual levels are often not in harmony or aligned with each other, and states of disequilibrium and disease are created.

3. We have an innate drive or instinct toward wholeness, integration, and equilibrium. There are unconscious patterns that set up a morphic resonance so that whatever is necessary for integration is brought into our lives. From this perspective, life itself is holotropic, that is, moving us toward wholeness.

4. Pain and disharmony focus our attention on the non-aligned aspects of our psyche so that we are eventually forced to create a homeostatic balance, whether it be pathological or healthy. On a spiritual level, movement is toward karmic homeostasis.

5. Past-life therapy enables a therapist to help a patient explore deeper parts of the psyche. The process allows a patient to understand his inner myth and the attitudinal matrix that unconsciously influences his emotional, physical, and motivational system.

6. Because these life scripts, problems, and life-type patterns are replicated on many developmental levels, a therapist can approach the resolution of these patterns in many ways and at different levels, such as in current life patterns, or in the peri- or prenatal experience, or in past-life experiences.[5]

7. Past-life therapy's concern is not only with the alleviation of symptoms but also with the dynamics and attitudes that support the symptoms. Often mental, emotional, and physical levels all need to be examined for complete symptom relief.

8. Past-life therapy helps us to understand more profoundly the mind-body-spirit connection and how we, as evolving souls, are responsible for creating our universe (and patterns) for our own spiritual growth.

9. The primary aim of past-life therapy is to help the individual to live a more integrated life style, to live in the here and now, to realize his connection to the universe and to participate in the creative process that gives meaning to each moment of awareness.

## Therapeutic Assumptions

1. Presenting problems, symptoms, and situations are not what they appear. Problems often have metaphorical, symbolic, or compensatory significance related to more primary or core issues facing a patient.[6]

2. Insight does not necessarily bring change on all levels. Symptoms are often expressed in a matrix of emotional and physical patterns that do not necessarily influence change on all levels. For example, a person with an obesity problem can come to an understanding of the dynamics of an overweight problem or to a removal of the emotional factors behind overeating, and yet not lose any weight. The patient would have to be guided through some type of behavioral therapy for weight loss or for a change in lifestyle.

3. Past-life patterns are utilized to understand more deeply and broadly the dynamics of existing problems and situations. They are part of the "implicate order" behind the "explicate order" that David Bohm addresses.[7] They also allow the patient to become aware of unconscious motivational factors behind the choices he makes in his everyday life.

4. Resistances are reactive patterns and boundaries that develop to maintain a certain integrity to the life scenario that the person is playing out. Resistances are to be examined within the context of secondary gains and can also occur within past-life patterns. Selective awareness occurs on all levels in altered states and a skilled therapist needs to lead and pace

with questions in order to understand the underlying patterns of emotional resistances and reinforcements.

5. Physical, emotional, and mental patterns, whether pathological or healthy, are functional for the development of the individual. All patterns work within a unified field of consciousness and are part and parcel of the entire journey that a patient takes in his spiritual development.

6. In the past-life therapy process, three stages appear to unfold:[8]

**Stage I: Identification.**

Here the patient relegates control to his own unconscious process so that he can begin to experience an internal scenario, a mythic journey, an identification figure perceived as a personal projection or sub-personality.

**Stage II: Disidentification.**

Nothing is what it appears to be. Re-living a past-life experience is like going into the backstage room of a theater where the player removes or puts on the accoutrements of the role. In this special room one realizes his/her true nature as distinguished from the role being played. It is this realization that is at the heart of the disidentification process.

**Stage III: Transformation.**

Life takes on a different perspective as the patient becomes both a participant and a witness to life processes. Seeing life as holotropic, a patient begins to shift attitudes and perceptions regarding past traumas and events, psychological scripts, particular parents, and attraction or repulsion for certain individuals as necessary factors for growth. Past-life scripts can be rewritten or released, depending on the choice of the patient.

7. There is a transcendent or noetic function within the psychological makeup of the individual that knows the origin of the problems and the resolution of those problems. This function can be activated by the therapist to assist in the development of self-awareness and resolution.

8. There are usually paranormal aspects to a problem.[9] As one sees the operation of a patient's behavioral and emotional patterns working within a field of other individuals in that patient's life, one becomes increasingly aware of transpsychic communication between the individuals. The phenomenon of transpsychic communication is most evident in the early developmental period between a child and his parents, a period that provides the foundation and imprint for the later development of a person's life script.[10]

9. Unconscious projections and processes on the part of the therapist play an important role in the therapeutic context and affect the responses of the patient. Transference and counter-transference take on greater significance since a patient often becomes highly sensitive to the issues of a therapist in an altered state.[11]

## Indications and Contraindications for Use

I do not consider the primary concern of any therapy to be only the alleviation of symptoms. Far more important is an examination of the dynamics and attitudes that support the symptoms, and this must be explored on physical, emotional, and mental levels in order to encourage symptom relief. Simply pinpointing the origin of a symptom in a past life and re-living it does not necessarily bring about complete change. Therefore, I do not undertake regression therapy with patients whose primary motivation is the alleviating of a symptom without working on the underlying matrix. It goes without saying that I can see no point at all in going into a past life merely as an interesting "trip."

Since the primary goal of any therapy is to help the individual live more fully in the here and now and realize increasingly his connection to the universe, regression work seems beneficial primarily to patients who understand and endorse this goal and wish to deepen and expand understanding of basic patterns in order that they may participate more fully in the creative process of living. It is not necessary for them to endorse a conscious spiritual goal, but some concept of their involvement in the universe and of the fact that they are playing out a pattern in their lives that has deep roots, is necessary if the deepest value is to be derived from regression work. For such people there are no contraindications. But, also, there is no particular preference as to the level on which a problem or pattern will be explored.

Past-life therapy is contraindicated as an escape or denial system of current realities. It is contraindicated for individuals who exhibit poor ego structure and who are not able to integrate symbolic material and create change in their lives. This includes borderline personalities.

# Induction

## Preparation

In my patients the preparation consists of all that is included in the beginning phase of therapy. This is usually not undertaken with the goal of past-life work in mind but as the thoughtful initial work on whatever problems the patient has brought. Interview and dialogue allow the therapist to understand the dynamics of various patterns that support the presenting complaint or symptom. The patterns are often supported and replicated in various areas and developmental periods of a patient's life. As a general therapeutic procedure these various periods are explored, including any circumstances known in the pre- and peri-natal periods, in the earliest memories and traumas, and in the self-image in the socialization period around puberty.

It is important to have profiles of the parents and especially of the injunctions and non-verbal messages they project onto the patient. Attitudes in the areas of sex, power, money, success, dependency and independence need thorough exploration. Gradually interpersonal patterns and defensive reactions emerge, as well as feelings regarding the levels of intimacy with the same and opposite sex, and these can be examined as far as possible on a conscious level.

It is important to know the history of any physical problems, and this history includes not only so-called objective "facts" but, even more importantly, attitudes toward these problems. In general, one of the things I want to find out is what is the script and the attitude that supports any problem. One may get the script, "I don't know," "I was so victimized," "People keep on discounting me," "I just can't make it," or "Poor me." These are the phrases that the patient repeats over and over again and that supply key words to use in an induction into a past life where they originated or where they have been repeated.

In considering problems that are brought into therapy, there are some basic truisms to help one become aware of the patterns involved. The first is that *the answer lies within the problem.* Examination of how and why the patient has created the problem reveals the true nature of the problem, and he can realize that the answer is often not outside the problem. Thus, the patient realizes that the symptom with which he comes in is not the real problem, and that situations are not what they appear. Often when, at the close of therapy, I take the first day's notes and see how the problem was stated, the issue that we have really dealt with is quite different. It is later obvious that there are all sorts of secondary gains and consequences covering up the real issues.

The above leads to a second truism, that *opposites are inherent in the situation.* For every victim I will find a persecutor and for every persecutor, a victim. I will always find the opposites emerging from past-life regression material, and that provides a guideline and a framework for what I want to look for. The battered were batterers and the person with an eating disorder has not only starved but has starved others.

The third truism is: *in order to see, you must not look.* If one does, one will see only with preconceptions. You have to allow your deep intuitive knowing self to determine the authenticity of any material. That is true of patients, also. They have to let images and lives emerge from their own energy and unconscious matrix. Past lives can be fabricated, too, and not necessarily unconsciously. The more past-life material resembles a dream, the more likely it is to be valid. If the theme of the past life has no relevancy to where the patient is, its reality is to be questioned. This process of letting the unconscious emerge without restraint facilitates work both on the current life process and past-life patterns.

Finally, in the preparation it is important to observe one's own attitude toward the patient. Helen Wambach said, "When your patients come into your office, the first thing they want to know is, 'Do you love me?'" Acceptance and empathic listening are very important factors in allowing the patient to disclose himself. The depth of exploration with patients seems to correlate with the degree of unconditional regard one gives. Working with altered states, patients develop a highly intuitive degree of sensing the feelings of the therapist. If a therapist does not examine his own fears and internal blind spots, these factors will create an emotional impasse between therapist and patient.

## Induction Techniques

I have three major approaches for getting into past lives, but there are certain processes that precede all of these inductions. In order to move a patient into an altered state, some relaxation process is in order. How deep or extensive this is depends on the situation with the specific patient. Some need a great deal of relaxation in order to get into an altered state and others are there almost without more preparation than an exploration of their feelings and attitudes. Sometimes I simply have the patient image each part of his body becoming relaxed, beginning with the feet. Most of the hypnotic techniques I use are Ericksonian. In general I focus on body awareness and this leads into a linguistic approach. Sometimes I use the image of a ball of light over the head opening up and erasing all tension. This is an especially effective image when I am using the third, the transcendental approach.

Throughout the regression there are techniques and approaches that will facilitate recovery of memories and will help to deepen understanding of them. In the first place, it is important that power be given to the patient to be in control of his altered state. Using the key words that have been identified as pertinent and repeating them where appropriate helps deepen the state. It is also helpful to remind the patient frequently that his Higher Self or Inner Mind knows the answers, knows where he needs to go. The patient can also be asked to focus on his body or his problems, such as needing to be loved. Give permission to the patient to go beyond conventional boundaries of the mind.

## *Extended Induction with Bodily Relaxation*

Preparatory to the induction, structure a safe healing place with the patient.

*Take a deep breath. I want you now just to let your mind's eye go to your body and become aware of where your feet are and your ankles, coming up to your calves. As you become more aware of your body just release all the tension you have brought into this room so that you feel relaxed and released, releasing all tension and relaxing at the same time.*

*Bring your awareness up to your knees, your thighs, be aware of your seat. Even notice that you can become aware of the texture of the cushions beneath your body, of your lower back, your upper back. Be aware of your limbs and how your arms are flared out. Be aware of your upper arms, your elbows, your hands, even the texture of the cushion beneath your hands and fingers, so that at each moment of time when you hear my voice you feel yourself drifting deeper and deeper into relaxation.*

*Allow another part of you now to emerge, bringing those images, those memories you need to look at in order to understand why it is in this lifetime that (describe problem).*

*Now become aware of your breath and the moving up and down of your diaphragm and chest. Just allow your body to breathe for you now. It's as though in just watching your body you don't have to do anything, exercise any conscious control. Each breath takes you deeper and deeper into a state of relaxation. Allow yourself, give yourself permission now to simply let go, to simply be.*

*Be aware of the back of your neck, the back of your head, the top of your head, and the band around your forehead, so that as you increase the awareness of your body you also increase the depth of your relaxation with each moment, with each word. Become aware of your eyes. If there is any tension around your eyes, around your forehead, just simply let it go now with awareness.*

*Now become aware of the movement of air in and out of your nostrils. Feel yourself breathing in calm, breathing out tension. In and out. In and out. Breathing in the calm of the universe, breathing out tension. Just allow your body to come to its natural state. Just simply be. Be here now. Be relaxed.*

*Be in touch with your feelings, beginning to be in touch with the part of you that you need to look at. Because there is a part of you that really yearns for understanding, for reconciliation, for a broadening of awareness of why it is that perhaps on another level you (state problem).*

*Now become aware of your mouth, of your chin and jaws, and if there is any tension there, just simply let go. Now become aware of your ears. And then just gently scan your body from the top of your head all the way down.*

*And now that you've increased the awareness of yourself, allow yourself to deepen the state of relaxation by going into your healing place (describe the situation set up earlier in the interview). Allow yourself to be there and allow all your senses to be open to all the things there, looking around, being aware of the textures and colors of the flora around you, even being aware of the smells, the fragrances that seem to permeate this special place. So with every breath you take, with every sensing of this place, you seem to feel yourself going deeper and deeper, feeling the ground under your feet, so that with every step you take you release more and more of your bodily tension.*

*You even begin now to look around. You're noticing whether it's warm, or cool. Is the sun shining on your head? Be in touch with that. Put yourself in a day where the sun is shining. You can feel the sun coming down over your body, penetrating your skin to the very bone, releasing all tension, feeling the warmth, the nurturance, the comfort of being in this place so that as you walk through this place you become more and more aware of being relaxed. What sounds are in this place? Even the sounds seem to add that deep sense of calmness that is coming over you. Become aware of the sounds, the insects, the birds, the wind. Become aware of these factors. They seem to be added to the feelings and the fragrances so that you are now beginning to let your imagination take over as if you were really there. Release all the tension in your body now, allowing you to get into the qualities that are inherent in this place that communicates to you a sense of deep peace and deep relaxation.*

*You will be noticing your breath now and your breathing is becoming more and more calm. You are breathing more slowly now as you begin to release all the tension.*

*Again see yourself walking through that special place, and as you walk you begin to see a shift now, a shift of seeing. It's almost as if as you walk through this place you begin to walk through another dimension of space and time. Your unconscious mind is now allowing you to go beyond this place, to know that beyond this place is another place, is a time that you were once familiar with. In it is the answer to the question we ask about (same problem). Go back now. Where is the energy coming from?...*

## Deepening and Supportive Techniques

Patients need to be reassured that past lives do not emerge like television shows. Encourage any small impression to be reported and then allow the past-life events to unfold, using the various sense modalities. Begin with an open question: Where are you? What are you experiencing? Then ask questions to develop the context of the experience: How? where? and what? (How old are you? What does your father do? What is your area called now? How long have you been ill?) Have the patient describe the experience in the present tense. Do not use the "why" question, as it shifts the patient into an analytic mode of experience. It is only appropriate if the question directs the patient to find the answer within the context of his experience.

After developing the context, formulate questions in order to understand the dynamics of what is happening. Once the patient finds the experience that anchors his feelings and attitudes, it is then important to ask questions that allow understanding of the perceptions, feelings, and attitudes associated with that anchor. Then move the patient forward or backward in time in order to understand the context of the past-life scenario, or to a significant event that will allow better understanding of the problem or issue. "Go to the scene or event that you need to examine in order to understand. Move ahead in time to see what consequences develop from that decision or behavior." Focus on the antecedents and on the physical, emotional, and decisional consequences of the event.

Event—>Subjective interpretation—>Conflict—>Decision made in order to resolve conflict—>Script

It is important to note that it is not the event that creates the problem but the decisions and interpretation of the event. Within every event a subjective interpretation follows. From the interpretation comes a conflict of a sort, and then, because of the conflict or the dissonance, there is an ego decision that becomes the posture that the person takes. For example, an event could be an absent father. An interpretation might be that men are not there when you need them. The ego or survival decision that follows might be, in order to not feel vulnerable, never trust a man to support your emotional needs.

e.g. (Event) Father goes to war—> (Interpretation) Men are not there when you need them—> (Conflict) Men will abandon you—> (Decision) I will work toward emotional independence and never allow myself to depend on a man for emotional support—> (Script) Men are never there for you.

The dynamic phase of the regression manifests when, through a dialogue with the patient, the therapist helps him to focus more clearly on these perceptual and emotional issues. By empathically identifying with the characters in regression, the patient begins to understand how the psyche draws from the world the necessary situations, persons, and props to develop the drama for its own personal spiritual growth. This is the state of identification, and its success can be measured by the ability of the patient to see the past-life experiences as a metaphor for the present life and to see how past-life experiences act as matrices holding the energy patterns of our life scenarios, that are repeatedly being played out.

## *Processing*

### Psychotherapeutic and Transformational Techniques

Once the patient is identified with the roles he has played, the next stage, where therapy and healing and transformation can take place, is one where he goes through a process of dis-identification in order to comprehend the patterns that the patient has set up and the lessons he has chosen to learn. Nothing is what it appears to be. Life mirrors paradoxes and other levels of meaning. A patient comes to the paradoxical realization that "I'm all that I experience and yet I'm not that, either." Seeing the function of various roles in the spiritual development of one's being or soul, a person begins to release the investment of energy into rigid roles. He begins to free himself to a point where he can play with that energy, not taking himself so seriously. The patient can begin to choose whether or not he wants to articulate that role. Also he begins to feel the freedom to choose and to integrate the energy with other parts of himself.

How can the therapist facilitate this process of dis-identification? There are a number of steps, and often it takes a long time. It is helpful, and sometimes necessary, to go to antecedent lifetimes in order to understand the decision-making process. For instance, one may suggest, "Go back and see why you made this decision, to choose a mother who is unloving. What did you do to her in the past? Like a bridge, go back to another time when you knew your mother." It is necessary to go back and forth between the lifetime experiences in order to understand the pattern of cause and effect. The therapist needs to help the patient see the aspects of past lives that are mirrored in this present one. Why did he need to bring that feeling into this lifetime? How does this lifetime serve the experiences of the past? What is the patient hanging onto in crossing over into this life? It is extremely important for the patient to see that he has set the stage and at some time made a decision that he needed to experience what he, in this lifetime, is now experiencing. When the patient can see what is being examined as functional for his spiritual growth and that his interpretations are all ego, all self, all narrow, and often inappropriate and unnecessary, when the patient can get to the event and see it for what it is, then he can bring in other dimensions and see what happened and its happening as a spiritual event. Then it becomes a lesson and the whole experience becomes transformative.

Techniques that are helpful, depending on the receptivity of the patient, are to suggest that a puzzling situation be presented to a Guide, or to the Inner Mind or the Higher Self, for understanding. But it is going through the death process that is most productive of insight. The patient should be encouraged to see the circumstances of his death and particularly to identify his last conscious thought, which, because it occurs in a heightened state of consciousness, often becomes a script for future lifetimes. The patient then goes through the death process, sees where he is in relation to the body he has left behind, and reviews his whole life. The patient should particularly identify the lesson or lessons he learned in past lifetimes and their effect on the current lifetime. Whenever possible memories should be healed with a transformational technique, such as setting a stage for forgiveness. Calling on guides to help understand the process of other personalities in a past life can facilitate forgiveness. The death process acts as a bridge to relate various aspects of the past-life experience in order to reframe the present lifetime experience. Past-life experiences need to be tied to the present time in order for changes to take place as the result of the reframing.

In the reframing process, painful and unwanted experiences can be recast as valuable and potentially useful lessons. To see pain as a vehicle for learning is a different way of viewing and confronting a painful situation. In this way a situation considered a liability can be perceived as an asset. It is also valuable to identify characters and events occurring in past lifetimes as isomorphic or equivalent with those individuals and events that characterize the present life situation or problem.

## Integration into the Total Psychotherapeutic Process

The freedom, lightness of spirit, and process of dis-identification achieved in a competent past-life exploration leads to a further process of transformation. This is not a one-time burst of insight but a continuing recontextualizing of the patient's life. That life is now perceived from a different perspective and a different realm of consciousness. The patient begins to re-vision his personal life, his psychological scripts, how he perceives his parents, how he has been attracted to or repulsed by certain individuals. During this stage the therapist takes the opportunity to guide the patient through his past-life experiences in retrospect in order to bring him to an awareness of the necessity of that life's experiences in relation to his personal spiritual growth. Past-life scripts are rewritten and worked through, and in that change of patterning the present life becomes transformed. Released from the past unworkable patterns, the patient becomes more attuned to living in the present and seeing the importance and meaning of what is in his world.

When a patient begins to understand his own past-life scenarios, his own inner stories and his own inner life, he begins to understand his existing scenarios. When that happens, the world becomes his teacher. Relationships carry a deeper meaning when it is realized that all relations are opportunities for growth. Seeing life as moving toward wholeness reinforces the shift in attitudes and perceptions regarding past-life traumas and events and facilitates a change in psychological scripts.

One salient characteristic of this stage is that patients begin to experience more synchronisitic events in their lives. There are no rational explanations for these situations in which a person has a thought, intuition, or inner psychological state that coincides with an event, but these events are intuitively experienced as significant. In this transformational stage patients often also exhibit a greater sense of self-esteem and worthiness. Their inner life increases in value and becomes a gyroscopic beacon for personal growth and direction. The patient begins to see more deeply the significance of life and its evolutionary process. It is as if past-life therapy affords patients an opportunity to remove the spiritual cataracts that have prevented them from perceiving the unitary nature of life.

## Failures

I would consider looking at failure within the context of whether or not relevancy of past-life material is established for the patient and of whether or not a patient can integrate and utilize the material for personal change. Borderline patients and other types with ego-deficit and object-relations problems often present a paradoxical dilemma. They are often very much in touch with their primary processes and can easily gain access to past-life material, but with poor ego strength they find it difficult to make the necessary changes. Such a case can be exemplified by a person who can easily gain insight into an overeating problem but finds it difficult to exercise discipline and change of dietary habits to lose the necessary weight.

Rather than focus on the cases that seemingly fail, I think that it is important to look at the elements that seem to foster failure in utilizing past-life material. One personality element that creates resistance and possible failure is the need by the patient to control the situation where that control is basically cognitive in nature. Such patients usually are so beset by anxiety and the need for control that they find it difficult to enter into a light trance or to allow imagery material to take prominence in their internal experience. Another factor that strengthens this tendency is the need to be attached to or to hold onto certain perceptions and feelings because of secondary gain.

Fear of change, of intimacy, and of taking responsibility for one's own life can also foster failure. When one becomes identified with a victimized position that generates sympathy and rallies attention from the outside world, there is general reluctance to give up that posture. The intimacy that results from being seen for what and who one is can also be highly threatening. Fearing judgment and experiencing overwhelming shame and guilt can also be inhibiting factors to the success of the past-life therapy process. Individuals may have to avoid responsibility for fear of the implications that responsibility brings.

Failures that result from the above emotional elements bring a sense of humility to the therapeutic context and a realization that, at best, therapy is a collaboration, with tacit agreements and mutually held assumptions as to what direction one takes in the therapy process. To prevent failures, there is a need for greater appreciation of the importance of therapists accepting patients as they are without setting unrealistic therapeutic goals, and to maintain a lead and pace approach in the therapeutic relationship. In that way, one focuses on and gives more importance to process rather than to goals, even though it is recognized that the basic goal for therapy is to move toward personal integration.

A therapist also needs to look at the counter-tranference issues, the inner projections, feelings, and expectations that are brought to the therapeutic relationship. Failure can be an indication of unresolved counter-transference issues interfering with the therapeutic relationship. Also, the need to have a past-life regression occur can exert undue pressure on a patient. In an altered state, patients are usually highly sensitized to these issues and if they feel threatened by the unresolved issues or expectations of a therapist, they will withhold and resist surrendering to the process.

# Cases

## Reframing

Of the transformational tools used in past-life therapy, reframing is one of the most powerful. It was first described by Bandler and Grinder in their 1979 book *Frogs into Princes*, where the focus of reframing is either to separate the intention behind a specific set of symptoms and to reframe that intention in a more beneficial pattern, or to reframe an inappropriate behavior pattern so that it occurs in a useful context. Within the past-life therapy context, reframing is broader than the definition given by Bandler and Grinder. Besides intention and inappropriate behavior patterns, many basic life patterns, such as relationships, talents, handicaps and physical illnesses can be reframed within a past-life scenario in order to provide a different and meaningful perspective to a patient. Such a perspective can not only offer insight into a situation but can allow a patient to have cathartic release and freedom from self-defeating patterns. Thus, reframing is the act of changing a frame by which a person perceives and experiences events in order to change the meaning. When the meaning of an event changes, the patient's behaviors and responses also change.

### Case 1. Reframing an Intense Mother-Child Bonding

Dawn was a professional woman, concerned because she was in her forties and had never had a loving and supportive relationship. Her experiences with men had turned out to be toxic and frustrating. She had felt a need for a child to complete her experience of being a woman, and five years before she had chosen to have a baby, even though she had to support and care for him alone. Though the experience was satisfying and fulfilling, she longed for someone to love, someone with whom to share the child, and she retained a nagging feeling that somehow she had failed as a woman. She also came under criticism because of her extremely close bonding with her son. She had had other regressions and in each of them she had found herself alone. This aloneness was repeated in the present regression when she moved from the garden setting she had chosen as her special place and which had been used for the induction into another lifetime.

> T: *Your unconscious mind is now allowing you to go beyond this garden, to know that beyond this garden is a place, a time, that you were once*

familiar with. Why is it that you have not made any significant relationships with the opposite sex during this lifetime? Where is the energy coming from? Why has that energy been reinforced throughout this lifetime. Go on back now.

P: The only place I'm getting to is sort of autumn, almost winter, by a forest, not in a forest but alongside one. That's all I see at the moment, not me but the place and the time of year and the wind is blowing.

T: Is this a forest you are familiar with?

P: No, I think it's someplace in the past—Europe or farther east.

T: I want you to focus on that. As you begin to focus on the forest, you can allow the nature of the forest to deepen your experience. Allow your mind to open up and develop the context of this forest scene and whether this is the place that you should look at in terms of understanding the lack of positive and loving experiences. Allow yourself to move either forward or backward in time in the scene into significant events connected with this lifetime.

P: I just see it large and in more detail but it's still the same.

T: Continue to look, and while you look, are you there somewhere? Is there a relationship between your sense of intensity and this forest?

P: I don't see any. I just sense me looking.

T: Is there a path through the forest?

P: I see now one of those little Nordic kind of horses that are smaller than ponies. They're wooly. Nobody's with it but I don't think it's wild.

T: Do you have the feeling this horse belongs somewhere to someone?

P: I have some connection to it.

T: See if you can allow this horse to lead you to its own home or to its connections.

P: I just see its carcass and maggots eating it.

T: What kind of feeling does that bring up?

P: (Crying.) Sadness.

T: Is there a feeling, that this pony is yours?

P: It was mine, yes. He was sold. He wasn't mine anymore.

Dawn then recovered earlier years in that lifetime when her parents were killed and she was taken to live with a rather silent and uncommunicative man and woman. The only relationship she had was with her little horse.

T: What's the special relationship you have with the horse?

P: It's just that it's my friend. My only friend.

T: What do you do with this horse?

P: Go into the woods, walk with it. It's more like a dog—no saddle or bridle.

T: How are you experiencing yourself in that family context? I want you to look. Just be very much in touch with your feelings and also the relationship between yourself and this family and yourself and this horse.

*See yourself as moving into scenes that will help you illuminate the nature of this relationship.*

Dawn described her feeling of isolation. She felt no love and no hate. She did her share of chores so she was not a burden. She was very connected with nature, with the woods and hills and seasons, as well as with the horse. The man went out in the woods one day and didn't return.

T: I want you to move forward in time and see what it is between you and this horse that deepens the relationship.
P: Just the joy of being together.
T: There's a deep sense of communication, isn't there?
P: Yes, I feel like we're soul partners. (Sobs.)
T: Is there connection just with the horse or with the things around you?
P: Yes, with the woods and the wild animals, even though we don't get too close. But they're not afraid of me either.

Dawn moved ahead and saw that one day while she was away, the woman, hard up for money, sold the horse. Sometime after that Dawn was swimming in a river and was caught in a bad current. She made no effort to save herself and was drowned.

T: Go to the time that led to your death. What is the feeling in your body? What are you experiencing, now that you have lost your good friend?
P: It was shortly after I found his carcass. I think he had been abused...to death. Nature wasn't enough to make me want to hang around. I can see what the work of that life was now. I knew there was something, but I wasn't focused on it. I couldn't see it and I felt I didn't want to try anymore.
T: So you just sort of resigned...or gave up.
P: I gave up. I didn't do it thoughtfully. I was just swimming in the river. I knew that the middle was very dangerous and I didn't really care that it was. It was sort of like Russian roulette. I had to see what happened and it was too strong for me and carried me over some rocks. I guess I hit my head.
T: And when you see yourself in that river and hit on the head, what are your feelings and the last thoughts prior to your becoming unconscious?
P: Maybe next time it will be clearer. My purpose.
T: Maybe next time it will become clearer. Any other feelings here?
P: Just sadness.
T: What does the sadness say?
P: It's as though I lost so much but I did okay as long as I had the horse. Even though I'd lost my parents. But that was too much. And even loving nature wasn't enough to sustain me.
T: I'm going to share a feeling I have here and I want to see if you resonate with it. The feeling is that you made a decision that there is "really no one

> there to help and support and take care of me." Or, "I can never really trust in having someone take care of me."
>
> P: That's definitely so.
>
> T: And when I can't find anyone to take care of me, the places where I find solace are not really ever enough. You can't depend on life to be there for you because other parts of life like that forest can be taken away from you.
>
> P: Even the city takes nature away.
>
> T: The city takes nature away. If you look back, with these feelings we've just explored see how that relates to where you are now, how it relates to your relationship with people, finding a significant relationship.
>
> P: I see it's related to the pattern. It seems like once again I've done what I've done in a lot of regressions—I've gotten to a very lonely life. I don't get lives with relationships.
>
> T: Let's go back. What you're saying is that in this life now and in that life people are never there for you. You can never really depend on people to be there for you, and if one lives life, one must almost live it alone. Is that the sense?
>
> P: Yes.
>
> T: I want you now to allow your Higher Mind to go deeper. Find out where, upon what basis you had to have this kind of lifetime of non-dependence on other people to be really supportive of where you are. I want you to move now to a lifetime responsible for this decision or this experience. I'm going to count back from 10 to one. When I reach one you'll find yourself in that lifetime.
>
> P: I think I know where it is.
>
> T: Already? I don't have to count? What is coming up for you?
>
> P: It's Egypt.

Dawn told the story of how she had been betrothed to a cousin almost from birth. They grew up together and developed feelings of attachment and love that blossomed into strong sexual feelings in adolescence. They took it for granted they would be married, but suddenly, overnight, when she was 16, she was sent away to become a priestess in the temple. She was given no explanation and in thrusting around for an explanation she decided the young man she loved had betrayed her. Pervasive anger at him covered over the former feelings of love.

> T: I want you to go back and look at that situation and see the circumstances of that love and also the change of plans. I want you to go to that scene where you decided that somehow he had betrayed you and I want you to see if that really was the case. There was his energy in loving you and feeling very much in touch with you and having a great deal of joy in expressing and experiencing his and yours both, both your energies. I want you just to see another scene now...

Dawn very easily went into such a scene and realized that her father owed something and had his choice between giving his daughter to the temple or having his entire family killed.

> P: To accompany whoever it was who had just died. Either our whole family went with him (died) or I went as a priestess.
> T: You became the sacrificial one.
> P: Yes. And I never saw or heard from this boy or his family again. I knew nothing about them. But now I'm seeing that he killed himself. (Deep crying.)
> T: Because he really loved you, too, didn't he? He felt the loss.
> P: (Crying.) He took poison.
> T: Uh huh. It seems almost as though both of you became victims of filial duty here.
> P: (Deep crying.) I don't know why I felt his family had done it, because I see now it wasn't so.
> T: Seeing it now as it is, where is that energy, that anger? Do you feel that you're releasing it, now that you've seen this as it really is, that there was no one who really wanted to reject you.
> P: I feel the anger at the religious power that things could be done like that.

Dawn went ahead in that life and saw that she grieved for a few years and then competently took up her duties as a priestess, which were connected with moon worship. She became the wise woman of the temple, one to whom people came for knowledge. When she was quite old she just stopped eating and let herself die.

> T: What are your last thoughts and feelings just before your spirit passes from your body?
> P: They're sort of double. One is that I've done a good job at what I was supposed to, what it appears I was supposed to do. And another was that something was totally unfinished. With the relationship I feel the pain a little bit again that I had felt on that last night of the year when I was 16.
> T: So that on your departure there's really the feeling on one level of satisfaction but on another level there are unresolved feelings.
> P: Yes. I both succeeded and didn't succeed. I succeeded in that I allowed myself to bend to the purpose that they gave me and flow with the wind.
> T: I have a feeling that there's more here. I want you to take this life and see yourself moving out of it and into a space where you can look and view that entire life and compare it to where you are now and see how the energies and the unresolved relationship had an effect upon the decisions you have made in this lifetime. What do you see? Take a moment and see yourself now reviewing that entire scenario and look at what you're unfolding right now. What is it that you see?
> P: Somehow it seems—I don't know—that I had some reparative work to do in having my son, that I cannot have my son and have a relationship, too.

> *That's the feeling that I have, that I've chosen in this lifetime to do something with my son.*
> T: *With your son. Do you feel any of your son's energy from that lifetime?*
> P: *(Voice breaking.) Well, I'm almost thinking he was the man. (Crying.)*
> T: *You feel that?*
> P: *I think...at least from my sadness...this time it was safer to have him as a son.*
> T: *Because in this way you could protect him, love him, love him in a way that would not have any intrusive factors coming in.*
> P: *It seems that he won't hurt me this way.*
> T: *He can't hurt you as your son.*
> P: *I have to look at my relationship with my son. I'm making it so there wouldn't be room for a man.*
> T: *That's right. There wouldn't be room for a man. It's almost as though you have created a very sacred space and that's part of your decision, and that space between you and him is not to be violated.*
> P: *Yes. Well, I get that feedback from people, too, and I don't know what's right and what's wrong. I don't know.*
> T: *I think it will be more clear to you as he grows up.*

Other connections were explored, such as Dawn's deep affinity with the moon, and she was brought back into the peace of the garden, where she saw her son dancing, and then came back into her body.

The major piece of work in this second lifetime lay in the reframing of her interpretation that no one cared for her and that the young man she loved had betrayed her. This reframing made it possible for her to re-experience the deep love she had felt for him and eventually to connect him with her son. She realized that the reason a significant, loving man doesn't come into her life is that her son is her significant loving man, the one with whom she has a deep but unfinished relationship. Other work remains to be done regarding the choice of her as a priestess, that appeared not to be a random one but one based on the potentials she must have manifested as a child in that lifetime.

An interesting sidelight to this regression was the insistence of Dawn's son, when he was three and a half, that he and his mother had lived together in California "before there were buildings." He remembered being a girl of 15 married to a young brave (his mother). He described fishing together in a wide river and times when the young brave went hunting and he (as the wife) made cakes of corn. He was able to describe the dwelling they lived in and many of the details of their lives as Indians, none of which Dawn had as yet recovered. As he neared five, the memory dimmed and is now almost gone, usual when young children recover past lives spontaneously.

Another factor in my experience of the regression was that as I went into a deeper altered state myself I began to pick up things in scenes and think, "Oh, okay, there's that factor." For instance, when Dawn was describing the loss of the young man, I was in the lead and pacing with her because when she said, "I was in love with this guy," I had already shifted and could feel the love. I sort of said, "Wait a minute." Then I got her back into that space prior to the resentment, and the tears came. I had already experienced that while she was still in the anger. I was continually picking up things in the various scenes. For instance, I thought there were other things that involved her being the sort of child who was selected to be a priestess. I was picking more information up and was becoming more and more connected with her and seeing her life. This capacity, while in an altered state, to tune into the field of the patient, extends one's ability to know what is the most helpful area or direction in which to move. I believe that past-life work can be done without it, but to me it seems a helpful adjunctive tool. It is necessary, as in this regression, to make a judgment as to when possible directions must be postponed for later sessions in order to focus and integrate a particular insight.

### Case 2. Reframing the Anxieties of a Past-Life Experience Recovered through Dream Flashbacks

A 19-year-old man came back to his university dorm after a drinking party and while sleeping went into a past-life memory of a Vietnam experience that was so vivid that he wrote out the entire memory upon awakening. He was referred to me by his mother because the memory or dream had created a great deal of anxiety, persistent flashbacks, and obsessional behavior that affected his ability to concentrate and function normally.

He had a desperate quality of trying to make sense of the experience, and he manifested this by reading as much as possible about the Vietnam War and buying an *Apocalypse Now* movie poster.

In his dream he found himself in Vietnam. He recounted the experience with a great deal of vividness:

> P: *Jungle, endless miles of jungle, interspersed with rivers, marks this place at the Mekong Delta. The air is sticky and sweet. The jungle seems to radiate the intense heat that is pounding down. From the helicopter, I see the jungle speed beneath me. I lean up against my shiny weapon of destruction that I am to operate. Sitting like some sort of perverse dragon in its rotating carousel, my M-60 Gatlin' gun gleams in the afternoon sun. God, the air is so heavy here. Everything is so damn sticky and humid. I wish*

> *I could take off my shirt, but then immediately I become an instant lunch for all of these damn bugs.*

His dream focused on a mission where, as a soldier in the war, he confronted the havoc of war.

> P: *The helicopter makes a wide arc and starts back toward the target. Suddenly the jungle explodes. Fire in huge ugly black and red balls curls upward from the jungle. It seems as though the whole world has been enveloped in some unholy flame. Oh, sweet Jesus, have I done that? I pray not. Charred and burning trees are all that remain. Everything is gone. What once may have been a home to people is now just scorched black ground. God, what have we done? I can't take my eyes off it. We just keep circling above this charred land. The sight transfixes and haunts me. I am hypnotized by the vioience that I have helped bring down. The Captain speaks through the intercom: "Let's take it home, boys.... There's nothing left for us here."*

His dream ended with his death when the helicopter was shot down and he died in the crash. It was at this point that he awakened from his dream, sweating and feeling the horror that he had just participated in and witnessed. For the patient, the dream became a living reminder of what he felt he took part in. Even though he was able to rationalize his feelings as part of a dream sequence, there was a part of him that experienced depression and a sense of guilt that would not leave him.

The dream was unfinished and was experienced as an artifact of his unconscious. The young man could not understand the significance and yet could not release the overwhelming feelings of discomfort and anxiety that resulted from the dream experience. The dream was used as an induction.

In an hypnotic state, he was asked to re-live the dream from which the above comments were taken. After he re-lived the entire dream sequence, he was then asked to go to an earlier period of that lifetime, prior to going to war. He found himself as a young man who grew up in a very insecure home environment and escaped to the army as a means of getting out of an intolerable situation. The army provided structure and a means to develop an identity. He found himself fascinated with the use of arms and the sense of power they gave him. In this situation he didn't have to acknowledge his feelings or to ask questions regarding his assignments. It was only after a long period of time in the army and after the experience of killing that he became reflective of his position and the consequences of his behavior. In reframing the dream sequence within the context of the entire life scenario, he saw a life where empowerment was given to outside authority figures. In relinquishing his power, he betrayed his own feelings.

In the integrative portion of the therapy session, he was asked not only to review the entire past lifetime and to see the lesson involved, but to see how it related to his present life. In reframing his dream sequence even further within the larger perspective of the current life, he could see the relevance of the Vietnam experience to his present situation, where he was dealing with his father and confronting other people's authority. He realized how important it was to not relinquish his own power in making decisions, and to make choices in his life based on his own values and feelings. The challenge now was in facing his father and taking up a university major that he wanted, and not a major pushed upon him by his parents.

After this session, which was taped, I asked him to listen to the tapes and to begin integrating the material. After a month's interim, I talked with the patient to learn that the obsessive behavior had gone and that flashback experiences were no longer haunting him. He felt he still needed time to confront his own issues and to deal with his father and other authority figures.

This patient did not have a belief in past lives, but it did not matter, as he was able to look at the entire experience as a parable describing the issues of his present situation. This patient had no history of previous emotional dysfunction. I surmised that the pressures from home, the transition of entering a university program, and the unresolved issues with his father precipitated the experience.

### Case 3. Reframing an Experience of Loss

Barbara, a therapist in her forties, volunteered to be the subject in an APRT training session. She reported recurring feelings of being desolate and abandoned when her husband, a man with whom she felt very bonded, was away on business trips. He was a workshop leader who traveled a great deal and was often gone for periods of several weeks. Especially in the middle portion of the two-week absences she experienced negative feelings of despair that bordered on rejection, even though she knew rationally that she was not rejected.

I used these feelings as an induction and asked Barbara in what part of her body she experienced them. When she indicated that they were predominantly in the heart and solar plexus area, I first did a brief general relaxation and then had her center on the feelings in the solar plexus and asked her to go back and remember a time when her husband left and allow the scene to come to her mind.

Barbara returned to a recent scene when her husband called and told her that he wouldn't be home according to schedule, wiping out her plans to have a good time with some other couples.

> P: All the connections are gone and I am powerless. It's just not fair. It hurts. I feel a real emptiness and darkness and despair.
> T: Could you stay with that profound sense of loss? What are the words that are coming into your mind over and over again?
> P: It's dissipating. It's going away. It's gone. It's empty.
> T: The connectiveness.
> P: The connectiveness. The wonderful connectiveness is going. It feels like it stretched so much that it suddenly just popped.
> T: I want you to stay with that sense of disconnectiveness in thinking to yourself, "It isn't fair." There have been other times that you have felt this, and I want you to go back to another time when you felt this same kind of feeling.
> P: It is just grayish and darkish, not distinct. Maybe some sort of hallway.... It's dark.
> T: Now focus on that and allow your mind to enlarge on that so you become more aware of where you are...with the feelings.

Barbara found herself as an old woman left behind while her village moved to another place to find food. She accepted the fact that she would have been a burden and courageously lived out her life alone.

> T: Now I want to know. Are you married?

Barbara avoided this question and described village life further and then told about her son, an energetic and brave young warrior.

> T: What I want you to do now is go either forward or backward and see if there is any other significant relationship that you need to look at during this time in order to understand the pain that you often feel from the disconnection.
> P: I think it is about my husband. I haven't quite gotten to it, but I have a real sense that he is not present because he has been gone for a long time. He was there for a while and we had this son.
> T: Let's look at that relationship. What happened?

Barbara then went back to when her husband was living and described the wonderful joy of being with him. Her heart was singing. She remembered her exciting marriage and all the connectiveness she felt with him afterwards.

> T: I want you to move forward now and see if those feelings stay or if they become broken. What happens as you become older?
> P: (Crying.) No! It can't be! It's not fair!

She described how the other men from the village came back and told her that her young husband had been killed. He was doing tricks on horses, leaping and cavorting around from one moving horse to another, and he slipped and fell and broke his neck.

> P: *(Crying.) He wasn't supposed to die that way! He was just having fun. I didn't even get a chance to say goodbye!*
> T: *Knowing that, did that influence your feelings in the way you raised your son? Knowing that your husband died because of his wanting to be free?*
> P: *I want my son to be free, fun, and cavorting, too. And he is. And I love that about him. And, also, I have really tried to impress upon him that he is not to take ridiculous chances like his father did. Ridiculous. It was a stupid thing to do, to leap from one running horse to another, just for fun. It wasn't even necessary. I am really angry with you because you did that! (Crying.) Too many chances! And in this life, too, I am so afraid! (Crying.)*
> T: *You are afraid it will end the same way.*
> P: *I am so afraid now in this lifetime. It's the same man and I am so afraid with all of his airplane trips. I am so afraid that he is not going to come back. He might even come back dead.*

I then took Barbara back over that lifetime, exploring how she raised her son, who became the village leader and led the group away.

> T: *Now move to the moments before your death. Where are you?*

Barbara recounted how she came back to the house feeling pain and lay dying.

> T: *Are there any last thoughts as you began to feel yourself dying?*
> P: *They are about my husband. When I think about my husband I feel very sad and alone and that it wasn't right that he wasn't here all of the time. It has been such a long life without him. And I feel that feeling again.*
> T: *Those feelings are?...*
> P: *I'm lonely, desolate, drained. He should have been here. He robbed us both of what was so good. What we had was so short compared to all of his friends. It's dangerous to be in love with someone who is so exciting. And I did that and I lost so much.*
> T: *Barbara, I want you to move to your death and tell me what is happening. Where are you?*
> P: *(Cries.)*
> T: *Right now could you review this whole life? Why is it that you have chosen to go through this scenario with this man? I want you to look at this entire scenario, one of loving a man who is fun loving, who loves to cavort, and*

who precipitated you into that sense of loss. What was this to teach you? What did you learn from this?
P: That I was going to be okay anyway. It was as though he touched the core. I felt lonely at first and desolate but I tended my little fire, went into the fields and came back, saw the sun and sky.
T: So what you are saying is that even though he left you, you realized that it gave you a sense of self-reliance and that self-reliance gave you strength and also gave you a sense of appreciation for all of the things that were around you. I want you to make that bridge. I want you to see how all of that has been instrumental in the choices and the situations you now find yourself in and in the relationship you now have with your husband. Can you see the connection?
P: He comes home and is loving, so nice. But he is the one who leaves. I feel desolation and fear that somehow it is over and he won't come back. Each time it happens I go through that fear. It seems that there is a purpose in having to face the fear.
T: Can you see that his not being there really is a time, an opportunity for your own self-empowerment? For that other lifetime you felt this total sense of fulfillment and wholeness in his presence, and when he was gone you realized that you had the power to find that wholeness within yourself, even when you had suffered that loss. Can you see now that in this lifetime you have taken a path of self-empowerment? You can have both—allow him to cavort and do all those stimulating things, while it is still okay for him to leave and come back. You don't need your power because of him.
P: It's a challenge, but it feels like a power issue, too. When he goes and I get into that bad state, I think to myself, what have I done? Have I given all my power to him? And I think that I've got to take that power back. I definitely see that I am consistently connected with men who are active, creative and stimulating, and with each one is the issue of giving away power. I don't mean power over them but over myself. I have to keep playing it over and over again.
T: I am going to leave you with this and allow it to filter in. When you love this man, it isn't so much that you love him out there but you are loving a part of yourself that he represents. And that part is always there in you, whether he is there, or not.
P: Oh!
T: So even with him gone, he is always there. It is a matter of connecting with that part of you that likes to be razzle-dazzle and fun. In that other lifetime your husband represented your own potential, so you acted out through him. But if you remember the source, then leaving is not a taking away.
P: All that rascalness, all that creativity is me.
T: I want you to keep an image of him now, in this lifetime. Sort of make your husband into a little man and put him in your right hand...and feel that feeling of rascalness, that excitement. Do you feel it?
P: Yes. It is warm.

T: *When he goes away and you begin to feel bad, take your right hand and put it there on your heart as a reminder that he has always been there. You will find yourself coming back to full center.... Now, when you are ready, take a deep breath and come back into the room and feel energized and centered.*

P: *(Opening her eyes after a few minutes.) I lost everybody, a whole community, a whole world of people, but it was all right. I have a changed perception of that loss. I was okay. The old lady, me, was lying there and she was okay. When I told everybody it was okay, they left without me. That was a pretty gutsy thing to do when you think about it, when everyone in the whole world leaves you and you are there and not sick and not dying, and they leave you there all alone with however it is that you are going to die. That is pretty darn brave! You know, it really is. (Laughs.)*

In a follow-up discussion several months after this regression, Barbara indicated that the intensity of her fears had diminished to the point where her feelings didn't intrude on her daily life. What came out of the session for her was an awareness of a decision point, where before there had been none. The truth is that we do die. We lose our friends. But that isn't the issue. The issue is that it can be perceived so differently that a different response is possible. The regression illustrates how change occurs when a patient has the opportunity to reframe an experience as a result of seeing the dynamics of a problem within a past-life context.

In working with patients I tend to hold back in the beginning and wait to see how things develop, but mid-way I feel connected and then it as though my internal television set goes on. I tend to get more directive later when I make the connection. This comes as a result of feeling clarity about what needs to be done. However, any directiveness is modified because it is communicated with a heart connection. If the therapist doesn't feel connected when he is doing that kind of clarifying, even though he is positive he is right, what he says becomes technique oriented, a sort of going through a protocol sheet, that prevents what he says from being effective. There must be an energy connection with the patient for transformation to take place.

Chapter XII

# Hazel M. Denning, Ph.D.

## *Biographical Data*

**Personal Background**

I was born on March 1, 1907, in Woodstock, Illinois, in the home of my grandparents, with my grandfather, a physician, officiating. I was considered to be a strong-willed child, but I became stubborn only when I believed that something was wrong or unfair. I felt driven to help anyone in trouble, from my classmates at school to the children in the neighborhood. I dreamed of becoming a doctor, a nurse, a religious education director, and when psychology came on the scene, I felt strongly attracted to that profession.

When I was nine years of age I had a profound experience that left me with a strong sense of destiny but which also led to years of uncertainty and confusion about myself because I could not understand why my thinking remained so different from that of those around me. In my early twenties this discrepancy increased, for I had grown so disillusioned with Christian orthodoxy that I became involved in study and research in the parapsychological and metaphysical fields, striving to find answers that seemed to me to be more appropriate to life as I observed it.

At the same time that as a perennial student I was involved in reading, attending workshops, and taking extension courses and classes, I began a career of public service. This started when, at 19, I was elected president of the Riverside County Christian Endeavor Union, serving for two terms and lecturing in a different church every Sunday. Later, in my late twenties, my studies in parapsychology and metaphysics convinced me that the answers I had been seeking about life and man's purpose could be found in these disciplines, and I began to teach classes and lecture on these subjects. At the same time I maintained a full-time volunteer career in church and community activities. For 38 years I directed a full-scale drama program in the Methodist Church and for 14 years was actively involved with the Riverside Community Players, using drama as a therapeutic modality with both young people and adults. I served two terms as president of the Riverside Branch of the American Association of University Women and later became president of the Riverside Branch of the National League of American Penwomen.

In 1931 I married for the second time, a marriage that lasted 49 years and increased in quality with each passing year. I consider the secret of the success of this marriage to have been the willingness of each of us to allow the other total autonomy in the process of self-actualization. We adopted three children and with them I now have five grandchildren. My husband died doing his favorite thing, playing tennis.

In 1952 I decided to complete my formal education and graduated from the University of California in Riverside in 1956. In 1962 I earned my first graduate degree, in educational psychology, from the Claremont Graduate School. Since neither of these degrees recognized my experience and interest in parapsychology, I took my second master's degree in humanistic and transpersonal psychology in 1981 from the Johnson College at Redlands University. A doctorate in clinical psychology followed in 1984.

In 1961 I encountered my first spontaneous case of past-life recall. A young lady was sent to me by her physician following a suicide attempt. In an altered state of consciousness she recounted the details of a life during the Civil War, and she connected events encountered there to her life of today. At that time I accepted reincarnation as a practical and workable philosophy but had no idea that anyone could actually recall past experiences. When the young lady had gone I felt excited and challenged and began serious research in past-life recall as a tool for therapy.[1] The positive results were incontrovertible and I began a new career, which since then has consumed the major part of my time. I am convinced that regression techniques will play an important role in the therapy of the future.

My interest in the paranormal field led to the organization in 1971 of the Parapsychology Association of Riverside. In 1977 this association served as the recipient of a quarter-million-dollar grant to provide evidence that the mind can literally heal the body of physical problems.[2] The design of this project, which I directed, involved seeing clients for three years and then continuing with a five-year follow-up. The results are now being computerized and will hopefully be available soon.

Because I recognized the need for an organization to serve the increasing number of therapists who were already incorporating past-life regression into their practice, I assisted in the founding of the Association for Past-Life Research and Therapies, Inc., serving for three years as president and later as Executive Director.

My work has required a great deal of traveling. My first trip in 1977 came in conjunction with the International Psychotronics Congress in Monte Carlo. In 1978 I visited Sweden for the First European Congress of Hypnosis in Psychotherapy and Psychosomatic Medicine. A Mediterranean Peace Cruise in 1979 took me to Greece, Turkey, Egypt and Israel. My only vacation just to rest was a Caribbean cruise in 1981. In 1982 I was invited to lecture in Holland and England. The Association for Religion and Parapsychology invited me to deliver the keynote address at their Eleventh International Conference in Tokyo in 1983. India came next in 1984, where I spoke in Madras and Bombay. The first International Conference on Alternative Therapies was held in Brazil in 1985 and I lectured and led a workshop in Sao Paolo. I made two trips in 1985 with the Noetic Science Institute to Russia and China, and in 1987 I was co-leader of an APRT workshop and tour in England.

As I glance back over my life I feel most blessed. This has nothing to do with the events in my life, for some of them have been very painful; but through the depression, the family problems, the deaths, has run a thread of satisfaction and inner joy which no outer circumstances can counteract. I know who I am, why I am here, and where I am going, and my one purpose is to help others discover the wonder of themselves.

## Personal Past-Life Experience

It is difficult for me to accept that, with the understanding I have of psychosomatic illness and the belief in "bottom line" causes, I should have taken so long to recognize my own blind spot, in this case a malfunctioning liver, which began when I was fourteen.

My graduation from eighth grade in 1921 was a major event. At the picnic, where the boys challenged the girls to a baseball game, I ate too much, played too hard in the sun, and had a splitting headache by the time I reached home. But since this was a special occasion, I had been given permission to go to a movie with a girl friend. I suffered through about two hours of "flickers" and staggered out of the theater. Unfortunately, my friend's father worked in an ice-cream parlor and had promised us a treat, and after eating a chocolate sundae I could scarcely walk home. At midnight I began screaming in a delirium—hallucinations, illusions, and all—undoubtedly precipitated by the toxic condition I had created in that graduation binge.

During the next twenty years I did not suffer a great deal except for infrequent headaches. Then in 1938 my children gave me a two-pound box of chocolates. For the first time in my life I decided they were "mine" to enjoy totally. I had been well indoctrinated in the art of sharing and self-restraint and up to that event would have given most of the goodies to the family. I was typing some articles that day, and as I sat typing I reveled in the thought of eating all I wanted. Accordingly, I set the box by the typewriter, removed the cover, and proceeded to intersperse the typing with the delectable See's creation.

The next morning I awoke early with a violent headache. I could scarcely stand as I tried to get out of bed. I had never before or since felt so physically fragmented. My entire body felt as though it were flying apart. I called my doctor, and a few hours later in her office she set to work testing me. When I asked her what could possibly cause so much physical anguish she said very calmly, "too much fatty food or chocolate." I stopped her and confessed that it was chocolate.

For about 45 years I lived under the shadow of chocolate. No pain ever served to diminish the pleasure in the delicious flavor, but if I wished to avoid the bilious attacks I had to control my intake. I was a chocoholic and constantly played the odds. Most of the time I could eat a small amount, but through those years I had dozens of headaches and suffered the loss of many a good meal. Fortunately, all tests showed no liver degeneration, only that my liver malfunctioned when abused.

So much for the background. I am a Piscean and enjoy water, whether it is swimming or the shower, where I do some of my best thinking and meditation. One morning as I was reveling in the joy of the water pouring over me, a powerful thought intruded: "Why have you always accepted your liver problem as physical: You know better. You don't let anyone else get away with that explanation." I felt somewhat overwhelmed with the enormity of my own blindness and I said, "God, I've had it with this problem. I want to know the real reason for it. I mean it, whatever it is, I am ready to know."

Instantly, a clear, sharp, and colorful vision filled my mind. I saw a soldier in full Crusade regalia lying on the ground. His white garment displayed a bright red cross on the front, his hands were guantleted with silver mail, and on his head he wore a silver mesh helmet. He lay on his back on the ground, with his right leg flexed. Clear and stark was a long spear at an angle upright from his body, and the spear had run through his liver.

In an instant I understood why I had always been drawn to the Crusades and at the same time felt an abhorrence for them. The Crusader had set off with religious zeal and after arriving there had been revolted by the bloodshed and violence. He was furious at dying for a cause he could no longer espouse. As he lay dying, he lifted his hand and touched the locket he wore around his neck. It contained a picture of his wife. He had two sons, and his thoughts rested on the three he loved and would never see again.

In that moment I knew the cause of my liver problem. I had held my rage in that organ. I also realized why I had always had such a temper and experienced such rage at anything I considered unjust.

That insight came several years ago. I now eat foods I could not tolerate for many years, and I have not had a liver upset since. A second very real benefit has been a marked increase in my tolerance for frustration. Since that insight, I no longer experience rage.

In retrospect it is possible to find many interesting aspects to such a case. Was I supposed to hold on to that handicap for reasons unrecognized by me? It certainly forced me to take better care of my body and to study nutrition, a fact that has served me well in keeping my body fit for so many years. It forced me to understand how as human beings we can be unaware of our own blind spots, and how important it is in therapy to recognize and be tolerant of clients who can't see something in themselves that is obvious to the therapist. In addition, it served to further substantiate my belief that there is always an event, an incident, a trauma that is the true antecedent of any problem we have and that originates in a past life.

I believe we must recognize that rage, fear, and guilt are all manifestations of energy used negatively and that the positive aspects of these three powerful emotions can be, and *are*, the forces which propel us toward constructive expression. In my case, for example, the rage at injustice served as a powerful motivation in my life and pushed me into working tirelessly to help individuals find their own autonomy, their own freedom, unfettered by the opinions of their peers or their culture.

# *Theory*

## Philosophical Hypotheses[3]

1. Man is a spiritual being with unlimited creative potential, endowed with the capacity to know who he is and where he is going.

2. A broader understanding of the universal principle of life as a spiritual reality with a creative purpose will eventually reduce the pain and suffering that are so much a part of life as we know it today.

3. We are not our bodies, and the spirit, energy, or soul within each of us continues to exist after the body dies and at some time in the future may come again to expression in another physical body.

4. Since the soul comes back, it must have been here before, so therefore it has had other life experiences prior to the present one.

5. All experiences are subconsciously retained or recorded, so that every individual is a composite of all previous experiences. When the mind is in touch with the inner wisdom of the self, memories of hundreds of years in the past are as easily recalled as events of present life.

6. No one has the right to coerce or attempt to control another.

7. Individuals consciously or unconsciously program their lives. The behavior in each life determines in some way the experience of the next. We make our own destiny and create our own environment. We purposefully choose parents, life settings, and lessons to be learned in each lifetime, all the events and relationships that are necessary for our growth and development.

8. Childhood traumas may actually be the extension or continuation of patterns that originated in some past experiences.

9. Whatever strong and destructive energy is generated at the time of death is carried over into the next incarnation. Unless there is change in the attitude or thinking of the individual, any sort of healing can bring only temporary relief.

10. Events in themselves are often inevitable because of the previous patterns that determined them, but we never lose our free will.

11. Every person is responsible for himself/herself. For every simple act there is a consequence or result. Nothing can occur without a cause, and this makes for an orderly and dependable universe. In the dimension of the mind or energy or spirit, law and order prevail as dependably as in the physical world. If we act contrary to a law, it causes us distress or disease. Pain is a teacher and carries a message.

12. When an individual recognizes his own role in determining his experience or his destiny and assumes responsibility for his role, then his own self-image is enhanced. All of his relationships improve, psychosomatic symptoms are generally eliminated, and the individual enjoys improved health.[4]

13. Guilt is the key factor in a personality that drives an individual continually to repeat mistakes. Guilt is a recognition that we have made a mistake or acted in a manner inconsistent with the deeper knowledge of the soul. In order for the soul to become free of guilt or to come into balance with its spiritual or higher nature, it launches on a path that it believes will result in making amends.

14. We cooperate in the universal purpose by assuming personal responsibility for all of our behavior and recognizing that such responsibility requires us to treat all other people with the acceptance, consideration, and the love that we desire for our own happiness and fulfillment.

## Psychotherapeutic Assumptions

1. The purpose of psychotherapy is to alleviate human suffering by helping individuals to change inappropriate behavior patterns, mitigate psychosomatic symptoms, promote acceptance of the self, improve interpersonal relationships, and achieve balance and integration in their personal lives.

2. Total well-being can be achieved only when the individual can be brought in touch with his or her inner processes. The person must also understand his own dynamics and accept the responsibility for his own life. Nothing short of insight into the cause can bring relief to the person in the present, and no amount of verbal exhortations in any form can accomplish more than temporary relief.

3. All services programmed to relieve pain must recognize and deal with three primary aspects of the individual: the physical, mental-emotional, and spiritual. Concentrating on only one of these aspects alone is fragmenting to the personality, and it is necessary to bring meaning and purpose to the *total* individual in order to achieve true healing. After any purely physical matter has been analyzed and taken care of, the reason for the problem and the purpose of it in the life of the individual should always be included in the analysis.[5]

4. Neuroses develop in the personality when the individual, exercising his ability to choose, makes the wrong choices and avoids the task he has set for himself, thus failing to implement his good intentions and inevitably arousing feelings of guilt. The individual continues a pattern of self-punishment until he discovers the original deed for which he is punishing himself. The regression experience is a search for the source of the problem. It is understood that the therapist does not have the answers but instead recognizes that the answers are always known by the client.

5. The therapist's attitude should be such that the client feels safe and confident in verbalizing anything at all that is seen in the subconscious while in an altered state. Unless the therapist is able to convince the client that these safe conditions exist between them, there will be much valuable and important subconscious material that will never surface.

6. When individuals are able to trace their own destiny patterns and realize that they are responsible for a particular learning experience, their orientation changes and they become less prone to blame God or their parents for what is happening in their lives.

7. Taking time to explore with the client the cause, and particularly the purpose of guilt, is often essential to success. When there seems to be a series of events unrelated to the present, in order for the person to detach the significance of these events from the present subconscious, it is necessary that the cause or purpose be understood.

8. The client does not always make a complete resolution of the problem just by reviewing what seems to be the original cause. It is imperative that the therapist assist the client in exploring the event and bringing about a satisfactory resolution before the client can totally release guilt. Also, everyone who encounters a past life that seems to explain the present is not automatically free of that problem. While some cases can be resolved totally in a few sessions, many individuals require long periods of time to integrate the new understanding into their lives. However, the insights gained from the regression provide a supportive framework as well as a sense of knowing where one is going and why, even though one is not there yet.

## Indications and Contraindications for Use

Regression therapy, more than any other therapy known at the present time, effectively and in a short time puts the individual in touch with his or her unique processes and unravels skillfully the tangled threads of the past. It seems to have an especial potential for promoting insight. There is mounting evidence that regression therapy experiences do change attitudes, remove guilt, build self-esteem, and free individuals from stress, fear, irrational behavior, and rage that are the result of past injustices. It is especially effective with clients who have lost all sense of self-worth or who experience strong personality clashes in their relationships. It can at times dramatically erase physical symptoms such as migraine headaches, allergies, arthritis and, in fact, all disease syndromes.

However, regression therapy is not for everyone. When life is going well and there are no apparent problems, there is no point in exploring past lives.

The important thing is living now, in the present, and doing the best one can with that. Only when life is not going well or when there are obvious unsolved problems should one investigate or seek a regression experience.

Also, if the individual is unwilling to be honest and blocks attempts at self-revelation, there will be no significant result. In such cases, the skills of the therapist may overcome the resistance, but until the individual is ready to face the truth about the self, there is probably no therapy that will be effective. Fear of exposure, religious conflicts, an inability to assume responsibility for oneself and one's actions and feelings and situation, or a feeling that one has a predetermined destiny to suffer, all contraindicate regression therapy.

# *Induction*

## Preparation

Before regression therapy is actually begun, it is important to discuss the client's philosophy of life. This therapy is transpersonal in the truest sense of the word, and much of it will make little sense to the client who has no knowledge of mind dynamics. There are a number of areas that should be explored, and this exploration can take anywhere from a half hour to a number of sessions to satisfy the therapist that the client is ready for actual regression. Until this readiness is recognized by the therapist, it is not only a waste of time but unwise to lead a client into traumatic material when he is unprepared to deal with it. There must be a willingness on the part of the client to try out various areas during the regression and evaluate the results later.

The areas that particularly need to be discussed include the following:

1. Every person is responsible for himself/herself. Individuals consciously or unconsciously program their lives.

2. For every simple act there is a consequence or result.

3. All experiences are subconsciously retained or recorded so that every individual is a composite of all previous experience.

4. Everyone has the capacity to communicate with the unconscious.

5. We make our own destiny and create our own environment.

## Induction Techniques

From the very beginning of my training, the degree of control exercised by the hypnotist caused me considerable concern. Since I place a high premium on personal freedom and have always held the firm belief that we have no right to coerce or control other persons, I carried grave doubts about using this therapeutic tool, even though its potential was obvious. I continued to read, attend lectures, and observe its use and the results over a period of six or seven years before I felt comfortable about using it. By that time I had restructured the technique and applied the term "altered states of consciousness" to describe the evolving experience. I found this term to be far less threatening to clients, and the results met my personal criteria for more control by the individual and less control by the therapist. Now I believe that hypnosis and entry into altered states represent two different processes. In hypnosis it is possible to program a person not to remember what has taken place, but this is not possible in an altered state as I use it. I make it very clear to clients that they are in control of their experience and I serve only as a guide or facilitator.

I gear induction techniques to the personality of the client. I begin the induction by having my clients breathe deeply, breathing in energy on the inhale and seeing it flood every cell, then breathing out toxins. I have them breathe in energy through every chakra and flood all their cells with universal energy.

Then I begin a deep bodily relaxation, meanwhile telling the clients that there is a part of them that knows everything about them and knows the answers to their questions. I have them follow affirmations such as, "My brow is at peace. My brow is serene and I am ready to explore something that is very important to me."

Then I instruct them to bypass their birth and when they are ready, go to the beginning of the pattern. I state the problem and ask for the source of it. Then I count to five, taking them back through time and space to the beginning of the pattern. I intersperse the counting with instructions to the unconscious mind to recover whatever incident or trauma is directly related to the problem, and at the count of five I ask that whatever is being experienced be shared.

### *Chakra Induction*

*Close your eyes and take a deep breath and just let go. I'd like you to take a second deep breath and this time bring energy into your body. With your mind send energy to every cell in your body.*

And now with a third breath bring energy to all the chakra centers. Image that you're sending energy to all the chakra centers and feel them come into synchronicity, each center vibrating at its normal rate so that all of them are vibrating like the cogs of a watch, each of them is vibrating at its own special rate. When you do this there is a synchronization of all the energy of all the energy centers, which is a very wonderful feeling. So feel yourself balanced, centered, and when you do this, feel yourself in tune with universal energy. Like tuning a violin to an orchestra, you are tuning yourself to universal energy. You are vibrating in harmony with the energy of the universe. When you do this, it is a very easy thing for you to slip into a deep altered state and get in tune and in touch with your own deeper all-knowing self.

So feel yourself getting in touch with this, going deeper and deeper into the altered state. Feel your mind expanding, down into your subconscious, out into your superconscious, expanding like the circles in a pool when you drop in a pebble. Your mind expands and expands, bringing into the conscious self all that wonderful knowledge and information that is available to you about the rest of your lives.

Let us focus now on (describe presenting problem) and say to yourself—out loud if you like—(name affirmation in question). And with that thought, putting all the energy into it that you can, let that thought take you back in time, through space to some incident, some event, some trauma, that occurred a long time ago that you are still expressing in life today. Go back and back and back to where you find yourself saying (repeat affirmation in question).

And as soon as you sense something or feel something or hear something, tell me and then I'll know the question to ask you to help you see more of it. (Repeats affirmation in question.)

## Supportive and Deepening Techniques

Following the induction, when I feel that a client is in an altered state, I suggest that he tell me whatever it is he's experiencing, even if it's only minimal. I suggest that he describe the time, place and experience that is directly related to his problem. I ask him to identify his age and sex early, because this often makes retrieval of other facets of the experience easier.

When the first incident has been to some extent recovered, I suggest that the client move forward to the next significant event. Sometimes I count to five to help the shift to this incident. I find this technique better than asking a lot of questions. As far as possible, I let people go through their experiences, asking a question or making a comment only when this promises to help the retrieval of the memories. When a client seems to need support, especially in the case of a disturbing or traumatic situation, I might hold his hand or touch her head.

When a situation is too painful, I remind the client that this is a past life and I suggest that he imagine he is looking at a movie of his past, so to speak, and he need not experience pain. I may suggest that the mind is like a great library and that the client can move through it and find a book about this particular incident. Though some people do not need to abreact, others do. Certain types of personalities need to express the feelings being re-lived. This is especially true of those who have strong feeling natures.

Sometimes clients in a deep altered state talk so softly that it is difficult to hear. I find that it is not disturbing or intrusive if I ask, "Do you mind repeating that last word? I'd really like to hear what you have to say. Could you speak a little louder?" Such a question gives clients the feeling that what they are saying is important and valuable to you, and as a rule they are glad to comply.

In the process of the regression there are many times when a pertinent life is recovered but its significance is not realized. Then it may be necessary to go through a number of lives before reviewing the first one and exploring its significance in greater detail.

Extensive experience with regression has suggested that groups, especially family groups, often reincarnate together, and there is a level on which the client will know which current relationship appeared in an earlier lifetime, even though the actual role is different.[6] Usually I do not ask about this, but if it does emerge, I explore it and ask about patterns from that lifetime which are repeated in this.

## *Processing*

### Psychotherapeutic and Transformational Techniques

The therapeutic goal is to restructure understanding of our current life in the light of our extended experience from other lifetimes. When we have only the present lifetime on which to base our interpretations, it is like trying to understand the theme and plot of a play when we have only one scene by which to go. Therefore, all therapeutic and transformational techniques are focused on extending perception of the lessons and limitations which the individual has chosen to help along the journey toward higher consciousness. Incidents are not recovered for their intrinsic interest but only to implement this understanding.

The wise part of us that does know everything is able to focus in on whatever lifetimes can contribute to this understanding. That is why the client must be able to trust that this selective process exists and will take place. All questions and comments on the part of the therapist should hone in on the problem under consideration, keeping in mind that the unconscious is cooperating by bringing up the relevant material. Questions, comments, and reflections can be rephrased in various ways until it is clear that similarities, relationships, and lessons are integrated by the client to the maximum degree possible at the time.

Much of the work of insight and integration from any lifetime can best be uncovered and expressed at the time that a person leaves his body in that lifetime. Also, the last conscious thought before a person has actually left his body often sets an intention that he carries into the next lifetime, and possibly through subsequent lifetimes, often being amplified by each new lifetime until that intention programs behavior and attitudes in the current lifetime. Therefore, I always ask that the situation of the death in the earlier lifetime be described, including the last conscious thought.

After that I take the client out of the body of that past life and ask him to consider what lesson was learned in that lifetime and what else could have been done. My objective is to help the client take responsibility for programming and implementing that life. I also explore the effect of that lifetime on the current one.

If the client feels that in the lifetime under consideration something has been done that can never be forgiven, this attitude must be explored until it is clear that this event is a part of the soul's growth, that it, too, is an aspect of being on the path to self-discovery. Both the incident and the judgment about it must be reframed. Sometimes, when there is deep anger at another person, it is helpful for the client to identify with that person, get inside his head, so to speak, in order to reach an attitude of forgiveness. Often clients must be reminded that they are not responsible for others' lives. Just as they are not entitled to control or influence others, so they cannot take responsibility for others.

A technique that I often use to help tie things together and integrate and consolidate a client's insight is to ask the client to imagine an altar with a presence behind it surrounded in light—the client's guide or Higher Self, whichever seems appropriate. I have the client approach this guide and receive a message. The guide will often summarize or heighten the understanding gained from the regression.

After that, I ask the client if there is anything further that needs to be seen or dealt with. Sometimes there is, and time must be allowed for this. If there is nothing further, I bring the client back by suggesting that he image an enclosing bubble of white light and visualize all the colors of the chakras. I ask if there is any part of the body that needs extra energy, and I suggest that all the wonderful energy of the bubble melt into the body for healing. Then I slowly count back from five to one, observing the body response in order to determine the pacing of the return.

## Integration into the Total Psychotherapeutic Process

Integration in succeeding sessions is built upon and reinforces insights and integration that have taken place during the actual regression, when every effort has been made to establish connections between incidents, attitudes, symptoms, and personalities from the past life and the current one. Many times these connections need to be reinforced, and this can be done by scrutinizing current happenings for their roots and meaning in other lifetimes that have been recalled.

Many times during a regression it seems that the basic cause has been recovered and that the problem or symptom should go into remission, but this does not happen. In such instances, further regression is indicated until the true etiology of this situation can be recovered and integrated.

There are other instances where past lifetimes have exposed a longstanding personality pattern that has been reinforced in this lifetime. Such a pattern will not disappear immediately but must be identified continuously as it reappears, when further work on integrating the insight can go on. Often during the actual regression a new perspective has been reached, resulting in a new statement of purpose or a revised understanding. Old patterns often resurface and carry sufficient energy to obscure or push back into the unconscious the insights and new perspectives that have been reached regarding the judgments of the self made in other lifetimes. These recriminations must be brought out again, and the insights and new perspectives must be reinforced. This reinforcement process may require numerous additional sessions.

## Failures

If the client is motivated by problems such as a physical difficulty or neurotic behavior, and particularly if such a person has lost a sense of self-worth or is embroiled in strong personality clashes, there is sufficient motivation to expect that positive change from regression work will take place. However, failures do occur even with such clients. They seem to be related to one or more of the following factors:

**Patient failures:**

1. The patient refuses to accept responsibility for his/her life. This may occur especially when the regression work uncovers qualities that the individual feels threaten his worth, or when he maintains a pattern in this lifetime of dishonesty or evasion in order to protect his worth.

2. The patient remains stuck in a role, such as "victim" or "guilty" or a predetermined destiny to suffer, which he feels committed to fulfill or live out.

3. The patient identifies with a religious system that contradicts insights that emerge under regression work.

4. The patient holds a preconception that regression work should be rapid and miraculous and does not allow enough time for a satisfactory working through of the problem.

**Therapist failures:**

1. Failure with clients is due not so much to inadequate techniques as it is to the therapist's adherence to a faulty philosophy of life, one that ignores each individual's responsibility to himself and his destiny in the universal scheme. When the therapist does not hold to a theory of individual destiny that is in conformity with some sort of ultimate purpose, any therapy is destined to fail with many people.

2. The therapist may fail to help the client feel secure enough and free enough from judgment to voice valuable and important subconscious material.

3. There is a series of events in the regression material that is seemingly unrelated to the present, and the therapist has failed to help the client understand the motive or purpose of these events.

4. Even though the original cause is reviewed, the therapist may not press far enough in understanding it to bring about a resolution or to satisfactorily integrate it into a patient's life process.

# Cases

## Family Interrelationships

Many of our attitudes toward significant people in our lives—spouses, parents, children, even close friends—apparently stem from incidents and relationships incurred in other lifetimes. Traditional therapy often results in little ameliorating effect. The affect seems to resist strongly the usual interpretations and conventional understanding of its etiology. Sometimes these attitudes have influenced many lifetimes, especially if there are patterns of anger or deep attraction, and searching them out takes time. Occasionally, however, a client is able to go to a source lifetime immediately, and significant shifts can take place in what seemed to be locked-in, destructive relationships. The following three cases illustrate shifts requiring various degress of exploration.

### Case 1. Obligation from Another Lifetime

Edna came for help in dealing with anger that she felt she could not express but which was so intense that her long-standing habit of gritting her teeth to control it had resulted in damage to her jaw and she had recently had to have oral surgery. At the time she came to me she was 42 and had been married 19 years and had three adolescent children. Her deep anger seemed to be a response to her husband's constant verbal abuse of her and the children. In addition, she carried inexplicable feelings of animosity toward a sister-in-law, feelings that led to embarrassing moments of acting out her rage.

Although she had become a successful business executive in her own right with a more than adequate income to support herself and her children, she could not bring herself to separate from her husband. For some reason, in spite of her children's urging, she found it impossible to leave him, so she repressed her anger, having found that expressing it only made things worse. She explained that her only reason for staying was that something within her would not let go; she had inexplicable feelings of guilt whenever she decided that leaving was the thing to do.

One regression proved to be enough to tap into the source of this problem. The moment she reached an altered state she began to cry violently and to speak in a young child's voice, sobbing so hard that she had trouble verbalizing.

She saw herself as a five-year-old girl locked in a closet for three days without food or water because her mother thought she had eaten a piece of cake, when in fact it was eaten by her seven-year-old brother Edward. Her brother told their mother that he ate it, but the mother did not believe him. Finally the father, who had been away, came home and discovered the situation. By this time the girl was unconscious. She never recovered from the incident and was bedridden for the balance of her life. Her father arranged for her care or took care of her himself until his death. After the father's death, her brother Edward took over her care.

T: How old are you when your father dies?
P: I am about 18, I think, and then Edward takes care of me, and he won't leave me. He wants to get married to Beatrice. He loves her, but he won't leave me because he thinks it is his fault that I have to be in bed all the time. Beatrice doesn't want to live in our house. She wants a house of her own, so he gives her up for me. I don't want him to do that, but he does it anyway.
T: Go to your own death now, please, and tell me about it.
P: I get real sick, and they don't know what is wrong with me. I have a high fever. The doctor tries a lot of things to help me but nothing seems to do any good. I—well, I just die.
T: Can you tell me, please, your very last thought before your spirit leaves your body? What is your last conscious thought?
P: I feel very sad. I think I can never make up to Edward for all the years he took care of me.
T: Now look at this very carefully. What does that life have to do with your present one? Is there any relationship between the two, that one and this one?
P: Oh my goodness! My husband was Edward before—no wonder I can't leave him. I have to take care of him now. *He is having a terrible time in this life and he doesn't mean to be the way he is...(long pause)....* Oh, no! My sister-in-law was my mother! No wonder I hate her so. I feel as though I can never forgive her.

Edna came for two more sessions and the time was spent discussing her feelings and exploring the problem further in an altered state. Though on one level it seemed as though she could not make a marriage work without her husband's cooperation and that more problems would be in store for them in the future if she remained in the situation and continued to be unhappy, Edna was determined to do everything she could to help her husband. As often happens, with this radical change in perception and her altered attitude, her behavior toward him also changed. Her sincere desire to help him and to understand him markedly changed his behavior so that the marriage began to manifest health and pluses for both of them. Edna was happier than she had ever been, and her husband, sensing the sincerity of her desire to help, had even consented to go to a psychologist for a few sessions. Father and older son were enjoying fishing and camping together.

Another striking relief for Edna came in her feelings about her sister-in-law. She now understood her rage from that earlier life and that the sister-in-law was a different personality now, having learned something in the intervening time and worked through what in a further altered state Edna could see had been a mental illness. This understanding dissipated her anger, though a great deal of work went into reaching this more dispassionate and forgiving position.

**Case 2. Under Mother's Apron Strings**

A client in her late thirties, married, the mother of three, came with an unusual reason for seeking help. She was on reasonably good terms with her husband but quietly resented his authority over her, though it was an authority she recognized she had given him. But her major problem involved her mother.

She explained that she had always felt that her mother was right and she was wrong. At the time of the session, her mother was living alone in the former family home and almost daily called upon my client to come over and clean the house or run errands, though her mother was well and strong enough to do these things for herself.

However my client's problem did not seem to be the requests made by her mother but the fact that if she did not comply she felt tremendous guilt. She summed up her feelings with this statement: "It is the constant feeling of guilt because I am 'wrong' that bothers me so much. And I realize I have always felt that way about her even when I was a small child. And somehow I have transferred that authority to my husband, even though he has never been assertive."

I assured the client that her mind knew exactly why she had these feelings about her mother and that her inner self could release this information to her outer self if she would be still and get in touch with it. She was open to the idea that the problem could be explored in an altered state and she went easily into one. She took a few minutes to allow her inner mind to produce and process information and then began to speak in a shocked voice.

*P: I am being dragged behind a wagon.*

With prompting she recovered the following incident. She was riding with her mother in a wagon. She was five years old and liked to watch the wheels go round and round, so she leaned out to watch them. Her mother told her to get back in. The second time she leaned out to look, her mother scolded her and insisted that she sit back in or she would fall, but she just had to look another time and leaned way out so she could see more of the spokes.

> P: *Just as my mother hollers at me to get back on the seat, my long hair catches in the spokes and I am thrown out onto the road. I guess I hit my head on a rock because I am lying in my mother's arms now and there is a lot of blood on my head. I think I am dead.*

I asked her to re-live her last thoughts.

> P: *If I had minded my mother, this would not have happened.*

The client then volunteered that she had died so young in that lifetime that she had waited only about three years before coming back. In the current lifetime, from the time she was very young she had always felt that she would be all right if she minded her mother. Her family had often remarked in her presence about her unusual obedience and what an easy child she was to raise.

Three weeks after her experience, she called to report that her feelings were changing and she had visited her mother and gently but firmly told her to stop being a helpless hypochondriac and find some activities that interested her. She felt freer after that than at any previous time in her life.

**Case 3. An Exchange of Roles**

Another situation where current family interrelationships were influenced by experiences from a former lifetime involved a husband and wife, a brother, and a small daughter. The marriage was in fragile shape because, as the wife reported, in spite of her best efforts she could not control her emotions toward the two men in her life: she responded to her husband with the type of affection she believed would have been appropriate for her brother and continually fought the love feelings she had for her brother, well aware that they were the kind of emotions she should be giving her husband. Moreover, her little five-year-old daughter continually treated her as the daughter instead of the mother. When she cried or felt depressed, the child patted her, stroked her hair, and assured her that everything was going to be all right.

She experienced herself as a beautiful young Japanese girl. Her male relatives had just passed a death sentence upon her because she had fallen in love with a young man of a different clan and thus had disgraced her family. Her mother pleaded for her life but was unheeded, and her brother took her into the garden in her ceremonial robes and disemboweled her.

As she worked on the connection between that life and this one, she realized that the mother from that life was her current daughter. Her past-life lover is her present brother, and her brother from that previous time is now her husband. This insight brought her great relief, and in a few sessions of follow-up and integration she was able to detach herself from that previous pattern. A follow-up three years later found her reasonably happy, and she and her husband were involved in plans for purchasing a new home.

## Guilt

If it were possible to step back and take a long penetrating look at life as it is lived out by most people, one would be appalled at the wasted time and energy unwittingly spent in trying to absolve guilt. That same energy spent in purposeful, creative pursuits could make a great deal of difference in individual destinies, as well as contribute to a more productive civilization.[7] When one considers the evidence that the guilt not only stems from the errors in the present life but is an accumulation of the guilt from an untold number of past lives, the burden is staggering to contemplate. It is no wonder that creativity is stifled in many people and that the world is full of those who do not feel worthy of loving or being loved.[8]

A pervasive type of guilt, called "trait guilt," is often so deep-seated that it does not respond to any current therapies, including psychoanalysis.[9] This sort of guilt is entrenched in a past-life episode, carried in the unconscious mind through one or more physical experiences, and manifests in the current life from early childhood, polluting the individual's entire life experience. The assumption by the traditional therapist regarding this sort of guilt is that an early childhood trauma (in the current life) is responsible. However, past-life work indicates that feelings of guilt have been brought in from other lives and are merely triggered by some early childhood experience.

It must be pointed out that even if the guilt is appropriate to the past-life behavior, which it often is, it still has to be released. The individual's need to bring about punishment and suffering in lifetime after lifetime has to be concluded so that the soul can get on with its journey toward higher consciousness. The process of canceling the expectation that one should have behaved differently is often difficult, but facilitating such a process is one of the responsibilities of the regression therapist.[10]

The following two cases deal with different aspects of guilt. The first concerns unjustified guilt programmed in by powerful outside authorities. The second deals with guilt at first considered to be the result of an action but discovered to be the consequence of an attitude, which is a frequent situation.

### Case 4. A Case of Misinterpretation

Lois presented her problem as a feeling of guilt that she could not identify. She believed she had done something so evil that she could never be forgiven for it, but she had no inkling of the source of the feeling. Her current life seemed otherwise fulfilling and optimal. She had caring parents, a good marriage, two normal children, and a strong faith expressed in a satisfying church affiliation. After she had gone into an altered state, her first words were spoken with deep emotion:

> P: *I didn't do anything wrong. I was only trying to help. I do love God and I was not doing anything wrong. But they are burning me. Oh, I didn't do anything bad. I only wanted to serve God. I didn't know I was doing anything wrong.*

She explained that she was only 15 and had been taught by her mother to heal with herbs and the laying on of hands. A mother brought a very sick baby to her and insisted that she heal the child. Even though she could "see" that the child was dying, she agreed to try, and the baby died. Lois sobbed heavily as she tells this part of the story.

> T: *Relax now and release the pain so we can talk about what happens next that is important.*
> P: *They come and get me. They drag me out of my house and are screaming at me and saying I am an evil witch, that I killed the baby. But I didn't, I didn't kill her. (Again she begins to cry in deep sobs.)*
> T: *You know you didn't and I know you didn't, so why do you feel so guilty now?*
> P: *The priest is telling me that I am a witch and witches are bad. But I thought I was doing what God wanted me to do. My mother told me it was God's gift to be able to help people. But the priest says it is always bad and witches are the devil's handmaidens.*
> T: *Do you believe that?*
> P: *I didn't at first, but he says the Church knows the truth and when people take this power, as I did, it is the Devil working through me and that is why the baby died. So it is my fault, you see.*
> T: *So they burn you?*
> P: *Yes, and I tell them I am sorry, but they say I can never be forgiven; that I am the Devil's handmaiden now and I will always burn in hell. I did a really bad thing and I can never be forgiven.*

T: Go to the last moment before your spirit leaves your body. What is your last conscious thought?
P: I have committed an unpardonable sin. I can never be forgiven. My soul will burn in hell forever.
T: Looking at it now, do you believe they were right?
P: Of course not. I was right.
T: Let's look at why they did that cruel thing to you. Use your intuition and get into their minds and feelings at that time and see what prompted their actions.
P: I feel their fear (surprised). They are afraid of me. They really believe that I am working with the Devil. That is why they are screaming at me the way they are. They are terrified of me. I thought they hated me, but they don't. They are just afraid of me.

Here the technique of getting into the minds of opponents and persecutors and seeing the situation from their perspective is introduced. It brings an insight to the client that seems to facilitate the process of releasing the accumulated negative energy surrounding the traumatic event. While the technique is very simple, the dynamics are very complex. Whatever explanation satisfies the skeptic, whether it is philosophical, psychological, or metaphysical, the fact remains that this technique is a valuable therapeutic device.

As a result of this insight, Lois saw that though she had at the time considered herself guilty and deserving of punishment, she now saw clearly that the priest was wrong and what she had was a gift and a good thing, that she was really doing what God wanted her to do. She was able to leave the guilt back where it belonged. She believed that it was gone. She felt much lighter, sensing that it had all been a big mistake and she was never bad. She verbalized her relief that she had not done anything awful in the past.

Usually guilt cannot be cleared in one regression session, but in this case, as with many fixations on a single idea or feeling, the answer seemed to derive from one specific traumatic event that had occurred in the past. If the client is able to identify it readily, as Lois did, the negative energy from the unintegrated past experience is dissipated almost instantaneously.

**Case 5. How Much Responsibility Must We Assume?**

Margo's case was somewhat more complicated, though it, too, stemmed from a single incident. Her story would have convinced anyone that the world held a vendetta against her. She had had two failures in marriage, with bitterness and anger accompanying their terminations. Her employment record was replete with personnel clashes and numerous dismissals. She had an estrangement of long standing with her parents and siblings. Her primary objective was to discover why her life was such a disaster when she tried so hard to live up to the rules by which she had been raised. In a strained voice she asked where she had gone wrong, and a flood of tears followed the question.

In such cases the cause is almost always found in a previous life, and more often than not, it reflects a past experience in which the person made an error of such scope that numerous other people were harmed.

Margo was open-minded about past lives and quite willing to try anything. She had always tried to be a "good Christian," but prayers and church attendance had not solved her problem. In an altered state she quickly regressed to an ancient culture and saw herself in a fortress with a crowd of people. She was in charge but she resented her position.

> P: I don't want this responsibility. What if I make the wrong decision?

When I questioned her as to who she was and what decision she had to make, she informed me that this was her castle and these were her people and they must not know that she was afraid. Her voice was filled with pride and authority.

I asked about the problem and she told me that her castle was being invaded and the opposing force had a lot more people than they had. She knew that in an open fight they would not have a chance but perhaps behind the walls they could hold out. There was a long pause and her expression indicated a struggle going on in her mind.

> P: They have offered to let us live if we submit to their rule. They want us to surrender.

When I asked her what this would mean to her and her people, she replied angrily that it would mean slavery and they would no longer be free. She thought they might win if they stayed in the castle and fought their opponents as they approached. That was the decision she finally made. After she informed me of this there was a long pause, and then she cried out in anguish.

> P: Oh, my God! I made the wrong decision. They're dying all around me. They're being brutally killed and it's all my fault. My people are all dead. I should have listened.
> T: Listened to what?
> P: Listened to them, my people. They begged me to surrender, but I couldn't. To them it would be changing masters, but to me it was giving up my freedom. I was too selfish to give up my freedom. I have killed them. My stubborn pride has killed them all.

For a while she cried and sobbed incoherently but finally composed herself and we reviewed what she had experienced.

P: *That explains why I won't take responsibility. I am always afraid I will fail or goof up. I am a responsible person, really, but I always want others to make the decisions. (Long pause.) Am I really punishing myself for that? Oh, this is unreal, really unreal.*
T: *Are you still punishing yourself?*
P: *It sounds crazy, but I feel like I am. But I was wrong; it was my fault. I was selfish and responsible for all those people being killed.*
T: *You thought you were making the right decision, so how can you blame yourself?*

I asked this question to help her realize it was not her act but her attitude that was important. She responded as I had hoped she would and in her own words explained how it was the motive behind her decision that was so wrong.

P: *My pride stood in the way. I didn't care about those people. I cared only about myself—that is, until I saw them all being killed. Then I knew it was all my fault.*
T: *Did you die with them?*
P: *Oh, yes. It was after I died that I looked at the horrible scene of all those dismembered bodies and realized how it was my fault. But is was too late. I had to live with that guilt and it seems that I am still living with it.*

I assured Margo that in the next session we would explore ways by which she would dispel her guilt. She was skeptical. She said she felt better about herself, just knowing why she had so many problems, but she didn't see how she could get rid of the guilt when obviously she was guilty.

The following week the answer came to her in a most unusual way, a way that gave her a whole new concept of the human scene as it is responsive to the universal plan. In an altered state she had the insight that man is not meant to be enslaved, that his efforts to achieve freedom inevitably include the death of the body many times but that the soul gains from each experience in its sojourns along the way to perfection. Therefore, in her case, the physical event was just another experience for all of them, and each gained or developed individually according to the attitude at the time of the event. In other words, each individual in that battle gained from the experience whatever he/she put into it.

Margo, as the leader, could have gained much in soul growth if she had been motivated solely by a desire either to protect her people or to keep them free. It was her own motivation of selfishness that had been the cause of her long-standing guilt. This became clear to her, and she was then able to forgive herself for that error and leave it where it belonged—in the past where it had occurred.

The physical event can never be eradicated, but since we live only in the now, the guilt generated then, which had continued to manifest in Margo's present life, became wiped out and she could function as if it had never occurred, except, of course, that now she is a much wiser person.

## Past-Life Precursors of Current Physical Conditions

Sometimes guilt is tied in with physical problems that are carried through one or more lifetimes, and the guilt and physical difficulties are resolved together. The next case involves guilt over an unacceptable attitude where the client came to consciously accept physical restrictions he had put on himself to transform that attitude. The second case deals with the remission of cancer after years of work on its meaning, during which time the client's personal self went through an extended transformation (which might be considered the purpose of the cancer). It would be unrealistic to leave the impression that all physical symptoms are readily removed by past-life work. However, when clients are ready to deal with a problem and are strong enough to face whatever they are hiding, the results can be rewarding and even seem miraculous.

### Case 6. Unconscious Choice of a Disability

Chet's case is unique in that it illustrates how the individual handles guilt over what is considered a flaw in the personality. This middle-aged man was born with one arm and managed quite well with an artificial limb. He married and fathered four children, the youngest of whom was still at home and soon to graduate from high school. He was a kind, sensitive man, the principal of a private school. His rapport with the students was well known to be one of the reasons for the large enrollment in the school.

When he came for counseling, it was for the purpose of improving his relationship with his wife. She was a demanding woman, and from appearances it seemed that she took advantage of his sensitivity. He was beginning to have feelings of resentment which he recognized and chose to deal with directly, rather than allow them to escalate.

He had three sessions in which he dealt with his marital problems at a conscious level. His purpose in seeking help was to talk out his feelings with an objective listener. During the fourth session I felt prompted to ask him if he ever resented his birth defect. He replied that he tried not to, but he often wondered why God had so punished him, and at times he felt resentful. I explained my work briefly and asked if he would like to know why he had chosen to be born with this handicap.

Chet was incredulous at the suggestion that he had chosen his handicap. When I reiterated that I thought he had, and told him that many others have come to understand why they came in with various problems, he agreed that it was worth a try and asked what he had to do. At this point I had him close his eyes and I took him through a very brief relaxation experience, instructing him to clear his mind of all thoughts and simply follow my words. Then I used a counting technique and suggested that he move into his past and find the meaning of his handicap. Almost immediately he grasped his left shoulder. His face contorted and his body doubled up in pain.

T: *Oh, please take me out of this. I can't stand the pain. The pain, it's killing me.*
P: *All right. Release the pain, but remain wherever you are so that we can talk about it. What is happening to you?*
T: *I am pinned under my car. It—we ran off the road. It's dark and I didn't see...*
P: *Move forward in time. What happens next that is important to you?*
T: *I think I die. My girl friend is not hurt so bad, but I—yes, I die.*
P: *Let's go to the moment of your death, just before your spirit leaves your body. What is your last conscious thought?*
T: *I did it again. I did it again.*
P: *What did you do again?*
T: *Oh, my God, I see it all. For five lives I have been arrogant, and I was doing it again. I was bragging to my girl friend, and my soul said, "You're doing it again. Let's knock it off and start over." So I caused the accident...*
P: *Yes?*
T: *Well, that was it. I evaluated the situation and decided that this time I would come back a cripple so I couldn't be so arrogant. I had to overcome this flaw in my personality.*
P: *Well, how do you feel about your decision now?*
T: *I think I have succeeded. I have plenty of faults but arrogance is not one of them. Looking at it from here, it seems that if you are guilty of breaking universal laws you have to suffer the consequences until you learn the lesson. Hmmm, that smacks of religion, which I don't much go for. But that is the way it looks from wherever I am now.*

Chet reported later that he had a much different feeling about himself following his regression, that it had deepened and strengthened his religious beliefs, giving them new and more profound meaning.

## Case 7. Dialogue with Cancer

Ten years ago Ruth Larson became a participant in a research project designed to test the hypothesis that the mind can heal the body of illness. At that time she came because her entire body was covered with psoriasis. For three years preceding our contact she had tried every known remedy but with no relief. She had six sessions using altered states of consciousness to explore the reasons for the problem. By the end of that time her body was clear and the lesions did not return.

In May of 1986 she sat in my office and with a tremor in her voice said that her doctor had told her she had inoperable cancer and had three to six months to live. She had nine lumps, in the glands under both arms and in the lower groin, and dark spots on her lungs, in addition to a back problem that kept her in constant pain. The doctor told her that there was nothing that could be done about the back and she would have to find medication for relief, and he advised chemotherapy at once for the cancer. When he told her she would lose her hair and be ill, she told him that if she had to die, she would at least do so without putting her body through such discomfort. She made an appointment with me and said confidently, "With your kind of help, I know I can be well again."

In our first session we talked about her situation. Ruth admitted that perhaps she was tired of life. She had an invalid daughter who was now in an institution and she felt she was no longer needed by anyone. She maintained a particularly acrimonious relationship with her step mother-in-law. Her deepest subconscious self would have liked to be free, but consciously she had decided to get well for her husband and other children. We discussed the obvious causes of her problem and the probability that hidden rage and resentment were connected with the cancer. She responded readily to the suggestion that she look for some event in the past that was directly connected with the cancer and its purpose in her life.

In a regression she described herself as a young girl of 16 with a white cap to cover her hair as she cleaned a rough wooden table. She lived with her father and older brother in France. Her mother had died a number of years before. The father and brother forced her to cook and take care of the house, and they often kicked and beat her. She described how she died at age 24 from a beating which broke some bones in her neck. I asked her to go through her death and recall her last conscious thoughts.

P: *I'm glad it's over. I'm still angry at them for what they did to me.*
T: *Can you see how that experience is connected to your present situation?*
P: *I feel a great deal of guilt. I'm surprised about that. I should have done better. I though I was trying, but...*

T: *Go back to a lifetime before that one and see if you can find out why you attracted one with so much abuse and pain.*
P: *I am seeing a lifetime where I was a beautiful person with many jewels, a haughty person, not a nice person.*

She described herself as a basically evil person, self-serving in every phase of her life, who used people because she had the power and money. She was killed with a knife by her jealous husband.

T: *Re-live your death in that lifetime and tell me your last conscious thoughts.*
P: *I am sorry, real sorry. My life was one of indulgence—I feel as though it was almost pushed on me. I had it all but I used it wrong. I can see that now.*
T: *Look at the connection between that experience and the present.*
P: *The woman did so many evil things that she had a lot to make up for and after she died she decided she had to make up for that and so in that next life she had nothing and was mistreated; she was a nothing.*
T: *If you paid for being evil in the miserable life as the young girl in France, why have you needed to hang onto the problem?*
P: *It was her attitude. She just built up more karma because her attitude was bad. If she had done it with the right attitude, her father and brother would have been different.*

I asked what her cancer was expressing, and she said that it was expressing resentment and negative thoughts. I asked her whether she thought her anger at her stepmother-in-law had anything to do with the cancer, and she replied that the cause lay in the past, but the stepmother-in-law had triggered it in this life.

I asked her to image the two women she had been in these other lifetimes. She saw them clearly and I suggested that if she felt comfortable, she could approach them and tell them she was sorry for those past lives. They could not be changed at this point, but she needed to come to love those two aspects of herself unconditionally and leave the events in the past and forgive them. After she did this imaging, she reported that the wealthy woman was sad but responded to her embrace. The peasant girl responded to her love but was not ready to give up all her feelings of guilt, reiterating her feeling that she had been a "stinker and rebellious" and that it was her fault that her father and brother had mistreated her.

Following this session Ruth felt so pleased with her insights that she announced she would not need another session and knew her cancer would soon be gone. As I evaluated her session, it was obvious to me that she was far from ready to be on her own. She was a compulsive perfectionist, living in constant fear of not measuring up to her own standards, and her self-image was low. But her determination to measure up to what she thought she ought to be and her courage were attributes that could lead to success. After a few days I called to inquire about her progress and she conceded that she needed more help. Thus began months of weekly sessions.

The next sessions were spent discussing her frustrations over her stepmother-in-law and a brother-in-law from the Middle West who had a history of dropping in unannounced for extended visits once or twice a year. The man smoked incessantly, drank beer, and listened to hard rock on TV. I helped her identify with both her brother-in-law and her stepmother-in-law and become aware of their feelings and why they had behaved the way they had. This approach helped her change her attitude toward them.

Deeper understanding of her anger at her stepmother-in-law unfolded through subsequent regressions. In one, where her stepmother-in-law from this life was her servant in the other, Ruth gave her away because of a rebellious attitude. This act angered the servant. In a subsequent life Ruth was a stepdaughter who at 12 was abandoned by her father and raised by this stepmother, who abused her constantly and called her stupid. Ruth cried as she re-lived the pain of that childhood in the former lifetime.

She saw then that she and her stepmother-in-law had to work out this problem and had agreed to come back into this current lifetime together in order to do it. After years of being pleasant in this lifetime the stepmother-in-law had become ill and was confined to bed, and her entire attitude changed and she became a tyrant. At this point Ruth realized that the woman was terrified and helpless and afraid of dying. The realization made it possible for Ruth, while in an altered state, to let go of her resentful attitude, a release that she duplicated with her brother-in-law when she discovered his loneliness and feeling of worthlessness.

Meanwhile, the lumps had noticeably decreased in size and she became aware of a pulsing sensation which she attributed to positive activity as her body was recovering. I suggested that she investigate the past-life connection between herself and her invalid daughter.

We found that the daughter had in an earlier 17th century lifetime in England been her sister, a slut who was eventually killed in an alley at an early age. Ruth tried in vain to change her, but these efforts only alienated her sister more. Ruth was able to see that she was not at fault for her sister's death in that lifetime. She felt sure that she had come into this lifetime in order to help that soul, who was now her daughter, a commitment she felt she had not fulfilled.

In further sessions she explored her back pain, which had persisted, and found that she was holding onto it because she wanted an excuse not to do her stepmother-in-law's cleaning on her days off.

We then returned to the origin of the guilt which cropped up in every experience, and we found it in the French life in which her father and brother had beaten her. She became aware that her father from the French life was also her present father, an alcoholic who, while he had not abused her, always made her afraid of him. This fear was a carryover of her fear of him in the French life.

Ruth's realization of this connection was followed by improvement in her back and lungs and decrease in the lumps in the lymph nodes. On the 8th of July her lumps were gone except for a slight swelling in one spot under the left arm, which the doctor said might be scar tissue. He had been so nonplussed when new X-rays revealed that her lungs were clear that he ordered the nurse to take pictures three times because he was certain there was some mistake.

We searched next for the reason she was holding onto that one last small lump under her arm. She described in detail a life in Korfu in which her small country was invaded in a war and she jumped off a high bridge to keep from being captured. She believed that suicide was a sin and that she would have to pay for it, a karmic debt which she felt she had not quite paid. As we talked about this, she faced that girl, forgave her, and said she could now let go of the guilt.

By September, the 11th session, her lungs had cleared up, her back was improving markedly, but that one little lump remained. I confronted her with this physical evidence that she was delaying her recovery. In an altered state she confessed that she was not sure she wanted to stay because she felt there was nothing significant to live for and she was bored. Her life seemed to have no significance or purpose. I agreed that if she really wanted to leave and it was time for her to go, I would help her to do it with the minimum amount of discomfort, but I suggested we could look at her life from another point of view. It seemed to me that she could have an important destiny because of her experience and her compassion and sensitivity to people. She could be an inspiration to others who had cancer and perhaps help many toward recovery. This appealed to her but she protested that she was afraid to talk to groups of people. She could talk to one person, perhaps, but more than that was frightening.

A dialogue with her Higher Self showed her standing before a small group talking about how cancer could be overcome. It was real and she believed she could do it. The next week there was no evidence of the lumps, and the doctor had declared her body free of cancer. She asked for a statement to that effect and he gave her a copy of his report but added, "Of course, you know it will come back," to which she responded, "Well, if it does, I'll get rid of it again."

A week later her husband collapsed in intense pain and was diagnosed as having advanced cancer in the digestive tract and died a month later. Ruth faced not only the responsibility of settling his estate but of providing for his father and her stepmother-in-law, but before she could work out arrangements, they both died.

I decided not to do the traditional sympathy routine with her. She had too much insight by this time for that, so I reminded her that the Universe was taking good care of her, that she no longer had to care for anyone and could get on with her life's purpose from that point. She was relieved that she did not have to feel guilty about being glad her responsibilities were over, and she felt ready to look forward to helping anyone she could to understand that cancer need not be fatal. Dealing with the husband's death was more difficult because she discovered she felt responsible, believing that he had contracted cancer because she had it. In an altered state she was able to see clearly that his departure was totally his responsibility and his desire, and from that time on the tears stopped.

On the third visit after his departure she reported that the lumps had returned, but she was optimistic in spite of this, just annoyed with herself for being so vulnerable. She had settled the two estates with her usual efficiency and recalled both the progress she had made over the preceding months and the power that she had demonstrated in controlling her life. We then spent half an hour dissolving the lumps with mind energy, knowing that she no longer needed to express her feelings in this manner. When she sat up at the end of the session, her hands went immediately to her armpits and her facial expression changed to one of amazement as she told me the lumps were gone. Now, seven years later, they have not returned and her back no longer gives her pain.

This report is a condensed version of her thirty-odd sessions, but it illustrates four major factors in regression therapy. First is the primary importance of education in assisting a client to gain a new perspective on life and its purpose. When the client responds to a carefully designed pattern of questions, he/she is led into remarkable insights and is capable of analyzing and evaluating his/her own situation.

Second, it is imperative that the therapist never lose sight of the goal, which is to find the activating cause of the problem. When the desired results are not forthcoming, something has been missed or avoided, and often it is necessary to return to the same past event a number of times, as well as to explore other events, before the core issue is revealed. At times, only two or three past lives are necessary, but often the client has carried a core issue through many personalities, and out of the review comes the realization of the futility of continuing the part. When an adequate review has been completed, a dramatic change occurs in the client. Simply stated, the client forgives the self. This is the bottom line and always brings relief.

Third, if the complaint is a physical problem, it is important to recognize the physiological involvement and the interrelatedness of the psyche and the soma. Ruth's case is a classic example of past traumas being retained in body tissue, and the importance of treating the symptoms as well as working on the remote causes. It also illustrates how tenaciously a symptom is retained in spite of medical intervention if the psychological cause is not found and resolved.

Finally, Ruth's case illustrates the primary importance of recognizing the role that guilt plays in cases where repeated insights fail to accomplish the expected results. Where there has been a series of lives all contributing to guilt responses, it takes more than one or two insights to free the personality of this crippling emotion. Along with the relieving of guilt, there must be a restructuring of the personality in order for the client to achieve true autonomy. Ruth worked hard at this restructuring and now functions with an expanded freedom and acceptance of herself that in the beginning of her therapy she had not thought possible.

Chapter XIII

# Roger J. Woolger, Ph.D.

## *Biographical Data*

### Personal Background

I was born in England and grew up in a free-thinking household with a strong exposure to music and the arts. I attended a traditional public school near Stratford-on-Avon during one of the Royal Shakespeare Company's most creative eras. As a student I took part in many amateur Shakespearean and classical theater productions. I also sang for many years in Renaissance and Bach choirs at school, at Oxford, and later in Zurich.

Always an omnivorous reader and an auto-didact, I had already dipped into Freud, Eastern religions, Gurdjieff and the occult by the time I started college at Oxford. In religion, though nominally Anglican, I was at that time essentially agnostic, my champion in skepticism being Bertrand Russell. At seventeen, shortly before starting at Oxford, I got a job with a volunteer organization in southern France. While in the Pyrenees I had a profound religious experience that shattered my skepticism once and for all. I began meditating and praying regularly and was strongly influenced by Aldous Huxley's *The Perennial Philosophy*. *The Bhagavad Gita, the Gospels*, and *The Imitation of Christ* (Thomas à Kempis) were eventually to become my regular contemplative guides.

At Oxford University I fulfilled the necessary requirements for the BA and MA in experimental psychology and analytic philosophy but generally found the content and approach quite deadly. Fortunately I was able to turn to the theater, music, and my private pursuit of mysticism for spiritual sustenance.

Disillusioned by academic psychology, I worked for two years with the British government as a language teaching advisor in West Africa. I then returned to London University where I completed a two-year doctoral qualifying degree, the M.Phil. in the psychology and philosophy of religion. My thesis, later to be approved for a Ph.D., was on the mystical psychology of Simone Weil, the French Jewish Marxist intellectual (1909-1943) who had an awakening to the mystical life inspired by medieval Christianity, Plato, and the Gita. Around this time my own unhappy married life and depression took me into psychotherapy with the rather unorthodox Jungian analyst, John Layard, who was also an anthropologist of some repute.

As my focus cleared as to what I wanted to do, influenced by Layard I went to Zurich in 1975 to complete five years of training as a Jungian analyst at the C.G. Jung Institute. After that I came to the United States to practice and began a careful study of recent developments in psychotherapy, notably bodywork, Gestalt therapy, psychodrama, Ericksonian hypnotherapy, and birth release work. I stumbled upon past-life therapy from reading and found that it worked well as a complement to birth work: the interface between death and birth work was not difficult to integrate with the Jungian concepts acquired during my training in Zurich. Gradually I became aligned with the movement for transpersonal psychology, with its recent research in past lives and its stress on holistic approaches to healing.

Simultaneous with this period of experimentation was my undergoing and learning the technique known as rebirthing, which uses intensive breathing and hyperventilation to stimulate the cathartic release of birth trauma residues. Finding myself moving in and out of birth trauma material and past-life deaths almost simultaneously led me to the realization that they are intimately connected. Later consultation with Dr. Morris Netherton and exposure to the work of Dr. Stanslav Grof confirmed my growing findings that this is a common experience at the deeper level of this kind of work. I found *The Tibetan Book of the Dead* a useful overview of the total process. After meeting Dr. Netherton and experiencing his particular method, I realized that I had arrived independently at many similar principles and findings. I had been struck from the outset, from my own body work and Rolfing, by the fact that certain past-life traumas appear to be buried in the muscle tissue. Because Netherton seemed to work at this level, I was encouraged to work in this direction. Later I came to understand this phenomenon in the light of the Yogic doctrine of the subtle bodies or energy fields that surround the body.

Although I was familiar with the Vedanta as a graduate student—Hinduism was my comparative religion focus—the question of reincarnation had never been emphasized in my courses or my reading. However, I have always had a mystical bent and found the idea of some kind of survival of consciousness after death self-evident. So I continued to work with past lives and struggled to understand their validity and, more importantly, their therapeutic value. In the process I became more and more impressed by the speed at which many patients experienced relief when I led them through past-life dramas. I began to use the techniques more frequently until today over two-thirds of my practice entails past-life work. After eight years of experimentation with colleagues, select patients, and students, I came to regard past-life regression as a specialized form of active imagination that is extremely valuable for integrating certain kinds of unconscious material.

During the past years I have presented my findings and techniques to professionals and the general public throughout the United States, Europe, and Canada, particularly at Rhinebeck's Omega Institute, the Open Center of New York, Esalen Institute at Big Sur, the more open-minded Jung groups on the east and west coasts, and to groups of therapists in Montreal, Toronto, New York, and Colorado, as well as in London, Zurich and Munich. University affiliations include appointments as Visiting Professor at the University of Vermont and at Concordia University, Montreal, and at Vassar College. My broader teaching activities have included leading tours to Indonesia and southern France and giving film seminars. For 14 years I have had a private practice in Vermont and New York. My publications range in subject matter from Greek goddesses to meditation techniques, with focus on mythology and spiritual disciplines. *Other Lives, Other Selves* was published by Doubleday, 1987, and a second book *The Goddesses Within*, co-authored by my wife Jennifer Woolger, was published by Bantam Books in 1987 and 1989.

My basic perspective in all this remains close to Jung's approach with his important distinction between the personal and collective levels of the psyche and his far-reaching conception of the process of individuation. Past-life work is so dramatic in its intensity and overwhelming in its implications that I am being led to re-vision in less concretistic ways our received views of ego, personality, complex, karma, and more. The picture that is emerging is complex. It has to do with the evolution and devolution of "soul" as a series of compensatory dramas in which, as Coomeraswamy puts it, "the Self is the only true transmigrant." I am currently practicing psychotherapy in upstate New York and travel extensively giving workshops and lectures in Europe and the United States.

## Personal Past-Life Experience

My first encounter with past-life therapy and regression was a purely skeptical one. As a member of the British Society for Psychical Research I was asked in 1970 to review the book *The Cathars and Reincarnation* by Arthur Guirdham.[1] I was not a believer in reincarnation at that time and, striking as Guirdham's case was, I nevertheless reviewed the book skeptically, citing Guirdham's obvious counter-transference to his patient and his patient's unexplored relationship with her father, a Medievalist. My impression was that Guirdham had fallen in love with his patient and enabled her to tune into her father's deep love of the Middle Ages. Today I am not so sure. All three may have interacted in a medieval lifetime.

My first personal experience of past lives was purely spontaneous and occurred during a two-week intensive Buddhist meditation retreat in 1976. During this time I underwent a mild cardiac crisis accompanied by horrible visions of what seemed to be witch burnings. My meditation teacher from Thailand informed me that they were simply past-life fragments and I should let them go. I followed his instructions and wasn't bothered further.

A year later in Burlington, Vermont, I agreed to experiment in a simple form of past-life regression with another therapist I knew personally. From my Jungian training I had done a great deal of "active imagination," which allows images from dreams and visions to be reactivated while one is in a receptive state not unlike meditation. From this experience I found it very easy, with the guidance of my friend, to go into a state where I would seemingly experience past lives. The very first memory to surface was the medieval story with the burning. It turned out to be the Albigensian Crusade and therefore was concerned with the burning of heretics and not of witches. I was a soldier taking part in the massacres and later converted to the Cathar faith. I was captured and burnt. My story was not remotely like Guirdham's, though his book may have influenced it. The process of bringing this memory to consciousness was painful emotionally, and following it I began a personal exploration that continued for nearly two years. In the process I learned to regress not only fellow therapists but a number of other friends who were also intent on learning its therapeutic benefits. For another two years I continued my own past-life remembering and did private experimentation with other colleagues.

# Theory

## Philosophical Hypotheses

1. The personality consists of conscious and unconscious areas. The ego is presumed to be the center of consciousness, while the self is the center that integrates both the conscious and the unconscious.[2]

2. The unconscious psyche is multiple: it is made up of many energy nodes or archetypes that may be conscious or unconscious. Aspects of the

archetypes that are activated during our lives are called "feeling-toned complexes," following Jung.[3]

3. Complexes are experienced in three major ways:

   a. *As projections*, involving others in neurotic dramas and acting out ("games" in the language of Transactional Analysis).[4]

   b. As *somatizations*, such as aches, pains, musculature rigidity, organic dysfunction.[5]

   c. As *personifications*, such as dream and fantasy figures and sub-personalities.[6]

4. Every complex has six aspects to it. Therapy may begin with any one of these aspects, which are all available to consciousness when appropriate techniques are applied:[7]

   a. The *existential* aspect of the complex: problems bothering a person in his or her life *now*.

   b. The *biographical* aspect of a complex: infant, childhood, adolescent or more recent unfinished business.

   c. The *somatic* aspect of a complex: physical manifestations such as illnesses, chronic pains, rigid muscular patterns, breathing and sexual dysfunctions, etc.

   d. The *perinatal* aspect of a complex: all intrauterine experiences and birth trauma residues, following Grof.[8]

   e. The *past-life* aspect of a complex: what in Hindu terminology are called the *samskaras* or psychic residues from previous lifetimes.[9]

   f. The *archetypal* aspect of a complex: these are the universal structural patterns which include mythic and religious motifs such as the sacred marriage, the hero quest, the scapegoat, the wise old person, the mystical union, etc. (These last three aspects, the perinatal, the past-life and the archetypal are also *transpersonal* phenonmena.)

5. No one aspect of a complex is either temporally prior to another aspect or psychologically more fundamental. From the viewpoint of the psyche each aspect mirrors all the other aspects according to holonomic principles (Grof).[10]

6. The *past-life aspect* of a complex arises where there was an event producing pain, hurt, loss, grief, bitterness, etc. in that lifetime; this would be the psychological equivalent of karma. A complex may also arise from fresh events in the current lifetime, the *biographical aspect* of the complex, hence creating new karma.

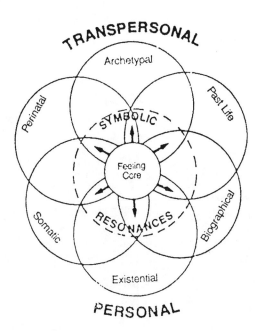

7. There are three distinct levels of subtle energy: thought, feeling, and life energy which can be conceptualized or clairvoyantly perceived as subtle bodies or energy fields:

a. *The Mental Body*: This very broad energy field is the most subtle of the three and is the locus of all powerful mental contents or fixed thoughts. These thoughts may be conscious or unconscious and can radically influence an individual's overall life patterns or self-image. Such thoughts can be the residues of negative past-life experiences.

They do not necessarily affect the lower bodies, but if they do, their influence is extremely strong.

b. *The Emotional Body* (sometimes called the astral body): This energy field is the locus of the *feeling* residues from past events, including, as with the mental body, past lives. These feeling residues may be sadness, rage, disappointment, apathy, etc. This energy level may be strongly affected by the negative thoughts from the mental body. The emotional body is more dense than the mental body. When its feeling contents become highly charged and are not released, the lack of release will affect the lower etheric energy body adversely.

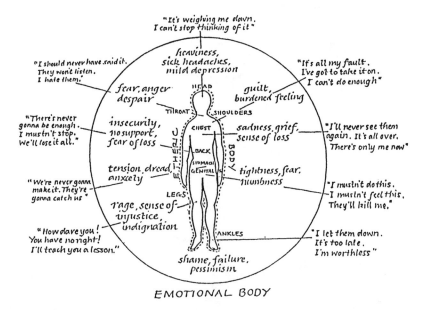

c. *The Etheric Body* or energy field is the most dense of the three subtle bodies and is physically perceptible to many people as heat emanating from parts of the body. It is the field worked with in such healing practices as therapeutic touch and hands-on healing. Residues from physical traumas such as accidents and surgery, as well as past-life traumas, restrict release in this body. Repressed feeling from the emotional body will lodge at the etheric level to produce organic problems.

7. The imprinting of past-life traumas onto the body (violent death, mutilation, disease, rape, starvation, etc.) is transmitted at a subtle level to become part of the *somatic level* of a complex in the current life. Emotions associated with the physical trauma in the past life will also be imprinted along with the somatic residues.

8. Opposite types of past-life memories frequently occur sequentially. One memory simply constellates or brings forth its opposite, as a pair of psychic opposites (master-slave, parent-child, persecutor-victim, profligate-ascetic), they reverse into each other according to the principle of *enantiodromia* described by Heraclitus and by Jung in *Psychological Types*.[11]

9. Integration of the opposites or wholeness is preferred to a goal of perfection or of "overcoming" negativity. Following Jung, the dark or shadow sides of the personality are to be integrated into consciousness and not banished or exorcised as if they are possessing entities.[12]

10. Until a person can acquire a witness point outside patterns of opposites on all levels of the complex, he or she may experience a continuing spiral of lives of action, reaction, and counter-reaction that elude any resolution. The aim, therefore, is non-attachment to the complex.

11. Ultimately all opposites are to be united with the psyche, leading to a state of non-duality or oneness of being. This principle is directly derived from Advaita Vedanta, Mahayana Buddhism and Tantrism:

> *The Great Way is not difficult*
> *for those who have no preferences.*
> *When love and hate are both absent*
> *everything becomes clear and undisguised.*
> *Make the smallest distinction, however,*
> *and heaven and earth are set infinitely apart.*
> *(Sengstan, hsin hsin ming)*

12. It is not considered important whether there is an individual soul that reincarnates or whether it is merely personality fragments or samskaras that are passed on to form new personalities; the work of psychotherapy is to deal with inherited residues, regardless of their origins. Since the archetype of reincarnation is traditionally a wheel, the search for a "first cause" of karma is seen as fruitless. Recourse could more profitably be made to archetypal doctrines of a fall from a higher state of being to a lower.

## Psychotherapeutic Assumptions

1. Past-life therapy is like Gestalt and psychodrama in emphasizing the healing power of catharsis and re-enactment, but it goes deeper, following Jung and Grof, into ancestral dramas that seem to be imprinted on the psyche at birth, revealing unfinished business or karma derived from the multiple lives of the soul. Past-life therapy offers a highly concentrated depth process that can free up and transform the root metaphors or archetypal patterns that can govern our lives.

2. By using a straightforward induction process it is possible to arouse ancestral images from the collective unconscious and vividly recall detailed memories of other eras through an ego consciousness different from our present identity. This ego consciousness has all the characteristics of a full autonomous secondary personality or part-soul. This other self can be of either sex and complements the living ego psychologically in the same way as the familiar shadow, anima, and animus figures from dreams. The difference is that these secondary figures reveal, when asked, detailed and consistent historical biographies, the content of which is often mundane, rarely glamorous, but always full of situations where the subject's complexes are vividly enacted within the constraints of that historical period.

3. The regression technique expands the Jungian injunction to "stay with the image" by adding to it a metapsychological framework that allows more than one reality in which the individual's complexes can be played out imaginally. Moreover, it includes the crucial archetypal "rite of passage" experience of the death transition from one reality to another.

4. The past-life approach entails using a therapist to focus the story and ask questions "as if" it were a literal lifetime and not a fantasy, thus subjecting the story to the constraints of time, space, personal identity, and history. It acknowledges, also, the limitations of the death experience and treats this, too, as a literal, bodily event when it occurs. The psyche responds with great facility to the "as if" of such suggestions and frequently gives quite spontaneous and surprising historical data.

5. Past-life remembering entails a deep projected identification with an inner or secondary personality. This involves imagination, as all remembering does, but in the fullest sense, so that the current personality must put itself in the place of the earlier one.

6. Past-life remembering brings our own inner cast of characters to the surface of consciousness with remarkable clarity, detail and consistency, by allowing a drama to surface among the personified complexes.

7. To acknowledge and to experience the other in ourselves is the first step toward genuine psychological reflection and toward knowing for one's self that in deeper or fuller consciousness we are multiple beings, that we have many personalities within us.

8. It is essential for effective cathartic working through in past-life therapy that the subject fully re-experience the bodily sensations of the past-life trauma for emotional release to be complete. This means staying in the imaginal body of the other lifetime while being aware of this lifetime's body sensations as one remembers the other life.

This overlay is the original cause of psychosomatic symptoms. Bringing the body image into a past-life scenario de-concretizes imprinting of the imaginal body and frees up energy for creative and spiritual purposes. Thus, in the sessions we move from the literal to the symbolic for release. Backache becomes a "broken back," becomes a discovery of new impetus for life. Migraine becomes a "head injury," becomes a freeing from burdensome and painful thoughts.

9. Remembering anger and other emotions and releasing them has a therapeutic effect but the more important release is at the level of understanding the symbolic nature of the complex.

10. There are three levels of experience in working with past lives:

> a. First is the re-living of past lives as though they were real. In this level there is real pain. Real executions are experienced, for example.
>
> b. In the second level the symbolic or metaphorical content is explored. The pains in the neck, in the first level experienced as beheading, may indicate a feeling of being cut off from life. Feeling crippled and being starved for love may now be seen to be metaphors for our current life patterns.
>
> c. There is also a third level which is symbolized by the well-known series of Zen ox-herding pictures where the person who has received enlightenment returns to the market place. Insight is here understood to be in the service of creative productivity and service. It does not exist as an end in itself.

11. When the patient has identified with the opposite personalities in past lives, either in the after-life review stage or at the end of a session when their symbolic meaning is explored, a major piece of the work is done. A shadow figure becomes integrated, a split is healed, a lost part of the soul is redeemed through love and acceptance.

## Indications and Contraindications for Use

In considering the suitability of past-life therapy for different patients, I have come to regard it as a short-term intensive therapy that is best reserved for patients who have already made considerable headway in conventional psychotherapy. It is particularly helpful for someone who feels blocked in certain areas in ongoing therapy to have a new modality to help finish fragments of unfinished stories where the psyche seems, as it were, to be stuck in a groove. Many issues of abandonment and separation, for example, even though they have resisted conventional therapies at the infantile, primal, or birth trauma level, are seen to open up dramatically as soon as scenarios of infant death and abandonment from other lives are re-lived. Often a deep-seated phobia or a sexual blockage can be released catharti-cally and psychosomatically when scenarios of rape, torture, and violent death are re-lived by the secondary ego. Parental complexes reveal themselves in a different light within the power dynamics of entirely different family constellations in another age. Complexes surrounding issues of power or money take on another dimension when memories of famine, oppression, slavery, etc., come to consciousness.

Another group of subjects who respond well to past life therapy are therapists of many orientations who wish to deepen their own process and to become more able to recognize fragments of past-life memories that may surface in their patients. Many therapists, body workers, and healers frequently observe material from their patients that seems to be connected to past lives, perhaps a function of the strong stresses that are being borne by the collective unconscious at this very difficult period of humanity's growth. Past-life therapy can be considered a "therapist's therapy," since it requires openness and commitment of persons who are very advanced in their own psycho-spiritual development. Jung recognized that only the wounded heal, and the therapist needs constantly to work upon himself.

Whether the person is trying to move from a stuck position or trying to deepen generally, the work is best done within the context of some broader frame of ongoing therapy or spiritual discipline. Much of the material that emerges may take many months to integrate fully, and some of it may require a lifetime of meditation and reflection.

My regression work consists of a series of two-hour sessions. Most patients complete their work in from five to ten of these intensive experiences. The longer sessions give adequate time for various stages of the process, and so integration is actually a part of each session rather than being a separate process following regression experiences.

Problems responsive to past-life therapy include most of those commonly brought into psychotherapy:

1. **Anxieties, fears, phobias, and depression.**

Insecurity and general fear of abandonment are often related to past-life memories of literal abandonment as a child, separation during a crisis or a war, being orphaned, sold into slavery, being left out to die in times of famine, etc. Phobias and irrational fears stem from every kind of trauma in a past life: death by fire, water, suffocation, animals, knives, insects, natural disasters. Depression and general low energy can result from past-life memories of loss of a loved one or parent, unfinished grieving, suicide memories, despair and rage as a result of war, massacre, deportation, etc.

2. **General behavior problems.**

These include sado-masochism, a pattern of accidents, violence, and physical brutality, guilt and martyr complexes, eating disorders. Sado-masochistic problems are usually related to a past-life memory of torture, often with loss of consciousness, usually with sexual overtones. The pain and rage seem to perpetuate hatred and a desire to revenge oneself in the same way. Guilt and martyr complexes may stem from past-life memories of having directly killed loved ones or from feeling responsible for the deaths of others, as in a fire, human sacrifice of one's child, having ordered the deaths of others, etc. The entrenched thought is most often, "It's all my fault. I deserve this."

Accidents and violence are often a repetition of old battlefield memories from warriors' lives or from unfulfilled quests for power. These can re-emerge as an *adolescent* neurosis in the current lifetime because this age period is historically where many soldiers met deaths during other lifetimes. Eating disorders are often the rerunning of past-life memories of starvation, economic collapse, or inescapable poverty.

3. **Relationship difficulties.**

Frequently problems of frigidity, impotence, and genital infections have past-life stories of rape, abuse, or torture behind them. Many incest and child abuse stories turn out to be reruns of old patterns where emotional release was blocked. Marital difficulties in general derive from past lives with the same mate in a different power class or sexual constellation: e.g., mistress, slave, prostitute, concubine relationship, often where the sex roles were reversed. Family struggles occur where there are old past-life scores to settle with parents, children, or siblings: betrayal, abuse of power, inheritance injustices, rivalry, etc. Most of the Freudian dynamics emerge here.

4. **Chronic physical ailments.**

These often stem from the re-living of traumatic injuries or deaths incurred in past lives, especially trauma to the head, the limbs, and the back. Headaches may also relate to intolerable mental choices in other lives.

Throat ailments, in addition to being caused by physical injury, may stem from verbal denunciations or unspoken thoughts. Neck aches commonly stem from hanging, strangling, or beheading. Re-living the past life often relieves the pain in these areas.

Past-life therapy does not work for everyone. To some the very idea of past lives is either intellectually bothersome or simply too alien, culturally speaking. But in addition to these cases in which the general attitude is the inhibiting factor, there are several categories of patients with whom I am wary about working at the past-life level.

1. I feel that regression therapy is contraindicated for patients with no therapeutic background because the material too easily feeds into a false literalism that upsets their ability to integrate the past lives as personified complexes. The ego becomes inflated or overcome with the glamor of the memories.

2. For some patients past-life work is too intensive, too overwhelming. They do not need to have the raw areas of their psyche exposed yet again. Instead, for them it is the personal factor in the therapeutic relationship that helps them rebuild their trust and confidence in life.

3. Others find imaging and working inwardly either too difficult or too dissociating. Even if they can remember past lives with ease, some patients do better to reinforce their connections with this life rather than to wander further off into another world.

4. Past-life therapy is not recommended for anyone seeking to confirm some prior metaphysical belief system. Usually it will provide experiences that are distressingly incompatible with fixed beliefs.

5. Past-life work is a moral problem that involves work with the entire ego-personality and requires a strong ego. Therefore, it is not indicated for anyone with psychiatric symptoms. In those with schizophrenic tendencies there is already a tendency for the psyche to become enamored, if not totally seduced, by the many sub-personalities within. It seems highly possible that many of the visions and voices that flood into the psyche of many a schizophrenic are indeed past-life fragments, but such a sufferer will be tempted to over-identify with such fragments and fall into a state of inflation. Such patients also attempt to turn readily available theories of reincarnation and metaphysics into grist for their own personal philosophical mills. Their wonderfully appealing theories often end up being nothing more than a huge and elaborate defense against the simple fact of being alive and present on this earth.

# *Induction*

## Preparation

Usually I start with an interview to explore any current or recurrent problems. In the first session I take a detailed personal history from birth through childhood up to the present, noting illnesses, accidents, or impairments such as deafness, the need for glasses, high blood pressure, etc. I ask if any emotional upheaval occurred shortly before or around the same period of life. This is my procedure for all patients, whether or not past-life work is to be undertaken. Usually I work with an individual patient for two hours.

## Induction Techniques

After the initial interview to explore any current or recurrent problems, the patient is asked to stretch out and is gently guided through a relaxation exercise. In a relaxed state of light trance a number of simple guided imagery exercises or thematic phrases will lead easily and effortlessly into a past-life story where the patient is the protagonist. Sometimes I encourage the patient to focus on a recent memory or a person and start to say whatever comes to mind as if that situation were being confronted. I may feed them, Gestalt-wise, a phrase to sum up or intensify the affect, such as "I've had enough of this. Leave me alone!" Sometimes we may focus on a pain in the body, such as backache or stomach cramp, and allow images to emerge from that area.

As soon as images, words and feelings start to intensify, I suggest they be followed into any story that emerges in this or another life. I tell my patient, "It doesn't matter whether you believe in reincarnation, or not. Simply follow the story as if it were real for the duration of the session." The unconscious mind automatically produces a story that reflects current life issues.

I do not use formal hypnosis in my practice, as I find it quite unnecessary for getting people into past-life memories. From years of dream work I can easily get patients to focus on their inner images, feelings, breath, or body sensations. No doubt this is trance inducing in the Ericksonian sense, but I do not offer it as such or claim it to be hypnosis. I would prefer to call it a kind of guided meditation.

## Four Brief Inductions

### 1. Using Images

We may begin with a dream fragment, part of a waking dream, or guided fantasy, or even a subtle *déjà vu* feeling, such as, "It's as if I had lived in that castle."

> T: *Find yourself back in the dream again with your eyes closed. Good. So you are standing on this bridge?*
> P: Yes.
> T: *What is the bridge made of?*
> P: Seems to be stone.
> T: *Are you crossing it, waiting or what?*
> P: I seem to be crossing into this town. There are people all around me.
> T: *Describe them and their dress.*
> P: They seem to be Oriental, maybe central Asia. Peasants.
> T: *And you, how are you dressed?*
> P: I'm wearing a long robe. Heavy material. A sort of cloth wrapped around my head, like a simple turban.
> T: *How old are you, roughly, What kind of body do you have? Etc.*

### 2. Using Words with Feeling States

If during the interview there is evidence that the presenting complaint is bringing up strong feelings, the patient can focus on those feelings and go immediately into the past life.

> T: *Give words to the feelings you have.*
> P: I'm so sad. I feel totally alone.
> T: *Say that again: "I feel totally alone."*
> P: I feel totally alone.
> T: *Keep repeating that until an image, or the sense of a story that belongs to these words, comes. Maybe you will find yourself in a story earlier in this life, or maybe you will find yourself in a past life. Etc.*

(This approach derives from psychodrama and Gestalt and is influenced by the Netherton method. It also has elements of indirect suggestion derived from Ericksonian trance induction.)

The basic principle is to contact the image, whether it is easily available to consciousness, split off, or somaticized. Once the image is contacted, awareness should then be directed in such a way that affect is expressed *within the context of the image.* Once the image is enlivened by affect, a story is easy to elicit. This amounts to giving the unconscious full rein to express itself on all the levels necessary: symbolic, emotional, and somatic.

### 3. Using Feelings with Breathing and Posture

Sometimes the patient can only talk about feelings in a detached or split-off way. When this is the case, the direct use of words does not work. Breathing is used to activate the somatic level of the complex. Suggesting postures that mimic attitudes that normally belong to the feeling state also facilitates a connection.

> T: *I want you to breathe fairly fast, as though you are out of breath. Now clench your jaw and your fists. Good. Now start to let yourself feel really angry. Angry at anyone or anything. Good. Just keep going.*

The patient may do this for five minutes or more. If it is uncomfortable, this is helpful, since the discomfort will usually trigger the split-off affect. Once the body seems fully involved in the exercise, the addition of words can be made by the patient.

> P: *I don't want to do it. Leave me alone. Don't you come near me.*
> T: *Keep saying that until you seem to be saying it to someone.*
> P: *It's a slavemaster. He's beating me. Etc.*

### 4. Using Bodily Sensations and Pains

All somatic disturbances probably contain deeply repressed feelings that either symbolically express themselves or else mirror a past-life trauma. To access them requires taking sensate consciousness into the area of the disturbance. This may involve one of several approaches:

> T: *I want you to close your eyes and take your awareness right down into your hips, right into the painful areas. Good. What does it feel like down there?*
> P: *It's as though I'm wedged, as though I can't move from side to side.*
> T: *Does it feel like anything is constricting you from the outside, or is it held on the inside?*
> P: *It feels like I'm stuck between something like rocks. I can't move.*
> T: *Good. Repeat: "I can't move," and stay with the image of the rocks.*
> P: *Oh, it hurts! I've been thrown down here. It's a crevasse! They wanted to kill me. Etc.*

Or

> P: *My necks feels tight. I'm tensing my shoulders.*
> T: *What are your shoulders trying to say, if they could speak?*
> P: *No, don't do this, don't do this!*
> T: *Exaggerate your shoulders—bring them up higher. Now say that again.*
> P: *Don't do this. No, no, no! They're going to cut my head off. Etc.*

## Supportive and Deepening Techniques

With these relaxation and imaging techniques and the repetition of loaded phrases, the patient will soon find him/herself in a different body and personality, recounting the story quite dramatically *as that other self*. Then, following the principles of psychodrama, I encourage the re-living, in their fullness, of the major events and turning points of that other life, assuming that the catharsis and release will tend to come at these crucial points of conflict. Whatever arises, however confusing, incoherent, or bloody, I take the patient through to completion. If a particular story involves a violent death, I will ensure that it is fully re-lived at a physically conscious level on the same principle that has been used successfully with shell-shock victims, namely, that only a remembered trauma can be released.

If we read the stage directions to any play we find that everything is written in the present tense, linguistically speaking (e.g., "It is night. The old barn has a small lamp shining dimly above the door. The farmer and his son enter downstage. They are arguing fiercely.") In guiding a past-life session it is extremely helpful to follow this model of keeping the subject firmly in the present, having him recount the story as it happens, event by event, very much as if he or she were in the middle of a drama. Whenever the therapist poses a series of questions in any past tense, this acts as an unconscious trigger which can easily distance the subject from the events of the story so that imagery quickly loses its vividness.

Often during a past-life session, when a subject is being moved forward in time, he or she will overshoot large sections of the story and will spontaneously begin describing the events in the past as over and finished. More often than not, this indicates a strong resistance to re-living the painful core of the event. To counter this, the therapist simply needs to refocus in the present. A simple technique is to ask the patient to go forward to the next significant event. Then, when the habit of relating what is happening in the present is re-established, it is possible to go back to the traumatic event and remain in the present.

Sometimes the opposite resistance occurs. The subject does not want to go forward in time at all because the unconscious is already anticipating painful scenes. Here it is common for an earlier scene to be dragged out moment by moment almost in slow motion so that the subject appears frozen in time. To counter this kind of blocking, it is helpful to use connectors with the present tense, such as, "What do you find when you go up the stairs?" or "What happens when you go into battle?" An even more subtle linguistic way of dissolving this kind of block is to use the conditional tense, "And what would you find if you went upstairs?" or "What would happen if you rode into battle?" The reason these techniques work so effectively is that although the conscious mind interprets a hypothetical situation, the unconscious nevertheless produces an image. It is the image that encapsulates the feared event so that once in consciousness the scene can be worked with.

"How?" questions are among the most valuable for bringing the zoom lens right in close to the traumatic event. Therapists in training often avoid this type of question if a particularly gruesome scene of torture or mutilation is involved (usually the avoidance is because some past life of their own is unresolved on these issues). Nevertheless, in order for a trauma of this nature to be released fully at a psychosomatic level, the details of exactly how will have to be elicited by the therapist with all the precision of a surgeon removing shrapnel from the tissue of a bomb victim.

In addition to verbal cues, such as "how" questions and the use of the conditional tense or going backward or forward in time, I often find it effective to use rebirthing breathing and massage. Refocusing awareness on the bodily experience will frequently open up blocked or buried feeling states.

## *Processing*

### Psychotherapeutic and Transformational Techniques

I always insist that the past-life story be experienced fully in the body, not from the viewpoint of a detached observer. There will often be quite intense bodily convulsions and contortions that are part of the somatic process of spontaneous release—sweating, hot and cold flushes, cramping, temporary paralysis, sharp pains, and other sensations, such as numbness, trembling, shaking, or tingling. I tell patients that this is the release of blocked energy associated with an old trauma. The trauma at a physical level may be from birth, a past life, or a surgical operation in this life, and often all three. Whatever it is, the body is encouraged to express and let go of the shock and the trauma. Although to an observer seeing a session for the first time, this may seem frightening or even a little crazy, it has been my repeated and consistent finding that such release at a somatic as well as emotional level is absolutely crucial to the full healing process.

In general, if bodily sensations and their concomitant emotions are not fully experienced, the complex seeking to express itself will remain lodged in the body because of the imaginal imprinting. No amount of methodical understanding of the meaning or symbolic content or the "karmic" ramifications of the experience will help unless this bodily imagery is allowed to surface as well. On the other hand, if the physical and emotional levels of the trauma are released without a full understanding of their meaning, in whatever framework the subject is open to (psychological, karmic, spiritual), then the subject will tend to remain stuck in a meaningless repetition of the emotions of the past-life scenario and the recurrence of whatever psychosomatic symptoms exist.

In most sessions I attempt to complete the memory of a life story by taking the rememberer through the death of that particular personality. When a death agony is unfinished and is recorded in the imaginal body memory, it becomes re-imprinted in the current life body as if it were any other physical trauma. Also, going through the death brings a sense of completion and, more importantly, of detachment. The death transition is an opportunity to let go consciously of the obsessive and repetitive thoughts, feelings, or fears of that other self. In the after-death period there is usually valuable comparison of the themes of the other life with unresolved issues in this one. Every patient is encouraged to see the story as now finished, as a pattern that need not be repeated.

To start out, in guiding sessions it is necessary for the therapist to take all experiences as completely real—*as if they were literal experiences.* This is the first or *literal* level of past-life work. There can be no questioning of whether this is fantasy or imagination, only absolute respect for the psychic reality of the experience in order that this other life can be reconstituted and relived in all its fullness. The therapeutic "as if" provides an attitude of unconditional concern that is the basis for all successful therapy. Whatever embroidering, distortion, or reworking may occur, each patient's story needs to be heard totally without judgment or interpretation, fully encouraged to be told *as real*. Naturally, there will be painful, even shameful aspects of the self that may have to be faced. This is what is called shadow work—looking at unpleasant and often negative qualities in the self but accepting them as a moral challenge and not repressing them further.

To know the shadow when it has surfaced is a process of constant inner dialogue with this secondary consciousness. I am convinced that our past-life identifications with personalities whose lives have been far from illustrious or creative are a profoundly helpful extension of this process. Past-life remembering is possibly the most vivid and extensive way of facing the shadow—seeing and knowing the murderer, the prideful priest, the cruel soldier, the abandoning mother, the greedy merchant, the sadistic slave-owner—that we may carry in us. These are personifications of the darker but necessary parts of the psyche that all stand in need of acceptance, forgiveness, and redemption. Jung said that we do not become enlightened by imaging figures of light but by making the darkness conscious.

Not all shadows of the ego personality are dark, however. A person with a poor self-image—an abused wife, or a violent rapist—may find in their shadow personalities creative and fulfilled images of self. They may remember successful past lives as artists, leaders, innovators. The psyche compensates the ego personality as part of its tendency to seek balance and stability within the psyche as a whole. Persons who feel powerless or inadequate may be shown lives with extremely powerful political or religious status, power that may have been abused and for which the ego in this or another life feels a need for atonement.

At the first level of past-life work, in which we take all stories literally, it is as if there were a linear cause-and-effect sequence that operates within and across lives. Here the story behind the complex is seen as absolutely real, a product of hidden trauma that is in need of healing through being brought to consciousness. Such past-life complexes arise where there is an area of hurt or loss, of grief, anger or bitterness. By bringing the traumatic incident to consciousness in all its horror and pain there is often a strong cathartic release and complete remission of symptoms.

However, for some patients this re-living is not enough. The causal, literal mode gets them unaccountably stuck. For such patients it is necessary to shift gears and go to the second level of past-life work, which involves therapeutic and transformational approaches on a *symbolic* level. This second level is a total reversal from what is real to what is metaphorical. The aim here is to detach from the stuck place by deliteralizing the complex, by asking for meaning rather than catharsis. As the formulation goes in Sufi literature, "There is nothing in this world but is a symbol of something in the invisible world" (Al Ghazzali). By making use of the after-death state, it is possible to detach from the sub-personality or the complex and see what has been re-lived as more like a dream pregnant with meaning. By standing outside the whole story one can see exactly how one is caught up in the drama of one's complex, and that it *is* a drama. At a psychological level this use of a detached or "discarnate" perspective facilitates the development of what certain meditation disciplines call the witness point.

In effecting these integrating and transformational processes I have drawn from many modalities. Most important have been the contributions of Jung,[13] especially his view that all complexes manifest as sub-personalities that can be envisioned and dialogued with. Moreno's psychodrama has been extremely helpful because it aims for the catharsis of conflicting complexes.[14] I have taken a great deal from the Gestalt theories of Fritz Perl because of their insistence on the contiguity of all complexes to awareness,[15] which was a reinforcement of similar ideas I had practiced in the Buddhist Vipassana meditation.[16] Finally, Reich's insight into bodily armoring and how the body holds attitudes at an organic level confirmed my impressions of how trauma is imprinted into the imaginal body and helped me work out techniques for releasing this.[17]

## Integration into the Psychotherapeutic Process

Most of the work I do is short-term, intensive psychotherapy intended to relieve persistent symptoms that have resisted other therapies. Often it is enough to work only at the first or literal level of past-life remembering. Many patients, however, seek longer-term therapy in the broader perspective of Jungian analysis. For these patients a transition to the symbolic level is helped by dream work and by maintaining a certain attitude to the unconscious that Jung called "living the symbolic life." Such patients often return periodically for substantial periods of intensive work while they continue elsewhere in regular hourly therapy of a traditional Jungian sort.

For patients who have integrated a number of major complexes at the initial level and have begun to understand those "other selves" as part of the larger symbolic patterning of their inner and outer lives, a third level may emerge. This is what I call the *integrative level*, and it closely resembles what Jung called the individuation process—the process of becoming who one uniquely is. A subtle and almost indescribable movement of the recentering of the personality is experienced, which often brings spiritual openings and manifestations of the Greater Self in dreams and meditation. The human comedy of all lives past and present is then seen from a perspective of understanding, compassionate acceptance, and non-attachment. From this standpoint one begins to understand that there is in the end no real division between a literal and a symbolic world. There is simply the one world where "God is a sphere whose center is everywhere and whose circumference is nowhere." This is a point of view that would not have been possible without going through the first two stages.

When we can achieve such a consciousness, all is both one *and* many, and everything is in its place in the ever transforming play of creation. We are called simply to know and embrace our part of this whole, to know that this part is perfect in and of itself. From such a perspective there is no reincarnation because the individual soul that is said to be reborn has no separate reality except as one of the billions of sparks of the greater mind.

This is the realization that many of those who have had near-death experiences have reached. Regression therapy is challenging and many do not want to go all the way, even if it is possible, but however far any individual goes, the regression process can increase the level of freedom within which he functions.

## Failures

Because past-life therapy does not work for everyone, it is important for the experienced clinician to be aware of categories of patients who have little chance of success in this modality (see contraindications). But even when patients for whom regression work is contraindicated are eliminated, there still can be failures. Three groups can be identified:

1. There are patients who are able to image other lives comfortably enough but do so rather flatly and with a certain rigidity in their bodies. They dutifully recover lifetimes and nothing changes. If the body is not alive and sensitive, the past lives that are reproduced will merely mirror back the emotional and somatic deadness of that patient with stories of characters like monks, hermits, outcasts, or others whose lives symbolized detachment, emptiness, and a reluctance to be embodied. In their case I usually prescribe a course of body work or some other kind of experiential work.

2. Stuckness and failure is sometimes a major metaphor in a patient's life, and therapy may be just another place to say, "There, I told you so." For instance, in some cases past-life therapy fails because a person is so deeply identified with a complex that neither in this life nor in any other does he seem willing to relinquish it. A man who had brutally killed in other lives and who had left his wife in this one when she was dying of cancer was so deeply entrenched in his guilt, being convinced that he deserved to suffer, that I could not bring him anywhere near the point of self-forgiveness. He had a negative inflation, seeing himself as "the greatest of all evil-doers," who felt he deserved to suffer to the end of time.

3. A third category of patient with whom I have limited success includes those who are psychologically healthy but who come to me with all kinds of theories about their past lives, possibly derived from Cayce, Seth, Theosophy, or a psychic they have been to. It is not the origin of the patient's beliefs that I find myself suspicious of but a certain obsessiveness in their attachments to these beliefs. This kind of patient, a little like the schizophrenic, is already somewhat intoxicated, if not quite inflated, by some secret and glamorous fantasies about his or her past lives. *It is the ego that seeks to benefit, not the personality as a whole.* Past-life stories and personalities that emerge in the regression process are often far from

flattering to the ego of the experiencer and produce characters that are rarely illustrious or famous. Because of this the regression experience is seen by the patient as a failure, even though the pattern which is exposed might be maximally helpful if it could be observed and transformed.

# Cases

In all my past-life therapy work I aim to clear negative samskaras or past-life patterning at three levels: mental, emotional, and physical. There is no particular order to this process, but the key principle is that the client must fully experience the bodily sensations as well as the emotions until they are completely released. In addition to this, full mental understanding of the karmic or symbolic meaning of the patterns must occur or else the symptoms will simply recur in physical and/or emotional form. Directing the patient to re-live a seeming past-life story *in the body of the past-life personality* amounts to enabling the patient to become aware of the subtle body of the subpersonality as if it were his or her present body.

Being aware of one's previous life through the subtle body is a two-pronged process. Staying in one's body has the dual meaning of (1) staying in the imaginal body of the other lifetime and (2) being aware of this lifetime's body sensations as you remember the other life. Therapy has to be sensitive to this overlay, since it is the cause of psychosomatic symptoms. Bringing the body image into a past-life scenario de-concertizes the unconscious imprinting of the subtle body and frees up libido (or orgone energy, or chi, or prana) for creative and spiritual purposes.

**Case 1. Arthritis-like Symptoms from a Bomb Explosion**

The first case will illustrate the necessity of getting into the actual experience of trauma in the body and show techniques used to accomplish this. It will also illustrate the importance of working both on the level of bodily sensation and at the same time on the metaphorical level. This is a situation where a young woman recovered the memory of a bomb explosion. In her current life the physical feature that was most salient was the arthritis-like pain in her arms and legs that was the expression of the particular stage of lupus erythematosus in which she was at that time. A colleague of mine who is both a Jungian analyst and a physician with considerable knowledge of alternative healing practices, was treating her and was somewhat pessimistic about her chance of recovery. When I met her, the slow spread of infirmity through her limbs had already become a serious threat to the pursuit of her career. I worked directly from her feeling of anxiety about this.

> T: *Close your eyes and simply find yourself at any part that is vivid to you.*
> P: (The whole of her body is trembling violently and tears well up in her eyes.)
> T: *Where are you?*
> P: *I don't know. I think I've died. I know I've died. I don't know what happened.*
> T: *Repeat those last words.*
> P: *I don't know what happened.*
> T: *What went wrong?*
> P: (Her body begins to twitch and convulse and she writhes from side to side.) *I know what went wrong. The bomb went off too soon. I'm dying. Oh, the pain. Oh! Oh! My limbs...it's black. I'm not there.*

I recognized that we were in a death experience of some violence in which, as the victim of a bomb, she kept losing consciousness. From the way her body reacted it appeared that, whoever the past-life personality was, he or she was horribly maimed. From many such experience I knew that the body needs to reproduce the whole of the event for it to be released. Painful as it is, the victim must not become unconscious in her memory.

> T: *Go back and re-live the events leading up to the explosion.*
> P: *I'm with a group of young men. I'm about 19, a man. It's Russia. We're going to kill them. We hate them. They killed my father!* They killed my father! *Several of our group has been killed but we go on fighting. No more of this tyranny. It's time to fight back.*
> T: *What are you doing now?*
> P: *We're carrying bombs. They're for those bastards (soldiers) who killed my father.*
> T: *Go forward and tell me what happens.*
> P: *It's all black. I'm not there. I don't know where I am. But my body hurts. Oh! Oh!*

Edith continued to groan as her body writhed from side to side in a state of utter terror, agony, and confusion. Was she dead? I kept urging her to get an impression of the situation, though she was in tears and resisting.

> T: *Go back and tell me how you died.*
> P: *I'm looking down from outside my body. Oh, my God! It has no arms and legs. There's been an explosion. It's still moving.*
> T: *Go back inside your body and tell me exactly how it feels.*

> P: *I'm dying, lying here on the street. The pain is terrible. No arms, no legs...(Cries.)...Now I'm dead. No more movement. I'm leaving my body.*
> T: *Be aware of your last words as you are dying and go to the point where your heart finally stops beating.*
> P: *My arms and legs will never work again. Oh, no!*

At this point Edith wept bitterly and I knew the possibility that her arms and legs would never work again lay behind her fear of progressive deterioration from the lupus. I guided her to becoming precisely aware of the last few seconds of being in that maimed body.

> T: *Were there any other thoughts you had been holding in your arms and legs before you left them?*
> P: *Yes. I wanted to kill them. I wanted them to suffer like my father. (Crying.) But now I'm hurting.*
> T: *Are you willing to let go of your anger at them?*
> P: *Yes.*
> T: *So let go of the anger and let go of all the pain and tell me when you are finally out of your body.*

Edith took a deep breath and her body went limp. Then, to reinforce her awareness of what had happened, I proposed verbal affirmations to counter all the pain and negativity.

> T: *Make this affirmation: "These arms and legs are strong and healthy and can work for me perfectly."*

Like most victims of explosions, the young anarchist had gone out of his body even though he was not yet dead. The death agony had been unfinished and was recorded in the imaginal body memory of the anarchist life that had, so it would seem, been imprinted on the young woman's body in this lifetime as part of the lupus symptoms of pain in her joints.

Letting go of the physical memories also entailed for her letting go of the vengeful feelings she (he) had carried as the young anarchist, which had symbolically turned against her as "explosive" rage. What is remarkable is that after this one session all the arthritis-like symptoms disappeared. Her doctor, who was present at the session, attests that the symptoms have not returned over two years later. In the case of this subject, it was just as essential for her to understand the symbolic meaning of the explosion as rage that had backfired against her in that lifetime, as to re-experience the death. But both were necessary for healing to occur.

## Case 2. Death in a Gas Chamber

Not being in the body is another version of the defense we described earlier as the temporal distancing a subject will perform to avoid painful emotions. Such subjects have to be taken backward or forward to the crucial existential moment of the trauma and then drawn fully into the body, even to the extent of exaggerating the imaginal psychodrama. An illustration of this was a young woman who described a previous life when, as a 12-year-old girl, she had been killed in a Nazi gas chamber.

This patient's initial account, in her first session, of her deportation to a concentration camp and subsequent death, though detailed, was extremely flat, detached, without catharsis. Painful as it was, we decided to re-run the memory, this time focusing both dramatically and physically.

T: *Where are you now?*
P: *We're in a line outside this building. I'm no longer with my mother.*
T: *What exactly are you doing?*
P: *I'm holding the hand of this older woman.*
T: *How do you feel?*
P: *Terrible!*
T: *Do you cry?*
P: *No, I can't.*
T: *All right. Then breathe very deeply and let any feelings you may be holding back come to the surface. (Coaches breathing.)*
P: *(Breathes deeply.) I don't want to go in there (trembles, heaves).*
T: *Say that louder.*
P: *I don't want to go in there! (Sobs loudly.)*

From then on a flood of emotion emerged and she described in detail the gassing: how it tasted, smelled, and which parts of the body it affected. For several minutes she went through the convulsions of choking, vomiting, and doubling up as she relived her death. By the end of the session, she had released so much fear, grief, and despair, as well as physical pain, that her chest had opened up to a much fuller pattern of breathing, similar to the release experienced in Reichian therapy and rebirthing. Later she reported that a deep-seated depression, that had affected most of her life, was gone and that her breathing was permanently changed. In her case, there had been no particular indication of the bodily blocks. Her breathing had been shallow, it was true, but not exceptionally so, so the clue to the block was the lack of affect.

### Case 3. Suicide

There are many cases where the body images advertise "trauma" very loudly, and when they do, direct intervention may be appropriate. An example of this is a woman of 34, a professional artist, who sought out therapy to deal with a confused bag of complaints about her marriage, about the bad feelings she had about her mother, from whom she had moved, and her notion that it was all connected to a fragment she had glimpsed of a past life as a painter in Holland. As she told her story I was struck by how rigid and tense her shoulders were. It was as though they were held two or three inches higher than necessary.

During the relaxation part of my induction procedure she had great difficulty in letting go, so I offered to massage her neck and shoulders. She agreed, and I worked on the tight trapezius muscle and on her neck. Very soon she slipped into a male life as an impoverished Dutch painter during the seventeenth century. The painter had a wife and a very young baby whom he could barely support. In his obsession with finishing a certain painting he severely neglected both wife and baby, even when the baby became sick. To his horror, the baby grew worse and died and his embittered wife deserted him. The key scene in our work was as follows:

T: *Where are you now?*
P: *I'm wandering along the canals. I can't find my wife. She's left me for good.*
T: *Where do you go now?*
P: *I think, back to the house. Oh, no! I don't want to go back there.* (Her shoulders begin to tense up noticeably.)
T: *Breathe deeply and go back to the house and see what happens.*

At this point the young woman, who had been lying on the couch, shot up to a sitting position, grabbed her neck, and began to scream.

T: *What has happened?*
P: *Oh, God! I hanged myself.* (Sobs deeply.)

For a short while we worked on letting go of the death experience and the emotions connected with the loss of wife and child. But this was not all. When asked to move forward she spontaneously found herself re-experiencing her birth in this life with the cord wrapped around her neck.

Full understanding came moments later when, as a baby, she looked up to her mother, having survived the second trauma.

P: *I know why I'm here.*
T: *Why are you here?*

P: To be close to my mother (sobs). I know who she is now.
T: Tell me who she is.
P: She's the baby who died. I see that I've been trying to make it up to her all these years.

The guilt about the neglect and the death of the baby had been lodged, as an imaginal imprint, at the moment of the Dutch painter's remorseful suicide. It was reinforced in the birth trauma and carried in her body language to the present day. Also carried forward were her feelings about the baby, and these had colored her feelings about her mother. In subsequent sessions she was able to release her feelings of guilt and despair and felt enormous pressure taken off her marriage, to say nothing of how her shoulders noticeably dropped a couple of inches!

### Case 4. Origin of Ulcerative Colitis

As more and more therapists are discovering, there are all kinds of neurotic complaints of both an emotional and a physical nature that simply refuse to be resolved through exploring infantile stories, no matter how far back we trace them. Many children are obviously born fearful, depressed, rage-filled, withdrawn, unable to eat (i.e. starving), desensitized, and so on. It is precisely in such cases that past-life exploration is proving particularly effective, now that we are free to ask the very questions that Freudianism and the *tabula rasa* doctrine of development have proscribed for so long.

Every part of the body, it would seem, has in one person or another revealed some old accident or wound. Past-life traumas always have a *specific* and *not a general* relationship to the current physical problem. Not all migraines derive from head wounds or all throat problems, from strangling. A similar throat complaint in several people may carry quite different stories; in one it may be a death from a beheading, in another, a choking death, while someone else may remember having been hanged. In different people a painful chest or pains in the heart region will bring up memory traces of all kinds of stabbings, gun wounds, lances, arrows, shrapnel, etc. Sore legs and arms remember being broken in accidents or war, crushed by fallen trees, shattered by torture or crucifixion or the rack, or else ripped off by wild animals. A weak or sensitive belly area may recall cuts, slashings, and disembowelings, or else starvation or poisoning. Sensitive feet and hands have in past lives been subjected to every kind of accident and mutilation, to say nothing of performing horrible acts on others.

A young woman, whom I will call Heather, had suffered since early adolescence from ulcerative colitis. Naturally, every kind of dietary therapy had been tried and in more recent years, psychotherapy. Her psychotherapist, who referred her to me, admitted that she could find no cause of anxiety to account for the ulcers in Heather's present life, despite many months of probing, so we agreed to try a past-life session.

The story that immediately surfaced took us to Holland during World War II at the time of the Nazi invasion. Heather found herself an eight-year-old girl in a Jewish family living in the Jewish neighborhood of a small Dutch town. In the first scene to surface she was happily helping her mother bake bread when the sounds of explosions reached their ears. The Nazis were systematically blowing up and setting fire to the terraced houses to "flush out" the inhabitants onto the streets. The mother, panicking, pushed the children onto the street, telling them to run. The street was full of townspeople running in all directions. There were armored cars and jeeps following them, and everywhere the sound of gunfire.

The little girl ran down an alleyway, thinking it to be safe, and watched for a time from behind a wall, seeing some neighbors and friends shot, but mostly rounded up by the Nazis. Fleeing farther from the smoke and explosions, she turned a corner and almost ran into a van commandeered by the soldiers. They caught her and shoved her into the back with other captives.

Later, she and the others were herded out and lined up in front of trenches that had been dug as mass graves. Standing and watching lines of people being machine-gunned as she awaited her turn, she reported that her stomach was totally knotted in terror. Eventually her turn came and she fell back, shot, onto a pile of dead and dying victims. She didn't die immediately; other bodies fell on top of her, and she finally died of suffocation and loss of blood. Her stomach remained knotted in terror throughout this appalling ordeal. My approach during our session was to direct her to breathe deeply and to let go of all the fear and anguish as much as possible. Given this permission she broke into convulsive sobbing, screaming, and keening. As the young Jewish girl she had died, so it seemed, unable to express the terrible shock of losing her parents, seeing mass slaughter, and facing her own premature death. Phrases such as, "I'll never see them again," "Help me!" "I can't get away," "It's too late," surfaced spontaneously and her body went through violent convulsions and dry vomiting for a while.

When it was all over Heather was exhausted and depleted, yet she felt unburdened of a fear she had always dimly sensed and that she now understood. Her stomach condition improved radically after this and a couple of follow-up sessions.

The important principle that may be gleaned from this highly condensed description is that there is a descending order of influence from higher to lower among the three subtle bodies. In Heather's case the following pattern can be discerned:

1. The unconscious thought: "I am in danger" (mental level) makes Heather feel perpetually anxious (emotional level);

2. Heather's perpetual anxiety (emotional level) creates constant tension in her abdominal region (etheric level);

3. The constant tension in Heather's abdomen (etheric level) affects the gastro-intestinal (somatic) system to produce ulcers.

In many cases, once we shift our focus away from supposed early childhood traumas in this life and give the deeper unconscious permission to express itself, we find that, as in this case, the presenting symptom seems to be derived from a past-life memory. There had been no event in Heather's current life experience remotely severe enough to induce fear symptoms as heavily somaticized as ulcers; in fact her complaint was quite out of proportion to the relatively untroubled course of her current life. Yet immediately after the past-life story of the Dutch Jewish girl emerged, we found traumatic images that were entirely consistent with her symptoms.

**Case 5. Stage Fright**

The subject, Mike, was a social worker who suffered terrible panic attacks every time he had to make any kind of presentation to his colleagues at meetings. About an hour before the appointed time of a meeting he would become uncontrollably nervous. His chest would tighten, his breathing would become constricted, and he would experience severe heart palpitations. In Mike's case I did not need to encourage him to be aware of his body as he described his problem: "My palms are starting to sweat as I talk about it," he said. He also described his tight chest and stomach.

Were these reactions new? By no means. Mike recognized them from childhood, where he remembered a painful experience at a talent show in which he had been forced to perform. The overriding feelings then as now were of fear and shame. And yet, neither as a child nor as an adult could he find any memory of anyone actually doing anything to humiliate or shame him.

Here is a condensed extract of how our exploration of these feelings and somatic reactions proceeded:

T: *So what does it feel like every time you go into one of your staff meetings?*
P: *Terrible panic. I feel like I'm gonna die. (Touches his chest.) Everything feels like it's gonna shut down. I can feel my heart beating like crazy when I talk about it now.*
T: *So what thoughts go with this? You're clearly in a huge conflict.*

P: I've got to do it, but I don't wanna do it. Oh, my God! No! How do I get out of it? *(His stomach seems to be tensing up and his arms are becoming rigid.)*

T: What does your stomach want to say?

P: I don't want to do it. How do I get out of this? Oh God! It's this terrible sinking feeling. My chest is all tight and my stomach feels like it's gonna drop out.

T: Stay with the feelings and what your stomach wants to say and just follow it.

P: I don't want to. I want to be left alone. Please don't make me! No, not in front of them all! I'm trapped. I can't get out of it. *(He is noticeably writhing from side to side now.)*

T: Let yourself go into any other life story these words apply to.

P: I get a church. And a crowd. Yes, lots of people. Oh no! I don't want to. Don't make me!

T: Say that to them, not to me. Stay with the images and your body.

P: It's terrible, I'm afraid. I'm not gonna show my fear. They're making me go there. Oh help! My hands and neck! They're really hurting.

T: What seems to be happening to you?

P: They've got my wrists bound behind me. Something touching my face. I can't see. Now it's my neck. Oh help! They're gonna hang me!

T: I want you to go all the way through it until it's over. The pain will pass, but it needs to be released. Keep saying exactly what you feel as it happens.

Mike's breathing became intense as he lay writhing on my mattress. He reported tingling in his hands and feet and increasing panic in his stomach. His struggle increased until the end. He was obviously fighting the execution all the way. I encouraged him to do so, since this was where all his tension was locked up.

P: I can't get out of it. I'm really stuck now. I don't wanna be part of this, but there's no way out. *(There are clearly elements of birth trauma in this part of the story.)*

T: What is your stomach saying?

P: I don't wanna do this. I don't wanna do this! I hate this. I can't get out of it. I wanna leave.

Mike continued his death struggle as the hanged man for some while. He experienced strong electrical tingling in his hands, face, neck, chest, and stomach. He kicked violently, reproducing the desperate attempts to touch the earth that his former self has been deprived of doing. A comprehensive etheric release took place as the parts of the body that had held the subtle body imprint of the trauma relived the event. Finally, his body went limp as he reached the moment of the past-life death. He wept, his chest heaving;

"There was nothing I could do." There was more release and opening in his chest. His breathing expanded considerably when the trauma was past.

We took as long as he needed for the energy release to be complete and for all the feelings to be expressed and verbalized. Then we went back to the events that led up to the hanging. Mike remembered himself as an adolescent boy who had robbed a man and then in a tussle knifed him. He was caught by the villagers and brought to trial, where he was condemned to death by hanging.

Mike remembered the jail cell, his huge public humiliation, and above all the sense of doom and powerlessness that sat in his chest and stomach in the last hours before he was taken to the scaffold. Needless to say, as an adolescent in this story, his life force was very strong, which was mirrored in his physical resistance to dying. This was why I encouraged him physically to express all aspects of the struggle, to maximize the etheric release, aspects of which were clearly locked into his chest and stomach in the present lifetime.

The remainder of our work consisted of helping him dissociate the old trauma from its current-life parallels. I suggested affirmations such as: "I am on the earth. I am fully in charge (for his stomach). I am proud of my work. There is nothing to be ashamed of any longer."

One interesting corollary to his experience was that Mike then remembered that he had several times stolen unimportant things as a child, always feeling deeply ashamed and unworthy when he was caught. He realized how he had been unconsciously replaying the old story, testing to see if stealing would be as fatal as it had been in the past life. He did not, until now, connect it to his public speaking anxiety.

In later sessions Mike reported almost total absence of panic feelings at meetings and a sense of greatly increased vitality and power in his life in general. The trapped and humiliated adolescent in him had been freed and was now contributing energy to his life instead of draining it.

**Case 6. Symbolic Body Trauma**

There are many cases where the transformational and therapeutic aspect lies in the symbolic handling of the materials. In this sort of work, guides, who are representatives of a transcendent function, may intervene to assist in helping the person in regression to achieve the witness point. Such was the situation with a young man, a teacher, who had been experiencing an almost paralyzing stage fright whenever he lectured to audiences larger than a small class. A seemingly unrelated body problem was poor circulation in his hands and feet and constant stiff necks.

In a past-life session he relived a life as an influential wandering teacher in the Middle East, a man who had attracted such large crowds that he and his following threatened to disrupt the stability of a small caliphate. He was arrested and martyred, first by having his hands and feet cut off, then by being left crucified overnight on a gibbet, and finally by being beheaded in the morning.

For many months following this, he experienced an agonizing catharsis during massage sessions whenever his hands, feet, or neck were touched. But when he again went through the death in that lifetime, this remarkable experience occurred. He floated above the earth and was met by a loving group of guides, a phenomenon quite common in the after-death state. He asked these guides why he had died so horribly. The answer came back immediately:

*You lost your hands because you were out of touch with the people.*
*You lost your feet because you were off the earth.*
*You lost your head because it was too puffed up with knowledge.*

These words struck such deep chords within him that he spent nearly a year meditating on them. When he came to a resolution, synchronistically he was offered a job lecturing to a large audience and found that his stage fright had now disappeared. Gradually, also, as the circulation in his hands and feet returned, he began to show some talents as a healer.

In his case the breakthrough came in the after-death state when he was able to stand outside, detach from the sub-personality or the complex he had been dramatically reliving, and see the whole experience more as a story, a dream play pregnant with meaning. It is similar to a technique used in psychodrama where the protagonist appoints substitutes to play himself and all his alter-egos. By standing outside the whole story this teacher was able to see exactly how he was caught up in the drama of his complex and that it *was* a drama. In other words, he had reached the witness point. Guides, or a higher sub-personality, however one wishes to understand it, had given him wisdom and insight. In this past life was evidenced the polarization of the teacher's complex: it demonstrated how spiritual pride had constellated its opposite in an utterly humiliating death, in this instance within that same lifetime.

# Chapter XIV

# Edith Fiore, Ph.D.

## *Biographical Data*

**Personal Background**

During my growing-up years I lived with my father, a portrait painter and teacher, and my mother, a dynamic, creative person, and two younger brothers. I attended various denominations of Protestant churches, ranging from Dutch Reformed to Episcopal, whichever was closest to our farm at the time. However, in spite of this conservative background, I told people I was Egyptian, a self-evaluation tolerated on the ground that I was an imaginative child. In the world in which I lived at that time, the emphasis was on this life as our one and only life—anything else was considered heretical.

My unquestioning faith in God became shattered during my freshman year at Mt. Holyoke College when I was first exposed to agnosticism, which fitted in with my scientific bent. (This agnosticism persisted until I began to encounter past lives through my patients' regressions.) During my college period I used to sculpt and for a time entertained the idea of becoming a sculptress. However, my interest in psychology won out and I began conventional professional training and education in psychology with a heavy emphasis on the scientific method. Not once in the nine years I spent studying as a graduate student at the Universities of Maryland and Miami was the concept, or even the word reincarnation, used. Education in those days was strictly in the observables.

During those nine years, I found myself strongly attracted to the writings of Freud, despite the fact that they were down-played by my professors. His work convinced me that the way to help people was to bring to light motivations hidden deep in the recesses of their minds and I became fascinated with the potential of hypnosis as an answer to this need. Through my long years of training hypnosis had not been taken seriously. The only reference to it was a few paragraphs briefly reporting that Freud had used it initially and had later given it up. Nowhere was it mentioned that at the end of his long career Freud stated that hypnosis, because of its efficiency, was the key to helping people. Medical schools were slightly more open, and in 1955 the British Medical Association, and in 1958 the American Medical Association, gave official sanction to hypnosis and suggested that medical schools include it in their curriculum, a delayed concession, considering that hypnosis as a tool of psychological healing had been employed in many different forms since the beginning of history.

My first exposure to the techniques of hypnosis came almost by accident. On the spur of the moment, I decided to drive down the coast to Big Sur for a weekend seminar in self-hypnosis healing at the Esalen Institute. Little did I realize that this single seminar would change the course of my life. I returned home with new skills and soon asked a few patients if they would agree to learn self-hypnosis, which I was convinced would greatly reduce their level of anxiety. The success of those early patients who used hypnosis motivated me to learn more about this technique.

I had previously been in private practice in Miami but by the time I learned hypnosis I had opened an office in Saratoga, California, where I still practice. After further training in hypnosis, I joined the American Society of Clinical Hypnosis, the International Congress of Hypnosis, and the San Francisco Academy of Hypnosis. Through these contacts I was able to attend many excellent seminars and advanced workshops.

In my practice I found myself applying simultaneously what I had learned at hypnosis workshops, scientific meetings, and from my never-ending reading, and it had begun to reap rewards. Hypnotic techniques greatly speeded the therapeutic process. Problems that had in the past taken years to resolve were now often cleared up in a matter of months or less. For me, an even more gratifying development than the decrease in the number of sessions and time per case was the confidence that I could aid a person to help himself or herself, and that, using hypnosis, the problems could be solved and the symptoms removed.

When I first began using hypnosis, I, like many other hypnotherapists, asked my patients to comb back through the years, revealing events in their childhood that had caused present symptoms. The recall of these events often removed the symptoms. Problems could be traced back to the first months, even to the birth experience, which in many instances had left the person feeling guilty, unwanted, and sometimes with such lifelong symptoms as depressions, headaches, and asthma. Gradually I moved patients back even further, discovering emotional problems arising from the supposedly cloistered months in the womb.

During those years I had no interest in the idea of reincarnation, but my indifference was shattered by a patient who, when asked under hypnosis to go back to the origin of his sexual problems, said, "Six lifetimes ago I was a Catholic priest." We traced back through this seventeenth-century life, looking at his sexual attitudes as an Italian priest. I was unconvinced this was indeed a previous existence. But the next time I saw him, he told me that he was not only free of his sexual problems but he felt better about himself in general. Several other apparent "past lives" resulted in a similar remission of symptoms, and I became aware that this process was a new and effective therapeutic tool.

Currently I use hypnoanalysis exclusively in my practice because the roots of symptoms often lie in past lives, and we deal with those former incarnations that are responsible for the particular problems. I use hypnosis, but if there is a crisis, supportive psychotherapy is undertaken. In addition, I am finding evidence that many problems are caused by possession by earthbound spirits and I use depossession as a means for relieving those patients.

I have travelled extensively, lecturing on past-life therapy in England, Argentina, Egypt, Australia, Italy and Brazil. To date I have had three books published: *You Have Been Here Before (1978)*, *The Unquiet Dead (1984)*, and *Encounter, (1989)*.

## Personal Account of Past Lives

Several of my own past-life memories have come in dreams. In an early dream I found myself as a lady of Spanish nobility. I was wearing a tiara and black clothes and was riding in a carriage with my infant son and my sister. We were trying to escape and struggled to get the carriage through an agitated crowd. When we got through, I thought my son was damaged, but when I unwrapped him, I saw that his leg was not pulled off as I had feared. I fell to the ground and kissed it in thankfulness.

For many years I had trouble sleeping on my back and could never understand the reason for this. One night as I was falling asleep I had a flashback that took only ten seconds but changed all the former discomfort. I found myself saying aloud, "Oh, God, not another seizure!" Tears spurted from my eyes as I turned to my left side, ostensibly to keep from swallowing my tongue. It awakened me with a start. I recognized this feeling as a residue from another lifetime and the reason I had not been able to sleep on my back. After that I had much less difficulty. If I had completed the experience, I would probably be cleared of the symptom completely. That experience helped me shift from an intellectual skepticism to a more accepting attitude regarding the validity of reincarnation.

My late husband was a film maker. For many years he had a hard time leaving me to go on location, even when all his crew had been assembled and everything was ready. In a regression he experienced a life as a Roman centurion whose wife (myself) was Greek. He often had to leave me to go off to battle, and one time he left and was killed. In my grief I stabbed myself in the abdomen. After this regression my husband had no further difficulty in leaving me and I could understand our relationship better.

In a number of past lives I have found myself as a priestess in Egypt, and in the Yucatan I was a priestess-healer who astrally projected and healed while in my astral body. This helped me to understand my early childhood conviction that I was Egyptian and my deep draw toward Egypt, as well as my commitment to a healing profession.

# *Theory*

## Philosophical Hypotheses

It is not essential for the therapist using past-life regression to embrace a philosophical belief in reincarnation. Nor is it necessary for the patient to hold such a belief. I use the following as "working hypotheses."

1. I believe that we are born again and again in physical bodies in order to perfect ourselves.

2. We are always meeting ourselves. There are no accidents—ever. We are never victims. If a person is raped in the current life, he/she has raped in another lifetime. If a person seems to have a "lucky" life, it is because it has been earned.

3. We build into our lifetime the challenges and tests that we need, the karma that we need to fulfill, to meet, to accept. How we accept it, whether we handle it in a positive way rather than in a negative way, determines how much spiritual growth we achieve.

Some philosophers feel that we keep evolving until we become one with the universal mind, but I have not accepted or rejected this hypothesis at this point in my personal search.

## Psychotherapeutic Assumptions

1. If a patient deals with the memory of what has caused the problem, there is a therapeutic result, usually a total freeing of the symptomatology.

2. Through the process of remembering we discharge the energy tied up with the memory, and it does not continue to create a state of disease.

3. It is necessary for the person to deal with the causative event. It is not necessary for the person to forgive himself, to accept the incident, or to believe that it really happened. The therapy is achieved at the moment a person "looks" at the event and/or deals with it.

4. Beneath each symptom lies energy-sustained guilt. If the patient remembers a traumatic death as victim, then it is helpful, but not necessary, for him to go back to the karmic event which necessitated this outcome.

## Indications and Contraindications for Use

Any symptoms or problems that are not directly caused by current situations have their roots either in repressed memories or in possession by earthbound spirits. The memories are usually past-life memories involving traumas, often traumatic death experiences. I use past-life therapy with any problems that are brought into my office, from physical problems of all kinds, to emotional, mental, and spiritual problems. Many of my patients have discovered that the causes of their phobias, fears, and even aversions, are rooted in traumatic events of previous lifetimes. They have found that irrational fears of snakes, fire, being alone, flying, crowds, natural cataclysms (such as earthquakes and storms) are derived from traumas experienced in a past life. Fear of the dark, especially, seems to originate in some terrifying incident that happened in the dark during a former life. Insomnia and sex disorders can stem from horrifying experiences such as sexual molestation or murder that happened during sleep in past lives.

Headaches, pains, disorders, or weaknesses of certain areas of the body are often related to events that occurred in former lifetimes. Headaches, including migraines, have been found to be the result of a patient having been guillotined, clubbed, stoned, shot, hanged, scalped, or in one way or other severely injured, usually fatally, on the head or neck. Several people with chronic intractable pain have re-lived having been run through with swords, bayonets, or knives. Even the origin of menstrual problems has been traced to traumas, usually sexual, suffered in previous lives.

I do not work with psychotics because of the problem with sustained attention span. Nor do I work with the mentally retarded, for the same reason.

# *Induction*

## Preparation

Because of my extensive work in past lives, most of my patients come to me expecting to work in this modality. I see regression therapy as an extended form of therapy. Ample time is given for adequate preparation and for integrating perceptions into the patient's life experience to the extent that this is needed.

During our first session the patient tells me as much as possible about the symptoms or problems. I want to find out as many details as I can in order to develop "leads." This process generally involves a very precise history of the problem and its ramifications, including any measures that have been taken. It includes asking about recurrent dreams, especially nightmares, which are usually flashbacks to an important past life. Any notable one-time dreams, or dreams that have a scenario that could be construed as a past life, are also discussed. My assumption is that the mind is always trying to heal us as, for example, through recurring dreams. Unfortunately, the person usually doesn't allow the flashback to continue through to its conclusion, so the healing does not take place. From the start I structure the therapy as a joint effort of two "detectives." One knows (at a subconscious level only) the source of the problem. The other (myself) knows how to track down this elusive source. So we look for clues in details of the history.

I make it an article of faith to be totally open with patients throughout treatment. What I know or guess about them, they know. So, even in the first session, I share any hunches I may have about what kind of subconscious event or events may be causing the problem. If I am right, this openness helps to speed up treatment. If I am wrong, it seems to have no negative effects. I point out, also, the nature of the therapy and the role of resistance, and I answer any questions.

During the second session I explain the nature of hypnosis, especially emphasizing that the patient may not feel at all hypnotized, will not be "unconscious," and generally will have total recall of all that is experienced. I make it clear that there is no loss of consciousness; therefore the patient is not under the control of anyone else. Next, I outline my procedures for the regression, describing briefly the induction techniques, and present a viewpoint that is helpful in dealing with what will be experienced. I give the analogy of the court reporter who takes down everything the witness says without judging the material that comes to mind. With just such objectivity the patient is to report verbally everything that is experienced (body sensations, perceptions, thoughts, and emotions).

At the end of our first double session, or our second session (if the first two sessions are on different days), I make a self-hypnosis tape, using the induction that I will use in our work together. Imbedded in the induction are suggestions that the inner mind will bring up therapeutic dreams that will be remembered and understood the following morning, and that there will be particularly significant dreams that will actually be flashbacks to former lifetimes. I see this as an excellent preparation for ongoing treatment. After I finish the tape, I re-hypnotize the patient and ask the inner mind to select two fingers: a "yes" finger and a "no" finger. The inner mind is instructed to lift the fingers without any help or hindrance from the conscious mind. It must be noted that finger signals, though helpful, should not be relied upon to be always correct.

## Induction Techniques

On the first side of the tape made for the patient at the end of the double session are suggestions for well-being. On the other side is a depossession process in which I speak directly to the possessing spirits. I tell them that their bodies are dead, that they should have gone into the spirit world but instead they have joined the patient. I call their attention to loved ones present who will help them go into the Light. I then say a blessing. The patient is asked to use the tape daily during the days before the next session. Formerly I used a relaxation induction, but I have found this to be too time consuming and not necessary.

I have the patient lie in a reclining chair with a pillow and covered with a soft light blanket, as the body temperature tends to drop during hypnosis. I have the patient begin, with closed eyes, to concentrate on breathing and then visualize a miniature sun in the solar plexus radiating out through the body and beyond an arm's length in every direction, creating an aura of brilliant white light. I explain that this raises the frequency of the already existing aura, preventing anything of a lower vibratory nature from penetrating it, thus protecting from any negativity that is of a lower frequency. Once protection is in place, I suggest that the patient imagine himself standing at the top of a beautiful staircase, the staircase to his subconscious mind, seen as an actual staircase. Then a step down is to be taken with each count from 21 to one. I use this with almost everyone, the only exception being when there is some trauma associated with going down a staircase, in which case descent in an elevator can be substituted.

The second stage of the induction is modified somewhat according to the problems or symptoms of the patient. As the bottom of the stairway is reached, I say, "Your subconscious mind holds a perfect record of everything that you have *ever* experienced, exactly as you have experienced it. Every sight, every sound, every taste, every smell, every thought, every emotion, everything is faithfully recorded. Now your inner mind is going to take you back in time and space, back to the very event itself responsible for your problem." I then describe the problem or symptom and suggest that this event will come to mind at the count of ten. Without any more deepening work, I count directly to ten.

## *Quick Induction*

*Realize that you have the power to help yourself. Just as your body can automatically heal itself, so can your mind heal itself if you really want it to.*

*Lie on the chair/couch and relax completely. (If air is cool, place a light blanket over the client.)*

*Close your eyes and relax your whole body. Let every part of your body become limp and relaxed. Relax every muscle. (Therapist names each part of the body and suggests that it is relaxed. Make sure legs are uncrossed.)*

*Concentrate now on your own gentle breathing. Notice each separate breath as it goes in and as it goes out.*

*You will go deeper and deeper inside yourself with each out-breath... Each time you breath gently out, you will drop deeper and deeper inside yourself ...inside your own mind.*

*As you breathe gently, imagine a bright light in the center of your solar plexus, just above your navel. It is like a miniature sun shining in the middle of your body.*

*You are now completely protected by the white light of this sun, which is expanding softly to fill your whole body with bright light. It is expanding out to your fingertips and up to above the top of your head and down through the soles of your feet. Your whole body is softly glowing with protective white light. You are quite safe. You are deeply still.*

*Each breath is taking you deeper. As you breathe out, you feel yourself sinking deeper. Each out breath is taking you down, deeper down into an inner state.*

*Now you are at the top of a flight of stairs that are covered with a thick plush carpet of your favorite color. Feel its softness with your toes. As you stand at the top, take hold of the bannister railing to steady yourself gently.*

*You are now going to walk slowly down the steps, one at a time, and with each step down and each out-breath, you will sink even deeper inside yourself, even deeper into your mind.*

*As you walk down I will count slowly backwards from 20 to one, and you will go down one step at each count. Each step will be a step down inside yourself, into the deep self-center of your mind.*

*Now take the first step...20...Step down again. 19...(Therapist pauses between steps.) And again. 18.... Deeper down now. 17.... Still deeper. 16...down, down. 15...deeper inside. 14...13...12.... Step down deeper. 11...10...nine...still. Eight...seven...six...very deep now. Five...four...deeper still. Three...two...now you will step down the last step into your deeper inner self. One...and you are there now.*

*Now I am going to count to 10 and you will go to an event before you were born where you experienced.... (State symptom or troublesome situation.)*

## Supportive and Deepening Techniques

I conclude this two-stage induction by asking the patient to go to the event responsible for the problem (specifying what it is and what is being experienced). I avoid asking what is *seen* because this may bring up the whole problem of whether he is recalling "seeing" things, or not. If the patient comes up with something, my main role at this point is just to allow the theme to be developed. If blocking occurs, such as "I'm not getting anything" or "I'm right here in this room," I have found it effective to suggest immediately that the patient simply make up a dramatic story about someone, somewhere, doing something (often suggesting a theme relevant to the presenting symptoms) with a setting long before birth. Sometimes a little more help is needed to get into this, but almost always within seconds the patient is in the midst of a regression, although he would vehemently deny it if asked!

Because of the preconception many people have that past-life recall should be like a movie, there are many times when I have to reassure the uncertain patient that even if he is only "making it all up," it is really all right. I don't put any emphasis on remembering *per se*. I ask patients what they are aware of in their bodies, because I have become convinced that the body is always remembering. Whenever possible I ask that the patient go back to what the body is remembering with the particular sensation. I use the body a great deal as a way of getting the person into a past life.

I find finger signals helpful in guiding a regression. I ask that if events aren't being recalled correctly, the "no" finger lift. Sometimes I say, "When we get to the part that is causing the phobia or that is having the greatest impact on your current life, the 'yes' finger will lift."

The mid-game portion of the regression depends more on the skill, judgment, and intuition of the therapist than does either the beginning or the end. It is important not to miss anything significant, yet most of the time the truly significant event is the death experience. It seems important to move to this experience during regression, even if one has to skip over important events in that lifetime and return to them another time. It is important to avoid negative repercussions from the therapy. These can occur when a traumatic death experience has been approached but not experienced. The following suggestion can be given: "Now move to the moment after the spirit leaves the body." After the experience has been described, it is easier for the nature of the death to be approached by going back to a minute before it occurred. Some of the charge has been removed because the death has first been remembered after the fact. The death remembrance and the spirit's joining the light are usually timed to coincide with the end of the session, and the patient can be brought back to the present by counting from ten to zero and giving suggestions for well-being, etc.

## *Processing*

### Psychotherapeutic and Tranformational Techniques

I find that is not necessary to do any interpreting or to ask the patient to forgive others or himself. It seems that all that is necessary is simply recalling.

It is my contention that beneath each symptom is energy-sustained guilt. If the patient remembers a traumatic death as a victim, then it is helpful at some point for him to go back to the karmic event that necessitated this outcome. If there is time during the same session, this further recall can be done immediately following release from the body by saying, "Now move back to the karmic event associated with this death." If necessary, count back. This procedure presupposes some information beforehand on the concept of karma and the karmic or originating event. Those patients who do not accept the concept of karma or even of reincarnation can be encouraged to take these notions merely as working hypotheses, a framework for doing the work. Belief in either of the concepts is not necessary.

Before getting into the ongoing therapy process, or even during the early sessions, it is important to provide a way to understand the "bad guy" role.

I point out an analogy between school and progressive classes, lessons, and examinations, and the cycle of rebirth. I add that, in my opinion, we are never good or bad spiritually but are like students passing or failing tests. This analogy relieves the person of a feeling of being bad because something formerly was done that would not be done now. I show that actually the test has now been passed because the values coming up are different, though energy may still be tied up in the failure and can remain tied up until the event is re-experienced.

I consider that by simply remembering, the patient is getting rid of the problem and that is a transformation. The analogy I use is of a light bulb in human shape with a bulb inside shining perpetually, like the image of the sun in the solar plexus which I use in the induction. We are really lighted beings. This light is shining perfectly, but here and there on our bodies we have smudges. In therapy, through remembering, we are taking a sponge and wiping off the smudges so that the light can shine through perfectly. That is both the transformational and psychotherapeutic technique.

## Integration into the Total Psychotherapeutic Process

About two-thirds of the therapeutic hours are spent in actual regressions. The remaining sessions deal with how the material recovered is affecting the daily life process and what changes or lack of changes have taken place in regard to symptoms and moods and affects. I never initiate this type of discussion immediately following a regression. At that time I awaken patients with suggestions for feeling well, and then they leave the office. But in the next session I always begin by asking how they have been since last time and how they felt immediately after the session. If there were depressions or headaches or other symptoms, I can check on these and use them as a sort of thermometer. I don't limit myself to the main presenting problem. I see the overall problem as a jigsaw puzzle in which we have to work to get a number of pieces in place. I return again to my analogy of the two of us being detectives with different roles to play.

I ask all my patients to observe themselves carefully in between sessions, especially the rest of the day following the regression, and to write down anything notable and bring it for the next session. I urge patients to keep a journal of anything untoward that happens and also to write down their dreams and bring in their writing. We don't place emphasis on dream interpretation as such, but I may use the dream as the focal point in the regression. If there has been depression, I work with the patient to find out what precipitated it. These investigations and discussions help to open up the area of memory where the precipitating cause is located, and, therefore, the place where the source of healing lies.

I do not avoid therapeutic counseling, especially in terms of bodily well-being, and I suggest helpful books on diet and exercise. I reject the idea that some patients have, that people enjoy suffering, and I suggest that this idea of the need to suffer comes from being a "bad guy" in another life and that all that has to be done is to recover that experience.

I tend, also, to put to rest the whole issue of parental influence. Because people like to go around blaming their parents, one of my teaching roles is to help them to assume responsibility for everything that happens to them. There are no accidents and there are never victims. No one is the victim of parents. When we are responsible for everything that happens, we don't have license to be angry with other people or situations. We create negativity in our lives by being angry and we need to find out what is causing the anger, which I see as a projection onto others. I don't see anger as a natural outlet. It can be dealt with by knowing that we are responsible for everything and that we have to learn to accept things as they are, while changing what can be changed. This is a cognitive approach, based on changing the field that has initiated the anger.

# Failures

There are three areas where failures occur:

### 1. Realistic Limitations of the Method

Past-life therapy is not a panacea and it does not always work. It may be that symptoms have sources other than past lives—perhaps environmental pressures. Then, also, there may be people who have on an unconscious level chosen to suffer in order to grow spiritually, and they will not be deflected, any more than patients who have chosen unconsciously to die will allow healing to be effective. Sometimes patients stay in treatment without any alleviation of their symptoms, and it must then be decided whether continuing for purely supportive help is indicated. Moreover, entities can be the cause of symptoms, and nothing will be accomplished until they are dealt with.

### 2. Patients' Attitudes

Many patients have unrealistic expectations, and improvement is downplayed because it does not seem enough. It is important for therapists not to promise too much from the technique or to give assurance that there will be a magical cure in one session. The truth is that this is a therapeutic modality that often takes time and patience, just as does any other modality. Failure is often caused by the self-termination of patients resulting from this unconscious expectation. In my experience one out of four patients does not return for a second session, and only half of the rest remain in treatment long enough to be helped. Often these patients have felt upset because they did not "re-live" the experience, did not feel hypnotized, felt that they were making it all up, and could remember everything that happened, even though I had pointed out that all these things might be their experience.

There are patients who do not wish to give up their symptoms. They prefer to retain them and avoid looking at the real cause: there is some secret they won't face. Often patients are unconsciously influenced by the skepticism of others, such as their physicians. Sometimes problems surface at times when patients can't deal with them, as at the end of a session or between sessions. Symptoms such as headaches, depressions, and anxiety can surface and be construed as evidence that the technique is faulty. As in any other form of therapy, as problems get closer to the surface, suffering may occur. This manifestation is only one of the reasons that therapeutic training is a must for past-life therapy.

Failure can sometimes occur because of a patient's fear of hypnosis, a fear that at times comes from other lifetimes. Often "going under" hypnosis is subconsciously equated with going under anesthesia, going under the knife during surgery, or going under water in the process of drowning. The buried trauma may have been so frightening that it is avoided to prevent re-experiencing it. Other patients have been victims of mind control practices in various forms or were drugged in order to be controlled mentally and/or physically, often resulting in disastrous consequences, usually death. Still others have, during past lives, been gifted psychically and were scapegoated. For example, if a famine occurred or they were unable to heal someone and they were blamed, they might be afraid that their present hypnotic treatment could reactivate these latent abilities. If these resistances cannot be dealt with successfully, any regression attempt will usually end in failure.

### 3. Problems in Technique

One common technical error that may make past-life recall difficult or impossible is insistence on visual images. There is only one time to ask what is seen, and that is after the death process. This error may be remedied by asking what is being experienced. Patients often become even more blocked when they are allowed to retain an expectation that past lives are recalled in 3-D technicolor! Careful explanation of the true process is helpful. Failures are less likely when the patient understands that this form of therapy takes time and patience.

# Cases

## Clinical Symptomatology

**Case 1. Obesity**[1]

The problem of obesity is complex in its etiology. Often extreme hunger in another lifetime underlies a problem of compulsive overeating in this one, but there may by more than one life of starvation and there are also complex behavioral factors superimposed on and reinforcing the overeating. Support and hope are also important factors in making change possible.

One straightforward instance of compulsive overeating that stemmed from two earlier lifetimes occurred with William, who appeared for therapy with over a hundred surplus pounds that he had started to put on from the beginning of his life. He was the only overweight person in a weight-conscious family. He had tried the usual variety of diets but sticking to them had been impossible. He found himself eating food he detested and staring at the refrigerator during the times he was trying to diet. He had never been able to get down to 200 pounds, though he had come within five pounds of it once or twice. In addition to the weight problem, in my exploratory search I found that he had a host of allergies and had been asthmatic since birth. He was especially reactive to chicken feathers and cat fur, though never to the fur of wild animals.

The week following the initial two hours of interview, William reported that he had played the self-hypnosis tape diligently several times a day and felt much more relaxed and seemed to go deeper each time. His first regression recovered and released guilt that he had felt over the pain his mother had experienced during his birth.

The next week I regressed William to a significant event in the past that was related to his weight problem. His body began to tremble. His voice was so weak that I had to strain to hear him.

> P: *It's been very calm...no wind. There's not enough food. On the ship everyone is hungry, maybe even sick.... It's scurvy.*
> T: *How do you feel?*
> P: *(Voice wavering) Hungry.*
> T: *How long has it been since you've eaten?*
> P: *We have some food, but it's just a little porridge or something.*
> T: *Have you lost a lot of weight?*
> P: *Yes. I don't know how much in weight, but my arms and my ribs are sticking out. We're starving.*

Men were lying around in the crew's quarters starving, and some of the crew had apparently already died.

    T: *What is the name of your ship?*
    P: Sally.
    T: *Is there another name?*
    P: May—Sally May.

His name was Tom Jones. He was over 20 and came from Bedford, Massachusetts. He had a wife named Jean. The year was 1781.

    T: *Move forward to an important event. One, ...two...three.*
    P: (Lowering voice) I think I took something I wasn't supposed to.
    T: *What did you do with it?*
    P: I ate it.

It turned out that it was a live chicken. He had taken it from a pen of chickens intended for the officers.

    T: *Tell me what you did with the chicken. How did you take it?*
    P: (Breathes very rapidly.)
    T: *Stay calm and relaxed. There's no need to get upset. How do you feel within yourself right now?*
    P: A little scared.
    T: *What are you afraid of?*
    P: I don't know...maybe I'll get caught. (Trembles.)
    T: *What do you do with the chicken?*
    P: I'm sure I must have killed it somehow, but I don't know how.
    T: *See yourself killing it.*
    P: (Long pause) I wring its neck.
    T: *And then what do you do with it?*
    P: I skin it and...I tear it open with my fingers and...it's awful...the smell of the guts (grimacing). I feel like vomiting.... Finally I cook it.
    T: *How could you cook it?*
    P: I...don't...know.
    T: *The knowledge will come.*
    P: There was a lantern...I cooked it with that.
    T: *How did that chicken taste to you?*
    P: Good...(Smiles.)
    T: *Now let's proceed to the next important event...One...two...three (Pause) What happened?*
    P: I was punished.

One of the officers caught him and he was locked up and then lashed 30 times with a cat-o'-nine tails with the whole ship's company watching.

During his recital of the beating he flinched and squirmed, and it took many minutes of calming suggestions before he was sufficiently relaxed to continue. When I brought him back to the present, he shook his head in bewilderment, explaining that he hadn't really believed we live more than once, though he had an open mind.

The following week he reported that at a restaurant he had, for the first time, ordered something he really wanted instead of what would be the largest quantity of food. He realized that all his life he had been eating like a starving man. He had also researched the period and found that a type of warfare that involved stalking British ships had been going on at the date he remembered. Later, under hypnosis, his subconscious mind brought to light that he had been at sea most of the years during that lifetime and that he had lived to be an old man. Although he never starved again, an indelible impression had been left, one that persisted for almost two hundred years!

In a later hypnoanalytic session, William's subconscious mind disclosed that though some of his allergies and some physical intolerance to certain foods were due to emotional experiences in his present life, others originated in a past life. To find the event responsible for his allergy to cats and chicken feathers, he returned to his lifetime as Tom Jones.

P: *I was eating a chicken and the cat found me. It wanted some and I wouldn't give it any. I kicked it and it started to yell and scream...and people came and found me with the chicken (begins to wheeze slightly).*
T: *So it was the cat that caused you to be discovered with the chicken?*
P: *Yes.*

A check with his finger signals verified that his allergy to chicken feathers was conditioned by the fear he had felt as he caught the chicken and his disgust as he ripped off its feathers and disemboweled it, and that his allergy to cats could be traced to the betrayal of the situation by the cat.

After the first session William had meticulously plotted his weight on a graph, and we inspected this the first thing each time we met. He lost weight steadily and finally had reached 200 pounds when he suddenly developed an incredible craving for chocolate. He was drawn each day to buy several chocolate bars, which wrecked his 800-calorie diet and brought about intense self-recrimination. Under hypnosis I asked his subconscious mind if there was something at an inner mind level responsible for this craving. His "yes" finger lifted, and his "no" finger showed that it was not in this lifetime. I regressed him to an event a long time ago that had to do with his craving for chocolate.

P: *Well...there's darkness all around me. I can't seem to see anything.*
T: *In a few minutes it will become very clear to you what is happening.*

P: *(Sadly)* It's cold...it's dark and cold. I'm outside. It's snowing and I think...I think there's rocks and trees...and it's snowing and cold.
T: Just get in touch with who you are. You'll know your name and all about yourself.
P: I was hunting...and I'm lost and I think I'm going to freeze. I don't know my name *(Voice very raspy and shaky)*.
T: On the count of three you will. One...two...three.
P: Fred.

Fred had started out hunting that morning and had planned to get back by noon but became lost. He was 30, lived by himself, and on the hunting expedition he carried a rifle. He weathered the night, becoming very cold, and the next morning a person appeared on a horse and Fred called to him. The stranger put Fred up behind him on his horse and took him back to town. From there he made his way to his cabin.

T: What is the first thing you do when you get back to the cabin?
P: I look for something to eat, and all I have is some flour and some beans. I still don't have any venison, and I have to go out hunting again because I have to get some meat.
T: Did you eat anything in town?
P: Yeah *(Smiling)*. I had a cup of hot chocolate.
T: How did that taste?
P: It tasted good *(with obvious relish)*.
T: Do you like chocolate?
P: Yeah, I don't hardly get any because it's hard to get...They gave it to me because I was about half frozen and it helped me.

After this regression William remarked that now he knew why chocolate had been such an important thing. And a year ago when he had got down to 200 pounds, he remembered the same pattern—during a cold spell surrendering to his craving for chocolate. He realized that it was the cold snap that triggered the other lifetime events and that had set off the compulsion. After that regression he was able to resist chocolate, and, as of now, weighs 185 pounds.

One of the last times he came in he smiled broadly and reported, "Cats have really rough tongues! I let our neighbor's cat lick some butter off the end of my finger. I even enjoyed it! And the best part is that I could breathe. Before I would have cringed and started wheezing right away if a cat came anywhere near me. But so far I still haven't had an encounter with chickens. I still think they are stupid!"

It is not difficult to credit the remission of the allergies to the regression. The problem of William's weight loss is more tentative, and undoubtedly our good rapport, the reinforcing influence of the chart, and the hope given by use of a new and untried approach played at least a part in his success.

### Case 2. Insomnia[2]

Insomnia is a distressing and puzzling symptom for therapists. When Joe came for help he was desperate. Most nights he could not get to sleep until dawn unless he took four sleeping pills, after which he would sleep for 12 hours and be hung over for many more. Night after night he would lie awake resisting the pills, and his head would swim in a stream of inconsequential thoughts. His insomnia made it difficult to concentrate, which, in turn, jeopardized his chances to pass a real estate exam for which he had to memorize page after page of facts and laws. Worry over this situation made it even harder to sleep.

Joe had formerly come to see me for his three-pack-a-day smoking habit, so he was well prepared for hypnosis and an exploration of past lifetimes. As many others do, he resisted initially his very clear impression of a general store and street scene because he thought he had conjured them up. Gradually, however, he relaxed and trusted his initial impressions.

He began his first regression as a child, Dale, playing in front of his house. His father was a marshall.

> T: *How do you feel about him being the marshall?*
> P: I'm proud of him.
> T: *Now concentrate on your breathing. Your inner mind is moving you ahead to the next significant event at the count of five. One... two...three...four...five.*
> P: My father's dead.
> T: *How did he die?*
> P: He was killed...shot...I feel bad because of my mother and my little sister...I didn't think that...ah...anybody could beat him.
> T: *Was he a good shot?*
> P: Mm-hmm. He was very fast. (His chin quivers. Tears form.)
> T: *I'm sorry to hear that. What will the family do?*
> P: My mother makes dresses...I'm not going to worry.

He was 18 and the next experience he tuned into was a campfire with a lot of people, a wagon train going west. He had a certain amount of contempt for the others in the train because they couldn't defend themselves. They knew how to farm and were going West to get land without having any awareness of the journey's dangers.

T: *Do you feel you are prepared?*
P: Mm-humm. Not in every way but most...most ways.
T: *How would you defend yourself?*
P: Just with my gun.
T: *You're a pretty good shot? How did you learn?*
P: My father taught me.

I had him let a little time pass and he found his wagon train being ambushed by Indians. The wagons weren't in a good defensive position so the journeyers left them and ran for the trees. Nearly everyone was either shot or carried off. He escaped and made his way to California. I had him look back on the Indian raid and tell me how it turned out.

P: (Long pause) We held them off till that night...weren't very many left...told 'em to pass the word to try to just make it on their own...don't group up because the Indians would catch up and...they'd be better off alone. I left alone.
T: *You left at night?*
P: Mm-hmmm.
T: *Were you tired by them?*
P: No.
T: *How could you see the way?*
P: Just...just by the moonlight and...maybe the Indians would be tracking us the next morning. I don't think (deep sigh) the others stand a chance.
T: *Were you able to sleep that night?*
P: No. The Indians were sneaking around us...got a couple with my knife that night.
T: *Were you all trying to get some sleep at that point?*
P: No!
T: *Wouldn't dare take a chance on that, would you? About what time of night did that happen?*
P: It was all night.
T: *So all night long you were in kind of a camp with the others or just in one area with the others.*
P: In the woods.
T: *And you had to be really alert because those Indians could come up at any moment. They were all around you?*
P: Mm-hmm. Could hear someone scream every now and then because (sighs deeply)...Indian had gotten them with a tomahawk or a knife.
T: *That must have been a terrible night for you.*
P: I wasn't afraid.
T: *How did you spend your time before you left?*
P: Just listening...watching. There wasn't much you could see, though. Just the trees, no moonlight came through there...good fighters.
T: *Who were they?*

P: Crows. I knew there were Crows in that area...Crows were the only hostile ones. Other tribes were peaceful.

T: What you're saying is that you were there in the woods. You could hear screaming from time to time, but you weren't afraid. You were just being very alert. Because you knew that if you didn't pay attention that it would cost you your life, is that it?

P: Well, I was just thinking of protecting myself. There was no way I could help the group (voice sounds depressed).

We moved ahead and found that he got to California and then, as the result of holding up a stagecoach to get money ($1500 in gold), he fled to Mexico. After this he became a guard in Texas, a sheriff in Kansas, and a marshall in Colorado. Through all these jobs he was skillful with his gun and slightly arrogant when he considered the comparative ineptitude of others. Finally a bank was robbed and he set out after the men who did it.

While he was playing pool with a banker and the mayor in the pool hall of the town where he was staying for the night, he was shot through the open window and killed. He died feeling indignant that he had allowed somebody to ambush him. Guides came for him.

T: What are you experiencing?
P: The doctor's pulling the sheet over my face...I knew it was going to happen...I don't feel anything.
T: What can you see from where you are?
P: I can see the doctor...his nurse cleaning up his instruments...the mayor and the banker saying they're really sorry about it.
T: What do you see on the bed?
P: Just a bloody sheet...and me (indifferently).
T: Where do you feel you are as you're observing this?
P: I don't know. (Sounds very puzzled.)
T: It's going to become clearer and clearer. I'm going to count from one to three and on the count of three it will be clear where you are. One...two...three.
P: (Long pause) It's like I'm looking through the roof. From the sky.
T: You feel you can see their expressions and hear what they're saying?
P: (Nods.)
T: Are you alone?
P: No, there are two people. One's a woman. She's got on...like a nightgown.
T: What is the other person like?
P: He's got on like a suit. Very distinguished-looking. I don't know either of them.
T: Just see if you're getting any messages from them or any thoughts.
P: They're leading me and like consoling me but...not with words. But I know what they mean.

With the help of these guides he was able to give up his anger. The following transcript shows the gathering of insight, which is *not* the therapeutic process that cured his insomnia. Relief from insomnia came merely from the recall of the experiences themselves. I have included the insight experience simply to show another dimension in past-life therapy.

T: How do you feel within yourself right now?
P: I feel good. I...feel the lack of anger.
T: You were aware of being angry before—is that what you're saying?
P: Yeah. I've always been angry with people.
T: From this spiritual state, tell me why you have always been angry with people? I'm going to ask you to tell me at the count of three. One...two...three.... What comes to mind?
P: They go through life so unprepared. They're vulnerable. (Short laugh.) And then I get killed!
T: What were the events that have resulted in the sleep problems in your life as Joe? What are the significant events that contributed to that or caused that? Whatever comes to mind?
P: (Long pause.) Most of my awareness had to be at night, alert.... Someone was always trying to make a name for themselves.
T: In what way?
P: They...if they could say they killed me.
T: You had to be alert at night?
P: Mmmm-ummm.
T: Do you feel the Indian attack had anything to do with your sleep problem?
P: Yes, it did.... They chased me for several days...I couldn't sleep at night.
T: Did you sleep during the day?
P: No.
T: You just didn't sleep at all, is that it?
P: I'd grab little naps but...but only when they were quite a way behind me, when I'd get on a high spot.

After this regression Joe became aware of other patterns and characteristics of his present life that had repeated the former one—the fact that shooting was his favorite sport and he was good at it, that he was basically a loner, and that he had a knack for finding people's weaknesses. I suggested that for homework he notice the weaknesses he spotted in others so that he could look for them in himself. With a guilty grin he agreed to do this.

A few weeks later he reported that the night following the regression he went to sleep immediately and slept soundly. The following evening he told his family the story of Dale (his name in the past lifetime) and became so intrigued with the details that he couldn't get to sleep, but since then he has slept soundly without medication. He was also delighted to report that he passed his real estate exam!

**Case 3. Acrophobia**[3]

Mike used all kinds of excuses to cover up the anxiety he felt in high places, which escalated into terror at times. Getting into a high place was unthinkable. In spite of business losses due to his avoidance of social and business appointments that required driving over bridges or into mountainous areas, he managed to remain a successful attorney. Over the years he had unburdened himself to a host of therapists—one an orthodox Freudian analyst, another who conducted weekend marathon encounter groups, and a third who specialized in phobias (a practitioner well known for a special "confront and conquer" approach). Despite the efforts of all involved in his treatment, his phobia persisted unabated.

Mike was psychologically sophisticated and had hypothesized that his phobia must be connected with fear of dying coupled with a strong drive to destroy himself and a fear of losing control and harming himself or others. However, this didn't fit in with the rest of his life—his good marriage, good relationship with his children, a successful career, and his ability to make and keep close friends. In spite of his phobia he had retained a zest for living.

He was concerned that he could not be hypnotized but, following practice in self-hypnosis, he slipped easily into a deep trance and was able to see scenes in fine detail. At first they were kaleidoscopic vignettes, flashes of scenes that seemed to emanate from different lifetimes. One of these vignettes stood out from the other images—a roof of a large Gothic cathedral, followed by a casket. During the weeks that followed we investigated a number of these vignettes, and finally, following the lead of a dream that had come after a post-hypnotic suggestion that his subconscious mind would prepare him to look at material he needed to understand, we moved into the Gothic lifetime. In the dream he had seen a man's body with the head impaled on a wooden structure. Although the dream was just a flash and had been "unbelievably horrible," following it he had felt a surge of self-confidence and sureness that lasted until his next session, anticipating as it did some sort of change.

Slipping eagerly into an altered state he saw himself as a balding, dark-haired man with a beard who was talking to people on a sidewalk and carrying a bag of tools under his arm. It was a pleasant day. There were a lot of red and orange tile roofs on the tops of stucco or plaster buildings.

T: *You will become aware of what they are talking about at the count of three. One...two...three.*
P: *Well, the first words I hear are "broken tile." Those words just come to me. I assume that this is the discussion...and the tools in the bags are for*

buildings. And one building seems rather high—two stories, you know. It looks like a big old church...Gothic type.

He saw himself going to the church and talking to the priest, who pointed to the roof. Then he crawled through a little octagon-shaped window and was out on the roof.

P: *This is a...a...one of those wings...churches are designed in the form of crosses. You have your long entry way going up to the middle and then you have two side walls...and I've apparently crawled through one on the side on the left to get around up to the right, for what reason I don't know. Mm-hmmm. I don't know why my hands should be perspiring.*
T: *Just stay calm and relaxed. Now what do you see happening? What are you doing now?*
P: *Just working on the tile...with a...out of my bag.*

He described the way he repaired tiles and the tools he worked with. Someone told him that when he was finished with that side, he should go to the other side.

T: *How do you feel as you're up there working?*
P: *Well, it's sort of high and stratified and kind of...I don't...I had a feeling when I first came out that it...you know, it was high, to watch my step. (His face breaks out in beads of sweat.)*

He had something tied around his sandals to keep him from slipping, but it had begun to rain and the tiles were getting wet. He was working on the gutters and looking around at the hills and feeling a little anxious. Because the tiles were wet he was particularly cautious. The priest came out and directed him toward a certain tile.

P: *I'm just looking down at the...apparently trying to find the area. He's standing up at the ridge of the roof or slightly to the left, looking down at me. And I'm aware of the height. (Becomes visibly upset.)*
T: *How are you feeling now? I notice you're clenching your fists, rubbing your hands.*
P: *Ah, just a little...moist...whether it's from holding...I'm aware of losing some tools—rolling down the side...I don't know whether I'm reaching for them, or what.*
T: *Just get in touch with what happens. Just tell me what comes next. What are you aware of?*
P: *Well, somehow there's some loose tiles and that enters into this. Where the hell it goes, I...I don't know, it just seems to be that the part...the loss of tools is something, falling down reaching them...giving away and...my*

> hanging, dangling on the gutter and the tiles and...that's a...and it seems that it's three stories high...it's just high!
>
> T: Where are you now?
> P: I'm hanging on that...gutter and grabbing some of these tiles that are loose and broken—but they're not much help and they're falling.
> T: Where is your body?
> P: I'm off the side, hanging...just...I'd say, arm on the gutter or...one hand in the gutter and the other arm on top of the...but I stay right there. I don't seem to...fall (face bathed in sweat).
> T: You're still dangling, you're hanging onto the gutter and your body is dangling and your one arm is grasping for tiles.
> P: (Nods head.)
> T: I'm going to ask you to concentrate on your breathing. I'm going to count from one to three and you'll become much more relaxed and calm and your inner mind will let you proceed step by step so that you can see what happens to yourself. One...just becoming very relaxed as you experience what's happening...two...three. What are you aware of?
> P: There are some people trying to help...standing on the other side letting down something—a rope or something.

Mike seized the rope and tried to hang onto it. He swung back and forth as he grabbed the gutter.

> T: What emotions are you experiencing?
> P: Fear, fear and a...terror? I mean, I'm just trying to hang on the best I can (covering his face with his hands). One of them lets go and I lost...
> T: One of the people lets go?
> P: Yes. My whole weight went on the gutter and it broke. The whole gutter is coming down—with some tile pieces and fragments.
> T: What are you aware of?
> P: Well, I just see myself falling. At first it was me, then I...pulled away and saw somebody falling.

Mike described his body falling to the ground in the same position in which he had clutched at the tile gutter. He heard the body saying, "Oh, my God!" The body fell between two buildings and then he lost track of it.

> T: Just relax. Now I'm going to count from one to three and you will see the body. One...two...three. What do you see?
> P: I see his impaled face. Well, I see a look of agony...of death in its ...complete form. He is on this wood scaffolding...it's almost gone through him...it was the horrible part about it...I don't know...I mean this is (breathing rapidly), I can look back up.

For a moment more he observed the building, the broken drain, the sky that had turned white. Then he returned to the body on the ground, aware that people were around him trying to help. It became darker and darker and he was aware of the frightened people staring and recognized that it was the same scene as in the dream, the same body.

> T: *The same face?*
> P: *Pretty close...it's just not as vivid...just a...that was just a blinding flash. The thing was...on and off. This is the party I saw standing out front of it, I guess. It was the church, the buildings. Sort of friendly, blue eyes.*

As Mike came out of the trance he smiled weakly, emotionally exhausted by the trauma he had just re-lived. He wiped the sweat from his face with his hands and got up abruptly, confirmed our next appointment, and fled the scene of so much psychic pain. I realized that during the session he had switched from participant to observer-reporter in order to avoid facing the situation and so spare himself panic and pain. That was why he had so much difficulty experiencing the fall, which I felt was the incident responsible for his fear of heights. He needed to experience the feeling of falling in order to get the relief he sought and needed.

In subsequent sessions we returned to the experience, and he became able to stay in his body during the fall. Each time the fall caused him less distress until finally he felt no more reaction. From this time on fear of heights no longer troubled him. This greatly freed his ability to meet business commitments and also allowed more scope in experience with his family.

## Self-Defeating Patterns of Behaviors

### Case 4. Recovering Personal Power[4]

One of the most satisfying therapeutic experiences is the transformation of a basic life pattern in a series of regressions that both underline the underlying perceptive flaw and through the recovery of memories allow it to be released. Such a transformation was experienced by Roger, a flawlessly dressed young man with obvious talents and charm, whose life was being handicapped by his inability to make decisions, especially about his unrewarding marriage and about shifting to a more creative career. He came for therapeutic help at a time when he had to make a decision as to whether to end a 13-year career as a college instructor and pursue one as a film maker. Hypnosis was a last resort. He had tried many therapies, ranging from Reichian therapy to Transactional Analysis—even marathon encounter groups. He hoped to be able to make positive, well-thought-out decisions and act upon them. In addition, he was hoping to get rid of his headaches and back problems.

He was an excellent hypnotic subject and established clear, fast finger signals without difficulty. His subconscious mind made it clear that there were six events from six past lifetimes that were responsible for the problem. In his first regression, I suggested that his unconscious mind take him back to one of those six events.

Immediately he was in what seemed at first a carnival, but which turned out to be a jousting contest. He found himself as a participant.

P: *Well, ah...I have the feeling I'm going to be in it...and I have to select a...a...either a club with a—with a ball on a chain, or an axe.*
T: *And which are you going to select? Which do you usually use?*
P: *I usually use the club with the ball and chain with the points on the ball...but I think I selected the axe.*
T: *What made you decide to select the axe?*
P: *I thought it would be better.*
T: *And you've already made a selection, is that it?*
P: *Mm-hmmm. I'm in a tent waiting for my ah...turn (his voice trembles.) ...I'm sitting on my horse in my armor.*

He was 19, named William of Orr. The occasion was like a tryout to be a knight. He was hoping to go into service with his king, whom he identified as Henry of England, and the time was 1486. As he awaited the tournament, he felt anxious and his stomach was queasy.

He and his opponent had drawn for first choice of weapons, and he had won and chosen the axe, so his opponent had the ball and chain, and both had lances. In the very early stages of the tournament, William was knocked off his horse and had to fight on foot. His opponent, still on horseback, circled around trying to get behind him.

T: *And now what happens?*
P: *He keeps trying to circle around behind me and then charge in from behind and...(Dodging)...club me with his club. I try to—back—back at him with my axe, but he's on his horse and it's hard to get him with an axe.*
T: *If you had picked the other weapon, how would that have been?*
P: *I could have pulled him—I could have wrenched him off his horse with—wrapping it around his neck.*
T: *What are you thinking now—about the choice of weapons?*
P: *I would have been better off with the club.*
T: *You feel you made a poor choice?*
P: *(Nodding) I definitely made a poor choice.*

After this his opponent ran him down with his horse and hit him on the head with his club. He lay there on the green.

> T: *What are you aware of?*
> P: *I just feel nothing...just a kind of warmth, kind of like blood, red blood, a warm red blood running through my body...and I just kind of...I saw a white light and I just kind of floated away.*

We left this scene of his death and went on to another lifetime. The word "Germany" came to mind. He had a feeling of uneasiness along his spinal cord. Finally he broke through his resistance.

> P: *I can see, ah...German uniforms...and I have the impression that I was a colonel in the SS.*

His name was Karl Heiniman and his initial contact with that lifetime was one of being hanged by a wire because he was suspected of having divided loyalties toward Hitler. He was beaten, tortured, stripped, hanged by the neck with a wire, and photographed, as an example to others.

> T: *Stay calm and relaxed...calm and very relaxed. Tell me what you are experiencing.*
> P: *(Relaxing a little.) Well, what I was experiencing was my hatred toward the bureaucratic red tape and the—politics in the German army. I felt you couldn't be a good soldier in that structure.*
> T: *Now, let go of those memories. Just concentrate on your breathing. Your inner mind will take you back to the event responsible for your problem in your current lifetime. I'm going to count from one to five. (Counts.) What comes to mind?*
> P: *I'm at a meeting of high-ranking officers...in Berlin.*

The purpose of the meeting was to discuss Hitler's stupidity and to plan his assassination. There were five at the meeting and two others who were in on it but not there. The plan was to plant a bomb in a plane or bunker close to Hitler. Karl and the others felt that this was necessary to save Germany and take control of the war and to justify the fighting men who had died.

> T: *Is that the decision that your inner mind considers a poor decision in terms of its outcome for you? If it is, your "yes" finger will lift, and if it isn't, your "no" finger will lift.*
> P: *("No" finger lifts.)*
> T: *Was there another decision that you made that was a poor one?*
> P: *I think the poor decision was to enter a conspiracy of so many people...I think that was the real mistake that led to my demise.*

T: *Tell me how you feel about that.*
P: *You can't trust that many people...their loyalties change from day to day under stress. Someone talked.... Someone was tortured and the plan failed.*

Apparently they were all rounded up. Karl was caught in his office and his captors beat him and broke his back, then strung him up, even though he was probably dead at the time.

His next lifetime found him as a 19-year-old Tibetan tribesman named Tanakee. He joined a group of porters who contracted to help some Swiss climbers ascend a mountain called "The Terrible One." Twenty-nine people from the village had been offered a lot of money to carry the climbers' gear to a base camp, and the group was excited about the challenge and the money. In taking on this assignment they were going against the rule of the village that forbade such a climb because it was too dangerous.

They began the climb. Tanakee's feet and hands were cold, and his face was burned. They had been climbing for three days. They came to an ice bridge, and three of the porters, including Tanakee, were roped together and tried to cross the bridge, but it broke and they fell into the crevasse:

T: *Was there any decision-making about going across that ice bridge, or was it something that had to be done?*
P: *I think I wanted to go back. I didn't want to go ahead...but we were kind of forced to go.*
T: *And now I'm going to ask your inner mind at the count of three to give you insight about what it is, which incident is related to your problem of making decisions in this lifetime. (Counts.) What comes to mind?*
P: *I think I didn't follow my own judgment. My judgment was to go back, but I didn't—I didn't assert myself. I wanted to go back when my feet were freezing...but I didn't assert myself. I think I made the decision to go on rather than to assert myself...to speak up.*
T: *All right now. Are there any other decisions?*
P: *The other decision is that I don't want to cross the ice and I'm standing there. We talked about it...and I'm the first to go. I was bulldozed by the others—the other two.*
T: *Are there any other influences besides that—any physical characteristics or mental or emotional characteristics? What comes to mind?*
P: *Well, the only other things were that I was pulled backwards into the crevasse and...broke my back again—the back of my head was crushed in.*
T: *Has that affected you here in this lifetime?*
P: *Yes. Headaches starting in the back of my head...and back problems. And I often feel sensitive in my back when I'm in a group situation.*
T: *Any other ways?*
P: *(Deep sigh) The love of outdoors...a fear of mountains maybe, or...rather the fury of a mountain...I'm somewhat fearful of a great challenge.*

We moved from that memory to a lifetime in New Orleans where his name was Edward Tyrone. He went to visit a pretty girl called Eileen and together they were watching gambling on the boat. Eileen encouraged him to take part. She told him that all the men gambled and he stood to make a lot of money.

> T: How do you feel about what she says?
> P: I feel I don't want to. But I want to be like all the other men. I think I want to impress her...but I don't want to gamble (sounding disgruntled).

Against his better judgement Edward joined the game. He lost and began to argue that they had cheated him.

> T: What's happening? Just tell me about it, step by step.
> P: (Long pause.) I was arguing and...and...(his body flinches)...I was stabbed in the back! Another man came up behind me and grabbed me and...and stabbed me in the back (Breathing very fast).
> T: And what happened as he stabbed you?
> P: I think I...I died.

Still in a trance, Roger said that the poor decision he made in that lifetime was to gamble. As he put it, "...my inability to not do what I wanted to do. It cost me my life!" He was "compelled" to comply because of his need to please others, to maintain his image. His inner mind indicated that he had carried over that problem, too. In addition he had begun—or continued—a pattern of not trusting women.

In the next lifetime he was a 17-year-old Greek boy steering a fishing boat. The boat was approaching a fog bank. He didn't want to go ahead but his captain urged him.

> T: So you don't want to go into the fog. But your captain says you should go, is that it?
> P: (Nods head yes.)
> T: Do you say anything to the captain about the fog?
> P: I don't think so.
> T: Do you have a strong feeling about going into the fog?
> P: I think it's wrong and dangerous. (The pulse in his neck quickens.)
> T: Why don't you say anything?
> P: I think it's better to be brave...better to follow orders.
> T: All right, just move ahead in time to the next significant incident at the count of five. (Counts.) What happens?
> P: We hit some rocks and...and I was pitched out on my head...on the reef of rocks. (Grimacing as though in pain.) I was pitched out on my head and my back...on some rocks...and they grind against me.
> T: What happens?

P: ...and I died (his voice fading).

He explained while still in trance that again his need to please had superseded his own judgment. Again he found himself powerless to assert his needs and wishes. He realized his lifelong dread of fog originated in that life, adding that he always checked weather conditions before driving through areas where fog could be a hazard. Nothing else from that life seemed to be affecting him in his current one.

The sixth and final regression found him as a courtier in France who could not decide whether to support his king or join a plot to assassinate him because of the way he treated the people. So he did nothing. Phillipe, a man who worked for him, was planning to give information to a group of assassins.

P: His politics were not mine...and I didn't assert myself. I wasn't courageous. I should have stood up to him.

Then Pierre was blackmailed into giving information in order to avoid exposure, and in retaliation Philippe talked and exposed *him* and accused him of fomenting the plot.

T: What happened next?
P: Then I (wincing)...was decapitated.
T: By whom?
P: By the king's men and...Philippe. He just stood there.

We then reviewed how each of his decisions had proved fatal, and I asked him to take time in the interval before our next session to think back over each lifetime and see what role it played in his current life.

Two weeks later Roger appeared and told me enthusiastically about all the "monumental" decisions he had been able to make. He had resigned from his teaching position at the college and bought himself a new van and an exotic speedboat for a new movie he wanted to make on water-skiing. He felt clearheaded and relaxed, and excitement and vitality lit up his face. He had put his finger on more similarities between this life and various of the former ones, especially with the German life, and told me of a *déjà vu* experience in Munich in 1968 where he had experienced extreme anxiety. In his current lifetime he has a total distaste for gambling. He has always been fascinated with politics and with the clandestine maneuvering of rival power structures.

P: *The common thread was my inability to assert myself and my need to please others at my own expense, overriding my better judgement. It will be interesting to see whether I change these things. If I do, I'll be so normal I won't be able to stand myself!*

Roger's experience is an example of the power of regression therapy to expose self-defeating patterns of behavior. In Roger's case, dealing with his repressed memories seemed to be the only therapeutic process necessary for complete and lasting relief of the symptomatology and for the consequent enhancement in the quality of his life.

Chapter XV

# Chet B. Snow, Ph.D.

## *Biographical Data*

**Personal Background**

Like many Americans of my generation, I was brought up in a Christian home during the fifties, with regular church attendance and social activities. My mother even wrote Sunday School curricula for the Presbyterian Church, while Dad served as a congregational elder. Belief in God, the soul, and life after death underpinned family life without being fanatical or forced. I now realize that my mother's Quaker background, although never taught or practiced, doubtlessly contributed to this tolerant environment.

I vividly remember regular Bible reading at my grandparents' and learning to honor their daily custom of an hour's "quiet time" when they retired to meditate. Still, the word "meditation" was never mentioned, just as the word "psychic" was never used to describe my mother's uncanny ability to know of my brother's and my minor accidents, just who was telephoning, and which relative was sick or in danger. It was just "Mother's gift."

Reincarnation and past lives, however, were not part of my upbringing, and India never appealed to me as a civilization. Except for a fleeting intellectual attraction to Tibetan Buddhism while a freshman at Johns Hopkins, I found Oriental philosophies distant and impractical. So I majored in International Relations in hopes of making *this* world a better place.

My junior year in Paris and the Vietnam War intervened in the mid-sixties and wiped out my dreams of a diplomatic career, but while Vietnam destroyed my illusions about the changing of U.S. politics, Paris opened up a new world of European civilization and culture. I decided to switch to sociology and history, which became my major subjects at Columbia University Graduate School. I also found ways to return to France for holidays or research almost annually for the next 25 years, so that France has become as much home to me as my native America, and French is practically another "mother tongue."

By 1978, after a few years of teaching Contemporary Civilization at Columbia College while I was writing a Ph.D. thesis in French history, I found myself frustrated. Academic teaching jobs were almost impossible to find. With the advent of the Carter administration, working for the federal government ceased to appear as unpalatable as it had seemed during the Vietnam era, so I took the Civil Service exams and within six months found myself in California working as a historian for the United States Air Force.

I would probably still be writing government reports today and flying military air missions had not two singular events occurred. While moving into a new office, I incurred a back injury that left me in pain and made fulfillment of my duties nearly impossible. Also at this time my father's mother, who had become especially close to me after the premature deaths of both my parents, died suddenly. Losing her support was a major blow. I had not been prepared for it in the way that years earlier I had been prepared for my parents' demise.

But within a few weeks of her transition my grandmother began to appear to me paranormally, urging me to widen my spiritual perspective and virtually putting new books about faith healing and psychic phenomena into my hands. It was in such a way, for example, that I first heard of Edgar Cayce. His experiences opened for me the question of reincarnation, and I soon experienced a series of intense dreams of my own past lives. These dreams so unnerved me that I commanded them to stop—unfortunately, for since then I have never had such clear past-life memories.

The most important message I received from my grandmother after her death was that I should get in touch with a woman therapist in Berkeley who could help me. Shortly afterward, I heard of Dr. Helen Wambach, whose offices were then in Berkeley. I made an appointment with her, and this contact led to my becoming her pupil and eventually to being her professional associate.

After six months of weekly sessions, exploring a number of my significant past lives by hypnotic regression and discussion of my dreams, which I had learned to record, we both agreed that I should seek further training so that I could become associated with her research on progressing subjects into the future. Helen's health, already poor, was deteriorating rapidly, and she needed someone to carry on her research into these future progressions. Moreover, working with her had led to my conviction that I was wasting my time at the air force job, which had become impossibly stressful, and I was intrigued at the idea of helping others as I was being helped. Realizing that my persistent back pain was a message that I had outgrown the USAF job and that my back would not improve as long as I insisted on staying there, I quit in order to devote full time to regression therapy and to my research work with Helen Wambach.

With Helen's approval, I enrolled in clinical hypnotherapy training under Dr. Freda Morris, a licensed psychologist in Oakland. I also began studying the theory and practice of personal analysis and transpersonal psychology with Helen, reading and discussing books she recommended. A few months later I became certified in hypnotherapy. Since then, I've had the good fortune to study and work with a number of other outstanding pioneers on the cutting edge of contemporary in-depth psychotherapy, including Stanislav Grof, Robert Monroe, and Jose Silva. Throughout this process, Helen and I continued to explore both my and other subjects' accounts of future lifetimes beyond the 20th century. In connection with this project, I wrote and delivered a paper at the First International Congress on Alternative Therapies in Sao Paulo, Brazil, in February 1985.

Another project which intrigued me was the idea of comparing past lives related by Americans with those of people of different geographic, cultural, and linguistic origins.[1] At that time Helen's and my proposal on future lives had been rejected by a major publisher, so work on it was in limbo. With her blessing, I decided to return to France to collect comparative data. I had been gone only a few weeks, however, when Helen's health, already precarious, suddenly disintegrated, and she passed away on her sixtieth birthday, leaving me feeling like an orphan.

Nonetheless, she had taught me well and had shared deeply with me. I determined to continue what we had started together. Thus, I developed my Franco-American past-life study and began seeing individual clients in Paris for regression therapy. As hypnosis was nearly taboo in France, I had to modify Helen's standard techniques. Fortunately, I had become interested in yoga and bio-energy work, and these led me to alternative, natural methods for inducing the consciousness modification needed to elicit past-life recall. I developed my own group and individual trance inductions based on a combination of yogic-inspired breathing and clearing of the chakras. I continued broadening my therapeutic repertory. An association with the Belgian Transpersonal Psychology Association led to an opportunity to study holotropic breathing therapy techniques with Dr. Stanislav Grof in Brussels. I also went to the Monroe Institute in Virginia. Though these new involvements have influenced my therapeutic practices, I remain most deeply influenced by what I learned from Dr. Helen Wambach.

Living in Paris until 1989, I also gathered American past-life data to compare with my French data, using my own regression methods during semi-annual trips to the United States. I became an officer of APRT in 1987. The future lives project, which I had temporarily abandoned after Helen's death, found renewed interest and led to acceptance of my revised book proposal by the New York publishers, McGraw Hill, Inc. *Mass Dreams of the Future* was published in 1989.² Since then, I have moved to Scottsdale, Arizona, although I continue to divide my time between France and the United States, lecturing, giving workshops, and fullfilling my duties as the current president of APRT. In rare quiet intervals I work on the sequel to my first book. In 1993 I will be joined in Arizona by my new French bride, herself an experienced body worker and massage therapist.

## Personal Past-Life Experience

If I had to summarize the theme emerging from my past lives, the phrase, "learning to be a responsible witness of this human drama in humility and love," comes immediately to mind. To me, a witness is more than just a participant. He or she is also a recorder and a reporter of human experiences. This seems to have been my chosen task for as far back as I have explored the thread that links many different and varied experiences here on earth. I cannot say that this learning process is in any way one of linear chronological progress. As others have also noted, some of the earliest lifetimes seem to have been both spiritually and philosophically richer. Still, there seem to be both gains and losses in each experience. Furthermore, each reflects a facet of who I am in this current lifetime at some level.

As stated above, my first recall of my past lives came in a series of vivid dreams shortly after I joined an Edgar Cayce study group. In these kaleidoscopes of colors and feeling I saw myself at different times as a scribe and as a high priest in ancient Egypt, as a crafty, dishonest businessman in late 19th century California, as a curious but disobedient sailor on a Yankee clipper, and as a bureaucrat in what I presume to have been Atlantis. There were others, also, that I failed to note or remember. Twice I found myself between physical lifetimes working with other spirits or souls to foster mutual progress toward some desired yet undefined goal. My most recent life, by linear chronology, was as a British airman who lost his life in WWII.

Throughout this period of rather intense bombardment from my sleeping mind, I also received several curious bits of subconscious commentary on the effects of these lifetimes on my personal development. I remember once asking the question in my dream, "Why didn't this soul evolve further if the entry was so highly developed at this point so long ago?" I asked the question after experiencing a lifetime as an ancient Egyptian high priest who worshipped One God, a concept not yet widely accepted. The answer that I received was: "Fear of death was a stumbling block to wholeness. Despite faith, doubts were stronger."

After other similar adventures I was told of overbearing pride or irresponsible disobedience or lack of consideration for others as stumbling blocks to progress. Pride and a desire to receive personal credit (either incarnate or as a soul) were pointed out as among the most potent barriers to spiritual progress. Apparently, I must be a slow learner, for I seem to have had many, many past lives hindered by this attitude.

When I met Helen Wambach, we explored several of these lifetimes further through hypnotic regression, just as we investigated numerous others. Altogether I have explored around two dozen incarnations. Of these, two best demonstrate the theme of unassuming, responsible witnessing cited earlier.

In our first session together, Helen suggested that my subconscious choose the most appropriate among a series of dates she listed as I slid into hypnosis. As soon as I heard the year 1200 A.D., I had a most vivid impression of a large triangular shield with a big red cross emblazoned on it. I was male, dressed in a rather dingy suit of armor that even enclosed my hands. I sat astride a large horse on a promontory overlooking the Mediterranean Sea. Instinctively I knew myself as a young Crusader knight, but in Greece rather than Palestine. It was bloody hot under all that armor, and above all else I was bored. As the recall developed under her skilled questioning, I told a tale of leaving my native Guyenne in southwestern France for the Crusades "to defend the cross," which I somehow venerated. A long, arduous journey had led me to this lonely fortress at the tip of the Peloponnesian peninsula. There I helped the local garrison defend both the port and its ships bound for the Holy Land as they faced occasional pirate raids. Our main sport or amusement was riding our beautiful horses up and down the rocky crags around the castle and jousting among ourselves. I was considered a bit of a dreamer because I could also read, and thus I spent some time poring over the few manuscripts kept by monks who were attached to the garrison. Although I longed to fight in Palestine, a foolish accident ended my short life before that project could be realized—I was thrown headlong from my horse over the cliff. As my spirit left the broken body on the rocks below I thought, "What a waste; I wanted to do so much and I was still so young." I vowed never to slip like that again.

This was my first past-life regression, and although it may not seem very exciting, it led to a major healing experience for me. All my life (this one!) I had had rather severe acrophobia especially when outside on exposed balconies or rooftops. An unreasoning desire to dive headfirst over the side always seized me in such situations, and sometimes it took an enormous effort to contain the urge. As soon as I experienced that youth's body flying headlong over the horse's mane and saw those rocks flying up to meet me, I recognized that feeling and heard myself vow not to be caught like that again and something unclenched in my stomach.

The experience led me to research just where this incident could possibly have taken place. In the regression I knew it was in southern Greece and I had even "heard" a name that began with "Koro." Further, when Helen had asked me who was king, I'd proudly told her I served only the Pope and my order. It took some historical digging, but at last I hit pay dirt. A small town named Koroni still exists at the end of a long Greek peninsula. Moreover, during the 1200's it had been a free Venetian city, protected by a garrison of Templar Knights, whose main ensign was a huge red cross. The proud Templars served at the pleasure of the Pope and were recruited among the nobility of all Europe. Koroni was one of their supply depots enroute to the Holy Land.

A few months after this initial regression, I had the chance to visit Greece for a few days. Immediately I rented a car and struck out for the lonely Peloponnesian peninsula and Koroni. I had never seen a photo of it and wondered if there were cliffs there. As soon as I rounded the last bend of the country road, however, all doubts ended. It was exactly what I'd seen on Helen's couch in Berkeley, CA, with my eyes closed, except that the hilltop fortress lay in ruins. The next day I was investigating the promontory when a cold chill came over me. This was the spot. I was certain of it, though a thin screen of bushes hid the cliff's edge. Quaking, I walked slowly to the bushes. The awful scene once again flashed before my eyes and I sat down. Then it cleared and I felt more at ease than I could ever remember so close to a precipice. The unreasoning urge and fear had practically vanished and I became very calm. I could actually stand by the edge and take a souvenir photo looking down. It was a wonderful feeling.

Of course, as is often the case in therapy, subsequent past-life sessions uncovered several other similar deaths resulting from outdoor plunges. Working through each of them helped me recognize a karmic pattern I'd developed in a much earlier lifetime in ancient Athens when I'd been violently thrown off the Acropolis by an angry mob. Fear, contempt and egotistical pride were all mingled in those dying moments, and these feelings set up a psychic resonance that still echoed after two millennia—in the form of acrophobia.

Thus I learned firsthand a cardinal principle of regression therapy: that extremely emotional moments resulting in life-threatening trauma tend to repeat symptomatically from lifetime to lifetime, even though surrounding circumstances vary widely. The negative emotions associated with such moments are seemingly imprinted on the psyche and thus can resurface several lifetimes later as severe phobias or even physical infirmities unless corrective action is taken. Although reviewing or re-living one of these "echo" incidents may alleviate current symptoms, it is usually necessary to return to the source incident or trauma in order to effect a lasting cure. This incident will almost always be associated with a variety of strong emotions such as rage, lust, guilt, and pride.

The second example I've chosen illustrates another, more positive, side of the theme I see running through my past lives. This time when Helen took me into hypnosis, I found myself in a large woman's body with black skin and short frizzy hair, squatting in front of a primitive hut on a tropical island in the Caribbean. I was called Juana and was a plantation slave in the 17th century. Life was simple and direct, physically taxing but also strangely satisfying. Even though I had a husband and some children, my daily routine revolved around the other women of the small village as we gathered a kind of leafy plant, beat it into pulp, and used it to make cloth or dye. Communal singing supplied a rhythm for the work, and my mother, an old wise woman, would tell stories about our people and a philosophy of life known simply as "the Way." From an early age, I'd been selected as her favorite pupil and learned this oral African tradition by heart. Eventually I replaced her as the pupils' storyteller, the one who kept our history, and thus our ancestors, alive.

"The Way's" philosophy was simple and direct. Our people were a chosen people who had always kept in close contact with the spirit world. This spirit world, consisting of animals, humans, gods and natural forces, was just as real as the material world in which we found ourselves. It was more real, in fact, for this earth merely reflected the other as one's face is reflected in a still pond. Thus, conditions in this world mattered little (although we all resented being taken from our homes and deposited in this alien land), for the spirit world was always the same everywhere.

"The Way" included stories of our homeland and of how we'd been captured with the help of evil spirits and exiled here and made to serve others. It foretold a return to the spirit world at death and then a chance to deal directly with the spirits who controlled our lives, for good or ill. One could even seek "revenge" there on the bad spirits whose evil influence lay behind all disease, pain and misery. There was an underlying unity to "the Way" which described how everything seen and unseen was somehow linked together into one Whole. Our present confusion came from seeing only that part of the Whole that our physical senses could perceive.

It was basically a good "Way" and included a variety of rituals and chants and prayers by which we hoped to influence the spirits in our favor. Even sex was part of the "Way." Its ecstasy could open communication with the spirit world sometimes, but it also bound us to this material world through desire, and it kept us in service to other bodies—women to men and men to women.

Thus, despite the material rigors of poverty and slavery, I found this life as a black woman to be filled with spiritual riches and a peace I seldom experienced in my present life. Yes, there were hardships and unpleasant moments, but they were more than compensated for by family and clan loyalty, dedication to the positive ideal of preserving our heritage, and the certainty that basic needs would always be met. This, plus faith in the underlying Unity of all things, made it one of the happiest lifetimes I've ever recalled.

As Helen took me to Juana's death as an old woman surrounded by her people, I felt at ease, for she had been more than ready to enter the "real" world and leave the physical behind. Her mother's spirit came to help her make the transition, and I recognized her as my own dear grandmother, whose influence had brought me to this place today. I wept as I realized that "the Way's" simple yet profound faith was still mine, even if expressed in different, more sophisticated concepts.

This session taught me what I regard as another principle of past-life therapy. This process is at heart a profoundly spiritual one. It implies the existence and accessibility of deep spiritual wisdom within each of us. This wisdom may carry a myriad of names and faces; it may even at times seem contradictory on the surface, yet underneath all the apparent contradictions is a fundamental unity behind our definition of being human.

It can be profoundly healing to get in touch with this spiritual foundation of the collective unconscious as it has been lived through past personal experiences. Consequently, while I agree that many therapy sessions must be devoted to extirpating negative imprinting and symptoms originating in previous lifetimes, I also insist on the value of finding and raising the psyche's cache of positive spiritual resources so that the client can build for the future from as solid a base as possible.

# *Theory*

## Philosophical Hypotheses

The issue of reincarnation and the independent existence of a nonphysical individual "essence" or "soul" has haunted humanity since the dawn of history. While my personal experiences have convinced me that indeed the human mind can access information "paranormally," that is, in ways transcending the causality of linear time and space, I remain undecided as to whether we retain an individual consciousness throughout creation and, if so, just how this consciousness unfolds its self-knowledge across time/space boundaries. Perhaps it is the final mystery, one to be explored only outside physical reality.

The following theoretical ideas are relevant:

1. The issue of past lives is a profoundly spiritual question. Each past life that is genuinely recalled has a distinct spiritual existence. Moreover, as has been amply demonstrated, such experiences profoundly influence both the psychological and physical conditions of a person's current lifetime, seemingly independently of any conscious belief system such as reincarnation.

2. The development of transpersonal psychology and past-life therapy as recognized and distinct psychological modalities marks a watershed in the search for new patterns and hypotheses beyond the traditional Western paradigms of belief in evolutionary or linear progress and in the primacy of material over spiritual reality. The findings of these disciplines are substantiated by recent discoveries in modern physics, such as Planck's quantum mechanics, and in biology, such as Rupert Sheldrake's morphogenetic resonance.[3]

3. Regardless of belief in an individual, personal soul that continues from incarnation to incarnation, something remains physically alive after we die at the end of a lifetime. That "something" is then apparently transmitted back into the psychic makeup of a new living human being, thereby having profound subconscious impact on the individual's life patterns.

4. Moreover, there seem to be two privileged transition points in this cycle; the moment of birth and that of death. The condition of the individual's mind at each of those two points directly affects the entire life cycle. Reliving and relieving psychic residues of previous birth and death traumas, from this life or any other, is important for individual well-being.

5. My experience leads me to be skeptical of any simple concept of linear progress, either at the individual or collective human level. If we do progress as souls, then it is in ways as yet only dimly understood.

6. I feel that a theory of electromagnetic resonance best explains the psychic transmission of experience from lifetime to lifetime. According to this theory the basis of all reality is the interplay of cosmic waves of force of an electromagnetic nature. As these forces play together they vibrate energy. Irregularities in these vibrations manifest as what we call "life." Each of us participates at an energy level in this cosmic concert in some unique way, having his own particular basic vibration.

7. All of these vibrating waves of force coexist within a single United Force. Their core essence is therefore stable in a state beyond space/time as we understand them. Together they make up the original, uncreated Creative Force which formed the material universe. How this happened remains a

mystery for science because it transcends our subjective space/time reality. Nonetheless, by its effects we can deduce that this Unified Force has will and creative purpose. It creates through the interplay of its component energy waves, through their manifested irregularities, the basis for all "life" as we know it. These living irregularities can be compared to the harmonics of sound waves detectable when a taut guitar string is plucked. These energies manifest themselves into our space/time universe and also into other dimensions that we can only deduce mathematically. Within these created dimensions, and particularly that of our space/time, these living energy waves, our own energy "selves," continue vibrating, interacting together, and creating ever denser physical manifestations of themselves. This is the "cosmic dance" so poetically evoked in many ancient traditions. Through this we are constantly creating new life experiences.

8. Perhaps the most refined form of creating is that of emotional states. It is only through the medium of our emotions that we actually relate to consciousness. Therefore, it seems that we incarnate primarily to experience emotions. Why this is so, still remains a mystery. Perhaps it is to learn or to grow. It may be just because at some level we enjoy the many emotional experiences that a physical human lifetime generates. In any case, it seems that emotions, or particular vibrational patterns, connect different levels of creation. Obviously, in human experience at least, the most powerful emotion is love. Love vibrates in a special way and serves as a kind of universal lubricant. Perhaps it defines harmony among the relationships of irregular wave patterns, what Pythagoras called "the music of the spheres."

9. As we transit from one level of reality to another at death, all the emotional patterns previously created coalesce into a resonant energy field and survive. At the birth of our next incarnation in space/time, they are transmitted to the new individual's psyche according to a process still little understood. Apparently some choice is involved, as well as some determinism.

10. The emotional programming received seems to be independent of linear space/time. It apparently includes not only past-life data but also archetypical models, the particular irregularities of a variety of vibrational energy patterns (other life forms), and human genetic predispositions. Stored at various levels of the subconscious, this programming profoundly influences future emotional and even physical reactions. New experiences are created during each incarnation and are added to the program at death.

Past-life experiences may or may not have been actually planted in linear manifested time (i.e., history). Some may have been and some not. Nonetheless, their psychological reality is proven by their obvious impact on people's current lives. Finally, their social reality has been demonstrated by the statistical work of Helen Wambach; given large samples, the past lives recalled by her subjects conformed to known historical patterns.

What is our destiny as the energy manifestations of a bundle of electromagnetic waves? Is our kind of life eternal? Its material manifestation in space/time certainly is not. Scientists estimate the material universe's age at around 15 billion years and guess it will be around for about that long in the future. Is its spiritual manifestation eternal? Perhaps, although by analogy I would guess that the spiritual dimension also has its limits.

What then remains? A return to the uncreated, Creative Force? Or perhaps another, different kind of life, i.e., new irregular energy wave patterns? What does that imply? Is it linear progress in some disguised form? I don't know, but I doubt that progress in our accepted Western definition of "gradual betterment" applies. Maybe it all boils down to whether or not human beings can conceive of eternity. I have the sneaky suspicion that we're going to be around together for a long time finding out.

## Psychotherapeutic Assumptions

As in the case with any present-day therapist operating in a Western setting, my therapeutic assumptions have primarily been shaped by the great pioneers of modern psychology, Sigmund Freud and Carl Gustave Jung. I subscribe to Freud's analytic dictum that "making the unconscious conscious" underlies effective therapy. Moreover, I agree with the psychoanalytic school that anyone who wishes to practice therapeutic analysis with others really needs to have undergone extensive analytic work himself. It was the self-analysis that I undertook with Helen Wambach that led me into this field. I also have been profoundly influenced by the seminal and pioneering work of Stanislav Grof,[4] whose principles of holotropic therapy reflect much of my own personal experience. Finally, I have been influenced by the life and psychic readings of Edgar Cayce, whose *Search for God* group study books have given me a solid spiritual foundation for understanding human relationships.[5]

My therapeutic assumptions include the following:

1. At some (usually hidden) level of awareness, each therapy client already knows what underlies his or her current distress and how to alleviate it. Accessing and activating this innate wisdom lies at the heart of the therapeutic process.

2. Consciously held symptoms and patterns are often related to deeper primary issues in symbolic or metaphorical ways. These patterns frequently have origins in a series of past-life traumas and are an expression of the

individual's unconscious attempt to uncover and resolve the underlying issues.

3. The therapist-client relationship is especially crucial in regression therapy. Such altered-states work necessarily connects *both* parties at several energy levels. Regression therapists play a more active role in eliciting hidden past-life issues and patterns from clients than do surface-level analysts. Therefore they must remain especially open and accepting of whatever material emerges from the client's subconscious and must not allow transference and counter-transference problems to interfere with the healing process. The regression therapist must remain an active yet flexible participant. His or her loving empathy allows the client to establish enough self-trust to permit transformation.

4. The regression therapy process is usually three-fold. First comes identification with and replaying of significant past-life issues and/or traumas. Emphasis is placed on the key moments of death and rebirth. Second, there follows a search for recurrent negative emotional response patterns between past and current lifetimes and their release through mutual forgiveness, when appropriate. Finally, positive, affirmative emotional patterns are discovered and integrated as alternative models for past and/or future responses. During both the second and third phases, the client's "Higher Self" or "Counselor Part" is called upon for its innate wisdom in seeking creative, lasting solutions to the problems uncovered.

5. Some cases involve spiritual or paranormal events such as entity "attachment" or possession and must be handled accordingly. In general, to be most successful, these issues need to be dealt with before past-life memories are uncovered.

6. Regression therapy may be successfully integrated into a broader transformational context. Its results are often enhanced by the alternate use of other techniques such as holotropic breathing, Gestalt, sensitive massage, or primal therapy.

## Indications and Contraindications for Use

The decision to use regression therapy must be reached jointly by client and therapist after discussion, so that each understands its possibilities and limits. Past-life insights have their greatest impact on those clients who are ready to begin assuming greater responsibility for their lives and who sincerely wish to understand how current problems relate to deeply embedded emotional response patterns that they have long been avoiding or denying. Although no specific religious or philosophical belief is required,

I explain that for me it is a spiritual process. The ability to suspend disbelief, at least during the session, is more helpful than any specific belief held.

I have found regression therapy to be useful in dealing with the following kinds of specific problems:

1. Emotional over-reactions to the ordinary kind of stress-producing situations encountered in life. Symptoms may be purely psychological or may include physical impairments or distress. Long-standing and/or disabling phobias are included here.

2. Psychosomatic complaints such as persistent headaches, sexual dysfunctioning (frigidity, impotence or premature ejaculation), and "phantom" back pain. (These are just a few of the many such complaints that can be alleviated by regression therapy.)

3. Inexplicable and enduring relationship difficulties such as excessive fear or dislike of a fellow worker, family member, or people of specific ethnic or cultural groups.

4. Certain creative blocks.

5. Persistent or seemingly innate negative character traits such as chronic tardiness, compulsive eating, drinking, or smoking.

6. Psychospiritual breakdowns, including feelings of lack of self-worth, anomie, hopelessness, and excessive grieving for a deceased loved one.

Regression therapy is contraindicated for:

1. Clients whose symptoms indicate clearly psychotic or borderline personality disorders.

2. Clients who reveal themselves as incapable of integrating the traumatic or symbolic material that may arise and who therefore risk severe ego confusion or a psychotic break.

3. Most children under 16, unless there has been a spontaneous eruption of past-life material that is disrupting their ego development. However, children are appearing now who need to remember past lives—especially as we enter the Aquarian Age.

4. Clients obviously seeking to escape personal responsibility for their current behavioral or attitudinal problems or who seek ego aggrandizement by association with a past-life heroic figure.

# Induction

## Preparation

I conceive of the interview as the first part of the induction. In a sense, the induction starts the moment a client sets up an appointment. Because I believe the therapist-client relationship to be particularly important in regression therapy, I place significant emphasis on the initial interview, which usually occupies nearly all of the first session. I usually see people for at least three sessions, which range from an hour and a half to two hours, as regressions require more time than conventional therapy.

The interview process helps me get a concise picture of the problem as a client currently understands it. However, things are seldom as they appear to be at first, and what seems to be the symptom or the distress is often only a surface issue masking something deeper. Whatever is first presented needs to be related to a larger pattern in the client's present life. Therefore, during the interview, in addition to the standard questions about motivation, previous experiences, family and personal background, and significant current-life physical or emotional trauma, I inquire about special areas such as birth memories or feelings, recent or strongly-felt deaths of family or friends, and any paranormal experiences or unexplained reactions to ordinary stressful events. In past-life therapy we search for patterns of attitudes and behavior that manifest both in the present lifetime and in past incarnations. It is logical to begin this search with the current situation via a thorough interview.

Another function of the initial interview is to establish trust and rapport with the client. Rapport is a key concept in altered-states work. It involves reflecting clients' concerns and ways of dealing with the world back to them so that they feel understood and so that they sense that the therapist is sympathetically in touch with their distress and with their outlook on life. This requires great flexibility on the part of the therapist, who will be seeing clients with a wide variety of viewpoints and life experiences. The therapist's own preconceived values, expectations, and judgments must be set aside if the process is to work. In a sense, this is also true for clients. It is permissible, after listening to their viewpoint, to ask clients to set aside some of their own biases or expectations that might get in the way of achieving past-life recall. For example, if clients believe they must have a certain kind of experience for it to be "valid" and then don't have it, they have set themselves up to fail because of their preconceived judgment about what a past-life experience must be like.

When people ask if I believe in past lives myself, I tell them that I am neutral but that I have had personal experiences that have led me to believe I have had other earthly lifetimes. I may give them an example from one of those experiences and explain what it did for me or why I thought it was meaningful. I always go on to explain that though such was my experience, their own experience may be different. I tell them that one can look at these experiences from many different viewpoints and take different philosophical approaches to them. They may consider past lives as personal histories, archetypical or genetic memories, psychologic metaphors, or even pure imaginary fantasy so long as they clearly understand that the material recalled is a product of their own unconscious minds and therefore therapeutically valid.

In some sessions clients do not return to past lives. The origin of their problem may lie in the perinatal period or in early childhood, as Freud thought. In any case, these are key phases in an individual's development in which energy can by psychologically blocked.

It is important to realize that past-life therapy is not a universal panacea, though as we look further and further back, we often come to incidents where unsatisfactory patterns developed. It is important to remain as value-free as possible with clients but not to hide one's opinion, to be flexible but loyal to one's values. The more honest and real the therapist is, the more acceptance he will get from his clients. This is the key to building successful rapport and worthwhile regressions.

When sufficient rapport has been established, and during the first session only, I usually proceed to offer a short "energy reading" for a client if I think it is psychologically suitable. This reading, which involves my briefly entering a light trance and using that state to access information about the client's current energy patterns, serves two purposes.

> 1. It provides me with information about the kinds of underlying problems and energy blockages with which we will have to deal. Occasionally what I say during this period of about 10 minutes will trigger a profound response from the client, even before a past life is accessed.
>
> 2. It provides the client with a safe, tested model of trance work performed in a non-threatening manner. It thus permits him to go smoothly into an initial light trance shortly afterward.

After this "energy reading" I explain my induction technique, which consists of controlled breathing accompanied by visualization of energy being channeled through the physical and etheric bodies via the chakras. Then without regressing we practice the technique a few times for familiarization. Finally, if there is time remaining, I will take the client on a short guided imagery trip to test how well he responds to different sensory stimuli and note any personal symbols or metaphors that arise. Occasionally, if I feel the case warrants it, I will test for the presence of external entities or parasitic energy at this time. I usually start the first actual past-life regression at our second therapy session.

While still in the interview stage, the therapist can and should reassure clients that the process of going into an altered state will not take away control or personal power. This is an issue for some and should be resolved whenever it seems appropriate. In addition, the therapist needs to make sure clients understand that they are not going to be "put to sleep" during the regression but will be active participants and will remember all that they experience. Many people, having seen stage hypnotists or deep-trance channeling, think they must lose consciousness to have a "real experience." If they anticipate this and then do not achieve that sort of trance, they feel that they have failed or they invalidate the experience they did have.

Therefore, as I go over the regression process I like to describe some of the physical characteristics of altered states which nearly all clients perceive. These include rapid eye movement or REM, the eye's tendency to produce tears, a feeling of lethargy and body heaviness, some twitching, and possibly chilly hands and feet. Knowing of these in advance helps prepare the client to accept the altered state more easily.

Everyone who does past-life work needs to know about karma, which in its simplest form can be described as the law of cause and effect. Regardless of philosophical or religious beliefs, clients need to have a working knowledge of this concept because it often comes up in regression sessions. Therefore I alert clients to watch for lifetimes where they played roles opposite from what they are playing today. Much like Newton's first law of motion, the karma of energy equilibrium indicates that for every emotion-causing action there is an equal and opposite reaction in one's past. This reaction may have been expressed directly and physically, or indirectly in attitudes or emotions felt. Thus, behind every present-day victim a past-life aggressor or indifferent witness to aggression can be found.

Therapists and clients alike also need to recognize that there is a karmic continuity of life scripts or patterns, which functions like the grooves of a record. Often one gets stuck in a particular groove. Clients need to understand that when they come into their present life, they may have been unaware of alternate choices and so picked up the established unsatisfactory pattern that they are replaying. This karmic "law" is similar to Newton's second law of motion, that anything thrown continues along its line of force unless an external agent such as friction or gravity intervenes. Some clients may find themselves repeating similar disastrous patterns of suffering and self-deprecation across the ages, each time ignorant of other possible ways to deal with the underlying problem. Regression therapy offers them an "external agent" by bringing the unconscious origin of the unsatisfactory pattern back into conscious awareness where it can be dealt with and released. I find that explaining these two fundamental laws of karma in terms of basic laws of physics is helpful in presenting the underlying ideas to Westerners without using Oriental philosophical terms or metaphysical overlays.

There are two final considerations in the preparation process. First, at the end of each regression session I request my clients to note any remarkable dreams, insights, or daydreams that occur within the following 24 hours or during a day or two *prior* to our next scheduled session. I have found that much important information spontaneously rises into conscious awareness this way, often just *before* succeeding sessions. This is especially true after one or two past lives have already surfaced. Second, it is appropriate to ask for higher guidance at any point during a therapy session, wherever and however one feels such guidance operates. During the first session I explain to clients that in altered states they will have greater access to their own innate wisdom, or their "Higher Self" or "Counselor Part" or "Spiritual Guides," however they wish to define it. I encourage them to get in touch with this special wisdom to assist in the healing process.

## Induction Techniques

There are various ways to help a client move into an altered state. The most usual is a relaxation technique. Almost diametrically opposed to this technique is the use of arousal. A metaphysical technique which I find works especially well involves deep controlled breathing combined with concentration on moving energy through the chakras.

### Induction through Relaxation

The relaxation technique, which I use about 80% of the time, often in conjunction with breath and chakra work, involves seven steps or key issues. Two approaches thread through the entire relaxation process: pacing and leading statements, both used in a permissive manner. Pacing statements recall physiological facts using neutral words. Some examples would be: "You are lying on the couch. You feel your body against its cushions. You are breathing normally. You hear my voice and the words I am saying to you." These statements are often combined with transition words such as "and" or "while" into a rather soothing and repetitious patter. They are interspersed with leading phrases whose purpose is to guide the client gently into perceptions desired by the therapist. An example is: "You may find your breathing becoming deeper and more regular as your body relaxes more and more." The higher percentage of leading statements, the more directive the therapist's style.

Every therapist has his own personal style. It falls somewhere on one continuum between directive and permissive and on another between assertive and non-assertive. Permissive style means using words such as, "Now you can find...you can allow...you can discover...new feelings in yourself." Directive phrases are more forceful: "Your thoughts are quieting.... You release all tension in your body...." The interview usually determines what mix of directive and permissive phrasing will work best with each client. Often initial resistance to directive suggestion can be overcome with a more permissive, client-oriented approach.

The steps involved are first eye closure, then body stillness, followed by a mental shift and the stimulation of imaging through as many sensory modes of perception as possible. This leads to a deepening of the relaxation level. Then a transition image is employed, such as a stairway or door (or descent down a flight of stairs and then finding a door). Finally there is the actual move into a past life.

**Induction through Arousal**

In this type of induction, the interview has established a specific problem or symptom, such as pain, a behavioral pattern, or an intense phobia. It is necessary to blot out the rational, analytical aspect of the problem. Then the suggestion is given that this symptom or problem can be released by retrieving the same situation from the past. The perception of the symptom or problem and its accompanying feeling state become the vehicle that takes the client into the past. It is a welcome suggestion because of the compelling need to work through the pain, phobia, or symptom.

In almost every case, focusing on the symptom will take the client back to a traumatic experience in his body, which results in yelling, crying, or reacting strongly in response to the past situation. Then the therapist's skill comes into play, and the situation is dealt with in its past manifestation. It may take a few minutes to build the arousal mode so that the client feels the situation or the pain, but the knowledge that re-experiencing the past trauma will release it, usually will take him there. The technique, known as an "affect bridge," using a similar current-life experience or symptom to evoke the past-life trauma, is often useful here. The therapist can help by asking the client visual and kinesthetic questions to stimulate sensory perception. This induction usually requires a more directive approach.

As the story unfolds, the client needs to be taken backward and forward, repeating the nexus of the problem until he can observe it without emotional abreaction. If the emotion is too strong or there is a death struggle involved, as there often is, the client can temporarily be taken out of the body memory into an observer position until he is able to deal with the pain. In such cases, nonetheless, it is important to deal with all reactions and feelings as fully as possible, taking the client in and out of the past-life body and incident several times in rapid succession so as to "desensitize" him progressively. Then background material can be gathered and eventually similar incidents in other past lives or in the perinatal state, can be uncovered.

**Induction through Breathing and Harmonizing the Chakras**

In this induction, deep, controlled breathing and progressive relaxation are integrated into visualization work with the chakras. It is a metaphysical approach that I developed by combining breathing techniques adapted from a form of pranayama yoga, discussed in *The Science of Breath* by yogi Ramacharaka[6] and inspired by the research into human energy fields of Dr. Valerie Hunt of Malibu, California.

At the end of this induction, before moving into the past or the future, I have clients visualize themselves surrounded by a field of pure white light. This is a protective device to keep them in their own energy and prevent them from attracting some external energy source that may be around and might influence their perception. Similarly, as discussed in Francine's case,[7] using white light imagery and chakra harmonization can be helpful when dealing with "entity attachment" or "spirit possession" phenomena during therapy. The white light or other similar sheltering imagery can also be used in a deepening phase of the standard relaxation induction where a safe, comfortable place is being established.

In using this or any induction involving energy visualizations, and particularly chakra work it is vital that the therapist take each client back into his current body and energy field after each session. The same applies to group inductions. Whenever the chakras are opened and harmonized or worked on during a therapy session, they must be restored to their normal functioning by direct suggestion as the client is being brought back from the altered state. Thus, if a client or group has been up through chakras into an altered state during induction, the therapist needs to work back down the chakras in reverse order with suggestions of harmony and balance so that they end the session at a normal level again, fully reintegrated and in equilibrium. I find that washing my hands in warm water between clients is energy releasing and helpful in maintaining my own energy balance and integrity.

All forms of induction tend to become more effective when brainwave entrainment is present. This is a term that describes the development of a unified electromagnetic energy field between therapist and client during a session. This occurs in all inductions to some extent, almost as if there were two strings vibrating, with one picking up the vibrations of the other. I consider it a measurable manifestation of the interplay of the universal electromagnetic forces that I describe in my section on "Philosophical Hypotheses."

Experience has shown that if the therapist keeps his or her own field clear, he may begin to pick up the vibrations of the client as the client slips into an altered state. Conversely, if the therapist lets his own mind wander, especially to something emotionally disturbing, the client may pick this up. Helen Wambach related that once while she was taking a research group through their past-life death, she experienced a minor heart thrumb and eight of the 12 subjects reported a death by heart attack. Several of them awakened very perplexed and reported suddenly being projected into a different body as they experienced the heart attack death. Some felt they had been catapulted into another past lifetime where they then experienced a heart attack, matching Helen's distress. It was as if Helen's vibrational change evoked matching scenarios out of the subjects' own repertoires of life experiences and overrode the one they had been "playing" during the regression up until then.[8]

Winafred Lucas' and my own recent research with the Mind Mirror, showed that not all therapists' brain wave patterns tend to blend with those of their clients during therapy sessions.[9] Some therapists maintain a high beta level of conscious awareness throughout. Others seem to share their client's inner state more fully. There seem to be gradations in this process, which we are just beginning to understand. These gradations may be related to the extent to which the therapist focuses on and follows his client's story, in such cases enabling the therapist to witness what is happening simultaneously. Owing to differences in individual energy fields, entrainment occurs more readily with some clients than with others.

Every therapist experiences resistance from some clients at various stages of therapy. I feel that it is important not to break down this resistance but rather to use it to achieve a deeper understanding of the client's core issues. What resistance says is that the client has some deep-seated reason for not doing what is suggested. Resistance during induction may be a signal to use another induction technique. Or it may be that the time, imagery, or phrasing or approach needs changing. However, clients who resist a variety of inductions should not be forced, because ultimately they know better than the therapist that they are not yet ready to involve themselves in the process being proposed. Their internal wisdom knows what is best for them at this time. When the resistance begins after trance is already induced, finger signals or other ideomotor responses can be used to determine if it is appropriate or not for them to go on. It might be that they could be taken into another past life to deal with some other subject when they can't yet handle the issue that led to their request for therapy. Therapists need to use their own experience and intuitive wisdom carefully in this area.

## *Induction through an Affect Bridge*

*Now close your eyes and I want you to concentrate on the pain you're feeling in your leg.... Get in touch with that pain again, right now...you're very strong and you can do it.... What I want you to do is look at the exact point of that pain. Look at what is causing that pain, at what it evokes in your mind.... Let it talk to you, if it wants to.... What are you experiencing? As I count, I want you to go back to a situation in which you knew that same pain once before, in this life or any other, the same pain, the same place.... I want you to see yourself in that situation, in that pain again...."* (Begin counting one to 10. Observe the client's reaction as you count. At 10, or when there is a significant abreaction, continue the pattern.) *"Feel that pain again.... What's happening now? What are you experiencing?... Where are you?..."*

## *Chakra Induction*

*Let's start with a little yawn. And as you yawn, you may find that your eyes just let themselves close. Your focus shifts from the left sphere of the brain inward to the right hemisphere. And as your brain begins to shift the attention from the left to the right, your thinking may become more intuitive and more creative, more in touch with your imaginative capabilities. You're now beginning to energize the physical and mental energy field around the body, clearing the channel so that it can help bring your awareness into your conscious attention. As you energize the field, you may let your mind and body relax automatically, letting go of any tensions or critical feelings so that you can lean back and enjoy the experience.*

*Now we're going to breathe into the various parts of the body, starting with breathing into the left foot, letting the energy come through that foot and up and around the hips and down and out the right foot. Again, in at the left foot and around and out the right foot. Behind the left knee now. Up and around, down to the right knee and out. Let any tension out. Again at the knee, and around to the right and out. Behind the legs is the red energy of the first chakra. Let the energy move up in the body, circling around as it comes back and out between the legs. Red again. Circling around and back out.*

*At the abdomen is an orange energy, orange. The orange energy moves up the body and back out the abdomen. Again, orange. Back out. Moving now* into the solar plexus with the yellow. Back out with the yellow, again at the solar plexus level, letting the yellow energy flow out. Into the heart breathe a green energy. Again, open the heart chakra; let the green flow through. See and feel the green, cool green.

At the throat is light blue. Let that blue energy flow in and back out into the field. And again let the blue flow in and out. Let's breathe one more time at the throat to open it up completely, and then let it go out again.

Now move up into the brow, the Third Eye, with deep purple. Sink into the deep purple energy, letting it float and flow, and flow back out. Again, breathe the purple energy in. As it flows out, it opens the Third Eye to more inner visioning and intuitive awareness. Move into the crown and let the white light flow through the body, cleansing it, purifying and cleansing the body as it flows in. Now let it flow back out through the crown until it spreads out around your body as you breathe in and out through the crown. Breathe in the white energy, letting it flow into the body and back out. Again, breathe through the crown, breathing in the crown energy, feeling yourself becoming more and more in touch with the energy field as you breathe regularly and deeply, letting yourself blow in that energy, feeling more and more calm and comfortable.

You can allow your physical body to relax itself and as you relax you become aware of any tension that may remain in any part of the physical body and you release that tension, particularly letting the jaw relax. Let your jaw relax as your tongue settles at the base of your mouth. You are more and more relaxed, feeling comfortable and a little dreamy as you drift along, focusing on the sound of my voice, allowing each breath to take you further into the deeper space. Each sound around you does the same. Each breath takes you down into a wonderful, calm, relaxed, comfortable place. Your breathing is deep and easy. Your awareness is focusing more and more into your energy fields, and it's taking you easily and naturally to just the right level for you, the right level to respond to all of my positive suggestions.

The path is becoming more and more familiar to you. You let yourself go, allowing your conscious awareness to begin now, seeing the consciousness and awareness of your mind, letting it drift on down like a falling autumn leaf. Visualize that leaf for a moment and watch it, bronze and golden from the last rays of the summer sun as it slowly drifts from the branch of the tree, caught in the breeze, slowly drifting down, falling into a lazy forest stream. Let your conscious awareness follow the leaf on down as it swirls and eddies in the slow lazy current, drifting away from the stream, leaving you completely relaxed, to focus on my suggestions.

Now I'd like you to give me a signal with one of the fingers of your right hand, a finger whose signal will mean yes.... All right. That's good. Now are you feeling more comfortable than you were a few minutes ago? Feeling more relaxed and kind of drowsy? Now let yourself continue to drift, going deeper and deeper into the relaxed, comfortable state, opening all the channels, making them harmonized and clear.

Now I'd like you to picture yourself at the head of a staircase. When you have that in mind, just signal with the yes signal. All right. So you're there *now. At the bottom of the stairway I want you to walk through the corridor until you find the right closed door. There is a door that you will recognize as the right one today. You will find it easily and swiftly. When you reach the door and when you're standing in front of the door just give me a description of the door. Tell me how big it is, the color and shape....*

*All right, Now I want you to reach up to the doorknob. Open the door. I want you to take five steps, letting your subconscious take you to just the right time and the right place where you will get the information you need for today. When you've reached that and you've made the five steps into that time and place, signal me again with the yes finger. Go ahead now.... Very good. Now tell me about this place where you are. Look around you and describe the exact surroundings to me....*

*Return from the altered state. Good. Now you're floating in the light, feeling wonderful, allowing yourself to know forgiveness and acceptance. I want you to begin coming back to the here and now, whole, clean, while I count backwards from five. Moving back now, coming up, seeing that there's a beautiful bright ball of energy circling, coming down, surrounding you like the light. This energy is white and gold, silver and gold, sparkling, shimmering. The energy enters into the crown of your head, comes down into your face and your jaw. Take the energy down now into your neck and into your shoulders, moving down your arms, all the way down to your hands and your fingers, bringing back normal body sensations. Five.... The energy is moving down now, down the chakras of the throat and the heart, completing the final cleansing, giving you more compassion, new hope, going through the solar plexus, bringing inner peace through that chakra of the solar plexus, radiating warmth and love...four.... The energy moves down into the lower centers now, reintegrating the physical with the subtle bodies into your current body, bringing you completely back into this body.... Three.... The energy is moving down your legs from your thighs, all the way down to your feet and your toes. Your body is alive with vital energy and you're ready to come back, feeling fine, feeling refreshed and somehow lighter.... Two.... You're ready to come back. Ready, open your eyes. You're awake, all the way back.... Wonderful.*

## Supportive and Deepening Techniques

Every client builds the key to his own therapy. The therapist's role is to facilitate understanding and awareness so that lasting change can take place. The client has the solution to his problems at some level of inner wisdom but is not consciously aware of it. Through the regression process, the therapist needs to use his skill to help strip away those outer layers of consciousness that are hiding true inner wisdom until the client can become aware. This happens when deep rapport is established between the two, allowing the client to reach those deep levels of the mind where healing occurs. There are several general methods of helping this deepening to occur.

(It must be kept in mind that there will always be some clients with whom effective rapport will not develop. The regression therapist must be prepared to recognize this within the first few sessions and either move to another type of therapy that does not require altered-state work or recommend that the client seek help from someone whose personality or basic energy structure is more compatible.)

Repeating words or phrases gleaned from the client during the interview helps deepen rapport, as does repeating both pacing and leading statements and combining them with conjunctions to emphasize embedded suggestions. Positive, easy-to-follow suggestions are the most effective. Anchor words help maintain evenness of trance depth, especially for group work. For instance, toward the end of the induction, suggest that even if the client goes so deep into the trance that he falls asleep, he will continue to listen to your voice and that each time you use the word "now" (or any other word you choose) his mind will respond by following your suggestion or answering your question with an image, an impression, a thought. Controlling volume, tone, and pacing of phrases deepens altered states, as does using one suggestion to reinforce another.

Ideomotor responses are often helpful. Establishing "yes" and "no" finger response signals before the transition to the past life serves two key deepening functions: it bypasses the brain's temporal (word-producing) lobe, thereby reducing left-brain analytical interference, and it forces the client's mind to make a choice. I use present tense to heighten realism. Avoid open-ended questions or those such as "why" that require an analytic response.

Once the client is perceiving information from a past life scenario, my questions are guided by a combination of the original information gleaned from the interview and my own intuitive perceptions. At this point we are sharing an intensified energy field and often I find myself "led" toward critical issues. Experience has taught me to trust this guidance, which I feel develops from rapport.

As the session progresses, I pay close attention to the client's responses and use them to mould future questions. I feel that following the client in his internal scenario is essential for a successful regression. I do not perceive regression therapy as a "one shot" process; a scenario may require several sessions to achieve. Reactions and relationships perceived during each session will be used in succeeding ones until understanding brings release.

The initial past-life scene is rarely chosen by accident, so my first question usually attempts to amplify what is happening there and elicit any unusual or intense emotional or physical responses. In any case, I always use this scene for future reference. Unlike some colleagues, I do not "push" my client into intensifying emotional responses but nonetheless thoroughly support the externalizing and releasing of those manifestations that do occur.

Usually I follow a biographical approach, returning the client to the past-life childhood and moving forward via key events or decisions and their consequences in the past-life context. Often this uncovers crucial personal relationships (or their absence) and attitudes or perceptions that relate directly to current problems. Getting the client to identify with the basic motives and character of the past personality helps to conceptualize what happened and works to release inhibitions and self-judgment about the present. Obviously, in many cases the death scene is critical and I pay close attention to its unfolding.

## *Processing*

### Psychotherapeutic and Transformational Techniques

After death, I suggest advancing to a post-life review where any other key incidents or relationships can be examined. At this point I remind clients, now in "spirit," of their timeless connection to higher guidance and I ask that they be joined by their "Higher Self" or "Counselor Part" or "Guide," using whatever terminology seems appropriate for each client. With this assistance, the client and I proceed to widen the context of whatever trauma or "unfinished business" developed during the past-life scenario and to look for parallels in the current symptomology. In most cases obvious connections are perceived rapidly.

Sometimes it is necessary, with the cooperation of this higher wisdom, to return to other, earlier lifetimes in order to understand the impact of some decision or attitude. Usually such forays conducted at this stage of the therapeutic process are brief, as the client's subconscious offers him exact situations in which the trauma first developed. Also, at this point I may bring the client forward into the perinatal period of the current lifetime to help him understand how his predispositions to undue emotional response were imprinted by similar stimuli that occurred then.

The final phases of the regression process involve adopting a wider perspective than that of any one past-life personality or than the perspective heretofore held by the current ego personality. As the spiritual self displays the various parallels between events, emotions, and attitudes of the past-life character(s) and those of the current persona, support is given for releasing pent-up judgment, guilt, hate, and denial. Mutual forgiveness at the spiritual level is proposed, and the degree of acceptance is ascertained. This latter is often surprisingly mathematical as in, "I can forgive so-and-so 70 percent right now," or "I can let go of half of that." Such reactions should be noted and returned to in subsequent therapy sessions if lingering emotional reactions remain.

## Integration into the Psychotherapeutic Process

The regression therapist assists this integration process in a number of ways.

1. The client needs to be helped to understand that integration seldom develops immediately. It may take several sessions involving the examination of a number of related life themes from various past lives. It takes time for significant patterns to develop and impress themselves on the client's consciousness.

2. The therapist is a profoundly sympathetic yet disinterested companion, supporting the client in facing difficult emotionally-charged moments and facilitating safe passage through them. This gentle, empathic presence is often enough to permit a client to achieve the insight needed to end unnecessary suffering and find inner peace.

3. The therapist assists in bringing insights gained during regressions into the present through pre- and post-session discussions. These provide the client with a forum for testing new ideas and attitudes, and they help him or her to put such new viewpoints into practice in everyday life. Moreover, as inner healing develops, synchronous positive changes in surrounding conditions often take place. It is as if an energy level shift has occurred in the client's nexus of relationships.

4. The therapist encourages clients to note significant dreams, day-dreams, or flashes of insight that occur either just after a therapy session or within 48 hours before the next session. Frequently the client's subconscious provides material which, when correctly interpreted, penetrates long-standing psychological defenses.

5. During therapy the client is helped to build workable positive response patterns in daily life. Robert Assagioli, founder of Psychosynthesis, suggested that it takes about a month of conscious positive effort to alter a habit pattern.[10] Edgar Cayce, citing the Bible, suggested that fixing new thought patterns requires 40 days of conscientious attention.[11] Dialogue and feedback via the therapist is invaluable for such work.

## Failures

As in all such work, not every therapist is going to succeed with every client every time. The core vibrational energy patterns of therapist and client may be too far apart to allow sufficient rapport for an effective regression. Client expectations may be inflated and lead to premature withdrawal from therapy when dramatic results are not immediately forthcoming. There may be a "hidden agenda" of failure-seeking, thereby offering the current personality an excuse not to change. Some clients simply will not enter even a light trance state despite a variety of techniques. Others may achieve a trance, but their subconscious then blocks any surfacing of past-life material.

Dr. Helen Wambach once privately studied 20 such individuals who had been unable to succeed at her weekend workshops where she used hypnosis for three consecutive regressions. After several intense individual therapy sessions about a dozen of the group succeeded in accessing a past life. The others could be hypnotized but they consistently refused to regress beyond childhood memories. Furthermore, *every one* of those who did break through into the past was immediately caught up in a violent emotional struggle in their most recent past-life death. Once denial was released, none had any trouble with other regressions. "It was if there were a cork stopping up the bottle," she reported.[12]

Regression therapy is still new and unusual and perhaps also seen as glamorous by some. I have had a few clients, usually with long histories of therapy failures, who have sought regressions almost in defiance. "Do your best—you won't be able to cure me either," was the attitude. And of course I did not help them, for they refused to work on themselves. One female client had a clear objective of seducing me physically, just as she had successfully seduced at least two psychoanalysts, thereby proving her contention that male therapists could not be trusted. Although attractive, she had a low self-image and consistently resisted even a light trance state, so regression proved impossible. I was almost relieved to fail!

There is, however, one difference between regression therapy and traditional analysis with regard to failure. I often point out this difference to prospective clients. Regression therapy is an intense in-depth process. In all but the most unusual cases, progress toward symptom removal and dynamic cognitive reordering occurs within just a few sessions. Therefore, unlike many other modalities, client and therapist alike can detect differences quickly, thereby eliminating the possibility of years of weekly therapy sessions that result in no discernible progress. I tell my clients that if they do not find positive changes in their lives within six months of biweekly sessions with me, they need to try other techniques or another therapist. In practice, rapport failures are evident within three sessions, while more profound ego-defense problems typically surface within five or six.

## Cases

### Case 1. Rescripting

I include this case because of the controversy surrounding an important hypnotherapeutic technique called "rescripting." This is a device where, under the therapist's guidance, a regressed client intervenes at a critical point in his or her recalled experience to change that experience in such a way as to eliminate conflict and achieve durable growth. It is seldom used in regression therapy, but it can sometimes speed conflict resolution as victory replaces defeat in the client's consciousness. It should be used with caution and only when in agreement with the client's Higher Self or Counselor Part. As in this case, rescripting should be part of the client's integrative process to widen perspective.

Anne-Marie, a French woman of about 50, worked as a biomedical research assistant in a large Parisian laboratory. Her complaints involved a variety of personal problems, including uncontrollable procrastination. She simply put everything off until the last moment and then had to scramble to make experiment deadlines. She was a highly intelligent person, but repeated emotional attacks just before exams had led her to skip medical school, although in other respects she was ideally suited for such an endeavor. Instead, she found herself in a subordinate position to a new laboratory director, a medical doctor, of whom she was inexplicably terrified. From the first, just the sight of him panicked her, and she dreaded their weekly meetings. Her work was obviously suffering, as this panic reaction intensified her habitual tardiness. She wondered if the origins of these reactions could lie in a past life.

A good subject, Anne-Marie regressed swiftly to a past life as a male Italian page in the Renaissance era. Apparently from a rather poor noble family, Sylvestro, the page, had long despaired of ever gaining the riding skills required to become a knight until one of the daughters of the local duke took a fancy to him and helped him get the proper lessons. In gratitude he sought to become her champion. Unfortunately, in one of his first tournaments, he was opposed by an older, more experienced rival, who was apparently jealous of Sylvestro's upstart attentions to the high-born maiden. Feeling woefully unprepared, the young page put off the test as long as he could but at last had to fight his opponent. His inexperience led him to miss his enemy's shield with this lance, and he fell from his horse. Trusting that he had time to regain his own weapon, he turned his back on the other man briefly, whereupon his adversary ran him through as he turned to face the man again. Death was not instantaneous and before leaving his body he had time to dwell on his rival's glaring stare.

> T: Now, let yourself experience the spirit leaving the body...rise up out of that body.
> P: I can't seem to do that. His eyes are terrible, so dark. He's towering over me. I was a fool to think I could beat him! I needed more time!
> T: Move ahead until your spirit has left that body...
> P: (Sighing) It's okay now; I'm out of there.
> T: Continue moving forward and upward. Remember now that your consciousness expands again as you leave that body; your spirit's always in touch with your inner wisdom. Let your Higher Self come forward now and help you see how that experience related to what's happening now to Anne-Marie, in this lifetime.
> P: Yes, I see it now. Those dark eyes, they're the same as Dr. X's! Good grief, that's who it was! I didn't want to fight him—I wasn't ready but he made it a question of honor. I still feel that way! If only I'd not turned around; I was foolish.
> T: I'm talking to the Higher Self now, am I not? (Assent.) Good. Now I want to know if it would serve Anne-Marie to go back to that tournament, but this time with more training and experience, ready for combat. Could she learn the same life lesson from preparing for success as from failing?

After a moment's hesitation, her Higher Self agreed that she might "go further ahead" if she replayed the incident with more training and confidence. So I requested that she visualize longer training hours and find a feeling of being ready for the decisive test before taking the field again. As she did so, she recognized that Sylvestro's arms master was—in the present lifetime—none other than an overly severe nun who terrorized her in elementary school.

Finally, as Sylvestro, all was ready. This time he rode forward with his lady's handkerchief tucked in his sleeve for luck. When the two adversaries met, Sylvestro was strong. (Afterward Anne-Marie told me that she felt "three times bigger than the black knight!") A surge of power came over him. His aim true, the page knocked his opponent off his horse by a clean hit on the shield, thereby winning the tournament and the promise of knighthood.

With his victory secured, I asked Sylvestro to move ahead to the end of that lifetime. After leaving his body on a battlefield a short time later, my client told me that as he knocked the black knight off his horse, he felt a "rush of generosity" overwhelm him like a strong energy. It was a totally new feeling and something Anne-Marie had never felt possible in her current lifetime. There were no longer regrets about the rather rapid battlefield death. Apparently Sylvestro had learned the lesson he came to achieve. He realized that his earlier feeling of rivalry stemmed more from pride and ambition than from real love for the duke's daughter, and so he went away shortly after the tournament.

At our next meeting Anne Marie proudly announced that she had actually finished an experiment report a day early and that she could now face her new supervisor without undue fear and trembling, although their meetings still weren't exactly a pleasant experience for her. Future sessions revealed other past lives in which that same supervisor had played a highly judgmental role. Although rescripting of those lifetimes did not seem appropriate, we did work on mutual forgiveness and building positive relations for the future. Later, she told me that her supervisor's attitude toward her, initially rather stern and suspicious, seemed to have mellowed. By the time she left therapy for summer vacation, she had decided not to resign, something that had seemed all but inevitable when we had started two months earlier, and she was also investigating taking some night school management classes.

In reviewing this case, I note similarities with other rescripting I have experienced. First, only one key incident had to be changed to effect a more positive outcome. Second, subsequent changes in the past-life materials were minimal compared to the shift in emotional response and understanding. Finally, in Anne-Marie's case the attitude of generosity allowed her to recognize that pride and ambition had interfered with her spiritual progress. These traits were more readily given up by her other past-life and current personalities after the experience of victory rather than of violent defeat. That her former adversary seemed to acknowledge their changed relationship may be seen as an example of those "astonishing synchroncities in the Jungian sense," cited by Stanislav Grof as a characteristic feature of deep transpersonal change.

### Case 2. Balancing

Margot, a professor at a small college, gave as her presenting problem her constant anxiety that her husband was having an affair with a specific woman. This was Margot's second marriage. I knew little about the first one, which seemed to be obscured in a distant past. The current marriage, several years old with a dynamic young attorney, seemed to be a highly compatible match. Her husband was frequently away taking depositions, but he had never done anything to justify her pervasive anxiety. Usually very poised,

Margot often found herself precipitated into clinging behavior because of her anxiety. She felt that the source of her doubt might lie in another lifetime and that exploring such a source might free her.

When I asked Margot if she went into an altered state easily, she said that she generally did but she was feeling a little anxious because resolving her doubts was so important. I told her we could work through concentration as well as relaxation, but I started with a breathing induction using the chakra points. I had her breathe the colors in through the chakras, having the white go down as far as it would and then come back up like a fountain to envelope her whole energy field. Further chakra breathing was followed by a check for points of tension.

When she was feeling deeply relaxed in her entire body, I had her mentally go down a stairway and walk through a corridor until she found the right closed door and then signal me with a finger that we had previously designated as a "yes" finger. She described the door and then walked through it five paces and began to describe her surroundings. She found herself outdoors on the ground. She wore a long dress with little flowers on it. She described her physical body—a small waist, small frame. I had her touch her hair, and she was aware that it was honey-colored, wavy, and hung down her back. She was a young woman in her twenties.

She stood in a clearing with trees ahead of her and fields on either side.

> T: *Now stay in that same body and approximately that time frame and move to a moment when you are having some strong feeling, either feeling very good or very bad, something emotional, something that you're watching, that you begin to become a part of. Move there. Where are you?*
> P: *I'm there in the same place.*
> T: *Let yourself move into the moment you begin to feel. What's happening?*
> P: *Well, there's a man coming out of the woods. I'm holding some flowers.*
> T: *What's the first thought that comes through your mind as you see him?*
> P: *I'm excited.*
> T: *Get in touch with that excitement for a moment. Get in touch with the excitement in your body. Where does it come?*
> P: *Up around my heart and my chest. And my throat. And my thighs. My thighs feel real warm. Real quivery.*
> T: *Okay. Stay with that feeling. Feel it even more strongly.*

Such anchoring of feeling in the body intensifies and deepens the experience. Margot easily saw the man coming toward her and moved out toward him, feeling "all bubbly." They embraced.

> T: *Let yourself feel that. What are you feeling?*
> P: *Ah, it feels wonderful. And we shouldn't be doing this.*
> T: *Get in touch with that double feeling.*

> P: Oh...ahh...I think I'm going to swoon.
> T: He's whispering something in your ear just as you begin to swoon. What is he whispering?
> P: "I love you...Darling, I love you so much."
> T: Now I want you to move back from that moment, using that same energy force, to the first time that you realized that you had that feeling. Move there now.

This was the first of several attempts to help Margot move into another lifetime that had an impact on the one she was remembering. In each succeeding session she returned to the incident she had started to recount the first time. It seemed to be the one incident in which the trauma was focused. The second time she returned to her collapse and reported how she was overcome with feeling "as though I had no bones in my body."

Her lover carried her away to the woods to a little bower, where they made love.

> T: Let yourself move through until you've completed that sequence.
> P: He's made a wonderful little place. It's all sort of grassy and mossy. There's a little bower of branches, a little nest, off to the right. And I just feel like I have absolutely no will and no power.

Gently I kept moving her forward and she was able to describe all the steps of the lovemaking. The physical experience made her feel totally bonded with her lover, but she knew that they could not really be together, and gradually she realized that this was because he had a wife and children. She felt deeply guilty about this.

> T: Move through—touch exactly your feelings. Get into the guilt feeling that you're having there along with the wonderful sensations. I want you to let yourself flow into those now.
> P: I can't believe that I'm really his. It's like he wants me to be his but he can't really be mine. It's not fair, but it's so exquisite. It means so much to be with him but I feel conflict at the back of my neck.
> T: Okay. Feel that feeling at the back of your neck. Now I want you to move forward one year from that date. Get in touch. Now where are you?

From the vantage point of another year Margot was able to know that she continued to have an affair with the man, meeting him in the woods when the weather permitted or passing him silently in the village.

> T: Now I want you to move forward until something happens that affects that relationship. How much time passes?

Margot went forward another year and came to a final liaison in the woods, when, in the midst of lovemaking, she looked up and saw his 10-year-old son standing nearby looking at them.

> T: *Get in touch with exactly what happens at that moment. Move through it.*
> P: It's like everything just stops.
> T: *Where do you feel that stopping in your body?*
> P: In my chest. My breath and the whole world just stops. I stop, and he says, "What's the matter?" He looks and sees his son. The son stops. He's just looking at us.
> T: *You know there's something wrong.... Keep going.... At that moment what happens inside you?*
> P: I feel that terrible sinking feeling, that I've been found out...and we weren't supposed to.... (Deep sigh.)

Her lover pulled away from her, tried to gloss over the situation, and Margot had the sinking feeling that the boy would go home and tell his mother. She was distressed at the unhappiness she was bringing the other woman. She realized even more clearly that she shouldn't be there.

> T: *You know you shouldn't be doing it. Can you go back to that first moment when you knew you shouldn't be meeting him?*
> P: Yeah.... And that kind of light-hearted feeling like I just want to swoon.... It's ruined now. It's ruined. It will never be the same.
> T: *Say it again—with more feeling.*
> P: It's ruined! We can never meet again! It's all over!
> T: *Now I want you to take that energy and go back to the origin of "It's ruined!" Say it again, "It will never be the same!"*

Again I tried to take Margot back to an earlier source of the feeling, but evidently there wasn't one, for she remained in the experience of being found out. I moved her ahead five years and found her in the same village in wintertime. She ran into the wife as she was going into a store and became aware of the depth of the other woman's sadness.

> T: *Move forward until some other important event directly related to the feeling that it's ruined, it's over, you'll never have that again. In that lifetime.*

Margot described a scene in which a man her parents hoped she would marry came to call, but she felt she had no right to meet him and turned him down.

> T: *Okay, move forward until one year before the date of your death. And just look back on your memory of that lifetime. What stands out?*

It turned out that her parents tried several additional times to arrange a marriage for her, but she couldn't look anyone in the eye. Then she became sick and experienced death from some lung problem.

T: Let yourself go. Get in touch with what you're thinking about as you're lying there.
P: Just—what a wasted life. The only happiness was with this lover, and it was so mixed because it had so much guilt and fear and yet also such incredible delight.
T: Move on up out of the body. The spirit leaves the body behind. Get in touch with what your feelings are at this point—out of the body.
P: Just how sad! What a waste! Maybe I really made a very big mistake to not wait for one of these nice gentlemen I could have married. I could have had my own children with a relatively free conscience. But I let myself just be overcome.

Margot went on to regret her wasted life and her early death, which occurred before the death of her parents. Then she moved into the transformational aspect of the regression.

T: Okay. Now I want you to move up in spirit form to where you can get in touch with your Higher Self. Get in touch with more wisdom than was in that body and in that mind. I want you to get in touch with the main purpose of that experience.
P: To learn about what works and what really doesn't work in relationships. And I learned that doesn't work. It didn't work for me and it didn't work for any man who could have married me or was interested in me, and it didn't work for his children and it didn't work for his wife. And it didn't work for my parents—they were very sad that I could never somehow respond to other suitors.
T: So now, have you learned that lesson? Let yourself get in touch with that lesson but at the same time ask yourself the question, Do I need to carry doubt about myself in terms of that lesson? Will I forget if I don't?
P: I think I need to forgive myself.
T: Can you see that woman that you were? Let yourself see her the day she saw the other woman in the store. Can you move toward her the way you are now and forgive her?
P: I'll try.... I come up behind the woman I was then and I turn her around. I'm a little bit higher than she is and I take her face in my hands and I'm looking her in the eye. "I understand. Believe me, you've paid a price for this, a very deep price."
T: Tell her, "I forgive you. I let go of that feeling because I've learned that lesson." Can you let go of that feeling and still keep the lesson?
P: Yeah.... I'm just on the verge of forgiving her.
T: Go ahead. See yourself doing exactly what you need to do.

P: It seems to have something to do with the pain, the emotional pain, the loneliness—there's all that incredible hurt and that loneliness. And I didn't see him again. In fact, he just never came to the woods again. I went to meet him sometimes still, and he was never there. It just faded out.... (To self of that lifetime) "You've been very deeply hurt. You've hurt them, but you have been very deeply hurt yourself. You may have been even more hurt than they were (crying), because they got to have him the rest of their lives and you didn't get to really see him again.

T: Now I want you to move in the spirit. Look around and see others there that are in spirit, too. Get in touch with all the actors in that drama and see the role they played.

P: The wife and I are looking at each other. She has kind of a clear understanding look in her eye.

T: Not like she was in body. Can she forgive you—is there a clear understanding look in her eye?

P: She's just nodding and saying, "Well, we'll just do it another way around another time. Until we've both learned what we need to learn."

T: Is that acceptable? Can you forgive you and her for that?

P: It sounds frightening, but it sounds right.

T: What's frightening about it?

P: Because I don't want to have to experience what's she's experienced. I don't want to be the wife whose husband is with somebody else.

T: Can you find out if that's a need, if that's something you must live through?

P: (Surprised and startled.) I did experience it. I really did! And three children and everything. And they knew, too. And it's interesting because my son this time actually saw, not as clearly as that boy did, but he saw in this life my first husband with his young lover.

T: There's a balancing.

P: (Sadly.) Yes.... I need to stay here for a minute. That really is balanced. It's funny because I found it so hard to identify with the other woman, and yet now I know I've been the other woman.

T: I want you to move forward and go up in spirit until you reach the highest Guide, the highest one that's available today. Can he take the need for more balance off? Can you release that pain to him?

P: Oh, I'd like to.

T: See if you can. Take it as though you're reaching into your heart and giving that part back, giving that out because you do not need it anymore.

P: (Sigh.) Oh, I'd like to...(After long silence.) Okay, I see the first event and I see the event in this life—they look so matched, so nicely matched. It really helps.

T: Can you get in touch with the Guide?

P: It's not a person. It's a Light, yellowy, glowy.

T: Move into the Light now. Let the Light come and envelop you. Feel the feeling of the Light.

P: Yes. (Definite relief in her voice.)

T: *Feel the peace, the understanding, the acceptance. Feel the acceptance—just as you are. How is that?*
P: Good. (Great relief.) *There's still a little bit in my chest.*
T: *Let the light flow into it, flow it away, lift it off, sort of like spot removing.*
P: Yeah. It's coming out...out of my chest.
T: *That's right. Let it all go. Let it flow and flow and flow until there's hardly anything left—down to a trickle, a wisp. And when it's all gone, I want you to take a big deep breath and get rid of the last little bit. Big, deep breath.*
P: (Long silence. Then a deep sigh.)
T: *Very good. Now you're floating in the light, allowing yourself to know forgiveness and acceptance. I want you to begin coming back now to the here and now, whole, clean. Moving back now, coming up, seeing that there's a beautiful bright ball of energy circling, coming down, surrounding you with light.*

I completed Margot's return to her body by moving the energy down through every part of her body and concluded by putting in positive suggestions.

T: *Your body is alive with vital energy and you're ready to come back, feeling refreshed and somehow lighter. You're ready to come back. Ready, open your eyes. You're awake, all the way back. Wonderful.*
P: Thank you.

Following this regression Margot experienced a significant lessening of her anxiety over her husband and his assistant and came into an expanded sense of her own worth and her power to be sufficient in herself, no matter what happened. This had a freeing effect on her marriage. Further therapeutic work focused on this self-empowerment through subsequent regressions linked with careful attention to the current process of living.

### Case 3. Choosing from a Broader Data Base

Apparently relationships in other lifetimes initiate strong valences in this one. Many times this draw seems irresistible and inexplicable until one understands that it stems from an uncompleted involvement in an earlier lifetime. Such a balance may lead to inappropriate and even destructive behavior in this life, but recognizing its source can make a wise choice of direction easier. In Bea's case, karmic tangles had to be exposed in order for her to be able to choose a more fulfilling pattern for her current life.

Bea was a slender, attractive blonde of 42 who lived in an affluent Los Angeles suburb. Although she did not really need extra income, she had a part-time practice as a licensed body-worker. She belonged to a spiritual meditation group as well. Viewed externally, she seemed to be living the all-American dream: intelligent, pretty, married to a successful businessman, and mother of two pre-teenage children, all living together in a beautiful home. Yet, when she arrived for our first appointment in January 1989 she was a bundle of nerves and confessed that she felt conflicted and miserable. Within a few minutes in our initial interview she began spilling out her story.

In recent years nothing seemed to be going right in her relationship with her husband, Jerry, with whom she felt less like a wife than like either a mother or a daughter, depending on the circumstances. Then, about 10 months previously, she had suddenly met a younger man, John, in his early 30's, at her meditation group. Although John was not particularly striking physically, she had felt an instant passionate attraction toward him, and, despite her devotion to her family, she soon found herself involved in an extramarital affair. As the months went by and the affair developed, she felt increasingly divided over whether or not this mostly-physical relationship with a younger man who had yet to commit himself to a stable career and lifestyle was enough to sacrifice her fifteen-year marriage and children for. Could her immediate and uncontrollable passion be karmic, i.e., related to a past-life experience? She desperately needed to know whether she should continue to work on her marriage but felt helpless to decide.

I told her that it might well be a karmic pattern that would be more available just because she felt so desperate. Then I relaxed her to help her unwind so that we could begin our search.

After her body had relaxed sufficiently, I gently guided her back through time's corridors, asking her subconscious mind to direct her to the source of her infatuation with John. Looking down at her feet, she saw them in sturdy black shoes, the kind worn by little girls in the 19th century, with thick woolen stockings. A dark simple dress and apron covered her girlish body. Thick reddish hair and freckles completed her appearance. Apparently she was standing in a kitchen, peeling vegetables.

> *P: I'm in the kitchen fixing dinner; even though I'm just 10 years old, I'm somehow responsible for things here....*
> *T: Are you helping your mother with these household chores?*
> *P: (Emotionally) No, she's not here (hesitates); she's gone (a little sob); I think she's dead. Yes, that's it, oh, how I miss her! And only Father and I are left here in this big house all alone. Except for Miss Johnson, who comes twice a week to handle the scrubbing and washing. I'm not big enough to do that yet.*

My next question established that in this life Bea (then named Mary) lived alone in the Scottish countryside with her father, an educated landowner, who seemed to have settled into a rather melancholy retreat after the premature death of his wife. Although not materially uncomfortable, it was a lonely and cheerless existence. Mary seemed to love and respect her father, but his depression, punctuated by unreasonable demands for absolute obedience down to small details of dress and behavior, weighed on her. As Mary grew into young womanhood she felt helplessly trapped between her feelings of daughterly duty and the natural desire to lead her own life. Similar feelings had been echoed in Bea's remarks during the pre-induction interview.

One day, on a rare outing to the village church, Mary, now in her mid-20's and already fearing spinsterhood, saw George, a young lawyer from the city who had just inherited a farm in the area. Mary fell deeply in love. Here was the "Prince Charming" she had dreamed of.

Mary's father, however, had a different viewpoint. After allowing George to call a time or two, he took a violent dislike to the young lawyer, upbraiding him for his foolish political views and "lack of common sense." After a long argument, he told George not to return. Mary was distraught, but George persuaded her to meet him in town on Sundays, under the pretext of going to church. They soon became secret lovers.

> T: *I want you to get in touch with your inner feelings about this situation as Mary. Are you satisfied with this double life? How is it affecting you? And your relationship with your father?*
>
> P: *I feel so guilty, sneaking off to be with George when Father thinks I'm just going into the village for church. I know it's wrong but what can I do? Anytime they see each other they act like children, always sneering and shouting. I feel I don't have any say in it at all.*
>
> T: *You feel helpless to decide between them? How long does this go on? I want you to move forward now in that life as Mary until you reach the incident or event that tipped the balance for you and something happened. Just relax and move forward, now...*
>
> P: *(Slowly) All right; I guess almost a year has gone by because it seems like early spring again and it was Easter when I first met George at church....*
>
> *(Emotionally) Oh, my God, I think I must be pregnant or have missed my period or something like that. I know I am terrified that Father will find it out and know I disobeyed him and continued to see George. I've got to do something! I've got to do something!*
>
> *(Breathing hard.) I sent a message to George in town and he's coming out here to take me away. I'm so frightened; Father's been acting awfully strange lately, too. I don't know if he suspects something or not.*
>
> T: *Just move forward into the next scene. What happens when George arrives?*
>
> P: *(Sobbing now.) He's dead; he's dead. How could it come to that? (Sobs violently.)*
>
> T: *Just take a couple of deep breaths and let yourself detach slightly from the intensity of that scene. You can just be an observer for a moment. George is dead? What happened?*

P: *(Regains control.)* No! Father is dead! What happened?... Father was waiting for him when he came and they fought...and George killed him! It's awful—awful...I feel so helpless *(sobs again).*

T: *(After calming Bea/Mary with suggestions that she can merely observe the scene as it unfolds)* All right, now let yourself continue to move forward in time; go to what happens after your father dies in the fight. What do you do next?

P: *(More calmly.)* I think George panicked and ran away; I see him riding off on his horse, leaving me alone there. *(Pauses.)* I'm not sure I ever saw or heard from him again. I don't know how I know that, but it seems right. He was so frightened when he saw what he'd done, I think he just bolted and ran.

T: Do you see him again? Move forward in that life and see if you can find a time when you're together again?

P: *(After a pause.)* No...I just see myself in the same country house and I have a little girl with me. But I know I never forget him. And I don't feel angry at him. I just wish he'd turn up again so I could show him our child. I still feel helpless not knowing where he went, and I miss him terribly.

After taking Bea on through Mary's death, which occurred in 1890 from natural causes sometime after her daughter had married and moved away to a neighboring village, I asked her "Higher Self" if she could recognize anyone from that life as being back with her today. I was not surprised when she told me that her lover, John, was the reincarnation of George while her father from that life was now her husband, Jerry. Mary's interrupted relationship with George had rekindled forgotten desires when Bea met John at the meditation group, while her mixed roles as daughter and housekeeper to her Scottish father had returned in Bea's confused feelings about Jerry.

It would be both simplistic and inaccurate to imply that this single regression, dramatic as it was, was sufficient to restore Bea's equilibrium and enable her to choose between her family and younger lover. I continued to work with her during follow-up sessions, during which we explored other aspects of these two relationships as well as those with her children and her alcoholic father, who had at least once while drunk made improper advances to her in her childhood, thereby providing additional reinforcement for her helpless feelings and confusion over wife versus daughter roles.

Nonetheless, this session did provide Bea with enough insight so that she began to distinguish between what were remnants of Mary's frustrated desire for George and her own true feelings about John. Consequently, about five weeks later in a follow-up session she told me that she now knew that despite her mixed feelings about her husband and the problems in their relationship, she was no longer willing to risk her marriage for John. The affair ended shortly thereafter. Later, in a future-life progression session she found herself reunited with George/John as her lawful "partner" and shared the feeling that "this time we totally understand each other; we know who each other is."[13]

In a synchronistic development, Bea's current husband Jerry finally accepted marriage counseling and later entered a program of personal therapy for himself. This happened in spite of the fact that he had no knowledge of Bea's affair or of our sessions and Bea's subsequent decision to leave John. A year later the family was still together and Bea told me that she now feels more personally in charge of her future than ever before.

# Chapter XVI

# Rob Bontenbal, M.A. and
# Tineke Noordegraaf, M.M. (The Netherlands)

## *Biographical Data*

### Shared Background and Work

In the early 80's Hans ten Dam lectured and presented workshops in the Netherlands about his approach to reincarnation therapy. Shortly after this he initiated a Dutch training program. It was a structured, short, tough course of 10 intense eight-hour meetings. I graduated in 1984 and Tineke in 1985. Ten Dam's way of working touched us deeply. We enjoyed learning the methods and strategies he demonstrated, and even before finishing the course we started practicing, first with relatives and friends, and then with friends of friends, and even with people Hans sent to us.

In 1984 I explored the possibility of organizing an association of reincarnation therapists, and after a hesitant start about 20 graduates formed an informal group. Members came together in my house every three months to discuss different aspects of practicing therapy, and in 1986 participants in subsequent ten Dam training groups joined. When ten Dam left to work in Brazil, the association started a year-long training program in 1987, of which Tineke and I, together with Alexander Bund and Zoop Vanderhagen, were original trainers.

Subsequently the program was enlarged into an institute with a two-year curriculum, a 360-page manual, and eight trainers, averaging 45 new students each year. Since the beginning, over 130 students have graduated from the course. Many of them are members of a large professional group, the Association of Dutch Reincarnation Therapists, which currently has a membership of 200.[1]

In the past several years we have sponsored three-day training workshops with trainers from outside the Netherlands, as well as within. The most important of these outside trainers was Morris Netherton, who helped us develop our basic concept of the holographic model. Through his influence we came to see that any chronic problem has to be considered as the result of related biographical, perinatal, prenatal, and transpersonal events.

In 1985 I started a newsletter for the members of the original circle, and later with the help of an enthusiastic staff of editors I have been able to develop the newsletter into a professional journal, *Cyclus*, which is published three times a year.

Tineke and I had worked together in the training team for a year and a half when she lost her voice during a seminar. She wanted to continue with a distressed student and asked me to help, which I did successfully. Soon we started working together with clients who had severe problems. This has proven to have many advantages, especially when energy and body work are needed or different (male and female) roles have to be emphasized by voice.

Since then Tineke has gone to Germany and Switzerland, and Swiss and German students have shown great interest in her work, especially with young children. We fly to Germany and Switzerland five times a year to train and work with 25 students. Together we have attended workshops and conferences in the USA, and in 1991 we presented our first workshop in the APRT Spring Conference in San Diego. It still surprises us that two people who are both rather individualistic can practice, train, and travel together successfully.

## Personal Background *(Rob Bontenbal)*

I was conceived shortly after D-day when, after a surge of hope for a brighter future than we had experienced under the Nazi occupation, the Dutch people experienced a terrible winter of fear, cold, depression, and especially, starvation. The country's tension and my mother's desperation around food impacted me on many levels, including the physical one, where I experienced severe digestive problems. My birth on March 12, 1945 was a stressful experience because of lack of proper heating, hot water, and sufficient light. My pre- and perinatal war experiences left me as an infant reactive to the smallest sound or movement, a problem that was alleviated only later when my father took me with him to crowded and noisy soccer matches where I could yell with the crowd and begin to feel more comfortable in noisy situations.

My family lived close to the major airport next to Amsterdam, where my father did troubleshooting for the freight department of KLM, the Royal Dutch Airlines, a line of work that enabled me to travel abroad later in my life. I stemmed from an interesting and diverse background. My mother and her sister came from a family in which politics played an important role. My grandfather was an anarchist, while his sons held seats in the community councils of Amsterdam and Rotterdam for the Dutch Communist Party. My father and mother were more bourgeois in their convictions, liberals but with strong agnostic beliefs.

When I was 12 years old I visited the USA for the first time, arriving in Manhattan with a feeling of excitement, but my first view of the city put me in a state of sadness and confusion that I subsequently learned was a hangover from an earlier lifetime. My sister lived in Rochester in upstate New York, and subsequently I spent many holidays there until she and her husband moved to Colorado.

My father's business trips to Africa, the Middle East, and South America sparked my interest in history and geography, and in high school I decided to study political science at the University of Amsterdam, an intention that was delayed until I was 21 because of my being drafted into the Dutch Army for the regular one-and-a-half-year term.

Studying political science in the 60's was an exciting experience, and after three years I found myself spending more time on the streets demonstrating than in class getting my degree. Eventually I took a break from school to travel and work at odd jobs. In 1972 I went into a depression, because I was unable to find a goal in life and someone with whom I could share my search. I decided to leave the Netherlands and re-visit the USA. While utterly lonely and roaming the streets of San Francisco, I suddenly found myself again. I realized that wherever I was I would be the same person and that as a person I was a complete being, with stronger or weaker points and many things to work on, but complete. As a complete being I could find fulfillment with or without someone to share my life; without consciously knowing the concept, it was my first understanding of the polarity within me. Now, almost 20 years later, I am convinced that accepting that polarity in Haight-Ashbury saved my life.

I returned to Amsterdam and the university and earned my bachelor's degree in political science. Within six months I met Lydia Kimman, a wonderful, beautiful girl who has been my partner in life for 20 years. At the time I met her, she worked as a registered nurse in one of the Amsterdam hospitals and supported me through my M.A. in urban planning. By the time I was close to graduation Lydia was so impatient with the way the medical world was dealing with health and sickness that she decided to go back to school to become a natural health practitioner.

Later, at the same time that I was working as a researcher at the university trying to be as scientific and rational as possible, Lydia came home every day with a range of new concepts and ideas: astrology, vegetarianism, holistic health, palmistry, flower and herb remedies, reincarnation. My resistance was strong. Those concepts and ideas felt threatening to my position in the ivory tower of the academic world, but one concept pierced my armor—reincarnation. I made an effort to prove that believing in past lives was just another way of not being able to cope with reality. But reading Dick Sutphen, Gina Cerminara, Edith Fiore, Morris Netherton, Thorwald Dethlefsen, and Denys Kelsey and realizing that almost all of these therapists/authors had academic degrees, even Ph.D.s, made it difficult to prove my point. I started to understand that their analytically schooled minds had made it easier, instead of more difficult, for them to accept the logic of the reincarnation concept and to develop therapeutic methods based on that concept.

While my wife continued her studies toward becoming a holistic health advisor (she is now famous in the Netherlands for the way she uses palmistry and iris-diagnosis to advise people on matters of mental, emotional, physical, and spiritual health), I continued my research on reincarnation and during that period lost most of my resistance against many other new (for me in this life) concepts and therapeutic methods. I became a non-fanatical vegetarian, took a course in astrology with a Jungian whom I had met when we were students in urban planning, and went through a number of rebirthing sessions. I decided that if I wanted to become a therapist I would become a reincarnation therapist. I already was convinced that only insight could heal and transform.

Morris Netherton's book held an especial fascination for me. Although it was obviously written to inform the general public, its simplicity made me long for a training institute or program that could teach me and at the same time let me experience as a client the methods Netherton used. Shortly afterward, I ran across a book by a Dutch author, Hans ten Dam, *Een Ring van Licht*.[2] Here I found the Netherton methodology more elaborated but with ten Dam's down-to-earth approach. A few weeks later I was delighted to find that he was organizing the first Dutch training program in past-life therapy (reincarnation therapy as we prefer to call it). Though I was a procrastinator in most things, I didn't hesitate to call and enroll in the introductory course of the program.

## Personal Reincarnation Experience *(Rob Bontenbal)*

If my wife Lydia hadn't introduced me to the concept of reincarnation I probably would never have gone into therapy. I had a rather strong fear of rejection that made me procrastinate often, but to go into therapy for that? I lived in Amsterdam, not Manhattan or Paris, where in the seventies psychoanalysis was demeaned to the status of a pre-yuppy lifestyle. I had a dynamic and loving partner, a nice job, no health or financial problems, and, shortly before I decided to take a course in reincarnation therapy I had moved to a pleasant old house in one of Amsterdam's better neighborhoods.

The introductory course for the Hans ten Dam training program provided my first experience with recalling trauma. The course started with a group session. Before Hans began his creative imagination to bring us into contact with an important past life, I had told myself that even if I had to imagine it all I would come up with some story. And what a story it was! Weeks later in an individual therapy session I found that I had hit on my life prior to the present one. In my current life I look very Caucasian: tall, blue eyes and blond hair (what is left of it—I became bald early). Much to my surprise I found myself as a young black man in a room where an even blacker lady was cooking. She was obviously not too happy with me, warning me that if I didn't stop fooling around I would end up in the gutter.

When Hans moved us through the life to the next important incident, I experienced myself dancing through the night, a real ladies' man. I worked then, but it was the thirties and the Depression soon put me out of work. Standing in line for the soup kitchens, drinking the cheapest liquor I could get, picking the garbage cans of hotels and the houses of the rich, asking strangers to spare me a dime—it all seemed to come from a Hollywood musical. But no happy end for me. One last attempt to save my life failed when Uncle Sam didn't want me to fight the Nazis in Europe and I died in a Bowery scene.

When Hans moved us to our death-scene, I experienced myself lying on some snow-covered pavement. The night was icy, and freezing to death felt almost like a relief. Much to my surprise, I moved out of my body faster than I could have imagined and into a brilliant white light where warmth returned. My last thought was, "Enough of that shit!" But somewhere in the back of my head was the nagging thought: "Why didn't they let me fight in Europe?" Of course, in this life I had read in the books I had studied about the light experienced after death, but I also had read in the books of ten Dam and Netherton that people who die in such a way as I just did much more often can't get away from their bodies or the death scene, and I did.

When we were brought back to the here and now I was even more surprised to hear that of the 16 people in the course I was practically the only one with such vivid and traumatic experiences! When asked to talk about my impressions I started telling the others that I probably had imagined it all. As a student of political science I had shown great interest in the Black Power movement in the USA. I had read books by Angela Davis, Malcom X, Martin Luther King, and Eldridge Cleaver. Therefore it was not surprising that my subconscious mind had created its own version of the Soul on Ice! Hans just smiled as I talked.

Later that weekend I had a private session with him. "Private" meant Hans working with me while the group watched. Using an affect-bridge he regressed me back to a life with my current wife, Lydia. Once more it was very cold, but this time I wasn't bothered by that. My much bigger problem was that my young wife was expecting to give birth at any minute. There wasn't enough food, oil, and fuel to get through the severe winter of Canada. I was so nervous about the situation that my wife sent me out to hunt and pick up some old trees for the fire, telling me the birth wouldn't come for another day. When I came back some hours later I found her dead, with the small head of the baby visible. She had obviously pressed herself to death while giving birth. Still in shock I wandered around for a few hours until I killed myself. This time there was no instant travel into the light.

It took Hans a good deal of creative talking to get me away from my dead body. When I finally left the scene and moved slowly into a lighter and safer sphere, I suddenly saw my wife. Before I could apologize, she smiled and told me that it was all right. I was still shaken by our encounter and her leaving so soon, when somebody in the group hissed out loud: "He needs green, he needs the color green for his heart." Before I could control myself I yelled at the top of my lungs: "No, no green, no green, green is poison!" and moved right into another lifetime in Burma, where I was forced to publicly poison myself after I had betrayed the authorities, a bunch of malicious monks, of whom I was one. If I still had any doubt about the validity of my own past-life recall this session convinced me!

These first sessions were followed by many more, and I am getting close now to the 200 hours on the couch that Morris Netherton thinks is a necessary minimum for any (reincarnation) therapist. I have recalled lives on all continents, as a member of all races and of all great and not so great cultures, experiences that put an end to thoughts of discrimination. The symptoms I worked on had mainly to do with my strong fear of rejection, which was my core issue. Therapy sessions helped me overcome that fear with clients, but my fears in front of a group of students or in intimate relations proved more stubborn.

Only when I started to understand the concepts of polarity and projection was I able to connect incidents in such a way that it became clear to me that my fears had less to do with rejection by others than with rejection by myself. I actually had a fear of success, which explained so many of the things that had happened to me, not in the least my procrastination.

With the help of colleagues I found that a number of lives in the 17th and 18th century all ended with severe disappointment in humanity in general and myself in particular. Among them was the life of a young composer in England whose great hopes that his church music would change the bigotry of his generation soon died, and he with them; the life of the already mentioned fur hunter whose young wife died giving birth; and the life of an influential informer of the King of France at the outbreak of the Revolution, caught between his loyalty to the king and his understanding of the inevitability of a revolution.

The chain of disappointments in these lives and others and the belief that was connected to it ("The world is rotten and so am I") made me find a personality and an environment that were really rotten: a slave hunter and trader who caught blacks and brought them from the west coast of Africa to America. I traded thousands of these animals after hunting them down and shipping them to Savannah and other ports. One day, hunting deep in the jungles of what must now be Ghana or Nigeria, I saw a young woman picking roots in an open spot. Her slim body with its black skin was gleaming in the hot sun and right there I knew this was not an animal but a human being and a beautiful one, too. She touched me deeply. I nevertheless hunted her down but took great care to bring her back to the beach unharmed. There I put her in a cage. That night I waited until everybody was asleep before I paid her a visit in her cage. The moment I reached out to touch her, her hands went right to my throat. I never had a chance to escape from those hands. They felt like steel claws when they choked me to death. Once out of body, I deeply regretted what had happened, but even in my distress I noticed that the young woman must have gone into a terrible shock because her hands never left my throat and she made no attempt to escape through the unlocked cage door.

It became worse. When my mates woke up the next morning she was still sitting there, strangling me in the cage. What followed was an absolute nightmare. My mates were outraged and killed her by cutting her to pieces. My guilt remained so intense that it took a number of sessions to accept that I had been that terrible man who not only humiliated thousands of people, killing hundreds of them, but who was also responsible for the horrible death of that beautiful young woman. In the last of these sessions I finally understood that after my death I had judged myself and found myself guilty. The self-inflicted punishment? Never to be intimate with another human being again.

After that came four lives, all lived in the USA and all of which had to do with the lack or loss of fulfilling intimate relationships. There was a young farmer boy, slightly retarded and therefore hated by a father who killed him for his clumsiness at the age of eleven. There was the much loved and arrogant son of a northern industrialist, who marched merrily into the Civil War, honestly believing that he was going to free the slaves, only to die slowly, just hours into his first battle, from a bayonet wound. Next was a young factory girl, hating her life and her restricting parents so much that she fled to the West, ending up in some kind of saloon. Hating entertaining the "gentlemen," she finally turned to her own sex for love, only to be punished for that by dying under the strangling hands of one of her unsatisfied customers. And at last there was the already narrated life of the young black in Harlem, who found out the hard way what the life of the grandsons of the slaves in America was like.

But my soul's flight into the light, my promise of "enough of this shit!" and the nagging thought of "Why didn't they let me go to Europe?" changed the pattern. I was able to find parents on another continent, although with business and family connections with the USA. They were bruised by the war, but D-day charged their optimism and made them decide to try for a second child, something they had postponed for years. During a prenatal session I recalled my father saying to my mother: "It can come now; the Americans have landed, the war will be over soon."

So there were feelings of joy and hope at my conception, but after three months these feelings changed into guilt ("We should have waited," a nice actualization of my procrastination), and fear and sadness and even anger, both from my father, chopping wood, and the doctor, fighting with the bad light at my birth. Recalling my pre- and perinatal experiences made me understand why I was so fearful as a young child.

My father, not the easiest man to have around (if he was not flying around the world), and my mother together helped me actualize my procrastination, he by scorning me often, she by spoiling me often. But they and my sister also loved me and cared and helped me with all my fear of success through high school and into university and even made it possible for me to travel alone to the USA at the age of seventeen. It was my wife and some inspiring colleagues who helped me to understand and resolve most of my fear of rejection, of intimacy, of success in life. Some traces of this theme are still there, no doubt, but I am satisfied with the progress I have made.

## Personal Background *(Tineke Noordegraaf)*

I was born on the 23rd of September, 1945—in a great hurry according to my mother. The assisting doctor was my own father, a plus for our bonding. He was amazed that, after having delivered many babies, he had the experience of his own daughter opening her eyes directly after birth. The war was over when I was born, so there was celebration and much hope for a brighter future. Since my father was a country doctor, my parents had not gone through the pressure of near-starvation during the notorious hunger winter of 1944 when, because of the combination of an extremely cold winter and no food, many people starved to death. My parents maintained a hopeful attitude, and my prenatal war experiences gave me the idea that no matter how bad things look, there remains something to be optimistic about.

Living in the countryside had advantages but it meant that education in the little town where we lived was dated in its approach. Because of this my parents moved to Amsterdam when I was three years old. It took me quite a while to get used to Amsterdam with its many houses and crowds of people, things I didn't like. I still dislike the memory of the huge dark house where we lived for four years before moving to the more rural suburb of Amsterdam, not far from the International Airport.

My childhood memories are filled with moments of magic, such as communicating with a frog whom I considered a friend when I was very young. School days passed without problems. When I was still rather young I decided to study medicine, a decision in part the result of an incident that occurred when my father discussed with me a situation of a small boy who suffered with a severe ear problem. My father had been deeply touched by the boy's suffering, and moved by his compassion I drew a beautiful, brilliant, shining, friendly sun to cheer the boy up. Then and there I decided that such illnesses should not happen and that I was going to be a pediatrician in order to help children get rid of pain and agony. About 40 years later I re-lived my pain and sadness as that earnest child during a session with Trisha Caetano in California. My father was moved when I told him my decision to become a physician and showed him the drawing I had made.

I loved my study of medicine in Amsterdam but my personal life was a melting pot of too much thinking and a lot of contradictory emotions. Something was missing, something that wasn't to be found anywhere in Holland. Five years later I passed my exams and quit my studies. I decided to make up my mind about what to do with my life next by traveling around the world in order to get acquainted with real people instead of learning about life through textbooks and patients. My parents weren't happy about the decision but they had brought me up to do what I could support logically, and I have never regretted the decision. I knew the impact it would have on my life.

I went to the Canary Islands for a year as an international hostess and then, after traveling through Morocco and Spain, ended up in Rotterdam married to another travel addict. My husband and I and our two-year-old son went to Asia later in a self-built motor home.

During our Asian adventures I noticed that my clairvoyant qualities, which I had had from childhood, were opening up so that I could no longer deny them. I had buried them during my medical studies but in India I met people who taught me a great deal, especially one sadhu who sat with me in front of the Taj Mahal making me promise not to give anyone short-sighted advice—still another moment of magic. From that time on my interest in reincarnation escalated—it seemed the only logical answer to questions I had always had, though after my return to Holland it still took persuasion from a friend of mine to get me to join an introductory weekend in reincarnation therapy that had been organized by Hans ten Dam, author of the only book I had read on the subject, *Een Ring van Licht*. In 1986 I realized that the perfect synthesis between my analytical skills and my intuitive talents was to become a reincarnation therapist.

Working in private practice I found I could extend this kind of therapy to children, and I began to look for more information concerning this particular field. Many colleagues tried to dissuade me, but eventually I developed my own methods for working with children that proved to be effective for young people from the fourth year on.

## Personal Reincarnation Experience *(Tineke Noordegraaf)*

I had my first spontaneous recall when I was eight years old. It was the night of the terrible storm of February 1, 1953, when the dikes broke in our southern provinces and there was a flood in all of the south of Holland, long before work was started on the famous Deltaworks. I remember lying awake in my bed that night, listening to the sounds of the fury of the elements and watching the searchlight of Schiphol turning round and round, disappearing and coming back again, a powerful beacon. Squalls tattered the windows of my room and my parents came in to tell me that as a precaution, because it was an old house, in order to keep the windows closed they would tie them with a rope to my bed. With me lying in my bed it would certainly hold, they told me; my weight would prevent the windows from opening.

My parents didn't realize that they did me a favor by this arrangement, but they did notice that it meant a lot to me that I could stay in bed to make the house safer. I was aware that using the weight of my body made me stronger than the hurricane outside. This was a perfect match, I thought. The more I observed what was happening, the more excited I got.

This excitement was probably responsible for my leaving my body to see what was going on. I saw myself lying on the bed with big enchanted eyes! That was even more fun, experiencing the whole setting while being out of my body. Since I had succeeded in leaving my body as easily as that, I thought it would be simple to experiment more. If the bed with my body on it could hold the windows by way of a simple rope, it should be possible to connect myself to my body with a kind of rope as well, in order to be able to come back no matter what happened. So I created a kind of umbilical cord and when I imagined it, it was already there! Magic, magic all over!

Checking twice before I went further and finding everything okay, off I went upward, tossing and turning like a cosmic plaything of the gods. I clearly realized that though this was the first time I was aware of doing this kind of thing, it was so familiar to me that I must have done it before. Before? Was there such a thing as before? And where was that before?

I found myself looking at a huge wild sea in which a volcano was erupting! It was an eerie thing to see while I was up there and the sea was beneath me producing huge waves. When I wanted to leave that scene and go back to my present body I followed the umbilical cord, that strangely enough could grow longer or shorter as I wanted, and ended up safely in bed, closing away the sounds of the subsiding storm.... Was it a dream after all? I am sure it wasn't, although when I said something about it the next day, my parents praised my fantasy but told me I had to be reasonable.... Now years later I know that it had something to do with Atlantis, which I hate to admit because it means some more work for me to do. And what about my postulate, *This is just a perfect match*, which brought me there in the first place?

I found myself back as a judge in England in the 16th century. The first thing that I experienced was the sight of rainy, dirty streets with little muddy rivers caused by unceasing rain. It gave the impression of extreme poverty and hopelessness. I happened to be a wealthy lawyer in the King's service. One day they brought in a dirty, hungry young boy, similar to the many who were brought in to be sentenced to prison or to be put in an orphanage or be locked up in a reformatory. There were many waifs in those days and they caused the establishment a lot of trouble with their stealing and pocket-picking in the streets. They were a real nuisance and the only thing to do with them was to put them away without any jurisdiction. They had no legal status anyway.

This boy had stolen some apples at the market, and he stood there without pleading guilty, just looking at me with something in his eyes that made me hesitate to condemn him to imprisonment or a reformatory. There was no fear at all, no hope for a better future, just waiting for the words that would tell him what he already knew would happen to him. It was resignation all over. He had just given up...desolation...nothing left to defend himself...he had just abandoned hope. He looked exactly the same as my father did in my *present* lifetime, with me sitting underneath the table looking at his face and hearing his words.

Something happened inside me at that moment. Was it his attitude that showed me he would, as stoically as he could, accept whatever the verdict would be? This boy needed help instead of conviction. I heard myself asking him what his motives were for stealing the apples. It was as though the boy were coming out of severe shock. He started responding to my questions and that did it. Fear that he had suppressed until then began to show itself, and the boy started trembling all over, telling me that he was hungry as never before. He hadn't eaten anything for three days...and so on and so on.

I really listened to a child for the first time in my life. I listened to his story, telling me that he had been hungry for as long as he could remember but this time was worse because everywhere he tried to get something to eat he had been chased away. He was starving and stole some apples in the end. This eventually led to my defending him instead of accusing him of robbery. It was quite a shock for the so-called "in-crowd." They first thought I had lost my mind, which was right in a way, but when they could not talk me out of it, they had to accept that I meant what I said. This situation revealed another theme of my lifetimes: *Accept the challenge so that you may feel the exhilaration of victory!* This situation saw this theme worked out for both the boy and me, though it took a long time for the boy to believe that I meant what I said, that it was not another trap, not set up, a betrayal from me.

I learned a lot from him by just listening when he told me about his life and the circumstances that made him steal. The more I listened to him, the more I got interested. This boy was no dummy. Not being able to have any kind of education was a shame, so I started to teach him how to read and write, and what started with one little boy ended eventually with my trying to figure out how to set up an educational program for similar youngsters. And there were many of them! I spend a great deal of my life trying to find the right answers to all the questions that arose during the development of an educational program that could give these unfortunate children a little more hope. It proved hard to convince my wife that this was important, that I felt alive doing it, but it was the result of that *particular magical moment* in which that boy had looked at me that caused me to re-evaluate my perspective.

I got pneumonia before the effects of my efforts were thoroughly established, the result of the kids calling for me on a rainy day to get help for a sick, feverish boy. I died thinking about being more effective next time. The situations in which these children lived were abominable and unhealthy and there was no doctor available to give a child what he needed. *If only I had been a doctor, I could have helped him in a more effective way....* Those were the thoughts I had when I died. Guess why I wanted to be a pediatrician in my present lifetime!

*If only I could have helped him in a more effective way....* The meaning of that life became clear to me when I processed another much earlier life in which my heart was torn out and I was fed to the birds who were already circling above me high in the air. The sun shone brightly, the sky was blue, there were no other sounds to hear than the sounds of the vultures waiting for their meal. I still feel their claws on my shoulders tearing me apart.... I went back to the incident and found myself one of a group of male dignitaries approaching some kind of Inca settlement. I was carrying my little two-year-old son on my shoulders on my way to a meeting with former enemies to establish a proclamation of peace. It was a magical moment for my son!

But things turned out to be quite different from what I had anticipated. The negotiations that had appeared to be successful proved to be nothing other than an attempt to create false expectations. They took us prisoners and the torturing began. The worst of it was when they molested my little son without my seeing what happened to him, just hearing him scream his lungs out of his little body. At least screaming meant that he was still alive. *Not* screaming was even more frustrating. Was he still dead or alive? They told me over and over that my revealing the things they wanted to know about strategic warfare would determine whether my son would die. Quite a dilemma. I would be guilty either way. If I didn't tell anything, that would be the certain death of my son. If I did tell what I knew, that would make me guilty in another way: I would betray my people and myself. Either way I was lost. I gave in only after they had murdered my son and showed me his slaughtered body. I told them everything I knew and when they were satisfied with the information, they fed me to the vultures. I didn't realize it then, but while processing that death I found that they tore me apart in order to give the vultures the opportunity to tear my heart out of my body. The last thing I felt were the huge claws on my left shoulder and the terrifying sounds those birds made. To realize that I was food for the vultures made me feel sick.

One of my last thoughts was that I had done wrong by telling anything I knew. If only I could have helped in a more effective way. I had betrayed my son's moment of magic. That shouldn't have happened. I just hadn't protected him well enough.... And I felt a lot of guilt, helplessness, and self-blame. I didn't want to leave my body and that place because I believed that my little son must still be there as well, and I didn't want to leave without him. When in the regression I eventually found him, I had peace of mind and could take him with me to a place where we could rest a while. I forgave myself for telling everything I knew, considering the circumstances of that moment, and could let go of the guilt that was still there when I died.

The third life that is relevant in this context is a short lifetime in Egypt that came up when I wanted to know the reason for having difficulty with writing. I found myself as a girl this time, approximately 10 or 11 years old.

I was squatting secretly on a roofed-in gallery, eavesdropping at the door to find out what was in there. I was in a terrible mood, furious and frustrated. No one was helping me to think in a way that would help me. I had a lot of questions and they refused to answer them because I was a girl. Well, I would teach them a lesson and find my own answers! I was very good at stamping my feet at that time. It was forbidden for girls to learn how to read and write. I saw hieroglyphics on every pillar that I saw and touched and could not understand what they said. I knew it was impossible for me to understand what was written on them unless somebody told me the answers. If only somebody would teach me! But that was strictly forbidden.

I still remember that magical moment when I decided to do something. I solved the problem by finding out where and when the reading and writing lessons for boys were given, and somehow or other I managed to overhear them. So I succeeded in learning how to read and write, and I practiced by wetting papyrus leaves and placing them over the hieroglyphics on the pillars in order to make copies of them. Afterward I took the leaves with me in order to dry them carefully in the sun and study them while I was hidden in the grass.

It was fated to go wrong eventually. The boys teased me often about their being able to read and write and I took up the challenge and told them I could do as well as they, maybe even better. They stopped teasing me and looked at me unbelievingly and then yelled at me to prove it. And I *did* prove it.

Magic, challenge, the exhilaration of victory—it was all there, but it didn't last long. When they told my father, he was furious and he hid his pride very well—I could see the pride in his eyes, but he couldn't afford to compliment me for my efforts. His words were a verdict. Although I knew what was going to happen when they found out, still it was a moment of shock, and the next thing I remember was lying in a boat while the poison spread slowly, causing paralyzing pain. *Don't show them how good you are, don't tell them anything, it won't help, it will do no good.... But I am still convinced that everybody should be able to read and to write.* These were my last thoughts before I passed away in pain. I was aware of dying that way only when I processed that lifetime very carefully and found out that reading and *writing* were connected with pain and dying. Talk about a writer's block!

I got rid of the poison and frustration and pain I took with me from that lifetime, together with other decisions I had made then, and this has resulted in my being able to write now in the way I want and about the things I want to write about. I am sure my working on myself isn't finished yet. There is still a lot to do and a lot to resolve, but life remains *full of magic* and I enjoy every moment of it. Is this what is meant by exhilaration?

# Theory

## Philosophical Hypotheses

We are convinced that the collective knowledge of the dynamics of both the human mind and the eternal spirit that we call the soul is still in a premature level of existence, and we assume that:

1. All beings on earth are here for a purpose. Life on earth is part of the universe. The universe is in a continuing process of transformation and our purpose as earthlings has to do with this transformation.

2. Why the creative force of this universe meant this to be both a personal and common odyssey is a question only the creative force can answer. Trusting that we are a part of the creative force, we asked our subconscious that question and got a simple answer: it's a universal law. We have volunteered, are chosen, or have been forced to be a part of the process of transformation.

3. From our first incarnation on earth we have all been confronted with polarity, which is intrinsic in a transforming universe, manifesting itself most clearly in "I and others." As long as we participate in the process of transformation we are at least subconsciously aware of this polarity.

4. The number of times we have to return on earth to be able to understand and accept the transformation of and polarity within ourselves and the world around us is strictly individual. The roles we play and the challenges we meet during our many lives on earth are a common experience, but the way we deal with them dictates the number of times we return. It is as though we come together to play with a deck of Tarot cards. When we pass the deck from hand to hand we are all in touch with all the archetypal roles we have to play and all the archetypal challenges we have to meet. Each time we draw a number of cards out of the deck, certain roles and challenges are emphasized. If we keep on playing with the cards and act out what they tell us, eventually all roles and challenges will come up, although it can take many draws to face all cards, largely because we find it difficult to accept what the cards tell us and to act accordingly.

5. Not being able to understand and accept polarity, especially our darker side, our shadow, creates self-judgments. These judgments of our mistakes and failures work as postulate: predicting what we should experience to balance what we think we did wrong. We project the polarity within ourselves into the environment, which reflects it back to us.

6. Facing our individual and the collective polarity and accepting it in its true sense ends the judging of ourselves and others and helps with our transformation, both individually and collectively. Awareness of this principle heals body, mind and soul and can end our individual cycle of rebirth on earth.

7. The subconscious mind has stored all that we have ever experienced. By proper methods all this can be recovered to benefit us.

## Psychotherapeutic Assumptions

1. Reincarnation therapy is not to be considered an alternative, complementary, or "New Age" therapy. In the holographic model it is a logical exploration of the subconscious mind, much in the tradition of Sigmund Freud, Carl Jung, and all other analysts who were and are dedicated to making the subconscious conscious.

2. Techniques used in therapy should obviate any control by the therapist over the client and the client giving his control away. It should always be the client doing the work, assisted by the therapist. The client has to know consciously what comes up from the subconscious mind, so the subconscious should be researched without shutting off the conscious mind—a state of the mind we call "elliptic consciousness." Awareness helps to avoid transference and counter-transference. Letting the client take responsibility in therapy for his or her problems is in accord with the principles of the process of reincarnation. A reincarnation therapist can be effective only when client and therapist feel safe and trustful with each other.

3. Problems show themselves as symptoms. These symptoms are evidence of past traumas in the patient. Clients with specific symptoms need only a short bridging induction to recall these traumas. Reincarnation therapy should not be called past-life therapy because it does not deal with traumas in past lives only.

4. All problems are merely symptoms of core issues. Each core issue or theme has its own character-postulate or basic belief structure. In its essence such a character-postulate is a self-judgment, usually formed in a prior existence which actualized connecting traumas in all four main areas of recall: transpersonal, prenatal, perinatal, and biographical. Diagnosing the core issue and its character-postulate during the initial interview, or at least during the first few sessions, is essential for a clear therapeutic process and helps to limit the number of sessions needed for the healing.

5. A reincarnation therapist is effective when he/she trusts that the cycle of reincarnation is a universal law, but the client does not have to believe this.

The client needs only to trust that the therapeutic model of reincarnation work promises beneficial results. The therapist does not need to trust that all past-life material is individually authentic.

6. Reincarnation therapy becomes most effective when therapist and client understand how polarity and causality work together to create specific individual reincarnation patterns. When in a certain lifetime, before, during, or after death, one evaluates his deeds and non-deeds in such a sense that he cannot accept what he did or did not do, he triggers the law of polarity. There may be a perfect causal reason for being in a position to make mistakes but one will not be consciously aware of that. By postulating, "I never want to be in a position again where I can do all this wrong," one keeps focused on what he thinks and what he did wrong. Because he cannot accept his wrongdoings, he starts projecting. Therefore in his next incarnation he will be dealing with the same aspects, but because of the projection will find himself in the opposite role, that of a victim. Having lost conscious contact with the polarity and feeling he is a victim of circumstances, he finds it hard to stop projecting.

7. Projection creates new postulates, which can keep one in the victim position for many lifetimes, causing a chain of traumatic victim events. Another pattern is called the "pendulum," a constant change of roles among perpetrator, enabler, and victim. In any of these patterns, although the source is a specific situation, new traumas will occur in a more and more non-specific way, accumulating postulates and connected emotions and somatics.

8. With the mental-emotional-somatic bridge (MES) one enters a present life looking on a subconscious level for circumstances and events that will confirm an established pattern. These circumstances and events become actualized in the pre- and perinatal periods. Without awareness of such a pattern the possibility of making conscious choices is severely restricted. After the client becomes aware of the programming he can perceive the core issues involved. He can process all the related traumas of the core issue, find the source of the character postulate, and by accepting it, can finally bring freedom of choice back into his life, and with that, transformation.

9. Traumas differ greatly as to the beliefs or postulates created or reaffirmed, the emotions and somatics involved, the intensity manifested and time involved, the kind of roles the client played, and many other aspects. By differentiating traumas and using a different model of processing and integration for each of the categories, reincarnation therapy becomes more effective. Various cognitive and creative integration techniques are essential instruments of the reincarnation therapist because not all clients have the

same ability to use insight for cognitive and creative integration of core issues.

10. People differ in the way they store information. Some use mainly a visual system, others an auditory system, a third group, a kinesthetic system, while there are also people who use two or all three systems to store and reproduce information. Shutting off commands (both internal and external) during or after traumatic incidents is responsible for shutting off these representational systems. For that reason, blocks during therapy provide vital information about which systems have been shut off. Different systems can be shut off in different lives.

11. The profession of reincarnation therapy requires proper training. Education or training in psychotherapy or counseling is an advantage when integrated with the above approach.

## Indications and Contraindications for Use

Though reincarnation therapy, like many other therapies, is appropriate for dealing with symptoms—mental, emotional, somatic, or spiritual—it is uniquely valuable when it deals with polarity as well with causality.

Sometimes the physical part of the healing process proves to be too difficult; the illness has already gone too far to stop. In these cases reincarnation therapy can help to find mental, emotional, spiritual and even some physical balance at the moment of death.

There are several instances where reincarnation therapy is contraindicated:

1. We have found it difficult to work with psychotic and borderline clients—reincarnation therapy requires a relatively rational mind, no matter how irrationally the past is influencing the present. On the other hand, people who have lost contact with their emotions have also proven hard to work with.

2. Clients who are not interested in insight should look for another kind of therapy. They are wasting their time when they actually don't want to know how they programmed themselves in the past.

3. Clients who prefer to remain clients often develop fast attachments toward therapists and bypass therapeutic gain.

4. Clients who are pushed by relatives or friends are reluctant to work on themselves. For that reason we insist that the potential client makes his/her own appointment with us.

5. Clients with severe hearing problems have trouble benefiting from reincarnation therapy because language is one of the main tools of a reincarnation therapist, and suggestions and feedback need to be heard.

6. Using addictions to escape the pain of reality often backfires, and one of the tasks of the reincarnation therapist is to confront clients with such problems so that the problems finally can become resolved. Because addicts block the finding of pain and other feelings, those addicted to alcohol, drugs, medication, work, need to show willingness to abstain from the use of the addictive substances for at least a couple of days before a session. When abstaining is hazardous to their health, a program with an MD has to be arranged.

7. Some reincarnation therapists believe age (too young or too old) can be a contraindication. Tineke's work with young children has proven to us that children aged four through 12 make the best of clients, though they may require creativity from the therapist.

8. Our experiences with older people (60+) are varied. Some seniors have the courage to explore new horizons, even if they look overshadowed; others have rather fixed ideas about their lives, about the creative force, about spirituality and many other things. Sometimes they refuse to give up these ideas, even when the information from their own subconscious indicates an opposite point of view. In this case it is difficult to work with them.

While practicing together we often work with problems and clients who have been labeled "difficult" by colleagues, by other therapists, by themselves, and sometimes even by us after working with them in our own private practice. But actually there are no "difficult clients." Even the term "contraindication" implies a question mark. All one can say about clients who cause problems for the therapist is that the therapist hasn't yet found or developed the tools to work with them. Since the two of us are woman and man, Virgo and Pisces, and a few other opposites, we form a good polarity force when we work together.

# *Induction*

## Preparation

The first contact between client and therapist is almost always by phone. By proper pacing and leading we usually can find out in ten minutes or less if the client is *both rational and emotional enough*, is *interested in insight*, and if he has one of the *symptoms we feel comfortable working with* and is therefore potentially suited for reincarnation therapy. If we are convinced that these basic indications exist, we make an appointment for the initial interview, or, in the last couple of years, due to the growing need for our work, we put the client on a waiting list for an interview. If these basic indications are not met, we make sure that the client is referred to a therapy and/or therapist better suited to deal with his/her personality and/or symptoms.

All our therapies start with an initial interview. Such an interview is held with the following goals in mind:

1. Finding out if our first diagnosis of the three basic indications for reincarnation therapy was correct and if there are any contraindications to be considered.

2. Creating a safe and trustful relationship with the client.

3. Determining the system(s) the client uses to store and reproduce information.

4. Linking symptoms to core issues (themes) and underlying character postulates (beliefs) so that clear boundaries can be set and both therapist and client can know where to focus at the start of the therapeutic process. For linking we use peeling down techniques and the META-Model of NLP.

5. Diagnosing the connected emotions and somatics of both symptoms and core issues.

6. Letting the client tell his/her life history in order to learn how the core issue has actualized itself in the present life. We also learn about particular traumas, experiences, and behaviors that are important within the frame of therapy. We listen to information heard from parents or other relatives about the prenatal, perinatal, and infancy periods. We learn about illnesses, operations, use of medication, about sexual problems and sexual traumas, about addictions, about occupations and hobbies.

7. Finding out which goals the client wants to reach in therapy and if these goals are congruent with those set by the therapy.

The initial interview is especially important for beginning the therapeutic process. In the Dutch training program the first three months of the first year curriculum are focused exclusively on teaching how to interview the client in the light of reincarnation therapy.

## Induction Techniques

### The Holographic Bridge

In the late 60's neurosurgeon Karl Pribram demonstrated that the way the mind stores information and the way it will reproduce this information resembles a hologram.[3] A special aspect of such a holographic photograph is that when a part of it is reproduced elsewhere, the whole picture is still visible, though it may be less clear. The mind stores information in seven ways: thoughts, images, sounds, tastes, smells, somatics, and emotions. Pribram found that by focussing on one of these elements the "hologram" of a trauma or of any unresolved experience can become available for therapeutic processing.

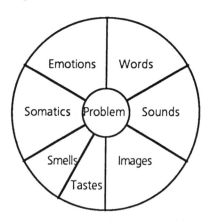

**The Small Hologram**

*This concept of the hologram underlies the phenomenon of regression experience.* It is manifested in the small hologram, where one aspect, such as an image or feeling, can trigger the other aspects, or in the large hologram, where one phase of soul experience, such as prenatal or past-life, can trigger all the other levels of experience.

This holographic approach is most effective when used in a two-step process, proceding from the small hologram to the larger hologram. We define one element, such as a thought or somatic or an image or an emotion, and then construct a "bridge" of at least three connected elements—a Mental one (very often words but also sometimes images or sounds), an Emotional one (fear, anger, sadness, etc.), and a Somatic one (pain, numbness, restriction, etc.). This *is the MES bridge*. Within minutes it can access the hologram of a traumatic experience, either the small hologram of related aspects or the large hologram of related levels, even when a client at first blocks.

The use of the MES bridge has several advantages. Bridging limits the control by the therapist over the client and prevents the client from giving his control away. It enables the client to know consciously what comes up from the subconscious mind—it helps to create "elliptic consciousness," the ability both to experience the trauma and to process it at the same time. Also, it encourages the client to take responsibility for his/her problem.

Bridging is a natural way of bringing the client into an altered state. While the client focuses on the MES elements of the symptoms and the first impressions of trauma or incident, the altered state deepens until an elliptic state is reached where the client can link past and present.

By focusing on the MES elements of symptoms in the small hologram, the therapist works efficiently and is goal-oriented. Because of the association with traumas, relaxation is unnecessary. Relaxation almost always is a detour. It is not effective to start relaxing away the mental, emotional and somatic elements of a symptom and then look for them again after the client is in a relaxed state. The client may then refuse to recall a trauma in an associative way. Because problems show themselves as symptoms and symptoms are proof of past traumas, it is easy through bridging techniques for clients to contact their source. It takes only a brief time.

**Somatic Entrances**

A vital underlying assumption of this MES bridge is that the physical body registers and expresses emotional feelings through somatics. Many people experience this phenomenon daily: emotional stress shows itself through headaches, stomach pains, tensed neck and shoulders, etc. In cases where symptoms seem to be purely somatic, not psychosomatic, the physical feelings activate emotions, confirming the tight connection between the E and S. Assuming that emotions and somatics also express themselves mentally (through words, images and/or even sounds), it is always potentially possible to locate the MES of a symptom in the physical body. This raises immediately the question as to where the mind is located: in the brain or in the whole physical body? This is a question many scientific researchers concern themselves with.

Clear physical symptoms suggest a somatic entrance. Concentration on somatics will then contact the E and M components of the bridge. To diagnose the nature of somatics we use a pain list, such as is used in hospitals in the Netherlands, with more than 60 different somatics and in addition two other categories: smell and taste.

**Mental Entrances**

One of the most usual entrances is the mental one. A form of this, the linguistic entrance, starts with the recognition of postulates, key phrases, or even single words, spoken with emotional or somatic charges while the therapist notes which are especially expressive or out of context. By letting the client repeat these words a number of times, the connected E and S will show themselves more strongly.

Sometimes it is appropriate to move directly into the trauma by repeating a chosen postulate, key phrases, or even single words, such as "It's all over" (M). This causes the E and S charges to become strong enough to move the client into the trauma. Clients often use a number of phrases in the initial interview to explain their symptoms, and in regression they can repeat these and decide which produce the strongest E or S. An alternate technique is to ask what words come to mind after the repetition of a postulate and then what additional words occur, until eventually a strong enough E and/or S is located.

If these techniques are not productive, linguistic techniques such as making sentences where the postulate is followed by "because," "if...then I feel...," or simply "is." These can be used until the client repeats the phrase and can't make another completion. Often the use of single words makes it easier to trace the E and S of traumas in infancy or childhood because single words or simple phrases, such as "scared," have been used at that time to express feelings.

Clients may have some sort of visual memory of or may live with various types of images. All of these visual impressions can be used for creating the MES bridge. Examples are visual memories of biographical traumas, spontaneous recall of past-life incidents, images from dreams, images stemming from psychic readings, and recent problems or symptoms.

**Emotional Entrances**

Often clients express emotion when they talk about their problems, and by letting them feel the emotion deeply, the S and M (sometimes words but also sounds and images) can be traced. The emotions usually experienced are fear, sadness, and anger. Guilt is important in therapy but is not primary because it expresses a reaction toward a trauma, not action during the trauma.

**Special Entrances**

There are several types of special entrances. Hans ten Dam developed one that he called *aura analysis*, which is a combination of the visual and somatic. The client is asked to move outside his body and study it carefully, noticing especially the light around it, any specific colors of the aura, possible wounds, objects, energy attachments, etc. When the client finds one or more of these, they are used to create the MES bridge. *Chakra analysis* combines emotional and somatic entrances. By letting the client focus on these energy points with regard to symptoms a MES can be created.

## Some Bridging Inductions

**Moving Directly into the Trauma**

In a small minority of the cases, when repeating a chosen postulate the E plus S charges will become so strong that the client moves right into the trauma.

> C: *It's all over (M).*
> T: *Say that once more.*
> C: *It's all over (repeats six times). (At the fourth time tears come up and at the sixth time C starts to sob heavily (E), his hands moving to his stomach, rubbing as if in great pain (S).) Oh, my God, it's all over; we are all going to die—we are all going to die!*

Recall and/or grounding instructions in such cases are hardly necessary and often even take the client out of the already contacted trauma.

## Tracing the E and S

More often, the therapist first has to trace the E and then the S, or vice-versa. After letting the client repeat the chosen postulate a number of times, the therapist asks what feelings are coming up. The emotions mentioned are then located in the body. Or, when the client points out somatics, the therapist asks for the connected emotions.

> C: It's all over (M).
> T: Say those words again.
> C: It's all over (six times).
> T: What do you feel?
> C: Fear, like something terrible is going to happen (E)!
> T: Where do you feel that fear in your body?
> C: Mainly in my stomach, but I also feel some tension in my hands (S).
> T: What do you feel in your stomach?
> C: Sharp pain! Growing stronger!
> T: Breathe into those feelings, feeling them as deep as you can, then move to the beginning of the incident where you feel this fear, like something terrible is going to happen, where you feel this sharp pain in your stomach and where you say, think, or hear the words, "It's all over."

When the client has answered the question, "What do you feel?" with "a pain in my stomach (S)," the therapist's next question would have been, "What emotion expresses this pain (E)?"

## Using "Chaining" or "Peeling-Down" Techniques

There are a number of linguistic techniques that can be used when the above mentioned fail. These techniques chain or peel down until phrases or postulates are spoken out that are charged with E and/or S. The three most used are:

A. The word "because" (backward chain):

> C: I am afraid of men.
> T: Repeat that and finish: I am afraid of men because...
> C: I am afraid of men, because they are violent.
> T: Repeat that and finish: They are violent because...
> C: They are violent because they like to dominate.
> Etc.

B. The words "if...then (I feel)..." (forward chain):

> C: I am afraid of women.

T: *Repeat and finish: If I am afraid of women, then...*
C: *If I am afraid of women, then I blush.*
T: *Repeat and finish: If I blush, then I feel...*
C: *If I blush, then I feel clumsy.*
Etc.

C. The word "is" (organization chain):

C: *I feel afraid.*
T: *Repeat and finish: Feeling afraid is...*
C: *Feeling afraid is like dying....*
T: *Repeat and finish: Feeling like dying is...*
C: *Like losing all control....*
Etc.

Keep on using these techniques until the client "circles," repeats him/herself, or doesn't know a next completion. Non-verbal signs often tell which completion is charged. If this is not clear, let the patient repeat all the completions a number of times to find out which one has the strongest E or S.

## Deepening Techniques

*The symptoms of a problem are the ingredients of the MES bridge.* Via that bridge these symptoms will give entrance to any unresolved experience (a small hologram). In the same way the basic belief or character-postulate of a core issue gives entrance to what we call the large hologram—all traumas, either biographical, perinatal, prenatal or transpersonal, that are chained together by such a basic postulate. For this reason, finding the core issue, the character postulate of a problem, is important in the early stages of therapy.

The large hologram has a number of aspects, all of which reflect the same pattern. The prenatal area consists of the so-called mother tape, on which everything can be found that the mother is experiencing during her pregnancy, and two types of tapes of the child: the tape of the embodied part of the fetus and the tape of the unembodied part that gives information on the state of consciousness of the new incarnate. In addition, birth is an extremely important area because almost all present problems have been actualized there. The moment of bonding has also proven to be essential, both for defining the perinatal area and for finding major traumas that have to do with intimacy, rejection, love, and other aspects of relationships. Following this, the biographical area covers the present life from the moment of bonding until the here and now. Therapy with Inner Children and other sub-personalities is an important part of the work in the biographical area. The transpersonal area includes past lives in the different kingdoms, higher death states, and archetypal and shamanistic experiences.

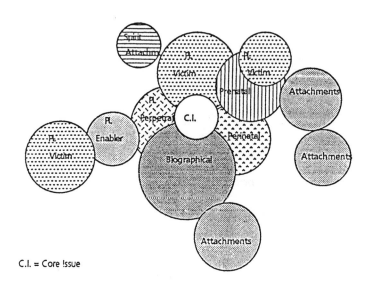

C.I. = Core Issue

### The Large Hologram

When viewing the possible complexities of a large hologram and the number of sessions involved, it is important to realize that for issue solving, processing the large hologram can stop at the moment the character-postulate transforms as a result of what has already been processed. At the beginning of therapy the different areas and traumas hide behind the core issue or character-postulate, but at the end of the therapy the chronology of the way that polarity and causality created the large hologram has become evident.

**Traumas**

Following the categories of Hans ten Dam, there are eight different kinds of trauma, each of which needs a different model of processing. These categories include the victim trauma, enabler trauma, perpetrator trauma, hangovers, unresolved death, alienation, attachment of living beings, and spirit-attachment.

In general we define traumas as unhealed wounds (emotional, physical, mental and/or spiritual). These wounds are the result of relatively short incidents that have a clear beginning and end. Both the enabler-trauma and the perpetrator-trauma are often involved and provide strong feelings of guilt, and out of this guilt arise strong self-judgments. We call these traumas *polar traumas* because they imply the non-acceptance of the basic polarity of good and bad. The victim's dominant emotion is usually fear; the enabler feels sadness, and the perpetrator, anger.

In the process of working through traumas, not surprisingly most clients will try to stay away from the physical, emotional, or mental pain of the trauma, much as they did when they first experienced the incidents. Clients try especially to avoid facing *polar traumas*. Those incidents that created the strongest self-judgments are most often lives in which patients played the role of perpetrator or enabler. When the character postulate does not transform after working for some time, instructions have to be given that will bring the client in contact with a polar incident or polar life.

Unresolved trauma means that the client on some level is still in shock. The challenges of the original incident were so great that the client tried to get out of the situation mentally, emotionally, or physically. Therefore recalling a trauma means bringing the client back to the moment that he or she went into shock. Shocks are blocks, which means that a recall of the past in which the client does not block in one way or the other should be mistrusted!

*Hangovers* (also called dirtskirts) are the result of long periods of tiredness, boredom, slavery, imprisonment, drudging, etc. They are an everlasting mortgage that becomes heavier and heavier to carry—the revolt against the situation has petered out. Sometimes hangovers begin as traumas, and in other cases there are so many traumas that the individual eventually loses the energy to fight. Hangovers should be processed differently from traumas. The client can be moved to moments in the hangover life where the hangover energy is most clear. Here breathing techniques and active bodywork can be used to support the cleansing of this depressed energy.

*Attachments* of various sorts are usually the consequence of severe trauma and violent, painful, or unexpected death on the part of an entity who stays in or with his body at the death scene or becomes involved in a negative afterlife, such as wandering or haunting.

*Alienation* is a term to describe strong feelings of not being at home in one's body, in one's family, in one's country, present culture, or even in the world. These feelings can be actualized by childhood traumas that have left the individual feeling unsafe, or they may be brought about by traumas in a past life, or in the moment of the first incarnation as a human being.

**Blocks**

Blocks can result from the misreading of contraindications (as neglecting psychotic and borderline symptoms), improper interviewing, and unclear inductions and processing instructions. Or one element of the small hologram can block traumas that may be present in a large hologram, as for instance, anger that is blocked during the recall of every trauma. There may also be blocks specific to one of the matrices. In general, such blocks can be circumvented by techniques such as having the patient move to the beginning of an incident or repeat words and feelings, or such commands as, "Breath deep into the feelings," or by asking for a single word to come up and then adding single words in a chain. Shock can be processed by going through the traumas a number of times while practicing breathing techniques or dissociation techniques such as birdseye view, higher-self intervention, symbolism, aura and chakra analyses.

## *Processing*

### Psychotherapeutic and Transformational Techniques

In individual sessions connected traumas and incidents that occurred within a certain time span are processed and integrated, but after a number of sessions it is important to make a chain of experiences from different lives and areas to clarify how a large hologram developed out of a polar lifetime, period, or incident. Such vertical sessions can have a strong integrating effect. The client begins to understand how, where, and why the large hologram of a problem has developed through time and space into the here and now. It is not always necessary to work through all the incidents of a large hologram before it collapses and before the character postulate no longer programs the client to experience consciously undesirable incidents. Quite often facing the polar incident produces healing and transformation.

There are clients who process a large hologram, polar experiences included, but still find no strong evidence of transformation, issue solving, or even problem solving. For them it is important to understand that integration and transformation often take time, especially when physical symptoms are involved.

Besides time, other aspects are to be considered. It will help clients, who may be waiting impatiently for their life to change, to realize that their core issue created participation in structures and networks (family, work, living environment, friendships, etc.) that are felt and seen as part of the problem. Some of these structures and networks will change with the client, others will even disappear, while others seem resistant to change. Often one can't just step out of the family one chose when incarnating. A new house, new work, new friends, or even a new partner, needed when it is obvious that the old ones are a product of a character postulate and slow down transformation, can't all be achieved at the same time. Quite often clients start feeling the final transformation taking place months after closing the therapeutic process.

*Renovation* techniques, doing what could not be done in the life itself, are often helpful. An example is defending one's family bravely against robbers, something that was not possible in the real situation because of severe shock or because certain situations were inopportune. The experience of being able to defend oneself when not in shock or when the opportunity is available can be deeply healing. Renovation can also be used when death has been painful or when the body has been injured in a terrible and/or humiliating way. Often a client can't leave his body behind without taking care of it by cleaning, healing, and/or burying it (renovating) it.

Actualization of old traumas often has resulted in the creation of traumatic Inner Children or other sub-personalities. These Inner Children are an important part of a large hologram. Gestalting a "sane" parent or adult is almost never possible without resolving childhood traumas. Integrating Inner Children in short- or long-term therapy is therefore essential for the healing process.

With behavioral problems, especially, an ecological check in the future can show client and therapist how successful the session has been for the short term. Going into the future and imagining a situation in which the problem would normally occur give insight into the progress that has been made. Any such future check has a two-fold thrust:

a. How do the other ego parts (Inner Children) react to the changes in personality?

b. How do relatives, friends, co-workers, etc., react to what has changed or is changing?

No client is happy to lose all his friends within two weeks because he has finally become more assertive! There is a good chance, also, that some Inner Child will protest with strong feelings of rejection or even with illness.

## Integration into the Therapeutic Process

Effecting integration and closure is more difficult than recovering the experiences themselves. Integrating previously unresolved experiences into the present personality in such a way that a person feels him/herself able to transform his life requires dedication, compassion, creativity, and patience on the part of the therapist.

The processing of trauma is often an integrating experience in itself. The literature about reincarnation therapy shows that even dissociated recalls sometimes integrate incidents that have previously remained unresolved and thus effect a remission of symptoms. In a few cases, even core issues are impacted. When the processing of traumas is done on a deeper level (the MES processing), this is even more likely. But even deep recall of traumas with ample focus on all MES elements does not always mean that the client is able to understand and accept immediately what has happened. As was pointed out, after working through death in a past life, feelings and thoughts about certain incidents during the life or about the death experience itself can prevent him from moving on to a sphere where integration, healing, and transformation can take place.

Part of the integration process involves removing the former personality from the surroundings, spheres, and places where it still feels pained, unhappy, restless, vengeful, humiliated, etc. When the projections change into ones in which safety, rest, warmth, love, and healing are experienced, the therapist knows that integration has started. This process should be extended to include an understanding of when and how the problem actualized itself in the prenatal, perinatal, and biographical areas.

During the opening phase of therapy often the feelings and new self-esteem that result from catharsis fail to last, but when integration takes place during or at the close of therapy the client will experience a cathartic release of long hidden feelings, together with insight into the working of individual postulates. This can result in a sense of relief, of satisfaction, of intimate happiness. When the polarity and causality of a large hologram is understood and accepted, projection stops, integration starts, and so does this healing process of transformation.

## Failures *(Rob Bontenbal)*

Tineke and I will write individually about failures because while working together we make few mistakes and have few failures. Working together has the advantage of one therapist being able to diagnose rapidly when the other is moving toward a dead end. We have each learned to trust the direction that the other takes but also to change that direction when it proves to be invalid.

I tell every new group of students that the success of a therapist and the satisfaction he/she gets out of working in reincarnation therapy depends largely on the way he/she is able to deal with disappointments, mistakes, failures. A therapist who is afraid to make a mistake or to fail does so because he has not processed some of his/her major polar traumas, such as incidents where mistakes have severely hurt others.

I have made quite a few mistakes, had a number of disappointments, and even failed a couple of times in the seven years I have been practicing reincarnation therapy. When I started out I felt eager and dedicated to my new profession, though a little insecure as well because the training had been short and I knew I still had a lot to learn, such as how to conduct a good initial interview, how to pace and lead, how to work with the pre- and perinatal experiences, how to integrate in different ways, and how to develop a model based on the concept of polarity and not just on that of causality. Besides making mistakes because of my inexperience and lack of knowledge, I was so eager to succeed during those first few years that I often neglected strong contraindications for this sort of treatment, such as borderline behavior, clients who preferred to stay clients instead of solving their problems, dogmatic spiritual beliefs, lying about addictions, and finally, clients who would not dream of facing a perpetrator life. Trusting my gut feelings could have saved me a number of disappointments.

One case that illustrates this failure is of a woman who felt life had cheated her—a glaring projection! We found one victim life after another in which she had been neglected, tortured, humiliated, killed brutally, starved, and suffered a few other unpleasant situations. After six of those sessions I knew it was necessary to find one or two lives in which she had done something unacceptable to others. No way. Victim lives kept on occurring, 11 or 12 in a row. No wonder the feeling of having been cheated became stronger and stronger. I tried desperately to unearth the other face of polarity, first by tracing a life in which life had been good to her; it was a relief when we found one! But the client wasn't relieved. One miserable life of happiness against twelve lives of despair and pain was no match. This taught me a painful lesson, not to go on tracing and processing victim lives without finding the polar life that explains the pattern of all those lives in despair. And if such a polar life is difficult to find, it is important to recover one or more positive lives to balance the victim lives.

I have made other mistakes as well. Once a woman came to me with the presenting complaint of a bad relationship with her husband. She felt she had lost his love and feared that the fact that they had had difficulty getting her pregnant had contributed to the disintegration of their relationship. The session went well and she began finding some answers to her questions. She left in good spirits, perhaps a trifle caught up in herself. That night she called to tell me that she had driven her car into a tree, probably because she had fallen asleep for just a second. I was shaken by her story and much relieved when she told me she was all right, though the car was a total loss. However, she assured me that she had hated that car and was happy because the car was brand new and the insurance money would buy her another car more to her taste. Then she said, "You know what is so good about all this?" In my shock I couldn't see that there was anything good but she explained that her husband had felt so frightened that he could have lost her that he had come to realize how much he actually loved her. Exactly ten months later I received a little blue card informing me that the couple was happy to announce the birth of a son.... Nevertheless, after that I paid more attention to proper closure techniques.

Blocks bothered me for some time. Often I didn't know how to work through or around them. Then Morris Netherton convinced me, not only that blocks are inherent when working with traumas, but also that it is possible to use the blocks. By asking a client to repeat the words that express the block and helping him understand that these words are part of the trauma for which we are looking, I have learned to deal with blocks more effectively.

Before I started training others, I had only one way of communicating with my clients. I was understanding, almost Rogerian, in my approach. This worked well with many clients, but not with all. Some were able to fool me (and themselves, of course) for long periods of time, leaving us both frustrated when the therapy was terminated.

Watching my colleagues and students doing demonstrations in the training program, talking with them about different "styles," reading articles and books of and about Frank Farrelly, Milton Erickson, Thorwald Dethlefsen, and Roger Woolger, and especially seeing Morris Netherton and most recently Trisha Caetano, working with colleagues, I was able to develop different ways of working with different clients: sometimes soft, almost tender, sometimes very rational, sometimes emotional, sometimes provocative, but always pacing (and then leading) the client's moods. This change not only has made me more effective as a therapist, but it has made and still makes both practicing and training others in this profession a joyful experience.

## Failures (*Tineke Noordegraaf*)

When I think of things I still consider I handled incorrectly, the first word that comes to mind is *boundaries*. Doing therapy without having established clearly what the actual goal of the therapy is, is the thing I have learned not to do. As a beginning therapist, starting was more important than finishing!

One of my first clients was a woman with many problems, which can best be described as "more or less depressive." The one question I should have asked her immediately was what her life would be like with her symptoms gone and with her able to do what she had always wanted to. It would have saved me, and probably my client, too, a lot of trouble and a lot of sessions. After a couple of successful sessions (or so I thought) she started to develop a therapeutic co-dependency—that is, she became a therapy junky and felt well as long as the therapy filled up her energetic battery, but the battery became empty again by the time she came in for the next session. I didn't know what was wrong. I thought perhaps she should go to another therapist, somebody who used techniques I didn't have as yet.

The moment I started talking about her ending therapy with me, she developed an instant black-hole depression, and there I was in a Catch 22. Whatever I did from that moment on was wrong for both of us, for the therapy and for the results that had so far been achieved. I didn't know much about transference and counter-transference then, but I have definitely learned about them since, through reading and talking and listening and watching my colleagues. It cost me a lot of blood, sweat, and tears before I was able to figure out what had happened in our therapeutic relationship—all I perceived at the time was that the therapy wasn't therapeutic anymore. I felt guilty that my results weren't any better and I continued to give my client hope that things would work out in the end. I worked for the two of us, feeling responsible for the whole process in which we were involved, with my client doing nothing except waiting for the next brilliant idea from me, the therapist. I considered myself a poor therapist because I could not help her, and finally I stopped the therapy, although my client resisted fiercely and tried many maneuvers to access my Florence Nightingale personality. However, I was well protected by that time (thank you, whoever it was that protected me), and she left furious, telling me that she would definitely die within one year due to her never-ending depression. I have never heard from her since, but the experience with her taught me a lot about making a contract at the beginning of every therapy and affirming that contract while the sessions are ongoing.

I had to learn, also, not to do therapy with the kind of people who always have an excuse for not showing up on the right day, or the right hour, or are too tired to work, or too etc., etc. When I first started as a therapist I accepted everything and was the most understanding and empathic therapist imaginable. I got out the tea or coffee and talked to the patients, assuring them that it didn't matter and that we'd find a new date for another appointment—until I learned what that said about me. Again, it had to do with *taking myself seriously as a therapist*. By convincing myself that I couldn't allow excuses anymore and that I couldn't make another appointment with such a person, I almost immediately stopped getting this kind of client. Experiencing what it is to have self-esteem as a human being and not only as a therapist is one of the things we discuss with our students in the Netherlands. One can deal with boundaries only when one knows what it is to have self-esteem and self-respect. One is not able to be a good therapist without at least having a glimpse of what these things are worth in life—in any lifetime, that is.

# *Cases*

**Case 1. Horrorscope** *(Noordegraaf)*

When I started working with children I considered it helpful to give the parents of the child the opportunity to stay with the child during the initial interview and following sessions. I thought that would take away somewhat from the child's feelings of insecurity while being confronted with this kind of therapy as a possible solution of his/her problems. But what I began to note was that during the time the child was asked to describe his problems to me, the parent (mostly the mother) took over and tried to correct the child by telling how she regarded the problem and how things and situations really were. What I at first failed to recognize was that this approach produced an impression of the problem as seen by the parents and not as seen by the child. That meant that while working with what the parents told me to be the problem, very often this wasn't what the child had to cope with. It took me some time before I noticed that I wasn't working with the child's problem but that I was trying to modify that problem in such a way that everybody *seemed* to be happy. After a while I felt uncomfortable, realizing that I needed to listen to the *child's* version of the never-ending-problem story.

I decided to change the situation. I started to work with the children without their parents present, and what I feared didn't happen. First, I asked the children if they knew what had brought them to me, and a lot of times the answer was no. Their parents often told them a lot, but not what they came to me for. So I worked out a standard formula for explaining to the kids what kind of work I was doing and how often in the beginning it might seem as though the problems were getting worse instead of fading away. "That is fairly normal," an earnest-looking kid told me once. "Of course you know what kind of wound is to be found under the bandage, but you want to keep it that way, because looking at the wound would remind you of the pain and the situation in which it happened and everything comes up again. The bandage hides an awful lot, even the memory of what really happened once. Maybe you are some kind of plastic surgeon for my soul." That seemed an undeserved compliment, but the boy didn't want to change his evaluation. There was no insecurity or blocking or resistance as far as that child was concerned.

The progress of the child's therapy became a new and unknown land, but since I had been a child myself and I shared this with my young patients, I had access to almost every child and to his problems. As a therapist I learned to listen to the children instead of to their trying-to-do-it-as-well-as-possible parents. My own children had been my teachers a long time before, and I had passed that class, but I had to learn to really listen as a therapist.

Some weeks ago Ludovic, a Belgian boy of 12 years, came to me, along with his mother. "Ludovic has a lot of problems," she told me, looking at him as if she wanted to apologize that she had a son who needed therapy.

When Ludovic came into my office his legs trembled so much and he was so afraid of falling that he was walking on crutches. He was a child with the label of "Minimal Brain Disorder." He couldn't sit on a chair without moving and touching everything that was at hand. His mother often told him to sit still, and he looked at me as if he wanted to say: "When do *you* start telling me that I am not all right the way I am? That I have to behave a different way?" He was unhappy, and there was a glimpse of sadness visible on his face as he waited to hear the familiar words of rejection.

Before his mother could take over, I asked her not to discuss things her son could tell me as well. He was the expert. He knew best what was bothering him.

That made a lot of difference to Ludovic! He sat up straight, waiting for me to score again.

> T: *I am sure that he can tell me quite well about what is worrying him, but if not, I will help him as much as possible.*
> M: *But you know, a lot of people don't know that he needs love and understanding instead of telling him not to touch things and sit still. He knows we all love him very much at home, but it seems as if he is locked up in a world of his own and I especially cannot reach him there.*

I told the mother politely that I wanted to work with Ludovic alone if he would let me. It had to be his decision and I wanted to hear his motivations about coming to me in Holland. I respected her concern for her son. It was a wonderful thing she had done to seek for therapy to help her son. I had no doubt about her being a good mother, but I wanted to work with the child alone.

The mother's insecurity about her role as a mother who is guilty because she produced such a son disappeared, since she felt there was no condemnation involved from my point of view, and she relaxed and started to listen to the questions her son wanted to ask me. After he asked me everything he wanted to know about the therapy I was offering him, he decided to give it a try.

When his mother left, he changed on the spot. Gone was the boy who asked the questions he wanted to be answered. Every question I asked him was answered with an "I don't know," that could be nothing but the truth. He sat there, trying to find adequate answers to rather simple questions. He began to feel upset and uneasy and his legs started to make shaky movements that he couldn't control.

> C: *It drives me mad, it drives me really mad.... I don't know what happens to me. I don't know how to stop this. But I can't. It just occurs to me. I have no control over it.*

He started to cry. When I asked him when these symptoms had started, he told me that he had had them all his lifetime. The doctors who had examined him had explained to his parents that these are the symptoms that belong to the MBD syndrome.

> T: *Do you accept that, Ludovic?*
> C: *Accept it? I have to, haven't I?*
> T: *So you gave up?*
> C: *What do you mean, I gave up?*
> T: *You're not fighting anymore, are you, just accepting that you've had it all your life, so it probably won't change anymore....*
> C: *You don't understand, you just don't understand what it's like to feel this way, you...*
> T: *Well, tell me all about it then. I am not one of those doctors. I don't know anything about what you're feeling, so start talking to me. You're the expert, remember?...*

Ludovic started to explain that this happened very often, especially after an outburst of rage against his mother.

C: *I don't want to, but it happens. I don't know how to stop it. I call my mother names, which I feel ashamed of.*

He repeated those sentences, telling me about his not being able to handle what happened, his knowing that it was never going to change, how dreadful and shameful it was to realize that his mother always tried to do the best she could while he put her in an awkward position all the time by making her angry. There was something going on between them that he couldn't explain, that he wanted to change if only he knew how to. His mother took him to therapists and doctors trying to find out what was wrong.

C: *And something is terribly wrong, you know. I am even terribly scared of a thunderstorm, of the thunder and lightning. I scream and I shout as if it were a nightmare, as if a disaster were going to happen. I tell myself over and over that I am not a little baby anymore and I don't have to be afraid, but it doesn't work. Something is wrong with me. I just don't know what it is.*

Ludovic sat there, a little boy who had lost his way in life, sitting in too big a chair, convinced that it was all his fault, that nothing could be done anymore. It was all wrong. Everybody tried to do the utmost, but it wouldn't work out. He was the wrong one. He was the one who had to change. If only he knew how to....

Ludovic sat there, the utmost example of despair, a poor little lonely lost boy.... They call it MBD, and in a sense naming it prevented this boy from being healed.

T: *Well, let's find out then what is wrong. And before we start working on being wrong, just tell me what you mean by "wrong"? How would it be to be "right" then?*
C: *(Shocked.) Are you crazy? Don't you know? Feeling at ease of course, feeling all right, not having to be alert all the time. Not to wait for the next time these tremors will show up...for the next terrible fight with my mother. (Sobbing.) I just want it to stop.... Please help me.... (Desperation is coming through strongly.)*

After repeating that sentence "I want it to stop" a number of times, the typical tremors started.

C: *I feel as if...*
T: *As if what?*
C: *As if everything is shaking. As if the whole world is falling to pieces. As if...I don't know what is happening anymore...I am falling...it hurts.... Oh,*

> God, please help me! What is going on.... This is too much. I don't know where I am anymore. (Panicking, sobbing, trembling.)
> 
> T: (Touching him to let him know I'll be with him, no matter what happens.) Feel what is happening there. Watch your body, watch your feet, just stay in touch with what is happening.... Let it happen. Let your body remember what happened so that your brain will start to understand as well. Stay with the feelings. Let your body do what it has to in order to understand why these movements make sense. Move through it. I will stay with you. Keep on moving through it.
> 
> C: It doesn't stop.... It doesn't stop. I want it to stop. Please stop it (pleading).
> 
> T: What do you want most to stop? What is it that you want most to stop? Just tell me the first thing that comes to mind.
> 
> C: The war...the light...the thunder...the screaming...everything...
> 
> T: Feel the shaking of your body and let go until you feel that the shaking diminishes.... Breathe through it if you can and help your body to release this shaking. And let's find out then what war... light...thunder... screaming...and everything you are talking about means.

He landed right in World War II at the moment that Hiroshima was bombed in August, 1945.

### A Hard Rain's A'Gonna Fall (Bob Dylan)

> Where have you been my blue-eyed son
> Where have you been my darling young one
> 
> I have stumbled on the side of twelve misty mountains
> I have walked and I crawled on six crooked highways
> I have stepped in the middle of seven sad forests
> I have been out in front of a dozen dead oceans
> I have been 10,000 miles in the mouth of a graveyard
> 
> And it's a hard rain's a'gonna fall....

Ludovic accessed the moment that was the most traumatic for him. He was a rather young Japanese boy playing around in the streets in full daytime when his whole world fell apart. Everything he cared for went to pieces in a fraction of a minute. He didn't even know what happened. All of a sudden things were not as they used to be. Everything was black and ugly and frightful.

> T: Let's move back just a little bit in time, to the moment when things are still quite "right," when you're playing in the streets.... What is the very first thing happening there that is "wrong"?
> 
> C: Black...it's all black....

T: Is your body black...is the sky black...is anything else black...what exactly do you mean by black?
C: Black...nothing else...it's quiet now...I don't hear anything anymore, no sounds, no nothing...I don't feel anything anymore...
T: Can you tell me anything about the noise that goes together with this blackness...the "wrong" noise...results in everything being black?
C: ...it's terrible...it's like the thunder...it's overwhelming...I can't hide myself...I can't protect myself against it...it hurts...it's driving me crazy.... I want it to stop...I don't want to listen to it....

> What do you hear my blue-eyed son
> What did you hear my darling young one.
> I heard the sound of the thunder that roared out warning
> I heard the roar of a wave that could drown the whole world.
> I heard one hundred drummers whose hands were all blazing
> I heard 10,000 whispering and nobody listening
> I heard one person starve, I heard many people laughing
> I heard the song of a poet who died in the gutter
> I heard the sound of a clown who cried in the alley

C: ...It's terrible...it's like the thunder...it's overwhelming...I can't hide myself...I cannot protect myself against it...it hurts...it's driving me crazy.... I want it to stop....
T: Move to the beginning of the most frightening thing that you hear...
C: Something is coming.... I hear something coming.... It is in the air.... It comes from above.... It is a kind of an aeroplane.... It is burning I think.... I hear people screaming and crying.... I am so scared I don't want to look at it.... I don't want to know.... I want it to stop, I want it to stop.... It is terrible.... I am so scared. I don't know what is going on and I don't want to look at it anymore.... Please help me...I am so scared.... It hurts so much.... My skin is burning.... My body is burning...I can't hold still.... The earth is trembling, or is it my body?... Oh, please help me!
  I don't know what happens to me. I don't know how to stop this. But I can't. It just occurs to me—I have no control over it.
T: Imagine that you can see it from a distance, some place where fear is not so frightening. See what happens to you and your body that makes you cry and scream. What would you see?

> Oh, what did you meet, my blue-eyed son,
> Oh, who did you meet my darling young one,
>
> I met a young child beside a dead pony.
> I met a white man, who walked a black dog.
> I met a young woman whose body was burning
> I met a young girl; she gave me a rainbow

> I met one man who was wounded in love
> I met another man who was wounded in hatred
>
> It's a hard, it's a hard, it's a hard rain's a'gonna fall.

Ludovic said there was no such place to be found, where fear was absent. Everywhere he went he took the fear with him, and the fire and the hurting and the trembling. Only in the blackness was he able to experience some kind of quietness.

T: *Tell me about the black. Is it all around you?*
C: *It's just black. I don't have to feel anything anymore. I don't have to think anymore about what happened.*
T: *What do you remember that you have forgotten while being in the black?*
C: *The fire, the hurting of my body before it was blackening.*
T: *Tell me about what your body looks like before the black comes that helps you to forget, the very last moment before the black comes. What do you feel happening?*
C: *I fall down. It's not exactly falling but being blown away. Everything trembling, the air, my body, the street, everything.... Then there is nothing left anymore.*
T: *How long does that take—from the moment you hear those terrible sounds of thunder and screaming and crying till the moment there is nothing left anymore...and you are surrounded by blackness?*
C: *I don't know...I think it never stops....*
T: *Listen to what you say.... It never stops.... What do you think never stopped then and there....*
C: *The pain, the trembling, the urge to get out of there....*
T: *Let's find out then what is still going on, things your body knows but your mind somehow refuses to believe....*
C: *I am scared.... I don't want to know...it's terrible...all those dead bodies...not looking like bodies at all...shining and glittering like fishes....*
T: *Try to find your own body, just to figure out what happened to you, before you concluded that it never stopped, that you couldn't stop it.*
C: *It's not a body anymore. It's black and burned. It looks terrible. It doesn't move anymore. It isn't me anymore.*
T: *What do you think happened to your body?*
C: *It's destroyed. It's fallen apart, torn to pieces. Something is wrong with me.*
T: *Do you think that that body is still alive?*
C: *No. That looks very dead. It can't be (Sobbing)...*

It took quite a while for Ludovic to release all the pain and shock that he had experienced during that couple of minutes before he died. He had not understood up until now that he hadn't survived that terrible bomb attack. He was totally unaware/unconscious of the fact. When I asked if he wanted to do anything with his body now that he saw how hurt it was and blackened, he answered that thinking about it and remembering what happened there was all he wanted now. Maybe later, but for now he wanted to leave the body untouched as a kind of reminder. I respected that thought. It would give him the strength he needed.

When we had worked through his death he got in touch with his anger, anger about the number of dead corpses he saw lying around everywhere.

C: It drives me mad, it drives me really mad. *We are all destroyed. All the people are destroyed, and the houses, and the trees, and...everything.*
T: *What would you like to do most now, if you were able to...*
C: *I wish I was stronger...I wish I could help them...I wish I could teach them a lesson by taking them apart...I wish I had that much energy.*
T: *Then you have to come out of that blackness of yours, to be able to do that, won't you? You have to come out of your safe hiding place into the open a little bit in order to do that.*
C: *Well, that would be worth it....*
T: *Give it a try then and tell them as loud as you're able to what you're so angry about. Start telling them, let nothing stop you this time.... Feel that you're right in doing that. Tell them* they're *crazy and wrong instead of you. Make clear to them that you know what happened there with you, with your body, and with the world, with everything.... Use your lungs, use your energy, use your body and use your muscles in the right way. Do everything you feel you need to do in order to get rid of all the things that are still bothering you. Come on! Do your utmost!*

Ludovic gave a very good try, and it worked. He screamed, cried, trembled a lot, and felt exhausted and relieved afterward.

T: *Look around you now, is it still black?*
C: *No, it's getting brighter, but I feel very sad now. I feel like crying for all the people who died there.*
T: *Feel what sadness is yours and what isn't. Feel all the sadness you are experiencing as your own sadness.*
C: *There are a lot of them.*
T: *Them.... Who are "Them"?*
C: *All the people who died and never understood it. They look so astonished, so scared. They are all holding on to me, not knowing I feel scared too, I don't know. They are shocked, all of them.*
T: *Realize that they are attached to you one way or the other.... It is their sadness, too, that you are feeling. It is their terror too, that you are experiencing. Can you get in touch with them, in such a way, that you are able to explain what happened to them...explain to them that they died? Just try it.*

> And what'll you do now, my blue-eyed son
> And what'll you do now, my darling young one
>
> I am going back out for the rain to start falling
> I walk through the depths of the deepest dark forests
> Where the people are many and their hands are all empty
> Where the pellets of poison are flooding their waters
> Where the home in the valley needs the damned dirty prison
> And the executioner's face is always well hidden.
> Where hunger is ugly where the souls are forgotten
> Where black is the color where none is the number
> And I tell it and speak it and think it and breathe it
> And reflect from the mountains so all souls can see it.
> And I stand on the ocean until I start sinking.
> And I'll know my song well before I start singing.
>
> And it's a hard, it's a hard, it's a hard rain's a'gonna fall.

Ludovic was part of a cluster of people who never realized that they had not survived that terrible disaster. We brought them all to a place where it was quiet and where they could process what had happened to them all. They didn't want to go to the so-called "Light" because Light and light and lightning meant something terrible to all of them.

When Ludovic sat back in his chair after this first session, he looked more mature. He was tired and relaxed but wanted to go immediately into a next session. He had understood now where the trembling came from, where the fear of thunder and lightning came from, why the thought "It never stops, it drives me crazy" had stayed with him for such a long time. What was still unsolved was the relationship with his mother and the anger involved there. When I asked him if it could come from that lifetime he denied it. "That is much older," he said, looking at me rather provokingly. "We have to go further back in time the next time—tomorrow, maybe?"

The only fact that could make sense in the context of his death in Hiroshima was the fact that, in considering mothers and relationships, the pilot of the plane that carried the bomb had called his plane after his mother, the "Enola Gay." We know what happened to that man when he realized what he had done. Maybe some of that energy was attached to Ludovic as well, but I was not sure.

**Second Regression**

In the next session, which occurred the following day, I asked Ludovic about the people he had taken to the place where they could rest and eventually feel at peace. He had referred to wanting to get away from the earth in order to feel at peace, and this had intrigued me.

T: *Is being at peace a normal situation for you Ludovic, is it wrong?*
C: *There is nothing wrong about feeling peaceful, is there?*
T: *That means that there is nothing wrong with what you want, is there?...*
C: *No, of course not.*
T: *What does that mean about being wrong or about being not normal then?...*
C: *Do you mean that there is nothing wrong with me then?*
T: *Well, do you?*
C: *No, actually not (Starts to laugh and can't stop).*

I tried to discuss this further, but Ludovic couldn't answer—and he was laughing his head off.

T: *What on earth is most different from the place where you are when you feel at peace?*
C: *On earth there is always something terrible going on, something wrong.*
T: *Which words are connected with that feeling you have, when thinking about earth?*
C: *Fear...anger...jealousy...hatred...not being able to defend myself against others...they want something from me....*
T: *Where does that come from? Did you take anything from them or did they take anything from you? Feel what it is you have to get back, what you left unfinished and has to be brought back in place...*
C: *They despise me...they laugh at me, they're making a fool out of me (anger is coming up, body is shaking).*
T: *Who are "they"? Move to the most important moment that can point out to you what you have done to lose their self-esteem, the moment they make a fool out of you, the moment that causes you to still feel so angry.*
C: *(Hesitant...) I see something I'd rather not talk about, I am feeling ashamed, I am so angry there. I think I despise a lot of people. I don't deserve to be loved anymore. I am some sort of arrogant...I am feeling a strange kind of anger.... There is something wrong with me there as well....*

He said that it started with doing a test of some sort. He was a 12-year-old male member of a clan who, along with the others of his age, had to prove to the elders that he was able to travel along with the rest of the group to escape hostile tribes. Those who were not able to pass certain tests were to be left behind. It was the survival of the fittest. There was no particular attack taking place at the time but the tests had to be passed. He felt he could pass the test if he didn't feel any fear. If he felt fear, he wouldn't trust himself to do what he had to.

There were many young boys and all had to jump over a canyon with a fast-flowing stream below. It was a test of their muscles and also of their capacity to exclude their feelings and just concentrate on jumping. He first reported that at the moment he started to jump the other boys yelled at him, screaming that he couldn't do it. Unable to concentrate, he tumbled into the canyon.

When I asked why they yelled, he said that he had always showed them up, telling them that he was the best and the strongest. He was arrogant and could not accept that the other boys were good and strong as well as he. Instead, he told them that they were all wrong if they didn't realize that he was the best. He had tried to concentrate but stumbled and hurt his foot so badly that he was unable to jump across. As he fell down he grabbed some bushes and braked his fall, but he couldn't get out of the canyon by himself and nobody wanted to help him. Instead, they yelled at him and said he was stupid and called him all the names he had called them.

He felt humiliated as he clutched at the bushes with his legs hanging in the air, searching with his feet for a ridge to stand on. He hated himself for not succeeding in what he had thought was easy, hated his body for not having the energy to jump across the canyon, hated himself for having had feelings of pain.

T: Is it "wrong" to feel?
C: Yes, it is, definitely....
T: Is it always wrong to feel?...
C: No, of course not.
T: Is there anything wrong about your feeling pain when you hurt your foot like that?...
C: No, of course not.
T: Under what circumstances is it wrong to feel then?...
C: The feelings I feel are awful.
T: I understand, but is it wrong to feel them, or what?...
C: It is easier not to feel them, I guess (Smiling).
T: You're right, only then and there you thought it was necessary not to feel anything in order to succeed, do you realize that?
C: Yes.... But I didn't fail because I started feeling anything. I failed because I stumbled and fell instead of jumping. And I hurt my foot. (He drew that conclusion on his own, which was good, considering he was only a kid of 12 years lying on a couch.)
T: Feel that there is nothing wrong with you or with your body about feeling pain.... Just allow yourself to feel the pain you have avoided feeling.... Breathe into it as deep as you can in order to release the pain.

Ludovic took some time to do that, but he did it thoroughly. Then he admitted that there was something worse, something too shameful to talk about. He finally described how he hung there listening to his comrades mocking him and feeling humiliated and despised, not worth anything anymore, and decided that he had better disappear. Deep sorrow came up as he related how he had mutilated himself with a knife he was carrying. Anger had come up in the form of self-hate. He had hated his body and wanted to get rid of it. He wanted to punish it before he fell down into the river. It was a shameful moment and it was some time before he accepted what he had done and why he had done it. He had cut his body in a kind of suicide gesture before he let himself fall into the river.

T: *What is the last thought you have before falling into the river.*
C: I don't deserve it to be loved anymore.
T: *Because...*
C: Because I failed.
T: *You failed what...*
C: I failed the test...
T: *If somebody fails a test, do you have to despise him, or does he need something else, what do you suggest?... Just imagine somebody else struggling there in that cleft for his life. What would you do the way you are now, when seeing that?*
C: I know how he must be feeling, so I think I would do my best to help him and get him out of there....
T: *Well, do as you say then and help that boy to overcome his hate for his body and himself. Start helping him the best way you can....*

And Ludovic wouldn't be Ludovic it he hadn't made one of the most beautiful rescue operation I have witnessed. He supported the hanging boy with all his heart and guided him by telling him exactly where to put his feet in order to be able to climb higher and higher and eventually get out of that terrible canyon. Both the boy and he started to cry intimately and the synthesis was there when they looked each other in the eyes. But that was not all. We finally came to understand his struggle with his mother.

C: My mother has something to do with it as well. I feel it.
T: *Let's find out then. Move to the moment that you feel her energy the strongest. With what emotional charge is her energy connected?*
C: Jealousy...attraction...humiliation.
T: *Tell me all about it, what do you see?*
C: There is that girl I like a lot. She is influenced by another boy. It hurts the way she reacts. I want to impress her by showing her I can jump as well as that other boy. I like her. She is very good looking. I want her to admire me. I didn't succeed. I did something terribly wrong.
T: *Repeat that please and listen to what you say....*
C: I did something terribly wrong. That thought again! (Laughing.)
T: *That girl, has that girl anything to do with your mother in this lifetime?*

> C: *Sure, she is my mother now. I told her I would come back to make it all up to her. To prove to her I could do it....*

He understood his anger toward his mother quite well by this time. I didn't have to explain anything. He opened his eyes.

> C: *Thank you for helping me jump over that canyon.*

We sat there for a while, the two of us, understanding well what had happened. He didn't need any renovation techniques. He had figured it out for himself. A little boy wonder instead of a little boy lost. And he knew that I knew, a wordless understanding.

He didn't need another session but just wanted me to read to him out of one of the many fairy tale books I have in my office. I chose *Alice In Wonderland*, Alice falling and falling in a rabbit hole, not knowing what was going on. He sat quietly listening.

Recent contact with Ludovic confirms that his world now appears to him to be less threatening. He has given up his crutches and his legs have stopped trembling. He even plans to learn to swim next year. His residual fear is that the old fear will return and he will become ill again, and he is working on that. His increasing confidence is reflected in a better self-image. Reports from his doctor confirm steady improvement.

> T: *Thank you for working with me Ludovic. Thank you for your ability to change your world. Thank you for your courage. You taught me a lot.*

### Case 2. The Rapist: An Example of Processing a Large Hologram *(Bontenbal)*

A couple of years ago Henny, a young woman of 25, consulted me about her anxiety over being raped. This fear had begun two years before when a man attacked her while she was cycling home after a night out (a conventional thing for a liberated young Amsterdam woman to do). The man had not been able to rape her because a young couple came to her rescue, but he terrified her. The bruises resulting from falling off her bike healed quickly, but the shock of the rape attempt lingered on. The words she used to described her fear were: "I am afraid a man will suddenly jump on me and rape me."

The initial interview exposed many other problems. Although college educated as a social worker, Henny had been unemployed since her graduation more than a year before, a source of unhappiness to her because, in order to earn money to supplement her welfare check, she cleaned houses. She had a number of physical problems: her overweight made her feel unattractive; she had allergies to certain foods; and she had had two abortions in the previous five years, both considered the only alternative but never fully accepted by her. Finally, her relationship with her current boyfriend was disintegrating, not so much because of fear that he would rape her but because his reactions to her mental, emotional, and physical disturbance made their sexual relationship difficult and painful.

In general she felt that her life was a mess, but her fear of rape upset her most. She still lived in the house to which she had moved as a student, where she should have felt secure, but when the other residents (mostly students) were out, she did not dare to open the door, afraid that there would be a man standing there who would jump on her and rape her.

Henny came from a large Catholic family, the fifth of eight children. She smiled when I asked her if she knew anything about her birth or anything that had gone on when her mother was pregnant, an anecdote, perhaps?

> C: *We never talked about those things. My parents are rather conservative and they never educated me sexually. I don't believe they had a very active sex life. I don't think my mother liked sex very much. I suspect that my parents only had sex when the parish priest came by to inquire if it wasn't time for a next child. As a student I had experiences with different men, my way of educating myself, abortions and all.*

In the first session Henny had no problem feeling the fear of being raped, especially after repeating a number of times: "Suddenly a man jumps on me." She experienced the fear as one of becoming suffocated. As expected, the first incident that came up was the attempted rape of two years earlier. Because the first impression was still nebulous, I grounded her in the moment she was cycling home feeling good after having some drinks with friends in a café.

> T: *You are cycling home, feeling good. What are you thinking cycling there?*
> C: *Thinking? Nothing special. It's rather dark and cold. I had fun, but I long for my warm room.*
> T: *Okay, move to the very first moment you see that man.*
> C: *(Panicking.) He is right there! He suddenly jumps out of the bushes, pulling me off my bike! I fall. Oh, god! I feel so frightened!... (Starts sobbing.)*
> T: *Feel how frightened you are, really feel it, as deep as you can...*
> C: *(Still sobbing a little.) And then those two people are there and he runs away...but I am still so frightened...*
> T: *Breathe into the feeling. Feel it once more as deeply as you can, then breathe it out, all of it....*

After a couple of minutes Henny seemed to have released some of her fear.

> T: *Move once more to the moment you are cycling...just before the man jumps...but move through it this time in slow motion...and just realize what you thought the moment he jumped.*
> C: *He jumps.... God it really startles me....*
> T: *What are you thinking right there. Right there.*
> C: *Oh God, he's going to rape me!*
> T: *Say that again, and feel what is happening within you, within you body....*
> C: *Oh God, he's going to rape me...I freeze....*
> T: *Realize that and then breathe yourself through that freeze, keep on breathing till you come out of that freeze....*

We went through the moment of shock two more times before she realized that there had been some time between his jumping out of the bushes and the moment he pulled her from her bike. He had even run some feet before he could touch her. And because of that she realized, also, how the exclamation, "Oh, God, he's going to rape me!" froze her into shock, which made it impossible for her to act at all.

As he came after her she became even more disturbed.

> C: *No, no, please...no, no, don't rape me! No...please...no...noooo!!!*

She almost fell off my couch while obviously defending herself against one or more attackers. She started moaning louder and louder until suddenly she started to jump from the bed, shrieked, then became motionless. At that time I questioned her:

> T: *What are you experiencing right now?*
> C: *(Deep sigh, still motionless.) I believe I am dead. They killed me.*
> T: *They?*
> C: *Those men. They came upstairs, jumped on me, raped me, then killed me.*
> T: *Repeat those words, listen to them!*

I moved her back in time, as far as necessary to be able to understand what was happening.

> T: *Where are you now?*
> C: *On my horse. I am riding my horse.*

In grounding this situation she told me proudly that she was a young woman, 18 years old, riding her horse all by herself in the woods.

T: *How do you feel riding your horse?*
C: *(Smiling proudly.) Very good. I love it. They don't like me to do it, but I love riding my horse and I don't want to wait till they are finally ready to go.*
T: *Who are they?*
C: *My parents! They are always so protective. They still think I am a little girl. But they never take time to ride with me. So I sneak out of the house once in a while. The stableboy hates me doing it. He's scared they will blame him when they find out, but I don't care....*

The parents proved right to be protective of their spoiled daughter because she lost her way in the woods. She became a little worried because it was dark, but finally she found a way out of the woods, which led her to the outskirts of a village. There she came across a small inn. Because it was dark by now and because she felt hungry and thirsty, she went inside.

T: *What goes through your mind when you go inside?*
C: *I don't like it, but I have no choice. I can't go back now! My God, it seems even darker inside. (Shivers.)*
T: *What do you feel?*
C: *Scared of course. All these men!*
T: *Which men?*
C: *Who do you think!? The men who are drinking there, of course. You sound like my father. He also asks such stupid questions!*

The inn fell dead silent when she entered. But the innkeeper was nice to her. He fed her, although she had no money, and protected her against the men. He even offered her a place to sleep. Because she had no choice she accepted the offer. He then led her upstairs where the "rooms" were.

C: *This is terrible! I can't sleep here! There are no rooms. It's just an attic, with some partitions and straw on the floor.*
T: *Do you say that to the innkeeper?*
C: *Of course! This is no place to sleep for a lady!*
T: *How does he react to that?*
C: *He just grins! He says: "Sleep well, my lady!"*

She made herself as comfortable as possible under a thin blanket, complaining all the time.

T: *Do you realize what makes you complain so much?*
C: *Because I am scared! I am not stupid! I know I am scared, wouldn't you be!?*
T: *Okay, feel that you are scared. Just feel it!*

Although she was scared to death and feeling guilty as she thought of her parents, she nevertheless fell asleep. Suddenly she was awakened.

C: *(Whispering, I can hardly hear her.)* Oh no! There are men coming!
T: What are they doing?
C: I don't know. I am so scared. Oh God no! Don't come near me! Stay away! *(She starts sobbing.)*

She then recalled being raped three times until the last of her rapists strangled her to death. Slowly we processed the rapes and the strangling on all levels (mental, emotional and physical), but she still seemed filled with stress.

T: *What is the most difficult to accept of what just happened?*
C: I don't know. The innkeeper was one of them. I trusted him. The bastard!
T: *Say it again! And let all the feeling connected to that word come out.*

(Henny repeated this 10 times, relieving a lot of anger, sadness, and fear.)

C: I think of my parents all the time. I feel so guilty about what I did. They must be worried sick. I was so stupid to go horseback riding on my own. I feel I am such a bad girl!
T: *Listen to how you judge yourself. Repeat those words and just listen to yourself!*
C: *(Repeats her last two sentences.)* I know, but that's the way I feel. My poor parents.
T: *Go to them. See how they are.*
C: I can't go there!
T: *Sure you can go! That's one of the nice things of not having a body. You can go where ever you want. Just try it.*
C: I wouldn't mind leaving this place.
T: *I hoped you would feel that way. Just try it. Think of your parents.*

She then moved without any problem out of the inn and back to the castle where she had been living for 18 years and found her mother in terrible distress, her father raging. This didn't lessen her guilt, of course.

T: *What would make you feel better?*
C: Telling them I am sorry. Telling them that I made a mistake with terrible consequences but that I am all right now.
T: *Okay, tell them!*
C: They don't listen to me. They can't hear me!
T: *Which of your parents can you reach more easily.*
C: My mother, I guess. My father is raging.

T: *Just concentrate on your mother. Just concentrate and reach out to her.*
C: *(Starts crying.) I am sorry mother. I really am sorry!*

She felt that her mother was somehow listening and understood, which made it possible for her to leave.

C: *She'll help my father. She is stronger than he is.*

She felt herself move away from her parents and into a light and warm sphere, where she wanted to stay for a while to rest and heal. After letting her slowly breathe in the lightness and warmth of that sphere until it filled her as completely as possible, I brought her back to the here and now.

T: *What does what you just experienced tell you about your fear of being raped?*
C: *That's quite obvious isn't it? Those men raped me! I was alone in that attic and three men raped me!*
T: *Does that mean that whenever you are alone and there are men that you get raped?*
C: *Of course not!*
T: *Good! Realize that! Because that's just what you believe all the time. You told me that yourself: "I am afraid that when I open the door and there is a man standing there that he will jump on me and rape me and that there is no one to help me."*
C: *(Very slowly.) Do you mean that I somehow subconsciously predicted the situation of two years ago?*
T: *Very likely. Such a belief, what we call a postulate, can only survive when it gets confirmation from time to time!*
C: *But...but...still...why do men do these things?! Are they crazy or so?*
T: *Men...they...you mean all men?*
C: *Okay, those men!*
T: *There was obviously something wrong with those men, as with the man who attacked you two years ago. There are men like that. It's a shame we can't take them into therapy. As long as we can't do that, what can you do to prevent this happening again to you?*
C: *What do you mean?*
T: *Do you want to stay a victim of rapists?*
C: *No! Of course not!*
T: *How can you change that?*
C: *If you want me to say: "by not going out alone," forget it! A woman has every right to be on the streets on her own, without having to watch out for every sick idiot! She has the right to feel safe.*
T: *You are absolutely right! Let's tell those rapists! But first of all tell yourself, really tell yourself, that you have every right to be alone on the streets and feel safe. Say it out loud.*

> C: *(After some hesitation)* *I have the right to be alone on the streets and feel safe.*
> T: *And at home and feel safe.*
> C: *And at home and feel safe.*
> T: *How does it feel when you say that?*
> C: *Strange! Like I have to convince myself that it is all right to believe that!*
> T: *Can you convince yourself?*
> C: *It's like something deep inside me is still protesting.*
> T: *Okay, let's find out in the next session what's the real source of that protest.*
> C: *Yes, I think that's very important.*

The third life in this pattern proved to be important in several ways. She recalled the life of a young woman married to a miner in what she believed to be Limburg, the most southern of the Dutch provinces, bounded on the east by Germany. The description of her surroundings suggested that this was the life prior to her present one. When I asked her what year it was, she said it was 1948.

When she moved into the life, she was sitting in her kitchen feeling utterly depressed. Somewhere in the background two children were asking for attention but she felt it impossible to take care of them. Moving back in time to find the cause of her distress, she found herself five years younger, living in the harsh times of World War II. What kept her spirits alive then was the courtship by a boy of her age.

> C: *He is nice and sweet and very protective. And he makes me laugh when I feel bad. I love him.*

When the war was over and the mines were operating again, her fiance became a miner like his father. They married shortly after he brought home his first paycheck. Within two years they had two children. The hard work in the mines and the responsibility of his young family changed the young miner's mood.

> C: *I miss him all the time. Before he started working we were together a lot. Because of the war there was no work. Now he is gone all the time, and when he comes home he is tired of his work in the mines. I try to make myself pretty but he does not seem to notice.*
>
> *I feel so utterly alone sometimes. It seems all love has gone out of our relationship. We don't laugh together anymore. The only times I hear him laugh is when he is with some mates drinking, which he does more and more often. When I complain, he gets really mean. He tells me to shut up, that he needs that after the hard work. At home there are only problems with the children, with money, with me. He has changed. He is really mean to me, while he used to be so nice.*

T: *Move to a moment he is really mean to you.*
C: *I am in the kitchen again. I hear him coming through our small garden. I feel scared. I pray he hasn't been drinking. He comes through the door. I avoid looking at him, turn my back on him. I hear him fall down on a chair. I feel his eyes on my back. He makes me so nervous.*
T: *Feel your nervousness, feel how it affects you.... What happens next?*
C: *He asks if dinner is ready. He sounds angry. I say, without looking at him, that it's not. He gets mad. Calls me names.*
T: *What kind of names?*
C: *Lazy no good...Slut...Ugly one...even Bitch...all kinds of names (Starts crying).*
T: *Repeat those words...so you can detach them from you....*

(Henny repeats the words until the crying becomes less.)

Because of her husband's lack of loving response to her, the perpetually returning clutter in the house, the children's constant need for attention, she slowly stopped taking care of herself.

C: *Look at me. I am still young, but I feel old already. I really look slovenly now. Everything is so dirty in the house. The mines make everything dirty. It does not make sense to clean it. I feel terrible.*

I moved her to the first situation she recalled, sitting in the kitchen.

C: *I feel so depressed! I don't want to live anymore. I don't want to hear the children crying, to see the dirt, to look at myself in the mirror, to wait for him to come home in a bad mood.*
T: *What do you do next?*
C: *I don't know. I am just sitting there. It feels like I am sitting in that kitchen forever.*
T: *Just move backwards a little bit in time. Until you feel you are moving again. Doing anything.*
C: *(After a minute.) I actually move very slowly, like a zombie. I feel very strange.*
T: *Move back a little more. Before the slow moving as a zombie starts.*
C: *I am standing now. In the kitchen.*
T: *What are you doing?*
C: *I don't know. I give up.*
T: *Repeat that!*
C: *What?*
T: *I give up. Say it again.*
C: *I give up (six times).... Oh God (Starts to cry.), I have pills in my hand. Oh God, no!*

Very slowly she recalled taking the pills. She was sitting at the kitchen table. She heard her children cry but she was not able to respond. The zombie feeling was already there.

> C: I can't move anymore. They are crying. I feel terrible. I have let them down. I want to stop it. But I can't, I can't anymore!

We processed the slow dying by moving through it a number of times. At the end she was crying freely, letting it all out, the distress, the fear, the anger, the guilt.

> C: Oh my God. This is really the worst thing you can do. Killing yourself. It does not solve anything. I know now. I am still having these feelings. Lately even more. With my boyfriend in this life it's almost the same. It started out all right, we had a good time together, but now the relationship has grown distant, cold, like all positive feelings have gone, I am just repeating it....
> T: Knowing all that, what does it mean for your present situation?
> C: First of all: never, never commit suicide again. And second: talk to my boyfriend about ending the relationship or give it a new try. It makes me feel better to say that. Like a new start. I now understand the abortions in this life as well. I was so afraid of having children again.

When Henny came for the next session she felt a lot better. Her boyfriend and she had had a long discussion. They had decided to separate but the feeling remained that they could stay friends and help each other.

Because her fear of being raped was still there, although considerably less than when we started the therapy, we focused this session again on her fear. Once again she surprised me with how her facial expression and voice changed with the MES induction.

> T: What's happening?
> C: (Rather harsh voice.) I am telling a buddy that they are expected to arrive today.
> T: Who are expected today?
> C: The new slaves. They will bring the new slaves today. There will be a big auction in a few days.
> T: Do you have anything to do with this auctioning of slaves?
> C: No, I am guarding the gates.

Henny found herself as a guard of the gates of a medieval town. In that life she was a strong man and felt very powerful because it was his job to decide which people to let in and out of the gates. He was excited about the arrival of the slaves.

T: *What makes you so excited about it?*
C: *I have a friend working at the warehouse. He guards the warehouse where the slaves are kept until the auction. Tonight, after they have arrived, I'll go there.*

She moved to the moment the slaves arrived at the gate:

C: *Just what I hoped for. Some nice looking female slaves. We'll have a party tonight.*

After the changing of the guards, he and his buddy waited until it was dark and then carefully approached the warehouse. His friend let them in quickly. The female slaves were in an iron cage. He felt excited when it was his turn to enter the cage first, pick out one of the women, and take her with him to the back of the warehouse.

C: *God I am so horny. I can't wait. I jump on her right away...and take her....*
T: *Say that again, please, and listen to the words you are saying....*

This went on for quite some time, the three men taking one woman after the other.... Suddenly the merry mood changed.

C: *Somebody is coming...more people.... Oh my God, soldiers...*

The three men were more or less caught with their pants down and arrested.... They were thrown into a dungeon. The once strong man slowly deteriorated into a skinny, white-haired wreck, who mostly felt sorry for himself. He died slowly.

C: *I feel so bad, I can't breath anymore...my lungs...*
T: *Move through your death, feel what's happening with your body...your breathing....*
C: *...Can't breathe any more.... (Choking severely.)*
T: *Move through this feeling till it's over...move through it, feel it...till it's over....*
C: *Finally...*
T: *Where are you experiencing now?*
C: *I am looking at my body.... I hate it...it caused me all this misery....*
T: *Your body caused that?...*
C: *Yes...I couldn't control it...it did those terrible things to those women...and because of that I lost my life...I had a good life...I was proud of being a guard....*
T: *If your body is to blame for all this, does that mean that you feel completely free of guilt now, being out of your body....*

C: *(Deep sigh.) No!*
T: *So whom are you really blaming?*
C: *(Another deep sigh.) Myself, of course.... My god, I have been really wicked...I deserve the worst....*
T: *Repeat those words! And listen to them. Really listen to how you judge and convict yourself....*
C: *I listen...I listen...but the guilt is so strong...I just can't accept what happened....*
T: *Take a little more distance...just a little more.... Survey this life and how it relates to the other lives you recalled....*
C: *I understand....*
T: *What do you understand?...*
C: *I have judged myself and convicted myself to experience the worst....*
T: *And did you?*
C: *Yes! Even in my present life!*
T: *And you want this to go on?*
C: *What do you mean?*
T: *You want to go on experiencing the worst?*
C: *No! It's enough!*
T: *Say that again.*

She was then able to move into a sphere of brilliant light where she experienced a growing acceptance of the polarity of her issue, which ended in a strong catharsis. Henny proved that it had been enough.

We did two more sessions, focused on the pre- and perinatal areas. Conception again proved to be the first moment of actualization of the pattern. Her mother felt forced by her father to have sex, which verged on rape when he neglected her strong protest. After those sessions Henny's fear was completely gone.

Within six months after the last session she found an appropriate job and not much later settled in a small house by herself. A year later she married a young lawyer whom she had met at work. When we danced together at her wedding, she told me she felt she had come a long way.

Chapter XVII

# Irene Hickman, D.O.

## *Biographical Data*

### Personal Background

I was born in rural Iowa, the eighth of nine children, two of whom died before I was born. We were very poor. Mother was not well throughout my childhood. My older sisters cared enough to teach me reading and writing before I entered kindergarten, and after my mother's death when I was ten, they brought me up.

School was a joy. From the beginning it gave scope both to my intense curiosity and to my drive to experience and learn new things. When I started junior high school the most direct route home took me past the library, where I frequently stopped to explore books on all subjects. One of the most interesting, discovered when I was 12, was *Palmistry for All* by Cheiro.[1] I tested the principles on my own hands and then on family and friends, discovering for myself the validity of palm reading. After that I earned small fees for palm reading, and in the process I met many interesting people.

My father openly opposed education for girls on the ground that girls only got married, for which they didn't need much school. During my junior year I found that in order to complete high school I would have to leave home. I supported myself as a mother's helper for a while. Then I was invited to live with the minister's family, one block from school, and for the first time I participated in extracurricular activities. Because there was no money for college to pay for my tuition, I first took a job as a maid. The following February I became the first beneficiary of the Poverty Award with government subsidy, which lasted for a semester. Getting through college became a precarious experience financially. I survived on odd jobs, a small scholarship, and for several years I worked as a lab assistant, which paid my tuition.

My first marriage was untenable, though I stuck it out for ten years and bore two sons in the process. Knowing that divorce was inevitable and that I would have to raise my sons alone, I decided to become a doctor. For my medical training I chose the College of Osteopathic Physicians and Surgeons in Los Angeles and graduated in 1949. At this time, with the help of a Jungian analyst, I became able to dissolve my marriage, knowing that I had done everything possible to make it work. Shortly afterward I met and married my second husband, Jack, on December 3, 1951 and gave birth to another son. My marriage lasted until Jack's death 40 years later.

During my undergraduate years at Simpson College in Iowa I had assumed that I would find answers to all the questions I had been thinking about. But I did not find them there, nor did I find them during my medical training in Los Angeles. There I was taught, as a first principle of medical training, that the human body operates as an integrated organism. Yet little was mentioned of the mind and nothing of the impact of emotions on bodily functions. Nor did I find answers to such questions as why some people are rich and others poor, some healthy and beautiful while others are deformed, ill, disabled, or in pain.

In 1949 during my senior year in medical school I read Thomas Sugrue's *There Is a River*, a biography of Edgar Cayce.[2] With this book answers began to fall into place. The publication of Gina Cerminara's *Many Mansions* in 1950[3] increased my understanding and excitement, and I felt compelled to test the hypotheses contained in them by trying hypnosis, which led in 1963 to the major experience of my life, my participation as a research subject in a project testing the safety parameters of psychedelics in an outpatient setting at the International Foundation for Advanced Study in Menlo Park, California. It was an indescribable experience and one that I would not exchange for a million dollars, but I have no inclination to repeat it.

After graduation I felt I was well enough equipped to present myself to my community as a physician. I expected to help my patients resolve their health problems with the therapies taught to me in medical school, but it soon became evident that only a few could be helped, even physically. The majority of patients who came to me remained ill, tense, worried, or unhappy, in spite of my best efforts. New and different ways of treating them had to be found. It became clear to me that tranquilizers did not provide a permanent or even a long-range solution. In 1950 I began to use with selected patients the techniques of hypnosis that I had learned. I found that many who had failed to respond to former treatments soon became well.

My patients taught me more about the human mind than I had been able to learn from other sources. By asking questions rather than giving suggestions, I learned that it is possible to probe surprising depths, a deeper level of consciousness that is a source of knowledge and understanding, not only of the nature of physical problems but also of causes of problems and their needed remedy. An extensive description of my methods and results is related in my book *Mind Probe—Hypnosis,* first published in 1983 and now in its fourth printing.

I found that if I asked my hypnotized patients to go to the source of their problems, they usually did so. Sometimes they would find that source in an earlier part of their present life, but often, with the same instructions, they would go immediately to a past life. During more than 40 years of using hypnosis in a non-directive way for therapy, I have become convinced that within the subconscious of each of us there exists a level of wisdom and insight that far surpasses the levels available in our usual state of consciousness. With the use of hypnosis it is possible to transcend both time and space and to recall and re-live distant memories.

I am now retired from private practice and am involved in writing and publishing books, instructing others in non-directive hypnotherapy, listening, and giving workshops. I designed and published the first issue of the Journal of Regression Therapy for the Association for Past-Life Research and Therapies.

## Personal Past-Life Experience

The past-life experience that was the most helpful to me was my first one in 1950. A friend, Patricia, and I, though reluctant to allow anyone to control our minds, had nevertheless become increasingly interested in every facet of hypnosis, and our curiosity had grown by leaps and bounds. We discussed the presumed danger of being "controlled" and decided that if we took turns being hypnotist and subject, the control would even out. We had just read *Many Mansions* by Gina Cerminara, and I, especially, wanted to test the reincarnation concept.

We acquired the book *Hypnotism Revealed* by Melvin Powers for a dollar and read the induction to each other in turn. After one of us reached the hypnotic state, the other suggested that if there was anything in a past life that could help us understand ourselves in the present life, it would be shown to us. Through this process each of us found an important past life.

For me, the opening scene appeared to be about the size of a puppet stage. At first I observed from my chair. In the scene were two people, a small boy of about eight, fancily dressed, and a blond young woman in a floor-length dress. The boy was stamping his foot and screaming, "I won't go to the party! I *won't* go to the party!" and began ripping his ruffled shirt open until the buttons flew across the room. The woman tried to calm him and get him dressed. Almost at once I began to feel his fury and very soon found that I was no longer a spectator but was suddenly inside the boy's body.

When I was asked by Patricia why I wouldn't go to the party, I answered that Joe wasn't going, so neither would I. In response to further questioning, I supplied more and more details. I, as the boy called Buddy (a name that I resented), was the son of a wealthy slave-owning plantation owner and politician during the years before the Civil War. My mother was occupied with social events. I was an only child, totally ignored by my parents and cared for by governesses, servants, and slaves. My constant companion was Joe, a slave boy born the same day as I. Joe was the only person who really cared about me, and a deep love existed between us.

When we were twelve, Joe was required to work in the fields and I was sent off to school for the sons of the rich. I missed Joe and grew to dislike the other rich boys and resent my parents for sending me to such a school. Books and learning became my only joy. School continued for five years and then I returned home. My father sat down and explained that I was now a man and that it was my duty to uphold the honor of the family name. After this one lengthy conversation, my father returned to his old pattern of ignoring me. When political colleagues visited, they and my father would walk right past me, giving no more attention to me than to a piece of furniture. My resentment grew.

Soon the States were at war. My father used his influence to establish a special assignment for me, including a uniform different from those the others wore. My duties were to carry messages for the officers, and I soon learned that most of the messages were invitations to ladies to join the officers in their tents. I grew to despise everything and everybody involved in my situation, and once I even mixed up the messages deliberately so that the ladies found themselves in the wrong tents. During one battle, perhaps Gettysburg, I stood on a hill overlooking the battleground and cursed the Southern soldiers and vehemently hoped for their defeat.

After the war I returned to the plantation and married a very able woman who cared for our two sons and managed the plantation business capably. Still bitter and resentful, I spent most of my time in study, my books being my only real pleasure. I died about the age of 60, still discontented and bitter.

This regression revealed the source of a number of patterns that a great many sessions with therapists and analysts had failed to reveal. In my current lifetime I grew up in a small town where the majority of people were blond and blue-eyed, and I never knew a black person until I went to college. But as I was growing up, whenever I saw dark or black people, I always wanted to go up and hug them. I didn't act out this wish but I remained intensely aware of it. I was also aware of quite an opposite reaction to rich people. If

I knew that a person or family was rich, I experienced an instant dislike, even before I had any idea what the person or family was really like. Also, as a child I gave some outstanding exhibitions of temper tantrums, often thinking, as I was throwing the fit, "You may not like me but you're going to know I'm here."

Joe was my reason for wanting to hug blacks. The rich kid's school explained my dislike of the rich and my love of books. The intense desire to be noticed, even if it took a temper tantrum, came out of Buddy's resentment at being ignored. This regression proved to be a great help in dealing with these irrational patterns.

# *Theory*

## Philosophical Hypotheses

I do not think of my approach as either hypothesis or an assumption. I have now gathered sufficient evidence in both my own experience and the experiences of my patients to satisfy my requirements of "proof." However, here are some basic principles:

1. The human entity is eternal in nature.

2. This present body is only one of a series of bodies we have worn.

3. We are here to learn the lessons that we failed to learn in previous incarnations.

4. Every experience is recorded and cannot be erased.

5. Within the deep level of the mind of each of us there exists a level of wisdom and insight far surpassing that available in our usual state of consciousness.

I think of the mind as having three facets or areas (each of which is intermingled to a greater or lesser degree with the other two): the conscious, the subconscious, and the superconscious. The conscious area is concerned primarily with sensory experiences, choice making, receiving impressions through the five senses, caring for the body and possessions, performing work duties, enjoying family and friends, or creating art and beauty.

The subconscious level manages all of the body functions not subject to direct conscious control, such as heart rate, body temperature, or glandular function. It is also the storehouse of memory, the part that survives bodily death, carrying with it the memory record into the non-physical realm between lives and bringing this memory again into the next body at rebirth.

The third level, the superconscious, is the level at which we experience a oneness with all things. When this level is touched, awareness expands without limits. Intuition, inspiration, creativity, have their sources at this level, and when these are freed up and made available, they can be used in any way the conscious mind chooses.

The subconscious-superconscious has a wider and deeper awareness of the entity's purpose and direction than the conscious self and wants to guide conscious choices in a way that will facilitate growth, consciousness expansion, and total health. Under hypnosis these wants from the non-conscious mind are dominant over contradictory wants of the conscious mind. What is revealed in these deeper levels facilitates self-acceptance and encourages choices that lead to greater awareness, harmony, and creativity.

## Psychotherapeutic Assumptions:

1. Our task as therapists is to guide our patients/clients into contact with the wiser deep part of their nature so that the guidance from within can reach their consciousness and aid them in making appropriate decisions and choices.

2. It is not the memory but the emotional charge on the memory that causes the problems. These emotional charges can stem from childhood, uterine states, or past lives.

3. These emotions can be vented, discharged, or expended so that they no longer cause a problem.

4. The deep level of wisdom and insight in the unconscious can be tapped by non-directive hypnotic techniques. The patient can be directed simply to move back through time to find the cause of distress. It is not necessary to give directions specifically to go back to past lives.

5. The clue to adequate emotional release lies in the subject's feeling of comfort or discomfort following the session. If discomfort remains, then the emotions have not been released sufficiently and further work is needed.

## Indications and Contraindications for Use

In my experience, the first requirement is the willingness of the patient. My personal impatience often urges me to premature expression or recommendation. I have learned to wait (reasonably patiently) for the patient/client to ask, or at least to respond positively to a gentle suggestion.

There seems to be no limit to the usefulness of regression therapy for all kinds of problems and for assisting in growth of awareness and creativity. Among the spectrum of presenting complaints that can often be dealt with effectively through regression therapy are panic attacks that have not yielded to more conventional psychotherapy, phobias, allergies, migraine headaches, inexplicable attractions and repulsions, sexual dysfunctions, and persistent guilt.

However, the benefits of regression therapy are really more pervasive and far-reaching than relief from specific problems. Patients learn to see how past mistakes still interfere with their optimum functioning and how they can make new choices to improve the old error-filled record. This therapy is particularly helpful to those who strain against life with an attitude that life is unfair, that in a sense God plays favorites and they are not the favorites. During regression they are led by the understanding that comes to them from deeper levels of their minds to accept themselves and their circumstances. They are also directed by their deeper wisdom to make the choices that will lead to greater awareness, harmony, and creativity. When people stop blaming parents, society, economic conditions, or other influences for their problems and begin to assume full responsibility for themselves, they take a step toward maturity.

The major contraindication to regression therapy is the unwillingness of the patient/client. This form of therapy is an approach wherein open cooperation is strongly linked to effective results. There are some other contraindications. Hypnosis is not appropriate outside of a hospital setting for someone who is clearly psychotic. Drugs, either legal or extra-legal, probably interfere with the effectiveness of hypnotic techniques and also with the ability of the patient to integrate insights. However, I know of no evidence that shows that hypnosis results in harmful effects to the mind or to the body.

# Induction

## Preparation

For the therapist's part the most essential preparation is to have as complete a concept as possible of what a human being is, to be willing to guide rather than to direct the subject during the session, and to remain flexible so that clues given by the subject can be followed at all times. It is important in the beginning to realize that responsibility for the outcome must rest squarely on the subject. The therapist must accept whatever happens as being both appropriate and proper.

As far as the patient is concerned, the first appointment should include a history and a short induction to see how the patient is likely to respond. This first induction may include a post-hypnotic suggestion that in the future, if it is desired (and only then), when I take the patient's left hand in my left hand and count slowly from one to 21, that will be the signal to relax and go into deep hypnosis. This usually works well so that subsequent sessions can be devoted entirely to therapy without having to take the time for a lengthy induction.

## Induction Techniques

There are hundreds of techniques to induce the hypnotic state. Hypnotists choose their favorite or favorites. It does not matter whether one or another method is used if the results are attained. More important than choice of method is an understanding of the process and comprehension that there are deep unexplored areas in every human consciousness.

I prefer a slow, permissive technique. When I am working with one person, I like to take my subject's hand in mine—usually left hand to left hand—and in a low monotonous voice induce deep relaxation. I always intersperse reassuring phrases and reminders that the person is in control and will remain in control and is free to reject anything or everything I say that becomes displeasing, disturbing, or conflict-producing. I add that the deep inner wisdom that is tapped will reject any suggestion that would be detrimental or damaging and will ignore any request for information that is best not known by the subject at the time.

Holding the hand has several advantages. It gives the subject—especially if it is the first experience with hypnosis—a greater sense of security. It also gives me a more accurate measure of the degree of relaxation. I can feel the hand and arm grow limp and heavy and this tells me how rapidly or how slowly the subject is responding. Some will relax very rapidly while others require several training sessions before they allow themselves to relax and respond. When I am working with more than one person at a time, I modify this from necessity. However, lacking hand contact during the induction, I am less able to determine the speed of response and therefore I proceed even more slowly with a group.

My favorite induction method is to ask the subject to close eyes and become as comfortable as possible, with hands unclasped and legs uncrossed. I then give directions to pay close attention to the body, beginning with the toes, and moving the attention slowly up and over the entire body, arms, and head. When sufficient time has elapsed for this to take place, I request that special attention be given to the breathing, feeling the air pass into the nostrils, up through the upper nasal passages, down through the large and small airways all the way to the bottom of the lungs, then to notice how the process is reversed as exhalation takes place. I suggest that the subject now imagine that what is being breathed in is pure relaxation and what is being exhaled is all the tensions, worries, irritations, fears, and pressures from all sources. I suggest that the relaxation that has filled the lungs be carried all through the body and that any tensions that remain anywhere in the body be allowed to flow up to the lungs and out with the exhaled breath.

While this is being done I keep up a steady patter, assuring the patient that he/she is relaxing, getting loose, limp, comfortable, calm, serene, and deeply relaxed. I watch for telltale signs of deep relaxation, such as increased pallor of the skin, slowing of the breathing, or lack of movement in any part of the body. When the subject appears to be deeply relaxed (I prefer using the term "relaxed" rather than "sleepy"), I usually give a few tests of depth. I first lift an arm and drop it. If it falls limply like a wet rag, then I know that deep relaxation has been achieved. I will probably then touch the eyelids lightly, stating that the lids are locked tightly closed. If the lids cannot be opened, I may go on to other tests in the following order: first, the rigid arm that cannot be bent, then the glove anesthesia. These tests serve the purpose of letting me know where the subject is on the depth scale and also letting the subject know that he or she is really in a hypnotic state. Whatever test is given must always be removed before awakening or at a given signal after the subject is awake. If this is not done the patient is likely to awaken in discomfort or feel uncomfortable for several hours after the session ends.

Whatever the presenting complaint, I will suggest, "Now go back to the beginning of this problem. Go back as far as necessary to find the origin and cause of what is troubling you now." The response may be almost instantaneous or may require additional time and guidance. Selection of the specific event is left to the Inner Wisdom's choice. Invariably, each contributing past experience is one of intense emotion, usually of a painful nature. Resistance may be encountered, but force is never used—rather, a gentle but persistent persuasion encourages expression of any emotion being felt.

If there seems to be an inability to find the requested information, it may be helpful to suggest that the subject is in a theater watching something on the screen where the images are appearing or that he is walking down a path in imagination relating whatever is noticed along the path. Another useful fantasy is to guide the subject down a long hallway that has many doors on either side. This method is preferable to directive or commanding hypnotic procedures, and it does not require the assumption of an omnipotent and omniscient position that directs the subject to do whatever the hypnotist decides is best.

Occasionally there will be a patient who resists any of the usual deepening techniques, and for such people it is effective to tell them that I am going to awaken them soon. Then before I awaken them I suggest that they allow themselves to relax as deeply as they can before waking. In this way they seem to bypass the resistance to being more deeply hypnotized because of their expectation of being awakened soon. A post-hypnotic suggestion regarding future sessions, when given at this time, usually becomes effective.

## *Hypnotic Induction*

*Close your eyes and get as comfortable as possible. Uncross your legs and unclasp your hands. Realize that you are in control and will remain in control. You are free to reject anything that I say that is displeasing, disturbing, or produces conflict in you. Your deep inner self will reject any suggestion that would be detrimental or damaging. It will ignore any request for information that is best not known by you at this time.*

*Now give close attention to your body. Begin with the toes. Move upwards to your knees. Allow them to be totally relaxed. Now go upwards towards your hips and pelvis. Feel relaxation moving through them, let the relaxation stream upward to your shoulders. Relax your shoulders and your arms and feel your hands lying limp on the arm of the chair. Move upward to your head.*

*Feel your breathing becoming slower and deeper. Give special attention to your breathing. Feel the air pass into the nostrils, up through the upper nasal passages, down through the large and small airways all the way to the bottom of your lungs. Then notice how this process is reversed as you exhale. Feel the air in the bottom of your lungs move upward, up through the nasal passages, out through your nostrils. Imagine that what you are breathing in is pure relaxation. You are exhaling all the tensions, worries, irritations, fears, and pressures from all sources. Allow the relaxation that has filled your lungs to be carried all over the body. Let tension anywhere in your body be allowed to flow up to the lungs and out with the exhaling breath.*

*You are becoming relaxed, getting loose, limp, comfortable. You are becoming calm, serene, and deeply relaxed. Your lids are locked tightly closed. Now go back to the beginning of this problem. Go back as far as necessary to find the origin and cause of what is troubling you now....*

## Supportive and Deepening Techniques

The most difficult part of regression therapy is the induction. Once the subject has reached a sufficient depth, the work becomes relatively easy. Then all there is to do is the gentle leading or traveling though the memory records to find and reveal the source of the problem. Each response becomes the basis for the next question. Like a meticulous archaeologist, I dig carefully for more information or further clarification. No matter how lacking in awareness a person may be during his usual waking consciousness, he becomes able to tap into great wisdom at deeper levels while in hypnosis. As emotionally charged events are approached, holding the patient's left hand in mine and giving assurance that I am there and will go through it is perceived as supportive. Most of the time that I am tuning in to the patient I am seeing the same scenes that are being described.

The time required to retrieve significant information varies widely. Some patients respond with surprising rapidity. Others may have to be led slowly and patiently to recognize and to describe scenes charged with great emotional pain. The reluctant ones are often helped by imagery techniques. It may become necessary to try two or three such techniques before finding one that is effective.

To move from one scene to another, or from one time period to another, is simple. I suggest that the subject go forward or backward in time to an important happening. Sometimes I count from one to five, saying that at the count of five the pertinent scene will emerge.

Sometimes I ask that the subject give me a signal when the move has been completed. This can be a nod of the head or the lifting of a finger. When the signal is given, or if I notice changes of expression that denote emotion, I will ask a question. "What's happening?" is one of my favorite questions and is totally non-leading and allows complete freedom for expression of anything that has come to awareness.

Although I do not attempt to direct a subject to a specific traumatic event, once such an event has been contacted it is necessary for the patient to stay with it until it is resolved. The re-living of old painful times is facilitated, not by force but by a persistent repetitious persuasion. Patients show increased resistance when the attempt is made to move them to or through a scene too rapidly.

The scene is repeated again and again until all intense emotion has been expended. After one scene is fully described and released, I ask whether there are other experiences that contribute to the problem or symptom under consideration. The patient/subject can easily move forward or backward in time to any such event. It is important to keep the question in present tense since most people actually re-live old traumas. For example, "What is happening?" is a more effective question than, "What happened?"

## *Processing*

### Psychotherapeutic and Transformational Techniques

Once a contributing event has been found and re-lived, I ask if the emotions expressed are still there. If any painful feeling remains, the subject is requested to go back over the entire happening again, adding any details that may have been left out in the first telling. Each time the incident is re-lived and retold, its emotional intensity becomes diminished until finally the story can be related with complete composure. All that remains is a memory; the painful emotion is neutralized and the cause is removed.

I feel it is essential for the patient to contact his/her own inner wisdom and allow that wisdom to give the guidance that is needed at the time. My experience is that this inner wisdom contains the memory of all past experience and functions as a patient and loving teacher or guide, using every opportunity to turn both the conscious mind and the physical body in the direction that they need to go on their journey of increasing awareness and physical health.

Each human psyche contains all the information needed to recognize, understand, and correct any human ill. The task is then simply to probe into the subconscious mind and recover the cause, call it into consciousness, and dissipate the buried emotions that may be attached to it. If the subject is filled with fear, then he or she is led to look for its cause and is provided support and guidance as required in the search.

It is interesting to compare these non-directive methods with more direct methods, which may be effective in removing a symptom but cannot deal with causes of symptoms. When causes are not removed, then symptoms usually recur. Users of directive methods assume that the pain or other symptom is the problem and that direct removal is the purpose of treatment, but in the non-directive method the pain is thought of as a signal of something deeper. Finding and dealing with the cause is the purpose of treatment. The directive method requires more extensive training and education of the hypnotist, who then removes the pain through the use of superior training and knowledge. The non-directive hypnotist is a facilitator who helps the subject discover, understand, and remove his symptoms through the subject's deeper wisdom, knowledge, and power.

This therapeutic attitude is compatible with the psychoanalytic method. It differs in that in the psychoanalytic situation the patient must struggle to bring forth the repressed material slowly and with great effort and without the aid of the hypnotic trance state. In successful psychoanalysis it is probable that deeply repressed material is recalled only when the patient spontaneously enters a hypnotic state. Therapeutic progress with the aid of hypnosis is many times more rapid than is therapy without hypnosis. Hidden memories are revealed more quickly and probably more deeply than in psychoanalytic experience.

There are therapists who resist the inclusion of religious discussion into therapy. I have found it imperative to deal with religious teachings, thoughts, and feelings. Most of my patients' problems have included serious conflicts regarding guilt; confusion regarding right and wrong; fear of punishment in the after-life, of Hell-fire, of isolation, of alienation, of the wrath of God. Such patients lack the inner security and peace that can come from a real understanding of our universe and of our relationship to it and to universal forces. Much fear is related to the overzealous or deliberately intentional use of fear by ministers and priests seeking to impress parishioners with the need for conforming behavior. The result is the production of all sorts of repression of feelings with a consequent clogging or binding up of these feelings along with the traumatic memories.

When strong feelings are long suppressed, communication with our inner selves is prevented. The primary thrust is to re-establish this lost contact with inner thoughts and wisdom. The subconscious mind, when probed, explored, drained of buried painful records, and restored to balance, becomes a source of strength and insight. Digging into areas of repressed feelings and thoughts enables us to purge the emotional charge from these areas. The memories remain when this is done, but the pain is gone.

## Integration into the Psychotherapeutic Process

Much of the integration work is done as past lives are recovered. The learning from each lifetime is examined in the context of the recall. Not all problems are solved as if by magic, but the problems that compelled the patient to seek help, even if not eliminated, can be reduced to a tolerable level. As patients integrate new-found knowledge, these problems fade into the untroubled memories of the past where, like the ripples of a stone dropped into water, they become lost in the larger and more recent ripples of living. Yet, like the ripples that are never really lost but continue to exert their forces, they remain forever a part of the ceaseless movements of the sea of life. These are the substances with which we each build our own eternity.

Past-life work can be interspersed with other techniques such as dream analysis. Through using non-directive hypnotherapy the inner wisdom can be asked to analyze the dream, to recall a dream partially or totally forgotten, or even to present a new dream during the hypnotic session and then give the dream's meaning. Other non-directive hypnotherapy techniques can enhance past-life work and can shorten therapy in any modality or discipline.

## Failures

Since my hypnotherapy is non-directive, and consists of asking questions rather than giving directions, and of leading gently where the patient wants to go, it is designed to avoid or prevent failure.

My principal assumption is that each patient or trainee with whom I work possesses a deep inner wisdom that is far better acquainted with that person than I could ever be and that this inner wisdom seeks to produce optimum growth, awareness, and creativity within the person. My second assumption is that whatever the subject does is "right" for that moment, even if it is nothing. Such an approach may not be necessary for every therapist. I felt that it is necessary for me, however, because I choose to insulate my subjects as much as possible from my overly-developed impatience to see great results and from my tendency to dominate those around me.

I do feel a sense of failure—or rather, dissatisfaction—whenever there has been less dramatic change than I would like to see. However, I also wonder if there would ever be enough symptom removal, resolution of relationships, or growth in awareness to enable me to feel that nothing more could be accomplished. The understanding that all of us are less than perfect while within our earth bodies helps me to accept, with only a mild sense of dissatisfaction, those clients who stop therapy while remaining "unfinished."

# Cases

## Family Karma

Patients often report that people with whom they are involved in the present life have been known to them in other lives. The relationships can change widely from lifetime to lifetime. Experiences reported in various lifetimes support the concept that unfinished business in one life must be finished in a later life with the same people. This is necessary in order to continue to work out various karmic problems. The soul often returns to those it has known before.

### Case 1. Repeating Widowhood

Rose Morgan (not her real name) was a recent widow. Her husband, a Boy Scout leader, had drowned during an outing with the Scouts. She had become deeply depressed and had considered suicide but had discarded the idea in order to care for her four-year-old son. Periods of depression recurred during which she would eat excessive amounts of food. Her weight kept increasing. She had always been heavy but had now become grossly obese.

She had consulted me about a digestive problem, but as I talked with her during the initial interview she revealed the real reason for coming to my office. She wanted help in dealing with her mood changes. We agreed to try hypnosis and ask for inner wisdom. She responded readily to hypnosis and showed little resistance to the material evoked.

During an early session Rose regressed to a former life in which she was very beautiful, ecstatic in her marriage, joyous, living on a warm, peaceful coast. Her husband fished at sea, at first only for short trips, and then for more prolonged periods. Finally one day the boat that carried her husband failed to return. She became totally distraught and inconsolable. She ignored her infant son and became increasingly despondent. She walked along the beach, looking out across the water, hoping for the sight of the boat that she knew would not come. Then she threw herself on the sand and sobbed uncontrollably. One day she walked out into the water to her death.

We reviewed periods of this former life again and again, as I urged Rose to express fully any emotions she had felt. To her, what had begun as a picture viewed from outside became a drama in which she participated fully, complete with all the sensations and emotions originally experienced in that life. With each repeated review the emotions diminished in intensity until she could talk about the incident calmly. Then we asked her subconscious mind to relate that life to her present life.

She realized at once that she was presently repeating the same pattern, with one major difference. In that life she had been beautiful. In this life, though she had pretty features, she was far too heavy to be called beautiful. In her sorrow and despair over losing her husband in the earlier life she had felt that it would have been better not to have known love and then to have lost it. If she had not loved, she would have avoided the hurt of loss, and if she had not been beautiful, she might have been spared the pain. At the end of that life she had vowed never to be beautiful again. However, the vow did not save her from meeting the same entity who had been her husband then, or from loving and being loved as she had been then, giving birth to the same son she bore then, the son whom she had deserted through taking her own life. Again she had been left a widow as before.

After all the old former-life emotions had been dredged up, fully expressed, and the old pressures relieved, she became able to see why the former pattern was repeating. She had given herself a failing grade for her reaction to her earlier widowhood and had chosen to repeat the course. Now she was almost failing again. Through regression she came to a new awareness that she had to learn the lesson of acceptance of loss and that her earlier non-acceptance and suicide had been for selfish reasons. "I don't want to hurt!"

Having gained this insight she became able to accept and live creatively and contentedly. Her weight became controllable. About two years later she met and married a man who suited her well and who became a good father to her son. I followed her progress for several years and was gratified to watch her life becoming full and more joyous. This was a case where, if we had tried to focus on the symptom of obesity, we might have missed the whole matrix in which the symptom was set. Weight problems are often very complex, as in this instance, and are derived from far more extensive maladjustment.

### Case 2. Bonded by Resentment

The wife in this case was a strong, vital, capable professional woman who had no physical complaints and was unaware of her personal contribution to the central problem, which appeared to be totally her husband's. The husband complained of various and sometimes vague symptoms, none of which could be linked with a known disease and which were usually diagnosed as hypochondriasis or imagination. His history included years of difficulty in keeping a job because of frequent absences, and low productivity. He appeared honestly to believe that he was physically ill, and he grew progressively more annoyed at a series of doctors, all of whom failed to locate and treat the cause of his discomfort.

Nor did I, when working with him, find what was causing his problem. He responded only moderately to attempts to use hypnotherapy. His resistance to developing insights about himself was pronounced. We were able to increase his relaxation, diminish his anxiety, and enable him to get to work on time almost every day but his failure to respond to any therapy method I could call upon was discouraging.

After several months of slow progress, it became evident that there was some problem between him and his wife that could not readily be elicited. I asked the wife to come in for a conference and she agreed. When I presented the option of her exploring her own mind using hypnosis, first to obtain direction from her source of inner wisdom and secondly to help understand the family situation, she expressed delight at the possibility. I had only one session with her, for a total time of 90 minutes.

Betty (a fictional name) quickly responded to hypnosis and gave no resistance to whatever was to be found in her memory record. She readily answered all questions and reported a remarkable series of former lives, five in all, each time with the same husband, each time with herself as the stronger partner and her husband weaker.

In one life they lived in a frontier wooded area in a log cabin. There was a forest fire. The husband ran for his life without attempting to save his wife and baby, who perished. In another life, the husband suffered continual miseries while she, strong and capable as ever, cared for him, provided the income, and even did the heavy chores outside.

The other three lives with this man proved to be slight variations on the same theme. In the last scene she described, the husband was sitting in the kitchen with his feet in a bucket of hot water with a warm shawl around his shoulders while she set out into a blizzard to chop wood.

When at the end of 90 minutes she was awakened, she took a long deep breath and said, "Oh, I am so glad we did this. I didn't know until just now that this was my fault." This was a surprising comment after the scenes that she had described. She went on to give her reasons. "I know now what has tied me to this man. I've resented him! I know that as long as I continue to resent, I will continue to be tied. I'm going to get over it this time, because I couldn't take it again."

Betty was delighted with her new understanding and was soon able to appreciate her husband rather than to continue to resent and endure him for the sake of their two children. As her efforts to "get over it" grew more successful, her husband also found it possible to grow in strength. His symptoms diminished and his personality brightened.

This was one instance where allowing my patient's own inner wisdom to emerge paid striking dividends, as my automatic clinical reaction had been somewhat wide of the mark. This experience deepened my own confidence in the ability of each person to find the particular answer that is appropriate and effective for himself/herself. My experience has been that in family relationships it is particularly important to trust the patient's inner source of wisdom to provide insight and suggest a solution because of the multivariant nature of the family interaction, which makes it especially difficult to know what underlies the difficulty.

This case also illustrates the often surprising phenomenon whereby a change in one family member evokes a change in another without apparent insight on that other person's part. It requires, as was true in this instance, that the first person be willing to work toward a change in the hope that the family system will shift to a new balance.

**Case 3. The Origin of a Triangle**

Sudden and strong attractions that may be highly inappropriate often have their source in other lifetimes. Until the strong emotional pressures that have been stored up from these previous lifetimes can be relieved, it is difficult for rational decisions about the situation to be implemented. Kitty Brown dramatically illustrates this dilemma.

Kitty came to me asking me to help her resolve a troublesome conflict. Among her acquaintances was a man for whom she felt intense attraction alternating with equally intense revulsion. Kitty was married to a dependant and somewhat immature man, but she felt content in the marriage and was not seeking out another man. Neither her attraction nor her revulsion to the acquaintance made sense to her. She could find no explanation for either feeling, both of which were becoming so troublesome that she felt she must obtain help to resolve the ambivalence.

The first three sessions with Kitty failed to produce any relevant material. During the fourth session she related feeling herself standing on a hilltop overlooking a valley. She could describe the valley and feel the gentle breeze blowing back her long light brown hair. She also felt deep sorrow. No other details were given.

The following session found Kitty again on the hilltop. She said that she went to the hill because she wanted to think. In the valley was a small village. Session by session she would add details. She lived in one of the houses in the village. She had an illegitimate son, still a baby. Over a number of sessions she revealed that alone with her child she lived as a social outcast shunned by other villagers. The first real breakthrough came during a session when she re-lived a day in which she had gone up on the hill to commune with her inner self while leaving her infant son asleep in his crib as she had done countless times before. When she returned this day she found that the baby had wakened, had left his crib, had crawled across the floor and had fallen face down in the hot coals of the fireplace causing severe scarring. She felt terribly guilty about this accident, which added more weight to the guilt she felt for bearing him out of wedlock. She said she knew there was something more about this house she needed to know. She felt that if she could move to the house and look into the window, she would know what it was.

Several sessions later she was able to approach the house and to look reluctantly into the window. Then she started to scream. She screamed and moaned for several minutes. I calmed her as best as I could.

> T: *It's all right. You can scream about this, but you do not need to be afraid of it. Whatever it is, it is now in the past. Just relax and tell me what you see.*
> P: *(With tension gradually lessening.) I see my body hanging by a rope from the rafters. I see my baby crawling across the floor and reaching up toward the body. I see my real self over in the corner observing the scene and helpless to do anything about it.*

Further sessions filled in further details until the whole story was revealed. Her lover in that life was the man who now both attracted and repelled her. She had loved and hated him then. The feeling stored deep within her memory kept surfacing again and again. The old love was mixed with her distress and agony at being deserted when pregnant and left to fend for herself in a bigoted, narrow, and unforgiving village. The added guilt of seeing her child's scarred burned face left her with no solution, as she thought, except to hang herself. When her real self saw what she had done, that she had not really died but had merely deserted her helpless child, the guilt became even more overpowering.

As a result of our work together, Kitty was able to deal with the love-hate ambivalence and to understand the clinging dependency of her husband, whom she recognized as the child she had deserted in that life. This was one of the most difficult problems brought to me. Kitty had reason to resist knowing her past history.

## Allergies

The treatment of allergies is usually concentrated on a symptom and is therefore contrary to the general trend in regression therapy, which is to examine patterns. However, there is no area where results can seem more miraculous than in the exploration of an allergy. Allergies, and also some phobias and compulsions, seem often to be tied into one specific past-life incident or even a sequence of incidents of a repetitive nature. The relief experienced when these are unearthed is so great that at times such a limited focus seems justified.

**Case 4. An Allergy to Cats**

Allergies to animals are frequent, and the lives that have initiated them are often easily retrieved. They are frequently dramatic, and the remission of symptoms is surprisingly complete. Such a case was D.M., a young woman who could not remain comfortable in the presence of a cat. Her eyes would begin to itch, as would her skin. Then she would experience difficulty breathing. If she remained with a cat for a longer time, she would develop asthma. She liked cats and was unhappy that she could not play with them.

T: *Please now go back through time and find the reason you are having trouble with cats.*
P: *I'm walking.*
T: *Where are you walking? Where are you coming from?*
P: *The camp. Tents.*
T: *What is your appearance? What color is your hair?*
P: *Black.*
T: *Are you male or female?*
P: *I'm male.*
T: *What is your name?*
P: *Orgio.*
T: *How old are you?*
P: *Twenty-eight.*
T: *As you are walking tell us what you are doing and what you see.*
P: *I have a spear in my hand and a shield. I'm hunting.*
T: *What are you hunting?*
P: *Intruders. They're fair-skinned. North. There are a lot of birds. It's very quiet. I've got to be quiet.*
T: *How many of them are there?*
P: *Three dozen. I'm running back to tell my chief that there are intruders down by the river. Then right in front of me there is a tiger. I stop in my tracks.*
T: *What happens next?*
P: *He's lying down looking at me. He's crouched down ready to spring.*
T: *What are you feeling as he looks at you?*
P: *I'm trying to stay calm and figure out a way to get away.*
T: *How close is he?*
P: *Ten yards. He's ready to attack if I move. I stand there a long time and then start moving very slowly to my right. I've got my shield up and my spear in my hand. My chest is hurting so much. I'm almost around him.*

> He hasn't turned and looked at me or nothin'. I'm going to try and run. I'm going to have to do it just right.
> T: Go on. Tell everything that happens.
> P: I'm standing behind him. I stand for a little bit longer so he's not too riled when I leave. I'm waiting (Then she began to breath very heavily and rapidly.)
> T: What's happening?
> P: (Expressing great fear.) He's coming after me. (Then a great outcry of anguish and horror together with a flinging of her body violently back in the chair.)
> T: (Taking her hand.) It's all right. You're all right now. Everything is fine. Go back again to the time when you are walking in the forest and everything is quiet and peaceful.

This was the end of the first description of the incident. It seemed advisable to go immediately into a replay.

> P: (Now speaking calmly.) I'm going to tell my chief that there are strangers going to the river. I'm running. I come to a spot and hear this growling sound and it's a tiger—a huge thing. He's staring at me. I stand and watch him. He's watching me. I stand there for a long time. He's calmed down now. Somehow I gotta get around him. I can't leave very quickly. I move slowly around to my right until I'm around behind him. I wait for awhile. I'm going to drop my shield and spear and run. (Panting breathing again.)
> T: What's happening now?
> P: I'm scared. He's getting closer—and closer.
> T: Keep talking.
> P: He's breathing on me. I'm not going to make it. I'm not... (Another loud outcry but not so extreme as the first one.)
> T: Okay. Let go. (She quickly becomes more calm.) Now what's happening? Where are you now?
> P: I'm watching.
> T: What are you watching?
> P: I'm watching the tiger eat me.
> T: How are you feeling about this?
> P: It's a shame I had to go that way. I was a very good scout.
> T: Where are you watching from?
> P: The treetops.
> T: Is the fear all gone?
> P: (Shakes her head.)

Since there was still some fear, a third recounting became necessary and we went into this immediately.

T: *Let's go through this one more time.*
P: *I'm running and ten yards in front of me crouching down is a tiger. His hair is raised and his ears are up and his eyes are right at me. I stop right in my footsteps. I stand there for a long time lookin' at him—a long time.*
T: *Are you feeling the fear as you tell it this time?*
P: *A little.*
T: *Keep talking.*
P: *I'm frozen like a statue. I keep moving my thumb on my spear to keep me together. I make my decision to go around him. I start off to the right. It takes a long time to get around him. I'm going to drop my things and run.*
T: *Go on. You're running now. Each time you tell it will be much easier for you.*
P: *(Rather calmly.) He's catching up. I can't outrun him (A heavy grunt but no outcry.)*
T: *What happened?*
P: *He tore my back apart.*
T: *Are you still feeling the fear?*
P: *(No response at first.) I'm just sitting there watching him eat me. Face down on the ground. My back is all torn out.*
T: *How are your feeling?*
P: *A good warrior should die in battle.*
T: *Are you still feeling fear?*
P: *A little bit.*

The fourth recount was made without emotion. There was some upset that she had not been smarter at dealing with the tiger, but when this was talked about, she let this go, too.

T: *Is there anything that you have learned from this experience?*
P: *To take my time and be more like a cat when I hunt and try to out-think them before they out-think me.*
T: *Do you need to talk about this incident anymore (She shakes her head.) Is there any other time when you have had big trouble with cats? If there is go back and find it.*
P: *I'm a little girl.*
T: *Tell me all about it.*
P: *My parents have a barn in the back yard. And there is a whole bunch of cats out there. They told me to never get near them.*
T: *What kind of cats?*
P: *All kinds! There's a bunch of 'em out there.*
T: *What's your name?*
P: *Lucy.*
T: *Okay Lucy, tell me about the cats in the barn. What happened?*
P: *My daddy won't let me go out there because he says that they're not nice.*
T: *Do you want to go out there?*

P: Yeah! I want to play with the kitties. They just had a whole bunch of new kitties. I want to go out and play with them.
T: Do you go out there and play with them?
P: Shh! Gotta be quiet.
T: Do you go out there?
P: (Whispering.) Yes, I'm going to go out and look at the kitties. Shhhh. Gotta be quiet.
T: Okay Lucy, tell me what happens.
P: I'm opening up the door and a whole bunch of kitties are there but no big cats are around. I don't know where the mommies are. I'm going' in. Shh. Oh look at em—look at em. Aren't they cute? They're meowing.

Lucy took some of the kittens and put them in her pocket. When she got home she put them in a box under her bed. She planed to feed them with an eyedropper she had retrieved from her father's medical supplies. She didn't tell her parents about the kittens but fed them secretly after her parents had gone to bed.

T: What happens next?
P: I'm gettin' up in the morning. I go down and I have breakfast, and fool around. I'm not old enough to help with any of the chores.
T: How old are you?
P: Ohhh—five?—four—I'm about five.
T: What are you doing now?
P: Thinkin' about gettin' more kitties.
T: Is it about time to do that?
P: Yep. It always gets in the afternoon that Mom starts sewin' and doin' stuff inside. Dad's outside feedin' the horses—so I can go to the barn and get more kitties.
T: Where are you now?
P: Lookin' out the door makin' sure anyone's not around. Gotta be quiet. (Whispering.) I'm going to sneak out the door. Gotta be quiet. Don't make no noise.

She went to the barn and opened the door and was confronted by several mother cats. When she tried to take some more kittens they attacked her.

P: Ooo—They're clawing me all over. Ouch—ooo it hurts. I can't get to the door. They're clawin' me. Ohhh—Why are they doin' that? I'm just tryin' to help them. Owww—oooo.
T: Can you holler for Daddy?
P: I, I, I (stammering) He's not around. Mom and Daddy can't hear me. I'm not supposed to be in here. I can't yell. I gotta get out. Ouch! Owe! Oww—ooo. I'm trying to get to the door. I'm almost there. I open up the door

and I start runnin'. I'm all cut up. I'm bleedin' real bad. My dress is all bloody. I run in to Mommy and I told her that I went to see the kitties.
T: What does Mommy do?
P: She picks me up and holds me. She said, "You know better than that." I said, "I know. I just wanted to see em." And she cleaned me all up and I have scars. There are a couple of big ones on my face.
T: Are you feeling better now?
P: I don't feel very good.
T: Do you still have the kitties in your bedroom?
P: No, I took 'em to Mommy. Then she put me to bed. She said I'm going to have to get a shot or something—or take medicine or something. I don't know. I've got a big long cut down my face. She says that it'll be there for a long time. And the ones on my hands and my legs and my arms.
T: Did Mommy put something on them?
P: Yes, she washed 'em all out and put some ointment that she had on 'em.
T: How do you feel about cats right now?
P: I don't like 'em. I don't ever want to see one again.
T: Are you afraid?
P: Yes!

We immediately re-lived the scene, starting out where she went to the barn the second time to get more kittens. This time she went through the experience with much less affect.

T: Is the fear all gone?
P: Mommy will protect me. Yeah. She'll do sumpthin' about it.
T: Are you sure the cats can't hurt you anymore?
P: I just won't go near them anymore.
T: Are you afraid of cats?
P: Don't like 'em. They're not very nice. They're mean.
T: Is the fear all gone?
P: I'm not afraid. I just don't like em.

After one session on the cat problem, D.M. no longer reacted to cats as she had previously. She was now able to be around them, even holding them and petting them without discomfort. This is an example, not unusual, of the rapidity with which it is possible to remove the cause of an allergy. When the cause is found and the initial emotional charge released through re-living the incident as many times as is necessary for the relief of the emotional tension, the symptom will disappear and will not return.

## Case 5. An Allergy to Cold Water

Marge T. had suffered an unusual reaction to cold water for years. She could not be exposed to cold wetness without reacting violently. The inside of her mouth would swell if she drank something cold. If she held an icy drink in her hand, rinsed her vegetables under cold water, handled frozen food packages, or rinsed her hands in cool water, the skin of her hands would become swollen, cracked and oozing, as well as painful. If she were caught in a rain shower her skin would erupt in great red swollen blotches wherever a rain drop touched her.

She had been to many doctors. The latest (before she came to me in Sacramento) was the University of California Medical School in San Francisco. There she was presented to staff and student classes as a rare case. Her condition was given a name, she was given medication with which she was to inject herself daily, and she was warned of the danger of showering when alone in the house, as cold shower water might prove fatal. The injections helped a little, but she was still required to avoid cold water as much as possible. She was given no hope of recovery or remission of her allergy.

When she considered consulting me she was hesitant, even reluctant. She had heard that my patients sometimes talked of former lives, which was totally contrary to the religious doctrines she had been taught. Therefore, it was not surprising that she reacted uniquely to hypnosis. When I would ask her to find the cause of her illness, she would spend several minutes describing designs—irregular patterns and colors, even disjointed bits and pieces of scenes she might have gleaned from distorted dreams.

Then suddenly, as if the scene had come into focus, she began to describe actual events. During the six sessions I spent with her she re-lived what she said were four different past lives, all of which were traumatically linked with cold water. One was a drowning; another, a near drowning. The third, reported gleefully, was a description of how she (then a galley slave) and others had overpowered the captain of a ship and keel-hauled him. Her glee changed abruptly to dismay when she recognized that captain as the man to whom she was now married. The most dramatic of these lives was one during which she and her four children were on their way to colonial America from Europe in a wooden ship.

As the ship neared shore it struck rocks and began to take on water. She was a good swimmer and was able to swim to shore with two of her children. She stood on the shore watching the ship break up and knew it meant the loss of her remaining two children.

She expressed in the regression all the emotion appropriate to that situation, and only after I helped her re-live this exceedingly painful experience several times did she become able to talk about it calmly. After the final calm, matter-of-fact relating of the incident, her allergy left and did not return.

A few days after the final regression, Marge went trout fishing with her husband in a cold mountain stream without the slightest reaction or discomfort. I saw her regularly for years following her therapy. It was one of her delights to go with me for coffee so that she could show me she could drink from a glass of ice water—something we all take for granted but which she had not been able to do before our work together.

Chapter XVIII

# Edward N. Reynolds, Ph.D.

## *Biographical Data*

**Personal Background**

There are two aspects of my personal development that are crucial to my interest in past lives. One of them was my mother. She was nominally a traditional Christian and her own father was a Methodist minister. I was brought up a mainline Protestant. But what my mother really believed had to do with more esoteric processes. For example, during her life she had believed in Unity and subscribed to its publications. Most important, she had what she considered to be psychic experiences, including what seemed to her to be past-life recall. Another factor that influenced my life was growing up in a college town, Oberlin, Ohio, which emphasized independence of thought and an inquiring, questioning attitude toward dogma.

When I was in high school, the book about Bridey Murphy[1] was published and caused quite a stir. I remained fascinated by it, began to read a great deal about past lives, and found myself drawn into a study of Eastern thought. During my freshman year in college I was drawn to the writings of Aldous Huxley[2] and Gerald Heard[3] and the philosophy of the Vedanta,[4] and later I began a personal relationship with Heard. He was an old man when I met him, but he seemed to possess an infinite curiosity. He was himself a believer in past lives.

Through my graduate school years I took courses in hypnotherapy and hypnosis and began to explore past-life recollections and their relevance to contemporary problems. I became rather taken with the vivid quality of the recollections and the intensity of emotions experienced in past-life recall. At the beginning I had no notion that such recall could have therapeutic relevance; I was much more interested in it from a philosophic point of view.

During the period of my post doctoral studies with Abraham Maslow,[5] I was encouraged to think in new ways about new potentials and possible directions in mental health, but Maslow's skepticism about the validity of past lives caused me to stop pursuing this line of inquiry for a period. After seven years of full-time college-level teaching—five years at Boston College and two years at Evergreen College in the State of Washington—I moved to Los Angeles and combined my interest in teaching with the development of a practice in clinical psychology. Living in Los Angeles in the middle seventies with Southern California's more liberal attitude toward transpersonal matters stimulated and renewed my interest in past lives, particularly in their possible relevance to psychotherapy.

Between 1980 and 1981 I worked with two graduate students in a project designed both to explore past-life memories under hypnosis and to determine what validity could be ascribed to these experiences. More than 30 volunteer subjects were placed in a deep hypnotic trance and meticulous notes were taken of their most recent past-life experience, in the hope of determining the nature of such recollections. As I now know is typical of such explorations, the findings were both complex and contradictory. Much of the material appeared to be a result of projection, and particularly projective identification. However, there was also present some material that seemed truly unexplainable in this form.

From 1979 on, relationships with friends and colleagues who felt that regression work had relevance for the practice of psychotherapy further stimulated my exploration of past lives, both with the goal of better understanding the phenomenon and developing ways in which it might become a therapeutic adjunct. In 25 years I have moved from being a total believer in past lives, to a total skeptic, to having a position somewhere in between. It is undeniable to me that much of what people consider to be past-life recall can more parsimoniously be explained in terms of projection. However, certain experiences remain that are strongly suggestive of the authenticity of true memories from past lives.

One such experience was a 35-year-old San Fernando Valley teacher who under hypnosis explored a life in Victorian London with unusual vividness of detail and precision of information regarding the identification of people involved. An exploration of records in London provided some verification of personal vital statistics as well as validation that my subject had a considerable knowledge of London of that period, in spite of the fact that she had never been there. The agoraphobia which had characterized her in that lifetime, and had also characterized her in this one, totally disappeared following the past-life sessions and has not recurred in the years since then. (See Case 1).

Edward N. Reynolds, Ph.D.

## Personal Past-Life Experience

An examination of my own past lives reveals the presence of a major philosophic thread. The less I have been involved with others, the stronger and clearer this thread appears, so my task seems to be to gain the ability to hold onto this thread while being involved with the world. Also, in looking over these lifetimes, it seems as though I work on one facet at a time, holding onto insight in each facet as carefully as possible while going on to something more difficult. It has sometimes appeared that the earlier lifetimes proved to be more harmonious, but a more careful scrutiny of them shows that these lives held fewer challenges, so that staying centered and philosophical was easier.

In an early life in Rome I found myself as a woman, a poetess, who witnessed Rome's decline and felt both angry about it and powerless to do anything. It was a feminist feeling. I was privileged and educated and had achieved some recognition for my talent, but I felt dissatisfied and started questioning why poetry did not cause people to change their lives; people appreciated what I wrote, but they stayed the same. Yet I harbored a sort of recognition that the decline of my world was really part of the order of things, and that everything occurred in its own time and one had to let go. My relationships, although harmonious, were rather distant ones and I never married. I remained well-to-do and had all the comforts I needed provided for me. It was a perfectly responsible position to be in but without any human closeness. I died of old age. Death was like a leaf falling from a tree, a sort of natural end, serene and harmonious.

I lived a more recent lifetime as an American Indian in the 1400's, in Kentucky, I think. I was part of a hunting tribe whose members also engaged in a little agriculture. Things I now think of as horrible did happen, such as being attacked by animals and disease, and the lifetime included both rest and strain. However, I was involved with a small band of people who cared about one another and lived in harmony with all of life, so any tension became absorbed into the concept that it was all right. My present-day conscious impression of American Indians is very different; it is one of tribal warfare and struggle to survive. In contrast, the past-life experience was rooted in knowing that we were all part of a plan and that the important thing was staying in touch with the Center in sort of Zen-like state. Death and life and loss were not seen as tragic because of our deep integration with nature.

In a Civil War lifetime as an idealistic young soldier, I experienced much more intense interaction with my world, and I could not hold onto my philosophic stance in the face of it. I belonged to a Southern Ohio family with three sons, of whom I was the youngest. We all entered adulthood as the Civil War started, and we were eager to go to war in spite of the protests of our parents. I was 14 and was precipitated into the Battle of Gettysburg. I became horrified by what war was really like; it was much worse than anything I could have imagined. I became separated from my company for a time, and I wandered around hungry and devastated but eventually found my companions. Even though the North won, I had become so disoriented that when I returned home and tried to become a farmer, I couldn't adjust. I died with TB when I was 18, My last thought was that we need to have a peaceful world, but I was still too young to process this concept. Throughout all these lives I remained deeply committed to peace. The lifetime in the Civil War especially influenced me and set my commitment to pacifism. My conviction about our need for peace has become so strong in me during this lifetime that I have converted most of my family to it.

In my most recent lifetime I was the only child of Italian immigrant parents in the late 1800's. My father had worked his way up to being a professor of chemistry at Syracuse University. My mother, however, found herself unable to adjust to the new culture and remained a withdrawn and joyless person. As a child I lived an isolated, unhappy life, marginal, with no satisfaction with my parents and no aptitude for fitting in with people. When later I studied at Syracuse University I did better socially. I was fairly smart and it helped to be in a more intellectual environment, so I felt I had a fresh start in relating.

When I graduated, I didn't know how to move on. I became a perpetual student and hung around the university for another five years, taking extra courses in physics and chemistry. I lived for my girlfriend, who remained my only interest. She grew weary of my extreme attachment and the dependent quality of our relationship, which she felt was neurotic. When she became pregnant, I wanted desperately to get married, but she wanted equally desperately to break away, so I insisted she have an abortion. I did not go with her but instead stayed at home, very worried and guilty. I was waiting for her to come back when I heard an ambulance, and, thinking that she had been killed, I rushed upstairs to my father's lab and took poison. After I died I realized that she was still alive.

In reviewing this lifetime from the after-death state, through tapping into the wisdom I had developed during my other lives, which had been carried on by my basic essence, I realized that my life had remained unbalanced. I projected an intention that in a subsequent life I would understand emotions and become a more caring person. I realized from that expanded vantage point that my own self-centered life in Syracuse had led to a disastrous ending. I had not understood my family's dynamics well enough to see how my own personality had been formed by the unhappiness of that childhood. I needed to understand people more in depth. My intention became a commitment never to be that selfish again. I understood that even suicide had been a selfish thing and that my reason for suicide had not been valid; I had never taken my girl friend's needs and feelings into account. My whole life had been external and superficial.

During the last two lifetimes I was not able to hold onto the philosophic centeredness that I had gained in the earlier lifetimes because the impact of the environment was too strong, so I see my task as being able to do this, to stay centered in the midst of pressure and disaster. Certainly my after-life perceptions of the last lifetime and my wish to understand emotions contributed to my becoming a psychologist in this lifetime.

Past lives are like threads in a skein. All my threads have worked toward increasing my ability to become an integral and competent part of the fabric of humanity with all its stresses and strains.

# *Theory*

## Philosophical Hypotheses

It is difficult to be effective in regression work without some philosophical stance, and a choice must be made between postulates that carry an authoritarian implication and those with a humanistic flavor. In every stage of regression work there is a choice between these two approaches. The contrast between them is salient before the patient ever enters the picture. When I explored possible hypotheses, I found myself returning to two simply stated but profound humanistic assumptions that were first stressed by Maslow:

1. Human beings harbor an innate desire to grow on many levels.

2. Love in some form facilitates the growth process.

## Psychotherapeutic Assumptions

The humanistic approach to therapy, as developed by Carl Rogers and Abraham Maslow, shifted the focus in the therapeutic process from the patient as an object to be "fixed," to the relationship between therapist and the patient as a powerful agent in producing therapeutic results. Nearly half the research in psychotherapy and five years of observing and documenting the process have grounded this shift in focus. In a new modality such as regression therapy, where the dominant legacy comes from the authoritarian approach of hypnotic induction, it is important that these gains in psychotherapy as a total field are not overlooked or lost. The humanistic therapist moves strongly away from classical hypnosis in the formulation of his therapeutic assumptions. Some of the most salient of these follow:

1. The relationship between the therapist and the patient is a crucial dimension of change. As Carl Rogers pointed out, a central dimension in effective therapeutic work is the companionship offered to the patient as he walks into a frightening corner of his life. This relationship appears to be even more significant in regression therapy where the intensity of fears and critical self-judgment can be overwhelming. The real transformation occurs within the energy field between the patient and the therapist.

2. Analysts' models of how to perform therapy interfere with openness to what is actually happening. Through the process of using regression techniques there must exist a great sensitivity on the part of the therapist to the experiences of the patient, above and beyond technical considerations. The good therapist draws on all knowledge in a way that keeps the focus on the patient rather than on the technique. The use of techniques as such seems fundamentally to interfere with the transformation that is sought. In the foreground is the relationship, and in the background are the techniques. Just as humanistic therapeutic principles raise traditional therapy to a higher spiritual plane above mechanistic approaches, similarly an emphasis on caring and sensitivity appears important in maximizing the transformation hoped for in regression therapy.

3. There exists an inextricable relationship between emotional development and understanding.

4. The cathartic aspect of past lives (emotional re-experiencing) seems to play a role in release of tension and possible resolution of conflict. This appears to hold true whether we assume we are working with metaphors or with actual past-life experiences.

5. The cumulative nature of experience is such that until a problem or conflict area is resolved, it recurs in every lifetime.

## Indications and Contraindications for Use

Regression therapy should be used only when the therapist has a relatively complete background on the patient and has evaluated the nature of the problem in more traditional ways. It may be helpful in the following circumstances:

1. For people who have a strong belief in past lives and wish to use regression as a modality to explore present problems.

2. For those for whom it is difficult to formulate the problem in terms of anything that is understood from their present lifetime.

3. For certain people who are blocked.

4. For those situations wherein the origins of symptoms cannot be explained in the light of their present circumstances.

5. For those patients for whom working in the current lifetime leads to superficial results when they need help to further alleviate their symptoms.

The decision to use past-life therapy has to be an emphatic response to the client's sense that it would be a helpful approach and that the origin of the problem is more accessible through this technique.
Contraindications are:

1. For people who have psychotic or borderline symptomatology.

2. For those who are clearly trying to flee the necessity to explore problems in this lifetime.

3. For those in crisis who need traditional methods of patient-therapist support.

# *Induction*

## Preparation

The general objective in the preparation for regression therapy is the development of good rapport and a working alliance that seems solid. Once this relationship has been established, familiarization with deep relaxation and light to moderate levels of hypnotic states is also helpful. An open discussion of the beliefs and assumptions that the patient holds regarding past lives, as well as disclosure regarding the therapist's own views, is also a desirable preliminary step. Since regression sessions often cannot be contained within the traditional 50-minute hour, it is advisable that sufficient time be available at the end of each session to discuss the content.

## Induction Techniques

I believe that hypnotic trance is the most effective method of working with past lives, and I use the traditional inductions that are thought to promote deep trance, often using ocular fixations, such as a candle, or hand levitation and similar traditional procedures. At times techniques that draw on guided imagery and autogenic procedures are effective. I take a good deal of time for the induction. I play a fairly authoritarian role in the process of guiding a person into a deep hypnotic state, even though generally I am not an authoritarian person.

### *Classical Hypnotherapy Induction*[6]

*Let us start by having you focus your attention on this candle. (Lighted candle is nearby.) As you focus on it you will be aware that your eyes are getting heavy. Your whole body is beginning to relax. As your eyes close you will be drifting into a state of deep relaxation.*

*We might start with a few autogenic sentences to help you relax even more deeply. If you are willing, I'd like to begin by focusing on your right leg. The sentence is, "My right leg is heavy and warm." Just listen to me and say the sentence along silently to yourself.*

*My right leg is heavy and warm (repeated 10 times).*
*My left leg is heavy and warm (10 times).*
*Both of my legs are heavy and warm (10 times).*
*My right arm is heavy and warm (10 times).*
*My left arm is heavy and warm (10 times).*
*My arms and legs are heavy and warm (10 times).*
*My entire body is heavy and warm (10 times).*

*My forehead is cool (10 times). Visualize a very gentle, soft light right behind your forehead. Let it become brighter and clearer as you go into a state of deep relaxation, which is the ideal preparation for our work together.*

*My stomach is warm (10 times).*

*You are safe and protected in every way. As I count back from 19 to one you will feel increasingly relaxed, safe and protected. 19...18...17, etc.*

*You are safe in every way. Let your thoughts move back in time. You are safe and relaxed, quiet and comfortable. Move back to a very quiet and happy time, a time in the past year. Let your thoughts move back in time. Let* yourself enjoy again a pleasant time in the past year. Relax very deeply. And when you are ready, let those thoughts dissolve. Let those memories disappear.

Letting yourself relax, move back in time to a happy time in your early twenties. A pleasant memory, a relaxing, pleasant time in your early twenties.

When you're ready, feeling safe and relaxed in every way, let your thoughts move back in time to your childhood, to a pleasant, happy time in your childhood. Just accept whatever the unconscious gives you as a memory or an impression. (Pause)

Feeling safe and relaxed in every way, let those thoughts dissolve. Let yourself move back in time to that comfortable period of total relaxation and safety when you were still in your mother's womb. Feeling totally safe and relaxed, recover that feeling of well-being. (Pause) Remember that at any time you can return to this place of peace and calm and safety.

Now, letting your thoughts move back in time still more, move to a significant incident in the lifetime before your present lifetime which will help us understand the issues we spoke about. (Name core issues which have been discussed.) Safe and protected in every way let the unconscious take you back to a time that will shed some light on those issues. When you begin to get an impression, let me know what comes to mind.

## Supportive and Deepening Techniques

Hypnotized people are highly responsive to subtle nuances of language so that it is important to be soothing and to give maximum support throughout the process. I try to use images and language that have been identified as particularly useful and helpful to the individual patient. For instance, some people feel threatened by going into a "deeper trance" because the word "deep" suggests "death," so words such as "more profoundly relaxed," which seem stilted for some people, work better for these patients. Avoiding language that the individual has identified as jarring seems to deepen the trance.

When questions are presented in clear and preferably either/or fashion, the trance is not disturbed, in contrast to open-ended questions. It helps to start with more descriptive issues, rather than those involving affect. What I generally do during the first session is to get an overall picture of the total past-life experience. In subsequent sessions we work on specific problem areas, in order to better understand the issues that were dealt with and the relevance of each experience as it pertains to the current lifetime.

I work almost exclusively with memories of the most recent past lifetimes until the material presented is resolved. If there is an indication at that point, I may go on to the lifetime preceding. I always assure the person that he can discontinue the experience anytime he chooses. I structure ahead of time a safe place, such as the mother's womb or a particularly happy memory, where the person can go if he becomes disturbed or exhausted.

# *Processing*

## Psychotherapeutic and Transformational Techniques

For me the foundation of past-life therapy is Rogerian—unconditional positive regard and congruence—and helping that to bear on material that might be frightening and strange. I try to pace the sessions so there is initially an overview of a past life. I try to create an atmosphere that is essentially unrushed in its exploration of past-life memories that the patient sees as important. I have found that emotional release seems to play a part, and I offer support, encouragement, and reassurance during these times.

Routinely I ask about relationships in past lives in terms of their relevance to relationships in this time and what possible karmic issues are present to be resolved. I have found it helpful in instances of extreme distress or anger to trace the origins of those emotions to the context of a past life, and I have found that frequently release comes with understanding. Many times this cannot be done in one session but is worked on over a period of time.

In considering what effects a positive change in a patient, it appears that support helps people face frightening aspects of their lives. This support plays a role in helping them examine and resolve material from a past lifetime, much as it does in the present. Being accompanied and supported by a non-judging companion often allows a person to look at how harshly he has judged himself, even without knowing the long series of specific events that have perpetuated this attitude of self-judgment. Freedom from the distorting effects of intense emotion and self-judgment helps a person to gain a clearer perspective on past events and relationships. This increased perspective can be generalized to significant people in this lifetime who have been involved in unresolved issues in past lives, where they may have played different roles.

## Integration into the Psychotherapeutic Process

There is always a discussion at the end of each session about the meaning of the material, and in these discussions it is never assumed that the experiences are either real or metaphorical—that is left up to the patient's belief system. These discussions center on the relevance of underlying themes from past-life memories to current-life problems. Sensitivity to the client always entails protecting him from feeling overwhelmed and giving him control over the content that is to be worked on in any session. Sufficient closure after a potentially successful session is equally important. Patients need to talk about what happens in a session. This time of discussion is important, both to integrate new information and to attain a sense of emotional synthesis. I try to do a thorough exploration of past-life material when it is presented, and I generally return to it in future sessions only when the patient initiates it.

## Failures

I seldom have failures because I use regression therapy with discrimination and not until I feel that a patient is entirely ready, that the problem is clear, and that the regression work promises an added dimension of insight. I particularly eliminate ahead of time any exploration of past lives by patients who want to avoid problems in this life. Also, I watch my own enthusiasm and do not let it precipitate a regression that the patient does not really want.

In spite of this, failures sometimes occur. An example that comes to mind is a very creative and imaginative young woman who was well prepared for regression work and gave elaborate and detailed accounts of various lifetimes, but the quality of what she produced had the flavor of a creative writing project. There was little affect, and little insight emerged as a result of our past-life explorations. It was as though she remained in a closed room.

# Cases

## Conventional Clinical Pathology

In regression therapy it is usually more appropriate not to focus on specific symptoms. However, in certain cases there seem to be exceptions to this general guideline. Such exceptions are cases in which the symptoms turn out be connected to specific traumatic events, either in early childhood or in past lives. When more general approaches have not proven effective, early childhood or past-life exploration of the symptoms to determine their underlying connections is often a rewarding approach.

The following cases failed to yield to more conventional approaches and regression work was initiated.

### Case 1. Agoraphobia

The patient, a 35-year-old married mother of three children, lived in the Los Angeles area. She sought treatment for a vague cluster of symptoms, including periodic but mild feelings of anxiety and mild agoraphobia. Traditional explorations of a possible cause of her agoraphobia proved fruitless. This patient, while a member of the Catholic faith, also held a belief in reincarnation and suggested that the modality of regression therapy be attempted. After a session in which there was exploration of the nature of past-life therapy techniques and the patient's beliefs about past lives, she was placed in a deep hypnotic trance in which she was asked to recall the lifetime immediately preceding the present.

She found herself as a frightened six-year-old in Hyde Park in the 1900's. She appeared to be in the grip of such terror and anguish that some thought was given to taking her out of the hypnotic state.

P: *Why doesn't my daddy move? I want him to move (very distressed).*
T: *Tell me what is going on as if you are watching it in a movie.*

In a more calm voice the patient then described that she and her parents were taking a ride in the park.

P: *I dressed just like my momma. It was such fun but the horse was frightened by another horse.*

She was instructed again to become the observer. In spite of her distress, moving out to the position of observer seemed to relieve her enough so that we could proceed cautiously and gradually uncover the outline of what she believed that life to be. Apparently she was the only child of a prosperous merchant and his wife and accompanied them on a Sunday outing. There was a serious carriage accident that immediately killed the father and left the mother seriously injured. The mother died two months later, and the child was taken to an orphanage run by Anglican nuns, where she remained until age 16. This orphanage appeared to have been an unusually secluded and almost cloistered environment.

At 16 she left to care for two children of a businessman whose wife was seriously ill. After the wife's death she continued to care for the children and eventually married their father. The marriage appeared to be primarily one of convenience and it provided her with little love. Her seclusion continued and became further complicated by drug use, either through contacts her husband had to procure opium or through medical treatment. She died suddenly, without prior illness, of a heart attack at the age of 47.

We covered the general dimensions of the lifetime during the first session and reviewed each part, segment by segment. During the second session we explored recollections of the time in the convent school, a period filled with hard work and devotion. Even at that time she experienced great anxiety whenever she ventured outside. This anxiety had been present ever since the time of the accident, primarily because the presence of horses in the streets reminded her of the loss of her parents. Her sense of anxiety intensified when she realized that she was going to move into a new home with her husband—leaving her safe convent haven was very difficult for her.

P: *It's frightening to have to go outside. There are horses in the streets.*
T: *Why is that important?*
P: *You'll never know what they'll do.*
T: *Why does that upset you so much?*
P: *Because they killed my parents.*
T: *Let's talk about the connection between going out of the house and the pain you felt when your parents died.*
P: *(Crying.) My life was never happy after that. No one ever loved me again.*

This was the second day's work. We spent the entire next session in further exploration of the connection between the fear of going out of the house and the experience of the loss of her parents so suddenly and at such an early age. One of the last sessions explored her death in that lifetime.

P: *I am having normal afternoon tea when my cup falls out of my hand and I see my body on the floor.*
T: *What are your feelings when this happens?*

P: Surprised but in many ways very relieved.
T: Move away from surprise to the point of understanding the meaning of that lifetime.
P: Yes.
T: What were the major lessons you were working on then?
P: To understand about love and fear.
T: Did you gain the understanding you needed?
P: It's not really resolved but I know more than I did at the beginning.
T: What's the meaning of those experiences for your present lifetime?
P: I've got to let go of the fear of loving people.
T: Is there anything else?
P: Taking risks in life is not nearly as painful as always living in fear. I need to do more of that—taking risks.

We worked with this material over eight sessions. Time and care were given to the particular emotional aspects, without using desensitization through repetition. The therapeutic agent was assumed to be the supportive stance that made it possible for her to explore this material. During this period there were times in her normal waking state in which there was mild discomfort, which she associated with the past-life memories. By the conclusion of this series of sessions, however, all symptoms of agoraphobia were absent and six years later they have not returned. Another behavior change that occurred after the therapeutic work involved her attitude toward taking medicine. Her lifelong resistance disappeared entirely, a change that she ascribed to dealing with the opium addiction of that earlier lifetime.

Several years after this regression I spent some time in London, and while I was there I checked on some vital statistics the patient had disclosed. I did find the record of a child born with the name she had reported, and in the year that she said was that of her birth. The name was not an unusual one, but it was interesting that the birth occurred during the assumed birth year. I also found a record of an Anglican orphanage and school with the name the patient had reported and in the part of London in which she said it had been located. It was no longer in existence, but there were records of its functioning during the time that the patient felt she had been there. I did not find a record of her death in the year that she said it had taken place, but this is possibly because I had not asked her married name.

### Case 2. Cigarette Addiction

The patient was a 28-year-old married woman living in Ohio, mother of one daughter. She sought treatment as an aid to overcoming a five-year cigarette addiction that violated her convictions about good health practices. Because of her orthodox Protestant beliefs, no thought was given to the possibility of using past-life therapy in her treatment. However, what appears to have been a spontaneous past-life regression contributed to overcoming her present problem.

In the process of exploring the history and the emotional significance of her cigarette smoking she spontaneously recalled a past life in which she had been a teacher in a one-room country school in Kentucky in the 1840's. It appears that that lifetime was a fairly happy one and relatively uneventful until her traumatic death as a result of typhoid fever. She re-lived this experience with much emotion, describing the tremendous relief she felt at the time of her death. In this current lifetime she had begun to smoke cigarettes after the birth of her daughter, during which she had nearly died of complications. She claimed to have been reminded of her death from typhoid in the other lifetime. I then put her under hypnosis to see if we could determine the connection.

> T: *How long have you smoked?*
> P: *I smoked occasionally for a short while when I started college, but I really became addicted to cigarettes after my daughter was born.*
> T: *Why do you think it happened?*
> P: *(Evasively) I guess I was just bored. (Pause) No, actually the smoking started because I was feeling a lot of anxiety about what I went through when Susan was born. I was in terrible pain and afraid of dying.*
> T: *Let's explore where the anxiety really began.*
> P: *(In great anguish) I'm on fire. Someone please help me!*
> T: *Are you in a fire?*
> P: *No, I'm sick. I have the fever.*
> T: *What kind of fever?*
> P: *Typhoid fever.*
> T: *Leave that and go back to a happier time in that lifetime.*

The patient then moved back to a time during her uneventful and relatively benign earlier years.

> T: *You're gradually coming back to the present moment but you are remaining deeply hypnotized. You're calm and relaxed, but you will remain in a deep hypnotic state until we decide our work is finished for the day. What do you think is the meaning of what you just experienced?*
> P: *That kind of fear was what I felt when Susan was born, that feeling of being close to death. Smoking seemed to push it away.*
> T: *How did it push it away?*
> P: *I guess I was so terrified that I needed a pacifier, and memories of my father in that other lifetime smoking his pipe by my bedside comforted me. Now I see that kind of comfort can't push away death.*

Following this session, the patient realized that smoking was associated with the comforting presence of her father. Her desire for cigarettes disappeared and has not returned during the eight years subsequent to the experience. Immediately following this session, the experience seemed to the patient to be an authentic recollection of a past life. However, a week later she dismissed it as sheer fantasy.

## Resolving Difficulties in Relationships

All therapists working with relationships have encountered cases that do not respond to traditional intervention for reasons that appear mystifying. In these difficult cases past-life work can often yield deeper insight into the tangled nature of the relationships.

**Case 3. Fear of Men**

This patient was a 40-year-old clinical psychologist who was concerned about her relationships with men. She had grown up in a strict religious group in the East, a Mennonite family, and had felt oppressed and restricted as a woman in a male-dominated cult. Vowing not to repeat the restrictive life patterns of the women in her family, she fled to a more liberal-thinking college in her late teens and followed this by living for several years in Europe. Her interest in studying medicine was replaced by intense interest in psychology as a result of being exposed to feminist thinkers, and she completed a Ph.D. in this field in the late 1970's. Her personal relationships with men were limited and unhappy, though she seemed able to sustain warm and intimate relationships with women friends. After many years of traditional psychotherapy, including several years of clinical analysis, she was still troubled by her difficulty in relating to men and sought past-life therapy as a method of exploring this problem in a different way.

I used a classical induction, including establishing a beautiful spot in the desert as a safe place to return to if she needed to do so.

The patient rapidly found herself in a state of terror, feeling that she was being pursued by a group of angry men. She realized that she was male in that lifetime and was living somewhere on the west coast of Africa.

P: *They're going to get me. I just can't get away (very agitated).*
T: *Who is going to get you?*
P: *The men with clubs. They followed me to the big water (Starts shaking violently and crying.)*
T: *What's happening now?*

P: *(No response but more crying.)*
T: *Imagine you're looking at it on a movie screen and just describe it without emotion.*
P: *(Unable to do this.)*
T: *Would you like to come out of this for right now?*
P: *Yes.*
T: *Let your thoughts go to that beautiful spot in the desert where you used to camp. (Pause.) Now on the count of five, feeling fully refreshed and alert, awaken in the present moment.*
P: *I was so terrified.*
T: *What was going on?*
P: *I don't really know but I felt as if I had been pursued for many days by people who wanted to do me harm. They might have been slave traders but I'm not sure.*
T: *Do you want to do more work on it today or resume it in our next session?*
P: *Let's wait until our next session.*

I initiated the next session by taking the patient to the beginning of that lifetime that had been so frightening. She suffered from severe physical defects and when she came to the time of initiation into manhood, her father, as the spokesman for the group, informed her that she would never really be a man and could not go through the initiation rite. This led to denunciation of her father's authority.

P: *It's not right.*
T: *What isn't right?*
P: *They're all against me.*
T: *What do you mean?*
P: *My father doesn't take my side. (To her father) You're wrong. I am a man. I was born to be the chief and I'm going to be the chief (yelled out with vehemence).*
T: *What's happening now?*
P: *They're all chasing me but I get away.*

During this session the patient recovered many additional impressions. Her physical handicaps had been the result of being mauled by an animal as a young child, and she had never felt fully accepted. The group had constantly told her that she would never be a man in their eyes, and her father only reflected the general attitude of the whole tribe. She violated a tribal taboo when she resisted her father's decree. She was pursued for many days and was eventually captured, clubbed to death, and thrown into the ocean.

It was the patient's impression that the vengeful father of that lifetime was the stern, fanatic, rejecting father of her present lifetime. This understanding was accompanied by a flood of tears and deep catharsis when she voiced it in the therapy session. She also felt that though her fear of involvement with me stemmed from her troubled relationship with her father in this lifetime, its origins were truly in the past life that she had recalled in this regression.

This belief led her to use a variety of techniques in order to resolve this deep wound. The Intensive Journal technique was used for a time, followed by a couple of months of Jungian therapy. Within a three-month period the patient visited her family and attempted to resolve with her father many of the conscious conflicts that had stood between them. While this was not wholly successful, in attempting to clear up the problems of their relationship she experienced a feeling of great relief just from the attempt, and gradually she began to include more male friends in her adult life. She was now able to separate the problems of her childhood from the overlay of fear that had come from the other lifetime when her father had wanted to murder her. Within a year of this past-life work she established a committed relationship with a man, and this relationship has continued up to the present.

**Case 4. Ambivalence toward Mother**

This regression was with a 40-year-old legal secretary, Janice, who was divorced and living in Los Angeles with her 12-year-old son. Before becoming a legal secretary she had been an actress, and at the time of the regression she was in training to become a psychologist. Her problem had to do with a lifelong antagonisitic relationship with her mother. When she was away from her mother she could see her as a basically kind, intelligent, and empathic person, but when she and her mother interacted she felt overpowered by feelings of resentment, anger, and a conviction that her mother had let her down. During her childhood she had had an especially close relationship with her father, but she had never trusted her mother, though she could not put her finger on anything that her mother had done that was injurious and that could justify this lack of trust.

She went back to a lifetime as a little girl in Connecticut in 1870 with a widowed mother who was trying to keep up a rundown tobacco farm. (Later research showed, to my surprise, that tobacco was grown in Connecticut at that time.) She started out with a good relationship with her mother, but the mother was ill from the time of her birth.

When the child was five years old her mother began to deteriorate from TB. The little girl became frightened and endeavored to nurse her mother back to health. During the regression the patient remembered making tea in a special way that her mother liked, but the mother's health kept on declining until she became too weak to leave her bed. The two were destitute by this time and survived only with the help of the neighbors. One day the mother asked her to make a cup of her special tea. Before the child could return, the mother died.

> P: *(In the tone of a small child) Here's your tea Momma!... She's so still. (Screams) Drink your tea. Momma!...She's dead. (Deep sobbing) I made it just right! (Continuous crying.)*
> T: *What are you feeling?*
> P: *She left me all alone (beginning to be angry)! I made it just the way she liked it!*
> T: *Did she leave you on purpose?*
> P: *(Angry and sad) I did just what she told me and she died anyway.*

Janice stayed beside the bed for two days before she and her dead mother were discovered. There was no option for her other than to enter an orphanage. She felt abandoned by her mother and determined that she would never trust anybody again. When she was 14 she was taken from the orphanage to work as a maid for a wealthy family. She made no real friends and died in 1917 in the flu epidemic.

> T: *Go to the time of your death in that lifetime.*
> P: *I am sick. I get sick suddenly. I can't work. I have to stay in my room. I get worse and worse until I die.*
> T: *What do you feel at the time of your death?*
> P: *Relieved.*
> T: *What is your last thought as you leave your body?*
> P: *Now I can find my mother again. I have missed her so much.*

Out of the regression this patient realized both why she had wanted to attack her mother and why she was afraid to do so. She soon found out that she was able to invite her mother to visit her from the East and later had her come and live with her. Currently the relationship is a completely comfortable one. The change probably came about because what had been unconscious became conscious, and with that, a certain freedom was restored. The anguish of a child's feeling of abandonment at the time of the mother's death was perceived in a new light and from an adult perspective. The anger on the top could be skimmed off, and the longing and love could finally emerge.

# Chapter XIX

# Barbara Findeisen, M.F.C.C.

## Biographical Data

**Personal Background**

I was born and spent a rather uneventful childhood in the balmy atmosphere of southern California beaches and orange groves. During those pre-smog days one could see the snow-capped mountains behind San Bernardino, and from a hill behind our house we could sometimes look across Los Angeles to the Pacific Ocean. World War II was being fought—a time of gas rationing and food coupons, of older brothers and some fathers in the service, a time of feeling united, and also shaken up when our gentle Japanese neighbors were considered dangerous to national security.

My parents had grown up in New England and had brought with them to more free-thinking California their puritanical work and social ethics and even the Bostonian cuisine of baked beans soaked on Friday and baked on Saturday. Counteracting their influence was that of my maternal grandmother, a student of New England transcendentalism, who lived with us until she died when I was seven. She read me metaphysical books and left them to me when she died. Still another trend in my life lay in my aptitude for dancing. I know now that I had been a dancer before and that was why I never had to practice and even as a child performed in various places, such as the USO's, but this lifetime was to have another purpose. Also from earlier lives came a proclivity for religious experience, at first in a Protestant Sunday school, then later in Christian Science, which resonated strongly with my grandmother's New Thought.

After high school I enrolled at Stanford and almost immediately stopped dancing, feeling that I was being drawn instead into a life of service, though at first I did not know just what. I tried teaching, and through this I was assigned to the woman who in a sense became my "master teacher," Lucille Nixon, the first Westerner ever to win the emperor of Japan's haiku poetry contest and the co-editor of *The Choice is Always Ours*.[1] All along my way I met master teachers of various kinds, often hidden in ordinary clothes and occupations—a dance teacher, an elementary school teacher, a friend, an enemy.

Meanwhile, my life moved along on two tracks; first, the conventional feelings; second, a subtler, almost imperceptible transpersonal road. Just before beginning my teaching experience in Palo Alto, I married and within a few years had a house, two sons, and a daughter. But into the conventional process of life an old thread of transpersonal thinking returned when I heard Edgar Cayce's son talk on TV about reincarnation. "Of course!" I thought, much to my surprise. From then on I read and thought about this area, but it remained separate from the working part of my life until years later. Meanwhile, as my children grew, my husband and I became involved in the community, working with teenagers, families, and groups toward peace. Five years later I went through a divorce, my "dark night of the soul." During these years I returned to school, this time to study psychology and complete my training and licensing as a Marriage, Family, and Child Counselor.

During my training in psychology I worked with Gestalt, Jungian, Freudian, Reichian, psychodrama, and primal therapy approaches. After graduation, as I began my experience as a therapist, I found past-life memories and memories of birth and the uterine world spontaneously occurring, but at first I accepted them more as metaphors than realities. The shift to practical application of them required further investigation and training, so I studied with Dr. Morris Netherton and Dr. Edith Fiore. With them I found that birth and uterine memories, as well as past lives, contained keys to neurotic patterns.

Throughout those early years of the seventies I found very few colleagues with whom I could discuss pre- and peri-natal psychology, let alone past-life therapy! My own uterine and past-life recall had jolted me into an arena for which I had no formal educational training, and much of what I was learning and experiencing conflicted with my university education. I found that either I had to deny this personal experience of myself and others or greatly expand my model of consciousness. Since I could not deny what I had experienced, I chose to incorporate the new parameters into my model, and I began to seek and find other professionals with whom to share and learn.

In 1982 I became an active participant in the formation of the Association for Past-Life Research and Therapy and I have been involved with this group ever since. Shortly afterward I attended the first North American Conference in Pre- and Peri-Natal Psychology in Toronto, and the organization *IPPANA* was formed at that gathering, largely as a result of the work of Dr. Thomas Verney, author of *The Secret Life of the Unborn Child* (1981). It remains rewarding to join others who are exploring these realms of consciousness, to share with them how these areas affect us, and to work with them in a therapy setting.

Throughout the past 10 years I have videotaped many sessions and gathered data in the pre- and peri-natal area. In the summer of 1986 some collaborators and I made a film documentary, "The Journey to be Born: An Introduction to Pre- and Peri-Natal Psychology," which combined clients' regressions and interviews with international experts. This film was shown at the Congress of Pre- and Peri-Natal Psychology in Austria in September of 1986 and at many other conferences. It is my hope that through materials such as our film an impact will be made which will expand consciousness and extend opportunities for people to become free of negative echoes from the past, whatever that "past" may be.

Any personal background summary would be incomplete without including two other powerful influences in my life. In 1976 I attended a seminar on what was originally called the Fisher-Hoffman Process, developed by Dr. Ernest Pecci and Robert Hoffman.[2] Since then I have been teaching and growing with that tool, which I call the STAR process (Self-Analysis Toward Awareness Rebirth), a powerful experience designed primarily to clear repressed material from childhood, beginning with the prenatal period.

The second influence has been my work in Sweden. In 1977 I was invited to go to Stockholm to lead a STAR group and practice therapy, and this experience became a further vehicle for teaching and learning and loving, challenging me to risk, to grow, to give, and to receive. A part of my heart will always be in Sweden, my second home.

Currently, the core of my teaching, workshops, and practice is at the Pocket Ranch, our center in Healdsburg, California.

## Personal Past-Life Experiences

Looking at one's biography in the light of one's past lives is much like looking at an entire landscape—horizon, sky, hills, fields, and flowers—as opposed to looking at one small patch of flowers narrowly focused through a camera lens. There have been a number of trends and aptitudes in my life which, from the standpoint of this life alone, are inexplicable but from the broader context of many lifetimes form definite and understandable patterns.

One of these trends is my attraction to a spiritual life, hard to understand from the limited perspective of my essentially non-spiritual family.

However, regression work has unveiled lifetime after lifetime spent in spiritual disciplines. In a comparatively early lifetime in Egypt I was given to a temple to be raised, and my duties included both dancing and caring for flowers. Later, I spent a lifetime in Greece as a gifted oracle who marred her talent by displaying a possessive and insanely jealous temperament which caused the death of the man she loved.

I lived many lifetimes in Catholic orders, one as a mother superior in a French convent during the Black Plague. When I had no more to give, I willingly died of a heart attack. After recovering that lifetime I had to explore further back to find the origin of my compulsions to give to the point of bodily sacrifice. I found two terrifying lives, one among the Incas and another in Egypt, where to be sacrificed was regarded as a great honor. Then later I uncovered a life as an American Indian shaman where I misused my powers, was found out, and died by being skinned alive, a death which left me with great caution in the use of power, so much so that in this lifetime I prefer to *not* be special or be singled out or honored in any way. In fact, any special attention makes me acutely uncomfortable. In my work as a psychotherapist I emphasize the empowerment of my clients and I stay away from anything that feels like a misuse of my position to control or manipulate.

Another pattern in my life which I have explored in therapy is that of the nature and consequences of, and the reason for, the emotional neglect by my unemotional and unaffectionate Yankee parents. I often wondered why I chose them. The answer came to me during two separate regressions, one involving my father in another lifetime and the other involving my mother. In the lifetime with my father, he and I had been Masai warriors. One time in battle my father risked his life to drag me to safety, and then he cared for me in his hut (he was not my father in that lifetime, only a fellow warrior). I behaved with bitter and ungrateful complaining. During my recuperation, the hut caught fire and I died, loudly expressing blame that he had not rescued me a second time. In the present lifetime the roles were reversed and I gave affection to a father who, as I had in that other lifetime, felt unable to receive it. Understanding the karmic rightness of this, I became able to accept him and even to care for him deeply without needing return of my affection, to be with him tenderly when he died, and to mourn his passing. Perhaps the pattern is now worked through enough so that we can share a lifetime in which we both care.

My mother in the other lifetime had been a nun in a convent in the Middle Ages. I, in that life, was a deformed male child, homeless and abandoned. She found me and took me into the convent, though it was against the rules, and she hid me and fed me and cared for me for several years. The only thing I cared about was that she fed me, and when she died, I was angry and felt no compassion for her or gratitude for what she had tried to do for me. In this lifetime I devoted my childhood to trying to make things up to my mother, dedicating myself to making her happy. True, this was a neurotic pattern, but it was also a karmic healing that I needed. The patterns, debts, vows, and incompleteness from earlier lifetimes, such as this need to make my mother happy, had to be brought into my conscious awareness so that the compulsiveness in my character could be released. Also, forgiveness, especially of oneself, frees one from the need to repeat one's history.

I have also looked at talents, aptitudes, and attractions that have grown from roots in other lifetimes. My aptitude for dancing, which I mentioned earlier, had its foundation in earlier lives as a dancer, once as a temple dancer in Greece and again in the 1900's where I lived life as a dancer. But when an aptitude is well lived out, it serves no purpose for it to be repeated; in this lifetime I knew I had to let it go and move on. I felt drawn into the new consciousness, aware that an evolutionary shift had begun to happen in humanity. I felt that the current age would be one either of destruction or of healing, and that I had to remain on the side of healing. I knew, also, that one must first begin with one's own healing.

My past-life history, like all others, is long, filled with drama, pain, struggle, boredom, wars and joys, times of spiritual awakening, times of sacrifice and martyrdom. All that matters about such lifetimes is what we learn from them. When we have truly learned, we do not have to repeat the pattern anymore. Now is the time to learn from the lessons from the past and use them to find a better way of living together on the planet.

One specific forward thrust in consciousness that has come to me as the result of regression therapy is the melting away of prejudices. How can I be prejudiced against men when I have been a man? Against Catholics, when I have been a nun? Against blacks when I have been a black? I have wailed at the wall as a Jew. I have spun prayer wheels in Tibet. I have been an untouchable in India's masses. I have lived the life of a French aristocrat, attending the queen. I have spent long, tedious, dusty, and uneventful lives, such as when I labored at a monastery copying books. So I cannot reject one who is like a part of my own past and thus a part myself. In loosening the bond of prejudice we make way for peace and a better earth.

# Theory

## Philosophical Hypotheses

1. Within each of us is a fragment of the whole, and each fragment reflects the whole (one of Pribram's holographic theories).[3]

2. Each fragment carries with it all that we need of truth and guidance to experience ourselves fully. We have within us all we need for our own healing.

3. The self does not begin at birth or conception, nor does it end with death. Life is like a string of pearls, the self being the thread and the pearls side by side are life experiences, births and deaths being a continuum, all opportunities for growth in consciousness.

4. At this time we are making quantum leaps in our knowledge and use of our human potential. Consciousness, the mind, is the area of this century's power, and it is imperative for our human evolution and for the peace of this planet that we make this shift in consciousness.

## Psychotherapeutic Assumptions

1. Re-experiencing past lives inevitably leads to an easier acceptance of others' beliefs, customs, and ways, and judgment and prejudice fall away like old dried mental cocoons.

2. Healing occurs in the space created within the relationship between client and therapist.

3. The major responsibility for creating that trusting space is the therapist's and so is the energy level. The emotional and spiritual well-being of the therapist is crucial.

4. *Therapy is a process of clearing away blocks, limitations, fears, and guilt that keep us from experiencing the self that we are.*

5. Our reactions and the way in which we respond to problems are rooted in the past. In therapy we work to bring old memories to consciousness so that repressed material may be seen in the light of the present and so that we may choose our responses, rather than be driven to react from old patterns.

6. Change must take place in the emotions as well as in the intellect.

7. Since the answers lie within the client, any authoritarian position with clients is contraindicated. The therapist's skills should be focused on positively empowering clients, enabling them to yield as deeply as possible to the wisdom within.

## Indications and Contraindications for Use

A much larger category of problems than one might suspect can be alleviated by regression therapy. Although many of our concerns and struggles in life relate directly to something that is happening in present time, our reactions and the way in which we respond to our problems are rooted in the past. I have found this modality especially helpful in four areas:

1. All phobias, compulsions, unexplained anxieties, and over-reactions of any kind that indicate past trauma. For example, a person who in a past-life experience suffocated and died in a cave and then had a long and difficult labor during his birth into this lifetime, will, if trapped in an elevator, certainly react differently from someone who has no earlier history of entrapment. *One has no irrational fear or phobia if there has been no previous cause.*

2. Problems in relationships. When we harbor negative repressed material we are not free to respond to individuals from a present-time perspective. Old fears, old expectations, old needs, ancient memory traces influence every aspect of our lives, especially when we find ourselves under stress or in crisis. Regressing to the original event enables one to release unconscious patterns of relationship and establish new and more positive ones.

3. Pregnant women or women planning to have children can greatly benefit from working on their own birth experiences. The experience of birthing, which is a time of stress, is a likely time for restimulation of repressed memories surrounding birth. In addition, problems of infertility, chronic miscarriages, phobias about birth or blood, have psychological as well as physical components and may be relieved by regressing to earlier experiences. Increasing research indicates that the baby is directly affected by the conscious and unconscious emotional state of the mother.

4. Various other forms of neurotic and psychotic behavior have proven responsive to intervention through the re-experience of pre- and peri-natal development. These problems include depression, suicide, autism, asthma, allergies, addiction, adult criminal behavior, and violence. Birth is a time

when imprinting occurs. If these imprints are adverse they may influence the total life pattern.

There are two major areas where regression therapy is contraindicated:

1. Those who have not arrived at the place where they are willing to assume responsibility for their attitudes and behavior. When clients expect the regression process or the therapist's magic to absolve them of accountability, this form of therapy will have no efficacy.

2. Chronic psychotics who are unable to care for themselves and are unable and unwilling to assume some level of responsibility for their lives. These are better served by more traditional forms of psychiatry.

# *Induction*

## Preparation

Rapport between client and therapist is vitally important, and therefore I take time to discuss my clients' general beliefs about reincarnation and their religious and psychological orientation. I answer their concerns and describe the process and suggest what can be expected. I try to allay any fears and make sure that the client is comfortable mentally and physically before the regression begins. Specific symptoms and problem areas that the client wants investigated need to be presented and clearly understood.

I assure the client of my support, that he will be able to communicate with me, that he may come back any time he chooses, that he can trust his own psyche, which seeks only his highest good. I invite him to allow any image that wants to come up, any feeling response or any physical sensation. I explain that past-life material often surfaces in any one of those ways and we will work with it as it appears. I request that any perceptions be reported, and I let the client know that this can be done usually without interfering with whatever is being experienced. I explain that there are circumstances, especially *en utero* or in birth, which are non-verbal and very physical. I will not stop the client's experience to ask for an explanation of what is occurring. In the process, tensions, energy blocks, and repressed material may emerge and be released with virtually no words and no discussion.

## Induction Techniques

In my experience, hypnotic states, trance states, and altered states are very similar. Perhaps they are points along a continuum and are induced by guided imagery, deep breathing, counting, and other relaxation techniques. After bodily relaxation and breathing, the depth of the altered state can be intensified by using the image of an elevator or stairway that will take the person deeper into his own mind.

It seems that in this particular time in history, entrance into an altered state is much easier and faster than was formerly true. It is as though the veils separating the states have become very thin. Actually, many of my clients come into a session already in an altered state. Anxieties and emotions seemingly unrelated to the present-life situation may have precipitated this altered state, probably as a result of anticipation of the session. If this is so, I have the client lie down and yield to this state and we work from there. I often feel that there is no need for further induction. In fact, lengthy relaxation techniques in these instances often bring the client out of his altered state and inhibit the material. With an altered state already induced, all that is necessary is to suggest or request that the client move immediately to the source of the problem.

### *Space Ship Induction*

*I would like you to lie down and begin to relax. Close your eyes. Breathe deeply.*

*Breathe all the way in and as you exhale imagine any tension releasing with your breath. With every breath you take you will become more relaxed. Feel your body relaxing. Good.*

*Imagine you are in an elevator. Push the button. The doors open. Imagine stepping out into golden warm sunlight. Feel the sun shining on your head, warming and relaxing your scalp. Continue to breathe deeply. Imagine the warm energy of the sun as if it were liquid gold spreading down over your forehead, soothing, easing, and relaxing all the muscles it touches.*

*Continue to breath deeply, sinking deeper and deeper into your own inner mind where it is safe for you to go. Imagine the golden warm liquid energy spreading down over your eyes and eyelids, soothing, easing, and relaxing all the muscles it touches. Continue to breathe deeply. Feel the warm golden liquid spreading over your nose, cheeks, and ears, soothing, easing, and relaxing all the muscles that it touches. Continue to breath deeply, sinking deeper and deeper into your own inner mind. Imagine the warm golden liquid spreading down over your cheeks, your mouth, your jaw. Feel it soothing, easing, and relaxing all the muscles it touches.*

*Continue to breathe deeply, sinking deeper and deeper into your own inner mind. Imagine the golden warm liquid spreading down through your throat and neck. Continue this until the entire body has been touched with this warm, relaxing energy of the sun....*

*You are completely surrounded with this warm golden energy. It forms around you a golden space ship. You feel the space ship beginning to lift. It lifts you up.... It lifts you up.... It lifts you up.... It is taking you high above the planet and back in time, higher and higher. Perhaps you can see the planet turning in space. You are going back in time, back to an important time for you to experience. You feel a pull to a particular place, a particular time. You feel yourself going down to this particular place. You are beginning to see the terrain. Closer and closer you see the place. You see a familiar figure. You are very close now. The space ship has landed. At the count of three you will step out of the space ship and tell me the first thing of which you are aware. Step into that body. Look down at your feet. What is there? Are you standing, sitting, walking? Do you have on shoes? Look at your hands. What color are they?...*

## Supportive and Deepening Techniques

In general, I use my voice as a soothing and supportive agent. During most regressions I make suggestions to move forward and backward in time to specific events that it seems important to experience. Sometimes I do this by moving backward to an earlier time, or from a past lifetime to a still earlier past lifetime. I find sometimes that asking for repetition of a phrase that has seemed charged helps regression and leads naturally into the next phrase or phase to be explored. Clients are encouraged to express freely any emotions that surface, and I support them totally in this process. Feelings themselves have the potential to take one deeply into the subconscious mind.

In my work I have come to regard the uterine and birth experiences as perhaps the most important areas in which to work. These seem to be the times when past-life memories are restimulated and when old feelings of fear of separation, loss, and death are reinforced. I regularly explore the nine months before birth, the birth itself, and the period directly following birth for vital keys to an understanding of the later consciousness. The uterine world can be filled with physical and emotional toxins, past-life themes of being poisoned, trapped, or lost in dangerous places, especially frightening memories around water, drowning, etc., to say nothing of the old frequent theme of feeling rejected. Sometimes, in the case of unsuccessful abortion attempts, the person becomes frozen into a past-life image of being imprisoned, murdered, or attacked. These images and uterine experiences can become imprints for survival patterns, and generally they do not change with time. When they are re-experienced and brought up to consciousness, they can be modified and transformed, along with their accompanying decisions about the self, the universe, and how to survive in a basically inhospitable universe.

To the infant, its mother is the universe, not only her body, but also her mind, conscious and unconscious. The optimum contribution that the mother (and to a lesser extent the father) can make is to be aware of her mind on all levels and to clear or heal any fears or negative feelings and beliefs that she may harbor about pregnancy, birth, bonding, and children that she may have developed from her own past experience. This would include experiences from the recent past, such as abortion, a miscarriage, a difficult pregnancy or delivery. It would also include her own birth. Whatever feelings and convictions a woman retains around this subject at any level are apt to be reawakened during her pregnancy or process of giving birth.

In the regression of clients it is possible to discover life scripts within traumatic situations, if one focuses on these traumas. The traumas are often initiated or replicated in the pre- or peri-natal process. Therapist and patient working together can uncover the etiology of current scripting. During these early traumas where the organism imprinted on survival patterns, the client made decisions based on his interpretations of what was happening at the time, and these decisions came to form the core belief behind his current script.

In regression work I track themes back from the present to the past and regularly look for the first experience of a particularly troublesome theme in this lifetime. I then move to the pre- and peri-natal period. Even with clients who are not open to past-life regression, past-life images often emerge spontaneously while they work on the birth, and this phenomenon acts as a stepping stone backward.

Another transformational technique that I often use is to return to a lifetime of fulfillment in service or peace, where love is experienced. This sort of lifetime is just as real as are painful lifetimes, and memories of happy lives can act as a ground when we are struggling with lifetimes where we seem to have missed the mark badly. It is a severe limitation when working with past lifetimes to fail to notice the good decisions we have made, the love we have shown, and the transpersonal qualities we have slowly developed.

# *Processing*

## Psychotherapeutic and Transformational Techniques

When it becomes apparent that the pre- and peri-natal and related past-life connections have been experienced as completely as possible, I take the client through an imaginary re-living of the entire pre- and peri-natal period from a positive perspective. This process reinforces more constructive behavior and attitudes. There it becomes evident that the goal of looking at past experiences is to reach a place where we do not make the same errors but learn from both our tragedies and our successes. This change in perspective brings about a shift in priorities and new evaluation of what really matters.

In reviewing past-life experiences I encourage clients to look at crucial decision points in particular lifetimes in order to consider what other options are available, either in behavior or in attitude. These decisions are then applied to current lifetime options. When the unconscious matrix of a decision-making process is unearthed and examined, our minds and our wills become better able to function with greater power to influence our conscious lives.

Sometimes I intervene to change the negative beliefs and attitudes that form the life scripts. During regression to a trauma, I ask if there could have been other choices made, or how the client would have liked it to be. This suggests the option of rescripting or modifying relationships and communications. One could argue that this is not the truth. I would counter that the truth is that the past *is no longer present except in our minds.*

My own philosophy is that there is within each individual a central Core Self, a knowing Self—call it Soul, Conscious Being, or Higher Self. This Essential Self exists before and beyond concepts of the personal self. The process of psychotherapy and healing examines the scripts and roles, and it effects the necessary self-rescripting, bringing this personal self into synchronicity with the more profound and loving and wiser patterns of the Essential Self.

A word of warning. Work in the transpersonal domain can be used to effect further denial and repression if the therapist is not alert. It can cover up shadows and knots that lurk within us and that insure that we will be back later with an expanded need to be released and set free from the entanglements of the ego world. The guise of a "spiritual person" can actually *cover* the glory that genuinely lies within and that awaits our integration of all that we are, dark and light. One does not find the light by embracing it but by integrating one's darkness and reframing one's limitations. The therapist is one possible agent for this unfettering of the psyche and the finding of that genuine inner self. He/she is an effective modern day shaman who will help rescript and reframe the experiences of our childhood and teach us to come to a place of peace so that we can finally let go of our emotional fetters.

One of the ways that the therapist can help the shadow aspect to be revealed and integrated is by assisting the client to go back to a situation where he was not the victim but the perpetrator. This approach is not easy because most clients prefer to deal with lifetimes where they were the victimized rather than to take an honest look at lifetimes where they were the victimizers. Even in our supportive working through of the repressions and wounds of childhood we must still keep in mind this need to expose and deal with the polarity. Lifetimes where harm was caused can be processed in much the same way that the AA or 12-step programs look at particular events in the current lifetime.

The place of forgiveness, which can function as a transformational agent, is complex. It is certainly an essential ingredient in releasing guilt, but it cannot be hurried or forced. Release and understanding of our behavior and feelings from other lifetimes provide fertile soil for forgiveness to take place. Pressure for forgiveness, either of oneself or of others, before the soil is ready is at best ineffective and may even be destructive, especially as it tends to generate more guilt. Sometimes the struggle to forgive is a necessary component of the client's process that we must respect. Sometimes looking for lifetimes in which one experienced a problem both as a victim and as victimizer enables one to forgive more easily and let go of negative patterns. Karmic reaction is not to punish but to generate sensitivity toward and awareness of our actions, and when such awareness has been learned we can let go of judgments of ourselves and the guilt that accompanies them.

I believe that everything that happens to us is an opportunity for learning and for expanding our consciousness. When we approach living in this context, it empowers us and frees us from self-justification, self-righteousness, and abuse. What is this experience teaching me? Why is this situation coming to me? Why have I attracted this particular person? The more we get answers to these questions and the faster we learn, the sooner we can begin to live in the flow, trusting our experiences and our ability to be able to handle whatever it is that life presents to us.

## Integration into the Total Psychotherapeutic Process

During regression clients may experience altered states of consciousness either of a transpersonal nature or of such intensity and power that the experience may be disrupting. In either of these cases I arrange for someone to be with the client for as long as necessary, or I have the client remain nearby in a comfortable place until he feels completely back in the present time. Both types of experience need to be integrated into the ongoing process of living and growing and relating to others.

In general, though there are some regression sessions that seem almost to produce a magical cure, on the whole this modality is a psychological tool to be integrated along with other techniques in the therapeutic process. During the discussion that follows a regression, the meanings and lessons learned are evaluated, and ways are perceived in which the good of such lessons can be integrated into the current life process. This step is especially valuable after the experience of the birth process, a time when many life and survival decisions are imprinted. Uncovering the past is usually only the first step. Old habit patterns need to be confronted and changed. New ways of responding need to be discovered and tested. Resistance and fears of change need to be handled. Clients are encouraged to avail themselves of further psychological counseling for support and continuing growth.

## Failures

Not all past-life therapy is successful. Perhaps this is true because therapy is an art and occurs within a changing environment and between two people. Lack of success may be due to the client or the therapist or the environment. A client may not be ready or willing to learn from the process or to make the necessary changes in his belief system or attitudes or in the structure of his life. This lack of resilience may result from fear or from rigid adherence to religious, philosophical, or scientific dogma. Sometimes a client brings to a regression session a negative set of images about past lives, that have been given to him in a previous "reading" by a psychic. A closed mind that wants only reinforcement of already held positions does not provide fertile ground for genuine exploration of consciousness. This is particularly true when a client recovers a lifetime where he was self-righteous, manipulative, or tending to judge inappropriately. In such a case, corrections in attitude must be made.

Though results that look like miracles sometimes happen in past-life work, when a client expects the therapist to remove both pain and mental blocks magically and with no effort on his part, therapy is not effective. No matter how excellent one's swimming teacher may be, one does not learn to swim by remaining out of the water. Moreover, though the therapist is trained to deal with resistance, if a client's mind is fortified against its own release, it is difficult to help him change.

Another stumbling block is the therapist's unwillingness to confront his own demons. It is difficult to lead someone into territory where one has oneself resisted going. A compulsive need on the part of the therapist to control the client and the therapeutic process, or a therapist's lack of trust in the powerful thrust of each human being toward wholeness, limits the success of the therapy.

In addition, not allowing enough time to process and integrate insights may result in failure adequately to use lifetimes that have successfully been recovered. It requires creativity and innovation to discover ways of working together to produce a healing environment.

An example of a failure due to rigid insistence on a correction of a former traumatic situation was Clyde, a bright, personable, outgoing man in his fifties who sought therapy when he had been put on probation after being arrested for exhibitionism with young girls, many of whom were friends of his daughter. The past life that he uncovered was one in which he, a young man in a Middle Eastern country many centuries ago, had been turned into a eunuch. The pleasant life, which he enjoyed, became disrupted when he tried to manipulate some of the young women in the harem and he was discovered and killed. His determination in this lifetime to show that he had a penis had become an obsession with him. He never molested children; he only wanted them to watch him masturbate, and he found it difficult to accept that such an action might harm them emotionally.

Though the recovery of his lifetime as a eunuch led him to determine to give up his exhibitionism, he remained unable to do it. He decided to exhibit himself one more time and was caught and taken to jail. But even then, though he was released on bail and given probation, he could not modify his maladaptive behavior and was later sentenced to a prison term. The hurt and shame and offense to his masculinity experienced in the earlier life proved to be too strong to be modified during this one.

# *Cases*

## Mind-Body Healing

The mind-body dichotomy has been entrenched in Western thought for so long that most medical doctors have felt little need to concern themselves with the psyches of their clients. Conversely, traditional psychotherapy has shown little concern with physical problems. However, the recent popularity and effectiveness of body therapies have prompted the acceptance of a concept of partnership between body and mind and a realization that they are not separate entities.

The majority of my clients enter therapy for psychological reasons, only to discover that change in the psyche affects the body, also. To the extent that an individual denies or represses large areas of experience, the physical body is affected and creative life energies become limited or directed in pathological or neurotic ways. To the degree that an individual is open to all aspects of personal experience and has access to all different sensing and perceiving abilities, his interaction with his world will tend to be constructive, both physically and psychologically.

**Case 1. Somatic Symptoms to Avoid Failure**

Frequently a client will begin a session with a feeling or remark that is directly connected to an earlier lifetime. Beth, a beautiful, high-strung, intelligent woman in her 40's began an early session with just such an expression of panic and suffering.

> C: *I'm afraid I'm going to die. I feel like I'm at the bottom of a deep pit and I don't have the strength to get out.*

Beth had come for intensive residential therapy for multiple emotional and physical problems. Eleven years earlier and a few days after her son was born she had had an unexplained physical collapse, from which she never recovered. I had seen her periodically for about six years, during which time we dealt with many issues, including the disfunctionality of her family, satanic abuse, and several past-life tangles. During this time, in an effort to improve her health, she had tried numerous diets and health treaments, running the gamut from traditional medicine to faith healers. Her physical and emotional health had gone up and down like a roller coaster. But there were a few times while she was doing something she liked very much, such as taking a weekend dance or movement workshop, where she exhibited amazing physical strength and well-being.

On this particular trip Beth arrived in California in a wheelchair on her way to do cell-renewal therapy in a clinic in Mexico. She was weak and suffering from heart pains, one of her chronic symptoms. By the time she arrived at Pocket Ranch, however, the pains had disappeared, and she walked up and down the paths from her cottage to the dining room with relative ease. The purpose of her visit was to clear away any emotional blocks that might hinder the cell-therapy in Mexico.

I asked her about possible secondary gains from her long illness and her heart immediately began hurting. She looked afraid.

C: *I know it's not a justifiable reason not to have to do what I don't want to do, but if I got well.... Oh, it's an awful responsibility and I'm afraid I'll fail.*

In the regression to her childhood that followed, Beth revealed how she had learned to fake being sick in the second grade when she did not want to go to school.

C: *When my mother thought I was sick, she didn't get angry—she was softer. I was relieved.*

By high school Beth had migraine headaches and regularly missed school and other responsibilities.

These memories built up to the climactic session when she declared that she felt at the bottom of a deep pit and didn't have the strength to get out. We used that image to go into an earlier time when she felt like that.

T: *Go back to an earlier time when you had those feelings.*
C: *I'm in a deep pit and there's no way I can get out. I'm trapped.*
T: *Tell me who you are.*
C: *I'm a dark-skinned man. I am the leader of my island. My people depend on me (sounds upset and desperate).*
T: *Let's go back further to a time when you and your people are peaceful and happy, when you are safe.*

Mary described a peaceful, almost idyllic life, which was interrupted when men from another island came in canoes to their island paradise and proceeded to kill and destroy. She, as the chief, and his (her) people put together a plan, but it was too late and they were overwhelmed.

C: *I really hate those people. We had a plan. I was leader and got caught. I let my people down. Now I'm in this deep pit and they are slowly throwing dirt on me. We were so right, so resolute—how could we have failed?*

The experience of this death led into a memory of being a Cherokee chief on the Trail of Tears, that tragic epic march from Georgia to Oklahoma where so many people perished. As the entity Sequoia she had exhorted her people to have faith in the Great Spirit. She felt that she had had a mission to save the people and she had failed.

C: *I did something wrong or it would have worked. What is this terrible flaw in me? I had pure intentions and it should have worked. It's my fault. I told them, "They may take our lands but not what we have inside."*

She experienced dying on the trail, having lost faith in the Great Spirit and, of course, in herself.

Beth shed many tears that morning. The shame and guilt from those two experiences had influenced her on an unconscious level to find ways of escaping whenever she was about to embark on a career possibility or an emotional commitment where others were depending on her. Her fear of another possible failure was too great to risk repetition. As a child in this lifetime she had learned to fake illness to avoid the responsibility of school. Gradually the pretend illness became a somatic disorder.

As a result of processing these past-life events Beth was able to see the dynamics involved when we explored the birth of her son and her subsequent formerly unaccountable collapse.

> C: *He felt like a trap. I felt panic, that he was going to get tied up and stuck and couldn't get out.*

She understood that the arrival of a child for whom she would be responsible had restimulated the sense of failures from earlier lifetimes and had also restored the familiar mechanism she had learned as a child, of getting sick to avoid the possibility of failing her son.

Subsequent work with Beth dealt with restructuring her old beliefs so she would be able to take responsibility out of choice. She began to forgive herself for what she had considered to be unforgiveable failures in those earlier lifetimes. In this lifetime, from childhood on Beth had had a sense of mission, and she was now able to reconnect with that feeling of purpose and become filled with a sense of peace and direction.

### Case 2. Chronic Leg Pain

Denial and repression of old traumas often show up in a variety of physical ways. Lois complained of several pains in her legs, a symptom that had occurred sporadically throughout her life. Currently she was unable to support herself and at 30 years of age was still being supported by her father, as if she had no legs on which to stand. She noticed that whenever she began to strike out on an independent path, her legs would become painfully cramped.

In regression to her birth she re-lived feelings of suffocation and lack of support from her mother, who was drugged and unconscious. Unable to free herself from the birth canal, Lois gave up and felt as though she were dying. Finally she was pulled out of the birth canal with forceps. The mechanical intervention saved her physical life but left her emotionally dead and feeling that she was helpless, at the mercy of others and unable to stand on her own feet.

Lois's mother was a schizophrenic, which reinforced her birth feelings of mistrust, particularly of women. So she turned to her father, who became her "legs," her support. To understand the patterns back of these relationships, we recovered the following past-life experience.

Lois was running from a threatening group of people. Her legs became exhausted and she stumbled. The crowd fell on her and cut off her legs, leaving her bleeding, dying, alone.

Lois had been healing people in non-traditional ways in that lifetime, and the official church warned her to stop, but she continued doing what she thought was God's will. The church consequently condemned her and stirred up the mob so that it murdered her. She experienced her death as a release and an affirmation.

C: *Do you hear the music and see the lights?*
T: *I feel your peace.*

After that death she moved into a broader perspective where she could respect herself for her courage and faith. Since the regression the leg pains have not returned. Psychologically she now stands on her own two legs with a sense of purpose, expressed in successful administration of an arts and crafts shop. Several years later she told me she could still close her eyes and remember the music and the lights of the blissful death experience and recapture the feeling of self-appreciation.

**Case 3. Severe Allergies**

In dealing with the psychosomatic aspects of physical symptoms in regression therapy, I often suggest that clients personalize the symptom and give it a voice. Surprisingly, the message is often benevolent, giving wise counsel for changes that clients need to make in their lives. It is as if each person has a specific path to take, a "mission," and the body speaks out a warning when this spiritual path is neglected. Though it may be easy to ignore intuition and feelings of depression or anxiety, it becomes difficult to push aside somatic physical problems, which, like a hit from a two-by-four, are strong wake-up calls. It would be easier on us if we could heed the earlier promptings of the feather-like brushes of our intuition, but whatever way it comes, we are given the message. In the end we find that all our experiences are opportunities for healing and finding our path toward Home and wholeness.

Jessica was a 15-year-old girl with a history of allergic reactions that began when she was three months old. At that time she began the first of what turned out to be 14 years of visiting specialists. At the time I saw her medical shots no longer alleviated painful reactions, and her sleeping pills had become ineffective. In a single night she would scratch through a heavy pair of cotton gloves, causing bleeding wounds on her arms and shoulders. She was unable to do many things that normal teenage girls do, such as swim in a chlorinated pool, camp or picnic in the countryside, or wear makeup, and her diet was restricted. She was allergic, not only to chlorine and make-up, but to all grasses, most animals, and a long list of foods. Frequent headaches increased her discomfort.

When Jessica was conceived, her parents had not been married long, and her mother felt it was too soon to have a baby. During the first trimester of pregnancy she was ill with morning sickness and threatened to miscarry. Jessica felt her mother's anxieties during this time and interpreted them as rejection.

C: *I'm not so sure I want to be here. Maybe she doesn't want me here.*

Though the mother's morning sickness gradually disappeared, she remained anxious about her pregnancy. At the first signs of labor her husband drove her to the hospital, but the labor was false. Since she lived forty miles from the hospital, the doctor decided to induce labor, and after eighteen hours and a very painful delivery, the little girl was pulled out by forceps, facing the wrong way. Her mother reported later that the pain had been so intense that after it was over she was too exhausted to care about seeing the baby.

In the regression to this birth process, Jessica expressed rage and pain.

C: *I don't want to come out. I'm not ready! They're making me. I want to go back.*

She spent one session expressing her anger at everyone who dragged her out before she was ready. She was facing the wrong way and she knew it. But with the anger was guilt for the pain she felt she caused her mother.

C: *(Crying) I'm sorry. I'll take your pain. I'm sorry! I'm sorry!*

Pain was to become Jessica's avenue of connection with her mother. From then on she would unconsciously manipulate her relationships and her body to create the presence of those two demons in her life, pain and guilt, as if she had imprinted on them. She was caught between anger and pain in the situation and the guilt she felt for causing her mother's suffering.

Frequently clients feel responsible for their mothers before they are even born. In childhood they become the helping, understanding, supportive, adaptive children, and later as adults they become compulsive do-gooders or care-takers of some sort. Even at 15 Jessica was manifesting these qualities. She was compulsively drawn to other children with serious problems and sacrificed her own needs, time, and wishes to friends, spending hours trying to rescue them and feeling heartbroken and helpless at the results.

In an effort to get to the source of this guilt and the resultant feeling of responsibility, I asked Jessica to lie down and breathe deeply until she was relaxed. Then through guided fantasy I had her imagine a character responsible for her allergies. This is a technique I often use with physical problems.

> C: *His name is Mr. Red, and he's an angry, bumpy, crabby blob!*

We found that Mr. Red stayed with her literally to keep her in pain. His job was to remind her not to be happy. Sure enough, as we discussed later, Jessica almost always experienced an allergic reaction when she started to have fun.

> C: *He says that he is tired of his job of causing pain and he likes to go water skiing.*
> T: *Take him to the lake.*
> C: *(Laughing) He's just fallen in the water.... But he's up again.... He's not red and bumpy, anymore. He's turning blue. He likes it there.*

The change in color suggested a change in Jessica's energy field, and after that session her allergies began to fade.

During the time we were working together, Jessica and her family rented the videotape *Gone With the Wind*. At the scene when Scarlett fell down the stairs and lost her baby, Jessica became hysterical. Her mother sat by her as Jessica re-lived a past-life memory of being pregnant and losing her baby. We later worked with this memory and uncovered the guilt she had felt because she had not wanted the baby. In another life she had abandoned her family. The chain of guilt stretched back many lifetimes.

During this time I worked with her mother, also. She regressed to Jessica's birth and re-lived the pain and inability to bond with her baby. She was flooded with tears of release and forgiveness as she felt the love for the struggling infant and for herself, the suffering, exhausted mother. Since then the relationship between mother and daughter has become more loving and filled with understanding.

It has been a year now since Jessica's therapy, and her allergies have not returned. Whenever she begins to feel a little itch, she takes herself into her imagination and talks to Red, whose name has been changed to Blue, and asks what the problem is that needs to be settled.

T: *What sort of advice does he give you?*
C: *He comes to see me only when I'm unhappy. He's there only to help me.*

This is a total switch from Red, whose task had been to remind her to be unhappy.

Jessica now competes on the school diving team, wears make-up, and goes camping. Her propensity for choosing friends who have many problems or who are in pain has changed. The headaches that she had come to regard as having been born with have also disappeared since her work on the forceps birth. Her enthusiastic summary of the therapeutic process is:

C: *Mainly, my therapy has totally changed my life!*

Why was this treatment successful? There are three factors that underlay or contributed to Jessica's healing. First, both Jessica and her parents were willing and open to look at their experience and cooperate with each other and the therapeutic process. Second, after 13 years where only the physical symptoms were considered, they were motivated to find the *cause* of those symptoms and thus enable healing and change to take place. Third, the creation of Mr. Red, who turned to Mr. Blue, was an effective image to reinforce the healing and avoid slipping back into old destructive habits.

In this case the negative experiences in past lives were restimulated by Jessica's pre- and peri-natal trauma, which was then manifested in her chronic physical problem. Fortunately, the correction was made early enough in life so that her energy could be directed in a positive way and not be acted out as a mother or as an adult.

**Case 4. The Renaissance Man**

Dennis entered therapy because he felt that his creativity as an artist was blocked. He knew he had talent. He was a brilliant scholar and teacher, but when he was painting he often felt gripped by fear as he stood before his canvas. Whenever he embraced new projects or traveled to new places, he felt anxious. He experienced a feeling of impending doom, as if the "roof had caved in on him."

Dennis experienced a variety of lifetimes in the course of his therapy. The crucial one occurred in 15th century Italy. He was an architect, scholar, a Renaissance man, secure and confident. Scholars from many countries came to learn from him. He designed a new kind of dome for official buildings and churches.

> T: *Tell me more about your work.*
> C: *I see a huge workroom full of drawings and charts. There are students from several countries standing around. (At this point his body becomes rigid and he lies back in his chair. Blood drains from his face.) A workman is running in. Oh, my God! No! No!*
> T: *What is happening?*
> C: *No, it can't be! The dome has collapsed. (Sobbing heavily) Workmen have been killed. It's my fault.*

We returned several times to that lifetime and its emotional trauma, gradually lessening the guilt until it was gone and he was able to forgive himself. He said that his arrogance and pride were shattered along with the cathedral dome.

The connecting link to that lifetime came during his birth. Both he and his mother nearly died. He felt that she was purposely keeping him down and that her body was closing in on him with no way for him to escape. His uterine world was "falling down" on him. He decided that it was all his fault, that he was somehow to blame for both his and his mother's pain. The experience keyed in all the guilt from that 15th century life.

The guilt and fear of some impending tragedy and the feeling that forces beyond his control would punish or block him have gradually disappeared from his life. He has been able to forgive his mother and to see that really no one was to blame. He continues to be a gifted lecturer and teacher, an inspiration to his students, perhaps drawing on his talents as the 15th century Renaissance man.

# Chapter XX

# Thorwald Dethlefsen, Ph.D. (Germany)

## *Biographical Data*

### Personal Background

In 1968 I moved into the area of past-life work in much the same way that many others have done; I stumbled upon it while engaged in general hypnotic work. A patient had re-lived earlier portions of his present life and had recovered a few incidents from his childhood. Following this I wanted to determine whether he could remember his own birth and perhaps even re-live it. He was able, amid moaning and altered breathing patterns, to re-live his birth. Surprised by my success I suggested that he return to the pre-natal period and found that he was able to describe his impressions as an embryo.

Then I suggested that he go still further back until he came upon an event that he could picture and describe accurately. After a tense pause he began to speak in a choked voice and to describe the story of a lifetime as a man, Guy Lafage, in 1852 in Alsace. For much of his life he sold vegetables, and he died in 1880 as a stable hand.

My experience with this patient provided the grounding for later research and also for a revised understanding of life. Gradually, I recognized the connection between psychic symptoms in the current life and traumatic experiences in earlier incarnations. As this theory developed, the idea emerged that there might be therapeutic value in bringing earlier incarnations into consciousness. At first I attempted to do this through hypnotic techniques but eventually developed methods that made possible regression into earlier incarnations without the subject having to be hypnotized, thus bypassing some of the limitations of hypnosis, such as sleepiness and dependency.

In the beginning I was concerned primarily with symptoms. I felt that if one regressed far enough backward through lifetimes one would come upon a causal incident, and the remembering of this incident would release the symptom. Gradually I came to understand that the path of the soul is more complicated and involves experiences of polarity. What I found was that it was necessary to regress the patient back to the moment when he himself originally set up the cause of the chain of suffering and introduced the basic theme that was to emerge in many different forms. This is the step in which the individual confronts his own karmic guilt by which he himself has made necessary all the painful situations he has been through. With the recognition of guilt the individual can assume full responsibility for his fate and effect his healing. Reincarnation therapy then emerged as primarily a spiritual process.

# Theory

## Philosophical Hypotheses

The basis for an understanding of past lives lies in the classic three-part division of body, mind, and spirit, combined with an individual soul. The living soul is contained in a material body and is the information carrier whose objectives take shape within the body and become formally visible. Body functions are thus an expression of consciousness. The physical organs of our body are only the material equivalent of psychic sensual perception. The psychic process is the primary one, and the material happening is a product of consciousness.

The lifeless body is the shell or executive organ of what we call life, consciousness, personality. Death is the occasion of the separation of soul and body. An individual soul runs through a phase of corporeal existence, frees itself from this shell, only to enter into a new connection with matter after a period of noncorporeal existence. The soul constantly remains the same, while the bodies vary from life to life. Time plays a significant part in understanding the connection of present symptoms with past lives. A neurosis is created when a person is unable to place his emotions in the proper time sequence. Forgetting is only an apparent solution because it eliminates nothing; it simply prevents something from being seen.

The cause of all behavior and misbehavior lies with the psyche (or soul), which is not matter. If one wishes to heal, changes must be made in the primary system, namely, in the psyche. The body is something we can put on or take off at will, just as we are the same human being, whether we wear clothing or not and regardless of what clothing we are wearing. The sum of all incarnations forms our learning history, which makes us whatever we happen to be and stamps our conduct and emotions. The unbroken continuity of the human psyche that goes beyond individual lifetimes makes it possible to understand why symptoms experienced in the current life may have their origins hundreds of years earlier.

Reality exists independent of the passing of time, but one can see and experience this reality only within a time coordinate. What one sees and experiences does not come into existence at a particular moment. Reality consists of unities, which nonetheless reveal themselves to human consciousness as polarities. We cannot perceive unity as a unity. But from this we should not deduce that it does not exist. The perception of polarity presupposes the existence of unity. Two can exist only as a consequence of one. We always see unity only in two aspects, which appear to us as contrasting. But these very contrasts form a unity and are dependent on each other. From the law of polarity it follows that everything that exists has the right to exist. Within a cosmos that functions according to laws, we can never say of anything that it "ought not to exist." Only human beings have divided the world into things that should exist and other things that should not. Every manifestation has its purpose, otherwise it could never come into being in the first place. All things are in themselves of neutral merit. It is only our attitude that creates out of them the contrasting categories of joy or suffering.

Society is a product of humanity. Nobody is to blame for one's fate except oneself. Evolution in our frame of reference is intentional higher development, a law that is effective throughout the universe and that encompasses all creation. Fate is the collective concept for the many problems that beset the individual in the course of his life in order to present him with the necessary ingredients for his development. Problems are the lessons from which one must learn. A human being is always confronted by fate with those principles that he has hitherto not realized, those that have remained alien to him, those that are still missing from his experience. One has two ways of learning, the active and the passive way. To learn actively means to face each problem happily and to consider it an invitation to learning in order to get a step higher in one's personal development. The passive situation is always connected with suffering. The only one at fault is the sufferer himself, for he had a choice. The law does not allow "not learning," for this would be stagnation and would be damaging to all development. Free will would contradict the regularity of a cosmos, but choice is a product of the laws of polarity and does not endanger orderly development.

Fate is something extremely personal, the result of one's own doing, the regular auxiliary of evolution. Calling for help from the outside is futile because such assistance solves no problems. In the final analysis those who call for help suffer because they cannot solve their problems and do not want to learn. Development is one of the things one must do for oneself. Differences in the fate of various human beings can be understood because each is in a different specific state of development and in order to advance needs specific problems and experiences. The fate of this life is therefore a result of the previous "chain of lives," a consequence of what was previously learned or not learned. Everyone at times goes through problems that he did not conquer in the past through conscious learning, and in the future he will again be confronted with the same problems until he has solved them for himself. This regularity is known in India as karma, which requires that a problem be experienced continuously until it is understood.

The past of the human soul is a path of learning and must obey the higher laws. A learning process of this kind, whose goal is perfection, is a long road, requiring many steps and involving many mistakes and many corrections. Only the seemingly endless chain of incarnations guarantees ultimate success. The results of a person's behavior vary, depending on whether that person lives in conformance with the law or opposes it. These varying results will be experienced by an individual as reward or punishment, but this experience is purely subjective. Each new life is a fresh chance, containing every possibility, and yet at the same time it is only a further link in the chain of incarnation, a reflection of the problems, mistakes, and assimilated lessons of the past.

Through his release from the body, an individual releases himself from his ties and looks over his past life. With the recognition of his shortcomings, he recognizes his need to learn more. This he can do only in another earthly life and with a body. He realizes that he must return to earth and begin another corporeal existence. Only the overview of a life and the confrontation with reality will make possible the further development of man and prevent him from gettng hopelessly lost in a maze of errors. The learning deficit that man takes with him to the after-death state is what determines his fate during the next life. The soul will remain in the after-death state until a point in time arrives that contains a quality corresponding to the nature of the lessons he needs to work out. Humans continue to make contact with the same people as long as they have mutual problems to solve.

Humans belong to a specific kingdom of nature, the human race, which is a small group in the giant hierarchy of living beings. Once an individual has attained perfection within his own group, he is able to move into the next higher rung in the hierarchy and continues his development there. So the world does not change materially when it comes to the distribution of understanding because it represents only one segment of development.

Death cuts away from all earthly events and excludes any and all emotion. In this new existence a person learns to view all reality without any polar fixation. Emotion is created only by fixaton. The deceased does not mourn those he left behind. He finds himself in a new environment with new problems, outside the realm of love and hatred. After death the deceased possesses a pure consciousness.

The knowledge of former lifetimes effects an enormous increase in a person's conscious knowledge. The individual learns how to interpret and understand details of his present life in a new manner. He recognizes associations and receives insights that greatly expedite his learning process. When the experiences are recovered, he becomes able to see reality as it is now, without confusing it with feelings from the distant past. It makes it possible for him to live always, completely, and consciously in the present.

## Psychotherapuetic Assumptions

The goal of past-life therapy is to bring traumatic recollections of previous experiences into conscious knowledge with the same accuracy with which contents of the previous day are recalled. The search for a trauma or traumata is the basis for almost all deep psychological therapy.

Symptoms and complaints are caused exclusively by unknown material, not by known matters. Suffering is the friction that arises because of the discrepancy between the individual's true, prescribed path and the direction that he or she happens to be following at the time. Suffering becomes superfluous only when we make the effort constantly to increase our understanding of our own path and voluntarily to conform to it. The great majority of all symptoms have their origins in earlier lives and not in this life. One comes almost automatically upon earlier lives if one searches persistently for the actual cause of a symptom. Former experiences will rise to the surface of their own accord if the patient is asked to return to the true cause of his symptom or emotion. To do this he must passively yield himself to whatever happens to him, giving up conscious control and an analytical approach.

It is only rarely that at the beginning of past-life work the patient reports his earlier life in a way that corresponds in every detail to his actual historical experience. The psychic material of earlier incarnations is subject to the same psychological laws that are found in psychoanalysis. The story will be falsified by the same psychic mechanisms that falsify any other report he might give us, such as that of his current childhood or similar experiences, because facts that have too high an emotional charge cannot be confronted at first. Fantasy experiences usually distinguish themselves clearly from real recollections and can be differentiated with considerable accuracy. They are useful because they bring about a gradual discharge of energy and enable the patient in time to come upon the actual events. Fantasy experiences have a quality of unreality and fail to evidence a continuity of reporting or consistency. Reports regarding past lives do not change when they are true.

Reincarnation therapy is not a flight into the past but a way of using the past in order to guide the patient into its opposite pole, the present. As long as the past is suppressed and continues to work on an unconscious level, the individual will not succeed in living consciously in the here and now. He will continually be re-stimulated by past events and will confuse past and present. The goal is to attain a state of constant awareness in the present moment. The perception of a traumatic experience may be expelled but not its emotional portion, which remains in a freely fluctuating state after the perception is expelled. A later occasion may, through some similarity, recall the expelled experience, which becomes projected onto the new situation. Therapy must reverse this process. If the procedure of bringing back to conscious knowledge the experience that has been expelled and forgotten is successful, the symptom disappears because the patient can dissolve the symptomatic projection through recognizing that this feeling belongs to an event in the past. He learns to put his emotions, which were momentarily stimulated, back into their proper time sequence. A neurosis is created when a person is unable to place his emotions into such a proper time sequence.

In the beginning only the symptom is known, and this symptom is based in a trauma from some time in the past. The problem is to develop a technique that will aid in finding the unknown. In therapy only the traumatic event is important. It is not necessary to review completely every life from the cradle to the grave. A random emotional experience, as time goes on, surrounds itself with emotionally similar incidents and so becomes more and more laden with energy. The growth can escalate so far that it threatens to swamp the ego. Repressed and forgotten incidents each form complexes distinguished from one another by their charge. The greater the charge in a complex, the less likely the possibility that it can become conscious knowledge. An experience that in the past was so unpleasant or emotionally disturbing that it was repressed has to be viewed again in order to bring it back into consciousness. The viewing brings with it the entire emotional impression, which is exactly what the consciousness fears. Therefore the finding of the trauma we seek is usually not easy. Consciousness defends itself, and this resistance is a defense mechanism that protects the ego from an emotional overflow so that a too powerful complex does not suddenly explode.

If we picture our complex as a large molecule, the trauma we seek is located in its center as the nucleus, or original experience around which are grouped all similar experiences that have occurred meanwhile. We start with the outer shell, encouraging the patient to *re-live* less charged and more recent experiences rather than deliver an intellectual report. By going back along the time axis and re-living all the situations, seeing once again the component parts of the complex, the extensive neurotic reaction can be diminished. The patient learns in the process that not being able to remember is actually not wanting to remember: there is no forgetting. If this procedure of making known continues, sooner or later one must come upon the nucleus and reach the actual trauma. The incident can be made known because its charge has shrunk to a bearable size. At the moment that an incident becomes fully known, the patient often feels at ease and has no further complaints or fear, no matter how gruesome the experience was. Once he is aware of it, it no longer has any effect on him. What is known can no longer hurt.

The alleviation of symptoms is not the final goal. True healing depends on confronting the polarity behind the symptoms. By exploring the chain of symptoms, the sick person is continually confronted with similar situations until finally he discovers the originating source of guilt. Through his act of recognition, he can dissolve the guilt, turning it into a transformative agent and solving his basic problem. Psychotherapy embraces the entire human being and touches the deepest levels of his existence. Its goal is to help him find and understand himself and make himself a significant part of the universe.

## Indications and Contraindications for Use

Since anxiety to some extent is a part of everyone's life, past-life work is generally applicable. The more intense and conscious such anxiety is, the stronger the indication for this type of work. An individual never lives completely in the present but always somewhat in the past, and when the past obtrudes upon the present and distorts it, a return to the original distorting incident can release and free the present. If the experiences from earlier years are made known, the filter disappears and the person is able to see reality as it is now, without confusing it with feelings from the distant past. Such incidents as accidents, illnesses, tortures, and death are important targets of recall.

In addition to the treatment of symptoms by tracing their occurences in earlier lifetimes and unearthing the polarity involved, reincarnation therapy is especially indicated for those wishing to pursue the hard route of purification in order to reach that unity that we once left behind and to which every human being longs finally to return.

One contraindication is a desire on the part of the patient to recover past talents and abilities. One should rely confidently on fate and work with the talents that one has received, instead of glancing back at those that one no longer has and that have no role to play in the current lifetime.

Reincarnation work is also contraindicated for those who are merely curious. Usually such recall is attempted with the help of psychics, who are often inaccurate and frequently cannot control material that comes through. The *conscious* surveying of past lives has always been recognized as one of the steps on the path of development, a step that is self-initiated with the help of appropriate techniques or, occasionally, that takes place of its own accord. Information produced by a clairvoyant is of relatively little use, since it will not by itself give the person access to the past, and he will not be able to identify with it.

# *Induction*

## Preparation

In the beginning of therapy an exact diagnosis is not important. After a physician's examination has assured us that an organic disorder (such as a brain tumor, etc.) is not the primary cause of a symptom, the patient's own exact description of his symptomatology provides enough material for a starting point. Depending on the patient, this process can be completed in three sentences or it may require an entire biography.

It is not necessary at this stage to enter into major speculation regarding possible psychic connections or to attempt to classify each patient or his symptom too rapidly. What his problem may be is completely unimportant at this time. What is important is that he is here and needs help. The longer it takes to understand a patient, the better the chance that eventually we will understand him correctly. To force a case into some sort of classification during the first hour is in most instances doing the patient an injustice.

At the start of therapeutic treatment, the patient and the therapist must join together to begin the voyage into the soul. Neither one knows from the start what the trip will be like, what experiences await, or where they will lead. Joining together with the therapist strengthens the patient for his journey. But even if the therapist accompanies the patient as helper and advisor, it remains a trip through the realm of the patient's soul. For this reason I generally find an opportunity during the first session to tell the patient that everything that happens in therapy must be done by him and that I can do absolutely nothing for him. I shall simply try to be a good companion and guide.

Healing is our goal, and I mean this literally. Healing means recovery, getting better. To approach recovery is to develop. Only the patient himself can bring about such development. No matter what, this task cannot be turned over to the therapist. Such a discussion is often necessary at the beginning of therapy in order to draw the patient out of the passive state that he brings with him from his usual visits to the doctor, where his attitude is, "I hope the doctor can give me an injection to make me well again!" Waiting for the therapist to do something can bring the therapy to a standstill. Once the patient understands his task, he begins to enjoy participating in his own development. This attitude toward therapy should clearly indicate that greater expenditure of diagnostic time serves no purpose.

## Induction Techniques

Our diurnal consciousness is usually comparable to a wide-angle lens. When we concentrate, the focus narrows and picks out one point exaggeratedly. Then it may happen that our consciousness penetrates to a deeper layer and a new, previously unconscious dimension is reached. This breakthrough to a new level is the turning point where what was at first a narrowing of consciousness is transformed into a widening of consciousness.

In all ages there have been people who tried to induce this process at will in themselves and others, developing the most varied techniques for that purpose: concentration, meditation, hypnosis of various kinds, biofeedback, and so on. The common factor in these techniques is the narrowing of consciousness to one point, as if, when a wide-angle lens is replaced with converging lenses, the light is concentrated and a strongly focused lightbeam picks out a tiny point, plunging the surrounding area into darkness. The intensity of light at this point is far greater than when the light was diffused.

Hypnosis is just one of the possible techniques for obtaining access to an unconscious level. In the beginning it seemed to me a viable way, and past-life work became linked with the hypnotic approach. Gradually I saw that in hypnosis it is possible by suggestion to replace faulty programs with more desirable ones, but this can affect only the remission of symptoms. It fails to achieve healing in the real sense. Healing can take place only through an encounter with truth.

An associated difficulty with hypnosis is that it works by suggesting feelings of tiredness and sleepiness in the subject and thereby goes against the aims of increased awareness of those situations that have led to both "illness" and symptoms. Man's problem is precisely the fact that he is constantly in a state of sleep and moves about like a marionette, instead of waking up and becoming conscious. Everything that happens in a therapeutic session should represent on a small scale what is expected of the patient in everyday life. Our goal is therefore to make people more awake and more conscious, to teach them to see reality with ever-increasing clarity and not to encourage them further in their sleepiness and unconsciousness.

A further consideration is that hypnosis is bound up with the problem of power, which is the central theme of every therapy. Hypnosis turns the patient into a passive consumer who expects it to provide an instant answer to his problem. These considerations should suffice to show why I have tried, as far as possible, to dispense with hypnosis in applying regression for therapeutic purposes. The result is that in our reincarnation therapy we now make the patient aware of earlier lives without having to use hypnosis. The regression takes place in full waking consciousness. I have moved away from hypnosis into other means of entering an altered state, primarily through relaxation and visualization where the patient is allowed to generate his own images rather than being limited by what I suggest.

I begin with a short period of relaxation intended to put the subject into a meditative frame of mind. The relaxation serves to diminish external stimuli and allows the person to listen to himself. It switches the attention from the outer to the inner pole, without either fatigue or sleepiness entering in. Through the help of the therapist, sensations and images arise that the person learns to observe and describe at the same time. He must not immediately be forced into a performance. Most persons expect too much from their first session. Only when the patient realizes that nothing is actually happening does he relax completely. Electronic meditation music makes it easier for many people to sink more deeply into an altered state.

In subsequent sessions I begin to suggest color experiences.[1] The suggestion might be, "All by itself and without your help a color will develop within your inner eye—it will be your color!" From the beginning I am careful not to suggest any particular color in order to avoid the slightest activity or strain on the part of the patient. If I speak only of "your color" he is practically forced to wait and see what develops. Only when he is able to identify the first color clearly do I go through the color chart.

If the patient has difficulty seeing colors, I engage him in a symbol drama. Depending on his ability, I run through as quickly as possible meadow, stream, spring, and delta. This technique and succession of pictures were clearly described by Professor Leuner in the concept of the catathymic picture life.[2] All in all I use the symbol drama generously without depending on specific pictures.

With the symbol dramas I attain three objectives simultaneously:

1. A patient learns the technique of daydreaming, that is, seeing pictures with his eyes closed, experiencing them, telling about them at the same time. Since these inner pictures are projected without conscious assistance, the patient becomes accustomed to accepting material rising to the surface as it appears and reporting it without criticism or comment.

2. The nature of the pictures permits a good diagnosis of the actual state of the patient's psychic condition. The principle is similar to a projective test. Archetypal symbols are fed to the patient in the form of pictures that will then be shaped in accordance with his psychic structures. Since the symbolism is usually not known to the patient, an accurate diagnosis of this picture world is made possible.

3. The symbol drama method, which in itself represents a therapeutic technique, begins to decrease the charge on the symbol level. This is already the beginning of therapy. It is generally not recognized as such by the patient at this time, since the method is almost like playing games.

There are two basic ways of taking a patient into his past. In the first it is suggested that he go back further and further in time. In the second a particular feeling or emotion is selected from this life and is followed further and further back into the past, for example, the fear of people. We begin by letting the patient re-live and relate any experience in which the fear of people was present. Then we go back further in time and let him report another incident concerning fear of people. Thus the patient, on his own, reaches even earlier years, does not stop with his birth, but continues constantly to go back further in time. New experiences will begin to surface on their own, experiences that are from a completely different chronological era. In this technique the emotion serves as a sort of guide line, like a red thread, in that I ask the patient to go back in time with this emotion until he finds an incident or experience in which this feeling was present. This technique of going back along the path of an emotion is quite time-saving and productive. The patient himself comes upon events, all of which are similar because they have a central emotional theme.

With the first method we always reach an old life rapidly, which at first need not agree in every detail with historic reality, yet, as a whole, encompasses the incarnation. The reverse is usually the case with the second method. Since in this instance we are pursuing an emotion, a trauma is usually approached automatically so that there is a much greater likelihood of receiving a series of fantasies that help pave the way energetically to the actual incident.

If we are looking for incarnations, the first method leads us to our goal more quickly and more surely. For therapeutic purposes, the second method is frequently indicated because it generally leads to the trauma we seek without digressing to any great extent. But both approaches are similar in that they merely assist the patient to tap into earlier and earlier situations or incidents. The following induction is appropriate for the first method but can be modified simply by mentioning whatever emotion or situation is being pursued.

## *Induction by Age-Regression*

*We shall go backward through your life because time means nothing to us. Time is only a means of communication, a measure, but you will re-live the past as if it were happening now. The past will become the present. We shall go backward in your life. You are getting younger; you will be 25-years-old.... (Pause) We shall go back further; you will be 20-years-old.... (Pause.) Let us go back further; you are 15.... (Pause.) You are 10-years-old. Now is your tenth birthday. How do you feel?... (Pause.)*

*Let us dissolve from this birthday and go further back in time. We shall go further back in time. You are getting younger. You are now six years old. Are you going to school now?... (Pause.)*

*Let us go back further. You are getting younger—five, four, three, two, one. Let us return to the moment of your birth. You are just being born. What time is it? What happens next? You are just being born. Tell me all your impressions exactly.... (Pause.)*

*Let us go further back in time. We are now five months before your birth.... (Pause.) We are proceeding further back to the time of conception. Let us return to the place from which you came to the time of conception.... (Pause.) Now you will conintue to go further back in time until a new situation develops. There you will stop and show me...*

## Deepening

Once the patient no longer has any difficulties with imaging, I take him through his own birth. With the power of suggestion I take him back to the time of his birth and let him experience and describe the entire birth process. At this point we almost always find physical feelings making their appearance. The patient experiences shortness of breath, pressure on his head, bodily pain, and the like. He smells the hospital odors, sees the delivery room, sees the people present, and hears every word that is spoken. The patient glides almost imperceptibly into this situation even when he himself believes it to be impossible. I have had the experience repeatedly that the patient, when I suggest to him, "Re-live your birth," will start to explain why he cannot do it and suddenly break off in the middle of his excuse because he is already experiencing birth pains. The birth experience is repeated frequently because it becomes clearer with every repetition, and more and more details are recognized each time.

Once the birth has become known, the therapy enters a new state, since the patient has now learned of his own accord that there is nothing that is really forgotten and nothing that one cannot remember. He has now gained confidence and passively allows items to surface of their own accord without wanting to activate everything himself. It sometimes requires a great effort to convince a patient that everything will happen of its own accord only if he is prepared to let it do so. Many patients feel that they must enrich the therapy by clever analysis of their symptoms, their childhood, their upbringing, and the like. Our method requires that all attempts at rational analysis be bypassed.

After the birth we study the individual months of the embryonic state in order to determine whether any trauma developed there. If we then conclude the experience by examining the moment of conception, we shall have made known the greatest unknown portion of the current life. I make known to every patient his birth, his intrauterine condition, and his conception, regardless of his symptoms. Once the patient has reached this stage (an average of ten sessions), nothing will stand in the way of the final step into other lifetimes.

Resistance, which may appear occasionally, is either a sign of a too highly charged event that one has approached, or may be the result of another problem temporarily overlapping the procedure. Resistance is handled in the same manner as the symptom itself. Energy charges that are too strong may be diminished to a safe level by inserting symbol dramas.

## *Processing*

### Psychotherapeutic and Transformational Techniques

The treatment of symptoms must be differentiated from true healing. Symptoms can be dealt with by connecting an emotion with an incident in the present time that encourages its projection. When the projection finds its true place in the past, the projection is released and the symptom disappears. Such release of symptoms and freedom from projection often lead to feelings of well-being and serenity.

The transformative power of regression work in the matter of symptoms does not depend on any specific type of intervention but is inherent in the process itself. This procedure of recovering and living out repressed and forgotten incidents is frequently applied in behavior therapy under the designation of "systematic desensitizing," especially in the case of phobias. The core problem has gradually accrued energy in the form of subsequent experiences, and these subsequent layers must be released one by one in order for the final kernel of hurt and distortion to be approached and relived. The release of the nuclear trauma effects a complete release.

At the same moment that an incident becomes fully known, the patient suddenly feels at ease and has no further complaints or fears. It is comparable to the birth of a child. The difficulties pertain only to the procedure itself, not to the results. It makes absolutely no difference how gruesome the experience was; once the patient is aware of it, it no longer has any effect on him. This is an important rule: *everything that is known can no longer hurt*.

However, for true healing, for coming to the place where we perceive that we are cradled in a cosmos guided by meaning and purpose and that our sole task is to serve it, we need to go deeper. If we relate the thoughts we have developed in this life to an earlier incarnation, we find that the traumatic experience was certainly no chance occurrence but an expression of a pattern that was brought into this life. The soul of a person who drowns in one life is likely to have fear of water in the next, but we should not conclude from this that the drowning was the *cause* of the later fear of water. The drowning was itself a part of a meaningful pattern, a demonstration of an inherent problem. The more one goes back, the more situations one finds that would seem to qualify as the "primal" trauma. Thus, a patient with an arrow in his left eye will find many more events in which he lost that eye. All these events are links in a chain whose totality forms the problem common to all the situations. When we have followed a chain of symptoms back as far as it seems to go, we need then to take the decisive therapeutic step and regress the patient back to the moment when he originally set up the cause of the chain of suffering and introduced the basic theme that was to emerge in many different forms.

This is the step with which the individual confronts his own karmic guilt by which he himself has made necessary all the painful situations he has been through. Up to now he has always regarded himself as an unfortunate victim. When he is confronted with his own karmic guilt something quite different happens. The sufferer has to integrate his shadow. He experiences himself as an agent, doing to others the very thing that he complained was being done to him over several thousand years. To confront his own guilt is no easy matter for the patient, but it is a major step in the direction of healing if he is able to take it. If one wants to insist on looking for a "cause," then it is to be found in karmic guilt.

Nothing of which we are fully conscious can have a negative effect. In therapy the confronting of guilt is entirely free of value judgment. It involves looking into reality that is incorporated into the past, as a step in the learning process. With the recognition of guilt the individual can assume full responsibility for his fate—a step that opens the door to healing.

Within the process of therapy we follow up several chains of symptoms with their accompanying karmic guilt. All of these chains ultimately lead back to a nodal point representing the basic problem that so far the patient has failed to overcome, and if we analyze the basic problem we find that it always boils down to the same theme, namely, power. Man becomes sick with the disease of power. In earlier lives this was usually lived out in an obvious way, whereas in the present life it is veiled and refined. But it is always power that is man's downfall. The polar opposite of power is humility. Once a patient recognizes in what way he is insisting on power, he must decide either to remain "ill" or to renounce power, a difficult choice. Power is to be equated with ego-dominance. It is the attempt to impose one's will on others instead of subordinating oneself.

## Integration into the Therapeutic Process

Through integrating step by step into his consciousness all his hitherto totally suppressed shadow, a person becomes complete and whole. Confrontation with guilt is not the taking on of a burden but the giving up of a burden. Although the confrontation itself is frequently felt to be unpleasant, afterward the patient notices an unfamiliar feeling of freedom and relief. To suppress guilt or to project it onto others is to create sickness in oneself since one is thereby retreating from reality. We must learn that we are guilty because we are human beings and that this guilt is the price we pay for our learning process. *Without error there is no development.* There is therefore no single person who has not shouldered guilt at some time in the past. Only by going through the darkness can we reach the light.

Not until the patient has re-experienced, with full clarity, the power urges of his earlier incarnations will he begin to unmask them in the here and now. Only when he has seen how over thousands of years he has heaped suffering upon himself in order to buy power, will he slowly begin to be ready to understand the doctrine of humility. Such understanding does not come about through an intellectual process but through an experience of reality that produces a trans-polarization in the individual. The changes in consciousness take place in the present, and thereby the person becomes healed. The symptoms, having become superfluous, literally disappear of their own accord, although we may in fact have not treated them at all.

Reincarnation therapy is a hard route to purification. In repeated reincarnations we see no source of comfort but rather a challenge to develop toward completeness and thus become free. We must say "yes" to this earthly existence as long as it is necessary for our path of development.

## Failures

There are two sources of failure. In the first, the patient fails to trust the therapeutic process in a way that will allow unconscious material to emerge. The second source of failure lies in being content with one of the outer layers of experience, allowing the core of the complex, such as the experience of primal guilt and the power urges connected with it, to remain unresolved.

# *Cases*

### Case 1. Inge's Spectrum of Fears

Inge was 28 years old, married, and a housewife. In the beginning she did not want to know about her prior lives, even to become free of a large number of symptoms that had been troubling her for several years. Her symptoms were far-reaching and to some extent unusual. In addition to depressions, she suffered from attacks of fear so intense that she was unable to leave the house alone. She was afraid of people and particularly hated all women. She had the feeling that she had to beat pregnant women because "every pregnant woman is a murderess." She could not look into a mirror and had not been to a beauty parlor for years. When she passed people whom she did not like, she held her breath so that she did not need to share the air with them. All symptoms were mixed with religious ideas; she spoke of original sin, of the fear of being discovered, and suggested that there was "something that had to be said."

I began her therapy by selecting individual symptoms during the hypnotic state and allowing their emotional content to be experienced. This emotion served as a sort of guideline, like a red thread. I asked Inge to go back in time with each emotion until she found an incident or experience in which the feeling was present. This technique of going back along the path of an emotion is time-saving and productive. The patient comes upon events that are similar because they have a central emotional theme.

Inge, even with the best intentions, was not able to lose her fears until she recognized the real cause. This recognition occurred by restimulation of a feeling connected with an earlier experience, which somewhat resembled the current stimulus. When she consciously recognized that her current fear was actually the fear she had experienced at an earlier time, her projections disappeared: she could place her fear in the proper time sequence. At the start I knew only Inge's symptoms. I suspected that some traumas in the past had been the cause, but in the beginning neither of us knew what the traumas were.

In regression to the embryonic stage we touched on the cause of the aggression she felt toward pregnant women that made her consider all mothers to be murderers. Her mother had attempted an abortion during her third month of pregnancy. This powerful threat to life was the trauma we had been seeking, the one that gave the symptom its emotional stimulus. Inge experienced this abortion attempt with all its pain, fear, and feeling of hatred. When she recognized the reason for her attitude toward pregnant women, her hatred and aggression disappeared.

The analytic interpretations of other childhood experiences were not so successful. Though connections were recognized and confirmed and the connection with symptoms was understood, and although the symptoms slowly lost their edge and the patient felt better from time to time, most of the symptoms did not disappear.

The turning point came during the thirteenth session when Inge, of her own accord and without special suggestions, continued her regression and began to talk incoherently of disconnected items that did not pertain to this 28-year-old life. Her entire body was agitated. She moaned and cried and at times her voice was choked and full of despair. Sometimes she swore, raising her clenched fist again and again. After about a third of the session had gone by, her normal voice suddenly became a deep, coarse voice that sounded almost like a man's. Her new voice had not the slightest resemblance to her normal voice and appeared almost ghostlike.

The material reported pertained to ancient Rome. She had not learned Latin in school and had no knowledge of the historical facts. In her first regression she found herself imprisoned. She was involved with a man named Afrahmus, but for a long time it was unclear whether or not he was her husband and what part he played in the imprisonment. She was in prison because she had poisoned someone after having been told that person was a traitor, and at first she seemed to think that this man was Afrahmus, but gradually her perception cleared and she came to realize that the man she had poisoned was actually her brother.

This regression illustrates how the patient can move backward and forward, deepening and clarifying impressions and filling in blanks until a complete story emerges that allows the complex to be exposed and the karmic guilt encapsulated in it to be released. In Inge this led to a remission of her symptoms and to a state of self-acceptance.

P: *I am so hungry and thirsty (moans), I don't know, I think they are going to execute me.*
T: *First tell me what you did. Tell me everything very slowly.*
P: *What I did? Well, I don't know. I did something to Afrah, I don't know, Afrah-Afrah, Afrahmus.*
T: *What did you do?*
P: *Afrah, Afrah, I don't know, Afrahmus...*

She then saw Augustus.

P: *He is so tall, what is his name? He is slender—what is his name? Rrrr, with an R, no—that is the Imperator—he is an Imperator—he is (moans).*
T: *What is the matter?*
P: *I have trouble getting air.*
T: *Why?*
P: *I don't know, he is the one! He sent my husband, he sent my husband into the arena, he sent him into the arena, that I know.*
T: *What did he do?*
P: *Yes, he sent him into the arena.*
T: *Why?*
P: *Well, that is, because he was a Christian (moans). I don't know his name—Augustinus—maybe...there are so many...I am afraid.*
T: *Of whom?*
P: *I am afraid, I don't know.*
T: *Of that man?*
P: *No, I, I...they will take me...they will take me away, too...I am so afraid, I am terribly afraid.... Everything is so dark and smells musty (moans)...there is nothing on the floors, not even straw and they are throwing me in there.*

Throughout this regression there were many references to the persecution of the Christians by Augustus. In that life Inge had been a Christian, and many Christians around her were being killed, including Afrahmus, but her imprisonment was because of the murder.

P: *They are killed.*
T: *The Christians?*
P: *Yes.*

T: By whom?
P: Hm...they are legionnaires.
T: I beg your pardon?
P: Legionnaires...they persecute us.
T: Who is persecuting you?
P: The legionnaires...yes, they followed us to this house, and we like them.... This is a friend of my father's; my father is dead.... They carried my mother away...Afrahmus.
T: Who is that?
P: He is a young warrior.
T: From where do you know him?
P: I met him...at my uncle's house.
T: But this is not your husband?
P: I don't know, he is not, no, he is not yet my husband.
T: Do you love each other?
P: Yes, very much, and he wants...he wants to be baptized. They always baptize there.
T: Where?
P: They baptize every evening.
T: Where?
P: They baptize in my uncle's house, that is the secret, it's called...it is a villa...and everything is green, all around, and we meet under the pretext of having a banquet, but we celebrate the Holy Mass, no, a sacrifice, a sacrificial worship, not a mass.

Through interrogation it comes out that Inge has stolen poison, baked it in bread, and given it to her brother Sirenus because someone had told her he was a traitor. Sirenus dies. Then she realizes that Sirenus was not a traitor after all and she will die for his murder. She goes over and over the situation of the poisoned bread, and the details become increasingly clear. Her anguish grows as she realizes she has murdered her innocent brother.

T: And for whom is this bread intended?
P: For Sirenus.
T: Is Sirenus a Christian?
P: He is a Christian, but he is a traitor, he is a traitor.
T: And he is eating this bread?
P: Yes, I bring him the basket, a wicker basket. The basket is very small, but it has a long handle, a handle to carry it, and I stand before him and next to me are two little children. I give him the bread. He is standing in front of a big building. I don't know—I am standing before a huge vault...yes, now he eats the bread, he eats the bread and he is going to die. He looks at me questioningly, very questioningly and says nothing...he only looks questioningly and with big eyes...I don't know...what shall I do? What shall I do? (Cries.) Brother—I am...
T: Tell me everything you are thinking!

P: I am upset, I can't get air, and I can't breathe.
T: Why? Just keep talking.
P: I did not want to do it, he was not the one, he was not the one.
T: Just keep talking quietly!
P: I am afraid, but not for myself. What will happen to the others now? What will happen to them? And then Afrahmus, he despises me. He never wants to see me again, never again. The men are all so loud, asking me questions.

Her captors laughed at her and called her a brother-murderess and threw her into a dungeon in chains. There were other women, and the soldiers burned off all their long hair and tied them to crosses. She became very afraid.

T: You will be very calm and tell us what else is happening.
P: I am afraid.
T: You will feel nothing. You will only see it. You will breathe calmly and evenly and tell me what else is happening. Tell me!
P: They are gathering wood and putting it down, but they are not lighting it yet, because we have to stay there until the sky is colored red. But I don't care anymore, because...
T: Tell me more.
P: I am coming, I am going away, I am going away from myself, I am going further and further away...
T: Can you still see anything?
P: I don't know...no...it is beautiful, yes, I see our bodies, all of them, and nothing hurts anymore...it is beautiful!
T: What do you feel now?
P: It's just like gliding, always further away. The voice is world encompassing. It is freedom. I notice I am everything and nothing. I am here.
T: What are you saying?
P: I am here and I am there, but I am there. That is, I am something that escaped out of myself. Now I am pure and clean, now I am...it is a powerful feeling. I am, hmm, but I feel nothing, see nothing, hear nothing, only it is I, alone. It is nothing—I shall withdraw.
T: Where to?
P: I don't know, everything is music there, yes, in the sphere, I don't know. There is no name for it, but it is beautiful! I am waiting for something, I am waiting for something, because I feel it is becoming tighter, like a spiral.

Following this I took her ahead to the 20th century, where she experienced being born. As the birth took place I gave her suggestions for peace and happiness.

P: Yes, it is pleasant! Now I know, now I know!

T: *What do you know?*
P: *That I am becoming a human, I know, I know, I am about to become a being, I know it.*
T: *You will experience a deep calm from now on. There are no more fears.*
P: *That is true, I know.*
T: *What do you feel?*
P: *Yes, peace, peace and happiness because it is a sensation so wide and so large and so broad, it is not a feeling of space, it is difficult to describe, truly wonderful (laughs).*

Following this session the patient had no difficulties of any kind adjusting to and filing away her newly acquired experiences in a possible former life. Her final statement that "I am becoming human" and her expression of peace and serenity had replaced many of her presenting fears.

During her next session Inge complained about a remaining symptom that continued to disturb her. She sometimes had red marks on her face, and she was ashamed of them. They became particularly noticeable whenever she was about to leave the house. She was always afraid that people would be able to tell something from these marks, though at first she did not know what. We discovered during her therapy that she was afraid the marks would show that she had engaged in sexual intercourse, which was shameful, but her enlightenment about this did not help the symptom to disappear.

After the induction I suggested that she go back in time until she reached the incident during which these marks first appeared. She immediately went back into the same Roman lifetime, this time before she was burned at the stake for murder. The tortured relationship with Afrahmus clarified as she skimmed layer after layer of protective fantasies from what had actually happened.

During this session it emerged that she had had a sexual relationship with Afrahmus in a garden and was seen. Because of this she was marked prior to her burning.

P: *When I, well, my brother—that was enough but not because I did that, but because then he left, I got these marks so that everyone can see that I am guilty.*
T: *Of what?*
P: *Yes, that I am guilty, and I was not baptized. Because, it didn't work anymore. Those are the...I don't know why I am suddenly thinking of that.... With the marks, when someone commits a sin, then you are marked, and that is why we were burned.*
T: *Who are we?*
P: *I am not allowed to talk!*
T: *Why can't you talk?*

P: Because of my guilt, because I am always afraid, because I poisoned my brother and that is why I am afraid, and we could not get married, whether...I really am not allowed to say that.
T: You may say it.
P: His name is...I can't tell you or he will be arrested, too.
T: You need not be afraid to tell me.

She began to talk about two children and a big belly.

T: Are you pregnant?
P: I don't know. I really don't know.
T: Surely you know whether you are pregnant.
P: No.
T: Could you be?
P: No. I don't know whether I could be or not. Yes, but I am not pregnant. I am imagining that because I also imagine...no, it is not possible.
T: What is possible?
P: That there was something.
T: Let us dissolve to that point in time...

Slowly and reluctantly she allowed the memory to emerge of having sexual relations with Afrahmus in a garden before they could be married. This was seen and reported. After a number of denials of the resulting pregnancy she was finally able to face it.

P: We were not yet married. That's what I mean. And perhaps that is why he went away, and because I was guilty I get these marks in my face, and because I like it myself...maybe...and then I was so ashamed when I stood across the way from him, and we stood alone across from each other, and I was so ashamed—my face became so hot it felt as if someone was burning holes in my skin.
T: How do you know how it feels to have holes burned in your skin?
P: That happens when you feel guilt. Yes, when you are supposed to talk and you don't want to talk, they burn holes in your skin.
T: Has that happened to you? Return to that incident!
P: Hmm, that is the sun. I won't say anything—I know what it was. No, I was supposed to talk, but I can't...they brand you.
T: To whom were you supposed to talk?
P: They have little sponges. They burn your skin with them—sponges. They take them out of the water, and they burn them on your skin with something sticky. It's brown-red and partly yellow when they heat it, they dip the sponges into it, and then they press them on your skin.
T: Why do they do that?
P: So that you are marked for something.

We repeated the incident again and finally she was able to describe in detail just how the sponges were dipped in burning acid and pressed on her face. Following this she was put on a rack and tortured.

T: *Why is he doing this to you?*
P: *So that I will repent.*
T: *What are you supposed to repent?*
P: *That I did that.*
T: *Did what?*
P: *Because I was with...because I was with Afrahmus in the garden...because, because we made love there, before we were married and before the baptism and...*
T: *What is happening now?*
P: *He is burning my face. He is burning my face (cries and sobs).*
T: *What else is happening?*
P: *He is still pulling, pulling on my legs. He wants to tear my legs out. He is pulling my leg apart. It is getting all stiff, I don't know.*

She was further tortured and then finally left to the ministrations of some women.

P: *I am all confused. I didn't know that something, hmm...because it was so beautiful and not bad, I knew I must not do it, but, hmm...I didn't know they would punish me so severely. I didn't know that, but I know I will never do it again, never again. I don't want to see it anymore, either, because he, because the way he looked at me. No one helped me say anything....*

All that remained was to help Inge see that this event had happened in the past and was no longer pertinent. This was the transformational intervention that crystallized her work and allowed the symptom to be released.

T: *Good, we shall leave this time period, leave these events, and go forward in time. Your face is clean, completely clear and spotless. Your skin is clean and smooth. You can feel the marks dissolve, isn't that right?*
P: *Yes, they are disappearing!*
T: *Because they have no further justification.*
P: *True, they don't.*
T: *You don't need them anymore. You don't want them anymore. We shall simply let them disappear, very simply. These marks have made an error in time. They are two thousand years too late. All your fears, all your feelings of guilt, are errors in time. We don't need them anymore. You are now living in the year 1975. Guilt feelings from the past are no longer valid. How do you feel?*

P: *Very well.*
T: *Then we shall end this session promptly.*

This case illustrates how easily the patient slips into other lifetimes if the search for the actual cause of the symptom is persistent enough. There is always *a direct, specific, and related cause,* which, if one can recover it, will release the charge that initiated the symptom. Recovering the incident resolves the time confusion that has remained because the original incident remained unconscious. In Inge's case, the spots were not symbolical. As is usually the case, they emerged out of an actual incident.

### Case 2. Claudia: Leaving the Past Behind

This case illustrates how going backward through childhood, birth, and the uterine state can lead to a past-life source of problems. In this case the subject was struggling with various phobias and fears that covered a spectrum ranging from death to a fear of rats. In addition, she had physical problems involving her limbs.

Throughout therapy, dialogues are carried on whenever they emerge on their own in a particular therapy situation. Entire sessions may be devoted to such dialogues that serve to clarify questions that arise. These dialogues will give the patient insight into the basic laws of life and the universe as well as into his own specific problems. It gradually becomes possible for a patient to understand the connection between a specific experience and emerging patterns of behavior, since he will have experienced the practical application within the session even before discussing the nature of patterns.

Unlike many cases where recognition of a situation is in the beginning too painful for it to emerge clearly, this subject's material evidenced little distortion, but repetition of facets of her experience deepened it and brought out many new details. When requested to do so, she was even able to write as an unschooled child and to speak an appropriate ancient dialect. Again, in this regression we observe that symptoms have their source in specific situations. She went back into two previous lifetimes, first as Claudia and then immediately preceding that as Lena, and in these lifetimes we tapped the sources of her various fears and she was able to release them.

A brief scan of her childhood and birth led to a uterine experience that formed a direct bridge to the earlier life she needed to look at.

T: *We shall go backward through your life because time means nothing to us. Time is only a means of communication, a measure, but you will re-live the past as if it were happening now. The past will become the present. We shall go backward in your life. You are getting younger; you will be 25*

*years old. We shall go back further—you will be 20 years old. Let us go back further—you are 15, 10 years old. Today is your tenth birthday. How do you feel?*
P: Not particularly well.
T: Why not?
P: I have the flu.
T: Did you get any presents?
P: Not many.
T: What did you get?
P: My mother sent me a package—a red blouse and a pleated gray skirt with straps. It had red and blue dots on it. But they took it from me.
T: Who took it from you?
P: My sister. She said the skirt was too short, that it didn't fit me, so she gave it to some other girl. That was my birthday present (cries). She...she doesn't like me. Everything I get she gives away. She takes away everything, I can't keep anything (cries). I don't like her either—I hate her—oh, I hate her (cries). I hate her, I hate her (cries)!
T: Let us dissolve from this birthday and go further back in time. We shall go further back in time. You are getting younger. You are now six years old. Are you going to school now?
P: Yes.
T: Can you do arithmetic?
P: Yes.
T: How much is five and five?
P: I have two hands—10.

## Birth

T: Good. Let us go back further. You are getting younger—five, four, three, two, one. Let us return to the moment of your birth. Today is April 13, 1946. You are just being born. What time is it?
P: Four fifty-two.
T: Good.
P: It is a Saturday, it's Saturday.
T: You are just being born. What do you feel? What is happening?
P: Phew, something is forcing me out.
T: Out of where?
P: Out of what I was in.
T: How does it look?
P: I don't know, dark and warm, but how does it look? You don't see it; you only feel it....
T: What do you feel?
P: Quite tight, but warm and soft.
T: Good. What happens next? You are just being born. Tell me all your impressions exactly.
P: No, it won't work. I can't get out. I can't get out. I can hardly breathe...I...no, it's not that I can't breathe, but I don't know. I can't get

out. I must get out, but it won't work. But suddenly it's getting light and something is lifting me up. A woman is lying on the table. It's my mother, and another doctor is taking something out, and her stomach is open...and there I am, I got out.
T: From where did you get out?
P: Out of the stomach, the open stomach. It's bleeding and now I'm getting a...hmm (laughs) and the midwife, or whoever it is...yes, the midwife, keeps saying, "My God, what a beautiful child, with such beautiful blue eyes." I don't even know whether I have blue eyes....
T: Did something go wrong with your birth?
P: No, no, I don't think so, I can't imagine what.
T: Were you born by Caesarean section?
P: I don't know what they call it, but in my case, they cut open the woman's stomach and I came out.

**Intrauterine Experience**

T: Let us go back further in time. Let us return to the place from which you came to the time of conception. Why are you laughing? Tell me!
P: Hmm (laughs) nothing, but it keeps bouncing.
T: Tell me exactly. What is bouncing?
P: I don't know, hmm, hmm.
T: What is happening?
P: Yes, I am lying there and it keeps bouncing. I think, I have...no, that can't be, I have experienced it before, this bouncing, but I'm not even born yet.
T: Tell me what is happening. Describe all your experiences.
P: It is pleasant. It is wonderfully pleasant, warm and soft, and even when it bounces, it is soft, it doesn't hurt, and I keep thinking...but perhaps it's only my imagination—I have experienced this bouncing around once before, or I know what it is.
T: What is it?
P: Like being on a wagon, or on a wagon rolling over stones.

**Induction into a Past Life**

T: Good, dissolve back to the picture.
P: Yes, I (coughs)...
T: What's the matter, why are you coughing?
P: I'm sick; I was in a wagon with the gentleman—in a horse and wagon—I have to cough constantly.
T: What is your name?
P: Claudia. That comes from Claudine, because Mama says that way it won't be noticed.
T: What won't be noticed?
P: At the time when I was born, there were many Frenchmen in the area. They were Napoleon's troops, and Mama, Mama called me Claudine so that everyone would think a Frenchman was my father.
T: Why were they supposed to think that?

P: No one was to know that the gentleman was my father.
T: What gentleman?
P: Well, the gentleman, the baron.

By using extensive and careful dialogue I was able to help the subject reveal much about her lifetime as Claudia. She was conceived as the result of an affair with the Baron and was brought up with the legitimate daughter Charlotte. From early years she suffered from consumption and eventually died of it at an early age. She also was afflicted with a withered arm, the result of her mother having been kicked by a horse during her pregnancy when she attempted to embrace the Baron in the stable and he pushed her away. Her mother considered Claudia's withered arm punishment for her sin.

Extensive dialogue described a visit to Berlin to see the King. She described the King and told about the knickknacks he distributed to his guests. She was able to write a rough draft of her name.

**Birth in the Past Lifetime**

T: Let us go back further in time. You are getting younger, you are ten, eight, six, four, two-years-old, you are just being born. What is the date?
P: September 12, 1812.
T: You are just being born. What time is it?
P: I don't know that; we have no clock.
T: But you still know what time it is.
P: No, we don't have a clock. How can I tell, we have no clock.
T: The correct time—to the minute—it will come to you—what time is it? It is the moment of your birth!
P: Oh, I—it is so far away—yes, one minute to four.
T: In the morning or afternoon?
P: It is dark, it is dark, yes, I am being born now.
T: What's the matter? Tell me!
P: Well, she, she's holding me so strangely.
T: Who is holding you strangely?
P: This old lady, this woman, and she keeps saying, "Poor little creature, such a poor little creature." Well, I guess I look pretty scrawny.

**Regression to a Still Earlier Lifetime**

At this point I took the patient further back into a still earlier lifetime that, among other things, touched on her phobia about rats. Her name in that lifetime was "black Lena" because she had long black hair. She was born in 1697 and at the time period she tuned into she was 26 years old. She couldn't write but could copy her memory of how the number making up the year looked.

T: *Good. Let's go back a bit further. Go back until your present condition changes. Let's keep going back until you come across a new situation. What do you see?*
P: (Moans.) *My God—no, oh no, oh no.*
T: *What's the matter?*
P: *It disgusts me.*
T: *What is it?*
P: *Ha, the rats, oh, no—help!*
T: *First tell me where you are!*
P: *Oh, my God* (cries)—*I'm in a tower* (cries)—*I, no, the...*
T: *Tell me, what do you see here?*
P: *Rats, rats, phew...oh, no...*
T: *Why are you here in this tower? What sort of tower is this? How did you get in here?*
P: *They threw me in* (moans).

Lena's husband, who had been a charcoal burner, had turned revolutionary, and they had been hiding out in a leaky, empty cottage and living on the environment—vegetables, berries, and whatever game her husband caught with a form of bow and arrow. She sent her husband further away for safety and kept her children with her. Every day the duke's guards passed nearby. The children were hungry so she caught a rabbit in a snare.

One day while she was in the forest trying to find something to eat, the castle guards found her. She had been betrayed by a foreign visitor whom she had met in the forest and who had tried to seduce her. She was thrown into a tower and beaten to try to get her to tell where her husband was. Finally she was left in the tower with nothing to eat. The rats came closer and closer. At first she was able to scare them away, but as she became weaker from lack of food, she couldn't manage this anymore.

P: *I want them to go away.*
T: *I beg your pardon?*
P: *I want them to go away...the rats...they're eating at me. They're eating at my feet...bah...disgusting...*
T: *Describe what you see.*
P: *Oh, that* (moans)...
T: *Look closely!*
P: *You want me to look at that* (moans)?
T: *Look at it!*
P: *I can't look at it.*
T: *Tell me what colors you see.*
P: *They're black, black, oh...*

### Death Experience in That Lifetime

T: Very well, then continue. What else is happening? Tell me, what else is happening to you?
P: I am becoming unconscious.
T: How does that feel?
P: Fine. Now I don't feel anything.
T: Can you still see it?
P: Yes, I see it, but I'm not there. That is—I am there, but I see myself.
T: What is that? What does that mean?
P: Ah, I'm dead. Hah (breathes a sigh of relief)!
T: Come, tell me, what's happening?
P: They let me starve to death. Now they're coming down the steps. One is kicking me. No, not me, but my body, that's lying there. He's kicking me in the side with his foot and says he wants me to get up and come along, but of course I can't do that. I'm dead. Then one of them says, "I guess she's gone," or something like that, and the big rat is still eating at my body.
T: Now, when you watch the rats eating you, what do you feel?
P: Nothing. That's just the shell. They're eating my shell. That doesn't bother me. If they're always down there, they must get hungry. They don't get anything to eat, so let them eat. I don't feel anything anymore.
T: What are you doing now?
P: Well, I'm going to look for my husband. He's still in my friend's hut, and he has a girl or woman, I can't tell exactly. He has her in his arms. They're laughing and they seem to be having a good time. No more talk of killing the duke or insurrection. They're just having a good time and drinking and laughing.
T: How does that affect you?
P: It doesn't bother me at all. If he enjoys it, if he's satisfied and happy, let him be.

### Interlife Experience

In the after-death state she also checked on her children, who did not recognize her when she tried to comfort them. Then she went into the interlife.

T: Very well, what happens now?
P: Well, I can see and recognize everything, but I am everywhere and nowhere. You know, this is a state...how can I explain it? Everything is smooth and quiet and you can simply wish to be wherever you want and suddenly you're there, simply by thinking. After all, you no longer have a body.
T: Would you like to remain in this state?
P: I don't know.
T: What happens next?

P: I think...I think I will get a new body.
T: When will that be?
P: Well, for a human it might be a long time, but for us it's not long.
T: Who are you?
P: Well, we're—what are we? We, yes, I don't know what we are. We have thoughts. We are, we are thoughts. I believe we are thoughts without a body, but I can't tell you exactly.
T: Is it pleasant, this state?
P: Yes, but, pleasant, pleasant, you know, what is called life and what happens during this life, this is—how shall I say it—at present it's harmonious and smooth and quiet, but there are no highs and lows. You know, you might say it's monotonous. I think—you are human, and humans in this state...I don't know... I'm quite certain you would find it very monotonous.

She went on to describe more of the interim state.

T: I shall try to understand you.
P: Yes, but you know, I can't explain it so well, I...if I had a body now, I could probably explain it to you better. You know...but I am nothing now, I am only—what am I, anyway? Do you know what I am?
T: What are you?
P: Do you know what I am? Can you tell me what I am now?
T: Are you not simply yourself?
P: Yes, I am myself, but what am I made of? Out of, hmm, I don't know, out of air? or, hmm...
T: What could we call what you are made of?
P: Energy, maybe, I don't know whether you understand. It may be energy, but I don't know exactly. I...

## Rebirth into the Life as Claudia

T: Good, then you want to come back into the world once more?
P: Yes, I guess so, but I don't want another body that has to, that has to suffer so much.
T: Do you have a choice?
P: No, I don't.
T: What will the new life be like?
P: Short, very short.
T: Why short?
P: Well, I'll have to suffer again, just what I didn't want, the body will have to suffer again, but not the soul, only the body, but the soul will—I think—be pretty well smoothed out, or I, you know, what I am right now—when that's inside a body, the body may suffer, but that, what I am, won't suffer—it will remain at peace and...
T: Is that better?
P: Yes, much.

She proceeded to the point where she was reunited with matter and went again into her life as Claudia.

T: Is it difficult?
P: No, not difficult, but it doesn't hurt, either, at least it's not unpleasant, but I don't know how to explain it. Imagine, imagine this huge vacuum cleaner and it sucks you in or something like that, something like that, yes, but it doesn't hurt. It isn't unpleasant either, it really isn't.
T: What's happening to you now?
P: Well, now I'm entering into it. I'm making the connection.
T: What else is happening?
P: I still have no body, but the thing I am in is growing, but very slowly—it's as if, you know, as if somebody is slowly pulling on all your limbs, very slowly and suddenly. I wouldn't say it's unpleasant, and suddenly you have a shape again.

She again described her withered arm and gave more details of the incident in the stable.

**Death as Claudia**

The patient then briefly retraced her life and looked to see if she had known any of the people in it in another lifetime or in the current one, but she could not identify anyone clearly. Then she went on to her death.

T: How old will you get to be?
P: I will not get to be very old; I may have about another half year to live, not much more.
T: Very well, let us go forward in time until just before your death.
P: Yes.
T: Tell me what happens.
P: Well, I am lying on the bed and I'm terribly thin and frail, I... hmm...and the doctor is there and says he can't help me anymore—I'll have to die.
T: Very well, let's do that.

With a combination of support and insistence Claudia was able to remember the exact time of her death—January 13, 1826 at 4:28 p.m.

T: Thank you. What happens now?
P: I am going to Mama and stroke her hair. You know, she always used to say to me, "It won't be so bad when I die, I shall return and you will return," so now when I go to stroke her hair and she is crying so bitterly, I say to her, "Mama, you know I'll return," but she can't hear me.
T: What else do you see? Your mother and what else?
P: Yes, and my...she is lying on top of me, on top of my body, which is still on the bed, and she is brushing the hair out of my eyes and keeps saying,

"Dear God, why?" and keeps asking "Dear God, why did it have to happen to me? I did no evil," or something like that, because she has already been punished for her sin.
T: How?
P: Well, you know, that's why I got the lame arm.

### Interlife Learning

She went into the interlife again and deepened her learning there.

T: What happens to you now? Will you remain in this state?
P: No, I doubt that.
T: Why?
P: Well, it was much too short. You know, what I experienced now...what do you call that? Hmm, it purified me, but it was much too short, it was...
T: You will come back to earth?
P: I'm sure of it, yes.
T: What will you still have to learn?
P: Well, I'll have to learn to accept fate as it comes, you know, make the best of it, come what may, and not always say, you know...Let me give you an example. I have—when I'm very thirsty, yes, and I see a glass half-full of water. I must not say it's half-empty, but I must say, "Thank God, it's still half-full," you know, that's what I must learn. Do you understand what I mean?
T: Will you learn that in your coming life?
P: I think so, and I'll have to learn to swallow or put up with a great deal, or whatever you want to call it, but I really believe I will learn that in this life.
T: So you really want to be born again?
P: I don't want to, but I have to.
T: Good, let's proceed to the point in time where you are united with matter again.

In a repeat description of her current birth the patient again mentioned the Caesarian section. Questions about the return of any of the people in lifetimes prior to this one were answered in the negative. She felt that the Baron was alive in this lifetime but lived as a vet in Cologne and she would not meet him.

### Processing of the Regression Material

T: Let us go forward in time to the year 1975, all right?
P: Yes.
T: Let us stop on May 11, 1975.
P: Yes, today is Mother's Day.
T: Yes, today is May 11, 1975. You are sleeping soundly and peacefully; you are in a deep hypnotic sleep. We have spoken about many things and have taken a long trip, but everything we have discussed will attach itself to your

conscious being and will be known to you even after this session, everything we have talked about, everything that you have experienced, everything you have seen, all this will be at your disposal after the session. Is this agreeable to you?
P: Yes.
T: Look back over your previous development. Review your past that we have discussed. How does it feel to see the past close up, to recognize it and to look over it?
P: Well, it's a knowledge that everyone ought to have. Everyone ought to know what he was or is.
T: So you will find it agreeable and pleasant?
P: Yes, only—there is something...
T: What else is there?
P: The rats.
T: Hmm...what about them?
P: They...rats disgust me. When I see a rat, my flesh creeps.
T: Why?
P: You know that rats were once eating me?
T: Yes, and you know it now, too.
P: Yes, and every time I see a rat...
T: You re-live what you experienced a long time ago.
P: No, I don't know whether I re-live it, but, in any case, it disgusts me terribly.
T: And this aversion started at that time?
P: Yes.
T: Now every time you see a rat, you must coordinate the time correctly. You know that this aversion goes back two hundred years; it has no business in your current life. You will learn to like rats. You will find them pleasant, beautiful.
P: Ah...
T: This feeling belongs back two centuries.
P: Do you really believe that?
T: Where does this feeling belong?
P: Do you really believe that? Learn to like rats?
T: Rats disgust you?
P: Yes.
T: Very well, where does this aversion belong? Dissolve back!
P: Yes, 1725.
T: Return to that situation!
P: No.
T: You must learn to look at it—not so much disgust, not so much emotion. Don't show your feelings. Look at it and describe it. Look at it objectively. What is happening? The rats are nibbling at you, correct?
P: Yes, at my feet.
T: Yes, and why? Because they are hungry.
P: Yes, because they're hungry.

The subject was led into an overview of her relationship with the rats, realized that she killed a rabbit because she was hungry and saw that the rats did not actually kill her; she died from starvation. She also processed her aversion to their furless tails and came to see that from a different point of view they were cute.

T: Now make up with the rats.
P: Okay.
T: But you must really mean it.
P: I really mean it.
T: That's good, they're really lovable and sweet little animals.
P: Well, I don't know if I'd call them lovable and sweet, but...
T: You have to learn to love their kind.
P: No, but you know, I understand now—you explained it to me. It's not the rats' fault.
T: Then you are angry with the people who let you starve?
P: Yes.
T: And you transferred this anger to the rats?
P: I did. Yes.
T: And a rat will never bother you again?

**Release of a Current Physical Symptom**

P: And what about my arm?
T: What's wrong with your arm?
P: I don't know.
T: Well, move it. You can move it. What's wrong with the arm?
P: I don't feel it.
T: Let's go back to the arm. Where did this arm originate? When did you get this lame arm?
P: 1812.
T: And what year is it now?
P: Mother's Day.
T: 1975.
P: Yes.
T: What is this lame arm doing in the year 1975?
P: Yes, but I—my God!
T: What's the matter?
P: But I'm—of course—I'm already dead.
T: This arm has no business in this life. It doesn't belong in this life. It's an aberration in time. We're living in the year 1975 and the arm feels fine.
P: Yes, I had forgotten that.
T: Good, move your arm.
P: Yes, it's fine.

The final processing consisted of an overview of her understanding of the confusion of time frames.

T: *You now have the opportunity of surveying your entire past. It is always ready to be reviewed by you, which does not mean that you should return to the past. We have done that once in order to make it known to you. You will always be fully conscious of it, but never forget that you are living in the here and now. The events from the past, those experiences, have nothing to do with the here and now. That is an anachronism, an aberration in time, if you continue to live with emotions dating back to days long gone by. You will have the capability of immediately recognizing feelings that do not belong to the present as those that actually belong to the past. This will make you more and more aware every day. Your consciousness will become greater and deeper. You will be able to review your past completely, but you will realize that it is the past, that you are living in the here and now, completely in the present and not in the past with emotions attached to events of the long ago. Do you agree?*
P: *Yes.*
T: *And so all events of the past have lost their power over you because you know them, you recognize them. They have no further influence over you because everything that is known has no influence. You have influence over what is known and not vice versa. Only the unknown can have influence, and since the past is now fully known to you, it can do nothing to you. You are living entirely in the present—you are feeling well. Do you feel this new well-being throughout your entire body?*
P: *My feet still hurt.*
T: *Where does this hurting of the feet belong?*
P: *1725.*
T: *And what year are we in now?*
P: *1975.*
T: *And how do your feet feel now?*
P: *Well, yes...I...you know, I keep forgetting, or I think I keep forgetting to simply leave it behind.*
T: *Let's leave the past behind us, where it belongs. We are living in the here and now, and in the now, you are feeling very well. You feel well, happy and satisfied. You have no problems. On the contrary, your entire body feels as if it's had a vacation—well rested and recuperated, as if you had been sleeping for hours, or even days, completely refreshed. Can you feel that throughout your entire body? Do you feel it?*
P: *Yes.*
T: *Yes, really feel it. How does it feel?*
P: *Hmm, not bad, comfortable, somehow.*
T: *Now we shall bring this session to a conclusion—you will then be completely awake, and even in your waking state all the information you have gained in this session will be at your disposal and you will feel very, very well.*

Chapter XXI

# Winafred B. Lucas, Ph.D.

## *Biographical Data*

**Personal Background**

When I was three my 90-year-old grandmother came to live with us. She was a scholar and also a theosophist, and I can remember her telling me about Annie Besant when I was five. Her death when I was seven left me with no one to talk to about things that were important to me. Though my hometown of Seattle welcomed new ideas, people were of the conventional variety, so I grew up willing to look at new things but also cautious about being different.

As I turned 20, with majors in Greek and philosophy and writing, I came upon novels by L. Adams Beck[1] that recovered for me the perceptions I had shared with my grandmother, and with them as my instructor I began to practice Raja Yoga. The work with yoga and the reading that accompanied it encouraged me to recover my knowledge of Sanskrit, which, though I was not aware of it, I had known in other lifetimes. After a year of graduate work in Greek, with Sanskrit as a minor, I reversed their order and in 1934 went to Munich to work with Professor Alois Fischer. Hitler had come into power that year, and before I could complete my doctorate in Sanskrit, this great scholar under whom I was studying was seized by the Nazis and killed in a concentration camp.

Meanwhile, I had been working in a Jungian analysis, an exciting experience that made me realize that I wanted to be a clinical psychologist. This new profession had just begun to emerge in Germany and in several major cities in the United States. I shifted my doctoral work to psychology and took an internship at the Seif Clinic, the first child guidance clinic in Germany. Before I could complete my degree, feeling the pressure of the

Nazis, I left Munich to study dance in Vienna. During these years in Europe I deepened my understanding of Eastern philosophy, both during the Jungian analysis and through the Wandering Bird movement, which stressed these concepts, especially in the widely read books of Hermann Hesse.

Several years later, having acquired two young children to support, I went back for my doctorate and completed it at UCLA in 1955 under Bruno Klopfer, whose assistant I was for seven years and with whom I explored many of the holistic concepts that later were to surface in the intellectual climate of the seventies. In the late 50's and 60's, following my training with Klopfer, I was a Rorschach specialist on the faculty of Los Angeles State University and also started a clinical practice. I continued, in both teaching and clinical work, to sort out and synthesize the concepts of the East and the West. It was during this period that I took part as a control in some LSD research in the Medical School and made my first extended contact with past lives, an enlightening and healing journey. It was also at this time that I joined a Japanese American group with Senzaki, the first Zen Buddhist monk to come to California.

In the seventies, as concepts of energy opened up, I cautiously exposed myself to holistic ideas, trying out expanded parameters in healing, self-health, and various forms of transformational imaging, again pressing toward a synthesis of modern science and Eastern thought. A workshop experience during this time extended my perception of past-life experiences, and from that time on I moved easily into a philosophy of life that I had touched upon during my childhood, which perceived the soul as on a journey and the body as a vehicle for this journey.

My years on the core faculty of the California School of Professional Psychology in the mid- and late seventies offered me opportunity to examine more deeply my new horizons, to trim off areas of thinking that lacked adequate conceptual justification, and to ground in many of the new scientific thrusts some of the concepts I retained as viable hypotheses. Initially I did not carry these new thrusts into my psychological practice, with the exception of transformational techniques that were becoming generally accepted (at least in California). I had not intended to include past-life therapy, about which I still had many questions. An experience with a patient whose separation anxiety threatened gravely to handicap her life, and that I could not seem to help her dissolve with any of the spectrum of clinical approaches I felt comfortable in using, made me willing to try past-life recall. This initial experience took less than half an hour and completely released the patient from anxiety around separation; the remission has held for more than eight years. It convinced me that, used appropriately, this therapeutic modality is both justified and helpful. Since then there have been further experiences of positive therapeutic outcomes, not only in the remission of symptoms but in the opening up of long-standing destructive patterns so that these patterns have become available for transformation.

It would be a grave omission if I did not say that the recovery of past lives has changed and deepened my own life by exposing patterns and focusing relationships so that a process of transformation could take place. The critical, scientifically trained part of me remains properly skeptical and unsure that past lives exist at all, and this approach I honor. At the same time, the intuitive part of me moves back and forth, making a scan of the pathways of my inner development. Seeing the pattern unfold, I become increasingly patient with the steps of my own personal journey, a journey that extends far backward into very early ages. Meanwhile, as I gradually withdraw from teaching and clinical practice, these older years, the best of my life, are perfused with meditation and filled with writing, bringing to whatever flowering is possible all that I have come to understand through many lifetimes.

## Personal Past-life Experience

Intimations of past lives flickered around me from childhood on, but the conditioning of my culture made me blind and deaf to them. At times I wondered about my aptitudes, addictions, deep interests, ancient thoughts; but remaining loyal to the thinking of my time, I denied that they had unseen roots. Still, I found myself puzzling about why contact with any animal, wild or tame, always moved me so deeply that I was choked with tears, and how at eight could I take an unrideable horse and without experience manage it competently. And it was totally inexplicable to me when I was 15 that I became haunted by the excruciating feeling that I had committed a terrible crime and would be found out and executed, a fear I could leave behind only when I made it to my 16th year.

Looking back later, I wondered that I, whose family, though scholarly, had nothing to do with the Classics, began to study Greek at 14 and found myself able to read Plato at 17 at a time when Greek had almost disappeared from the universities. And when I began to write a biography of Socrates, I questioned uneasily where all the certain knowledge about him came from that I had not read in any book. A few years later I learned Sanskrit by myself and found that it, too, was my language, and I made my way to Europe during the early 30's to earn a doctorate in it so that I could read the Vedas—not the most practical thing to do in a depression. Intimations of past lives were present constantly, but, not wanting to be out of step with my time, I carefully looked the other way.

Eventually I had to look. The first quick glance occurred when I was a control subject in an LSD experiment in the Medical School at UCLA at a time when neither I nor anyone I knew had ever heard of LSD. With no forewarning I was plunged into the deepest perceptions of my life. Included in these was a series of other lifetimes, as a child in India hearing a song so beautiful it seemed to come out of the heart of being; as a wife of a ruler in a small principality near current Pakistan in the ninth century, struggling to help rule from the unenviable powerlessness of a woman; death in an English cathedral in the fifteenth century. Even then I did not embrace this experience, putting it instead on hold because in no way could I fit it into the frame of reference in which I functioned.

My next encounter with a past lifetime occurred in a workshop with John Richard Turner on the aura (which at that time I wasn't at all sure existed). We worked in dyads to scan the edges of our auras, a process that made me feel slightly ridiculous, but it must have put me in an altered state, for when my partner reached my throat area I found myself back in Paris at the time of the French Revolution, lying with my neck on the guillotine in the process of being beheaded. I tried to scream but no sound came, and carefully I pulled myself together and went on with the workshop as though nothing had happened. However, at that moment the walls of my limited one-lifetime world were shattered, and nothing has ever been able to build them up again. Standing in a corner of that unattractive classroom with other dyads working all about me, I knew in a way of knowing that is difficult to comprehend or explain, that in that life I had been a young woman of 29 and that my daughter of this lifetime was my husband in that one. He had deserted me, and the soldiers had caught me and brought me to my death.

A few weeks later, when I had recovered from the shock of this experience, I lay down in my meditation room, put on some music, breathed light for a while to get into an altered state, and went back to the period just before the execution. I found myself as a young matron in a villa outside Paris, agitatedly walking up and down on a marble walkway in the garden. I could see the white clay pots of plants and the short bushes and the doors into the villa. I was waiting for my husband, who was to have come and rescued me, but he did not come, and instead I was taken by the soldiers.

Sometime later, when I was on the phone with my daughter, somewhat piqued with her over something, I remarked lightly, "Well, after all, you deserted me in the French Revolution and I got beheaded!" It was said flippantly and was meant to be a joke, the more so because I had no idea she had ever thought anything about past lives. To my total surprise she replied in an agonized voice, "Don't you know I was locked up in a dungeon and couldn't get to you?" She had gone back into the same experience and

Once the walls that blocked my perception had fallen, past lives were everywhere about me for the looking. My next experience came during a workshop that was part of a larger conference. The leader, experienced and skillful regression therapist Barbara Findeisen, was actually working with someone else, but listening to her induction I found myself back in the 16th century as a crusty old judge, complete with wig and gavel. A young woman came in, obviously agonized, carrying a baby. She had stolen food for her child, a serious crime in England in those days. I reminded her of this and told her that she would get the maximum penalty, and I sentenced her to a life in the workhouse and sent her baby to an orphanage. As she was led out she screamed at me that her son would revenge her. I became paranoid and at times sneaked over to see what she was doing at the workhouse and how the baby was. In a short while, to my relief, they both died. This time I became aware that the young woman of that lifetime was my daughter in this one, and I experienced remorse and regret and a beginning understanding of why our relationship has had so many ups and downs.

When I could find Barbara alone, I told her about the experience and asked her how I could come to terms with the sort of character that I had been, about whom I felt both shame and consternation. She suggested that I go back and find out why, as the judge, I became that way. So one night I got on the mattress in the meditation room again, put on some music, and mentally stated my intention to go back to the experience from that lifetime that had led to such a crusty, self-righteous attitude. Immediately I was back in England 20 years before my judgeship, and this time in a town called Ponticherry. I knew of no Ponticherry in England, only in India, though I realized that the one in India could have been named after an English town that now no longer exists.

At the beginning of this scene, which took place in a comfortable house on the outskirts of the town, I saw only my young wife, who was heavily pregnant and awaiting my return. Two men came to the door and forced their way in and demanded a set of jade Buddhas that I had collected from sailing ships. It seems that I had been talking extravagantly about them, and thugs had heard about the Buddhas and determined to steal them. My wife was equally determined to save them and struggled against the men. They attacked her brutally and took the Buddhas and ran away. When I returned, I found my wife, whom I deeply loved, dying, and of course the unborn baby died with her. At that time I was a young barrister and I vowed that if I ever became a judge and had any power, anyone who came before me and had stolen anything would get the limit.

As I lay in the meditation room thinking about this experience, all I could do was have compassion for the aspect of me that had been the young barrister. It did not absolve what he chose to do, but it did make it understandable. That was the only thing I could do at that time, but I began to see that the transformation of old patterns is the chief purpose of recovering past lives and that we are only at the threshold of understanding how to effect such a transformation. I did recognize that my daughter's anger at me at times in this life started a long time back, and this understanding made me more patient with her. And since I recognized that my wife of that lifetime was now my son, I understood my lifelong need to protect him, which is inappropriate now and which I struggle to release.

The spontaneous recovery of that past life in 17th century England, and especially my ability to move back into it and pick up earlier parts of it, made me realize that the curtain that hung between my waking perception and these other times was surprisingly thin and I could go back whenever I wished, but in spite of the ease with which this could take place, I did not attempt it very often. Once, however, I did go back to a very old lifetime, perhaps a core experience, as it is sometimes referred to, when, as a 16-year-old woman in a rain forest in South America, I left my village and my parents, who were dependent on me for care, and went off by myself in the jungle to avoid responsibility. While I was busy enjoying this forest life, a band of hunters came and one of them persuaded me to go back to his village. I later bore two children to him—the two children of this lifetime—but fretted under my responsibility to them, also, and eventually ran away from the village to resume my old life as a forest nomad. This time I was chased and killed by a big cat, and my last thought was that I had come into disaster because I had refused to take responsibility. Apparently this became stamped in as a deep karmic script and I have been making up for it ever since by trying to take responsibility for everything.

There are some lifetimes that expose a spectrum of threads that are restated in following lifetimes. For me one of these encompassing lifetimes, which contained both the seeds of personality patterns (one could call them sub-personalities) and core relationships of this current life, was an Egyptian experience that ended for me about 1205 B.C. I regressed into that lifetime because of my wish to understand my deep and almost compulsive involvement with Salukis, an Egyptian-Arabian sight-hound breed that my daughter and I had built into a famous line during more than 20 years of breeding and showing. Puzzled as to the intensity of my dedication, which had absorbed much of my energy and money for many years, I asked about the origin of this interest during a workshop with Edith Fiore.

I found myself as the nine-year-old youngest daughter of the Pharaoh of that time (about whose identity I had not the slightest inkling, as my knowledge of Egyptian history was scanty). I was on a barge going up the Nile with my father to the Valley of the Kings where he was supervising his tomb, having been told by an oracle that he would die in five years. For some reason, which I later came to understand but at first did not know, I did not live with the rest of my extensive family in the main capital but in another almost empty city, which apparently had once been the capital, where I was being trained in a Mystery School. Except for my very early childhood I never saw my sisters, the eldest of whom (my daughter in this lifetime) was being brought up to become a co-Pharaoh after my father's death. I had no human companionship other than my nurse.

My father had a Saluki (a breed called at that time the "Royal Dog of Egypt") who stood by his throne at times and accompanied him on the barge. This golden, far-seeing regal dog named Ra, who became my companion, was the only friend I had. Sometimes my father let him stay with me instead of requiring him to attend court.

As predicted, my father died and had a splendid burial, which lasted weeks but in which I did not take part since I was in the other city. I made a desperate try to get Ra back but was finally told that he had been strangled and embalmed and taken to the tomb to keep my father company in his long watch over Egypt. I went completely to pieces, experiencing the abandonment to which I had subjected others in other lifetimes. (At that time, however, I could only feel the terrible injustice. I think that in a long-time perspective one would have to say the abandonment was just.)

In a reaction of desperation I went to the temple and asked to be allowed to stay there and become a priestess, remembering my father's assurance that the priests knew how to go to the Land of the Dead, where I intended to go in order to find Ra. In the temple my assigned teacher was a young man Menephet (my son in this lifetime) who was so kind that gradually my distrust of people lessened and I began to relate to him. However, just before his initiation he left the temple suddenly, in spite of my pleading, feeling he did not understand good and evil and lacked the wisdom to survive the intense initiatory process. Word then came that he had died in a sandstorm while trying to cross the desert. Many of these details I recovered in a regression with Ed Reynolds.

Soon after this, intent on finding Ra, I asked for my own initiation. I was not ready for it, and in the process of it I was not able to evaluate objectively. I became undone when I went to my father's tomb and found him there, his ka or essence and his body, but not Ra's ka, only his body. Losing all centeredness because of the intensity of my anger over the fact that the sacrifice of Ra had been in vain, I put out my intention to find Ra wherever he was and, as happens when one is out of the body, I was immediately there. I became joyous at seeing him, and feeling that I never wanted to leave him, I severed the golden energy bond to my body, which was lying in the sarcophagus in the pyramid. Without the connection to my essence or ka, my body died immediately. However, I did not get to stay with Ra but found myself in a land of mist and tears.

Not only was nearly every important core person of this lifetime present in that one, but most of the basic karmic threads were exposed: my despair over abandonment; my deep problem with anger; my ease at going into the land of the dead; my tenacity in pursuing what I want; my involvement with meditation and the spiritual journey; the recurrent wisps of anger at my current daughter, who as my older sister then had no time to bother with me; the deep relationship with the priest who cared about me and tried to help me and who has played such a role as my mentor in many lifetimes, from Atlantis to Greece to the present time; the feeling of helplessness in keeping my son from difficulties.

When I decided to write a novel about our dogs, I had no idea into what depths I would be plummeted. I had meant to describe Ka-Nesmet, the girl, in an introductory paragraph or two as a fantasy, but as I wrote, putting myself in an altered state by touching the typewriter and setting down what I saw, I realized the layers beneath layers of karmic weaving that underlay this current experience with our kennel, how every facet of it had roots in that Egyptian lifetime. In this current lifetime the patterns and relationships had been thrown up again, to be understood and dealt with more wisely. I finally had to find a strong center in myself so that a feeling of abandonment could not wipe me out again. I had to become willing, after all the lifetimes of being stubborn, to give up anger for love, no matter how unjust a specific situation might seem. And I had a deep responsibility to our great dogs, who all stemmed from the progenitor Ra, called Siva in this lifetime.

Some patterns that could have been a problem in this lifetime were not, because they had been dealt with well in previous lifetimes. I have never had a problem with power, for instance. However, I have had an over-investment in "justice," which I have finally come to see has no meaning except as one looks through all the skeins of karmic patterns. To be abandoned was "just," not as punishment for having abandoned, but as a way of helping me understand what abandonment feels like so that I would not abandon again. Learning in that Egyptian lifetime that death as we think of it does not exist has made it easier for me than for most people not to give it too much meaning. So I separated death from abandonment until I could come to the place where I could see that on one level neither of them has any enduring reality.

# Theory

## Philosophical Hypotheses

1. We are on a journey of consciousness, and each lifetime is only one phase in our learning.

2. Each person chooses a lesson or lessons for a particular lifetime and determines the personalities and setting that will most effectively help him learn his chosen lesson.

3. What happens in each lifetime sets up energy fields that are carried forward to other lifetimes and determine their patterns.

4. Relationships weave back and forth through lifetimes until the emotional entanglements are resolved.

5. We are all androgynous, having experienced lifetimes as both men and women.

6. Memory, including that of past lives, is stored in the mind field and can be more or less easily retrieved. There is a feedback system so that as we change our energy fields this change is registered in the mind field.[2]

7. A change in the emotional field precipitates or is identical to change in the energy field and explains how we can resolve patterns and become free of them.

## Psychotherapeutic Assumptions

1. Energy fields generated in previous lifetimes occur in a current one in the form of sub-personalities or repeated patterns. Since they are all one field they can be worked with and transformed on any level—by going back to a past life, by dealing with a sub-personality, or by working with pre-birth experience or a current pattern.

2. Working in a past life can be especially effective because it amplifies the awareness of the patterns involved by showing their continuity and repetition.

3. Remembering past lives is generally not enough to produce change. Some form of transformational intervention is usually necessary.

4. Change must take place in the emotions. Emotions are the special characteristic of physical experience and the reason why the individual must seek to reincarnate. Intense emotionality heightens the vibration frequency of the energy field, and affirmations made in such a state are imprinted and carry over from one lifetime to another. This energy shift may occur at any crisis but is commonly manifested during the dying process and is the reason that exploration of final thoughts and affirmations carries such potential for transformation.

5. The most powerful energy is love, both for oneself and for others, and love is the most effective intervention.[3]

6. To be most effective the therapist needs to be in an altered state along with the patient.

7. Therapeutic change may eventually be found to lie in the interaction of the energy fields of the therapist and the patient in a sense that we cannot as yet understand. Such a shift in field may be found to characterize successful therapeutic intervention of any sort, probably including much physical healing.

## Indications and Contraindications for Use

1. Past-life work is indicated when other methods of treatment have proven inadequate, as when there is blocking and the patient is caught up in a pattern of behavior that resists change, or when there are relationship tangles that seem to have no meaning. It is also helpful in tracing the origin of physical symptoms, weight addiction, phobias, compulsions, and transforming the patterns in which these are set.

2. Even more important than its ability to effect symptomatic relief is the potential of regression therapy for deepening and expanding the spiritual perspective of a patient by aiding him to see his current life as set in a matrix of patterns extending back through many lifetimes. There are times when it is valuable to explore the origin of talents and aptitudes so that these may be better used or to touch on experiences of integration and balance in order to anchor a personality involved in stressful experiences.

3. Regression work is of little value when the belief system of the patient is rigid and impermeable so that the concept of past lives lacks meaning, or when it is apparent that the patient is looking to past-life experiences as a form of ego gratification. Such a set blocks perceptions of less glamorous roles.

4. Careful, supportive, reality-oriented techniques are preferable when the patient has a fragile ego structure. When there is abundant material within the frame of the current life, as when there is evidence of strong subpersonalities, it is usually preferable to work with present patterns.

# *Induction*

## Preparation

Therapeutic preparation in the form of focusing on current-life patterns is needed as groundwork for exploring past-life patterns. To facilitate this, I begin by taking an extensive case history, allowing the patient to initiate the order of his material but insuring that he includes information about his parents and siblings, what is known about his birth, a complete physical history with dates of surgeries and illnesses, and particular problems in adolescence. I explore his self-esteem and ask about his belief systems and his goals for his life. Some of this material can initially be worked on with techniques such as sub-personality work or journal writing.

In my general approach to psychotherapy I use many imaging experiences, usually open-ended in the sense that the patient finds his own images rather than following ones I suggest, though I may structure a setting or focus. Prior to a regression I first make patients comfortable in other altered state experiences, introducing such imaging with a short period of breathing in light, as I have found this to be the most effective way to enter an altered state. As a rule, each experience of moving into an altered state makes the next experience easier so that by the time we move into past-life work, attaining the requisite level of consciousness is an easy and natural experience.

In addition to this induction preparation, I like to talk about past lives and give some cognitive grounding and especially make it clear that past lives do not immediately surface in the form of a vivid and complete television show but have to be fished out by concentrating on any details that do appear and inviting deepening to occur. I point out, especially, that the patient does not make the past lifetime happen—he simply allows the images to come in.

# Induction Techniques

Formal hypnosis seems unnecessary to induce past-life recall because the veil between us and these states of awareness is often thin. I go immediately into an altered state myself and draw my patient with me, using the breathing of light as an amplifying agent. Sometimes I use very soft meditation music, such as Georgia Kelley's harp music.[4] Most of the time I follow the breathing of light with the building of a golden core up through the center of the body—both for me and for my patient. The core is raised an inch through the top of the head with each breath, and then the patient moves up through the core to the top and finds himself in a white tunnel, and I move out with him. He walks along, breathing in light and feeling light shimmering all around him until in the side of the tunnel he comes to a gate or door, which he describes.

After describing the gate or the door he opens it and walks through and finds himself in a Garden. This is an old Tibetan meditation. It is representative of the patient's unconscious, and what is found in the Garden can give many clues to his life process. I allow plenty of time to explore the Garden and then check to see that all colors of flowers are there—red, orange, yellow, green, blue, violet and white—as well as greenery and some form of water. I say that the Garden is the patient's and he can make it what he will. I ask him to go up five hundred feet above the Garden and look down and see if he can tell what time and place it is set in, as this often gives a clue to an important past lifetime and one that may appear in that experience.

When the patient has examined and enjoyed his Garden, I have him put a deep pool in the center and kneel and look into it, putting out his intention concerning what it is he would like to learn about his life. I ask him to report whatever he sees, even though it might be only a shred of color. At the same time I encourage him to let the images float through, not feel that he has to be active in producing them. Almost always, the image of a person gradually appears. I ask if he feels that it represents him. Usually it does but if not, I ask who it is and where *he* is, and I have the person whom he identifies as himself walk into the scene. As soon as this occurs, I ask what he is wearing on his feet. This almost always provides a strong lead into whatever lifetime we are going to examine.

The Garden induction is effective for several reasons. For one thing, it is a very old image of an altered state and seems to carry additional drawing power. But more important is the fact that there is a definite path into it and, correspondingly, a definite path back out into the body and normal consciousness. There is never a time when the patient need feel any anxiety about this other level of awareness or how he is going to return to his usual space-time state. As important as the induction is the return, and I guide this by bringing my patient back from the lifetime, which we usually have ended by moving through the death process, into the Garden, enjoying the flowers again. When he is ready, I suggest that he leave the Garden, go through the door, and walk along the white tunnel to where he can slip down the golden core into his body. There I have him in a leisurely way feel his hands and fingers, then his feet, then his breathing, and open his eyes when he is ready.

Probably this much induction is not necessary, though it actually takes only about ten minutes and gives a framework to the lifetime and is healing if the lifetime has included pain and suffering, which most do. A shorter induction is to count five after the patient (and I) have breathed light for a few moments, and the patient will usually be in another lifetime. In my perception, it is my sharing of the altered state with my patient that makes the experience safe and comparatively easy.

## *Garden Induction*[5]

*Image yourself floating on a slow river, drifting amongst a water garden of lotuses of all colors. Lean back in the boat. Let all the tension slide off you into the water.... Feel the motion of the boat, a gentle rocking. Hear the water as it makes a splashing sound against the side of the boat.... See the radiance of the sky and feel the air as it moves against you in a wisp of breeze....*

*Observe a particular lotus. Choose one of all those around you that calls to you. Become that lotus. Feel the color of it. Feel yourself floating on the river. Feel your green leaves reaching out on the surface of the water. Be aware of your rootedness in the mud of the river. Be aware of the number and arrangement of your petals. Become one of the petals. Feel your participation in the being of the lotus. Feel the joy of being one of the petals.*

*You, the lotus, are now full of light. All your petals and leaves are light. Light vibrates in your leaves and petals. You are this light. And if you listen, you may hear a flute on the river. Become this flute song. Let your notes vibrate across the river. Float on the sound current. You are one of the petals of the lotus. You are the light in the leaves. You are the flute on the river. It is the morning of the world.*

*Now your body is made light. In the center of it is a golden, shimmering core. Breathe in deeply, and as you exhale, raise the golden core an inch above your head. Breathe several times more, each time raising the golden core higher.*

*Now go up through the golden core and find yourself in a white tunnel. Walk along the tunnel, feeling it vibrating around and through you with light. As you walk along you will see a door on the side of the tunnel. Look at it carefully, noticing its size, the material it is made of, its shape, and how it is* opened. *(Allow time for patient's response.)* Open the door and go through and you will find yourself in a garden. Close the door behind you and look around.

What is the shape of your garden and what are its boundaries? *(Allow time for responses to all questions.)* What flowers does it contain? Are they in beds or are they growing informally? What colors are the flowers? It is your garden to change if you wish, so if there are no red flowers, put some in if you wish. If there are no orange flowers, add them. Put yellow flowers in if there were none when you came in. Put in whatever greenery you would enjoy having—bushes and trees and ferns. Don't forget blue and violet and white flowers.

Now walk amongst your flowers, touching and enjoying them. Reach down and touch the earth. What does it feel like—moist or dry? What water is there in your garden? Add a fountain or a stream or a waterfall or a river if there is no water. Add whatever is beautiful to you. Are there birds in your garden? Can you see them, or, perhaps just hear them singing?

In the center of your garden put a clear pool. Surround it with golden flowers if you like, or let it be set in some grass. Then rest. Rest deeply in your garden. After a while look deeply into your pool. You will see a star shimmering in its depths and as you look at this star it will blur and become the lotus on the river, you, the lotus, permeated with light. Gradually this image will thin and you will see yourself at the bottom of the pool, but it is a long time ago, before you were born.

It is the lifetime where you were concerned with (name core issue or pattern to be explored). Images are coming up. Share with me what you are seeing, even if it is only a flash. Who is there? Do you see yourself? What are you wearing on your feet? *(If images are slow to appear, ask the patient to make up a story in order to help him move through this initial blocking.)*

### Closure

And now move up through the pool to your garden. The image in the pool fades and you become aware again of the flowers. Your garden is very still. Bird song floats in the air like thin silver leaves drifting down slowly. There is light everywhere.

Slowly you walk back toward the gate. Know that whenever you wish to return to your garden, you may. Go through the gate and close it behind you and walk back along the tunnel of light. You have made a long journey and are bringing back joy.

You come to the golden core and slip through it into this body. Feel your hands and your fingers. Feel energy and joy coursing through you. Feel your feet. Feel the joy you have brought back shining through you. Be aware of your breath. *(Pause.)* And when you are totally back in your body, open your eyes.

## Supportive and Deepening Techniques

For many people, recovering the details and feeling of a past life are a little like rubbing off the surface of a lottery ticket to find the numbers or images underneath. The depth of the altered state may influence the initial clarity of recall: the curtain between individuals and their unconscious memories is of different thicknesses, and for some the procedure of pushing it aside is more difficult. Part of the therapist's task is to give skillful aid. Once the details are recovered, like the images on the lottery ticket they remain completely clear. Unlike general flights of imagination, they are not susceptible to change: if the child seen in a past life had a blue dress in a certain situation, no effort can turn it into pink. One of the most convincing differences between past-life recall and creations of the imagination is the stability of the image.

Where light is used in the induction and where the therapist is also in an altered state, most patients experience very little trouble getting an initial image, though usually this is amorphous and undifferentiated. My most successful approach to bringing it into clarity is to ask what, if anything, is on the person's feet. This grounds the image, and subsequent questions can elicit sex, age, clothing, environment and perhaps the country and time in which the lifetime is set, though this may be difficult for some people. The best way to help is to suggest that the patient say the first thing that occurs to him. Some patients will go immediately into an incident and need little help other than an occasional question, if pauses are too long, as to what the person is feeling and what is happening. In the beginning many patients are slow to fish out an image and happenings, and it helps to ask for an image in that lifetime of an evening meal. If there is a family, these other persons emerge at this time, perhaps with a little help through questioning, and family relationships begin to establish themselves. Sometimes what emerges instead is a pattern of isolation and loneliness, the origin of which can be probed.

When as many details as possible have been uncovered, the recall can be deepened by asking the patient to go forward (or perhaps backward) to the next significant incident. Sometimes it helps a patient who is moving slowly to count to five, after giving the suggestion that at five he will find himself in the next significant incident and can report it to you. When questioned, many patients will at the time say that they don't know the answer. Following one's conviction that there is a part of us that knows all the answers and has all the memories, one can suggest to a patient that he ask the part of himself that knows everything about that lifetime to provide the answer. It helps to suggest that he take the first thing that occurs to him as the answer. This avoids an intellectual trip that is unlikely to yield much.

Sometimes my reflection of feelings experienced in the past life helps to move recall along, much as it helps move along current material in therapy.

For the most part it is not difficult for therapists working with past lives to accept what is recounted just as it is, and without judgment. This unconditional positive regard, which is so important in more conventional therapy, has the same effect here in giving the patient support for what he is going through. There is some controversy as to whether the patient needs to experience all the feelings in order to work them through. I have found that the experiencing of feelings deepens the psychotherapeutic effect. However, there are times when the material is so agonizing that it seems as though the patient will disintegrate in the process of experiencing, and at such times I state that it is another lifetime, it is not happening now, and the patient can step outside of the situation and become an observer. From this vantage point he can describe what is happening, and later we can go back and work with the feelings again.

## *Processing*

### Psychotherapeutic and Transformational Techniques

Sometimes past-life recall alone is therapeutic and can effect change, especially in cases of physical trauma and phobias, but usually the therapeutic process can be aided by transformational techniques. These range from simple acceptance and reflection of feelings to stronger forms of intervention. One of the simplest techniques is to conclude a recall by pointing out that it is another lifetime and that the deep feelings of disturbance in it do not have to be brought forward into this one. This approach provides an especially effective minimal intervention in trauma, phobias, and separation anxiety. Following such an observation, the therapist may suggest that the problem will no longer interfere with the current life and that the patient will come back confident, joyous, and free.

Some therapists working with past lives feel that in order for the patient to become completely free he must go back to the lifetime in which he started the karmic thread, where he did to someone else something for which he is now suffering. They feel that recovering any number of lifetimes in which the patient has been the victim will not be enough. I have not found this to be true. Somehow the energy field that has been disturbing to the patient does get changed by initiating a new look at it and implementing some transformational techniques. I have also seen patients get back to an apparent source memory and then have a remission not hold.

Another variable is the energy of the therapist. It is difficult to understand how therapeutic success can depend on such a variable, but we can't rule this out as a possibility. There is no doubt that people react to the energy fields of others and are influenced by them—one can easily feel an angry field or a joyous one, for instance. A balanced field is therapeutic, and a strong balanced field in a therapist tends to pull the weaker and more uneven field of the patient into balance and increases his capacity for insight and resolution.

One technique of past-life therapy that seems especially transformational is the process of taking the patient through his death. It is a way of making a clear-cut ending to the examination of a lifetime. After the main patterns of the life have been uncovered, the therapist can suggest that the patient move forward to an hour before his death and tell how old he is, where he is, who is there, how he happens to be dying. He is then taken to the moment of his death and asked to describe what is happening and state his last thought or feeling and affirmation and then say where he is immediately afterward and what he is seeing. From this vantage point he can look back on the lifetime and see what lesson he wished to learn and whether or not he learned it. Patients often need help in this. For some, it is a new idea that we choose a lifetime and in a sense are therefore responsible for it, but for most it is a relief, and perhaps this is one of the most healing aspects of past-life recall.

An important transformational experience is forgiveness. If the person chose a lesson that he was able to work at successfully, the forgiveness is usually of others who have harmed or neglected or rejected him. I use the forgiveness sequence of psychosynthesis. It has five steps, very simple to state and often very hard to work through.[6]

1. The person describes his anger and indignation and sense of injustice, confronting his image of the person in that lifetime who has hurt him.

2. He states what he would have preferred that the person do.

3. He realizes that the person did the best he could, regrettable as it may have been, and cancels his expectation that the person should have done differently.

4. He accepts the person just as he is.

5. And in this place of acceptance he sends out his love to the person.

This process often takes time and requires support and help on the part of the therapist. Sometimes a patient is simply not ready to let go of his expectation that his abuser cannot be different. Then the therapist must allow him to hold onto his anger, knowing that it is a burden on his back that eventually, some other time, he must work through. But usually the patient is able to let go, and the forgiveness and release of anger is deeply transformational. It is easier to do this regarding personalities from another lifetime than with people we know now, though the necessity to change this destructive energy field is the same.

An equally, or perhaps more important, working through comes when the lifetime has not seemed successful, when a too-difficult lesson was chosen and was not learned. The patient looks down on that lifetime and senses that, according to his own space-time evaluation, he has failed. This is the time to introduce self-forgiveness. The process is the same as for forgiveness of others except that all the disappointments must be expressed to the self as that self existed in that lifetime. Expectation that he should have done better is first voiced and then canceled. He accepts himself just as he was and surrounds himself with his own love, knowing that there will be other chances to learn the lesson. Sometimes I suggest that perhaps next time he will understand how to set up a lesson that is more appropriate to where he is, knowing that he has unlimited time. For many patients the idea that they can love themselves is a new and healing one. In our society we are not very good at loving ourselves. Profound changes can take place in our lives when we are able to appreciate and love ourselves more.

There is a new transformational concept that is being introduced into past-life work that needs to be tested. Its inclusion cannot in any way hurt anyone, but we need to try to establish whether it contributes anything. This is the process of healing a body that has been damaged, mutilated, or even killed, a frequent experience throughout history. This can be done by both the therapist and the patient running healing light through a body, his own or someone else's, and seeing that body restored. Past-life therapy protocols indicate that many current physical problems stem from damage suffered in other lifetimes. It is as though in the anguish and fear of a traumatic event or death an energy field is set up that continues on. If one uses a transformational technique to heal the other-life body and make it whole again, will that heal or help to prevent stress and damage in this life in the part of the body originally affected? I find that often physical symptoms are lifted without any direct healing interventions being performed in the lifetime where they are originated, perhaps due to indirect factors causing a shift in the energy field. We need to explore this area. It may provide a powerful potential for certain types of healing.

There are times when in the final exploration of a lifetime one comes upon closely related people who have been killed and do not know where they are and have continued on, clinging to the patient through subsequent lifetimes. These beings emerge quite clearly and state that they are lost and do not know where they are, and the patient will report hearing them say so. In this case it is easy to have the patient offer to help them to the Light, calling on guides if necessary. This is a simple procedure, not often required, but usually it effectively ends any further shadowing of the patient.

## Integration into the Total Psychotherapeutic Process

One lifetime carefully recovered and thoughtfully integrated into the patient's life skein is often more effective than a number of lifetimes dealt with superficially. The paramount work lies in the tracing of patterns, including relationships. During the regression there are usually a number of places where the patient can be helped to see if someone with whom he was involved in other lifetimes is also present in this one, perhaps in quite another role. It seems that we tend to come back in clusters and have certain lessons to learn from one another. Though the other person may be the patient's mother in one life and his child in another, if one considers the relationship carefully, the same factors are usually clearly present at the current time. The patient can then be encouraged to consider how he sets up a repetition of the pattern, and this perception will help him move from the position of victim. One of the great advantages of past-life therapy is that it exposes clearly the tendency of the patient to behave in a certain way over and over again—an extension of the "repetition compulsion" that Freud proposed. The patient may be holding onto anger, or he may be afraid to take the responsibility for his life, or he may carry an underlying need to be a victim because he has been one so many times or because he is guilty and feels he deserves punishment. Or he may cling to a lifelong conviction that there is something wrong with having abundance because he (or usually she) has been an impoverished religious person so many times in the past.

As patterns are established and tied into the relationships and events of this lifetime, the therapist can clarify that repetition of certain patterns is not necessary, and he can encourage the patient to put out affirmations for change. Sometimes continued work on forgiveness is necessary in order to change an intense anger that has continued through many lifetimes. Always the patient needs to be encouraged to take responsibility for change. This is facilitated by the fact that he has seen patterns continue until he realizes he must do something about them. Often lifetimes emerge where power has been a problem or has been misused. In the current lifetime the patient may shun power, afraid he will abuse it again, and the therapist can work with him on how he can begin to use power in a productive and responsible way by pointing out that the correct use of power, as anything else, has to be learned and is a hard, difficult lesson.

Once in a while a patient will recover a life that is marked by competence, love, and joy. Sometimes it is a good idea to try to find such a lifetime in the first regression. When such a life is retrieved, the therapist needs to underline it and help the patient integrate it into himself to be used as a grounding and centering energy to hold him in times of distress and buffeting and to remind him that he is more than the suffering of his current lifetime. These balanced and harmonious and productive lifetimes help the patient to identify with the development and integration that he has attained over various lifetimes but cannot remember. (We tend to identify ourselves with the struggles or the lessons on which we are working.) Sometimes lifetimes are recalled wherein talents for languages, art, or science were initiated and their development was begun, and it becomes clear that the patient is building on them in the current life. These lifetimes can be treated with respect and appreciation. Sometimes talents are uncovered that do not concern the patient in this lifetime. Then one can work to observe whether those talents are sufficiently lived out, in which case other things are to be learned this time. It is just as much an error to neglect good and helpful patterns as to fail to see the connection of more troubling ones with this lifetime. The therapist needs to know that whatever comes up is for the self-actualization of his patient.

## Failures

There are times when regression work fails to accomplish its therapeutic goals. I have found that these instances fall into three categories.

1. Some patients cannot retrieve *any meaningful images* (past-life or metaphor), no matter what sort of induction or deepening techniques are used. Many of these patients arrive with a pervasive anxiety that somehow they won't be able to perform. Assurance to them that most people do not see a full-blown video script in the beginning but work from small details does not bring reassurance. Sometimes such patients will shift from a few details in one lifetime to a few in another lifetime and will not be able to deepen in any one experience.

Most of these patients have had little experience with introspection and tend to be extroverted in their approach to things. The wall that separates them from inner experiences is far less permeable than it is for those who are naturally introspective and who are able to participate in other types of imaging experiences. The solution would seem to be to work on general deepening of imaging potential in less-charged material, such as with some psychosynthesis exercises. For the time being therapeutic work can be done more profitably in the here and now.

2. One of the most perplexing types of failure occurs when *the patient cannot recover patterns or find any connection to this lifetime,* even when the past lives are apparently rather easily recovered. Such a patient finds one life after another, often with many details, and none of them seems to have anything in common either with another past life or with the current lifetime. The regression experience ends with a feeling of deep dissatisfaction and often resentment.

Though no pattern is evident either to me or to the patient, it is possible that we have both been blind to the pattern, but it is more probable that what comes up is devoid of meaning because the patient has not dealt with a dark pool of anger. The patient has learned how to cover the anger with conventional behavior and even with acceptable thinking and feeling, though it may be only a thin layer. This cover-up pattern screens out lifetimes where the stored up anger lies, and allows only innocuous and essentially meaningless material to emerge. For such people the treatment of choice is to begin to extirpate the anger through more conventional therapeutic modalities such as Radix.

3. Sometimes lack of connection happens when *the patient has entered the regression carrying unrealistic or inappropriate expectations.* Often such expectations are holdovers from a former conception that past lives are times of power and glamour. Such unsuccessful regression can often be turned around in the context of ongoing therapy.

A Jewish patient, who was sent to me by a fellow therapist to recover a lifetime as a Pharaoh, was deeply disappointed when on his first regression he recovered a life as a tinker in Ireland a hundred years ago. He was married to a woman whom he disliked and with whom he had no relationship, and his life was empty and meaningless. When that wife died he married a blind girl and gradually began to fall in love with her and to find meaning in life because of these stirrings of love, but she, too, died, and he regressed to living in a bitter, isolated way.

When this patient tried a second regression, though again I assured him I had no idea where it would lead, he found himself as a Roman centurion in Beth-Sheba at the time of Jesus. Again he found himself as isolated and frozen, but when Jesus came to talk in the town he was deeply moved. The statement of Jesus that he would be crucified in a month by the patient's fellow centurions led to a violent protest. As the patient narrated the events of this lifetime the prediction slipped his mind, and when his centurion friends came to Beth-Sheba and told him of the crucifixion, he went to pieces. He sat in the therapy room openly sobbing. He saw himself getting on his horse and starting across the desert and then being killed by a great boulder that rolled down a hill on him and his horse. This regression, also, left the patient deeply disappointed, though the pattern was evident: in each lifetime he had known isolation and loneliness, and each time when tendrils of feeling started to break this up, the tendrils were crushed before they could get a good start.

The experience with this patient helped me to see that maximally effective regression work must be set in the context of extended therapy so that there is an opportunity to help the patient contact and use the real meaning of his experience. Fortunately this patient had a perceptive therapist, and when I communicated his experience to her, she was able to work with him and told me later that he had eventually made a good relationship and was married.

We can have no expectations when we move into a regression. Humbly we have to try to see whatever pattern is shown to us. Past-life recall is seldom an ego-enhancer, though at times it may reconnect us to sound and joyous sides of ourselves or to potentials that may have been covered over. Lifetimes of higher status often—and I might say usually—turn out to be those of the deepest suffering. Power and affluence are not easy to handle well, and most of us take a lot of learning before we can manage them. At that point we have grown beyond the need for ego-enhancing.

4. The fourth group of failures consists *of patients who have recoverd lifetimes well and have understood the patterns, and who then fail to change.* Sometimes it is as though no therapeutic work had ever been done. Regression work was used, as dreams often are, as an intellectual escape from dealing with the problems that have been openly presented. Such a patient usually retains an unwillingness to take responsibility for his life. He may harbor a deep unconscious conviction that somebody should take the responsibility for him—mother, the universe, God, a spouse. Such a conviction disconnects his understanding from his will and leaves him standing still as far as transformation is concerned. In such cases, working with this "dependent" expectation as a sub-personality is necessary first.

# Cases

## Dealing with Loss and Separation

Loss and separation in earlier lifetimes often involve intense emotion and strong affirmation that cut grooves in an individual's psyche. Succeeding lives are forced to play these grooves over and over. In order to smooth out the grooves and release the pattern, it is necessary, while in an altered state, to eliminate the grooves and put in new and more appropriate patterns, just as one releases one program in a computer and substitutes another. The following cases illustrates how more positive grooves can replace negative ones that have been installed in the anguish and loss of a previous lifetime.

**Case 1. Separation Anxiety**

My first regression of a patient involved a relatively simple smoothing out of grooves made after the death of a father. The grooves had been carried forward into this life and had been generalized.

Ann was a young woman who worked as a clerk in a bank and had married a kind and conventional young man who was a junior manager in a large chain grocery store. They had two children, both under seven. Because they could not afford to buy a home in the Los Angeles area where they were then renting, they made a down payment on a house in a suburb far south of the city and were due to move in three months, changing their jobs and the children's schools and leaving their neighborhood and Ann's mother behind. A former attempt to settle elsewhere several years before had ended disastrously, and Ann had had to be brought home and for several weeks skirted the edge of hospitalization. She wanted to avoid experiencing such distress again.

During the first five or six sessions with her I tried a number of different approaches to get at the separation anxiety, and none of them helped. In frustration I suggested that perhaps the difficulty started in another life. Once the suggestion was out of my mouth I felt it to be inappropriate for a patient who seemed to be conventional in her thinking, and I expected her to reject the idea. To my surprise, Ann seemed relieved to have some new road to try and she wanted to start immediately.

I did a brief induction, having both of us breathe in light. Then I entered an altered state with Ann and simply told her that I would count to five and she would find herself in the lifetime where the difficulty had started. I sat behind her and put my right hand on her left shoulder to continue the energy flow and to deepen the altered state for both of us. I counted to five slowly, and at the end of the counting she immediately spoke.

> P: *It's a hundred years ago and I'm in a little town in Montana and the wind is blowing (spoken in a little girl voice).*
> T: *How old are you?*
> P: *Nine years old.*
> T: *With whom do you live?*
> P: *My grandmother—my father's mother. She's a terrible lady!*

Further questioning elicited information that her mother was dead and that she was unhappy. I counted to five again and told her that at the end of the counting she would move five years ahead in time. I asked her what was happening.

> P: My father is telling me that this is not a good town for me to grow up in and I must go to St. Louis. He wants me to stay with a cousin there and go to school.
> T: How do you feel about that?
> P: I tell him I won't go because if I do I'll never see him again. But he says that is foolish. I can come home any time I want to. *(Her voice drags and she speaks with reluctance.)*

I moved her ahead to her stay in St. Louis. Eventually she finished school and got a job as a companion to a wealthy old lady who lived in a beautiful house. After several years the old lady, who had become very fond of her, died, and since she had no heirs she bequeathed Ann the house. Ann felt ecstatic and described the house in detail. (This was interesting because she had never been outside of California and I had just returned from St. Louis, where I stayed in the neighborhood of these beautiful old houses.) In an effort to move the regression along, I counted to five again, telling Ann that she would go to her next meeting with her father.

> P: *(Heavy uncontrolled sobbing.)* It's too late. My father has already died. I'll never leave anybody again!
> T: *(After allowing the grieving to spend itself)* This experience is another lifetime. It does not belong to this one and does not need to affect it. You will come back into a current state of consciousness knowing that you do not any longer have to be controlled by what you said then. You will be able to separate from your mother and your neighborhood easily. As you come back into this lifetime you will be joyous and full of energy and able to handle all the changes in your life.

Ann felt such relief after the recovery of her father's death in that lifetime that our work seemed to be coming to an end, so I was surprised when she told me at the beginning of the next hour that she had one more problem she had not mentioned. It was with embarrassment that she admitted she had never had an orgasm. She had been married for ten years and her husband was a skilled and patient lover, but she could not let go. She felt distressed because her husband blamed himself and was sure that he was doing something wrong.

In the early session I had taught Ann how to breathe into the various energy centers and then allow an image to come in, and I suggested that she work in the second center, which is considered to be connected with sexuality, and see what image came up to help us. Almost immediately it became apparent that she had moved into another lifetime.

P: I'm standing in the doorway of a cheap hotel here in the West, and two men are pushing in after me.
T: How old are you and how do you happen to be here?
P: I'm 15 and I've come to try to find work. My mother has just died and I'm afraid of my stepfather. This is a rough town but I don't know where else to go. I don't know who these men are! (Increasing panic in her voice)

She became silent and very still. There was a long pause.

T: What's happening? Are you dead?
P: No. (Flat tone) They've both raped me. I'll never have anything to do with sex again.

We went back through the episode with the men, so that she experienced it fully, and then again I reminded her that it was another lifetime and she did not have to bring into this one the affirmation she had made then. We looked at the fact that various men are different—she did not need to generalize from that experience, painful as it was; she could come back into this lifetime and appreciate and respond to the lovemaking of her husband. I brought her back with affirmations that she would be responsive and joyous in her current sexual situation.

During both regressions, since I was feeling my way in a new modality, I used simple therapeutic interventions: a low level of cognitive restructuring and emphatic suggestions similar to those made in hypnotherapy. They bypassed any karmic pattern but proved to be sufficient to bring about change. Ann went home after the second regression and found herself able to achieve orgasm, to the relief of her husband. She moved to her next house without difficulty, integrated well into her new neighborhood, and has continued to grow in confidence and initiative. I have kept in touch with her for eight years and she has maintained her gains and has even gone back to school in an effort to prepare herself for more rewarding work.

## Resolving Anger

Sources of deep anger are conventionally assumed to lie in current life experiences or, looking further back, in childhood abuse. Stanislav Grof traced patterns of anger to severe frustration in prenatal and birth events. But these levels of prenatal and birth anger seem often to be replays of past-life interactions, the repetition of ingrained patterns of feeling. This is especially true when anger toward current parental figures is involved. The patterns of angry reaction live on, whether these figures have been parents in other lifetimes or involved in some other relationship, such as that of spouse or child.

In the following case a mother in a current lifetime was a husband in an earlier one. In a second case a father-daughter relationship was replicated. Whatever the roles, there seems only one solution, a transformational one in which anger in both the previous life and in this one is transformed by increased understanding and eventually by the energy of love. This is a form of reframing, a therapeutic technique that provides healing for the anger. Following reframing and the subsequent release of the disturbing feelings, positive synchronistic events often take place.

**Case 2. Anger at Mother**

Rosemary was a journalist in her early thirties who initially had two presenting problems on which she wanted to work. One was an irrational fear of suffering an early and untimely death without accomplishing anything. The other was a lifelong anger against her mother, who in their childhood had abused Rosemary and a younger brother, both physically and verbally. At the earliest time possible Rosemary had left home, but she remained haunted by regret that she could not love her mother, who had recently died without Rosemary having been able to mend the relationship with her.

As Rosemary's therapy progressed, it became apparent that there was another problem. She had entered into a living arrangement with a young attorney with whom she was very much in love, and though at first the two had seemed compatible, gradually the man, who to her knowledge had never been characterized by such behavior before, began to mistreat her verbally, refuse sexual relations with her, and finally even hurt her physically. She felt bewildered and confused as to what she should do.

Rosemary was already interested in past lives, and she suggested that we try this method of finding an explanation and perhaps a resolution, at least of her anger against her mother. Her mother's behavior (when Rosemary was a child) seemed on one level to be an explanation for Rosemary's deep feeling of anger, but she was still not satisfied and kept sensing that there was something more.

**First Regression:**

It was easy to draw Rosemary into an altered state through breathing light, creating the golden core, and walking down the white tunnel.

T: You will see a door or gate on the side of the tunnel. Can you describe it to me?

P: It's white—looks Victorian—with stained glass. A beautiful pattern, a flower trellis.

T: Go into the Garden and shut the door behind you. Look around the Garden and tell me what it is like.

P: It's full of roses. Red roses outline the Garden. One part is surrounded by red brick with ivy on it. Everywhere are red roses. Around the corner is space, not cultivated, open, with daffodils and wildflowers.

T: What other colors do you see?

P: It's mostly red and yellow. I see some tiger lilies. Oh, there are lilac trees around the corner, purple and white—and iris, blue and purple and gold. I'll put in a little brook—it runs down a hill so it makes a noise over the stones. I'll put some fish in there, too, and some big old trees, tulip trees.

T: Now go up five hundred feet and look down at your Garden. Can you place the country and the period?

P: England—Victorian—an English countryside. In the 1820's or 1830's. It looks like a painting of Constable.

I then asked Rosemary to call her mother to come into the Garden to talk with her. This is often good preparation for a specific past-life recall and tends to bring up feelings that need to be looked at. This time I overlooked suggesting that the entity who had been her mother this time around appear as she was in this lifetime, so I was for a moment taken aback by what followed.

P: There is a man here, a tall man with dark brown hair and whiskers. He has a coat with long tails in back and shorter in front. He has a riding crop and boots. He looks like a young English gentleman, a country squire. I have a feeling of anxiety.

T: Ask if he is you.

P: I'm getting a lot of tingling in the lower part of my body. It's my husband, not me. His name is John.

T: Now see yourself.

P: I'm a small blond woman. I have a high-waisted dress, white with a blue ribbon. These's something round my neck, not quite a cameo, some picture. It's a romantic moment. We haven't see each other for a long time. We both seem amazed, not exactly happy, but our pulses are heightened.

T: I will count to five and at five you will go to the next significant incident in that lifetime. (Counts.)

P: I'm starting to feel fear. It's in London—on the street at night. The fire! It seems to be a panic and a lot of people are running. Everything's on fire (very excited and disturbed) and the sky's red. There's a panic. I can't find John anymore. I'm running and running—I seem to be running down to

> the river. I have an icky feeling in the pit of my stomach—I'll never find him.
> T: Are you married to him?
> P: Yes, but I get the feeling it's not all peace between us—he left me alone. I feel abandoned. He was supposed to meet me but he stood me up. He's a proud and arrogant man. He felt I was smothering him. We have a nice house but it wasn't enough. I feel he stood me up and I'll never see him again. People are screaming. I don't want to escape. I only want to find him. He's probably already escaped. I seem to want to get to the house but it's where the fire is. I can't make any progress because I'm going against the crowd—they keep pushing me back. I'm being pushed along, and soldiers and policeman have seized me and are dragging me back to the river.

At this point I took her ahead a half hour and she found herself in a crowd by the river and everyone was talking about the people they had lost. An hour later Rosemary was being taken care of by the equivalent of the Red Cross.

> P: It's as though there were no future.

I took her ahead five years.

> P: It's as though I couldn't have any children and John got impatient. Feels like—ah, it is, it's a cemetery. I'm looking at tombstones. I don't seem to be alive. I think that girl committed suicide.

Five years was evidently too long a span. She was already dead.

> T: Go backward to an hour before your death in that lifetime.
> P: It's a knife. I hate to say this—it's in a room. It's almost like John killed me. It's in a study, in a library. I see his hatred. I'm pleading with him to stay, not to leave. I'm not old, not ugly. I just can't have kids. He needs kids for social prestige—he needs an heir. He stabs me in the stomach and walks out of the room.
> T: Go through your death and tell me where you are.
> P: I'm a little above her body and to the side.
> T: Was there a lesson you had planned to learn in that lifetime?
> P: Something. A sacrifice of self? It feels so totally empty. I don't know why I'd connect with that sort of person who didn't like me. I don't know why he hated me. I feel I didn't learn what I should have. It is almost a victim situation—ah, I didn't like myself and he didn't like me. It was a fatal choice.
> T: What was your name in that lifetime?
> P: Effie.

T: *Look down at Effie and tell her what you would like her to have done better.*

P: *I would like you to have been more independent and not clung to your husband so much.*

In small steps I then took Rosemary through the forgiveness process, helping her to realize she had done the best she could at that time and canceling expectations of herself, then accepting herself as she was and loving herself that way. Rosemary thought seriously about each step and went through the process slowly and carefully.

T: *Do you recognize John as being anyone you have known in this lifetime?*

P: *It was a very familiar feeling. John was my mother in this lifetime.*

As part of the transformational process I suggested that Rosemary go through the forgiveness routine for John in that lifetime, then return to the Garden and go through the process again for her mother in this lifetime. (If she had had difficulty with either process, I would have left it and returned to work on it in another session, but she seemed eager to forgive and free herself of the burden of anger she had been carrying for so long.)

T: *When you are ready, you can say farewell to your mother and thank her for coming and surround her with your love and light.... Look around the Garden, knowing that you can come back whenever you wish.... Go out through the door, close it after you.... Go down the white tunnel until you reach the golden core. Slip down it into your body.... Feel your hands and fingers.... Feel your feet.... Watch your breathing for a while.... And when you are ready, open your eyes.*

This session had several hoped for results and one entirely unexpected one. The latter had to do with the fact, which I had not known, that Rosemary had suffered all her life from stomach pains for which the doctors could find no explanation. The next time she came in she told me about those pains, which she had taken for granted as a permanent condition, and reported that they had ceased after this regression, and to date they have not come back. The pain had evidently been imprinted at the time of the stabbing and carried forward. As often happens with physical trauma, just remembering the situation released it.

It was clear from the memory of her murder why Rosemary had carried an irrational fear of an early and untimely death before she could accomplish anything. It was also a first step in working through the anger with her mother. But the most surprising result was the information that the session gave her regarding her current problems with the man with whom she was living. When I had first heard of his behavior toward her, especially the physical abuse, it was hard not to feel she was an innocent sufferer (in spite of knowing that there are no innocent sufferers), but the regression suggested that in a sense she had drawn the current partner to behave toward her as the husband in the other lifetime had. It suggested that so-called victims draw those around them to repeat old behavior, or they choose them because they have such potential.

One thing that was especially interesting in this regression was that, though I had meant to suggest that Rosemary call in her mother of this lifetime to talk with her in the Garden before trying a regression, I neglected to stipulate this, and the mother appeared immediately in the role she had played in the previous lifetime. This bypassed the usual intervening induction methods. It is also interesting that both the door into the Garden and the Garden itself were seen as Victorian. My experience is that the setting and time period in which the Garden is seen give clues to an especially significant past lifetime, though not always the one that is explored at the time.

Something could be said about the transformational techniques used here, namely the cancellation of expectations that seems to be behind nearly all anger, and the acceptance of the person through an understanding of where he is coming from. Rosemary came to understand the intensity of her husband's frustration at her childlessness and the strong social pressure around him. The understanding of the situation from that lifetime made it possible for her to cancel expectations about her mother in this lifetime, something she had not been able to do before, being caught in the assumption with which all of us start, that we are entitled to perfect parents! Much more work was spent in her subsequent therapy uncovering new details, deepening perceptions, and lessening the anger toward her mother until finally it thinned, like mist being dissolved in sunlight. Releasing expectations and accepting the person as he is allows love to come in, and love seems to carry an incredibly high and transforming vibration frequency. It is deeply healing.

**Second Regression:**

As Rosemary gradually left the position of victim, her native creative potential and high competence began to move into her consciousness, bringing with it a vague fear of power and the reactivation of strange fantasies of orgies, slave girls, and torch-lit underground mazes which had inexplicably obsessed her when she was a naive eight-year-old Catholic child. She was afraid of what she would find but eventually suggested that we explore and see what was there.

She found herself as a young Roman Senator, Demerius, orphaned at four by an epidemic carried by returning soldiers. It was the time of Rome's decline, and to avoid the plots and counter-plots against Caesar, the senator initiated a series of playful and creative orgies in underground tunnels that he had constructed and through which he and some of his friends chased almost nude girls. It was intended simply as fun and to create a high, but eventually the others became sadistic. When one of his fellow senators cut into the breasts of one of the girls, Demerius exploded and attacked his friend. Others pulled them apart, but the innocence of the subterranean pleasure hunt was over.

In the middle of the night Demerius left on horseback for the mountains with a pouch of gold and some papyrus and writing instruments. Here he changed his name to Lavo, which means "cleansing," and settled down in a simple shepherd community, eventually getting a young peasant girl to live with him. He spent his days writing a sort of journal, which he realized no one would ever read. Writing had been his only other pleasure in Rome, and part of his frustration there had been that no one valued what he had to say. Now it ceased to matter.

> P: *I was alone in that life. What I did was unheard of. I liked flute music—there were the little pipes that shepherds play that were so beautiful.*
> T: *Move ahead to just before your death in that lifetime.*
> P: *I am very old. I grow a grey beard. One morning I just can't get up, but finally the woman who lives with me helps me outside. I can feel the sun on my face.*
> T: *Move on through your death.*
> P: *The sun on my eyelids becomes a white light.*
> T: *What is your last thought?*
> P: *Now I'm coming home. I say this to my parents who are nearby. Strangely enough we are all the same age. We have so much to say to one another. They are well-educated and thoughtful people. Losing them at four made my life more difficult. I knew them in this life as my grandparents. We have always known one another and always will.*
>
> *My woman mourns my passing but she believes in the nature gods, like all people in this region. She accepts it as perfectly natural that I just went "up" somewhere, back to where we all come from. She and her father and the neighbor men prepare my body, dressing me in my best clothes for the grave. They dig a shallow grave and put a loaf of bread, an earthen jug of red wine, and a bunch of flowers along with my body. They cover it all with dirt, then mark it with a plain stone. In time the stone gets moved and we are back to nature.*

Rosemary was able to see what she had wanted to learn and accomplish in that lifetime: to share knowledge about the meaning of life and to teach and instruct in a positive and loving way. But it was the wrong lifetime—the avenues were too closed and too dangerous. This time it is not as difficult, though as Rosemary laid the two lifetimes side by side it became evident that she perceives the Hollywood beat on which she works as in some respects the modern equivalent of decadent Rome!

The recovery of the Roman lifetime gave her great relief. She realized that as the Roman Demerius/Lavo she had courage and insight and sensitivity and a developed sense of both morality and humor. The release of the underlying guilt opened new options for her, as well as the recognition that she is worthy of love.

Through the months following these regressions Rosemary was able to look more objectively at her man friend. Meanwhile, she brought herself to hear from his former girlfriend that the abusive behavior she had experienced merely repeated his previous pattern. With relief she allowed the relationship to terminate. During the process I did not interfere in decisions she made but instead gave her support by reviewing with her what she had learned from the regressions and encouraging her to act according to her new understanding. Synchronistically, in the course of her journalism work she met a sensitive man who seemed capable of intimacy, and she has entered into a relationship in which all her life now seems to be blooming.

**Case 3. Anger at Others**

Carrie was a successful internist on the staff of a large teaching hospital when she returned to me 15 years after her first therapeutic experience with me. She had come originally when she had been in the throes of a hostile divorce and had no means or plan for going on with life with two sons. The only daughter of dominant and successful professional parents who had told her what to do all her life, she found it difficult to find out who she was or what she really wanted or to move out on her own, but after a stint of therapy she became able to do this. With the funding from the divorce settlement she began the long trek toward a medical career, which she successfully completed as one of the top students in a good medical school. Somewhere along the way she met and married a physician about her own age who was engaged primarily in research and was a quiet, kind person who had no intention of telling her how to run her life, though he enjoyed sharing it.

At the time that Carrie decided to return for further therapy she had become aware of a strong drive to make money and be successful. This impulse had become so all-consuming that it threatened to swamp her exploration of her inner self, to which she had been committed through the years. Also, she had not been able to work through a pervasive dislike for her father, which hovered on the verge of anger most of the time. Other than these two areas, her major personality dynamics remained reasonably in balance and her outer adjustment in work and with her husband, satisfactory. She felt that she would like to explore past lives so as to understand herself on a deeper level.

**First Regression:**

During the first regression she moved into her Garden with obvious delight, passing though a white iron gate adorned with an intricate pattern of circles and straight bars. The Garden was filled with avocados and fruit trees and red and orange flowers. Gradually she saw daisies and irises, orchids and blue jays, a bridge over a stream, and plush grass to sit on, representative of the fullness of her current life. I asked her to look around and see if anyone was there.

> P: Bowman, my old nurse. I miss her...I love her. She's smiling and she's fun. I miss her guidance, her company, her support. (To Bowman) Were you my mother in another lifetime? She says she was.
> 
> T: Now sit down beside the pool and look through it and tell me what you see.
> 
> P: I see myself in wooden shoes, a long blue skirt, short white blouse. Looks like Holland. I'm outside. Someone is near, my mother. She's very unmade-up, very natural; her hair is pulled back. She has a sweet-looking face. She's in a wool jersey—a heavier garment, not a summer dress. She's holding my hand but she's near me. We're not in the city—we're in the county. I have a sense of peacefulness about life.
> 
> T: Go to your house at dinner time and tell me who is there.
> 
> P: It has a large eating area for such a small house. The table is wooden. The chairs are high-backed. The bowls are metal. There's a man there, my father—he's sitting at the end of the table. My brother and I are facing each other. My brother is ten. My father is quiet.

I asked if she liked her father and she said she didn't know him very well but recognized him as Bowman's brother in her current lifetime. Her mother then was Bowman in the present lifetime. The family dinner was a quiet affair because the father, a farmer, was very withdrawn and nobody dared to talk.

> P: I'm going to school. I want to do something special but I don't know how. I don't want to stay at home.

The Carrie of that lifetime did go out and became a secretary. There was a fire in her group of buildings, and though she escaped, her boyfriend was burned to death. A few years afterward she married someone else and had two children and felt happy about her life.

T: Go ahead to your death in that lifetime.
P: I'm in bed and my son is beside me. I can't breathe...(Pause). Now I'm above my body. It was a good lifetime. I think it was the importance of relating happily and peacefully in a positive manner, not negatively.
T: Spend a few moments appreciating that lifetime and integrating its harmony and balance.

Carrie then went back into the Garden and found Bowman still there and thanked her for being her guide. She left the Garden and slipped down into her body and opened her eyes and seemed relaxed and joyous. I asked her what she learned from that lifetime.

P: I learned that you will be happy and can be happy no matter what the circumstances. You make your life.

In working over the material of this session we concentrated on its positive aspects and how Carrie could return to her experience of that lifetime and use it as a centering and balancing experience when her current lifetime seemed stormy.

**Second Regression:**

Several weeks later we asked Carrie's Inner Mind to bring up what was most needed. She talked about her desire to become more spiritually oriented and realized that this desire was being sabotaged by her compulsive wish to make money. She appeared relaxed and open as we talked, and she shifted easily into an altered state.

P: The Garden looks different. The flowers are all there but there's a waterfall and a bench made out of stone with carved stone legs. Everything is a lush green. There is a small lovely waterfall. Bowman is here. I want her to know it helps me tremendously that she is a guide for me now. I have a great feeling of peace.
T: Lean over the pool and look deeply into it and tell me what you see.
P: A flash of blue, like a shirt. There's a young man in a blue shirt. He's in his twenties, big, well built, blond, blue eyes. Looks like a workman but he's not dressed like a workman. Maybe he's my father.
T: Walk into the scene now.
P: I'm young, a woman in my twenties, brown hair.

As she told the story we learned that the young man in the scene was her brother, and in the present life he was her husband. In that life he was not happy in the family and wanted to leave because their father always belittled him. Carrie had not married during the past life because her father thought the man she wanted to marry was not good enough. She recognized that her father from that lifetime had come back as her father in this one.

She then described a scene when she was in her thirties in that lifetime and her father was lying dead in the snow from a heart attack. Her brother had been gone for some time and had married, but now he came back with his wife and child to take over the farm. Carrie felt superfluous. The brother died shortly afterward. The two women tried to run the farm, but they lost it through poor management. After that, Carrie worked at a boarding house for rough drinking men, cleaning and waiting on the tables.

> P: *I'm not real old but I'm not young and I feel unable to take care of myself. I'm not happy. I feel trapped. It's very unpleasant here. I'm lonely and the drinkers are vile. I'm tired of being slapped on the fanny. I don't know what else to do. I have no skills and I can't take care of myself.*
> T: Go to an hour before your death.
> P: *I don't feel very well and I don't really care to go on. They put me in a grave, not even a coffin, just an open grave.*
> T: What is your last thought?
> P: *That I must be responsible for taking care of myself or I'll end up in a trap. I never want to be poor again.*
> T: Do you learn this?
> P: *I was working on it. I felt I did the best I could but I was afraid to do very much. I was concerned about convention, too concerned with what society felt.*
> T: Where could you have made a different choice?
> P: *I should have married the man I wanted to marry, even if my parents disapproved.*

After sending some compassionate and forgiving energy to the self of that lifetime, Carrie returned to the Garden. Later we talked about her situation of destitution in that lifetime. The fact that she had not been able to earn money might underlie her current compulsion to make more and more money, and she could release this and be more comfortable in her striving.

**Third Regression:**

To my surprise, the next time Carrie came in was when she wished to go back into that lifetime where her father had bullied her. That session had thrown light on the problem of her over-concern with money, and I wondered what more we needed to examine.

She started by looking down on her father dead in the snow from the heart attack. This time she brought in many new details, as usually happens when a lifetime is entered a second time. With distaste she held her dead father in the sleigh. Neighbors were helping. Eventually her brother came back with his wife and child to take over the farm and she felt like an outsider.

> P: I'm very angry that I didn't make my own decision for my life because now I feel cast off. With the child I'm even more an outsider—it's a new family and I'm only a branch.

Her brother and his wife began to experience tension, but suddenly the brother died of pneumonia. His wife, whom Carrie recognized to be her bossy sister in this lifetime, began to order her around. After they lost the farm Carrie left to work in the tavern.

> P: I resolve never to let anybody take over my life again. I'll never be a little mouse again. Not a little mouse. I hate myself for letting my father terrorize me. If I hadn't allowed that I would have been independent.

By this time Carrie's anger had begun to boil up against her father, and it became clear that this anger from an ancient source had kept her antagonistic and critical of her current father. The old relationship had been re-constellated in this lifetime, so it was evident that it needed to be worked on. I suggested that she identify with her Inner Mind and look down on her father of that lifetime and see if she could understand why he was the way he was.

> P: He didn't have a family that stayed in one place. No roots. So he came to feel that if you are ever going to get ahead you have to work through your family, and that's why he didn't want me leaving. He was angry at his mother for being so weak. I can see that his own father took everything and ran away—he even forced the mother to sign the deed so that he got the land. He learned to get what he wanted through physical violence, and that was a way of life in his household. My father then learned from him to get what he wanted by being angry.

I repeated her explanation of the dynamics of the father and his anger, and I asked if she could release her expectations about him, since she now understood why he had acted as he had. Carrie was not ready to do this, so I asked her to look down on that father at the time of his death in the snow and understand why he had died then and what he had been thinking.

> P: He knew he was making his family unhappy and didn't know how to do anything different. He felt he couldn't control himself. He knew he had caused a terrible breach with my brother and that this hurt my mother, and he didn't know how to stop from hurting us so he decided to die.

T: *How do you feel about him now?*
P: *I see for the first time that he really was trapped. I respect him for his early death. That feels nice. I see it differently.*

After this, Carrie's attitude toward her father in this current lifetime softened considerably, and she became able to use techniques of gentle confrontation that modified her father's brittle treatment. This work with her father continues, but the unrelenting anger she has felt toward him is gone. We need to do more work with this and also to explore other lifetimes in order to connect more fully with her thrust toward spiritual deepening.[6]

Chapter XXII

# Ernest F. Pecci, M.D.

## Biographical Data

### Personal Background

I was born in 1930, during the Depression, to parents who had minimal education and could provide only marginally for the material things our family needed. They were Catholics, but not overly conscientious ones. I paid only routine observance to church and Sunday School and instead explored many byways. When I was nine I sent for Rosicrucian material and studied it diligently. By the time I was 12 I had worked up to the Seventh Degree. In junior high school I studied hypnosis and put on a demonstration of it, but my outer world, including my three younger sisters and my parents, considered this a "weird" endeavor, so I dropped it.

My interest in parapsychology and past lives goes back to that time more than 30 years ago when I tried these unacceptable experiments. I continued to read anything I could get my hands on, in much the way that people read science fiction today. In those days there was very little to read other than uneven contributions about the occult, the Rosicrucian writings which I had discovered at nine, and eventually, the experiences of Edgar Cayce.[1] I became intrigued by Cayce and dreamed of a time when this kind of information could be used to help people and not just satisfy curiosity.

Since my ideas were considered bizarre in the conservative suburb of Boston where I was raised, they were gradually suppressed. I soon became brainwashed out of them and was compelled to seek a more conventional education throughout high school and my undergraduate work at Harvard and Tufts. By the time I had finished four years as an intern in the Chelsea Naval Hospital, then a short stint as a stockbroker, and had entered the Tufts Medical School, I had become imbued with the world of materialism.

For a while I became intrigued with what I learned in medical school, and I believed that science had all the answers. We could see right into the cell; this is the disease and this is what happens, and these are the white blood cells that are running to combat the disease. The scientific instruments and the theories that we used sounded impressive. Everything fit nicely together—the way the body works and the way a pill helps it to heal.

Then I began working in clinics, and things didn't fit together as well. I saw a lot of suffering people, and I delivered a lot of babies. I soon found that there was more going on in the mind than had been described in physiology books. It seemed to me that other factors might exist that would prove to be more important to health in the long run. I gained little satisfaction in curing disease of the body when the cure left a person in a depressed and anguished state of mind. I wanted to explore the total person and try to answer the question, "What is a human being all about?"

I decided to enter the field of psychiatry and served three years of psychiatric internship and residency at Langley Porter, followed by a year at Mt. Zion, two years in community psychiatry in Berkeley, and staff positions at large centers for handicapped children in Contra Costa. I remained intrigued by the supposed vast wealth of material, but again I became disillusioned. There was a lot of impressive psychological jargon but little in the way of useful tools to bring about change within a reasonable period of time. I concluded that concepts and ideas of early founding psychiatry were innovative and ingenious and probably valid, but they also remained limited in their understanding of the totality of man, of what a human being is really about, and they offered few methods of bringing about genuine change.

Following a series of career shifts and settings, I entered private practice. Here I continually sought new ways of exploring various aspects of the mind, especially its super-conscious aspects. I sought for a meaning in life. What was life all about? Did it have a purpose? Are there patterns in this life that might reveal that particular purpose?

My attention became directed to studying the importance of early childhood experiences, and I developed a number of techniques to regress people back to early childhood and then further back to intra-uterine experiences so that clients could experience the whole period from conception on. I found that each child was unique from birth and that the newborn is actually aware of its surrounding to an extent previously considered impossible. For instance, the baby can tune in on how the mother feels about having a boy or a girl and becomes aware of the attitudes and personal feelings of the doctors. In short, an unborn child soon gains comprehensive understanding of the entire environment. It thus became apparent to me that the child is programmed psychically by what he picks up from the parents; the feelings and attitudes of the mother form an important part of consciousness from the beginning of conception.

During the sixties I worked with Robert Hoffman on a method for healing ambivalent and wounded relationships with parents, a process which he had channeled and which led to my development of the Integrative Therapy Process that I conduct at my own school. Out of this work, which fit well with my understanding of the dynamics of parent-child interaction from conception on, evolved a series of workshops and my book *I Love You/I Hate You*.[2] Later, through my work as a staff psychiatrist in the Intensive Treatment Center of the Youth Authority in Sacramento, I found reinforcement for the hypotheses that had unfolded for me over the years. At the Youth Authority, participation in treatment of the one percent of the most severely disturbed children extended my understanding of the powerful impact of pre-natal, birth, and early childhood affirmations. I have recently retired from this work, having gained, perhaps, as much as I have given.

During these years I found that guiding people to remember the past as far back as conception was often effective, but for some people it proved ineffective. When I pressed them to go further back to find the source of the problem, they suddenly described another identity in another place. At first I was startled and wondered what was going on, what the symbolism was, but gradually I began to accept these as valid experiences, whether past lives or profound metaphors, and as I learned to work with these images, changes, often far-reaching ones, began to occur. From that time on, I began helping people through these past-life relationships.

In 1978 I opened a small graduate school to combine the transpersonal approach with more conventional psychological ones. During the last 12 years the program of this school, now known as the Rosebridge Graduate School of Integrative Psychology, has continued to unfold and evolve and has become a setting for continued exploration in many areas. In the matter of past lives, for instance, I have passed through different phases in my understanding. First, I tried to show that one deserves what is happening. Then I tried to show how phobias and fears are related to previous traumatic deaths. In my current phase I have spent some time looking at basic patterns that determine the task that the individual wishes to complete in this lifetime. I am sure that there will be other phases of understanding as I keep observing.

# Theory

## Philosophical Hypotheses

1. Consciousness is more unlimited than we have formerly thought. It is continuous, has no boundaries, and has the potential for knowing all things.

2. We can gain a great deal by studying the vivid pictures that emerge as past-life memories. Each one of our lives contributes to the tapestry of consciousness, and it is important to fill out the tapestry as much as possible in order to understand our lives as a whole.

3. Out of past-life work patterns begin to emerge that give special meaning to existence and a timing to all trauma, suffering, and life challenges. All of these experiences come to be seen as unique opportunities and make a shift in our attitude toward current life patterns.

4. An appreciation of our patterns takes the sting from our pain and makes of life an interesting adventure and one in which a new sense of harmony with the flow of universal life energy becomes possible.

5. There is a primordial essence characterized by unconditional love, joy, serenity, and wisdom, from which we have become separated and to which we can return by moving out into the vaster reaches of awareness. Movement toward this universal life flow of energy is the meaning of spirituality.

6. Coming to a place of peace and harmony with the self allows us to live a more full and complete life. In the process we must reactivate our capacity to love and to accept the universal love that continually nourishes us and awaits our recognition of it.

## Psychotherapeutic Assumptions

1. Each child is unique from birth, has a specific personality, and is aware of his or her surroundings to an extent previously considered unthinkable.

2. The child in utero and the neonate possess a comprehensive understanding of their entire emotional environment. They are programmed, not by what the parents say or do, but rather by the kind of energy that parents put out—the acceptance or rejection, the feelings and attitudes they project toward the child. Thoughts and feelings are as real to the child as are things. The feeling of the mother for the child she is carrying, imprinted at

this early time, becomes the background for all of that child's future feelings.

3. Most important in terms of the transition of the growing child into an adult are the ego decisions made at each stage of development, decisions that go back to those made in the early stages of life. These decisions about withholding, not caring, not feeling, involve the entire organism at the time that they are originally made, and the decisions continue to function on a subconscious level.

4. Ego decisions determine the basic attitude a person takes when the suffering happens (e.g., "I'm not going to feel," or "I'm not going to care," or "I hate the world"). These ego decisions were made early and tend to continue throughout life.

5. These ego decisions determine one's basic state of mind, which is always present no matter what happens. For instance, one may carry a constant feeling of being overwhelmed (usually characteristic of perfectionists) or of never having enough time or enough money or enough books, just not enough for what one has to do. Another pattern is one of feeling fearful and apprehensive, wondering what is going to happen, or feeling lonely and unloved, no matter what is done by others to be helpful. Each person carries a state of mind that he or she brings to each life experience.

6. This state of mind creates the atmosphere in which all experiences take place. The individual retains a compulsive need to create such an atmosphere.

7. The ultimate goal of all therapy is to alleviate crises, problems, and conflicts through an extension of awareness, which raises one's consciousness to a new level above the problem.

8. All problems are really perception problems, which blind us to the true meaning and purpose of each experience.

9. Present-day problems, experiences, and "symptoms" are significant because we need the focus they bring us in order to gain a point of recognition that enables us to understand the next lesson needed to become a whole, integrated person.

10. As each problem or "symptom" is experienced, it is not so important that we learn to alleviate the symptom as to understand what it is we need to know to bring us to that place of peace and harmony with the inner self that will enable us to live more fully.

11. We reach stages in our life journey where we feel blocked or unable to understand what we need to know, and at this time we need teachers and therapists who can show the way from a perspective of spiritual growth.

12. The mood that characterizes a person in this lifetime has been set up in other lifetimes. Current parents were drawn to play out this script. Then the child reacts with the environment that he has drawn or chosen, and he makes ego decisions that fit it.

13. If we detach ourselves from our egos, letting go of all ego decisions we have ever made about everything, we can become able to meet each new experience in a fresh way and with an optimistic and positive attitude.

14. There appears to be a super-conscious "orchestrator" that supervises everything and helps us to learn what motives and attitudes really work in terms of greater happiness, and guides us to make the changes indicated. We must learn to live out with courage these experiences presented to us.

15. One of the most effective methods for modifying these ego decisions and states of mind is regression therapy, because it expands the concept of consciousness and shows it as being continuous, engaged in repeated dramas with repetitious themes, playing out its myriad parts until it ultimately reaccepts itself and all its prodigal fragments come together.

16. Regression therapy is helpful because it loosens the rigidity of the intellect and opens the door to a new experience of reality. In it one experiences a body that has been conditioned by a somewhat different personality configuration, so that one becomes able to see the arbitrary nature of the current personality. This heightened awareness makes possible a review of current life from a more objective perspective. It also reduces survival fear, enabling us to be more comfortable with the current life, since we are reminded that there will be others.

## Indications and Contraindications for Use

I attempt to regress into past lives only a very small percentage of the patients with whom I work. I use this modality only when I become convinced that it would be of some use and when my patient has explored to the fullest all of the experiences from this lifetime. Also, I feel that it is necessary for my patient to have contacted an inner spiritual guide or teacher who can retrieve the understanding of the inner mind and who can serve an important function in helping to direct the course of therapy.

If the readiness is there, the patient will move along very quickly, as if the power to move is facilitated not by me but by the spiritual guide. I feel as though I am merely an instrument to help effect the change that a person needs. In the process I learn a great deal myself. Spiritual growth, in terms of a never-ending heightening sense of self and the discovery of our true nature and purpose, must necessarily remain the principal area of concern.

I do not regress patients whose focus is on alleviating isolated symptoms by conjuring up a past-life experience for each (as one would treat pain with aspirin) and who do not have a unified approach to understanding the relationship of that symptom to the whole life process of that person. Other patients for whom the experience is contraindicated are those who maximize the importance of past-life experiences, using them to justify all present symptoms and conflicts, thus missing the full significance of present-life circumstances.

When a past-life regression distracts from lessons supposed to be learned during this lifetime, it becomes difficult to produce significant results. We are here in this lifetime, and the life opportunity is set up for us to study our basic attitudinal patterns in the here and now. I do not want to encourage people to flee from present problems to search for a more glamorous role in another lifetime.

# *Induction*

## Preparation

I have found that extensive preparation is necessary if patients are to gain the most insight and impetus for change from regression experiences. Most of my regressions are done when patients already possess a great deal of therapeutic experience and have formulated clearly their current ego stances and the direction in which they want to go. During this initiatory therapy period I assess their ego strength, their coping ability, basic health, life stress points, and support systems. During the process I establish rapport, build up a bond of trust, assemble general information about their lives, and gain a sense of their expectations. I get an impression of what their self-image is like and what sort of cognitive coping abilities they possess.

An effective way of facilitating understanding of these areas is to have the patient write out 10 questions to which he or she seeks answers in his life. Occasionally a highly developed person will seek deepening through a regression experience, and in such a case this person's questions will greatly condense the amount of time needed for preparation. The questions may even be assigned over the phone when the appointment is made. The questions are not assigned in order that they may be answered but rather to show on what level the person is functioning, as well as something about his belief systems and the nature of his goals and areas of focus in general. There is a great deal of difference in the type of experience that can be anticipated between a person who has questions about financial goals or personal involvement, and another person who seeks to develop unconditional love or a relationship with the universe. The type of guidance suggested for the regression experience will vary accordingly. The sort of questions asked also provides clues about the general type of resistance characteristic of the person, whether he or she uses embracing, opposing, denying, or fleeing techniques to handle his anxiety and anger.

During the preparation period, whether extended, or, for those who are spiritually more ready, brief, the therapist needs to keep in mind the general purposes of therapy. First, the therapist wants to guide his patients to a level of understanding that is deep enough to bring compassion. This leads to the second goal: acceptance of oneself and others. Then with an understanding that all of life experiences have been a lesson, forgiveness follows. Eventually, the patient finds unconditional love of self and others. Anything short of this increased insight and deepened feeling that serves to open the heart is selling psychotherapy short.

Needless to say, if the preparation period reveals motivation for a regression as being ego-enhancement or even the limited relief of a symptom, regression is contraindicated. One sound reason for this contraindication is that I find regression experiences to be greatly facilitated by the use of spiritual guides, and patients with more limited motivation or blocks to accessing their inner mind often experience difficulty contacting such guides or using them in ways that are maximally helpful.

A technique that enables me to more adequately access a patient's ego-state, general feeling level, motivation and goals, is to mentally get inside that person's head and ask myself, "What is going on? What would I be feeling and wanting if I were this person?" It is possible in this way to achieve a deep empathy and to assess fairly accurately what I need to know in order to be maximally helpful.

The preparation period should conclude with both patient and therapist having gained a fairly clear idea of the basic pattern of the patient's life, his ego stance, and his basic state of mind, which lead to projection and transferences onto all the aspects of his life, including, interestingly enough, his guides.

## Induction Techniques

At the beginning of an induction, the life pattern and the questions about it, which have been carefully explored in the preparation period, are restated. Many patients are fearful of losing control or of confronting scenes too ego-dystonic, and so I reassure them by reflecting this anxiety, letting them know that the control at all times is theirs, and reminding them of the value of the work they are about to do in opening up their lives and making them more joyous.

Hypnosis and regression can be misleading terms if they imply that something is being done to someone else who is in a state of helpless passivity or sleep. On the contrary, my own technique, which often elicits very vivid scenes of past-life recall, involves an active participation by the subject. To increase a patent's confidence that the control is his, I ask him to hold a crystal pyramid and look up through the base to the apex, noticing how the crystal allows him to focus one-pointedly, using all of his consciousness, all of his awareness, as though nothing else existed but that one point. I point out how this process will allow him to let go of everything—worries, cares, fears, everything on the earth plane, matters that will still be around him while he goes deep, deep, deep within to a place within himself.

The next part of the induction uses general hypnotic techniques to release muscles and increase deep breathing. At the same time, suggestions are made that patients will go deeper but will continue to hear my voice, and that when they awake they will feel extremely well, deeply relaxed, and will remember everything. When the relaxation is sufficient, I take them to a sanctuary of the mind where they see themselves standing on top of a grassy hill with a panoramic view of beautiful scenery all around. This early visualization is a helpful prelude and training for the later visualization of past-life scenes. I then tell them that at the bottom of the hill is a special sanctuary, where they will make contact with spiritual teachers. I ask them to elevate the right arm and hand about a foot and, as they walk down the hill toward the sanctuary, to allow the arm and hand, which will feel heavier and heavier as they go deeper and deeper, to return to normal position. When the arm and hand are down, I will know they have reached the bottom of the hill. I then count slowly, interspersing the counts with suggestions for deeper and deeper relaxation.

At the bottom of the hill I ask them to see a brilliant golden light and say that in it is the form of their teacher or teachers, who come forward with a greeting. I ask for a description and names, and I suggest some conversation with the guides. I suggest that the guides will protect them and that nothing negative, no thoughts or influences of any sort that are negative, can get through the light into which the patient has entered to meet the guides.

Next I have the teachers present a large, shimmering, darkly-fogged mirror with a white circle on it, in which a number will appear that estimates the current state of relaxation, 10 representing the deepest state and one, the waking state. When a number is seen, I have it erased, and successively higher numbers are written in. When the state that represents each number is experienced, a nod of the head confirms it and the next highest number is written in. Meanwhile, discussions are encouraged with the teacher as to whether there is enough depth to recall other lives, a depth difficult for many people to attain. A depth of five will probably be sufficient for much regression work. Extremely deep regressions to the origin of consciousness and to ancient lifetimes in Atlantis and Lemuria may require a deeper state.

Bringing a person out of an altered state becomes an important part of the whole process. When the transformational techniques are complete and patients signify their readiness to return, I bring them back slowly through the mirror into their sanctuary. Then I count slowly from one to 10, giving them a chance to come back into their bodies and align their spirits with their bodies. I suggest that they will be totally relaxed and will feel a sense of healing throughout, as well as a sense of balance. I point out that they are resolved on many levels and that their life can now take a new direction with enthusiasm and excitement. I restate what they feel they have learned during the regression experience. I also routinely suggest that they will remember everything. At the close I ask how they are feeling, in case there may be any lingering problem of returning into the body.

## *Transpersonal Induction*

*You can help me to hold this crystal (crystal cut in the shape of a pyramid). As you look up through the base of the crystal to the apex, you notice how the crystal allows you to focus one-pointedly all of your consciousness, all of your awareness, as though nothing else exists but that one point. It allows you to let go of everything, worries, cares, fears, everything on the earth plane. The next hour the world will run itself very nicely without your having to think. The pyramid will be around you while you go deep, deep, deep within to a place deep within your past.*

*Even now you are beginning to let go. Allow your body to be very heavy. Your eyes are getting very tired. Your eyelids are very heavy. In just a few moments you will be closing your eyes, going deep, deep within. You will continue to hear my voice very clearly, and yet you will go deeper and deeper and deeper, letting go of all worries, fears, and cares, allowing yourself to surrender, letting go of all tension in the muscles, breathing freely, letting the superconscious mind now take care of your body while you go deep, deep, deep into an inner world. Deep, deep, deep into the inner world. You will continue to go deeper and deeper and yet you will continue to hear my voice and you will remember everything. No matter how deep you go, you will remember everything. When it is time to wake up, you will wake up and feel wonderful. I want you to experience the wonderful sensation of letting go, surrendering, relaxing, accepting, peaceful. You will sense that inner peace, deeply relaxing, but you will maintain contact with me.*

*Now I'd like you to go to the sanctuary of the mind. See yourself standing on top of this grassy hill, beautiful scenery all around, all the kinds of beautiful scenery you love, a panoramic view, very beautiful, all around you. And there's a special meeting place, a special sanctuary, at the bottom of this hill where you are going to make a contact with your spiritual teachers that will be stronger than ever before. So bring yourself to the top of this hill and when you are ready to begin to walk down this hill, nod your head and let me know.*

*Very good. In order for me to know when you're at the bottom of the hill I'd like you right now to stretch out and raise up your left arm and hand. Let it elevate about a foot. Now as I count you down this hill your arm and hand are going to become very heavy, and as you relax and go deeper and deeper, it will descend. When it reaches the original position, then I'll know that you have arrived at the bottom of the hill.*

*Take one step—it's a letting-go feeling. Then two. Looking forward to actually meeting your Guides. And three. Becoming heavier and heavier, deeper, deeper, and deeper. Four...Five. Getting deeper and deeper. Letting go. More and more peaceful. Six...And seven...Eight. Peacefully relaxing and letting go...Nine. Deeper and Deeper. 10...11...And 12...13. Deeply relaxed and all of your energy is flowing freely through your body. Your circulation is improved. This is a very healing rest for your body. Your blood flows freely through the relaxed muscles. Your energy flows freely through your body so you'll feel healed when you awaken. Let your body now be taken care of totally by your superconscious mind. As the mind relaxes you go deeper and deeper. (Continues until arm is in resting position.)*

*Now you're walking along the bottom of the hill feeling very comfortable, very safe. It is very beautiful. You pause and a little way off is a blinding golden flow of light and you begin to see the form of your teachers. Perhaps there is one. Perhaps there are two, coming to greet you with a smile on their faces, knowing that today you're going to have a very special experience. They are very important. They are going to help you with this experience. You may wish to give them permission to come forward and embrace you, joyfully embrace you. Are there one or two Guides? (Patient answers.)*

*Good. Take a deep breath. You might want to say a few things. Or ask questions. Or you might be embarrassed and think you don't deserve all this attention. That's okay. You could say, "I'm ready. I'm open. I trust. I'm willing to experience whatever I need to experience."*

*Now, for the work we're going to do, you're going to give them totally your support and your willingness and openness to learn. You're going to go deep, deep, deep. Let's put white light around you now. They're going to protect you.*

Nothing negative, no thought or influences of any sort that are negative would have a chance of getting through this white light.

Now your teachers show you that there is a large shimmering, shining, darkly fogged mirror that has a white circle on it. In a few minutes you are going to see a number in that circle that will be an estimate of your state of relaxation right now on a scale of one to 10—one is wide awake and 10 is a deep state where you can go into soul travel. Right now you're deeply relaxed. Have your subconscious mind put a number in the center of that circle to estimate how relaxed you are. You can tell me the number you see (For example, three). Okay. Now I'm going to help you to increase that number. You have an eraser in your left hand to erase that number and very slowly chalk in a four. As you do so, you will feel yourself actually sinking deeper and deeper into the spiritual realm, letting go of your hold on your body, deepening your whole sense of relaxation. When you have a four, nod your head. Very good.

Now erase the four and very slowly begin to chalk in a five. And as you're chalking in a five, know whether you have any anxiety about going deeper, if there is any fear about going deeper. So we'll chalk in a five. Feel yourself going deeper. When you have a five, let me know. You might ask your teachers, is it all right if I go very deep today? Can you help me go very deep? Erase the five and slowly chalk in a six. As you become more relaxed, you are open to the energy of your teachers. You are available to them, more receptive of their energy, more trusting, letting go, letting go of all the patterns of your thinking, letting go of the tensions, deepening into your inner world, relaxing completely. When you have a six, let me know. Are you feeling a little difficulty getting a six? There may be a little anxiety of letting go so completely. Let me know when you have the six. I think you may find that because of something that happened in a past life that is unconscious there is a fear of letting go totally and being in another place without some control. Your Guides are here. They are loving you. You are feeling their love. If you talk to them and they feel it's all right, we'll move on. Do you have a six? All right, erase the six. We're going on a very special trip today. We need to go very deep. Chalk in a seven. Got the seven already? Beautiful! Erase the seven and chalk in an eight. I hope your Guides are reassuring you that nothing terrible is going to happen. It's going to be a wonderful experience for you. You're going where you can learn a great, great deal. Therefore you don't have to be afraid. You can be totally open, totally exposed. You need to be exposed to go deeper. You'll like where you are going. So when you have an eight, let me know. All right, erase the eight and chalk in a nine. Got the nine already? Okay, erase the nine and slowly chalk in a 10. And as you do, your spiritual body becomes very ethereal and you are going through the mirror on a soul journey. Your teachers are taking you on a special trip, way back into time.

I am going to very gently hold your right hand. Keep the contact with me. Know that I am here. Go way back. Your teachers are all taking you on this journey, to bring back to memory that time when (describe area of understanding which patient wishes to contact). Share with me where you are.

## Supportive and Deepening Techniques

I give support primarily by voice and by my attitude of respect for the patient's process. Sometimes when the regression moves a long way back, I will hold the patient's right hand for reassurance.

To deepen, I focus on the problems brought in during the preparatory work and on the nature of the ten questions. Using this as a base, I work to expose the pattern of the lifetime more and more clearly by asking other questions that will help to bring clarity. When I am not sure just where the patient ought to go, I suggest questioning the guides for direction. Patterns begin to take on forms, such as rejection, abandonment, death of people close to the patient in various lifetimes; being a repeated target of blame, experiencing material loss or physical abuse, etc. The goal is to see that we have power beyond our current conception to modify all of our experiences and to unify all of the disparate elements that seem so chaotic.

When a scene is too traumatic, I move the person ahead through the death in that lifetime to the after-life plane of teaching so that the events can be viewed with greater perspective. Sometimes the broader view following extrication from the disturbing incident becomes enough to relieve the tensions, but if not, guides can be summoned to help.

# *Processing*

## Transformational and Psychotherapeutic Techniques

The common denominator of all psychotherapeutic techniques is undoubtedly the expansion of perspective that allows us to see our lives as a sequence of meaningful and significant patterns that act as teachers for our growth in consciousness. We see repetitious themes of misdirected energy, misuse of power, and, most important, the loss of love through selfishness. This loss is felt most painfully within as tragedy strikes over and over again because of stubbornness and self-judgment.

There are various ways of extending this perspective and learning to perceive things in a different and more self-accepting way. Some of these involve using deep sources of inner wisdom, such as our Higher Self or spirit guides. A technique that is often helpful, when there is an impasse in judgment within a lifetime, is to bring in the current self in the guise of a teacher or a guide. Whether one has regressed back to childhood of the current lifetime, to an experience *en utero*, or to other lifetimes, whenever one feels stuck in an old belief system often the current self can come in tenderly and offer helpful advice.

Seeing the event or attitude in the broader context of another lifetime tends to give it a different meaning, and the therapist can point this out and extend its impact through comments and questions. This can lead to a reversal of the ego decisions that have been running one's life. However, such a reversal should not be taken for granted but should be carefully explicated within the therapeutic process. As the pattern from the various lifetimes becomes more and more clear, there can also take place a disidentification with negative states, giving the person more room to make positive and helpful decisions.

Regression to childhood and tracing interactions with parents in the roles they played in other lifetimes can and must eventually lead to a re-evaluation of the parents. As we come to see that we have chosen our parents in order to play out complementary roles and that we failed in love for them just as they failed in love for us, we gain an expanded perspective that makes possible both compassion and subsequent re-evaluation. Old patterns of anger can be loosened and eventually released as we understand both the roles we played and how we brought anger about. In the end, we learn to be grateful both for the lessons we have chosen in order to help us grow in consciousness and to the people who have clustered in our various lifetimes to help us learn them. It is the work of the therapist to take an active part in this process of re-evaluation, facilitating a letting go of old attachments to negative states and yielding to the process of inner growth.

## Integration into the Psychotherapeutic Process

In therapeutic contacts following a regression, further exploration is helpful in order to see the way that the current life reflects past lives. Current difficulties can be reviewed within the setting of the broader perspective now available, and new choices can be considered. Patients can alert themselves as to how they are drawing things to happen. Meanwhile, with the material and compulsions of the unconscious so much loosened, it is possible to work on the development of the will. Gradually the patient becomes more aware that one attitude doesn't work and another does, and his will can implement a new choice and a new direction.

## Failures

It is my experience that failure in regression therapy occurs when the patient is not sufficiently motivated or prepared. I do regression work sparingly and only after the current life experience has adequately been explored and a need is felt for deepening of patterns that in the limited perspective of one lifetime emerge without clarity. I need to know that a person can contact a deeper level of himself and that he has guides to protect and help him before I am willing to try such an exploration. If these conditions are met, failure is improbable.

The one exception is when colleagues who have had a great deal of analytic work and self-exploration and whose therapists are not trained in regression work and often do not even consider it a modality, come to me asking for regression because they wish to deepen their understanding of themselves. I find it difficult to refuse them, since they often have no other recourse, but the results are not always satisfactory. Without knowing clearly the basic patterns they are working on, it is difficult to tune in intuitively to where they need to go and the way they can best be helped. After several regression sessions—and sometimes only one—there are times when neither of us has the feeling that we have worked on significant material. When the majority of our healing profession is trained to use regression techniques, it will not be so necessary for the few of us now doing regression work to risk such a situation.

## *Cases*

### Guilt and Self-Forgiveness

Out of all the themes that have arisen during my 20-plus years of doing past-life therapy, the most pervasive is that of guilt and of the resultant need for self-forgiveness. We feel responsible or guilty, not only for our motives and intentions and our negligence, but also for our legitimate helplessness. It is as if we cannot accept the limitations imposed upon us by a three-dimensional reality and so feel responsible for everything that goes wrong or that leads to the pain and suffering of others within our environment. The sins of omission often press more heavily upon our soul than do the sins of commission.

In the examples that follow we can see how the soul, in its learning, punishes itself for hurting others, for cowardice, for being inadequate, and for negligence. Once we have deemed ourselves guilty, the cycles of self-imposed punishment seem never to end until we have consciously arrived at an understanding that permits self-forgiveness. We are disciplined by guilt, we are taught by comparisons that engender guilt, and we have religious institutions that heavily reinforce guilt. The average person, in the natural condition of daily activities, feels subconsciously like a condemned criminal, awaiting fearfully the inevitable moment of exposure, as in Camus' *The Trial*.

What we cannot forgive in ourselves we cannot forgive in others. Thus our own guilt becomes projected upon others, resulting in judgments that perpetuate the emotions of anger and rage. This, in turn, results in progressive self-isolation, feelings of alienation, and fear. Guilt, anger and fear create a locked triangle which cannot be broken without self-forgiveness and forgiveness of others. Unfortunately, in our most intimate relationships, such as the family, our communications tend to reinforce each member's sense of guilt.

This is the foundation upon which I have based my model of therapy. I strive for a depth of understanding that will lead to compassion for self and others within a given situation. We need to accept others as trying desperately to work out their own salvation in the only way they know. From this understanding we can arrive at both self-forgiveness and forgiveness of others, a position that will open the gate to self-love and brotherly love.

### Case 1. Separation from the Source as an Initiator of Guilt

I have always believed that fragmentary therapy, working on symptoms, retrieving an exciting past life here and there, is not particularly helpful in achieving evolutionary growth. We need to look for patterns. The awakening of consciousness and the alleviation of fear and guilt begin to take us on that journey home to awaken our true self, an awakening that forms the basic evolutionary path. With various therapeutic tools the therapist can move a person from one place to another, releasing difficulties and blocks as the client moves forward and bringing the energy field of the patient into increasing balance.

Joanne's core issue was guilt. During our years together she passed through one barrier after another in her search to understand this guilt and release it. As often happens, the search took her back finally to her original guilt over separation from the Source, and in the understanding of this she became able not only to release that guilt, which was tied up with her low energy, but to find tools and understanding for working further in her life.

Joanne came to see me six years ago. At that time she was a pale, frail housewife who seemed to have a relatively simple life as a compulsive mother taking care of her children. She had always resisted help from anyone, but her son had allergies and other problems, so she came to me seeking help for him. Only after she had met me and felt that she could be comfortable talking about the disturbing feelings she had been having did she suggest sessions for herself.

We first discussed together her limited energy and feelings of extreme fatigue. Laboratory work showed that she was suffering from hypo-adrenal corticoidism, an adrenal activity so debilitating that she could not tolerate a single adrenal capsule. When in a following session I suggested that sometimes such physical states and feelings could relate to emotions one has experienced in childhood, she resisted the idea so strongly that I decided to bypass childhood and go directly into a past lifetime to search for the cause. Usually I do not do this until the patient has a fairly integrated sense of his life, but, as I intended, this suggestion startled her and got her attention so that she dropped her resistance, and shortly afterward she allowed herself to be taken into an altered state.

T: *Let yourself focus on that feeling you've been telling me about. Describe what you're feeling.*
P: *Remorse...I am astonished. The word is just there, a word I rarely use, and it fits precisely!*
T: *Okay. We're going to trace the roots of this remorse...deep down feelings of remorse. Now I'm going to count down from 10 to one and I want you to see a scene in which you had this feeling of remorse.*
P: *Children. Children hurting. (Tears are streaming down her face so that it is difficult to speak.)*
T: *Gradually you'll get a sense of what this means. Follow those heavy feelings. Dare to let yourself...*
P: *Babies.... Children being killed.... God! In the Holy Land.*
T: *Do you mean when Jesus was born and Herod had all the children killed?*
P: *Yeah.... I must be making all this up!*
T: *What are you seeing? Describe what else. I'm going to count from 10 to one and you will see more vividly where you were in that period of time.*
P: *I am in the middle of a village and there is a battle going on. It is night and very dark. The people everywhere are terrified and running around. I am a young man, 18-years-old, on a horse. I have just killed a young child.*

*The scene becomes more vivid: screams...horse hooves...shouts ...clinking metal...terrified screams. I am looking down from my horse into the face of a mother whose child I have just killed. She is a beautiful woman, very dark eyes and dark hair. I'm sure if I met her today I would know her, the vividness is so intense. And I am aware that the mother sees in her child something precious and valuable and important—all the things*

>    *I didn't see in children in that lifetime. I thought, "What difference do a few kids more or less make?" There is something in that eye contact with her that stops me in my tracks. I am painfully aware that my sword is still red and wet.*
> 
> T: Go back and see how you got into that situation. Go back an hour.
> P: *I am young...wild...I have terrific energy...wild. The colors are vivid. The sounds are sharp. I am a young man, constantly preoccupied with my own intense energy.*
> T: Look at that wild, terrific energy. Is it the antithesis of the energy you feel now? Are you keeping down that wild energy, afraid of what that wild energy can lead to?
> P: *I don't know.*
> T: All right. Go to the end of that lifetime.
> P: *I'm an old man now, and it won't be long until I die. I'm just doing my job. My spirit is broken. I'm haunted. I carry guilt and remorse and I don't know what to do about this, so I just keep carrying it. I die, but the guilt and remorse, like some celestial hot potato, go on.*

After this session we processed the material of that lifetime by working on self-forgiveness and stressing the wisdom and compassion that she had gained, and she became less stressed and felt better physically and her energy level increased. Then she dropped out of therapy for a while, but dreams began to flood her and some of the old feelings returned, so after a while she made sporadic appointments. At times we dealt with current-life issues and childhood experiences, which she was now open to looking at, and at other times past-life regression provided clues—and also surprises!

In one lifetime she was a professionally well-accepted but lonely male American doctor in colonial times. In another she was a highly intelligent African woman who because of her snobbish attitude toward less bright neighbors became isolated from them and died in childbirth alone. In the 13th century she was a monk, murdered after unjustly being accused of mismanaging funds. This life was also basically one of solitude. Still earlier, as a charismatic Atlantean leader with great authority and greater insensitivity, she misused power by separating and exiling families who displeased her.

The most recent lifetime, as in her first regression, was that of a soldier, a young man who was ambushed, captured, and tortured to death.

> T: Why, at some level of your being, did you choose to experience this terrible death?
> P: *I thought if I suffered enough I could be rid of my deep guilt. But I realize that the guilt was not moved and my pain was useless. Is it all hopeless, trying to release this guilt?*

It seemed that we had to go still further back to find the guilt, and as we pressed backward after these lives, Joanne began to wonder when all the earth lives began. Was there a time when she had existed before Earth? Without a body? She kept saying that she didn't feel wholly comfortable on Earth and wanted to "go home."

Meanwhile, her energy level had dropped again and we concentrated on trying to discover the reason for this. Her repeated complaint that she wanted to "go home" led into a significant session. The material came out in small driblets but has been condensed and summarized into the following:

T: *All right. Go all the way back before you were on Earth. Go home. What's it like? Go back before you were the Roman soldier, before you were the Atlantean leader. Go back as far as you can go.*
P: *I'm not in a body. I've never been in a body.*
T: *Where are you?*
P: *I seem to be a beam of light. I am like molten gold but indescribably more brilliant. I am a flowing of energy more powerful than all numbers can express, more concentrated than the greatest laser light and utterly pure. This light bends and curls like delicate plants at the bottom of the sea in intricate harmonies, expressing each subtle nuance of all that exists in the universe. Yet, in some way everything existing in the universe is encompassed in this beam of light.*

*I am a point of consciousness surrounded by other points of consciousness. Between us all exist perfect awareness and a symphonic harmony. I can direct a portion of this energy, and in doing so, I can express and arrange new harmonies. I can direct. I can control. I can imagine the power is me.*

*I become preoccupied with wielding the power. Gradually this subtle, exquisite immense energy begins to seem heavy and obliterates all awareness of those other points of consciousness. I am alone...trapped.*
T: *How could you return to awareness of the beam of light?*
P: *I have to see the point of error and acknowledge it. That is the key, acknowledging the error. Punishment is of no use. Nor is merely being "good." One has to acknowledge error and then turn around. That is all.*

*But I can't do that. Pride prevents the acknowledgment. My energy continues to feel heavier and heavier. And now I become aware, some time after this, that I am in a body, though some part of me still remembers the beam of light. But I have not acknowledged it nor have I turned around, and I am filled with guilt. I see that the separation from the Light because of my obsession with power was the beginning of the guilt that I have carried through so many lifetimes. Finally being able to acknowledge my error has released it.*

She summarized the experience in her Journal:

*After that session I knew that all the life experiences I've had here in this body and on this earth came after the first experience. I knew beyond all doubt that we, each of us, are more than beings in bodies. We are beings of awesome potentiality. We are beings whose heritage it is to live in harmony and beauty that exist beyond our present ability to perceive. I knew that each of us is more than we have believed ourselves to be. And my view of myself can never be quite the same.*

This awareness brought Joanne into a new balance and significantly increased her peace of mind. Her physical energy showed an almost unbelievable increase. She wrote to me a few months later;

*I still have down days and bad moods. I get impatient with my husband and grouchy with the kids. I work in my husband's business, cook meals, dust the furniture, and drive lots of miles. And like most mothers of teenagers I answer the phone a lot! But I am still growing, still discovering more about myself. It seems to me that my life is like an episode of an adventure serial, i.e., "to be continued."*

Our complexity as personalities stems not only from our experiences in various lifetimes but also from the decisions we have made about them. Joanne had a vivid experience of separation from the Source, which because of the feelings of power that she experienced in that process, she interpreted as selfish—and therefore "bad." This experience became the perpetuator of chronic guilt, which influenced lifetime after lifetime. Her "fall" from the beautiful and brilliant Light resulted in a diminishing of energy as she moved into a self-system different from the Source. This seems to be the inevitable course of the journey of self-realization of the soul, and probably there is no turning back if the process of self-realization is to be completed, but Joanne interpreted this individual process as a refusal on her part to turn back due to pride.

This pride and its accompanying guilt led to lifetimes characterized by an increasingly aggressive yang type of energy, in which she was inconsiderate of others and even totally selfish. She experienced the culmination of this yang energy in the killing of babies in the time of Herod. What she felt at that time was an adrenal rush, and so violent was her reaction when she finally was able to perceive the pain of the mother that at that moment she renounced her yang energy. Through subsequent lifetimes she struggled with the result of this renunciation. Unconsciously she remained determined not to experience an adrenal rush, because of the disastrous insensitivity she felt it had led her into during the lifetime in which she killed the babies.

Much of the energy Joanne did have she used in cutting back feeling because she didn't want to feel. She closed off all feeling—of guilt and also of pain. She had dreams of being iced below the waist and not being able to communicate with other people. She was afraid of her own power, of her own energy, and found herself trying desperately to hold her world together and not go crazy. This closing off of feeling became especially visible in the

African lifetime in which she lost her baby. She refused to let anybody know her pain. Her attitude was that nobody should know; she wouldn't utter a sound. This attitude was what made it difficult for her to come into therapy.

Her original experience of separation from the Source, which she interpreted as "the fall," led her to going deeper and deeper into a materialistic egoism and power until the experience of the shock and horror on the woman's face started a re-evaluation—"My God, what am I doing?"—and turned her in another direction, the striving to be good. After that she led a succession of altruistic lives—as doctors, monks, but always without feeling, so that the altruism in itself could not effect healing in her because it was not concerned with true love. When she came to me, her body was permeated with fear. She had become paralyzed with an expectation of what she was going to suffer next. She was afraid of herself and of her life decisions.

In Joanne's therapy it became important for her not just to elicit scenes but to look at these scenes in terms of forgiving and understanding herself. I needed to be there to help her change the scenes, to work with traumas, either in this lifetime or in earlier ones. I needed to say the things she needed to hear, to regress her to a time when she was filled with guilt and fear and say, "Look, it's not your fault. You're all right." When she felt acutely vulnerable, she had to have someone there showing her a way out.

Sometimes I would play low music and work with various chakra areas, especially with her third chakra, the solar plexus, in order to help her recover her lost feeling. She began to believe for the first time that she could trust the universe. She developed a sense of being grounded and wanting to be on the earth. She became more comfortable with her feelings, her sexuality—she had been terrified of sexuality—with her power, as well as with spirituality and love.

Gradually, as we progressed through the regressions and the peripheral work associated with them, her energy systems became re-integrated and she became able to accept and love all of them. To do this we had to go back through the different ego states and love the child at every level.

Joanne came in thin, pale, with cheeks sunken in. Her vital energy was almost blotted out—a compulsive housewife wearing blinders. In terms of her own experience and the observations of her friends, there's been a total transformation. But there is no ending to her growth. She, like all of us, can never say, "I've made it!" because every time she thinks she has reached a final balance, something else comes up. She has begun the endless study of herself, and there is no greater joy than ongoing self-discovery. She feels now that she is in a place where she can begin to be truly wide awake.

### Case 2. Opening the Way to Healing

Often the emotional state of a patient closes doors to allopathic and other forms of healing. In such a case, any approach that attempts to relieve or reverse physical distress will usually fail. It is the expression and healing of the emotions that change the energy field of the patient so that allopathic healing can finally come through. This does not result in a sudden "cure," but conventional ways of healing open up that are effective after these have formerly appeared to be unavailable.

Emotional reframing can take place on any level—through examining current relationships, through looking into childhood or birth distress, or through experiencing memory of other lifetimes. In the latter case, the reframing of the emotional situation that existed in other lives makes possible a more effective intervention in this one.

Les, a young man in his twenties, demonstrated how working through blocked emotions from earlier lives can open up healing where none had previously been able to take place. At the time he came to me, he had begun coughing up blood, and the pleural cavity on his left side filled up. Extensive medical tests could find no cause for this. One of his friends suggested that the condition might have karmic roots, and Les came to explore this. He was eager to try anything that would help, and he put up no psychological blocks to the regression process. Because he was so open and motivated, induction into an altered state was easy. I told him I would relax him gently, and I suggested that he let his thinking mind take a vacation. I had him take a deep breath and close his eyes, suggesting that his eyes were very heavy and that with each breath he would let go more and finally surrender totally. Then I proceeded through my usual induction, which took him into a medium depth of trance, enough for the work we were to do. At this point, using the feeling and discomfort in his chest as a bridge, I went directly into a past life.

> T: *Get in touch with the anxiety and the discomfort. Put them both into one strong feeling and let this feeling build a scene that will give us a clue about your present condition. I will count from one to ten and while I do this, let your feelings take you into that scene.*
> P: *There's a room, a great empty cold kind of room. A low light. There seems to be nothing in it but a table.*
> T: *Does any year come to mind?*
> P: *18...1822.*

At first Les thinks he as alone but when he looks at the table he sees a person and recognizes him.

P: He's a friend (heaving). He's dying. I'm a doctor. He's on the table and I can't help him (crying).
T: What's he dying from?
P: (Sobbing) Something with his chest. (Gasps for breath.)
T: Why are you so upset?
P: He put himself in my hands.
T: You feel responsible. What are you experiencing?
P: Guilt. He counted on me. I did all I could all the way, but it wasn't enough.
T: You feel guilt even though you did the best you could. He really thought you could save him?
P: It's all dark. His breathing is sharp. He's gasping for air.
T: Get in touch with the emotional connection you had with this man.
P: (Sobs too deeply to talk.)
T: Try to listen. You've taken on God's responsibility without having God's power.
P: I let him die.
T: Come to this doctor as Les in this present lifetime and be his helper.
P: He doesn't want to hear me.
T: He needs to listen. Guilt will not help his friend. Guilt is going to cause him to take on the suffering of his patient. Can you explain that to him? The results are out of his hands. He is only a channel. Tell him. It's important you do this until he realizes he can't be responsible. He needs to be given to and helped. He's lost a friend. Have him put his hands on his friend and know his friend is going to his peace. He's really helping his friend now to leave. His friend doesn't want to leave when this doctor is so guilty. Make a love bond, not a bond of pain and suffering. Can you feel this?
P: Yes, a little.
T: Now I'd like you to take a deep breath and relax and go back even further to where you began with this chest difficulty. Is there any other thing related to this chest difficulty?
P: It's a kind of open court within a building, a courtyard—Grecian or Roman. And there's a taper burning on the wall. There are two figures. One is a huge shining black man. He's lying on this bench. He's just huge, beautifully muscled, a gentle, huge man. Off in the shadows some distance away is a boy. The man is sick and the boy is holding his head in his hands and he's crying.
T: Is the boy you? How old are you?
P: Nine.
T: What century is it?
P: I think it's the fourth century A.D. The boy is the son of the owner of the house. The black man is a slave but the boy's constant companion, his guard.
T: What are you experiencing?

P: The man's dying. The boy is losing his only real friend. He can see him over there but he can't go near him because the priest came and said he had the "affliction."
T: Something wrong with his chest?
P: He can't help him. He can't even talk to him.
T: He's feeling helpless. Is his friend in pain?
P: He's in agony. He's gasping. How cruel!! How can somebody so marvelous die?
T: Look and see if there is some special bond with his body.
P: The boy wants to help him, give him anything. He wants to take the pain away. The priest says nothing can be done but the boy doesn't want to believe it.
T: The boy actually wants to take his friend's pain. Get in touch with that. Get in touch with wanting to share that pain. Pain is a bond. You practically do take the pain on, don't you? It is a bond. You think you might be able to help him by taking on his pain. But taking on his pain doesn't help him. The black man wouldn't want to die thinking that the boy took on his pain, would he?
P: No.
T: He would like to die with the feelings of love but not with the boy taking on his pain. Go ahead in that lifetime. Was the boy ever concerned about his chest in any way?
P: He had a physical distortion. He was shy about exposure.... A strange thing happened in this lifetime now. I had a friend named James, the most beautiful man in town. He got a chest ailment at the age of 20 and died.
T: Is he related to the black man? Do you have a sense it was the same person?
P: There is a sense of familiarity. We were always very close and nobody understood it. He was about four years my senior. When he died was when my chest pains began.
T: You see the connection there. Go back into that lifetime and as Les talk to that little boy and tell him he doesn't have to take on a friend's pain, that you have learned to love, not bond through pain.
P: I can tell him that. I can see that it is true.

Les and I spent some time communicating this message to the boy.

T: I will count to 10. Come back into the room, feeling really good, realizing that the real bond is love, not pain.... How do you feel?
P: Such a deep sense of relief. Amazing. Amazing. I never thought about it, the connection with James' death. When I went to the hospital it was just months after he died.
T: Let's see how it goes from here. If it is necessary, we can work through it again later, intensifying everything you have done.

It is important to realize that what had to be reframed was the emotional state in which the physical condition existed, not the physical condition itself. The emotional attitude of wanting to take over his friend's illness grew in Les over several lifetimes. This attitude had to be exposed as inappropriate and then released and a more appropriate response developed instead, namely bonding with his friend through love.

Another thing worth noticing is how easily Les shifted back and forth from the consciousness of the other lifetime to consciousness of his current life. It is a good example of how time frames overlap without any loss of clarity. All states of consciousness exist simultaneously.

After this regression Les did not immediately lose his chest problem, but he was able to find a physician who could treat it, something he had not been able to do before. With this new medical intervention the lungs drained. Working through the emotional blocks set up in the other lifetimes had made it possible for treatment to be effective. A physician can heal only when the person is ready. Release to find effective help is just as truly healing as is a more magical remission of symptoms and is probably the more usual way that such healing processes occur.

**Case 3. Reframing Inadequacy**

In experiencing a sequence of past lives it becomes apparent that the only attitude that really works out is one of shared loving, caring, and gratitude. The greatest crime, and perhaps the only crime, is not loving and valuing ourselves. Cowardly passivity, the fear of being true to oneself, leads to anguish, disillusionment, and despair. We must learn to live with courage, to live what we believe. Otherwise, we insult the indwelling Self, which leads to guilt and the need to set up similar situations in the hope that finally we will prove ourselves. Thus arise our karmic patterns and we feel guilty and set up still another trial with one more hope on an inner level that we will do better.

Such a karmic pattern was exemplified by Jack, a young married man whose dominant emotional pattern revolved around feelings of inadequacy, cowardice, self-pity, and lack of commitment. He found it difficult to be responsible, committed, and faithful in his marriage, or a good father to his child. I asked myself about the nature of his emotional suffering and the patterns for dealing with it. What was the nature of his fear? I saw that his pattern was one of feeling inadequate, full of self-pity, cowardice, self-hate.

When we focused on these emotions, Jack regressed quite easily into a past-life scene in which he was a young soldier being severely reprimanded by the commanding officer before the entire regiment because he had deserted his comrades during an attack and had let them die before his eyes while he was hiding in fear. The reprimand was a deeply humiliating experience and left him feeling guilty, deserving of punishment, and wanting to die.

Jack seemed bogged down with this heavy sense of guilt, and so I suggested that he go back to another lifetime that would give added dimension to the emotional picture presented by the soldier. He moved further back in time and saw himself as a young Lutheran monk who had impetuously left the Catholic Church and had then become aware that he had made an error. He felt irrevocably trapped because he was convinced that the church would never take him back, so he covered his cowardice by superficially serving the Lutheran Church without real feeling or commitment, afraid to admit what he considered to be an error. His life dragged on until he became an old man who lived without enthusiasm or joy, going through the motions, until he ended up dying in a solitary room, crying out in fear and self-hatred that he had been untrue to himself.

Later we returned to his life as the soldier, and recovered details that added depth to that lifetime. He was British, and following the abandonment by his comrades he became an outcast from England. He went to New England, where the Americans despised him because he was British, and he finally died alone in a shabby hotel in New England in a sad repetition of the last days of his life as a monk.

During his next lifetime he was again a soldier, this time in the Civil War, where he watched horrified and transfixed by fear while Union soldiers burned down his house with his wife and children inside. He couldn't bring himself to do anything about it, just sat transfixed by fear while his family burned to death. After that, overwhelmed with guilt, he traveled west in an attempt to pull his life together. But he became unable to do this. His last days found him again alone, unloved, in a bare room in a cheap San Francisco hotel, where he sat lamenting his fate and wallowing in self-pity because of his inability to react in the way he knew he should have done.

I have patients do homework in an effort to deepen their understanding of their problem and strengthen their will so that affirmations they have made will stand a better chance of success. It was evident that Jack had to program his intellect and will positively in order to change. Here is an excerpt from what he wrote.

> *I have felt the presence of my Spirit Guide all around me, assuring me that I am not alone and asking me if I now see my task clearly, which I do. I am encouraged to have the courage of my convictions in this lifetime, to be true to myself, to demonstrate unselfishly the courage of my convictions, day by day, to break the chain here and now. My Guide assures me I can do this and that I now have the strength of purpose for this realization. I can see that my present lifetime does not provide the opportunity for a dramatic demonstration*

> *of loyalty and courage through giving up my life, as I was given the opportunity to do twice before, but perhaps that would be too easy. That would be like the fantasy I always have that I can win the game by throwing a touchdown pass in the last play.*

This new sense of conviction in his own ability to modify his life opened the door to a deeper, more devastating process that followed spontaneously several weeks later, which I can only describe as a total collapse of the ego. He called me in a state of despair, and with the voice of a frightened child he said that he had to go on welfare. Supporting him through this period taxed all of my therapeutic skills.

It gradually became clear that he was re-living the emotions of the dying derelict who left the earth plane without ever resolving his feelings of guilt, remorse, helplessness, and cowardice. In fact, my work with this patient was actually performing therapy with this derelict, who now had the ego strength to trust and work with me because of the growth he had experienced in this lifetime.

Eventually, as the result of surveying those lives and working through the guilt in them, Jack finally became confident that he really did have the strength to change the pattern.

In this sort of integrating procedure I often feed spiritual truths into the patient's subconscious mind to replace negative programming after that negative programming has been deleted by the patient's new awareness. After Jack had recovered his initial resolve and begun to integrate it into his life, he made a further entry in his journal:

> *Even a play that does not gain much ground, if devised and executed with conviction and courage, opens the way for the next play to achieve its objective. The game is won or lost every day in everything I do, at work or play or home with my family. I am determined to be true to myself, loyal to others, and have the courage of my convictions to face any situation in this life.*

Since Jack now understood the pattern of the various lifetimes and set this strong intention to transform it, a deep and permanent restructuring eventually took place in his life. The kind of affirmation he put out was powerful and was repeated often. The formulating of such an affirmation and the integration of its repetition into a life pattern is part of the follow-up work of psychotherapy.

As the affirmations took hold, Jack moved into a life of more definition and action and positive feeling. He started a computer company, and as his assertions of strength and self-respect took effect, he divorced his wife, who had dominated him and reinforced his feeling of inadequacy. He had found nothing left to sustain the marriage once he had moved beyond such negative self-concepts.

The question can be raised whether, if reframing of his attitude had been more adequately worked through when the lifetime of the derelict was recovered, there would not have been the need to go through such a painful collapse of the ego. Perhaps not, but perhaps the collapse was necessary in order to make room for new and more positive attitudes. At any rate, there is no doubt that adequate work on the death process is of paramount importance in regression work, and probably the restructuring of guilt felt at the time should be a major emphasis in each regression.

### Case 4. Releasing the Need to be Responsible

Lydia, an older professional woman, presented as her recurring problem her compulsive need to take responsibility for everything and everyone. As we discussed the 10 questions she had written for me, it became evident that she carried a conviction that she was not perfect enough or spiritual enough to be worth much and that in some way she was constantly failing. In a sense she exaggerated the dust of her humanness into a big molehill. This concern with being less than perfect, is, incidentally, characteristic of many therapists. It had never occurred to Lydia that perhaps she didn't have to be perfect; in fact, the very idea seemed to jar her.

Since Lydia had already experienced many regressions and yet felt she had never been in a deep altered state, I felt challenged to give her a special experience. In order to help her feel especially safe, I had her look into a crystal pyramid and focus her consciousness on the top, while giving suggestions for deep relaxation and peaceful surrendering to the Inner Mind. Following my usual induction, I walked her down the grassy hill to the sanctuary. Lydia works with guides, and this time she saw Jesus alongside the two with whom she usually works. This did not surprise me as it is my experience that her type of deep feeling of loss and failure usually occurs in people who were with Jesus in the Holy Land. When Lydia looked into the fogged mirror she saw a three, which indicated only a light altered state. It took a while, but she finally allowed herself to slip to the 10 which I felt would enable her to have the sort of experience she sought.

For certain people who can reach this depth and who have had sufficient inner preparation, I suggest a return to the origin of consciousness.

> T: *You are going way back into a time when you were one with the Allness, way back to the very beginning, eons ago. You are ready for this. I am going to gently hold your right hand. Keep contact with me. Know that I am here. Go way back. Your teachers are all taking you on this journey,*

to bring back the memory of that time when your consciousness was one. Soon you will be able to describe to me what that experience was like.
P: (Tuning in without difficulty) Streams of lights of different colors. Music. But it's all filled with love, like what I feel from my guides, only more.
T: A place of pure light.
P: It's not even a place. Kind of like a condition.

I suggested that time be speeded up like time-lapse photography, enabling her to understand the process of how she became an individual consciousness.

P: I feel like a seed in dark slime.
T: Think of why you came to that place. Why is it necessary to leave that place of love? How does it happen? Is it an accident or a decision?
P: A decision.
T: Okay. Let's get in touch with that.
P: I just seem to be...it just seems to be...
T: You just need to play?
P: (Grimacing) Play is a kind of a hard word for me but I need to experience...
T: Experience...?
P: Because I was just being before. Now I need to experience.
T: As a separate entity. Okay. Now I want you to go to the process of how it happens when you do that. You become individualized, and then what happens?
P: Then I just find myself a seed.
T: Separated from the rest?
P: That's right.
T: How does that feel.
P: It really feels okay. It's exciting because I'm doing just what I want.
T: Let's see what happens when it finally dawns on you that you can't go back.
P: You see, I'm aware that I never really left, that I have it all the time, anyway.

Sometimes in a regression to the beginning of separation, there is some guilt or regret or sense of loss, which can lead to later patterns of feeling one is "bad," but Lydia didn't seem to have any of these, so I suggested that we explore further the conviction that she was bad, that we go to a scene where she did something she thought wasn't very good.

T: All this power, all this fun, all this connection—yes, what happened? Suddenly you began the whole concept, "I'm not good enough."
P: (Long pause.) I am in a place that I never really thought existed—Lemuria. I am playing in a field—very beautiful. Streams run through it.
T: Are there other people?

P: No. In the distance there is a city—very advanced. People come out from the city and ask me to join with them but I refuse. I like my life here, playing in the fields, being part of the fields and streams. I'm not interested. I just want to play.... Now something is happening. Water sweeps over my meadow. Everything is covered with water, and I know the city is covered, too. As I am drowning, I think that if I had joined with the others, perhaps together we could have found a way so this wouldn't have happened. I cared too much about play. I should have joined with the others.

T: You felt responsible?

P: I never tried to help. Perhaps I could have. I only cared to play.

This lifetime gave premonitions of what we were looking for and I suggested that we move along the time track to the next significant lifetime in which she was more aware of herself. When a plethora of scenes came to mind, I suggested that she focus on Atlantis and see what she was doing during that extended period of time. At first she said she had never been there, but almost immediately she realized that she had.

She saw herself as a man on the eve of the destruction of Atlantis, distraught over her inability to convince anyone of the danger that this time she strongly sensed was so imminent. Finally, she gave up the attempt and angry over her failure, she descended the cliff side and found a ship from Iberia that was headed for Egypt and became a passenger.

T: You are one of the group that goes to Egypt.

P: I just got out. I didn't try to save anything or anyone, not even my family. I took care of my own skin.

T: So the pattern is repeated—abrogating responsibility and leaving and taking care of yourself. How are you feeling about that, looking at it now?

P: Well, I feel pretty crummy. I have a lot more feeling that that isn't the thing to do than I had before in Lemuria.

After this we looked at her life in Egypt where she became a healer in the Temple Beautiful, carrying a sadness about the country she had left and trying to make up for her desertion of it by working hard at healing. She continued to feel guilty about leaving but still could not see any other solution. I had the Lydia of the current lifetime become a consultant to the man she had been in Egypt. I had her point out to him how he had brought his knowledge to Egypt and had learned to care about everyone who came, and that he really was a good person. Lydia could concede that the man was not evil, only selfish, perhaps, though not as selfish as she had formerly thought. Her self-criticism began to lighten.

T: He'll be pleased to hear that. What is his name?
P: Who? Oh, it's Philomen—sounds different.
T: Philomen had to make a decision and the decision he made was the only one he could make—a little selfish, perhaps, but not all that bad, not a bad person to know.
P: No, and he does a lot of healing.
T: Good. Let's take a look at that. It might be interesting to introduce some of that today. What kind of healing do you do there?
P: Well, we make some kind of energy out of light. I don't know the technique of it.
T: A laser beam does that.
P: It is something like that, only you lie under these lights and it is as though the light changes the energy fields of your body so they are healthy and beautiful.

It then came out that earlier, while on Atlantis, Philomen had belonged to a group of healers and introduced a new idea, which was not only turned down but which caused him to be ostracized from his group. He felt unwanted then, and Lydia admitted that this is a feeing she often has in this lifetime, too.

T: Nobody's going to want you.
P: That's right.
T: Nobody's going to accept your ideas.
P: That's right.
T: Look at Philomen now. What do you think of him?
T: I know what is wrong. I feel selfish because of that other lifetime. So I doubt myself even though I was right. I kind of mixed it up.
T: Philomen needs a little therapy from someone. Let's have the Lydia of today come into the scene. Let's have her go to Philomen as his teacher. You can tell him, "Look, you've got it mixed up. You're really right."
P: (To Philomen) Don't mix up being right with the fact that you were uninvolved or self-involved. You're right, so feel good about it.
T: You're right, so you can even take it to Egypt or some other place. You can feel good about that, too. You couldn't hold onto it there because there was too much pressure, but you can't be blamed for taking it to Egypt and being helpful in the Temple Beautiful with your ideas. Right?
P: Yes, that's right.
T: Let that sink in. Now we're going to go to one more very important scene. Take a deep breath now. Your teachers are going to take you to a scene in the Holy Land when the Master walked the earth. See what your role is. I have the sense that you played an important role, and a lot of your pain and sorrow and feeling you're not good enough came from that period.
P: (Despairingly) When I was a girl I loved Jesus so much and I lost it all.
T: Good. Let's see that. It's important to look at it. Who are you in the Holy Land?... Let's go back and remember that. Let's take a look at that. It's

important to remember now. This is where the loss comes. This is where the sorrow is.
P: I go with him up the stations of the cross.
T: What is your relationship with him? Look and see...okay.
P: Well...one of the men with him.
T: What's your name?
P: (Remains silent but obviously knows.)
T: Do you think you could in any way have done anything different?
P: I just lost him (helplessly.)
T: It's all helplessness. The love is there and then the loss. But why were you so bad? Okay. I want you to get in touch with your grieving at the time of the crucifixion. What are you feeling?
P: The loss of a wonderful person...who had a new idea.
T: It's important that we understand why you must experience this over and over again. What are you supposed to learn? Let's go to the end of this lifetime. Let's see how you live. Are you persecuted?

Lydia related how she withdrew to a monastery later on and finished out her life writing and serving as a teacher, so filled with Jesus' love that it lasted all the rest of her life.

T: Let's move through this lifetime and get up into the inner world, to your death where you once again connect with the one energy. I want to know why the tears at the loss? What must you learn? Take a deep breath. I want you to hear Jesus talking. What is he telling you?
P: That there isn't any loss really. I set out to have an experience and that's what I've had.
T: Okay. Go deeper...about the loss. What do you need to know so the loss doesn't hit you that way, so that you don't feel it as loss?
P: It may be that even though it isn't my fault, maybe I feel all the losses were because of me. I feel responsible.
T: Because you were selfish? You wanted those experiences so you set them up. Let's ask. Get up into the spiritual plane. Take a deep breath. Ask, "Am I in any way to blame? Do I have any guilt? Over all these losses? Am I responsible?"
P: No, I'm not.
T: What's the guilt?
P: Maybe I could have stopped it.
T: You were part of a larger scene of events that were not meant to be stopped, were they?
P: Maybe they would have listened. Maybe there was something I could have done.
T: Ask the Teachers, "Is there something I should have done?"
P: They say it was planned.
T: Things have to take their course.

P: *That's right. Things have to take their own development and we can't throw everybody into the light. We can't be responsible for everybody.*
T: *This is the lesson you have to learn, that you have to be able to follow the grand plan. You cry and go into pain and feel responsible and yet it's all a grand plan. Can you trust the grand plan by which everyone is going to return? Can you stand by and watch the drama with compassion but without feeling responsible and without that feeling of total loss?*
P: *In one way I know there isn't any loss, really.*
T: *And there isn't any way you can change what is meant to be. It's not your fault. You didn't set up the grand plan. The grand plan was set up to help you, however you experience it.*
P: *(Slipping back.) It's all connected to the fact that maybe I could have done something in Atlantis.*
T: *Maybe you could have prevented the losses, but in saying that, you have again made loss real. Otherwise there would be no guilt. Stay with that a little longer. It's important. You have seen loss as real. What is the enlightened way of seeing loss?*
P: *What I see now is that it only exists if you think it does. Otherwise, it's just part of a procedure.*
T: *Like a dream. An important experience but when you wake up the dream disappears.*
P: *Yes. Like a dream. It seems as though it helps us to release attachments.*
T: *Okay. Just a few moments more. I want you to really get there.*
P: *We can't be responsible for everything. And when we lose things it's really okay. Its part of the life process.*
T: *Do you understand that? Have you got it?*
P: *Yes.*
T: *Okay. Now take a deep breath.*

I brought her back through the mirror into her sanctuary, then counted slowly from one to 10, making suggestions about relaxation, healing, alignment, resolution on many levels, and stating again that, instead of preoccupation with guilt and the inappropriate sense of responsibility that had burdened her in the past, she would look forward to the future.

It is apparent in this regression that recovering the memories of other life experiences is only the beginning of the work. The pattern has to be pursued and when it is clear, it is necessary to work cognitively to transform beliefs and their accompanying feeling states. Again, using the Inner Teacher is an effective way. All the therapist needs to be is a facilitator. The tenacious quality of belief systems was well illustrated here when Lydia could for a moment be drawn back into her old way of perceiving. Through the several years of contact with her since this regression, I have found that she is becoming less demanding and critical of herself and more creative and free, both in her life and in her work. The old feeling has faded—Lydia no longer believes that she is responsible for the fate of the planet!

# Appendices

# Appendix A

# *Profile of the Contributors*

We who contributed to this book were educated in conventional psychology or medicine. What was the impetus for us to make the quantum leap into an understanding of life so discrepant from that of our time? What moved us beyond accepted models of psychotherapy into an approach as yet lacking in acceptability? There is a surprising consistency to our life patternings, and this consistency, though it presents no dramatic answer to such questions, provides food for reflection.

## Parents and Home Background

Nearly all our contributors grew up in conventional middle-class families with religious affiliations that were more routine than heartfelt. Bontenbal and Woolger alone came from free-thinking parents. The others, with the exception of Hickman, whose parents were too concerned with finding food to have much time for religion, covered the spectrum of respectable Protestant and Catholic affiliations. Reynolds' father was a United Methodist minister. Snow's mother wrote Sunday School curricula for the Presbyterian Church, and his father was an elder. Fiore attended various denominations of Protestant churches, ranging from Dutch Reformed to Episcopal, whichever was closest to the family farm. Pecci's parents were not overly conscientious Catholics, and his observance of church and Sunday School was routine and minimal. Denning, Findeisen, and I had families who paid conventional religious lip service, but we involved ourselves intensely with our respective churches in an effort to find answers that weren't there and eventually left our churches in disappointment.

## Early Transpersonal Influences

A shaft of metaphysical experience impacted the early lives of nearly all of us in spite of the conservative framework of our childhood milieus, and this added influence leavened our questioning of the philosophical givens of the time. Sometimes this insight was stimulated by a person, sometimes by a book, and at other times by altered-state experiences that left the normal space/time world of childhood or adolescence frayed.

Among those whose childhood was impacted by a person was Reynolds, whose mother, in spite of being the wife of a minister, had her own quite different philosophy and quietly shared her transpersonal ideas with him. Fiore's parents kept their acceptance of reincarnation a personal secret for years, but such a hidden agenda must have diluted the impact of the conventional beliefs in which they tried to rear her. Findeisen and I both had grandmothers who appeared when we were three and brought with them a spectrum of new ideas, hers from the wealth of New England transcendentalism, mine from theosophy. They left us with no one to talk to when we were seven, but the heritage they had shared with us continued to draw us in a metaphysical direction. Snow was introduced to meditation in his grandparents' home and grew up bonded to a psychic grandmother who looked at the world with a spiritual perspective. After her death she returned to be a guide to him and assisted his transition from a conventional career as an air force historian to the uncharted territory, not only of past but also of future lives. Noordegraaf absorbed from her physician father a compassion for people and a dedication to relieve suffering.

Without exception, books provided impetus for all of us to move in new directions. Cayce's books made the curtain go up for many, and other books were specific to individuals, but all the books returned an awareness of something we had known before. The thoughts they stimulated came streaming through a veil so thin that it only barely concealed that previous knowledge. Edgar Cayce was the opener of the gate for Pecci, Findeisen, Hickman, and Snow. Jue was drawn by Yogananda's *Autobiography of a Yogi* when he was 12, and after reading the Katha Upanishads in college he found himself resonating with a new and deeper sense of self. Reynolds was first drawn into the concept of reincarnation by the story of Bridey Murphey. Later he read Aldous Huxley and Gerald Heard, and his interest in Heard's books escalated into friendship. Woolger credits Huxley, along with Bertrand Russell, Gurgieff, and Arthur Koestler, with propelling him into vaster arenas of awareness. Following a transpersonal experience at 15, Woolger moved deeper into transcendental realms as he accompanied Thomas à Kempis, Julian of Norwich, and St. John of the Cross on their explorations. My own understanding, gained in other lifetimes, returned as I read *The Tibetan Book of the Dead*, *The Varieties of Religious Experience* by William James, the Platonic dialogues (read in Greek remembered from another lifetime), and two novels by L. Adams Beck about yoga and eastern philosophy: *The House of Fulfillment* and *The Garden of Vision*.

## Transpersonal Experiences in Childhood and Adolescence

Pecci sent for Rosicrucian material when he was nine and by 12 had worked up to the Seventh Degree. He became spellbound by the phenomenon of hypnosis and put on demonstrations until his parents' and sisters' disdain forced him to go underground. Hickman discovered a similar enchantment in the mysteries of palm reading. No one in her family had time or interest to react, so at 12 she began to make money reading palms. Noordegraaf lived a childhood interspersed with magical moments, some of which involved early out-of-body journeys and later psychic encounters. Mystical experiences began for me at two when I, also, made out-of-the-body trips, a capability lost and never regained after a deep shock when I was four, though experiences of higher consciousness came at intervals. When Denning was nine, a transcendental experience left her with a sense of destiny that she has retained throughout her life. Woolger, on a walking tour in France in early adolescence, reported a transformational experience that changed his life.

## Educational Background

The educational foundations of our contributors were established in institutions entrenched in established, conservative thinking. Woolger took one advanced degree at Oxford and another at the University of London. Pecci divided his undergraduate work between Harvard and Tufts, and at Tufts he earned his medical degree. Reynolds studied at Oberlin College and then took two master's degrees and his doctorate at Western Reserve University, following this with a post-doctoral year at Brandeis under Abraham Maslow. Findeisen was a Stanford graduate. Fiore did her undergraduate work at Mt. Holyoke and took her advanced degrees at the Universities of Maryland and Miami. Hickman had conventional medical training at the Los Angeles Osteopathic College. Denning's first degree was from UC Riverside. She earned two master's degrees, one from the Claremont Graduate School in educational psychology and the second from Johnson College at Redlands University in humanistic and transpersonal psychology. She completed her doctorate when she was 76. Jue's undergraduate work was in biological sciences at California State University at San Jose, after which he earned a master's in education and a doctorate in psychology at International University in San Diego. Following his degrees he spent a year as a Fulbright Scholar. Our Dutch therapists both took their degrees at the University of Amsterdam, Noordegraaf in medicine and Bontenbal in urban planning. Snow took his undergraduate work at the Sorbonne and John Hopkins and a graduate degree at Columbia University. My own undergraduate work was at the University of Washington, and a number of years later, after three intellectually ineffective years studying Sanskrit at the University of Munich, I completed a doctorate in psychology at UCLA.

## Artistic Expression

Most of our contributors immersed themselves at some time in their lives in a form of artistic expression. Reynolds studied for eight years at the Oberlin Conservatory to become a concert pianist before deciding that psychology was a more viable profession. Many years later he combined his teaching and psychological practice with singing in the Roger Wagner Chorale. As a young man, Woolger acted in Shakespearean plays at Stratford-on-Avon, his home while he was growing up.

Denning was connected with the Riverside Community Players for several decades and served two years as president of the Riverside Branch of the National League of American Penwomen. Snow played the clarinet and starred in high school plays before deciding acting wasn't a serious career option. Jue, during his Fulbright Teaching Fellowship in Indonesia, developed not only a science program for the embassy school in Djakarta, but at the same time became involved with the spiritual traditions in Indonesian culture and made a film study of the trance dances of Bali. Findeisen and I spent some years in dance before becoming aware that we had done that before and there were other things we should do with this lifetime. In addition, I played the concert flute, puttered on the pipe organ, and wrote music.

## Early Work Experience

Nearly all of us either took our first degrees in areas other than psychology or had early work experience in other areas. Denning was Business Manager of the Riverside Community Players, one among many things in which she has been involved during her long and rich life. Woolger worked as a language teaching advisor for the British government in West Africa. Pecci, besides his experience in the Navy, was a stockbroker for a brief time. Snow was an air force historian until he shifted to regression work. Noordegraaf's first position was as an international hostess in the Canary Islands. Bontenbal worked for some years as a researcher in urban planning at the University of Amsterdam. Originally I supported myself teaching fencing while trying, unsuccessfully, to finish the great American novel. Later I combined teaching with editing several small magazines.

Most of our contributors have taught on a college level, primarily in departments of psychology. Pecci heads his own graduate institute, the Rosebridge Graduate School of Integrative Psychology. Both Reynolds and I served on the core faculty of the California School of Professional Psychology and have taught at other universities. Findeisen and Jue originally chose teaching as a vocation but were drawn into psychotherapeutic work as truer expressions of themselves, and Jue still has connections with UC Irvine. Snow's first position was as a lecturer in Contemporary Civilization at Columbia University. Woolger has taught at the University of Vermont, Concordia College in Montreal, and Vassar College and has led educational tours to France and to Indonesia. Currently Jue, Woolger, Fiore, Denning, Findeisen, Snow, and Bontenbal and Noordegraaf lecture and present workshops at universities and give conferences locally and around the world.

## Travel

Most professionals explore at least some foreign lands, especially if they offer workshops. Our group is especially well traveled and many have lived in other countries for extended periods of time. Findeisen spends a part of every year in Sweden and has a following of students and patients there. Woolger worked in West Africa and Rhodesia for several years, often vacationed in Southern France, and lived in Switzerland for five years while he was working with Jung. Snow is bilingual and for many years has divided residency between France and the United States. Currently he travels throughout Europe and America as a seminar leader. He is proud to have set foot on all the world's continents, including Antarctica. Jue has lived in India, Burma, Thailand, Japan, and Bali. Reynolds often spends time in Europe, especially in England and France.

Fiore travels widely and gives workshops in Brazil and Europe. Egypt, Greece, and Turkey have been on her travel itinerary. Denning travels delivering lectures or presenting workshops. Most of her addresses are invited ones where she is a featured speaker, as, for example, at conferences in India, Japan, Sweden, Russia, Brazil, and England. Noordegraaf, after her medical training, traveled extensively in the Far East, part of the time with her husband and son in a homemade motor home. She has a regular clientele in Switzerland and Germany and is frequently in the United States. Bontenbal spent a number of early years in the United States as a young man, and he works with Noordegraaf giving workshops in this country and throughout Europe. I lived for three years in Germany during the Nazi regime, traveling around Europe on a bicycle. Since then I have lived for brief periods in India, Nepal, Sri Lanka, South Africa, and Japan and have explored less known areas of South America, such as the Amazon jungle and the Andes.

## Family Life

What do the demands of avocations and professions do to the family life of our contributors? Eleven of us are—or have been—married and have children, many of whom are professionals themselves. Four had marriages that ended in divorce, an experience the participants considered necessary to work out karmic patterns. Several of the divorced remarried and experienced a mellow and fulfilling second time around. Congratulations to the many who had clear enough karma so that they could choose a more comfortable and permanent interaction!

## Involvement with Past Lives

The time at which each of the contributors became involved with past lives makes it clear that it is not the age of the individual but the *zeitgeist* that is important. Nearly everyone was drawn into regression therapy in the middle or the late 70's. Only Hickman, who moved into past lives in the early 50's and Denning, who began her practice in the 60's, anticipated the movement.

New directions in perceiving the world were opening up in the 70's and books in little-explored areas were daring to be written and published. Even more important, inner experience was becoming acceptable, especially when it was entered through one or another form of imaging, and interest in past lives followed. None of our contributors set out to do regression work—they were eased into it through various means. Seven of our contributors first developed skill in hypnosis and found that regressing a patient back to an earlier time frequently led to past-life recall. The rest of us found to our surprise that the soul path we had chosen included past lives—they were part of the package!

Most of us suffer some ambivalence about past lives. The trained, scientific side of us is reluctant to endorse them as being real, while our intuitive right brain cannot imagine that they haven't taken place. Hickman, Pecci, Denning, Findeisen, and the Dutch therapists have the least trouble. Reynolds was moving into an acceptance stance during his relationship with Gerald Heard but became skeptical after his work with Maslow and now stays stuck in a bipolar position, a stance that includes Woolger, Fiore, Jue, Snow, and myself. The one thing on which we all agree is the efficacy of regression therapy, whether the material retrieved is true recall or a metaphor.

# Appendix B

# *Group Induction*

## by

## Helen Wambach, Ph.D.

Editor's Note: Helen Wambach was the first psychologist to share the experience of past-life regression with large groups of people. She was interested primarily in research, but her regressions influenced many therapists who followed her. Her induction, though drawing strongly on images used in hypnosis, also makes use of the Christos Technique.[1]

*All right everybody, yawn—I want you to count backwards in your mind, starting with 100. Now count. (One breath, pause)... Your eyes are closed and it feels good to close your eyes (two breaths, pause)... The relaxation moves now from your facial muscles to your jaw muscles, and as your jaw muscles relax, your tongue falls to the base of your mouth (two breaths, pause). The relaxation moves now from your jaw muscles to your neck muscles, down to your shoulder muscles, down your arms to your elbows, down to your wrists, your hands and your fingers. Deeply and peacefully relaxed (two breaths, pause). The relaxation moves now from your shoulders to your hips, down your thighs to your knees, down your legs to your ankles, your feet and your toes.*

*You may stop now and just drift to the sound of my voice. You will focus intently on my questions and instructions. If you drop too deep, if you drop deeply asleep, you will hear my voice saying the word, "Now." You will respond to the word, "Now." It will sound loud and clear, but pleasant, in your ear and you will wake up just enough to focus once again intently on my questions. Pictures, images, impressions, feelings will float easily into your mind in response to my questions.*

*And now we're drifting deeper. One. Deeper and deeper (two breaths, pause). Two. More and more relaxed (two breaths, pause). Three...four... five... six...seven...eight...nine ...10...you are deeply relaxed now, focusing intently on my questions and suggestions.*

*I want you to go back into your memory now to a time you are standing in front of the front door of the house or apartment where you live now. Your eyes are seeing that door, your brain has registered it. You're there now. Look at your door. What color is it? (Two breaths, pause.) Are there any nicks or scratches on the door? (Two breaths, pause.) Is there any glass or grillwork or numbers on the door? (Two breaths, pause.)*

*Now take out your key. Let your hand remember how you insert the key in the lock. Do you turn it clockwise or counterclockwise? Now put your hand on the doorknob. What does it feel like in your hand? Now open the door and leave it ajar and look down at the floor on the inside of your front door. What color is it? Is it wood, carpet, tile? (Two breaths, pause.)*

*Now close the door and you're on the outside again and I want you to go to where you can see the whole front of the building of where you live. Where are the windows placed in relationship to the door? (Two breaths, pause.)*

*Now I want you to make a leap of your imagination. I want you to stand on the highest point of the roof of the building where you live. You're not afraid of falling and make it a bright sunny day and you can see for miles. Now you're standing on the roof and it's an interesting view of your familiar neighborhood from up here. First I want you to find the direction east. Remember where the sun comes in the windows in the morning and that's east. Look to the east now. What can you see to the east from the roof of your building? (Two breaths, pause.) What street lies to the east? (Two breaths, pause.)*

*Now look to the south. What can you see to the south from the roof of your building? Make it as detailed as you can. (Two breaths, pause.) Now look to the west. What can you see at the horizon to the west? (Two breaths, pause.) Now look to the north. What lies to the north? (Two breaths, pause.) Now I want you to make another leap of your imagination. I want you to lift gently off your roof and fly as you've done in your dreams and you're flying now, free and light, flying to the ocean, to your favorite ocean beach. (Two breaths, pause.)*

*Now you're flying above the beach and you can see the lacy patterns that the foam makes after the waves break on the sand, and it's a beautiful clear sunny day at the ocean. And as a wave breaks against a boulder at the edge of the beach and the water sprays high in the air, each droplet sparkles like diamonds in the sun. (Two breaths, pause.)*

*Now you're soaring up over the ocean. Higher and higher now and the air is very clear. Higher and higher you fly and when you look to the west, to the horizon, it seems as though you can see the curve of the earth as the sea meets the sky. Now you've been flying for a long time and it's a delightful feeling. You are weightless, like an astronaut. Free of gravity. Dip and soar. Turn somersaults if you like. Catch the corner of a breeze and glide on it like a seagull. (Five breaths, pause.)*

*Now a fluffy white cloud comes along and it's just your size and it's deep and soft and warm and secure and because you're weightless, it's wonderfully supportive. Fly over to your cloud and stretch out and relax completely now as I count.*

*One...deeper and deeper (two breaths, pause). Two...more and more relaxed (two breaths, pause). Three...four...five...you're floating on your cloud feeling marvelously relaxed and we're going to float back now through time. When I call out a time period let an image or impression come into your mind. We're drifting back now through time, and it's 1900. The time period anywhere around 1900. Let an image or impression come into your mind. (Two breaths, pause.) Remember that image or impression from 1900.*

*Now we're drifting further back in time. We're drifting back and it's 1750. The time period anywhere around 1750. Let an image or impression come into your mind. (Five breaths, pause.) Remember that image or impression for 1750. And now we're drifting* back in time. Far back in time and it's 1400. The time period anywhere around 1400. Let an image or impression come into your mind. (Five breaths, pause.) Remember those images and impressions from 1400. And now we're drifting far, far back in time. And it's 100 years after Christ. The time period anywhere around 25 A.D. Let an image or impression come into your mind. (Five breaths, pause.) Remember that image or impression for 25 A.D. And now we're drifting far back into time. And it's 500 years before Christ. The time period anywhere around 500 B.C. Let an image or impression come into your mind. (Five breaths, pause.) Remember that image or impression from 500 B.C.

And now I'm going to review for you the five time periods. And when I complete the review I want you to choose just one of these time periods to explore further. Choose the time period where the image came quickest, was the most vivid, and that your subconscious will choose for you. You will not go to a time period where you will experience any upsetting experience. Remember your images now as I review. 500 B.C....25 A.D....1400...1750...1900...now choose. You are alive in that time period.

Look down now at your feet. Become vividly aware of what you are wearing on your feet. Are your feet bare? Can you see your toes? If you're wearing something on your feet, what does your footwear look like? What material is it made out of? Can you tell?... Now, look down at your clothing. Become aware of what you're wearing. Is your garment below the knee? Above the knee? What color is your clothing? Now, take a piece of the material of your clothing between your fingers. Rub the material between your fingers. Is it rough, course, silky, smooth? Feel it now between your fingers.... Now reach up and feel around your waist. Are you wearing anything around your waist? If you are, what is it? Become aware. Now, cross your arms across your chest. You're hugging your body. What does your body feel like? Are you a man or a woman? Hug your body. Do you have breasts? Are you tall, short, stout, slender? Become aware of your body now. Do you feel vigorous, young, frail? (Two breaths, pause.) Now, look down at your hands. Become vividly aware of your hands. Are they short, stubby, long, slender? Are they well cared for or do they look rough and work-worn? Become aware. (Two breaths, pause.) Now look at the skin of your hands and arms. What color is your skin? (Two breaths, pause.) Now reach up and thrust your fingers into your hair. Thrust your fingers into your hair and feel the texture of your hair. Is it rough, coarse, wiry, silky, smooth, straight? Become vividly aware of what your hair is like. What color is your hair? (Two breaths, pause.) Are you wearing anything on your head? If you are, become aware of what it is. (Two breaths, pause.)

Now look around you. Are you inside or outside? (Two breaths, pause.) If you are inside, I want you to go to where there is a window or a doorway where you can look out. Now all of you, I want you to look around and see the land here. What is the landscape, the terrain, like here? Is it rocky, barren, rolling, green, black? Become vividly aware of the land. (Two breaths, pause.) Can you see any trees nearby? If you can, look closely at a tree. How tall is it? What kind of tree is it, do you know? (Two breaths, pause.) Now look and see if you can see a building nearby. If there is a building nearby, look at it closely now. Become aware of that building. What's its roof shaped like? (Two breaths, pause.) What material is the roof made out of, can you tell? (Two breaths, pause.) Now look at the walls of that building. What color are the walls? (Two breaths, pause.) What material are the walls made out of, can you tell? (Two breaths, pause.)

Now, feel the air on your skin. Is it hot, dry, moist, cool? (Two breaths, pause.) Is there a breeze blowing? (Two breaths, pause.) Glance up at the sky now. Is it cloudy or sunny? (Two breaths, pause.)

Now hear my voice and follow my instruction.

I want you to go now to the evening of that same day and that lifetime and you are eating your evening meal. (Two breaths, pause.) Where are you now? (Two breaths, pause.) Now, look down at the food you are eating. Become vividly aware of your food. What is it? Can you tell? (Two breaths, pause.) Now take a mouthful of the food in your mouth and taste it. Savor it. Is it spicy, bland, what flavor does it have? Become aware. (Two breaths, pause.) Now look down and see what you're eating with. If you are using an eating utensil of some kind, see it vividly there in your hand. Is it a knife, a fork, spoon, something else? (Two breaths, pause.) What material is it made out of? (Two breaths, pause.) How is it shaped? If it's a fork, how many tines or prongs does it have? (Two breaths, pause.) Now look down at what you're eating from. Is it a plate, a bowl, something else? (Two breaths, pause.) Is there any decoration on this? (Two breaths, pause.) What material is it made out of, can you tell? (Two breaths, pause.)

Now look to your right. Is there anyone eating to your right? If there is, become vividly aware of that person. (Two breaths, pause.) What's your relationship to that person? (Two breaths, pause.) How do you feel towards that person? (Two breaths, pause.) Now look across from you. Is there anyone eating there? If there is, become very aware of that person. What does that person look like? (Two breaths, pause.) Do you know that person? (Two breaths, pause.) What are your emotions toward that person? (Two breaths, pause.) Now look to your left. Is there anyone eating there? If there is, focus in on that person. (Two breaths, pause.) How is that person dressed? (Two breaths, pause.) Who is that person? (Two breaths, pause.) What are your feelings towards that person? (Two breaths, pause.) Now, someone calls you by your name and you hear the syllables of your name as they are spoken. What do they call you? (Two breaths, pause.)

Now hear my voice and follow my instruction. I want you to go now to a time in that lifetime when something interesting, something unusual is happening. An exciting event in that life and you are there now. Quickly now, look down at yourself. How are you dressed? (Two breaths, pause.) Now listen. What sounds can you hear around you at this exciting event? (Two breaths, pause.) Now watch and observe what's happening. What can you see? (Three breaths, pause.)

Now hear my voice and follow my instruction. I want you to go now to a time in that lifetime when you need supplies and you are on your way to get them. How are you traveling? (Two breaths, pause.) Now you've arrived at the place where the supplies are. Look around you. What kind of place is this? (Two breaths, pause.) Is it a town, a village, a marketplace, a storeroom, someplace else? (Two breaths, pause.) Become vividly aware now of the place. You are there now. Look around you. (Two breaths, pause.) What can you see? (Two breaths, pause.) Are there any distinctive smells in this place? Become aware. (Two breaths, pause.) Now look at the supplies you came to get. Become vividly aware of the supplies that you are getting. (Two breaths, pause). What is that you're getting? (Two breaths, pause.) Is there anyone waiting on you or helping you with the supplies? If there is, become vividly aware of that person. (Two breaths, pause.) What is that person dressed in? (Two breaths, pause.)

## Group Induction—Helen Wambach

Now, if you pay for your supplies, notice where you keep your money. *(Two breaths, pause.)* If you pay for your supplies, look down now at the money in your hand. Is it coins, bills? *(Two breaths, pause.)* How large are they? *(Two breaths, pause.)* What color are they? *(Two breaths, pause.)* Do you see any pictures or writing on the money? Become aware. *(Two breaths, pause.)* Let the images come clear in your mind now as you are looking at your money. *(Two breaths, pause.)* Now you are returning home with your supplies. You are coming up to the entrance to the place where you lived in that lifetime and you see it sharply and vividly. You see the outside of the place where you lived. *(Two breaths, pause.)* What does it look like? *(Two breaths, pause.)* How do you feel about the life that you lived here? *(Two breaths, pause.)*

Now hear my voice and follow my instruction.

I want you to go now to the day that you died in that lifetime. You will have no pain and no fear and if the experience becomes uncomfortable for you, you will go back to your cloud and not experience it.

Now it is the day that you die in that lifetime. Where are you now? *(Two breaths, pause.)* Is there anyone with you? *(Two breaths, pause.)* About how old are you? *(Two breaths, pause.)* Become aware now of the cause of your death. *(Two breaths, pause.)* Now you have died and your spirit is leaving your body. Now let yourself experience your spirit leaving your body. *(Two breaths, pause.)* What are you thinking and feeling after you leave your body? Become aware of what you are experiencing *(Three breaths, pause.)* Now you have died and left that body. I want you to think now. Did you know anyone in that lifetime that you know today in your current lifetime? *(Two breaths, pause.)* If so, flash on their face then and their face now. *(Two breaths, pause.)* Now you've died and left that body and into your mind will come a map and on that map will be pinpointed the place where you lived that lifetime and the name of that place in modern terms will flash into your mind. *(Two breaths, pause.)* Now the year that you died in that lifetime in modern terms will flash into your mind. *(Two breaths, pause.)*

Now go back to your cloud and as you stretch out on your cloud and relax, let all feelings of physical discomfort leave you. You block awareness of any physical discomfort and all tension drains from your body and you're floating on your cloud deeply at ease, feeling light and free. *(Two breaths, pause.)* One...deeper and deeper. Two...more and more relaxed. Three...four...five.... You're floating on your cloud deeply relaxed but you will remember vividly, vividly, everything that you experienced on this trip. The memory will stay vivid in your mind for months and you'll be able to remember it whenever you wish. When I say the words, "Open your eyes, you're awake," you will reach for the data sheet and your hand will fill out the answers to the questions, moving rapidly over the page as the full recall of what you experienced in response to my questions comes flooding back into your conscious awareness.

Now you're floating on the cloud and you're completely relaxed and there's a white light all around you, deep and pure and bright and growing brighter. There's a tightly budded rose in your solar plexus. Rays of energy from the light gently unfurl the petals of the rose until the heart of the rose is exposed. Rays of energy from the light flood into the heart of the rose, and through your solar plexus. And the rays of energy move smoothly and harmoniously throughout your body and bring deep feelings of harmony and peace. *(Two breaths, pause.)*

*It's time now to return to the here and now. Picture to yourself that ball of golden energy sparkling out in a far corner of space. Picture that energy rolling and flowing down from that darkness of space, penetrating the atmospheric envelope of earth, coming down to the western hemisphere, coming down to this room and entering the crown of your head. As the ball of energy enters the crown of your head, it brings with it deep feelings of well being, comfort and ease, and you awaken feeling profoundly refreshed, feeling in a very good humor, feeling cheerful, feeling great.*

*One. The energy is moving into the crown of your head and into your face. Two. The energy is moving into your jaw muscles and into your neck. Three. The energy is moving into your shoulders. Four. The energy is flowing down your arms to your elbows, down to your wrists, your hands and your fingers. Five. The energy is moving from your shoulders down your torso to your waist. Six. The energy is moving into your hips. Seven. The energy is flowing down your thighs to your knees. Eight. The energy is moving down your legs to your ankles, to your feet and your toes. Nine. Your body is alive with vibrant energy and you're ready to wake up now feeling great. Ten. Open your eyes. You're awake.*

Appendix C

# Mind Mirror Research on the Retrieval of Past Lives

By

Winafred B. Lucas, Ph.D.

## Introduction

In the mid-80's Dr. Chet Snow and I, in conjunction with the psychologists at the Brentwood Psychological Center in Los Angeles, became interested in the potential of the Mind Mirror, a biofeedback device which provides information on the brain waves manifested in meditation practice. The Mind Mirror was developed in the 70's in England by a creative scientist and researcher, Dr. Maxwell Cade, who proposed to extend the scope of biofeedback as a means of inducing relaxation response and contributing to bodily health and well-being.[1] In the process of investigating various aspects of meditation and healing, Cade developed a biofeedback mechanism, which he called the Mind Mirror, that could portray on a screen all four levels of brain waves in both hemispheres. Eventually he identified a brain wave pattern that correlated with a high level of serenity and centeredness, and he called this the Awakened Mind or Fifth State. Subsequently he established Mind Mirror biofeedback classes, and research became secondary to his teaching efforts.

On Cade's death his work was continued by Anna Wise, an English woman who had worked closely with him while he was developing his theories and techniques. In the early 80's Wise moved to Boulder, Colorado and there established a school for teaching meditation by means of the Mind Mirror. She lectures widely, popularizing the idea of teaching meditation states through the help of biofeedback techniques. At our request she brought a Mind Mirror to our Brentwood Psychological Center and spent several days lecturing on and demonstrating its potential.

The clear pattern of brain waves produced in meditation stimulated our interest in possible Mind Mirror correlates to past-life recall, and on the final afternoon of the workshop we attached the machine to one of our group who was undergoing a regression. In addition to the expected alpha and theta waves, a surprising pattern of strong delta flares emerged, which are not characteristic of meditation. We became curious as to whether the presence of delta was a stable characteristic of the regression process and, if so, what it signified. This led to a three-day research project that Chet Snow and I carried out two years later.

## Background

The effort to document physiological correlates of inner states is relatively recent. It began with various biofeedback instruments, such as the temperature meter and the GSR, which measures stress and relaxation through skin resistance. The third biofeedback instrument included in the investigation of relaxation and meditation was a simple electroencephalogram. The first electroencephalographic recordings picked up only one brain wave pattern at a time, the dominant one, and for a while it was not clear that the brain actually produced waves on different levels at the same time. The various feedback devices made it possible to measure and record bodily changes that before that time had been considered unavailable to consciousness. Their measurement and recording opened the door to an expanded understanding of psychophysiological self-control, and research moved forward.

In the late 1950's Dr. Joe Kamiya (1958) took some giant steps in understanding biofeedback research as it relates to meditation.[2] His postulate that underlies all biofeedback was that self-observation of a bodily event that can be associated or linked with a specific mental event, including those not usually available to awareness, will lead to control of that state. In a research design (1958) in which his objective was to enable subjects to produce alpha so that they might enjoy its calming influence, he attached electrodes to the subject's scalp to register the alpha brainwave frequency. The subject was asked to judge whether alpha was present, or not. Subjects became increasingly able to judge this and then proceeded to produce alpha (or lack of it) at will. Some subjects who previously had not been meditators, when trained in this primitive biofeedback technique, developed a pattern similar to that found in 20-year practitioners of Zen meditation.

Kamiya's research on the alpha rhythm showed that it promotes a calm state of awareness. Production of it at will increases the individual's capacity for maintaining such a state, the same goal that characterizes the meditation techniques of Yoga, Zen, the Sufis, and Transcendental Meditation. Without biofeedback, development of the capacity to effect such control requires a long period of effort, and such a well-known yogi as Swami Rama, who was a subject of extensive research at the Menninger Foundation, feels that years of training can be eliminated by the use of biofeedback devices (Green, 1977).

In the early 70's Drs. Robert Wallace and Herbert Benson of the Harvard Medical School explored the physical correlates of Transcendental Meditation and found that their studies corroborated the presence of alpha brain waves and borderline theta during the extreme stillness of mind-body in that type of meditation. They found that this meditation produced very different patterns from sleep or resting and described it as "an alert, hypometabolic state" and thought that it constituted a fourth major state of consciousness.

Meanwhile Cade, aware of the Harvard research, was moving ahead on his own. The goal of his research was first, a verification of the health benefits on strictly scientific lines, and second, the development of an acceptable theory of mind-body interaction. At first he measured depth of trance primarily through the GSR and confirmed Kamiya's finding that the shift from sympathetic nervous system activity to parasympathetic activity (namely, to alpha) effected a therapeutic result. He even postulated that much of the beneficial effect of psychotherapy, and even of psychoanalysis, might be due to the long periods of deep relaxation on the therapist's couch! As a result of his studies and those of Kamiya and Benson and others, a consensus of opinion gradually emerged regarding the nature of alpha.

Cade extended the possibilities of biofeedback when he developed the Mind Mirror. He designed a machine consisting of 24 rows of light-emitting diodes arranged in two banks of 12 rows each with each row comprising 32 diodes, 16 on the left bank and 16 on the right. Signals from both the left and right hemispheres of the brain appeared on the instrument at the same time. Separate amplifiers recorded signals in each frequency channel, and an integrated circuit converted these to an illuminated display of the total pattern formation. The instrument used electrodes attached to the subject's head to pick up the voltages generated by the brain. The 13th row recorded muscle monitoring from a galvanometer and so documented any intrusion of unwanted "parasitic" voltages, such as those from facial, jaw, or scalp muscles.

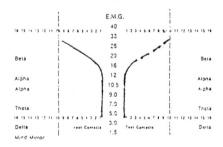

Figure 1. *Waking State* In this state the left brain shows activity, which may be accompanied by activity in the right brain, also.

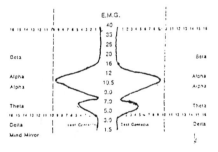

Figure 2. *Traditional Meditation* This state shows a significant narrowing of beta waves, large symmetrical bursts of alpha, and smaller symmetrical bursts of theta. As a rule delta does not occur.

Cade found that the alert state (beta) and the meditation state showed very different patterns. In the alert state, where attention is focused on the external world, the activities of the two hemispheres differ and the EEG pattern is one of asymmetry. In contrast, because the states of meditators are more internally focused, they manifest more integration, and the patterns of the brainwave levels tend toward symmetry. He found that experienced meditators, no matter what their background training, evidenced the same general pattern during meditation: bilaterally symmetrical alpha, the frequency of which steadily decreased as meditation deepened; and, following this, a steadily strengthening bilateral theta accompaniment.

The Mind Mirror has a sufficiently rapid response time so that even ephemeral brain-mind states can be seen. The patterns remain stable only so long as the state is stable: they scatter the instant the state alters or breaks up. The subject can see not only the pattern of his state but how long he holds it and what it becomes as it retreats. The great sensitivity of the Mind Mirror and its wide frequency range (from 1.5 to 40 hertz) combined with its ease of operation and ability to show both cerebral hemispheres at the same time, has made possible a deeper understanding of the brain and its powerful and complex involvement with the body and health.

Because the Mind Mirror provided a display that showed both transient patterns and stable states of brain activity, Cade found that it was possible to ascertain that brain rhythms were highly correlated with specific states of consciousness. Deep sleep, dreaming sleep, the hypnagogic state, and the waking state each concentrated in a single band of the EEG frequencies. In contrast, the meditation states appeared to be accompanied by several bands.

Cade made studies both of hypnotized subjects and of subjects experiencing guided imagery and found that the depth of the relaxation response was strongly related to the characteristics of the suggested imagery. A brief word picture of about 150-200 words of varied content produced a faster and deeper relaxation response in the majority of subjects than did traditional hypnotic induction methods.

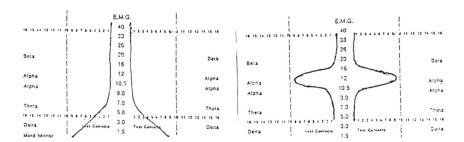

Figure 3. *Deep Sleep* In this state all brain activity is eliminated except delta. This is *not* the state where dreaming has been found to take place, but it precedes the REM or dreaming state.

Figure 4. *Hypnagogic State* This state, which includes daydreaming, lies just below the surface of alertness and is characterized by symmetrical alpha.

The level of brain functioning during dreaming (REM) has been controversial. Cade set it in theta, but many dream researchers, seeming almost reluctant to be pinned down, place dreaming in low alpha. All seem in agreement that production of dreams *follows* descent into the delta level of what for a long time was considered to be deep sleep. Since most dream research uses electroencephalograms restricted to the dominant level of brainwave functioning, it is probable that several levels may actually be involved, including a diminished delta. Investigation of dream states requires complicated laboratory equipment. Moreover, dreaming is obviously not (at least, as yet) a process responsive to biofeedback training, and therefore dream research was not high on Cade's priority list.

Cade's exploration of meditation states that were available for biofeedback, including the patterns of skilled meditators, such as long-time practitioners of Zen, Yoga, or Transcendental Meditation, culminated in documentation of the rhythms of a high meditative state, which he called the Fifth State or the Awakened Mind. This pattern showed reduced and rounded symmetrical beta, in contrast to the aggressive flares of beta found in the waking state, which tend to be asymmetrical. Alpha was strong and symmetrical. Theta was rounded and prominent, though not as intense as alpha. Occasionally, in some subjects, there were slight flares of delta. There was increasing evidence of brain hemisphere EEG symmetry. Cade stressed his Mind Mirror as a biofeedback device to help advanced meditators recognize the Awakened Mind state, enter it at will, and eventually maintain it.

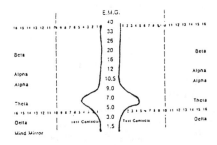

Figure 5. *The Dream State* (according to Dr. Cade). We do not know if this is an extrapolation (what he thought it probably was) or an actual brain recording.

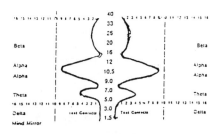

Figure 6. *The Awakened Mind (Fifth State)*. Note the softly rounded beta, the prominent alpha (similar to that in a general meditation state), and the symmetrical theta flares.

Cade was fascinated by the Mind Mirror patterns produced by successful healers. His early assumption (which turned out to be premature and later jeopardized the use of the Mind Mirror as a research instrument) suggested that the true healer inducts in the patient both psychophysiological relaxation and Fifth State Consciousness. Because he had observed these exceptionally symmetrical patterns in certain successful healers, such as skilled yogis, swamis, and Zen masters, he was sure that another important factor in healing, and one central to health in general, was the bilateral symmetry of brain functioning. The power of the healer seemed to be related to the amplitude, symmetry, and stability of the Fifth State that he manifested and that he was able to induce in the patient. Cade's final synthesis of his observations on healing was that the harmonization of both brain hemispheres, along with the Awakened Mind state that flowed from healer to patient, allowed the body to heal itself.

Further research indicated that Cade's assumption that a salient characteristic of *every* healer was the ability to transfer the Fifth State pattern to the subject, with resulting harmonizing of the subject's nervous system, proved not to be true. Various patterns of healing emerged later where successful healers appeared to blast their patient with energy that produced healing and in no way manifested the symmetrical Awakened Mind pattern. The fact that these healers did not fit into the given pattern led to concern that the Mind Mirror was not measuring what it purported to measure, and Mind Mirror research on healing went into an eclipse, very much as research with Kirlian photography on energy fields went into an eclipse after inaccurate negative publicity (Moss, 1979).[3] Gradually it became evident that it was not the Mind Mirror that was at fault but the interpretations that had been put on its data, namely, that there was only one valid pattern of healing. Currently it is not clear what is involved in energy healing, though one pattern has remained relatively constant: paranormal abilities of all sorts, not only healing of oneself and others but also self-control of pain, telepathy, psychokinesis, etc., are associated with an EEG pattern that manifests delta, often in strong flares, and moves toward a bilateral and integrated pattern.

The significance of delta emerges as a fertile area of investigation. Delta, once considered the sleep state, had earlier been reported by Luria (1973) to exist at times in conjunction with beta, a phenomenon not well understood at the time. Limited research at the Menninger Foundation has confirmed this conjunction of delta and beta. Swami Rama, a yogi with striking control of his physiological functioning, offered to produce delta waves at will.[4] After five minutes of meditation he went into a state of deep sleep and began producing delta waves, at the same time snoring gently! During the period while he was asleep, the researchers made statements near him in low voices. On awakening Swami Rama was able to repeat these statements almost exactly. Unfortunately, at that time devices for recording brain waves were limited to one amplitude, so there was no documentation of the presence of beta, though the implication is that it was present.

The underlying assumption of yoga is that dreamless sleep is necessary for contact with the universal ground of being, and when a person is deprived of such sleep he is thrown off balance. Each person needs this contact, just as he needs dreaming (expressed in alpha and theta) to process contents of his unconscious. We are becoming able in a process called lucid dreaming to become aware of our dreams and to influence them, thus combining beta with alpha and theta, and it should be possible to maintain awareness of the external world even while in the delta stages of sleep. In a truly integrated consciousness, according to yoga philosophy, consciousness of both dreamless sleep and the external world should be perceptible at the same time.

Cade observed that in healers delta frequencies were often found added to their Fifth State. Moreover, he found that in subjects engaged in parapsychological research, delta appeared in surprising flares, along with equally strong flares of beta, with variable alpha waves in between. The hypothesis that in some way delta was linked to the paranormal was also proposed in a paper by Dr. Joel Whitton of

Toronto.[5] As a result of the accruing evidence, Cade suggested that delta might be interpreted as a reaching out to the "not yet known in a passive way." Eventually those doing Mind Mirror research hypothesized that delta might be a radar state.

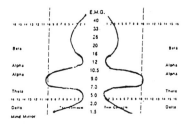 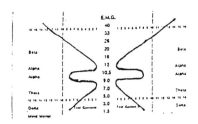

Figure 7. *Pattern of a Boy Bending Spoons Mentally.* Here beta is prominent but rounded. Alpha is extensive and also rounded, and there are distinctive delta flares.

Figure 8. *Pattern of a Subject Performing in a Parapsychological Experiment.* Here the beta is more assertive (shown by the flaring out), alpha is not so prominent and covers a narrower band, and delta is again dominant and strongly flared.

## Procedure

In the spring of 1987 Dr. Snow and I invited Peter Morrison, a senior staff member of Anna Wise's Awakened Mind Institute, to spend three days with us at our Center in further exploration of the pattern that had been produced by the Mind Mirror during the earlier regression. We requested two Mind Mirror instruments so that we could observe the patterns of the therapists as well as those of the subjects. All but three subjects and two therapists were senior professionals experienced in regression work. Some subjects who had no regression experience and two inexperienced therapists were included to test whether lack of experience would affect the brain wave patterns. Two of the therapists also functioned as subjects. Each therapist regressed at least two subjects in order to determine to what extent the therapist's brain wave patterns remained stable, responded selectively to different personalities, or influenced their subjects.

The subject lay on a couch at the back of the room and the therapist sat in front and slightly to the side. The two Mind Mirrors were set on a low table in front in clear view of a video camera, and between them were two galvanometers. All 17 regression sessions, a lecture, a group regression, and a group meditation were professionally videotaped.

The painstaking task of attaching therapist and subject to the machines provided time for the therapist to develop a focus for the upcoming regression. After attachment of the electrodes Morrison worked to determine proper amplitude for both therapist and subject and established a baseline on the galvanometers.

Videotaping began with the induction of the subject. The video record was supplemented by Morrison's extensive notes on each person and his series of Mind Mirror drawings made at intervals during the regression to freeze different patterns. Following each regression he spent about 20 minutes commenting on the Mind Mirror records and these comments were videotaped and recorded. In spite of the artificial situation—the attachment to electrodes and the presence of the video camera—the regressions appeared meaningful and therapeutic to those involved.

## Results

### Beta

A striking difference in regression experiences from usual meditation patterns lay in the presence of flares of beta, especially in the therapists' patterns but also in those of most subjects. This beta had an aggressive character, especially in the therapists, not softening or diminishing, which would have suggested a more peaceful and relaxed type of guidance. This distinguished it from the usual meditation state, where beta is absent, and from the Awakened Mind state, where beta is softer and more rounded. In a couple of the therapists who had practiced meditation for a number of years, the beta did at times become more rounded, which brought the total pattern into closer congruence with the Fifth State pattern, but even then beta was comparably more prominent. Most subjects showed strong beta, probably because it was necessary in order to process what goes on in regression. Such strong beta in the subject may suggest why many subjects do not feel they are in an altered state but instead are sure they are "just making things up." Apparently it is possible, even easy, to be in a deep altered state and still retain energetic control.

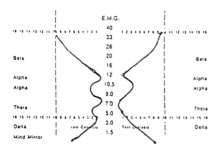

Figure 9. *A Therapist's Profile Showing the Presence of Aggressive Beta.*

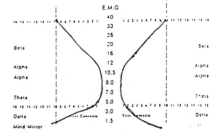

Figure 10. *A Therapist's Profile Showing Direct Progression from Beta to Delta, Largely Bypassing Alpha and Theta.*

When subjects who have been in a deep hypnotic trance are later unable to remember the events of the regression, the inference is that beta, and possibly high alpha, are blocked. However, the assumption that trance *must* involve a blocking of beta is, according to the Mind Mirror, incorrect. In fact, the Awakened Mind state strives to attain just the opposite: a bonding of imaging and perception from the unconscious with beta awareness.

The impression of the importance of beta, especially for the therapist, emerged early and remained consistent. Evidently the regression therapist controls the process with a strong hand. Morrison was disturbed in the beginning with this assertive beta, since he was accustomed to consider reduction of beta characteristic of an altered meditation state, but by the end of the research he conceded that flared beta was characteristic of the regression process.

## Alpha

Nearly all subjects and most therapists rapidly developed strong, rounded, and usually symmetrical alpha, which often started as high amplitude alpha and gradually moved downward to include lower amplitudes as well. The presence of strong symmetrical alpha is characteristic of the meditation state. Alpha is also an imaging state and the re-living of an emotional situation seems dependent on the production of alpha waves. As material is brought up from the unconscious (theta and delta) into images in low alpha, it percolates up through higher amplitude alpha into conscious perception in beta.

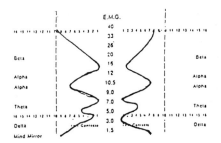

Figure 11. *A Subject Showing Rounded and Diminished Beta, Strong Alpha, Tentative Theta and Delta Flares.*

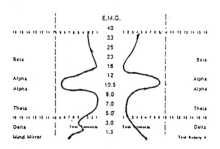

Figure 12. *Typical Profile of a Subject in Regression.* Note broad spectrum beta, strong alpha and theta, and flares of delta.

## Theta

Theta appeared along with alpha in most subjects and it was present in those therapists who went into altered states with their subjects. Theta is assumed to indicate contact with the unconscious. The question arose as to whether this emerging of alpha and theta states in therapist and subject is necessary for a successful regression. Several therapists and one patient seemed to be involved in a successful regression experience without significant alpha or theta, so these levels are not indispensable, but many subjects may need them to bring images up and re-experience emotions. Such subjects may be more comfortable including the altered state of alpha and theta. Other patients do not need this and may not want it, or perhaps are unwilling to trust it.

The approach to altered state work seems to be a personal matter. Some therapists evidenced an altered state that included alpha and theta automatically throughout the entire regression, while others touched on it at specific times. With our limited data we could only hypothesize that the therapist's involvement with alpha and theta enables the patient to feel empathy and support and so helps with the deepening and the recovery of material.

**Delta**

The presence of delta, which had been observed in the subject's pattern two years earlier, was strongly confirmed. Delta appeared in the therapist's pattern, also, though usually with less intensity. The delta of experienced therapists in our research was considerably more intense than that of the two inexperienced therapists, but with so small a sample this can only be earmarked for additional research.

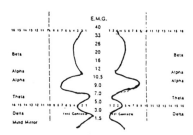

Figure 13. *A Therapist's Profile Showing Rounded but Still Prominent Beta, Empathic Flares of Alpha and Beta, and Delta.*

A number of questions arose concerning the nature and function of delta in the regression:

1. What is the function of delta in the regression process?
2. Can past lives be retrieved without delta?
3. Is delta necessary for both subject and therapist or only for the subject?
4. Is the presence of delta in the therapist a way of inducting the subject into a past life? Is it a form of tuning in to the subject?
5. Do skill and experience in the therapist increase the capacity to produce delta?

## Variations

The pattern that has been described was characteristic of all but two of the subjects. Both of the exceptions had been long-time meditators. During the induction they went immediately into the general meditation state—expanded symmetrical alpha plus symmetrical theta—and remained there. Beta disappeared and there was no occurrence of delta. The GSR fell to a low level and remained stationary, even during events that had emotional implications. Although apparent "past lives" were narrated, there was little affect. Details, and even major threads of narrative, were subject to revisions, which did not occur in the other regressions. These two meditators seemed little involved with their material and closure revealed minimal impact and insight. Both therapists manifested strong beta and delta, and one therapist appeared to be struggling to dislodge her subject from a stuck position, as manifested by her highly intense but unstable pattern.

## Discussion

The strong presence of beta in the therapist in regression work is easily understood as reflecting the need to keep the regression process in control. The presence of beta in the subject, especially in conjunction with altered states of considerable depth (strong alpha and theta) and the inclusion of delta, produces an unusual pattern that has been observed primarily in conjunction with paranormal functioning. It is hypothesized that such beta occurs in the subject because he must consciously work to understand and evaluate his material and reframe it. He must use conscious processes that are separate from altered states even though of necessity they take place at the same time. It is doubtful if transformational work could have been done in the older form of hypnosis where beta was often blocked so severely that memory was not retained. This points up the gap between merely recovering a past life, as was often done in hypnotic sessions in earlier times, and dealing with it therapeutically.

The emerging concept of delta as a radar state raises many questions as to the nature of past-life memories tapped in this radar state and where the memories are stored. That the mind does not exist within the brain is a hypothesis that is becoming more prevalent in scientific fields. The mind is beginning to be conceptualized as an energy field, a series of computer programs, that the brain, acting as a more or less efficient computer, brings into actualization.

The existence of such mind fields was researched at Yale for some years by Dr. Harold Saxon Burr, who published his results in *The Fields of Life* (1972). He and his colleagues at the Yale University School of Medicine hypothesized that all living things have electrodynamic fields—the "fields of life" or L-fields—that can be measured and mapped with fine voltmeters. Burr claims that "these field properties are not mysterious phenomena: they are measurable characteristics, not only of the universe but of the immediate environment of the earth." He concluded that the behavior of living systems is a consequence of the patterns of organization of the L-fields.

Burr's work was developed further by one of his colleagues, Edward R. Russell, who in his *Design for Destiny* (1976) added supportive evidence to Burr's work on the L-fields by making available the impeccable research on thought fields by L.L. Vasiliev, a professor of Physiology at the University of Leningrad (1973). Russell not only reinforced evidence for the existence of Burr's L-fields but took the hypothesis further by proposing that there is compelling evidence that thought is independent of the physical brain and exists in another kind of field, the T-field. This important concept provided a rational explanation, according to Russell, for the existence of the idiosyncratic ongoing component of a person. In other words, it insures a permanent storehouse for personal experiences over lifetimes.

The ready-made L-fields, as proposed by Burr, are always available in a common pool and can start to organize an embryo as soon as conception has taken place provided the right molecular conditions are present, which explains why human bodies are similar and have not altered their general design for 100,000 years. The T-fields, working in conjunction with the L-fields, are permanent electromagnetic fields that mold the ever-changing material of the cells and maintain the specific patterns of bodies and brains and store their experiences. Russell defines a T-field as "a field in space originating with—or the result of—a thought that can produce effects at a distance without any visible intervening means on any person or object that is receptive to its forces or influences." This is actually a definition of what many theoreticians call the mind field, though Russell rejects this term because he finds it ambiguous. The T-fields are individual and through them individual differences are passed on from one entity experience (or lifetime) to another.

Dr. Hiroshi Motoyama has been involved in Japan for some years in an exploration of what he calls the "subtle bodies." He, also, is convinced that the mind is an energy field (1978). One of his strongest supporters in this point of view is Dr. William Tiller of Stanford University, who proposes that consciousness can surpass its physical (sensory dependent) limitations. Motoyama's discussion of chi and the Chinese acupuncture meridian system throws light on the energy pathways of the individual mind field that are so puzzling to Western medicine. Using different instrumentation, the same concept was developed by Dr. Thelma Moss in her work at UCLA (1985).[6]

The potential for understanding the nature of delta and its radar qualities lies in the concept of morphogenetic fields proposed by Rupert Sheldrake, a biologist at the University of London. In his books *A New Science of Life: The Hypothesis of Formative Causation* (1981) and *The Presence of the Past: Morphic Resonance and the Habits of Nature* (1988) he postulated a morphogenetic field (his term for mind field) which forms a causative energetic field resembling Burr's L-fields but able to be influenced and changed in a way similar to Russell's T-fields. His assumption of a mind field in which experiences can be stored is relevant for understanding the nature of the material tapped by the delta (radar) contact. He feels that everything that is done and thought feeds into this morphogenic field. Though Sheldrake doubts that this field is electromagnetic in nature, he considers it to be a reality, not a concept.

Roger Woolger (1987) has extended the concept of a perpetuating mind field for each individual to include a differentiation of various aspects of the mind field. The physical or etheric aspects, which he considers the model after which the physical body is formed, influences what happens physically to the individual. It can be influenced, for better or worse, by what happens in this lifetime and by the choices made, such as reframing an old perception or changing one's attitude toward one's body. There is also an ongoing emotional constellation that influences the events in this life but can be modified by emotional changes and reframing. Mental scripts that we have made for ourselves during our lifetimes influence us strongly in this one but in turn can be modified and transformed by both conscious and unconscious intervention. All these levels of functioning are able to be contacted and mediated in regression work in the delta state.

Whether it is possible to contact past lives without delta remains to be seen. Were the experiences of the two subjects who seemed to remain stuck in the alpha-theta meditative state equally valid regression experiences? Subjectively they seem to have a different quality and to carry minimal impact. Much more extensive data is needed before the significance of different states, including others not manifested in this segment of research, can be evaluated.

## Conclusions

The pattern of brain functioning, as registered on the Mind Mirror, suggests an explanation for the recovery of past-life material. Memories may be stored in the mind field and be retrieved through a radar mechanism in the delta state. Material so recovered is brought up usually (but not always) into the personal unconscious (theta) and then is further propelled into alpha, where it manifests as images. From there it is drawn up into high alpha and beta where it is remembered and recognized and evaluated and transformed. This research must be considered exploratory. Documentation of many more cases is needed to confirm the pattern and explain the variations.

Further research to increase our understanding of delta is especially needed. What is the reason for the appearance of delta in the field of the therapist? Is delta helpful to the therapist in inducting the subject into a delta state? In the area of healing Cade (1979) found that if the healer manifested a strong Fifth State, the subject would begin to produce the state, even though he had never previously shown it. This is reminiscent of Thelma Moss's results with Kirlian photography (1985), which showed that the brilliant flares from the healer's fingers traveled to and engulfed the patient's imprinted fingers.

Does delta make it possible for the therapist to experience, at least to some extent, what the subject is experiencing and thus to be more effective in questioning and support? Perhaps the therapist's delta facilitates the recovery of past-life memories in the patient and deepens the understanding of their significance.

The primary question is whether the presence of delta is necessary for past-life retrieval. If so, what is the material produced by a subject who remains in a meditation state of amplified alpha and theta with no beta and no delta? Can the Mind Mirror distinguish between regression memories and active imagination? Certainly the current exploration suggests a more appreciative evaluation of beta, which has been formerly considered by meditators to be a chattering source of distraction. Now it can be honored as a necessary hard-working servant in the transformational process.

There are various other parapsychological areas where use of the Mind Mirror as a research instrument can give important information. Though a dream has to manifest through images in alpha or theta, possibly the actual retrieval comes during the delta state, which precedes the dreaming state (REM). There is also the possibility that some dreams do not emerge from the mind field but may be connected with alpha and theta processes independent of delta. Or all the states—alpha, theta, and delta—may be present constantly but in different intensities, so that when delta is dominant, that is what is registered on the conventional electroencephalogram, and this has led to the assumption that delta indicates deep sleep. What seems to be occurring is that in the current pursuit of lucid dreaming beta is added to the other brain waves, just as beta is now a conspicuous characteristic of the past-life retrieval process.

Similar considerations concern the field of healing. Granted that there are many healing states, ranging from vigorous beta blasting to the serene Awakened Mind State, do they all involve delta, and if so, what does this mean in terms of the source and nature of healing?

The ease with which delta is obtained by an increasing number of people is a recent phenomenon. If there is a mind field, it is changing rapidly in terms of availability—no longer is it limited to the elite in the Mystery Schools, nor is it necessary for a skilled yoga meditator to work for years to retrieve a past lifetime, as Paul Brunton suggested in the 30's.[7] He felt that remembering former embodiments required years of concentrated meditation using a technique of going backward in memory. We do not yet know how many people currently retrieve past lives, but the number is increasing. The Mind Mirror demonstrates how far we have come.

# Notes

## Chapter I: History of Regression Therapy

1. Sheldrake's concept of morphogenetic fields is clearly presented in a chapter titled "Morphogenetic Fields: Nature's Habits" contained in *Dialogues with Scientists and Sages: The Search for Unity* by Renee Weber, (1986).
2. Grof's description of the birth matrices is most clearly presented in *Beyond the Brain* (1985), Chapter I, page 92.
3. All of Ian Stevenson's books document such cases. One of his most popular books is *Twenty Cases Suggestive of Reincarnation*, published in 1974.
4. Brunton discusses this in *A Hermit in the Himalayas* in Chapter IV, page 41.
5. There are many acounts of Edgar Cayce's work with past lives. One of the best known is Gina Cerminara's *Many Mansions*. New York: William Devorrs and Co., 1950.
6. Morey Bernstein's *The Search for Bridey Murphey* was originally published in 1957 but was re-released in 1989 with a discussion of the vicissitudes of the first edition (see Bibliography).
7. A book that has contributed significantly to the rebirthing movement is *Rebirthing in the New Age* by L. Orr, and Sandra Ray, Millbrae, CA: Celestial Arts, 1977.
8. An excellent perspective on the paradigm shift is recounted in Stanislav Grof's *Beyond the Brain*, Chapter I, (1985).
9. Paul Brunton's *Search in Secret India* (1935) was followed by *A Search in Secret Egypt* and a number of general books on metaphysics such as *The Quest of the Overself* (1937). In the 50's Brunton withdrew to the Alps and lived a life of complete seclusion for 30 years. From this period emerged a series of 20 notebooks. All of his books have gone through many editions. They have now been gathered together by Larson Publications in Burdett, New York, which published his series of notebooks after his death in 1981 and sees that all his books are kept in print. Brunton, with his quiet, objective explorations of both the inner and outer worlds has had long-standing impact on the thinking of this century and has been a major contributor to the birth of the new paradigm.
10. L. Adams Beck was already well-known for her historical novels (under the name of Ethel Barrington) when she turned to an exploration of Eastern thought. Her novels enjoyed decades of enthusiastic reception and helped to bring yoga into the forefront of the thinking of those who were moving into transpersonal approaches. *The House of Fulfillment* (1927) spelled out the practice of yoga and proposed its potential at a time when even the word was almost unknown in the United States. A second novel, *The Garden of Vision* (1929), described Zen, an equally unknown area of consciousness exploration, and contained a careful exposition of Japanese martial arts. Her *Story of Oriental Philosophy* remains one of the most succinct expositions of a nebulous area.

11. Hesse's books appeared in Germany in the late 20's and were finally translated into English at the beginning of the 60's. Hesse won the Nobel Prize in literature. *Siddhartha* is considered to be his greatest work.
12. Elmer and Alyce Green in *Beyond Biofeedback* (1977) reported that subjects who were able to increase control of alpha and theta felt no wish to use drugs further (p. 143). They mention other researchers, such as Kurtz, who considers meditation and biofeedback far superior to drugs as methods for contacting the missing element of spirituality that is so much sought by many people (p. 192).

    Especially effective inductions into altered states emerge in various group experiences, such as Sufi movement, the serene chanting of those around Pir Vilayat Khan, and the lovely bhajan singing in Sai Baba's ashram. Those involved seldom realize that they have put themselves into an altered state. I remember years ago walking slowly in a circle for an hour and saying to each person moving in an opposite direction, "I am you, you are me, we are one." I felt foolish, but afterward I realized that I had developed a core of serenity. I highly respected Oxford-educated Pir Vilayat Khan and went to a weekend workshop to listen to him. When we ate cereal and apples three times a day and sat in a meadow chanting for ten hours, I wondered why I had come, but again, I came into extraordinary balance. Meditation provides steady deepening and centering, but these other altered-state experiences use shared group energy to contact a profound state very quickly.
13. Ramacharaka's book entitled *Hatha Yoga: The Yoga Philosophy of Physical Well-Being* was published in 1930, though his teaching had extended over several earlier decades. The book was published in Chicago by the Yoga Publication Society and along with the books of L. Adams Beck helped to stir up initial interest in yoga. Hatha Yoga, which deals with the body and health, was espoused by Ramacharaka, while L. Adams Beck stressed the lesser practiced and more difficult Raja Yoga, which deals with the control of energy.
14. The *Brain Mind Bulletin* reports on current alternative research and treatment and provides excellent reviews of new books dealing with the paradigm shift. Its address is P.O. Box 42211, Los Angeles, CA 90042.
15. This monograph is available from the Association for Past-Life Research and Therapies.
16. The proposal for this research is described in *The Journal of Regression Therapy*, Volume III, No. 1, 56-61, 1988. Maurice Albertson, William Baldwin, and Dan Ward. "Post Traumatic Stress Disorders in Vietnam Veterans: A Proposal for Research and Therapeutic Healing Utilizing Depossession."
17. The research with the Mind Mirror was first published in *The Journal of Regression Therapy*, Vol. IV, No. 1, 1989. It has been reprinted here as Appendix C. There is further discussion of the therapist-patient relationship in Chapter II, of this volume, and the place of delta in recovering past lives is proposed in Chapter VI.
18. References for prenatal theory and therapy are listed in the Bibliography for Volume II, Chapter I.
19. Chamberlain, David. *Babies Remember Birth*. Los Angeles, CA: Jeremy P. Tarcher, Inc., 1986.

20. Cheek, David. "Maladjustment Patterns Apparently Related to Imprinting at Birth." *The American Journal of Clinical Hypnosis,* Vol. 18, No 2.
———. "Techniques for Eliciting Information Concerning Fetal Experience." Paper presented at the meeting of the Society for Clinical and Experimental Hypnosis, Los Angeles, California, 1977.
21. For references to regression to early childhood therapy see Bibliography for Vol. II, Chapter II.
22. For references to death and dying see Bibliography for Vol. II, Chapter VII.
23. For references to interlife experiences see Bibliography for Vol. II, Chapter IV.
24. References to work with entities are listed in Bibliography for Vol. II, Chapter VI.
25. Crabtree, Adam. *Multiple Man: Explorations in Possession and Multiple Personality.* New York: Prater Publishers, 1985.
26. Lenz, Frederick. *Total Relaxation: True Accounts of Reincarnation.* New York: Bobbs-Merril Co., 1980.
27. Skrying is an age-old form of perception through looking into a crystal ball.

## Chapter II: Philosophical Hypotheses

1. Two informative discussions of karma are included in Thorwald Dethlefsen's *The Challenge of Fate* (pages 156-157) and Christopher Bache's *Life Cycles: Reincarnation and the Web of Life* (pages 62-104). Bache's discussion provides an invaluable underpinning for conceptualizing the parameters of past-life therapy.
2. Max Freedom Long has provided the most comprehensive account of the Kahuna tradition in *Growing into Light* (1955) and *The Secret Science behind Miracles* (1948), both published by DeVors of Santa Monica, California. However, a short clear exposition of working with the Body Self is contained in Enid Hoffman's *Huna: A Beginner's Guide,* Rockport, MA: ParaResearch, 1976.
3. See Bibliography for Sheldrake's works. Sheldrake offers a simple and clear presentation of his theory of morphogenetic fields in his dialogue with Renee Weber in her *Dialogues with Scientists and Sages: The Search for Unity,* (1986). Much of the material is a repeat of an excellent article that formerly appeared in *Revision.*
4. Thorwald Dethelfsen. *The Healing Power of Illness.* Sorset, England: Element Books, LTD., 1990 (English translation).
5. Simonton, Carl, Stephanie Simonton, and James Creighton. *Getting Well Again* (1978).
6. Achterberg, Jeanne. *Imagery in Healing: Shamanism and Modern Medicine.* (1985).
7. Cousins, Norman. *Anatomy of an Illness.* New York: W.W. Norton and Co., 1979.
8. ———. *The Healing Heart.* New York: Norton, 1983.
9. *A Course in Miracles.* Tiburon, CA: Foundation for Inner Peace, 1976.
10. Unpublished communication with Valerie Hunt.

11. Motoyama, Hiroshi. *Science and the Evolution of Consciousness: Chakras, Ki, and Psi* (1978).
12. Gerber, Richard. *Vibrational Medicine.* 1988.
13. The steps of transforming the energy of anger into that of love are delineated in Edith Stauffer's book, *Unconditional Love and Forgiveness* published by the Triangle Publishers in Burbank, California in 1987. The actual steps are noted on pages 167-170. An example of the use of these steps with a patient is contained in Volume II, Chapter II, "Reframing a Parental Image."

## Chapter III: Psychotherapeutic Assumptions

1. See especially Ring's *Heading Toward Omega* (1984). Near-death perceptions comprise an alternative thrust toward the changing paradigm with its concept of expanded consciousness. It is peripheral because it is limited to a specific population.
2. For an excellent concise description of these concepts see the conversation with David Bohm in Renee Weber's *Dialogues with Scientists and Sages: The Search for Unity* (1986).
3. An in-depth description of this process is included in Woolger's article "Imaginal Techniques in Past-Life Therapy," *Journal of Regression Therapy*, Vol. I, No. 1, 1986.

## Chapter IV: Indications and Contraindications for Use

1. See *The Creation of Health* (1988) by Norman Shealy and Caroline Myss.
2. Questions referring to economic or vocational issues or personal affairs suggest a focus in the lower chakras. Upper chakra questions would include concern about the meaning of life, the nature of existence, techniques for becoming more loving or more able to serve.
3. See Fiore, Chapter XIV, Cases 2 and 4.
4. Helen Wambach, *Life Before Life* (1978).
5. See Volume II, Chapter III, "Childhood Abuse" by Ernest Pecci. After several years of preliminary therapy this patient was able to resolve her psychosis by returning to its source in another lifetime.

## Chapter V: Preparation

1. See Chapter I, page 8.
2. See Chapter I, pages 8, 9, 14.
3. See especially *Dancing in the Light* by Shirley MacLaine, New York: Bantam Books, 1985.

## Chapter VI: Induction Techniques

1. The following are representative descriptions of lucid dreaming:
   Garfield, Patricia. *Creative Dreaming.* New York: Ballantine Books, 1974.
   LaBerge, Stephen. *Lucid Dreaming.* Boston, MA: Houghton Mifflin Co., 1985.
   A *Lucidity Letter* is published by Dr. Jayne Gackenbach, Department of Psychology, UNI, Cedar Falls, Iowa.
2. Cade, C. Maxwell and Norma Coxhead. *The Awakened Mind: Biofeedback and the Development of Higher States of Awareness.* New York: Dell Publishing, 1979.
3. Our research was first published as "Brain Wave States Underlying the Regression Process" in the *Journal of Regression Therapy,* Vol. II, No. 2, 1986. It has been reprinted in this volume as Appendix C entitled "Mind Mirror Research on the Retrieval of Past Lives."
4. See Bibliography, especially Renee Weber's *Dialogues with Scientists and Sages: A Search for Unity* (1986).
5. See section on dream research in Rama, et. al., *Yoga and Psychotherapy: The Evolution of Consciousness,* 1976, pages 142-171.
6. Alyce Green and D. Walters. *Biofeedback for Mind-Body Self Regulation: Healing and Self-Regulation.* Topeka, Kansas: The Menninger Foundation, 1974, p. 23.
7. See Appendix B for a group induction by Helen Wambach.
8. Leuner, H. "Guided Affective Imagery, a Method of Intensive Psychotherapy." *American Journal of Psychotherapy.* Vol. I, No. 23, 1969.
9. Jacobsen, Edmund. *Progressive Relaxation.* Chicago: University of Chicago Press, 1938; paperback, 1974.

## Chapter VII: Supportive and Deepening Techniques

1. See Woolger's section, Chapter XIII, Case 2.
2. See Fiore's section, Chapter XIV, Case 1.
3. See Fiore's section, Chapter XIV, Case 4.
4. See Volume II, Chapter I, "Rescripting Prenatal and Birth Patterns" by Barbara Findeisen.
5. See Reynolds' section, Chapter XVIII, Case 1. Also "Humanistic Consideration in Regression Therapy" by Edward Reynolds', *Journal of Regression Therapy.* Vol. I, No. 2.
6. See Denning, Chapter XII, Case 6.

## Chapter VIII: Psychotherapeutic and Transformational Interventions

1. These stages were first reported in "Imaginal Techniques in Past-Life Therapy," in *The Journal of Regression Therapy.* Volume I, No. 1, 1986. They are summarized in Woolger's section (Chapter XIII).
2. See Hickman's section Chapter XVII, Case 4.
3. See Hickman, op. cit., Case 1.

4. Release of anger through reframing appears in many of the cases in these two volumes. Use of the psychosynthesis technique of releasing expectations and accepting the person (another or oneself) is documented in Chapter XXI and also in the continuation of this case in Volume II, Chapter II, "Reframing a Parental Image."
5. Cases that illustrate this include Denning: Volume II, Chapter III, "Tracing the Source of Childhood Trauma" and Jue's Chapter XI, Case 1, in this volume.
6. This discussion of guilt is taken from Hazel Denning's unpublished doctoral dissertation, "The Exploration of Guilt in Past-Life Therapy," International College at Los Angeles, 1984.
7. See Volume II, Chapter IV, "Return to the Interlife as a Source of Healing."
8. See Volume II, Chapter IV, op. cit.

## Chapter IX: Integration into the Therapeutic Process

1. See Findeisen's article in Volume II, Chapter I, "Rescripting Destructive Prenatal and Birth Patterns."
2. See Denning's section, Chapter XII, Case 3 in this volume.
3. See Chapter XXI, Case 4 in this volume. Also Volume II, Chapter II, "Reframing a Parental Image."
4. See Chapter XXI, Case 2.
5. For a more complete discussion of the Shadow see Thorwald Dethlefsen, *The Challenge of Fate*, 1978.
6. Fiore's section, Chapter XIV, Case 1 in this volume.
7. Jue's section, Chapter XI, Case 1 in this volume.
8. Progoff, Ira. *At a Journal Workshop.* New York: Dialogue House Library, 1975.
9. Pecci's section, Chapter XXII, Case 1 in this volume.
10. There are many tapes that embed affirmations in altered state imaging. My tape "Moonlight Meditation" induces a deep altered state and incorporates affirmations largely selected by the meditator. Available through the Association for Past-Life Research and Therapies.
11. *90 Days to Self-Health* by Norman Shealy (1976).
12. Roberto Assagioli, *Psychosynthesis*, (1965).
13. Pecci's section, Chapter XXII, Case 3.
14. Robert Assagioli, *The Act of Will*, (1973).
15. An excellent discussion of subpersonalities is contained in *Synthesis, Volume I*, (1975). Edited by Susan Vargiu.
16. See Fiore, Chapter XIV, Case 1.
17. See Denning's section, Chapter XII, Case 4.
18. Chapter XXI, Case 2.
19. There are many meditations that enable us to identify with our Higher Self and observe our personal self. One effective image is floating down a river in a boat and seeing scenes from one's current life being played out on the banks.

## Chapter X: Failures

1. This research was described in "Past-Life Therapy: The Experience of Twenty-Six Therapists." It was written by Helen Wambach and after her death was edited and published by Chet Snow in *The Journal of Regression Therapy*, Volume I, No. 2, 1986.

## Chapter XI: Ronald Wong Jue, Ph.D.

1. Bohm, David. *Wholeness and the Implicate Order*. London: Routledge & Kegan Paul Publ., 1980.
2. Sheldrake, Rupert. *The Presence of the Past*. New York: Random House Inc., 1988.
3. Pribram, Karl. *Languages of the Brain*. Englewood Cliffs, N.J.: Prentice Hall, 1971.
4. Beahrs, John O. *Unity and Multiplicty: Multilevel Consciousness of Self in Hypnosis, Psychiatric Disorder and Mental Health*, New York: Brunner/Mazel, 1982.
   Talbot, Michael. *The Holographic Universe*. New York: Harper Collins Publ., 1991.
5. Grof, Stanislav. *Beyond the Brain*. New York: State University of New York, 1985.
6. Gilligan, Stephan G. *Therapeutic Trances*. New York: Brunner/Mazel, 1987.
   Horowitz, Mardi J. *Image Formation and Psychotherapy*. New York, Jason Aronson Publ., 1983.
7. Grof. *Beyond the Brain*. op. cit.
8. For a complete discussion of these three stages see "Imaginal Techniques in Past-Life Therapy" in *The Journal of Regression Therapy*, Vol. I, No. 1, 1986.
9. Mintz, Elizabeth E. *The Psychic Thread: Paranormal and Transpersonal Aspects of Psychotherapy*. New York: Human Sciences Press, 1983.
10. Schwarz, Berthold Eric. *Psychic-Nexus: Psychic Phenomena in Psychiatry and Everyday Life*. London: Van Nostrand Reinhold Co., 1980.
11. Langs, Robert. *Interactions: The Realm of Transference and Countertransference*. New York: Jason Aronson Publ., 1980.

## Chapter XII: Hazel M. Denning, Ph.D.

1. A significant book that appeared at that time was *The Case for Reincarnation* by Leslie Weatherhead, London: Samuel & Temple, 1961.
2. An outline of this research was presented in "Restoration of Health through Hypnosis," in the *Journal of Regression Therapy*, Volume II, No. 1, 1987.
3. For a more extensive discussion see Denning, "Philosophical Assumptions Underlying Past-Life Therapy," *Journal of Regression Therapy*. Vol. I, No. 2. (1986).

4. These concepts of the improved state of living for those who can take responsibility for their lives is thoughtfully presented in *Carl Rogers on Personal Power* by Carl Rogers, New York: Delacorte Press, 1977.
5. Many of these concepts are included in *The Will to Live* by Arnold Hutschneker, New Jersey: Prentice Hall, 1958.
6. A recent example of a group reincarnating together has been documented by Marge Rieder in *Mission to Millboro*, New York: Authors Unlimited, 1991.
7. See *Myth and Guilt* by Theodore Reik, New York: George Braziller, Inc., 1957.
8. An informative discussion of the consequences of guilt is contained in *Guilt: Its Meaning and Significance* by John G. McKenzie, Abdington Press, 1962.
9. An extensive discussion of state and trait guilt is contained in Denning's unpublished dissertation, "The Exploration of Guilt in Past-Life Therapy," Los Angeles: International College, 1984.
10. The psychotherapeutic treatment of guilt is addressed in Denning's article "Guilt: Facilitator and Inhibitor in the Growth of the Soul," *The Journal of Regression Therapy*. Vol. III, No. 2, 1988.

## Chapter XIII: Roger J. Woolger, Ph.D.

1. Quest Publications, Wheaton, IL, 1970.
2. Jung, Carl G. "Two Essays in Analytical Psychology" (Collected Works, Vol. 3) New York, Bollingen-Pantheon Press.
3. ———. *Structure and Dynamics of the Psyche: A Review of the Complex Theory* (Collected Works, Volume 8) New York: Bollingen-Pantheon Press.
4. Berne, Eric. *Games People Play*. New York: Grove Press, Inc., 1964 (Paperback Edition).
5. Jung. *Structure and Dynamics of the Psyche*.
6. Hillman, James. "Archetypal Psychology" in *Loose Ends*.
7. See Woolger *Other Lives, Others Selves*, Ch. 5, "The Multidimensional Psyche."
8. Grof, Stanislav. *Realms of the Human Unconscious: Observations from LSD Research*. New York: Viking Press, 1976.
9. Patanjali, *Yoga Sutras* (various editions).
10. Grof, Stanislav. *Beyond the Brain*. Albany, New York: State University of N.Y., 1985.
11. Jung. *Analytical Psychology*.
12. Jung. *Analytical Psychology*.
13. Jung, *Analytical Psychology*.
14. Fox, Jonathon. *The Essential Moreno: Writings on Psychodrama, Group Method, and Spontaneity*. New York, 1987.
15. Fagan, Joel and I.A. Shepherd. *Gestalt Therapy Now*. New York: Harper, 1970.
16. (On Vipasanna Meditation) See Dhiryamsa *The Way of Non-Attachment*. New York: Schoken Books, 1975.
17. Boadella, David. *Wilhelm Reich, the Man and His Work*. London, 1973.

## Chapter XIV: Edith Fiore, Ph.D.

Extended accounts of the cases in this section are contained in the following chapters of *You Have Been Here Before*.
1. "Obesity," Chapter V, pp. 85-108.
2. "Insomnia," Chapter VIII, pp. 171-189.
3. "Acrophobia," Chapter VII, pp. 159-170.
4. "Recovering Personal Power," Chapter X, pp. 203-227.

## Chapter XV: Chet B. Snow, Ph.D.

1. See Helen S. Wambach, *Reliving Past Lives* (1978) and *Life Before Life* (1979).
2. This book has now been translated into German, French, and Dutch.
3. Excellent discussions of their theories by both Planck and Sheldrake are contained in *Dialogues with Scientist and Sages* by Renee Weber (1986). Their books are listed in the Bibliography.
4. Grof, Stanislav. *Beyond the Brain*. Albany, New York, State University of New York, 1985.
5. Cayce, Edgar. *A Search for God*. Book I, Virginia Beach, VI.
6. Ramacharaka. *Science of Breath*. Chicago: Yoga Publication Society, 1904.
7. See Volume II, Chapter 6, "Differentiating Past Lives and Entity Attachment."
8. Personal communication.
9. See Appendix C, "Mind Mirror Research."
10. Assagioli, Roberto. *The Act of Will*. New York: Viking Press, 1973.
11. Cayce. *A Search for God*.
12. Personal communication.
13. The unfulfilled love that still lay at the root of Helen Wambach's psyche was exposed by the eventual bonding she experienced in a later session when she was progressed to a future lifetime. See Volume II, Chapter VIII, "New Age or Brave New World?"

## Chapter XVI: Bontenbal and Noordegraaf

1. For a more complete account of the movement in the Netherlands see Rob Bontenbal's article, "The Development of Past-Life Therapy in the Netherlands," *Journal of Regression Therapy,*" Volume IV, No. 1, 1989.
2. This book was translated from the Dutch by A.E.J. Wils and appeared in the United States as *Exploring Reincarnation*, published in New York by Viking-Penguin in 1990. It has also been released in Australia, New Zealand, and Canada.
3. Pribram, Karl. *Languages of the Brain*. New York: Prentice-Hall, 1971.
   ———. "Non-Locality and Localization: A Review of the Place of the Holographic Hypothesis of Brain Function in Perception and Memory." Reprint from the Tenth ICUS, November.

## Chapter XVII: Irene Hickman, D.O.

1. Cheiro, *Cheiro's Palmistry for All.* New York: Prentice Hall Press, 1964.
2. Sugrue, Thomas. *There is a River.* New York: Rinehart and Winston, 1942 (Dell Paperback edition, New York, 1967).
3. Cerminara, Gina *Many Mansions.* New York: William Morrow (Paperback edition: New York, The New American Library, 1967).

## Chapter XVIII: Edward N. Reynolds

1. Bernstein, Morey. *The Search for Bridey Murphey.* New York: Doubleday, 1965.
2. Huxley, Aldous. *The Perennial Philosophy.* New York and London: Harper and Bros., 1945.
3. Heard, Gerald. *Pain, Sex and Time.* New York: Harper, 1930.
4. Some books that are informative regarding Vedanta are:
   Sinha, J. *Indian Philosophy: Vol. I & II.* Calcutta: Sinha, 1958-1961.
   Taimni, K. *The Science of Yoga.* Wheaton, Ill: Theosoph. Publ. House, 1961.
   Swami Vivekananda. *Raja Yoga.* Ramakrishna-Vivekananda Center, 1955.
   Woods, James Houghton. *The Yoga System of Patanjali.* Delhi: 1914.
5. Maslow, Abraham. *Toward a Psychology of Being.* Princeton: Van Nostrand, 1962.
   ———. *Religions, Values, and Peak Experiences.* Columbus: Ohio State
6. Elements of this induction were first proposed by Schultz and Luthe in 1959 in their book on autogenic training. (See Bibliography.) They described the feelings of heaviness and warmth as characteristic of the hypnotic state.

## Chapter XIX: Barbara Findeisen, M.F.C.C.

1. Nixon, Lucille and Elizabeth Howes. *The Choice is Always Ours.* New York: Richard R. Smith, 1948.
2. Pecci, Ernest. *I Love You/I Hate You.* Pleasant Hill, CA: TL Publishing, 1978.
3. Pribram, Karl. *Languages of the Brain.* New York: Prentice Hall, 1971.

## Chapter XX: Thorwald Dethlefsen, Ph.D. (Germany)

1. For background in color imaging see Schultz and Luthe, *Autogenic Training: A Psychophysiological Response in Psychotherapy.* New York: Grune and Stratham, 1959.
2. Leuner, H. "Guided Affective Imagery, a Method of Intensive Psychotherapy," *American Journal of Psychotherapy.* Vol. I, No. 23, 1969.

## Chapter XXI: Winafred B. Lucas, Ph.D.

1. L. Adams Beck. *The House of Fulfillment* (1927).
2. See Rupert Sheldrake, *A New Science of Life: The Hypothesis of Formative Causation* (1983) and especially the conversation with Sheldrake in Renee Weber's *Dialogues with Scientists and Sages.* (1986).
3. See Edith Stauffer's *Unconditional Love and Forgiveness.* Burbank, CA: Triangle Press, 1987.
4. Two Georgia Kelley tapes that are especially appropriate are "Sea Peace" and "Tarashanti."
5. Stauffer. *Unconditional Love.*
6. For further in work Carrie's relationship with her current father see Volume II, Chap. II, "Reframing a Parental Image."

## Chapter XXII: Ernest F. Pecci, M.D.

1. There are many accounts of Edgar Cayce. One of the best known is Gina Cerminara's *Many Mansions.* New York: William Devorrs and Co., 1950. This describes Cayce's involvement with past lives and discusses some of the problems that he found originating in other lifetimes.
2. Pecci, Ernest. *I Love You/I Hate You.* Pleasant Hill, CA: IIT Publications, 1978.

## Appendix B

1. Taken from *The Wambach Method* by Helen Wambach and Leona Lee, 1978. Distributed by The Association for Past Life Research and Therapies, Box 20151, Riverside, CA 92316.

## Appendix C

1. C. Maxwell Cade and Nona Coxhead. *The Awakened Mind* (1979).
2. Kamiya, Joe. "Conscious Control of Brain Waves," *Psychology Today,* April, 1968.
3. Moss, Thelma. *The Body Electric* (1979).
4. Green, Elmer. "Biofeedback for Mind-Body Self Regulation: Healing and Creativity" in *Biofeedback and Self-Control.* Chicago: Aldine, 1973.
5. Whitton, Joel. "Ramp functions in EEG power spectra during actual or attempted paranormal events," *New Horizons,* Vol. I, No. 4, July 1974.
6. Moss. *The Body Electric* (1979).
7. Brunton, Paul. *A Hermit in the Himalayas* (1937).

# Bibliography

## Past-Life Therapy

This list represents the offerings of established psychotherapists who have developed regression techniques and recorded sessions with patients demonstrating their approaches.

Dethlefsen, Thorwald. *The Challenge of Fate* (Chapters 7 & 8). Boston, MA: Coventure Ltd., 1984 (English language edition).
———. *Voices from Other Lives*. New York: M. Evans and Company, 1978.
Fiore, Edith. *You Have Been Here Before*. New York: Ballantine Books, 1978.
Hickman, Irene. *Mind Probe—Hypnosis*. Kirksville, MO: Hickman Systems, 1983.
Hubbard, L. Ron. *Have You Lived Before This Life?* California: The Church of Scientology, 1958.
Kelsey, Denys and Joan Grant. *Many Lifetimes*. New York: Ballantine Books, 1987.
Moody, Raymond A. *Coming Back: A Psychiatrist Explores Past-Life Journeys*. New York: Bantam, Doubleday, Dell Publishing Group, 1990.
Moore, Marcia. *Hypersentience*. New York: Crown Publishers, 1976.
Netherton, Morris and Nancy Shiffrin. *Past Lives Therapy*. New York: Ace Books, 1978.
Oppenheim, Garrett. *Who Were You Before You Were You?* New York: Carlton Press, 1990.
Schlotterbeck, Karl. *Living Your Past Lives: the Psychology of Past-Life Regression*. New York: Ballantine Books, 1987.
Wambach, Helen. *Life Before Life*. New York: Bantam Books, 1979.
———. *Reliving Your Past Lives: the Psychology of Past-Life Regression*. New York: Ballantine Books, 1978.
Weiss, Brian. *Many Lives, Many Masters* New York: Simon and Schuster, 1988.
——— *Through Time into Healing*. New York: Simon and Schuster, 1992.
Whitton, Joel and Joe Fisher. *Life Between Life*. New York: Doubleday, 1980.
Williston, Glen and Judith Johnstone. *Discovering Your Past Lives*. Northampton, England: Thorsons Publishing Group, 1983.
Woolger, Roger. *Other Lives, Other Selves*. New York: Doubleday, 1987.

# Experiences of Past Lives

These books recount past-life experiences without a psychotherapeutic focus. Some were recovered spontaneously; others were remembered under hypnotherapy. They are a sampling of a steady stream of accounts that served to stimulate the interest of the public and to crack the rigid belief system that precluded an assumption of other lifetimes.

Bernstein, Morey. *The Search for Bridey Murphey*. New York: Doubleday, 1956.
  An updated version of the original book appeared in 1989. It describes the furor that the publication of the book aroused at the time it was first published.
Blythe, Henry. *The Three Lives of Naomi Henry*. New York: Citadel Press, 1956.
Cunningham, Janet. *A Tribe Returns*. Crest Park, CA: Deep Forest Press, 1994.
Glaskin, G.M. *Windows of the Mind: The Christos Experiment*. London: Wildwood House, 1974.
Grant, Joan. *Far Memory*. New York: Harper and Row, 1956.
——— *Winged Pharoah*. Ohio: Ariel Press, 1937.
  These are autobiographical.
Guirdham, Arthur. *The Cathars and Reincarnation*. London: Neville Spearman, 1970.
——— *We Are One Another*. London: Neville Spearman, 1974.
  This is an account of the regressions of a number of people, most of whom did not know one another but who found that they had shared a past lifetime in southern France during the 13th Century.
Iverson, Jeffrey. *More Lives Than One?* New York: Warner, 1976.
  This is a journalistic investigation into the work of the late Arnall Bloxham, who until his recent death was active in England as an author and conducting regressions on television.
Lenz, Frederick. *Lifetimes: True Accounts of Reincarnation*. New York: Bobbs-Merrill, 1979.
Moss, Peter and Joe Keeton. *Encounters with the Past*. New York: Doubleday, 1981.
Rieder, Marge. *Mission to Millboro*. Los Angeles: Authors Unlimited, 1991.
  This is a therapist's report of a group of people who appeared in her practice, most of whom did not initially know each other in this lifetime but who had shared a lifetime during the Civil War.
Ryall, Edward. *Twice Born*. New York: Harper and Row, 1974.
Stearn, Jess. *The Search for the Girl with the Blue Eyes*. Garden City, N.Y.: Doubleday, 1968.
Steiger, Brad and Lorin Williams. *Other Lives*. Arizona: Esoteric Publication, 1969.
Steward, A.J. *King's Memory*. Glasgow, Scotland: William Embryo Ltd., 1978.

## Theoretical and Research Background in Past Lives

Here are some underpinnings for a theoretical understanding of past lives. Ian Stevenson has produced most of the significant validation research. Joseph Head, Sylvia Cranston, and Carey Williams have provided scholarly background for conceptualizing reincarnation. Christopher Bache's recent book has set a model of elegance in thinking about the area of past lives and clarity in presenting conceptualizations. Ten Dam has assembled a comprehensive bibliography underlying therapeutic work.

Bache, Christopher. *Life Cycles: Reincarnation and the Web of Life*. New York: Paragon House, 1990.
Cranston, Sylvia, and Carey Williams. *Reincarnation: A New Horizon in Science, Religion, and Society*. New York: Julian Press, 1983.
Head, Joseph, Sylvia Cranston, eds. *Reincarnation: The Phoenix Fire Mystery*. New York: Warner Books, 1979.
Stevenson, Ian. *Twenty Cases Suggestive of Reincarnation*. VA: University Press of Virginia, 1974.
———. *Children Who Remember Previous Lives: A Question of Reincarnation*. VA: University Press of Virginia, 1987.
Ten Dam, Hans. *Exploring Reincarnation*. (English translation), N.Y.: Viking Penguin, 1990.

## Books Relating to the Development of a New Paradigm

Thrusts toward a new paradigm began as early as the 20's and 30's, lessened in impact for several decades, and then accelerated. Their documentation reflects this vicissitude in interest. The partial list below represents the books that have made the greatest impact on my own thinking. It is presented in *chronological order* to show the interweaving of the currents of Eastern thought, modern physics, and psychedelics.

Einstein, Albert. *The Principle of Relativity*. N.Y.: Dover, 1923.
Beck, L. Adams. *The House of Fulfillment*. New York: Cosmopolitan Books, 1927.
——— *The Way of Power*. New York: Cosmopolitan Books, 1928.
——— *The Garden of Vision*. New York: J.J. Little and Ives, 1929.
Hesse, Herman. *Siddhartha*. (Original German Edition). Berlin: G. Fischer, 1929.
Eddington, Arthur. *The Nature of the Physical World*. N.Y.: McMillan, 1931.
Hesse, Herman. *Das Morgenland Fahrt*. (Original German Edition of *Journey to the East*). Berlin: G. Fischer, 1932.
Morgan, Charles. *The Fountain*. N.Y.: Alfred A. Knopf, 1932.
Einstein, Albert. *Essays in Science*. New York: Philosophical Library, 1934.
Brunton, Paul. *A Search in Secret India*. New York: E.P. Dutton, 1935.
——— *A Hermit in the Himalayas*. New York: E.P. Dutton, 1937.
——— *The Quest for the Overself*. New York: E.P. Dutton, 1938.
Huxley, Aldous. *The Perennial Philosophy*. New York and London: Harper and Brothers, 1945.

Yogananda, Paramahansa. *Autobiography of a Yogi.* New York: Philosophical Library, 1946.
Hesse, Herman. *Siddhartha.* (English Trans.) N.Y.: Bantam Books, 1951.
Jeans, James. *The Growth of Physical Science.* Cambridge: Cambridge University Press, 1951.
Watts, Alan. *The Way of Zen.* N.Y.: New American Library, 1957.
Heisenberg, W. *Physics and Philosphy.* N.Y.: Harper, 1958.
James, Williams. *The Varieties of Religious Experience* New York: The New American Library, 1958.
Reichenbach, H. "The Philosophical Significance of the Theory of Relativity," in *Albert Einstein: Philosopher-Scientist* N.Y.: Harper, 1959.
Schultz, Johannes, and Wolfgang Luthe. *Autogenic Training: A Psychophysiologic Approach in Psychotherapy.* NY: Grune and Stratton, 1959.
L'Engle, Madeleine. *A Wrinkle in Time.* NY: Dell Publ., 1962.
Einstein, Albert. *Essays in Science.* New York: Philosophical Library, 1964.
Assagioli, Roberto. *Psychosynthesis.* New York: Penguin Books, 1965.
Kübler-Ross, Elisabeth. *On Death and Dying.* N.Y.: McMillan, 1965.
LeShan, Lawrence. *The Medium, the Mystic and the Physicist.* New York: Viking Press, 1966.
Hesse, Herman. *Journey to the East* (Translation from the German of *Das Morgenland Fahrt*). NY: Farrar, Strauss & Girgeux, 1968.
Planck, Max. *Scientific Autobiography and Other Papers.* Westport, Conn: Greenwood Press, 1968.
Govinda, Lama Anagarika. *Foundations of Tibetan Mysticism.* New York: Samuel Weiser, 1969.
Suzuki, Shunryu. *Essays in Zen Buddhism.* N.Y.: Mentor, 1969.
Huxley, Aldous. *The Doors of Perception.* N.Y.: Harper & Row, 1970.
Pribram, Karl. *Languages of the Brain.* NY: Prentice Hall, 1971.
Burr, Harold Saxton. *Blueprint for Immortality.* London: Neville Spearman, 1972.
Weil, Andrew. *The Natural Mind.* Boston: Houghton Mifflin, 1972.
Assagioli, Roberto. *The Act of Will.* New York: Viking Press, 1973.
Huxley, Aldous. *Island.* N.Y.: Harper & Row, 1973.
Mishlove, Jeffrey. *Roots of Consciousness.* New York: Random House, 1975.
Moody, Raymond. *Life After Life.* Georgia: Mockingbird Books, 1975.
Capra, Fritjof. *The Tao of Physics.* CO: Shabala Publications, 1976.
Grof, Stanislav. *Realms of the Human Unconscious: Observations from LSD Research.* NJ: Prentice Hall, 1971, Albany: State University of New York Press, 1976.
Rama, Swami, Rudolph Ballentine, and Swami Ajaya. *Yoga and Psychotherapy: The Evolution of Consciousness.* PA: Himalayan International Press, 1976.
Russell, Edward. *Design for Destiny.* New York: Ballantine, 1976.
Shealy, Norman. *90 Days to Self Health.* Ohio: Ariel Press, 1976.
Green, Elmer and Alyce Green. *Beyond Biofeedback* New York: Delta Publ. 1978.
Motoyama, Hiroshi. *Science and the Evolution of Consciousness: Chakras, Ki, and Psi.* Brooklyn, MA: Random House, 1978.
Progoff, Ira. *At a Journal Workshop.* New York: Dialogue House, 1978.

Simonton, Carl, Stephanie Simonton and Craig Stevens. *Getting Well Again*. Los Angeles: Tarcher, 1978.
Cade, C. Maxwell. *The Awakened Mind: Biofeedback and the Development of Higher States of Awareness*. New York: Dell Publishing, 1979.
Moss, Thelma. *The Body Electric*. Los Angeles: Tarcher, 1979.
Zukov, Gary. *The Dancing Wu Li Masters*. New York: Morrow, 1979.
Bohm, David. *Wholeness and the Implicate Order*. London, England: Routledge and Kegan Paul, 1980.
Ferguson, Marilyn. *The Aquarian Conspiracy*. Los Angeles: Tarcher, 1980.
Grof, Stanislav. *LSD Psychotherapy*. Pomona, CA: Hunter House, 1980.
Progogine, Ilya. *From Being to Becoming: Time & Complexity in the Physical Sciences*. San Francisco: W.H. Freeman, 1980.
Ring, Kenneth. *Life at Death: A Scientific Investigation of the Near-Death Experience*. New York: Coward McCann, 1980.
Verney, Thomas. *The Secret Life of the Unborn Child*. New York: Delta, 1981.
Dossey, Larry. *Space, Time, & Medicine*. Boulder, CO: Shambleale Publ. 1982.
Griffiths, Fr. Bede. *The Marriage of East and West*. Springfield, Illinois: Templegate Publishers, 1982.
Sabom, Michael. *Recollections of Death*. New York: Simon and Schuster, 1982.
Russell, Peter. *The Global Brain*. Los Angeles: Tarcher, 1983.
Sheldrake, Rupert. *A New Science of Life: The Hypothesis of Formative Causation*. Los Angeles: Tarcher, 1983.
Grof, Stanislav. *Ancient Wisdom and Modern Science*. Albany: State University of New York Press, 1984.
Ring, Kenneth. *Heading Toward Omega*. New York: William Morrow, 1984.
Achterberg, Jeanne. *Imagery in Healing: Shamanism and Modern Medicine*. Boston: New Science Library, 1985.
Grof, Stanislav. *Beyond the Brain*. Albany: State University of New York Press, 1985.
Weber, Renee. *Dialogues with Scientists and Sages: The Search for Unity*. New York: Routledge and Kegan, 1986.
Klimo, Jon. *Channeling*. Los Angeles: Tarcher, 1987.
Gerber, Richard. *Vibrational Medicine*. Santa Fe, N.M.: Bear & Company, 1988.
Hawking, Stephen. *A Brief History of Time*. New York: Bantam Books, 1988.
Shealy, Norman and Caroline Myss. *The Creation of Health*. Walpole, N.H.: Stillpoint Publishing, 1988.
Sheldrake, Rupert. *The Presence of the Past: Morphic Resonance and the Habits of Nature*. London: Collins, 1988.
Chopra, Deepak. *Quantum Healing*. New York: Bantam Books, 1989.
Dossey, Larry. *Recovering the Soul: A Scientific and Spiritual Search*. New York: Bantam Books, 1989.
Snow, Chet. *Mass Dreams of the Future*. New York: McGraw Hill, 1989.
Dethlefsen, Thorwald. *The Healing Power of Illness*. (English Translation) Rockport, Maine: Element, Inc., 1991. (American Edition) (The original German edition was published in 1983. English translation is by Peter Leureourier.)
Abraham, Ralph; Terence McKenna; and Rupert Sheldrake. *Trialogues at the Edge of the West*. Santa Fe, New Mexico: Bear & Company Publishing, 1992.

# Index

Abandonment (see **Past-Life Experiences**)
Abortion (see also **Past-Life Experiences**) 18
Abuse (see **Past-Life Experiences**)
Abraham, Ralph 12. 594
Abreaction (see also **Therapy**) 21, 39, 40, 41, 103, 104, 108, 110, 113, 126, 148
Achterberg, Jeanne 32, 581, 594
Active imagination 218, 219
Acupuncture 576
Age regression (see **Induction, Past-Life Experiences**) 518
Affect bridge (see **Induction**)
Affirmations 32, 140, 489, 519
Agoraphobia (see **Symptoms**)
Albertson, Maurice 580
Alienation 348
Allergies (see **Symptoms**)
Allopathic healing 40
Altered states (see also **Induction**) 9, 11, 18, 30, 31, 35, 45, 47, 66, 67, 76, 132, 133, 141, 156-158, 161, 193, 454, 483, 489, 554, 580
Altered states, sensitivity or vulnerability during 132, 133, 151, 161, 163, 170, 411
Ancestral dramas 224
Anger (see **Past-Life Experiences, Symptoms, Therapy**, abreaction)
Anima/animus 36, 224
Anxiety (see **Past-Life Experiences, Symptoms**)
Aquarian Age 292
Archetypal models 31, 220, 289, 346
Architypal symbols 454
Armstrong, Thomas 18
Assagioli, Robert 142, 584, 587, 593
Association for Religion and Parapsychology 186
Association for Past-Life Research and Therapy/Therapies (APRT) 157, 186, 282, 321, 379, 423,
Association of Dutch Reincarnation Therapists 320

Assumptions, philosophical 158
Assumptions, psychotherapeutic **35-45**, 159, 190, 224, 253, 290, 335, 382, 407, 427, 428, 449, 488, 520
Astrology 30
Atonement 117, 235
Attachment, spirit (see also **Therapy**) 291, 298, 347, 587
Attitudinal matrix 158
Attitude of therapist 45, 61, 86-88, 100, 150, 151, 152, 161, 163, 191, 198, 291, 299, 350, 389, 407, 408, 427, 429, 436, 452, 489, 496
Aura analysis 343, 348
Autogenic training 588, 593
Automatic writing 30
Awakened Mind 68, 569, 572, 578, 594
Awakened Mind Institute 571

Bache, Christopher 22, 581, 592
Baldwin, William 580
Ballentine, Rudolph 593
Barrington, Ethel (see Beck, L. Adams) 579
Basic self 30
Beahrs, John O. 585
Beck, L. Adams 10, 480, 554, 579, 580, 589, 592
Behavior modification 138
Belief system, and effectiveness of therapy (see also Religious beliefs) 51, 61, 147
Benson, Herbert 566
Berne, Eric 586
Bernstein, Morey 579, 587, 591
Bhagavad Gita 216, 217
Biofeedback (see also Mind Mirror) 12, 13, 156, 582, 583, 589, 594
Biographical aspect 220, 335
Birth (see also **Past-Life Experiences**) 42, 63, 96, 242, 243, 345, 423, 445, 504, 519, 584
Birth release work 217, 428, 441
Blind spots 187, 188, 500

## 596  Index

Blocks (see **Past-Life Experiences,
  Symptoms, Therapy**)
Bloxham, Arnall  591
Blythe, Henry  591
Boadella, David  586
Body Self  581
Bohm, David  10, 38, 158, 159, 585, 594
Bonding  345
**Bontenbal, Rob**  29, 45, 50, 52, 57, 58, 83,
  84, 95, 96, 103, 110, 123, 132, 135, 142,
  **320-376**, 553-558, 587
Braid  65
*Brain Mind Bulletin*  580
Brainwave (see also **Induction**, Mind
  Mirror)  35, 67-70, 298, 299, 582
Breathing (see **Induction**)
Bridge (see **Induction**)
British Society for Psychical Research
  218
Brunton, Paul  5, 10, 578, 579, 589, 592
Buddhism  223, 236, 280, 481
Bund, Alexander  320
Burr, Harold Saxon  575, 576, 593

Cade, C. Maxwell  68, 565, 567-571, 577,
  582, 589, 594
Caetano, Trisha  328, 352
California School of Professional
  Psychology  481, 556
Cancer  32, 49, 208, 210
Capra, Fritjof  10, 593
Catathymic picture life  454
Catharsis (see also **Therapy**)  39, 143,
  224, 225
Cause and effect  27, 39, 95, 189, 336, 446,
  458
Cayce, Edgar  5, 237, 281, 283, 290, 305,
  378, 423, 517, 554, 567, 588, 589
Cerminara, Gina  15, 323, 378, 379, 588,
  589
Chakra analysis  343, 348
Chakras (see also **Induction, Therapy**)
  14, 34, 47, 72, 126, 133, 582
Chamberlain, David  18, 580
Channels  148
Chaplin, Anabel  20
Character postulate (basic belief
  structure)  38, 58, 335, 339, 345
Cheek, David  18, 581
Cheiro  587
Childhood (see also **Symptoms**)  42
Child trauma as continuation of a pattern
  or trigger of old feelings  189, 203
Children, regression of  53, 292, 321, 329,
  338, 354
Children, spontaneous past-life recall in
  176, 292
Chopra, Deepak  13, 31, 594
Christos Technique  7
Clairvoyant (see Psychics)
Cognitive restructuring (see also
  Therapy, reframing)  41, 44, 138
Collective unconscious  36, 125
Compulsions (see **Past-Life Experiences,
  Symptoms**)
**Contraindications**  9, 46, 51-53, 161, 191,
  192, 226-228, 253, 291, 337, 351, 383,
  408, 428, 451, 489, 522, 524, 582
Contradictory roles (see also **Past-Life
  Experiences**)  29
Control issues  45, 58, 147, 159, 164, 170,
  193, 295, 336, 349, 525
Core experience (see **Therapy**)
Core issues (see also **Induction**)  37, 38,
  82, 148, 214, 335, 345, 346
Core self  25, 30, 32, 433
Cosmic consciousness  21, 65
Cosmic waves  31, 288
Countertransference (see also **Therapy**)
  45, 151, 161, 170, 219, 291, 335, 353
Course in Miracles  581
Cousins, Norman  33, 581
Coxhead, Norma  582  589
Cranston, Sylvia  592
Crabtree, Adam  20, 581
Creighton, James  581
Cunningham, Janet  137, 591
*Cyclus*  321

Davis, Russell  17
Death (see also **Past-Life Experiences**)
  18, 19, 31, 224, 496, 581
Decision (see also **Past-Life Experiences**)
  521
Deepening techniques (see also
  **Induction**)  39, 86-104, 164, 166
Defense (see **Past-Life Experiences**)
**Denning, Hazel M.**  15, 17, 26, 28, 30, 41-
  43, 45, 49, 52, 57, 61, 72, 74, 78, 100,
  115, 116, 126, 127, 128, 129, 131, 133,
  136, 142, 148, 150, 152, **184-215**, 553-
  558, 580, 584, 585, 586
Dependency (see **Symptoms**)
Depossession  255
Depression (see **Symptoms**)
Desensitizing (see also **Therapy**,
  repetition)  458
Detachment (see **Therapy**)
**Dethlefsen, Thorwald**  xiii, 9, 22, 27, 29,
  31, 40-43, 50, 57, 59, 60, 67, 72, 80, 81,
  95, 102, 110, 115, 118, 138, 147, 148,
  352, **445-479**, 581, 584, 588, 590, 594
Developmental factors (see also **Past-
  Life Experiences**)  156, 160
Disharmony (see **Symptoms**)
Disidentification (see also **Therapy**)  36,
  114-125, 160
Disequilibrium (see also **Symptoms**)  158
Dissociation (see also **Symptoms**)  148,
  350
Dialoguing with the unborn (see also
  **Abortion**)  18

Dianetics 5, 6, 83
Disharmony (see **Symptoms**)
Disidentification (see **Therapy**)
DNA 31
Dossey, Larry 13, 594
Dreams (see **also Therapy**) 36, 65, 68, 70, 73, 139, 163, 224, 251, 254, 342, 370, 568, 578, 582, 583
Drugs 11
Dutch school 29, 38, 42, 61, 63, 83, 84, 103, 113, 320, 323, 340, 587

Eastern philosophy 10, 155, 156, 216, 481, 479
Eddington, Arthur 10, 592
Ego strength 146, 147
Einstein, Albert 10, 592, 593
Electromagnetic resonance 31
Elliptic consciousness 335, 341
Ellis, Havelock 10
Emotional (astral) body 222
Empathy of therapist 45
Enantiodromia 223
Energy fields 31, 129, 134, 221, 298, 488, 489, 496, 497, 538, 576
Energy reading 294
Entities 147, 223, 260, 581, 587
Entrainment (see also **Therapy**)
  brainwave 69, 298, 299
Erickson, Milton 352
Eriksonian hypnosis 73, 217, 230
Etheric body 31-33, 40, 222
Existential aspect 220
Expectations 148, 170, 260, 500
Explicate order 38, 159
European Congress of Hypnosis in Psychotherapy and Psychosomatic Medicine 186

Fagan, Joel 586
**Failures 146-152**, 169, 170, 197, 237, 260, 306, 351, 353, 390, 413, 435, 460, 499, 531, 584
Farrelly, Frank 352
Fear (see **Past-Life Experiences, Symptoms**)
Ferguson, Marilyn 14, 594
**Findeisen, Barbara** 15, 26, 29, 30, 38, 41, 42, 45, 48, 49, 57, 63, 72, 77, 96, 97, 122, 124, 135, 136, 137, 149, 152, 422-444, 484, 553-558, 583, 584, 588
**Fiore, Edith** 8, 15, 20, 28, 39, 41, 44, 47, 48, 52, 57, 61-63, 71, 74, 77, 89, 93, 101, 103, 111, 112, 118, 130, 138-140, 142, 147, 148, 151, **249-279**, 423, 485, 553, 554-558, 582-584, 587, 590
Fisher, Joe 19
Forgiveness (see also **Therapy**) 137, 291, 496
Fox, Jonathan 586
Frequencies, energy 42

Freud, Sigmund 3, 4, 46, 68, 216, 227, 249, 290, 335, 423, 498
Future projections 8, 19, 29, 282, 587, 594

Gabriel, Michael 18
Gackenbach, Jayne 582
Garfield, Patricia 68, 582
Genetic predispositions 31
Gerber, Richard 13, 34, 594
Gilligan, Stephen G. 585
Givens, Alice 18
Glaskin, G.M. 7, 591
Goals, establishment of 149, 340, 353, 524
Govinda, Lama Anagarika 593
Grant, Joan 6, 7, 590, 591
Green, Elmer and Alyce 12, 13, 32, 583, 589, 593
Grinder 171
Grof, Stanislav 4, 11, 18, 217, 220, 224, 282, 290, 504, 579, 585, 586, 587, 593, 594
Group induction 559-564
Group reincarnation 137, 195, 498, 586, 591
Gurdjieff 216, 554
Guides (see also **Therapy**) 30, 121, 130, 131, 140, 149, 168, 196, 248, 249, 268, 296, 304, 314, 322, 524, 544
Guilt (see also **Past-Life Experiences, Symptoms, Therapy**) 41, 42, 118, 148, 191, 203, 215, 253, 389, 458, 460, 583, 586
Guirdham, Arthur 137, 218, 219, 591

Handicaps 208, 209
Hatha yoga 33
Hauntings 348
Hawking, Stephen 594
Head, Joseph 592
Healing 13, 14, 17, 32, 34, 65, 110, 197, 436, 446, 453, 457, 459, 497, 538, 569, 578, 583, 589, 594
  role of patient-therapist relationship in (see also Attitude of therapist) 45, 453
Health, attitudes toward 12
Heard, Gerald 403, 554, 558, 588
Heisenberg, W. 593
Heraclitus 223
Hesse, Hermann 10, 481, 580, 592, 593
**Hickman, Irene** 17, 20, 28, 30, 39, 44, 50, 57, 62, 71, 76, 81, 91, 100, 103, 112, 113, 139, 151, **377-402**, 553-558, 583, 588, 590
Higher Self (see also **Therapy**) 140, 164, 433, 584
Hillman, James 586
Hindu philosophy 155, 217, 220
Hippocampus 65

## 598 Index

Hoffman, Enid 581
Hoffman, Robert 424, 519
Holographic theory (hologram) 16, 17, 19, 158, 321, 335, 340, 345, 346, 348, 584, 587
Holotropic breathing 291
Holotropic theory 290
Holotropic view of life 36, 158, 160
Homeostasis, homeostatic balance 158
Horowitz, Mardi J. 585
Houston, Jean 11
Howes, Elizabeth 588
Hubbard, L. Ron 6, 590
Humility 459
Hunt, Valerie 33, 298, 581
Hutschneker, Arnold, 586
Huxley, Aldous 11, 216, 403, 554, 588, 592, 593
Hypersentience 7, 8, 590
Hypnosis/hypnotherapy (see also **Induction**) 139, 156, 250, 379, 383, 384, 403, 445, 554, 572, 581, 585
Hypotheses (see also Holographic theory, Karma, Soul) **25-34**, 157, 158, 188, 219, 252, 287, 334, 381, 427, 446, 453, 488, 519, 520, 581, 588, 591

I Ching 30
Identification (see also **Therapy**) 36, 160, 291
Imagery (see also **Induction, Therapy**) 47, 65, 66, 594
Implicate order 38, 158, 159
Imprinting 31, 143, 224, 225, 236, 429, 432, 435, 441, 489, 520, 581
**Indications** 161, 191, 226, 253, 291, 337, 383, 408, 428, 451, 489, 522, 582
**INDUCTION 65-85**, 147, 161, 163, 192, 193, 229, 254, 293, 339, 343, 384-387, 409-411, 429-431, 452, 490-493, 523-528, 559-564, 580, 582
affect bridge 63, 279, 300
age regression 6, 8, 80-82,, 456
altered state 9, 65, 72, 75, 76, 295, 341, 454, 489, 491, 505, 538, 580
arousal 72
auditing 5
blocks, using to achieve induction 352
body awareness 73, 163, 164, 179, 229, 231, 246, 385
brainwave frequencies 65, 67
breathing 4, 66, 71-73, 164, 193, 229, 231, 255, 296, 298, 385-387, 430, 490, 491, 502, 503, 505, 538
bridge, emotional-physical affect 6, 8, 58, 66, 82-85, 335, 538
bridge, holographic 340
bridge (MES) 336, 341, 345
catathymic picture life 454
chaining 344
chakras 72, 133, 193, 194, 196, 294, 296, 298, 300, 310
daydreaming 454
Christos technique 7
deepening techniques 39, 66, 86-104, 166, 194, 232, 257, 302, 345, 386-388, 411, 430, 431, 494, 502, 527
depossession 255
directiveness 297
dream 178
emotional charge 66
emotional entrance 297
energy of therapist 76
Ericksonian approach 73, 229
fear of 62, 261
feelings 179, 431, 455
Garden 491
golden core 491, 505
guided imagery 63, 229
guides 525, 526
holographic bridge 340
Hypersentience 7, 8
hypnosis 3, 5, 6, 9, 20, 52, 62, 65-67, 71-73, 193, 229, 254, 295, 384, 410, 453, 491, 525
imaging 7, 63, 66, 71-78, 164, 256, 297, 410, 430
light 66, 67, 71, 73, 164, 196, 255, 298, 300, 490, 491, 494, 502, 505, 525
massage 7, 242
mental-emotional-somatic (MES) bridge 336, 374
mental entrance 342
mental shift 72, 297
peeling down 344
permissiveness 71, 297, 384
preparation for 57-64, 162, 163, 192, 229, 254, 292, 339, 384, 409, 452, 490, 523, 524
rapport 61, 292, 302, 429, 523
rebirthing 7
relaxation 63, 67, 71-73, 163, 193, 229, 296, 341, 384, 385, 430, 454, 525, 559
resistance to 59, 60, 297, 299, 386
return from 132, 133, 150, 196, 298, 526, 564
scrying 21
stillness, body 72, 297
symbol drama 454, 455
tone of voice 76
touch 62, 76, 384, 387, 544
transpersonal 526
transcendental 164
turning memory backwards 5
unconditional acceptance 71
verbalization 343, 344, 431
visualization 67, 71-73, 454
Inner children (see **Therapy**)
Inner Mind 30, 41, 67, 121, 164, 168, 513, 515, 522
Inner self 41
Insight (see **Therapy**)

**Index** 599

Insomnia (see **Symptoms**)
**Integration** (see also **Therapy**) **134-145**
Integrative Therapy Process 519
Intensive Journal Process 140, 420
Interlife (see also **Therapy**) 581, 583
International Conference on Alternative
  Therapies 186, 282
Intervention (see also **Therapy**) 44, 45,
  **107-133**, 242, 433, 583
Intrauterine memories 63, 518
Introversive capacity 47, 52
Intuition 352, 440
  role of in therapy 62, 150, 156, 162, 169
IPPANA 424
Iverson, Jeffrey 591

Jacob, Lindsey, Dr. xii
Jacobsen, Edmund 73, 583
James, William 593
Jampolski, Gerald 33
Jeans, James 10, 593
Johnstone, Judith 590
Journal writing (see **Therapy**)
*Journal of Regression Therapy* 580, 582-585, 587
Journey of the soul (see Soul, journey of)
**Jue, Ronald Wong** 14, 15, 16, 26, 28, 30, 36, 38, 41, 43, 45, 51, 57, 59-61, 73, 74, 79, 87, 89, 91, 92, 102, 108, 114, 119, 121, 129, 130, 143, 146, 147, 151, 152, **155-183**, 555-558, 584
Jung, Carl 4, 29, 46, 117, 139, 144, 217-220, 223, 224, 226, 235, 290, 335, 420, 423, 480, 586
  "Active imagination" 4, 219

Kahuna 30, 581
Kamiya, Joe 566, 567, 589
Kaplan, Abraham 69
Karma (see also **Past-Life Experiences, Therapy**) 26, 27, 28, 60, 61, 115, 128, 137, 221, 223, 224, 252, 295, 448, 557, 581
Karmic core 115
Karmic event 118, 253, 258
Karmic guilt 118, 446, 458, 462
Karmic homeostasis 26, 158
Karmic patterns 115, 116, 128, 137, 285, 316, 391, 425, 426, 541
Karmic reaction 137, 434
Karmic residue 40
Karmic thread 495
Katha Upanishads 155, 554
Keeton, Joe 591
Kelley, Georgia 491, 589
Kelsey, Denys 6, 7, 590
Kempis, Thomas à Kempis 216, 554
Khan, Pir Vilayat 580
Kirlian photography 570, 577
Klimo, Jon 594
Klopfer, Bruno 481

Koestler, Arthur 554
Kübler-Ross, Elisabeth 19, 593

LaBerge, Steven 68
Langs, Robert 585
Layard, John 217
Lee, Leona 589
L'Engle, Madeleine 10, 11, 593
Lenz, Frederick 20, 581, 591
Le Shan, Lawrence 12, 13, 593
Leuner, H. 454, 588
Leuner symbol drama 72
Levine, Jason 15
Life review (scanning) 37
Light (see **Induction, Therapy**)
Limitations of past-life therapy 146-149
Linear model 28, 31, 33, 158, 235
Long, Max Freedom 581
Love 33, 134, 149, 164, 289, 407, 489, 496, 509, 520, 541
LSD 66, 481, 483
**Lucas, Winafred Blake** xii, 57, 66, 68, 69, 75, 78, 85, 92, 94, 122, 124, 130, 132, 136, 299, **480-516**, 553-558, 565, 571, 580, 589
Luria 570
Luthe, Wolfgang 588, 593

MacLaine, Shirley 60, 146, 582
Maslow, Abraham 107, 404, 407, 555, 558, 588
Massage 249, 291
Mahayana Buddhism 223
McFadden, Bernard 12
McGarey, Gladys 18
McKenna, Terence 12, 594
McKenzie, John G. 586
Meditation 20, 65, 68, 73, 118, 140, 143, 144, 155, 156, 216, 219, 226, 236, 243, 453, 482, 491, 554, 566, 569, 586
Mental retardation 254
Metaphorical significance 159, 225, 290, 408
Metaphysical influence 553
Midlife crisis and Jungian analysis 46
Miller, Alice 18
Mind-body-spirit connection 159, 185
Mind field 31, 70, 488
Mind Mirror 17, 68-70, 73, 74, **565-578**, 580
Mintz, Elizabeth E. 585
Mishlove, Jeffrey 593
Monroe, Robert 282
Moody, Raymond 19, 21, 590, 593
Moore, Marcia 7, 590
Moreno 143, 236
Morgan, Charles 10, 592
Morphic resonance 158
Morphogenic fields 4, 576, 579
Morphogenic resonance 7, 288
Morris, Freda 282

## 600 Index

Morrison, Peter 571-573
Moss, Peter 591
Moss Thelma 576, 577, 589, 594
Motivational factors 159, 207
Motoyama, Hiroshi 13, 14, 34, 576, 582, 593
Myss, Carolyn 13, 47, 582, 594

Near-death experience 19, 21, 37, 132, 237
Netherton, Morris 6, 8, 9, 15, 82, 83, 217, 230, 321, 323, 325, 352, 423, 590
Nixon, Lucille 423, 588
Noetics 160
Noetic Science Institute 186
Non-alignment 158
**Noordegraaf, Tineke** 29, 45, 50, 52, 53, 57, 58, 83, 85, 99, 101, 110, 111, 123, 132, 135, 142, 149, **320-376**, 554-558, 587
North American Conference in Pre- and Peri-Natal Psychology 423
Nurturing (see **Induction**)

Oppenheim, Garrett 17, 590
Opposites 29, 60, 118, 163, 223, 225, 295
Orr, L. 579

Pain (see **Symptoms**)
Paradigm shift 10-12, 14, 22, 33, 380, 592
Paranormal abilities 65
Paranormal aspects to a problem 160
Paranormal perceptions 65
Paranormal phenomena, research of 12
Parapsychology Association of Riverside 185
Parents, reaction to 42, 260
PAST-LIFE EXPERIENCES (see also **Symptoms**) 159
   abandonment 91, 117, 166, 172, 180, 212, 226, 227, 312, 421
   abilities 452
   abortion 431, 461
   abuse 4, 18, 162, 200, 227
   accidents 50, 451
   addictions 138
   age regression, past-life material retrieved during 66, 157, 250, 251, 456, 519
   affluence 501
   aggression 29
   alienation 347
   aloneness 171
   anger 48, 110, 148, 347, 364, 379, 380, 500, 515
   anxiety 177, 415
   arrogance 209, 327
   Atlantis 283, 330, 526, 546
   battlefield experiences 227
   beheading 117, 243, 483
   betrayal 119, 174, 227

birth memories 4, 18, 37, 96, 242, 456
bitterness 221
blocks 148, 284, 347
body feelings 39, 90
bomb explosion 239, 358
burning 465
charged material 100
choking 243
choices 228, 274
conflict 166
core issue 81
cowardice 127
crucifixion 117, 249
cruelty 117
**death** (see also suicide) 32, 37, 41, 42, 50, **94-103**, 109, 117, 123, **129-133**, 147, 148, 173, 175, 178, 181, 187-189, 196, 200, 201, 203, 204, 206, 210, 226, 227, 233, 239, 242, 244, 246, 249, 253, 258, 268, 275, 285, 297, 401, 404, 415, 417, 419, 425, 438, 440, 449, 451, 473, 475, 485, 486, 489, 496, 500, 507, 510, 513, 519, 534, 542
decisions 42, 166-168, 201, 206, 276, 277, 317, 324, 326, 331, 333, 347, 350, 360, 374, 432, 433
despair 227
deformity of body 475
deformity of etheric system 44
denunciations 228
deportation 227
depression 372
developmental factors 156
disappointment 326
drowning 401
drug use 415
drudging 347
drowning 115, 458
economic collapse 227
eliciting of 89-93
enabling 347
emotional charge 39, 382, 450
emotional complexes 31
energy fields, generation of
engram (original traumatic situation) 6
evaluations 42
executions 225, 228
fabrication of 163
failure 148, 308
falling 270-273, 284
famine 226, 227, 261
fear 108, 347, 542
feelings from 41
gassing 236
fire 393, 425, 506, 512, 542
greed 117
grief 221, 227, 325
guilt 90, 137, 243, 326, 332, 370, 451, 532, 534, 537, 539, 542, 545
hanging 243
hangovers (dirtskirts) 347

## Index 601

PAST-LIFE EXPERIENCES (Continued)
  harming others 127, 434
  humility 29, 364
  hunger 52, 139, 262, 472
  illnesses 50, 451
  imprisonment 347
  imprinting during stress 42, 44, 130
  inadequacy 149
  injury, violent 40, 227, 497
  injustice 49, 51
  intra-uterine memories 63, 80
  isolation 173, 494, 500, 534
  killing of others 227, 237
  kingdoms, different 346
  Lemuria 526
  loneliness 496
  loss 180, 221, 227, 325, 415, 431, 501, 540
  martyrdom 117
  massacre 219, 227, 267
  mistakes 383
  misunderstood motivations 121, 128, 204
  molestation 253
  murder 110, 117, 136, 211, 253, 318, 326, 327, 332, 462, 533, 534
  omission, sins of 127, 531
  oppression 226
  pain 221
  patterns 28, 29, 31, 41, 42, 60, 144, 158, 160, 197, 203, 543
  perpetrator 434
  poisoning 325, 333
  polar lives 347
  poverty 29, 227, 498, 514
  power, abuse of 51, 52, 117, 227, 498, 534
  power, relinquishment of 178, 278
  power urges 138, 148, 227, 459, 460
  perinatal experiences 29, 159
  physical injury 31, 187, 243, 508
  prenatal events 8, 156
  pride 117, 118, 284, 535, 536
  primal trauma 458
  programs, establishment of 44
  rage 188, 227
  rape 103, 226, 227, 252, 370, 375, 504
  rejection 91, 431
  responsibility for deaths 227, 242, 326, 425, 444, 461, 533, 541
  rivalry 51, 227
  sadism 117, 510
  seizures 251
  self-judgment 38, 347, 365, 412
  sexual torture 227
  shock 347
  skinning alive 425
  slavery 226, 347
  source lifetime 199
  stabbing 243
  starvation 139, 262
  strangling 243
  stuck 60, 161
  suffering 148
  suicide 96, 100, 113, 213, 227, 242, 374, 391, 395, 406
  tiredness 347
  torture 50, 226, 227, 332, 451, 467
  touch 101
  talents 452
  trauma 38, 39, 86, 118, 127, 148, 253, 290, 279, 336, 347, 414, 455, 461, 519, 537
  uterine 431, 432
  victimization 29, 137, 347, 351, 383, 434
  violence 52, 148, 226, 232, 306
  war 52, 227, 244, 358, 405, 406
Patanjali 586
Patterns (see also **Past-Life Experiences, Symptoms**) 34, 37, 38, 40, 46, 48-50, 64, 114, 115, 118, 119, 141, 144, 159, 161, 295, 336, 427, 458, 485, 498, 519, 520, 524, 583
Pecci, Ernest 15, 25-27, 30, 37, 41-43, 46, 47, 51, 52, 57-59, 64, 71, 75, 76, 78, 95, 99, 100, 114, 121, 124, 125, 127, 128, 131, 140, 141, 149, 150, 152, 424, **517-549**, 553-558, 582, 584, 588, 589
Pendulum 30
Pendulum pattern 336
Perl, Fritz 143, 236
Perinatal period 29, 42, 220, 321, 327, 335, 336, 339, 376, 423
Persistence, role of 47
Personifications 220, 224
**Philosophical hypotheses** 157, 188, 219, 252, 287, 334, 381, 407, 427, 446, 488, 520, 581
Philosophy of life 59, 61, 192
Phobias (see **Symptoms**)
Physical ailments (see **Symptoms**)
Physical reactions 31
Physical and energy fields 30, 34
Planck, Max 10, 288, 586, 593
Pocket Ranch 424, 437
Polar incident 347, 349
Polarity (see also **Therapy**) 29, 41, 42, 50, 60, 117, 118, 152, 322, 325, 334, 336, 337, 446, 447, 451, 459
Post-Traumatic Stress Disorder (PTSD) 17, 580
Possession 253, 291, 298
Power (see also **Past-Life Experiences**) 459
Power animal 30
Powers, Melvin 379
Prejudice 426
Prenatal period 18, 42, 96, 156, 159, 321, 327, 335, 336, 339, 376, 423, 424, 431, 432, 445, 470, 519, 580
**Preparation** (see also **Induction**) **57-64**
Presenting problems (see **Symptoms**)

Pribram, Karl 29, 42, 158, 340, 427, 585, 587, 588, 593
Primal therapy 291, 423
Primary issues 159
Procrastination (see **Symptoms**)
Progoff, Ira 140, 584, 593
Progogine, Ilya 594
Projection 220, 336, 404, 524
  from therapist 45
Protection 132, 133
Psychedelic experiences 11
Psychic Determinism 3
Psychics 15, 30, 46, 51, 52, 148, 435, 452, 554, 585
Psychoanalysis 35, 389
Psychodrama 143, 230, 236, 249, 423, 586
Psycho-somatic medicine 9
Psychosomatic embodiment of trauma 40
Psychosynthesis 141, 496, 593
**Psychotherapeutic and Transformal Techniques 107-133**, 167, 195, 258, 304, 348, 388, 412, 433, 457, 495, 529, 583
**Psychotherapeutic assumptions 35-45**, 159, 190, 224, 253, 290, 335, 382, 407, 427, 449, 488, 520
Psychotherapy, definition of purpose 35, 190, 451

Quantum Self 31
Quantum substrate 32

Radix process 148, 500
Rage (see **Past-Life Experiences, Symptoms**)
Ramacharaka 12, 298, 580, 587
Rama, Swami 70, 566, 570, 583, 593
Rank, Otto 4
Rape (see **Past-Life Experiences**)
Rapport (see also **Induction**) 139
Rebirthing (see also **Induction, Therapy**) 217
Reframing (see also **Therapy**) 41, 47, 119, 538, 582, 584
Reich, Wilhelm 5, 143, 236, 586
Reichenbach, H. 593
Reichian therapy 241, 423
Reik, Theodore 586
Rejection (see **Past-Life Experiences**)
Releasement, spirit (see **Therapy**)
Religious beliefs 60, 147, 155, 184, 192, 198, 209, 216, 249, 280, 295, 351, 389, 422, 429, 435, 460, 489, 517, 588
Reluctance to change (see also Resistance) 32, 149, 170, 171, 261, 353, 436
Renovation (see also **Therapy**, rescripting) 349, 366
Repetition compulsion 498
Repression, danger of 433
Repulsion toward others 160, 169
Rescripting (see **Therapy**)

Research 16, 44, 65, 68, 70, 137, 405, 445, 568, 580, 586, 592
Resistance (see **Induction, Therapy**)
Responsibility, personal (see also **Therapy**, responsibility for one's life) 447
**Reynolds, Edward** 26, 45, 49, 52, 57, 61, 75, 88, 97-100, 107, 108, 113, 115, 150, **403, 421**, 486, 553, 558, 583, 587
Rieder, Marge 586, 591
Ring, Kenneth 10, 37, 594
Rogers, Carl 33, 107, 407, 408, 412, 585
Role reversals 116, 117, 136
Rolfing 217
Rosebridge Graduate School of Integrative Psychology 519, 556
Rosecrucian writings 517
Russell, Bertrand 216, 554
Russell, Edward R. 576, 593
Russell, Peter 10, 594
Ryall, Edward 591

Sabom, Michael 594
Samskaras (psychic residues) (see also **Symptoms**) 28, 114, 220, 223, 238
Schlotterbeck, Karl 20, 590
Schultz, Johannes 588, 593
Schwartz, Berthold Eric 585
Scientology 6
Scrying 21, 581
Self-esteem 43
Senzaki 481
Sexual problems (see **Past-Life Experiences, Symptoms**)
Shadow (see also **Therapy**) 36, 41, 117, 138, 150, 152, 223, 224, 458, 484
Shadowing 497, 498
Shaman, therapist as 434
Shamanism 157, 346
Shealy, Norman xii, 13, 47, 582, 584, 594
Sheldrake, Rupert 4, 7, 10, 12, 31, 70, 158, 288, 576, 579, 581, 585, 587, 589, 594
Shepherd, I.A. 586
Shiffrin, Nancy 590
Siegel, Bernie 13
Silva Jose 282
Simonton, Carl and Stephanie 13, 32, 581, 594
Sleep research 70
**Snow, Chet** xiii, xiv, 8, 14, 16, 17, 19, 26, 28, 29, 31-34, 37, 38, 43, 45, 49, 57, 58, 60, 61, 63, 68, 69, 72, 74, 77, 87, 90, 99, 102, 113, 122, 123, 125, 133, 134, 139, 148, 150, **280-319**, 553-558, 565, 566, 571, 585, 587, 594
Somatic level 223, 341
Somatizations 220
Soul, journey of 21, 22, 25, 27, 33, 34, 160, 218, 446, 482
Spirit guides 47, 117, 141

## Index

Spiritual growth 28, 33, 51, 159, 160, 167, 168, 523
Spiritual search 46
Spiritual self 43
Spontaneous past-life recall 176, 177, 185, 329, 342, 417, 432, 442, 591
STAR process (Self-Analysis Toward Awareness Rebirth) 424
Stauffer, Edith 582, 589
Stearn, Jess 591
Steiger, Brad 591
Stevenson, Ian 5, 16, 579, 592
Steward, A.J. 591
Stress (see **Symptoms, Therapy**)
Sub-personality (see **Therapy**)
Subtle body 44, 576
Sufis 325, 566, 580
Suggestibility and therapist responsibility 87
Sugrue, Thomas (see also Cayce, Edgar) 588
Superconscious 382, 522
Supportive and deepening techniques (see also **Induction**, deepening) 86-104, 583
Survival fear 41, 522
Sutphen, Dick 323
Suzuki, Shunryu 593
Symbolic exploration 37, 38, 159, 225, 290
SYMPTOMS (see also **Past-Life Experiences**) 42, 47, **48**, 95, 110, 159, 161, 337, 342, 445, 447, 450, 451, 457, 459, 460, 478, 521
  accidents 227
  aches 228
  acrophobia 101, 130, 270, 285, 586
  acting out 220
  addictions 97, 265, 292, 338, 416, 489
  agoraphobia 100, 404, 414
  aggression 29
  allergies 48, 91, 191, 262, 367, 383, 395, 396, 401, 428, 440, 441
  anger 48, 49, 115, 116, 125, 126, 130, 152, 199, 212, 420, 498, 504, 505, 511, 532, 584
  anomie 292
  anxiety 48, 170, 178, 227, 261, 309, 366, 414, 428, 430, 451, 481, 495, 502
  arthritis 191, 238
  asthma 262, 428
  attitude toward others 115-117, 178, 179, 199, 242, 292, 316, 383, 393, 394, 420, 511
  attraction 115, 169, 199, 316, 383, 394
  autism 428
  aversions 253
  backache 225
  behavior problems 227
  birth problems 48
  blocks 51, 142, 226, 292, 294, 333, 443, 489, 522
  breathing, shallow 241
  breakdowns, psychospiritual 49
  brutality 227
  cause, removal of 388, 389
  chain of 458, 459
  chest pains 243
  circulation, poor 248
  colitis, ulcerative 243
  compulsions 48, 292, 395, 428, 489
  conflicts 59
  criminal behavior 428
  depression 49, 178, 227, 241, 261, 353, 391, 428, 460
  despair 179
  disequilibrium 158
  disharmony 26, 158
  distress, early childhood 18
  dreams 177, 220, 534, 536
  dysfunctions 49
  eating disorders 227
  emotional charge 39, 253
  entanglements, emotional 28
  exhibitionism 436
  family struggles 51, 178, 179, 199, 202, 227, 420, 511
  fatigue 533
  fear 41, 48, 49, 84, 85, 102, 115, 170, 188, 227, 253, 270, 326, 327, 357, 418, 428, 432, 438, 458, 460, 468, 519, 532, 537
  frigidity 227, 292
  genital infections 227
  grief, excessive 49, 292
  guilt 42, 48, 49, 52, 170, 178, 188, 190, 201, 203, 227, 228, 383, 434, 442, 444, 459, 498, 531, 532
  headaches 48, 191, 225, 243, 253, 261, 274, 292, 383, 438, 441
  heart pains 437
  hopelessness 49, 292
  humility 29
  hypochondria 392
  imbalances 47
  impotence 227
  inappropriate feelings 136, 202, 316
  indecision 93, 130, 207, 273
  infertility 48, 351, 428
  insomnia 110, 130, 253, 266, 587
  irrational behavior 49
  lack of self-worth 292
  lupus erythematosus 239
  menstrual problems 253
  martyr complexes 227
  mental problems 48, 253
  minimal brain disorder (MBD) 355
  miscarriage, chronic 48, 428
  neuroses 190, 197, 220, 227, 428, 446, 450
  obesity 66, 93, 112, 130, 138, 159, 262, 391, 587

## 604 Index

SYMPTOMS (Continued)
obsessions 130, 177
overeating 139, 169, 292
pain 26, 158, 189, 190, 220, 253, 439
panic attacks 383
parental complexes 50, 125, 169, 226, 260, 530
patterns 28, 31, 38, 42, 49, 159, 273, 489, 521
personality clashes 49, 197
personalization of 440
phobias 44, 48, 50, 130, 226, 227, 253, 270, 292, 297, 383, 395, 428, 458, 468, 471, 489, 495, 519
physical ailments 44, 48, 49, 95, 117, 130, 135, 186, 191, 197, 208, 210, 220, 227, 253, 437, 440, 465, 468, 489, 533, 538
poverty 29
powerlessness 235
pregnancy problems 48
procrastination 307, 326
psoriasis 210
psychosis 228, 254, 292, 337, 383, 409, 428, 429
rage 49, 116, 188, 199, 210
rejection 179
relationship problems 49, 119, 199, 202, 208, 227, 351, 418, 428, 489, 505
reluctance to give up symptoms 149, 170, 171, 261, 353, 435-438
repulsions 383
resentment 393
samskaras (psychic residues) 28, 238
self-punishment 190
self-recrimination 128, 434, 541, 546
self-worth perceptions 49
sexual problems 220, 226, 227, 253, 292, 339, 503
shame 170
spiritual problems 48, 253
stage fright 117, 245
stress 49
stuck, feelings of being 52, 148, 149, 198, 226, 237, 530
suicide attempt 185, 428
tardiness, chronic 292
traumas 339, 414, 495
tremors 355
unassertiveness 142
victimization 29, 142, 148, 170, 498
violence 227, 428
weakness 253

Talbot, Michael 585
Tantrism 223
Tarot cards 334
ten Dam, Hans 6, 9, 16, 83, 320, 323, 324, 329, 343, 347, 592
Theory (see also **Philosophical hypotheses, Therapeutic assumptions**)

23-53
Theosophy 237, 480, 554
Therapeutic assumptions (see Psychotherapeutic assumptions)
Therapeutic touch 222
Therapist-client relationship 45
Therapist, emotional and spiritual well-being of 45
THERAPY 107-133
abreaction 21, 39, 40, 103, 104, 108, 110, 113, 126, 148, 152, 195
affirmations 76, 140, 141, 504, 542
altered state, therapist's entry into 45, 69, 177, 434, 489, 492, 502
anger 126, 196, 225, 269, 348, 361, 497
assertiveness 350
attachment, spirit 20
attitude of therapist 87, 88, 163
balance 337
behavior modification 138
birth memories 63, 423, 429, 431, 435, 439, 441, 442, 469, 475
body feelings 39, 109, 114, 234, 238
blocks 32, 92, 163, 233, 257, 261, 306, 337, 348, 351, 524
boundaries 353
breathing 101, 103, 109, 236, 244, 347, 348, 358, 367, 371, 442, 503
catharsis 171, 235, 244, 246, 249, 350, 376, 408, 419
chakras 537
choices 383
closure 350, 351, 361, 412, 493, 495
core experience 188
core issue 38, 110
core problem 458
Counselor Part 43, 130, 291, 296, 304, 307
countertransference 161, 170, 353
counting 101
decision-making 433
deepening 86-106
defenses 62, 236
dependency 142, 151
desensitization 112, 458
detachment 98, 99, 235, 249, 414
dialoguing with the unborn 18
discharge of energy 39
discomfort 383
disidentification 40, 42, 113-125, 160, 167, 168, 530
dissociated recall 110, 236, 348, 350
dissociation 247
dreams 62, 63, 139, 177, 236, 259, 296, 305
eliciting of material 88-93
emotional charge 39, 389, 457
energy connection with client 183, 496
entering points 48
entrainment 69
equilibrium 158

**THERAPY (Continued)**
evaluation 435
fantasy 386, 442, 450
feedback 305
finger signals 62, 93, 255, 257, 303, 310, 387
focal memory 48
forgiveness 37, 42, 43, 125, 127, 128, 131, 137, 138, 168, 214, 253, 258, 304, 434, 496, 497, 508, 524, 531, 532, 537
Greater Self 236
guides 248, 249, 544
guilt, dissolving of 42, 43, 126-128, 258, 434, 458, 459, 511, 532, 536, 537, 549, 585
higher guidance 63, 100, 296
Higher Mind 174
Higher Self 30, 43, 121, 123, 130, 131, 144, 166, 196, 213, 291, 296, 304, 307, 308, 348, 529
honesty 52
identification 36, 37, 86, 108, 160, 167
imaging 69, 261, 387, 494
Inner Children 142, 345, 349
Inner Teacher 549
insight 30, 37, 41, 57, 102, 135, 159, 197, 269, 305, 392, 524
integration 37, 59, 110, 129, 132, **134-145**, 158, 159, 168, 170, 178, 179, 197, 220, 236, 259, 292, 305, 336, 350, 383, 389, 390, 413, 434, 459, 477, 479, 498, 530, 537, 543
interlife 19, 21, 132, 473, 476
intervention 100, **107-133**, 242, 433, 495, 504, 583
intuition 303, 440
isomorphic characters/events 168
journal writing 139-141, 259, 535, 543
life review 304
light 75, 76, 494
MES processing 245, 350
metaphorical exploration 37, 38, 40, 413
movement through time 94-97
observer position 99, 273, 298, 414
opening wedge 48
pacing 151, 170, 176, 194, 233, 352, 387, 495
pain 36, 76, 168, 209, 225
patterns 21, 27-29, 37, 38, 40, 43, 48, 49, 51, 114, 135, 136, 139, 144, 151, 152, 160, 167, 169, 171, 197, 198, 238, 305, 315, 392, 498, 500, 504, 530, 549
peace and harmony 43, 520, 521
personalization of symptoms 440
polarity 29, 42, 130, 152, 249, 351, 376, 434
possession 291
power 459
prenatal/perinatal memories 432, 433, 457, 468

preparation for 57
processing 167, 258, 304, 388, 436, 457, 529
psychosynthesis 496, 500, 583
rapport 100, 306
rebirthing 7, 241
reframing 37, 39, 41, 48, 102, 113, 119, 121, 128, 130, 138, 168, 171, 176, 177, 178, 183, 434, 505, 541, 544, 584
relationships 135, 136
releasement, spirit 20
reluctance to change 149, 435, 501
renovation (see rescripting) 122-124, 349, 366
repetition 101, 103, 388, 391, 397, 400
rescripting 122, 123, 307, 366, 433, 434, 584
resistance 52, 60, 93, 135, 159, 232, 299, 388, 435, 436, 450, 457, 524, 533
resolution 160
responsibility for one's life 149, 170, 189, 190, 192, 196, 198, 260, 291, 292, 335, 383, 429, 446, 459, 498,
return from a altered state 132, 133
screaming 100
script 166, 168, 169, 432
shadow 29, 43, 142, 152, 235, 434, 458, 459
shock 348
soul 144, 145
spiritual transformation 43
stress 86, **97-104**
sub-personality 29, 126, 142, 143, 160, 228, 235, 249, 346, 349, 488, 501
supportiveness of therapist 87, 100, 302
symbolic exploration 37, 235
techniques 167, 195, 233, 258, 304
touch 101, 194, 502
transference 101, 161, 353
transference cure 149
transformation 39, 42, 43, 48, 129, **134-145**, 152, 160, 168, 304, 313, 349, 432, 451, 485, 495, 496, 509, 537, 555
trauma 76, 450
venting of energy 39
wholeness 158
wisdom, sources of 21, 26, 30, 63, 112, 121, 160, 291, 381, 382, 385, 387-389, 393, 394
witness point 30, 40, 114, 129, 160, 223, 236, 248, 249
Tiller, William 576
Time management 150
Touch (see **Induction**)
Training of therapists 15, 16, 149, 150, 151
Trance (see Altered states)
Transactional Analysis 220, 273
Transcendence 30, 160, 249, 555
Transcendental Meditation 566, 569
Transcendentalism 422, 554

Transference (see also **Induction, Therapy**) 45, 101, 150, 161, 291, 335, 353, 524
Transference cure 149
Transformation (see also **Psychotherapeutic and transformational techniques, Therapy**) 36, 42, 107-133, 134-145, 156, 160, 304, 432, 481, 488, 495, 529
Transpersonal 27, 47, 48, 72, 121, 138, 140, 141, 156, 217, 220, 282, 288, 321, 335, 346, 433, 554, 579
Transpsychic communication 160
Trauma (see **Past-Life Experiences**)
Turner, John Richard 483

Unconditional positive regard/acceptance 33, 71, 88, 163, 412
Unity 403
Universal consciousness 70
Upanishads, Katha 155, 554
Uterine memories (see **Findeisen, Barbara**; Perinatal; Prenatal; **Pecci, Ernest**)

Vanderhagen, Zoop 320
Vargiu, Susan 584
Vendantic philosophy 10, 14, 216, 223, 403, 482, 588
Verney, Thomas 18, 424
Victimization (see **Past-Life Experiences, Symptoms**)
Vipassana meditation 143, 155, 236, 586
Visualization (see also **Induction**) 65, 66
Vulnerability in altered states 132, 133, 151, 161, 163, 170, 411

Wallace, Robert 566
Wambach, Helen 8, 15, 16, 19, 52, 61, 72, 74, 77, 148, 281, 282, 284, 286, 287, 290, 299, 306, 559-564, 582, 585, 587, 589, 590
Ward, Dan 580
Watts, Alan 592
Weatherhead, Leslie 585
Weber, Renee 581, 582, 587, 588, 594
Weil, Andrew 11, 593
Weil, Simon 217
Weiss, Brian 19, 590
Whitton, Joel 19, 570, 589, 590
Wholeness (see also **Therapy**) 158, 223, 440
Wilbur, Kenneth 594
Williams, Carey 592
Williams, Lorin 591
Williston, Glen 590
Wils, A.E.J. 587
Wisdom, sources of (see **Therapy**)
Witness point (see **Therapy**)
Woolger, Jennifer 215

Woolger, Roger 6, 13, 14, 16, 17, 20, 26, 28-30, 35, 39-41, 43, 44, 47, 50, 57, 58, 60, 83, 88, 90, 93, 103, 109, 113, 114, 117, 130, 138, 139, 143, 144, 145, 147, **216-240**, 352, 553-558, 576, 583, 585, 586, 590

Yoga 480, 566, 569, 570, 579, 580, 583, 593
Yogananda 155, 554, 593

Zen 10, 155, 225, 481, 566, 569, 579, 592
Zukov, Gary 10, 594

# Other Books by the Publisher

A wide variety of similar books may be found at the publisher's retail web site at www.Holistictree.com. Bookstores or educational institutions may order from their favorite wholesaler, or from the publisher directly by logging onto:
www.TranspersonalPublishing.com
www.BookSolidPress.com

BookSolid Press
PO Box 7220
Kill Devil Hills, NC 27948
(800) 296-MIND
252-480-0530
fx: 252-480-0510
Orders@holistictree.com

Pass on your Experience! ⬇

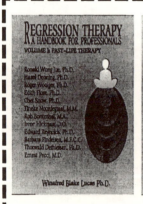

Order from your favorite wholesaler
or from the publisher:
1= $69.95
2-4= 10% discount
5 or more= 40% discount

Retail:
www.Holistictree.com
Wholesale:
www.BookSolidPress.com
(800) 296-MIND

Volume I: 978-1-929661-17-6
Volume II: 978-1-929661-18-3